New Approaches
to the Study of Religion
1

New Approaches
to the Study of Religion

Volume 1:
Regional, Critical, and Historical Approaches

Edited by
Peter Antes, Armin W. Geertz, Randi R. Warne

Walter de Gruyter · Berlin · New York

Originally published as volume 42 in the series *Religion and Reason*.

∞ Printed on acid-free paper which falls within
the guidelines of the ANSI to ensure permanence and durability.

ISBN 978-3-11-020551-0

Library of Congress — Cataloging-in-Publication Data

A CIP catalogue record for this book is available from the Library of Congress.

Bibliographic information published by the Deutsche Nationalbibliothek

The Deutsche Nationalbibliothek lists this publication in the Deutsche Nationalbibliografie;
detailed bibliographic data are available in the Internet at http://dnb.d-nb.de.

Printed in Germany
Cover design: Martin Zech

Contents

Section 3
Historical Approaches

Introduction

by

PETER ANTES, ARMIN W. GEERTZ, AND RANDI R. WARNE

It is particularly fitting at the threshold of a new millennium to reflect back on what has transpired in academic approaches to the study of religion over the last two decades of the twentieth century. The summary of developments and achievements in our field presented here follows in the footsteps of two former publications, namely, Jacques Waardenburg's *Classical Approaches to the Study of Religion*, first published in 1973 (paperback edition 1999), and Frank Whaling's two volume edited work, *Contemporary Approaches to the Study of Religion*. Waardenburg's *Classical Approaches* provided scholars with a comprehensive survey of the academic field of religion from its inception as an academic discipline in the nineteenth century up until the end of World War II, and is marked by a phenomenological and textual emphasis that reflects the concerns that animated the field during that period. Whaling's *Contemporary Approaches*, covering the post World War II period up until the early 1980s, was subdivided into two volumes: *The Humanities* (1983) and *The Social Sciences* (1985), reflecting a shift of intellectual and scholarly terrain. While the former was comprised of a selection of texts chosen by the editor from works not initially intended for a publication on methodology, the latter presented articles on methodology explicitly solicited from various authors by the editor. Our present two volume publication, published like the preceding volumes in de Gruyter's *Religion and Reason* series, is a sequel to both, but as with the latter, all the contributions have been explicitly written for this publication. *New Approaches to the Study of Religion* thus completes the survey of the study of religion in the twentieth century with a focus on developments characteristic of its last two decades, i.e., the period from 1980 to the present.

Though many people in Western Europe and the Americas experienced a kind of a millennium fever at the turn of the twenty-first century, historians of religions know that the periodization of an era is rather arbitrary. A glance at different religious calendars confirms that neither Muslims nor Jews, Hindus nor Buddhists shared the tension of the transition from one century to another and even less so from one millennium to another. It is thus not surprising that in terms of methodological approaches, the end of a century of our era does not necessarily mean a turning point in the type of scholarly work being undertaken. What can be described here, therefore, is less a retrospective consideration of methods used, *per se*, than a consideration of the promise of new approaches that are currently being undertaken and need further methodological consideration.

The present two volume publication maps the methodological terrain in the scholarly study of religion in seven sections—as outlined below—with volume one covering regional, critical, and historical approaches; and volume two covering textual, comparative, sociological, and cognitive approaches.

A Survey of New Approaches in Various Parts of the World

Academic studies may seem to be universal in their methods and results. However, a closer look at what is actually being done shows that these studies are context-related in many respects: linguistically, politically, religiously, and culturally.

The linguistic setting is of major importance for determining what might be considered "new," particularly when considered in a world-wide context. Philippe Ariès' *History of Childhood* may serve as an example to illustrate the problem. The book was originally published in French in 1960, and launched an intense debate in the French-speaking world. A German translation was published in 1975, and led to vigorous debates similar to those undertaken in the French-speaking world fifteen years before. Within the German context, Ariès' thesis was something new, while the French were astonished to discover that Ariès was still being discussed in this way. What may be new in one context does not need to be so in another, or—put somewhat differently—academic debates do not need to be synchronic. Numerous and different levels of discussion may occur simultaneously in academic debate world-wide. Even though English is increasingly becoming the common language for academic publications, the diversity noted above is not well represented in respective journals and reviews because of the tendency for editors to work from their own frames of reference regarding "newness" and the established framework for debate, rather than documenting the full range of discussion being undertaken globally. It is necessary to highlight these context-related particularities to assess "new approaches" adequately.

There are also political reasons why academic discussions vary from one context to the other. This holds particularly true for Eastern Europe. The fall of the Berlin Wall in 1989 and the consequent end of communist rule over most of the countries in Eastern Europe produced new academic discussions in these regions. Many scholars were confronted with the methodological approaches of Western countries for the first time, and approaches that seemed outdated in the West were both welcome and fascinating in this new environment. For example, a strong interest in the phenomenology and psychology of religion has recently developed in the academic study of religion in Poland, and is, within that context, a genuine methodological innovation. The waning of Marxist ideology has also been paralleled by a decline in the currency of the neo-Marxist worldviews of the so-called Frankfurt School (Theodor W. Adorno, Max Horkheimer, Jürgen Habermas) in the West. The political landscape clearly shapes the academic enterprise in an important way. What is "new" and relevant is context-specific, with academic debate having become increasingly multifaceted so that it is nearly impossible to determine with any finality what is "new" on a world-wide scale.

However, political conditions alone are insufficient to describe extra-academic influences on the academic debate. Religious factors can also be decisive,[1] as consideration of research within Muslim contexts gives evidence. The contributions in this volume make clear that within the Muslim world a number of different approaches are possible, from a very religious one in the Arab world to a laicist approach in Turkey.

Linguistic, political, and religious factors are thus without doubt of great importance for determining what constitutes a "new approach" in the study of religion in various contexts. However these are all external to the study of religion as such, and shape its structure in that way. There is, however, an intrinsic argument for defining newness in the study of religion, one related to disciplinary barriers. Specifically, a widely approved method in one discipline may be totally unknown in another. A great deal of courage is often needed to introduce a method from one discipline into another. Moreover, it may take years for the new methods of one discipline to be adopted in others. This is particularly relevant to the study of religions if we consider the classical understanding of the "History of Religions." In Italy and France, the sociology and psychology of religion are not considered sub-disciplines of the field, while they are in German and Spanish contexts. The turn towards the humanities and the social sciences described in Whaling's *Contemporary Approaches to the Study of Religion* thus was far more easily and widely undertaken in Germany and Spain than in Italy and France.

The aim of a survey of new approaches in various parts of the world is to draw the reader's attention to these context-related realities of research in the study of religion. The goal is not to enumerate all the different studies that have been undertaken, or to itemize a list of important representative scholars. Rather, the task at hand is to provide an orientation that will allow the reader to put all these studies into a proper context, to clarify what is being done, and why it is being done in the way that it is. Each contribution that follows should

---

1   Cf. *Marburg Revisited: Institutions and Strategies in the Study of Religion*, ed. by Michael Pye, Marburg: diagonal-Verlag, 1989.

thus be considered in relation to its originating context, as an indicator of the state of the discipline therein.

We hope that the work in this section will inspire more (and much more detailed) studies in this area, for it is indeed a new field of research that begs for further study. Ideally, in future volumes of this kind, this section will be considerably enlarged and will encompass all relevant research areas of the discipline.

Critical Approaches

The next section is dedicated to critical approaches. "Critical" refers here to critical reflections that are relevant to the study of religion(s), although the arguments themselves stem from other disciplines. Critical arguments engage two main concerns: 1) the problem of the relationship between reality and the study of religion(s) and 2) the socio-psychological conditions of the researcher and their impact on the results of research.

Regarding the first, new approaches taken from philosophy and semantics strongly suggest that we have no immediate access to reality. The time when people explained truth as the equation between what things are and what is said about them (*adaequatio rei et intellectus*, in medieval terminology) has definitely passed. It is clear to most, if not all, philosophers and linguists that reality *per se*, or seen "objectively" (i.e. what things are), is beyond the reach of human intelligence. From this perspective, all so called "objectively true" statements are nothing but agreements between people and are, as such, only certain within a given context of people who are willing to accept the agreement. Meaning and truth claims are thus neither subjective nor objective, but intersubjective insofar as they express convictions shared by everyone within the group. Consequently, truth is much more the equation between intersubjective statements made within a particular group (*adaequatio intellectus ad intellectum*, to express it in terms analogous to the medieval claim) than it is a statement about reality, objectively known. This is of particular interest in the study of "religion," which is claimed to have a non-empirical dimension and is thus even less "objectively" accessible than the empirical data of other disciplines. The ongoing debate in philosophy and semantics about the relationship between reality and what is said about it thus has intriguing consequences for the discipline and needs to be widely engaged both generally and in relation to specific areas of investigation.

A second range of problems needs to be considered as well. The first critical approach questions the possibility of objective access to reality as such and suggests instead that all human knowledge is more "human" (i.e. intersubjective) rather than "objectively" true. The second suggests that human access to knowledge is further conditioned by different socio-psychological factors that influence research and have an impact on its results. Consequently, it is not only "objective reality" that is under debate but the neutrality of the researcher as well. For instance, it has now become clear that male dominated, androcentric studies have ignored, distorted, and elided knowledge by and about women. Feminist and gender-critical approaches have led to highly significant insights in areas which were hitherto un(der)investigated. It is therefore important to understand that the way we look at the world and the type of questions we ask in our work are conditioned by socio-psychological factors to a great extent, i.e. that we are all "located knowers" whose specificity of perspective is relevant to the kinds of studies we engage in and the conclusions we draw.

It is important to note that critical studies such as these are not relinquishing "objectivity" for open-ended relativism. Rather, they must be seen in the context of the general truth claims put forward by religions. Theoretical explanations in the studies of religion(s) do not lead to dogmas but to explanatory theories that need to be tested and can be rejected if proven flawed or otherwise inadequate to the task at hand. Changes are always possible, including revisiting theories from the past that may now appear to have greater relevance and/or applicability than when they were previously superseded. Such comings and goings further underline the relativity of newness, from another perspective, in the studies of religion(s).

Historical Approaches

Historical approaches characterize the historian of religion's work best. This section, however, goes beyond classical historical studies and is more innovative. Here the focus rests upon consideration of the religion under study as a construction of the describer in ongoing response to and exchange with the described cultural phenomenon. Jørn Borup's contribution on *Zen and the Art of Inverting Orientalism* in this volume concludes the following:

> Studying religion is not like looking through a window. It is necessary to see with glasses, to use models and maps to see religion not as a metaphysical truth to be perceived, but as a cultural phenomenon, itself a construction, a living reality. Though both constructivism and processes of relational interconnectedness are also keywords within Buddhist discourse, our "constructions" need not be in harmony with theirs. But ideally they need to be potentially reflecting each other. Though a mirror can be used for reflection and illumination, the images reflected in the mirror are not the thing itself. Historians of religion are not supposed to reveal a "truth," but to reflect on an always ongoing discourse about their truths—and on our own discourse.[2]

---

2   See page 482.

It is, consequently, the characteristic of "construction" that is relevant to all types of descriptions of religions. It is not only the fact that religions, in the history of religions, are seen from the outside and that the outsider's view might be different from an insider's, but rather that the "images reflected in the mirror" are to a large degree constructions generated out of the observer's own mind. This is perhaps less significant in cases of established traditions such as Buddhism (though some would disagree), but it is clearly the case for more general classifications of contentious topics such as new religions, new fundamentalisms and Western esotericism. Here, the first task of the researcher is to delineate the subject, determining what properly belongs to the field to be studied, and what ought be omitted. Thus shaped, the subject is submitted to more detailed study. Clearly, initial assumptions will implicitly shape the conclusions that may eventually be drawn. If, for example, one is convinced that fundamentalism is an important trend that is noticeable in all major religions at present, a list of elements will be established to prove its existence in each of them. If, on the contrary, one denies this basic thesis, the same elements will not be seen as sharing a cross-tradition commonality, but rather will be understood within the specific framework of the religious tradition itself. The same principle can be applied *mutatis mutandis* to new religions and Western esotericism. Different results will emerge, depending on the breadth or narrowness of the observer's conception of these phenomena. Studies in these fields are not "like looking through a window." Even the comparison with the image in the mirror is imprecise for, what is seen in the mirror is not the image of what is, so to speak, "the thing itself," but an image of the thing created in the observer's mind as the subject of study. All the elements put under scrutiny and the methods employed to that end are consequences of initial decisions made about content at the outset of the study.

Textual Approaches

This section—the opening section of volume two—addresses one of the most classical approaches in studies of religion. For decades the most prestigious type of study in the field of religion was textual analysis and translation, for which philological methods were the most appropriate. A continuing concern for this way of engaging the study of religion may seem to imply a certain stasis in the field. The present volume, however, shows that there are theoretical problems with translation that studies of religion need to take into account. A further problem is the context of the process of translation, and the implications this may have for the adequacy of the translation itself. A good example of the problem is the German tradition of using the German mystical vocabulary of the late Middle Ages to translate the key terms of Islamic mysticism, a practice that leaves the reader with the impression that religious experience in Islamic mysticism has striking parallels with that of German Christian mystics. What has not been noted in these translations is that these parallels were intentionally chosen by the translators, but are not necessarily justified parallels as such. Language dictionaries are the best examples of translating terms from one cultural or religious context into another without any debate on how legitimate these parallels might be for academic use in translations.

Another field in textual approaches is the use of electronic media in the study of sacred texts. There are methodological implications and interpretive consequences in this area as well that require further study.

Finally, literary theory deserves serious discussion in its possible application to the study of religion.

All this shows the importance of extra-disciplinary developments to textual approaches within the study of religion, and assessments of their relevance to it. It may be tempting for scholars to neglect these developments, on the assumption that textual approaches will always be the same. They may find it difficult to imagine that innovative methods might be introduced or have any effect on their traditional work with texts. There is all the more need, therefore, to underline the importance of progress in this field, and to invite scholars of our discipline to actively engage in ongoing discussion of these issues.

Comparative Approaches

The section on comparative approaches covers a variety of fields of application from classical concerns such as syncretism and ritual, to new areas of interest such as dance and human rights. In the former case the main focus is on new insights and developments within traditional subject areas, while in the latter case more emphasis is necessarily laid upon arguments for integrating such fields of research into the study of religion. Here, the case needs to be made that these new subjects are too important for and relevant to the study of religion to be ignored. Conversations with colleagues from other disciplines are imperative, so that their research enriches our own as ours may theirs. The new questions thus generated may spur reinvestigation of our own source material in light of these different perspectives, to fruitful results.

Social Sciences

The section on social sciences touches upon one of the most important fields of influence on the study of religion since World War II. This section contains a survey of advances in the sociology of religion, as well as more specific topics such as the reassessment of secularization theory, urbanization and religion, religion in the media, religion and law, and religion in diaspora. The latter topic signals important and innovative developments in vocabulary in the study of religion. The section on historical approaches made reference to neologisms in the study of religion insofar as the word "fundamentalism," originally used for a certain tendency in American Protestantism at the threshold of the twentieth century, has now become a general term for antimodern tendencies in all religions. A similar expansion of meaning is occurring with the word "diaspora" so that we currently speak of Muslim, Buddhist, Hindu diasporas in Europe and do not reserve the term for Jewish minorities in Europe nor—as in traditional Roman Catholic circles in Germany—for Catholic minorities in mainly Protestant areas of Germany.

It is important to note that such expansions of meaning occur first in public debate, and subsequently find entrance into academic circles without any debate on whether or not this new terminology should be employed. The crux is that common parlance becomes academic terminology without clarity of definition for the purpose of academic study, thus launching endless debates about its appropriate use. Establishing clear definitions at the outset, as is done in the natural sciences, would arguably help offset the proliferation of later debates about a term's descriptive value.

Cognition and Cross-cultural Psychology

The last section of volume two focuses on cognition and cross-cultural psychology. Both are well-developed research fields outside the study of religion but have a direct impact on studies of religion as well. It is therefore highly desirable to investigate these areas further to determine the usefulness of these approaches for academic studies of religion.

The various sections of the present volume offer a wide range of approaches to the study of religion which are making, and can make, fruitful and important contributions to the study of religion. Each of these "lenses" has contributed significantly to the generation of knowledge within our field, signaling the fact that progress in academic studies depends deeply on methodological exchange with other disciplines. To encourage and advance this exchange is a key goal of this volume.

Bringing a work such as this to fruition would be impossible without a publisher's strong support. We, the editors, would like to thank de Gruyter Publishers for having accepted *New Approaches to the Study of Religion* for publication in de Gruyter's *Religion and Reason* series. We would also like to express our appreciation for the strong support of its general editor, Jacques Waardenburg, who was always there with help and advice as the volume progressed. We thank him in particular for his encouragement and hope that the results of these labors will be a volume that will be found useful by a wide range of scholars in religion across the globe. Last but not least, we greatly thank Dr. Karl-Heinz Golzio for compiling the indexes of both volumes.

Finally, we hope that our readership will be inspired to incorporate new approaches to the study of religion in their own work, developing and deepening studies in religion as a result.

Section 1

A Survey of New Approaches in
Various Parts of the World

New Approaches to the Study of Religion in North America

by

RANDI R. WARNE

Before embarking on an exploration of new approaches to the study of religion in North America, a cautionary note is in order. What follows is necessarily circumscribed. A key reason is the sheer numerical vastness of the institutional context for the study of religion. There are at least 1,265 undergraduate programs in religious studies and theology in the United States alone,[1] and approximately 50 undergraduate and graduate programs in religious studies in Canada. To treat all of these departments and areas of scholarly inquiry comprehensively would easily entail an entire book of its own.[2] Such a work would also arguably need to be produced by a number of scholars, given the range of subject areas contained within multi- and interdisciplinary fields of the study of religion.

It is also important to recognize that the academic study of religion is not undertaken solely in departments of religious studies. "Religion," and specific traditions like Christianity, or Buddhism, are studied in departments of history, philosophy, East Asian studies, Middle Eastern studies, psychology, sociology, and more. Tracking these comprehensively would be an undertaking of equally gargantuan proportions—although a study of how these institutional locations shape religion's academic study would be a timely and informative undertaking. Rather than pretending to have accomplished that task, this essay has the more modest aim of highlighting some of the important debates and developments currently taking place in the academic study of religion in North America. It is hoped that the unavoidable *lacunae* of this article will spur further work, bringing to the forefront other "new approaches" not addressed herein.

Yet another issue is the definition of the terrain itself. "New Approaches to the Study of Religion in North America" implies a homogeneity to North Amer-

---

1   Allen 1996: 31.
2   For example, see the *Directory of Departments and Programs of Religious Studies in North America*, published yearly by the Council of Societies for the Study of Religion, which has an average length of 500–600 pages.

ica that does not hold up under closer scrutiny. Put differently, what constitutes "North America" is, in practice, over-determined by the sheer cultural dominance of the United States; Canada, if it is considered at all, is incorporated only insofar as it reproduces or is consistent with the categories and questions generated from within that latter context. This essay will depart from that practice. Here, Canada will be considered as a distinct country with its own characteristic concerns and contributions to the study of religion, in recognition of the importance of position in setting scholarly horizons. Moreover, the different cultural and political contexts of both Canada and the United States shape the academic study of religion in distinctive ways that need to be acknowledged as well.

This being said, there is yet a further twist to the study of new approaches to the study of religion in North America, namely, the increasing permeability of national frames of academic reference as a result of the Internet. In the past, the best scholarship was arguably international. Accomplished writers and thinkers engaged the work of like scholars at prestigious international, multilingual conferences and colloquia. A certain hierarchy was in place; to participate in these venues a scholar had to be established, have an earned and long-term reputation, and the financial resources to represent his or her institution/ country. Today, discussion list-serves link scholars across the globe. As with the Andere-L list run out of University of California Santa Barbara, prestigious senior scholars debate on equal footing with graduate students, junior and mid-range professors, and part-time academic teachers, disrupting the conventional hierarchies of the past. While noting a distinctiveness to the Canadian scene on the one hand, I also wish to suggest that a dissolution of boundaries is simultaneously underway whereby scholarly interchange has become somewhat more fluid. Indeed, it may be just this recasting of the field of academic debate that has allowed "minority" players such as Canadians to gain greater profile than they might have had in previous times. What counts as a "national" approach is thus complicated, and a continental one perhaps even more so.

These *caveats* aside, there remains much that may be said about new approaches to the study of religion in North America. Let us begin with an overview of where practitioners in the field consider themselves to be.

The American Academy of Religion's[3] *Census of Departments and Programs in Religion and Theology* and the Canadian Corporation for Studies in Religion's[4] *State-of-the-Art Review* Series

The American Academy of Religion's *Census*

The fall 2001 edition of the American Academy of Religion's publication, *Religious Studies News*, proudly contained a special pull-out section summarizing the results of a multi-year, Lilly Foundation funded project to conduct a census of programs in theology and religion in North America. Undertaken via Lilly's "Strengthening College and University Programs in Religion and Theology" (SCURT) initiative, the census was intended to support departments; according to Edward Gray, the then-AAR Director of Academic Relations, the AAR was "better prepared to make the case that every student deserves an education that includes the study of religion."[5] Elements singled out in the survey included faculty profiles, student profiles, types of institutions, course offerings, and the like. It was claimed that "[n]early 900 departments and programs in the U.S. and Canada participated in the effort,"[6] with the result that the *"AAR Census of Religion and Theology Programs* has comprehensively mapped the academic study of religion (religious studies, theology, and Bible) in the U.S. and Canada. It achieved an adjusted response rate of nearly 80%."[7]

Particular confidence was expressed with regard to the breakdown of undergraduate course offerings in religion. Edward Gray notes:

> The Tradition section of the questionnaire reveals that Judaism is a subject of study at 40% of the departments responding. Islam and Buddhism are offered at nearly a third of departments, and Confucianism [sic] at a fifth. While curricular offerings are

---

3   The American Academy of Religion is North America's largest scholarly society for the general study of religion. It holds both regional and national meetings, in which a number of Canadian scholars participate. For more information, see the AAR website, www.aarweb.org.

4   The Canadian Corporation for Studies in Religion (CCSR) was formed in 1971 to promote publication of the works of Canadian scholars of religion. While not a scholarly society itself, its constituent members are the Canadian Society for the Study of Religion (CSSR), the Canadian Theological Society (CTS), the Canadian Society of Biblical Studies (CSBS), the Canadian Society of Patristic Studies (CSPS) , the Canadian Society of Church History (CSCH), the Société québécoise pour l'étude de la religion (SQER), Société canadienne de théologie (SCT). For more information, see the CCSR website, www.ccsr.ca. Links are provided to the several scholarly societies it serves.

5   Gray: ii.

6   Ibid.: i.

7   Ibid.: iii.

decidedly focused on the Christian tradition at most responding departments, almost half of all departments (46%) offer comparative courses as well.[8]

That "decided focus" on Christian traditions is represented in the percentage of respondents offering courses in Old Testament (78%), New Testament (84%), historical Christianity (71%), Christian theology (65%), and Christian ethics (54%).

By percentage of those responding, the following topic areas were also represented:

> American religion (42%), arts and literature (31%), ethics (47%), gender and sexuality (29%), new religious movements (18%), philosophy of religion (47%), racial and ethnic studies (21%), ritual and performance studies (16%), social scientific approaches and topics (23%), and (distinct from gender and sexuality) women's studies (33%).[9]

A number of observations might be made about the foregoing. First, the *Census* appears to reflect an advocacy agenda, not just for scholars who have chosen the study of religion as their professional area of inquiry, but also for all university students, who, as stated above, "deserve" an education that includes the study of religion. This advocacy stance is under-girded by SCURT's explicit agenda to "strengthen" college and university programs in religion and theology. This is not mere mapping; there is a stated purpose to gathering this data which is to fortify and enhance religion and theology in the university setting.

A second consideration is the fact that while scholars often must teach in areas in which they do not publish, the curriculum offered in the institutions by which they are employed is not irrelevant to their academic accomplishments, including how their contributions to scholarly debate are evaluated. Indeed, while new faculty are often hired to complement an existing set of specializations within a department, there is an equally prominent tendency for departments to reproduce themselves. In this regard, it is appropriate to note how Christian the general frame of reference of this *Census* is. The unproblematized lumping together of religion, theology and Bible, and the use of Christian-exclusive terminology (e.g., "Old Testament") suggests that for the AAR at least, the study of religion is still very much a Christian enterprise, although some space has been made for "comparative courses as well."

While the AAR is undoubtedly responsible for the areas it decided to track, the prevalence of Christian theological and cultural content may be in part seen as a product of those responding to the survey. Again according to Edward Gray,

> [o]f the responding programs, close to 25% were at public institutions and 20% were classified as "private non-sectarian." Catholic institutions accounted for 17%. The

---

8   Ibid.: ii.
9   Ibid.: ii.

single largest institutional type was "Protestant," representing over one third of the responding units (324 total).[10]

This being said, when broken down by type of institution (public; private non-sectarian; Catholic; Protestant), Christianity remained the most fully represented in the curriculum at both the undergraduate levels. While undergraduate courses in Christianity were offered by 97.9% and 97.7% of Catholic and Protestant institutions respectively, they were also offered by 86.2% of public institutions, and 89.1% of private non-sectarian institutions. Similarly, "topics" courses like philosophy of religion and ethics were offered at 72.6% of public, 67.9% of private non-sectarian, 57.1% of Catholic, and 66% of Protestant schools respectively.[11] This representation is mirrored at the graduate level as well, both with regard to Christianity, and to other religious traditions, the exception being Judaism and Islam, whose profile at the graduate level is significantly higher than in undergraduate programs. An additional interesting piece of data is the prevalence of courses in American (not North American) religion at about half or more of the programs surveyed, compared to racial and ethnic studies in religion, found in one-quarter to one-tenth of the programs involved.

There is a brief description given of the methodology employed by the company whose task it was to analyze the survey data.[12] At the final consultation meeting held in Atlanta, Georgia, on September 10, 2001 that I attended as president of one of the participating societies, great confidence was expressed in the reliability and general usefulness of the data gathered. However, while I will not be pursuing the matter in depth here, for a number of reasons the data on Canada is problematic.[13] Happily, other resources exist to map the landscape of Canadian scholarship on religion.

---

10   Ibid.: ii.
11   Ibid.
12   Ibid.: i–iii.
13   For example, Canada is treated in a separate, regional category, rather than being broken down and integrated into the categories employed to analyze programs in the United States. The category "American Religion" flags another issue/problem. When Canadian representatives (like myself, as then-President of the CSSR) were invited to comment on the initial questions generated for the survey, suggestions were made to allow for Canadian specificity. However, rather than "Religion in Canada" and "Religion in the United States," or even "National Religion," the category "American Religion" was employed. Canadian specificity is not recognized within this false generic. There were other difficulties related to accommodating Canadian/U.S. difference as well, such as Canada's official bilingualism and the francophone province of Quebec. Suffice it to say that to the categories and assumptions of the AAR *Census* remain fully American rather than North American in scope, and that it is necessary to look elsewhere for reliable data on the Canadian scene.

The Canadian Corporation for Studies in Religion's *State of-the-Art* Reviews

Canadian post-secondary educational institutions are predominantly public institutions. In contrast to universities in the United States, many of which were founded and/or are funded by private fortunes and endowments, generally Canadian schools have received their primary funding from government sources. Increasing pressure has been placed on Canadian universities in recent years to generate revenues through fund-raising, with implications that will be discussed more fully below. At this juncture, however, what is important to note is the practical effect public funding has on the constituencies to which universities are accountable. On the Canadian scene, a key player in this regard is the federally funded Social Sciences and Humanities Research Council (SSHRC).

As Ron Neufeldt notes in the first volume of the monograph series *The Study of Religion in Canada/Sciences Religieuses au Canada* (commonly referred to as the *State-of-the-Art* series), the impetus for the initiative came from SSRHC's observation in June 1979 that "the existing Canadian learned societies seem inactive in reviewing and communicating the state of research in their disciplines."[14] The Canadian Corporation for Studies in Religion (CCSR) and the Canadian Society for the Study of Religion (CSSR) were thus prompted to propose a series of regional reviews of the state of religious studies in Canada. With the province of Alberta proposed as a pilot project to this larger enterprise, a successful application was made to SSHRC for funding, and the work was undertaken in 1980. The proposal's initial key concerns were what areas of research needed to be developed, the steps needed to encourage interdisciplinary research, and the role of scholarly publications in the development of the discipline. In consultation with other religious studies scholars in Canada, these were recast as "teaching programs, research, community-related activity, and the role of religious studies in interdisciplinary research and activities."[15]

Setting the parameters for the study proved to be a subject of some debate. Over the objections of scholars elsewhere in the country, it was felt that the assessment of the study of religion in Alberta's post-secondary educational institutions needed to include theological and Bible colleges as well as universities, and liberal arts, community, and regional colleges. Neufeldt's introduction to the study outlines a pragmatic rationale for this decision, that pivots in part on the distinction between first-order descriptive studies and second-order analytic studies. Neufeldt argued that:

---

14 *A Proposed Five Year Plan for the Social Sciences and the Humanities Research Council of Canada,* cited in: Neufeldt 1983: ix.

15 Neufeldt 1983: x.

there may be, and sometimes is, little difference between religious studies courses in a university and courses in Bible colleges or institutions … particularly where the latter have insisted that their particular Christian context should not jeopardize scholarship. It should be pointed out, however, that only those courses in theological and Bible colleges for which a student might receive credit or an exemption in a university will be included as part of the present study.[16]

That is, rather than equating theological and secular university education in religion, the standards of the university were considered to be the benchmark for determining legitimacy within the curriculum. While clearly this distinction will not satisfy those who believe the university curriculum itself is "infected" with theology (and hence has tainted standards), it is nevertheless useful to note the difference between Neufeldt's approach and one that simply assumes the equivalency of (Christian) theology and the secular academic study of religion.

The success of this pilot study resulted in the publication of five more book-length regional treatments of religious studies in Canada, all published by Wilfrid Laurier University Press (for Quebec, Despland and Rousseau 1988; for Ontario, Remus, James and Fraikin 1992; for Manitoba and Saskatchewan, Badertscher, Harland and Miller 1993; for British Columbia, Fraser 1995; and for Atlantic Canada, Bowlby with Faulkner 2001). Each volume addresses the historical origins of the study of religion in each region, the curricula taught at various institutions, the areas of research undertaken by faculty, the degree programs available, the particular social and cultural context at the time of writing, and makes recommendations for the future.

Throughout, various degrees of tension are revealed with regard to religious studies and theology. For example, after making the distinction between religious studies ("a scholarly neutral and non-advocative field of study that is characterized by rigor and detachment in its approach, by a variety of methodologies drawn from the humanities and the social sciences … conducted in a public and pluralistic institution") and theological studies ("a scholarly committed and advocative field of study that is characterized by self-critical engagement in its approach, by a variety of methodologies in its research, and by results that intend to enhance participation in and contribution to the religious traditions and communities that govern the institutions in which the study takes place"), Brian Fraser, author of the volume on British Columbia, intentionally abandons the series' previous focus on "religious studies in the secular university" to attend to theological education, which he claims had been slighted as a result.[17] As noted with regard to the initial volume on Alberta, the inclusion of theological education in any particular was considered by

---

16   Ibid.: xii.
17   Fraser 1995: viii–ix.

some to be unacceptable. The inclusion of theology in discussions of religious studies is a matter of considerable and ongoing debate.

A final volume, external to the *State-of-the-Art* series but a CCSR publication that has made an outstanding contribution to mapping the academic study of religion in Canada is *L'étude de la religion au Québec: Bilan et prospective*, a multi-authored collection edited by Jean-Marc Larouche and Guy Menard, published by Les Presses de l'Université Laval (Laval University Press) in 2001. A compendium of the work of over thirty scholars, this publication provides an admirable overview of the state of the study of religion in Quebec. Departing from the format used in the *State-of-the-Art* series, *L'étude de la religion au Québec* focuses on research: who works in what field of expertise, what has been produced, and what directions are indicated for further study. The collection is divided into four sections: Religious Traditions (with the distinctive inclusion of two articles on Amerindian traditions, an article on Inuit traditions, and Afro-Brazilian cults, in addition to more commonly found foci like Catholicism, or Islam); Sacred Texts and Ancient Religions (Hebrew Bible, New Testament, the Coptic Collection of Nag Hammadi, Religious Traditions of Egypt and the Ancient Near East, and Religious Traditions of the Medieval Occident); New Religions in Culture (sects, new age, rituals); and Religion, Social Practices, and Cultural Production (with articles on feminism, sexuality, architecture, the environment, ethics, film, and more). The vitality of this work is amplified by the context; the rejection of Quebec's Catholic past has left a residual suspicion of religion's worth as a subject of academic study, a problem rendered all the more acute in the face of government cutbacks to higher education.

Given the range of time over which these volumes were published, and the detail provided, it is difficult to provide a succinct summary of all their findings. However, for our purposes here, it may be useful to compare some of the data gathered with the shape of the field in religious studies at the outset of the project. A survey was done in 1978 for the Canadian Society for the Study of Religion's *Bulletin* (vol. 2/2, 1978) outlining the areas of expertise represented in the society's membership. Not surprisingly, given the antecedents of religion scholars at the time, the areas of expertise most highly represented were philosophy of religion (80), phenomenology (64), and systematic theology (54). Buddhism (50) and "Hinduism" (47) follow, with 9 categories (psychology of religion, sociology of religion, church history, ethics, and related topics) in and about 35. At the bottom of the list were Islam (21), moral theology (19), "primitive religion" (17) and Amerindian religion (12).

A cursory glance at religion scholars at Canada's major universities in the first years of the twenty-first century suggests a very different landscape.[18] While the University of Victoria in British Columbia has no religious studies

---

18   This list is a sample, rather than exhaustive.

department, it houses an innovative program in religion and society initiated by Dr. Harold Coward, the purpose of which is to bring together scholars and community issues. This collaborative venue has a prolific publication record, and definitely meets the concern, voiced in the late 1970s, that academic studies demonstrate their relevance to the larger community. The University of British Columbia in Vancouver represents an increasingly familiar phenomenon—the merged department. Religious studies at UBC is undertaken within the boundaries of a department of classical, Near Eastern and religious studies, and reflects a thoroughgoing emphasis on the archaeological, historical, and scriptural. East Asian studies are housed separately, in an independent unit.[19]

Once a thriving independent unit with scholars in Islam, Judaism, Christianity, Buddhism, and indigenous traditions, religious studies at the University of Alberta in Edmonton was merged in the 1990s to form a mega-unit that included comparative literature, film and media studies, religious studies, and numerous language programs. This unwieldy arrangement was restructured into a smaller unit of comparative literature, film and media studies and religious studies, but the faculty complement was not replenished as faculty retired or left. Now housed as a program within the department of history and classics, religious studies has three faculty members in various areas of Biblical studies.

A more diverse and vibrant scene is evident at the University of Calgary, where scholars represent a range of expertise, in three streams (Eastern, Western, and the Nature of Religion). The University of Lethbridge, also in Alberta, lost its religious studies department in the 1990s, with scholars in sociology of religion, archaeology, and Bible absorbed into other units.

Elsewhere on the prairies, religious studies has survived in small pockets, building on diverse competencies, often augmented by courses offered in affiliated Christian denominational colleges. Religious studies at the University of Regina has just become a department, after many years as a program, while religious studies at the University of Saskatchewan affiliated with anthropology to form a strengthened joint department. The University of Winnipeg in Manitoba has a small department that teaches in three streams: Western religions in historical perspective, non-Western religions, and contemporary problems in religion and culture. These streams are echoed at the University of Manitoba (Western religions, world religions, and religion and culture), but with much more of a cultural studies/postmodernist inflection.

Large religious studies departments and programs are found in Ontario, with major undergraduate and graduate programs at McMaster University (in

---

19 The distinctive role of area studies deserves fuller attention than is possible here. Suffice it to say they have their own politics, dynamics, and strengths, and vulnerabilities within the university.

Hamilton) and the University of Toronto. Wilfrid Laurier University has a department of religion and culture, while at Queen's, the religious studies department is affiliated both with the faculty of theology and the faculty of arts and science. Numerous other programs and departments exist, at the University of Waterloo, where denominational colleges are central contributors, the University of Ottawa (a bilingual program that has strong offerings in the social sciences), Carleton University, and Laurentian University in Sudbury.

The study of religion in francophone province of Quebec has had a distinctive history, based in large measure on the former influence of the Catholic church on the educational system. Theological studies are thus still well represented in the several campuses in the University of Quebec system. In an interesting and exciting development, the University of Laval in Quebec City is becoming a world leader in the study of gnosticism. The major English language university, McGill, reflects a conservative, traditional emphasis on the philosophy of religion, Christian studies, Biblical studies, and other traditions such as Buddhism, Hinduism, and Islam, often with a strong textual emphasis.

The Atlantic region (New Brunswick, Nova Scotia, Prince Edward Island, and Newfoundland and Labrador) has a mix of offerings, reflecting the strong religious identities found within the region. St. Thomas in New Brunswick is a Catholic institution affiliated with the University of New Brunswick, whose religious studies department still teaches Catholic theology as well as thematic and traditions courses in religion. A concentration on Christianity is also found in religious studies at the University of Prince Edward Island, along with traditions and thematic approaches. In Nova Scotia, at the time of this writing, two out of the three religious studies departments/programs (at Dalhousie and Mount St. Vincent University) are in flux due to faculty resignations, while the third, at St. Mary's University, is flourishing and looking to expand. Acadia University closed its department of religious studies a number of years ago, but a flourishing department of religious studies exists at St. Francis Xavier University in Antigonish. Memorial University in St. John's, Newfoundland, reflects the province's Christian past with a concentration of faculty expertise in Bible and in Christian thought and tradition, adding some interesting dimension with scholars of popular culture and of Chinese religion.

What is striking in the foregoing is what appears to be a widespread abandonment of the phenomenological approach that dominated religious studies in Canada and elsewhere up into the 1980s. Also significantly diminished is the philosophy of religion, in its traditional practice as a largely Christian/post-Christian enterprise. As will be suggested below, this shift in demographics may be due to more than ideological or intellectual developments, specifically, to economic and political changes that wrested the power out of the hands of academic departments, placing it instead with administrators governed by a new agenda for university life.

The Canadian scene has been described in considerable detail for a few reasons. First, its size makes it possible to do so. The United States has so many institutions, of so many different types (see AAR survey above) that one could find an institutional location for virtually every approach to the study of religion. (For example, when I taught at University of Wisconsin-Oshkosh, it housed the only religious studies major in the UW system, with a completely separate program, within a merged unit of religious studies/anthropology. A religious studies minor was housed in a department of philosophy/religious studies at University of Wisconsin-Steven's Point, while a vibrant Asian studies program existed at University of Wisconsin-Madison, the main campus. Even a single multi-campus state system such as the University of Wisconsin, contains divergent program emphases and institutional embodiments.) A thorough study of institutional locations for the study of religion in the United States would take much more time and space than is available here.

Another reason is that attention is not generally paid to the Canadian scene in itself, except by Canadians. This venue provides the opportunity to offset that lack somewhat. Additionally, one of the main themes to be discussed below, method and theory in the study of religion, is notable for the significant participation of Canadians in its debates. It may well be that holding a minority position is useful for critical engagement of a larger scene; certainly, as in the case of feminism, it may affect what is taken for granted as normative. Finally, many of the areas of scholarship engaged in the United States are addressed in other sections of this volume. It is hoped that readers will make the necessary links to generate a better sense of the landscape for religious studies in North America overall.

New Approaches to the Study of Religion—Some Themes

The remainder of this chapter will focus upon some key themes that have shaped intellectual work in North America in the last two decades of the twentieth century. More in-depth engagement with specific issues and perspectives will be found elsewhere in these pages. Here, the intent is simply to flag some of the discourses and intellectual concerns that continue to shape debate about and inquiry into the academic study of religion into the present century. The topics to be addressed are: method and theory; feminism; post-colonialism; and religion and culture/cultural studies. A final section on the material conditions of knowledge production in the contemporary academy in North America will locate these themes within the political, social, and economic realities within which such scholarship is being undertaken.

Method and Theory in the Study of Religion

This heading serves as an umbrella for a constellation of interrelated issues concerned with the definition of religion and its proper study within the university. There are a number of axes along which debate is played out, each with its own merits. With no intent to privilege one over the other, we might begin with the problem of definition and the "anti-essentialist turn." The problem of defining religion is not new in itself. As Jonathan Z. Smith has noted, at the beginning of the twentieth century, Leuba outlined over fifty different theories of religion. Rather than this suggesting that it is impossible to define religion, Smith rejoins that "[t]he moral of Leuba is not that religion cannot be defined, but that it can be defined, with greater or lesser success, more than fifty ways."[20] However, he cautions that there is no such thing as "religion" *per se*; the term, indeed the concept, is a construct made by scholars. What people do religiously in their daily lives, and generic, invented "religion" are two different things. Trying to find some essence of "religion" is thus a quest doomed to failure. There are only particularities, and categories into which they might be placed, according to the scholar's disposition and perspective. Taxonomy, not ontology, is the order of the day.

Jonathan Z. Smith's influence upon a fresh generation of scholars has been persuasive, perhaps as compelling as that held over an earlier generation by a former colleague at the University of Chicago, Mircea Eliade. Indeed, eviscerating Eliade seemed to have become a preferred blood sport by the 1990s, with all traces of "the Sacred" to be expunged through the ritual cleansing of academic debate. Rather than approaching religion as a distinctive phenomenon that addressed deeply held human longings for meaning and transcendence, this next generation of scholars avowed a range of antithetical positions. Robert Segal argued for reductionism, and a strict circumscription of seeking truth through argumentation. Eliade's allegedly tainted political past (an association with a Romanian pro-fascist youth organization) has been used as a skewer to debunk Eliade's previously exalted status.[21] Some cautioned for a more nuanced approach,[22] but in general, in method and theory debates at least, appeal to "the Sacred" as "the essence" of religion is seen as evidence of having not paid much attention to the last twenty years of debate in the field.

But if "religion" is simply a construct, with nothing to do with an identifiable, extra-mundane realm, why use the term at all? Scholars like Tim Fitzgerald[23] have argued at length that the concept of "religion" adds nothing distinctive to the debate, and as such should be jettisoned. So too—it would

---

20   Smith 1998: 281.
21   See, for example, the discussion in McCutcheon 1997, especially chapter 3.
22   See for example, Rennie 1996.
23   Fitzgerald 2000. Fitzgerald currently teaches in Japan.

seem to follow—departments devoted to religion's academic study. If "religion" does not really exist, except in minds of scholars, why not locate those
scholars elsewhere, in departments like anthropology and/or cultural studies?
This would seem to be a pragmatic problem rather than an intellectual one. If
"religion" is *really* only academically significant as a product of material and
cultural forces identifiable by scholars across a range of disciplines and techniques, why privilege an otherwise empty category? As Laura Lee Downs
suggests, categories carry with them a practical power to shape human experience, however unstable they may appear under the theoretical microscope.[24]
Moreover, concepts like "psychology" or "politics" are equally human cultural
products, but no one would consider dropping those terms or closing down
departments that deal with them.

Advocates of separate religious studies programs claim they are necessary
because they provide an integrated, multi-disciplinary context wherein the
various aspects of what has been taken to constitute "religion" can be investigated. Moreover, religious studies engages many types of religious traditions,
not just Christianity, and considers phenomena that, while not recognized as
"religious traditions" *per se*, exhibit elements that may be deemed (quasi)
religious (such as the ritualistic aspects of Super Bowl Sunday). However, the
key distinguishing feature for some in this debate is that religious studies is
"scientific"—that is, it is objective, value-free, and at its best embodies what has
been called the "god's-eye-view," in contrast to the overt, value-laden enterprise of theology.

A striking element of the North American academic scene with regard to
religion is the extent of disagreement about who has the upper hand in the
"religious studies/theology debate." As will be suggested here, the persistence
and seeming unresolvability of this discussion may be due in part to the way it
has been constructed. Resources arguably exist for moving discussion in other,
more fruitful directions, yielding genuinely new approaches to the study of
religion, some of which are already emergent, though not usually placed at the
center of this debate. Here I will address the issue as it has played out in dominant academic circles, then suggest some ways in which the problem has been
and might be recast in the service of greater scholarly utility.

That the study of religion in North America is a highly contested terrain is
evident from the plethora of titles available on the subject. Tensions ran
especially high in the mid-1990s, with the publication of volumes lamenting the
loss of the "soul" of the American university, on the one hand,[25] and grave
warnings about religion's "overtaking" the university on the other.[26] Eventu-

---

24 Downs 1993.
25 See, for example, Marsden/Longfield, eds. 1992; Marsden 1994, 1997.
26 See, for example, Hart 1999; also Wiebe 1999.

ally, the issue hit the American mainstream media, with the November 1996 issue of the publication *Lingua Franca* featuring the issue on its front page. "Is Nothing Sacred? Casting Out the Gods from Religious Studies," by Charlotte Allen, laid out a problem all-too familiar to scholars of religion in North America. Foregrounding scholars like Don Wiebe, Gary Lease, and Jonathan Z. Smith, Allen articulates a perspective that holds that the teaching of religion in universities should be "academic" rather than "religious;" that methodological agnosticism (if not atheism) is required for scholarly rigor; and that inclusivity and liberalism are essentially covers for Christianity's continued cultural and intellectual dominance in the study of religion. While giving these and other like-minded thinkers a fair bit of ground, Allen points out that the clear lines of demarcation they advocate between religion's "scientific" and "academic" study on the one hand, and religious commitment and theology on the other, perhaps ought be reconsidered. One way of moving the debate forward, she suggests,

> would be to recognize that in this era of self-proclaimed postmodernity, the Enlighten-ment is over. Its hallmarks—philosophical positivism and the conviction that scientific methodology can explain everything—now seem dated, even to many hard and social scientists.[27]

The power of postmodernity to disrupt the old "Reason vs. Belief" standoff is significant.[28] However, it is unlikely that debate will disappear any time soon, in part because the triumph of the critics would be self-defeating. (Once the dragon is slain, whence the knight?) In any case, people do and will have values, including those who claim to stand outside of them. To the extent that the participants in this debate reflect majority culture privilege (and the degree to which this debate is undertaken by previously religious white males is quite conspicuous), they will be able to claim a certain degree of unmarked objecti-vity, but intellectual currents like postmodernity, feminism, and postcoloniality will continue to pose challenges to this stance.

For some, this foreshadows a tumbling into the abyss of utter relativism, and the loss of reliable knowledge altogether. Here, considerable resources exist to negotiate a more satisfactory conclusion. Despite repeated appeals to the inviolability of "science," there seems to be little appreciation for, or engagement with, the work of feminist epistemologists and philosophers of

---

27　Allen 1996: 39.

28　Indeed, it was precisely through the destabilization of previous discourses of "objecti-vity" via postmodernism that Christian theologians like George Marsden argued for the legitimacy of theological perspectives in the American academy. For an analysis see Wolfhart 2000. The impact of postmodernism on intellectual life in the late twentieth century is evident throughout these pages and will not be pursued in greater depth here.

science like Sandra Harding, Nancy Tuana, and Helen Longino.[29] In particular, Sandra Harding's notion of "strong objectivity" might serve well to move the debate beyond its current impasse.[30] The rich area of critical science studies would prove a further resource for moving beyond an ideology of science that appears, if not intellectually unsupportable, then certainly highly contestable. Science studies' emphasis on how science is actually *done*—by whom, within what politics, and for what ends—is a welcome antidote to the sacralized notion of "scientific objectivity" that functions ideologically in Western discourses. Here, the work of Muslim scholar Ziauddin Sardar is most instructive in outlining the colonialist disposition of this allegedly neutral enterprise.[31]

Regardless of whether these avenues are explored, a further reality is that theology as a (if not "the") way of studying religion is unlikely to disappear any time soon. For a variety of reasons, having a place for religious people to reflect on their beliefs—even in the university—seems to hold fairly widespread acceptance. The idea that people would want to spend their lives studying phenomena whose reality is in doubt and in which the scholarly ideal is disinterest is much less immediately understandable. Allocating already scarce resources to such a seemingly counter-intuitive enterprise is unlikely as well.

As the foregoing suggests, debates in method and theory exploded in the last two decades of the twentieth century. One of the more interesting venues for their exploration emerged out of the University of Toronto in 1989, when the journal *Method & Theory in the Study of Religion* was founded by graduate students at the Centre for Religious Studies. A particularly vibrant cohort, many of whom studied with Don Wiebe, took the initiative to generate a forum for sustained reflection on the business of doing religious studies. Eventually moving from the University of Toronto to Brill, while retaining Canadian scholars as its editors, [32] it remains an excellent resource for key debates in the field. Moreover, a number of past and present editors and contributors to the journal, graduates in religious studies at the University of Toronto, have gone on to make further contributions to mapping the field through publications

---

29 See Longino 1990; Harding 1998; Tuana, ed. 1989.
30 Feminist scholars were faced with a dilemma: How was it that the scholars/scholarship that claimed to be most "value-free" and "objective" nevertheless reproduced cultural biases about women (such as women's inferiority, women's "nature," etc.)? Harding suggests that by not recognizing cultural location, supposedly "value-free" scholars unwittingly reproduced them. See Harding 1991. See also the several articles in Harding, ed. 1993.
31 See, for example, "Fairytale of Science" in: Sardar 1998. For an overview of the field of science studies see Sardar/Van Loon 2001.
32 At the time of this writing these are Willi Braun, University of Alberta, and Johannes Wolfhart, University of Manitoba.

such as Braun and McCutcheon's *Guide to the Study of Religion* (2000), McCutcheon's *The Insider/Outsider Debate in the Study of Religion* (1999), and Darlene Juschka's *Feminism in the Study of Religion* (2001). The importance of categorization for "new approaches" to the study of religion in the late twentieth century is especially evident in Braun and McCutcheon's *Guide*, and a similar publication edited by Mark C. Taylor, *Critical Terms in Religious Studies*.[33]

Feminism/Gender Studies in the Study of Religion

The impact of gender-critical approaches to academic study was considered so significant by Cheris Kramarae and Dale Spender that they entitled their comprehensive assessment of the phenomenon *The Knowledge Explosion*.[34] A decade or more later, it is instructive to consider the status of both feminist and gender-critical approaches to the study of religion. As I have argued elsewhere, despite the ubiquity of gendering as a cultural practice, its significance within religious systems, and its foundational role in shaping human possibility and opportunity, gender has not been widely adopted as an essential analytical category by scholars of religion. Or put differently, "gender"—understood generally to pertain to studies of women—is tolerated, and perhaps even in some measure applauded as a necessary corrective, but it remains far and away "women's work."[35] The "expertise of the margins" thus created is arguably one of the reasons why feminist epistemologies have not been widely drawn upon by male scholars in the boundary debate over theology and religious studies.

Yet gender, and gender theory, remain enormously important areas for the study of religion. The category was deemed sufficiently significant that it found a place in both Braun and McCutcheon's *Guide* and Taylor's *Critical Terms*. Indeed, Daniel Boyarin produced the chapter for *Critical Terms*, giving an interesting reading of gender through the relationship between rabbinic Judaism and early Christianity, in contrast to the approach taken to my article on "Gender" for the *Guide*. As Darlene Juschka has noted, "gender" has become a frequently used term in the last decade and a half of the twentieth century, reflecting a paradigmatic shift. However, she cautions:

> ... what does this shift represent? The movement into gender analysis in the study of religion could be lauded for its apparent trend toward a more objective appreciation of gender as a facet of socio-historical change, particularly that related to religion (rather than using it either apologetically or politically), were it not for the suspicious juxta-

---

33   Braun/McCutcheon, eds. 2000; Taylor, ed. 1998.
34   Kramarae/Spender, eds. 1992.
35   Warne 2001.

position of this objectivizing tendency with the replacement of women and feminism by gender.[36]

The theoretical terrain that Juschka lays out thereafter may be challenging for the uninitiated, but it is precisely this kind of work that must be mainstreamed if gender-critical approaches to the study of religion are going to make an impact on critical debate in future. Happily, there are an increasing number of male scholars whose work reflects facility in the myriad debates this category generates. Whether Juschka's *political* point will be taken, however, remains unanswered (i.e., that gender has been adopted as a "safe" term that by implication naturalizes bodily sex and the hierarchies and disciplines imposed upon it). Even feminist scholars are vulnerable to this criticism. Unfortunately, given some of the theoretical baggage within feminist scholarship itself, widespread support for gender-critical and feminist studies of religion is not as strong as it could, or needs to be.[37]

These cautions should not be read as undercutting the significance of the work that has been done by and about women, men, and gender theory over the last twenty years. While much of that work has been done outside of the field of religious studies (see for example, the range of articles in Juschka's anthology), important new volumes have been produced within it.[38] What the vitality of the field requires, however, is that gender-critical approaches to the study of religion (as well as studies of particular gendered experiences and cultural dynamics) must be truly mainstreamed, so that competence in this area is no longer seen as an "Other," a particular kind of specialization, but simply one of the expected analytical tools of *all* practitioners of the trade.

Postcolonialism and the Study of Religion

"Religion" and its study are bound up with colonialism and imperialism, and the expansion of western Euro-North American culture throughout the world. Reflections upon this history, and its implications for the study of religion gathered steam increasingly through the 1990s, both within North American scholarship and elsewhere.[39] To the extent that academic conversation continues to expand its global parameters, the future impact of postcolonialism on the study of religion can be expected to continue in significance. In addition to historicizing and contextualizing foundational definitions in the field (what constitutes "religion"; descriptors like "primitive religion"), adopting a postco-

---

36 Juschka 1999.
37 See Warne 1995.
38 For two disparate examples, see Joy et al., eds. 2002; Haddad/Esposito, eds. 1998.
39 Chidester 1996.

lonial perspective requires a foundational reassessment of the theoretical frameworks of the "founding fathers," as bound up with parochial assumptions of Western cultural superiority. Further, the gendered character of such discourses and the assumed primacy of "the" rational invite scholars to explore, indeed, reinvent/recreate the field anew.

In keeping with the concern expressed above about the mainstreaming of feminist and/or gender-critical approaches to religion, postcolonial perspectives provide a logical avenue for drawing in scholars unfamiliar with feminist analyses. Recognizing the Other—and the feminization and exoticization involved in its creation—may be a more immediately appreciable intellectual process than, say, reading Mary Daly's *Gyn/Ecology* or *Pure Lust*. Postcolonialism is also interesting in that its task is not simply destabilization and/or deconstruction, but rather moving beyond disruption to produce more adequate constructions—something that is harder to do, but arguably of longer-term benefit to the field.

One practical effect of postcolonialism has been to undercut traditional Western formulations of both philosophy of religion and of phenomenology. It throws into sharp relief Western assumptions about rationality and its power. Determining the ultimate nature of the universe/God looks very different when building from a non-Western set of assumptions.[40] This is not to claim that "the West" is undifferentiated, or all bad—but rather than being an intellectual technique of an elite (as goes the joke, there are no postmodernists without paychecks), postcoloniality is foundational to the lived experience of non-privileged and privileged alike.

Postcoloniality also has an interesting inflection to offer the debate about religious studies "vs." theology, insofar as the primacy (and alleged neutrality) of Western knowledges is called into question. The volume, *Postcolonialism, Feminism and Religious Discourse* is illustrative of this point.[41] Biblical scholars and systematic theologians are included along with specialists in Jewish studies, Indian ritual and narrative, Arabic studies, sociology, and religious studies. While this kind of a roster may appear to some to be a result of inadequate boundary maintenance, such a constellation of interests may also suggest that disciplinary boundaries are themselves not innocent of the enterprise of colonialization.

---

40   A postcolonial perspective also poses a challenge to comparative approaches that assume that there are universal, culturally neutral categories that underlie the particularities of all religious phenomena and experience. For a sophisticated engagement with comparison in the study of religion, see *Method and Theory in the Study of Religion* (2004).

41   Donaldson/Pui-lan, eds. 2002.

A related issue is an increasing focus in North America on indigeneity,[42] including the religious and cultural traditions of North American indigenous peoples. The articles in the Quebec volume noted above are an example of this trend, as are the several texts assessed in the July 2003 (vol. 29, 3) edition of *Religious Studies Review*. The destruction of native cultures over the last several centuries, attempts to reclaim agency, and the dangers of romanticizing an idealized, non-existent past make this enterprise a challenging one, but also one that promised to generate important work of import for the profession overall. The recent work of Yale-trained, mainstream, established church historian, Justo Gonzalez, serves as an excellent example of the transformation effected by postcoloniality. Author of over seventy books, a number of them widely used as standard textbooks, Gonzalez dramatically describes how growing up as a Protestant in Cuba, his intellectual imagination was initially formed along Cartesian lines of "objectivity" and "universalizability":

> That was the mental map with which most of us grew up. It was the mental map of the modern age. It was the mental map that made it possible for me to read a book such as Hoffet's *Protestant Imperialism* and simply accept the judgement of an Alsatian pastor over my own culture, blaming all our political, economic, and social shortcomings on that culture, claiming that the Protestant North Atlantic was much better in all respects, and claiming further that the reason for this was the Protestant faith. In a word, I had been internally colonized by a mental world map in which there could be only one rational, objectively better, universally valid way of doing things, of seeing the world, and of organizing life. And that one rational, objectively better, universally valid way was the way of the Protestant North Atlantic.[43]

Relinquishing that map—a process of years of imaginative undoing—has generated, for Gonzalez and others, a more richly textured, polycentric cartography that does not completely jettison past constructions and dynamics, but rather recontextualizes and reinterprets them. Perhaps one of the most exciting aspects of postcolonial explorations is their capacity to bring fresh questions—and hence, intellectual life—to the conventional wisdom of the past.

Religion and Culture/Cultural Studies

Another growth area in the study of religion in North America is religion and culture, sometimes named as Cultural Studies. Studies along this axis range from the theory-driven-to-the-point-of-jargon pieces decried by Mark

---

42   See, for example, Olupona 2004.
43   González 2002: 51–52.

Hulsether to a plethora of texts on religion and popular culture.[44] Many of the articles and texts of recent years are the products of scholars not in the field of religious studies proper—for example, historians, literary critics, sociologists, and the like. There are important contributions being made by scholars like Colleen McDannell, whose *Material Christianity* is a masterful analysis of nineteenth century material artefacts of Christian kitsch.[45] Religion and leisure/ entertainment is another growth area, as with Lynn Marks' widely praised *Revivals and Roller Rinks: Religion, Leisure, and Identity in Late-Nineteenth-Century Small-Town Ontario.*[46] Identity (a theme also addressed by Marks) is at the center of studies by American cultural historian and religious studies professor Edward T. Linenthal, whose early work on American heroes has moved into studies of American sacred space, museum memorials, and more recently, the Oklahoma City bombings.[47]

Another area of exploration that has emerged is that of internet culture. Lorne Dawson's chapter in this volume explores some of the theoretical implications of this new reality. Exciting new work is also being done by newer scholars like Chris Klassen whose work on being a witch in cyber-space takes religious studies into a realm few could have imagined two decades ago.[48] Bruce Lincoln's sophisticated theoretical analysis of the implications of the events of September 11, 2001 presents yet another facet of the study of religion and culture, demonstrating both Lincoln's inestimable skill and the richness of religion and culture as an area for present and future scholarship.[49]

The Material Conditions of Knowledge Production

While it has not always been acknowledged in academic life, the conditions under which scholarship is undertaken materially shapes what is (and what is able to be) produced. The ideal of the academy as a "marketplace of ideas" in which "the free play of the intellect" is the order of the day is easily recognizable as an ideological fairytale for any but those at the uppermost reaches of privilege. In reality, politics, at both the macro and micro levels, govern much of academic life. Intellectual investigation is linked directly to sources of

---

44 See, for example, Mizruchi 2001; Garber/Walkowitz, eds. 1999; Williams 1999; Mazur/McCarthy 2001. For a useful overview of the value of cultural studies for the study of religion, see Sands 2002.
45 McDannell 1995.
46 Marks 1996.
47 See, for example, Linenthal/Englehardt 1996; also Linenthal/Chidester 1995; Linenthal 2003.
48 Klassen 2002.
49 Lincoln 2003.

funding and the "merit-market" they create, and important and intellectually sound perspectives are often forcefully resisted because their acceptance would disrupt existing academic hierarchies. It is useful, therefore, to ask what material conditions have affected scholarship in North America between 1980 and the turn of the twenty-first century.

At the outset, it is important to note that the conditions of academic employment vary widely throughout North America. Some faculty are unionized, some have faculty associations, and some have no collective voice at all, so that individual professors negotiate directly with administrators for salaries and the like. Remuneration for workload is by no means standardized, and salary differences of thousands (and thousands) of dollars for faculty at the same rank and accomplishment is not uncommon. Teaching loads also vary widely. For example, when I taught at the University of Wisconsin-Oshkosh in the mid-1990s, the standard teaching load was 4/4—that is, each professor taught four different courses—in each of two terms, to a total of eight. Because the department I was in was considered a "research department" (that is, the majority of department members were active scholars with strong publication records), the Dean granted a collective reduction in teaching load, to 3/3. A 3/3 load is at the high end for schools in Canada, where full-time faculty at some of the larger institutions may teach 2/2, or even 2/1 (these schools often have graduate programs, so that faculty have supervisory responsibilities over graduate students as well as course responsibilities).

Increasingly, there has been a tendency towards a "two-tier" model, where full-time professors enjoy considerably greater privileges than the part-time and/or stipendary scholars who end up teaching the high enrolment "bread and butter" courses, usually at the lower levels. In a competitive marketplace, the benefits of a salary and getting teaching experience are offset by having less and less time—and no institutional or financial support—to do research. Scholars in this position are faced with two equally unattractive options. Either they have the opportunity to stay at one institution, in permanent second (or worse)-class, or they can become "gypsy scholars," moving from place to place for short-term contracts, with the hope that they will find a department in which their expertise is sufficiently valued that their position may be turned into a tenure-track position—for which they can then compete.

Opportunities for faculty in North America to establish active and stable scholarly careers are thus marked by significant inequality. While the argument from merit may be mounted—that is, the "best and the brightest" are hired by the best schools, and rewarded accordingly, is a somewhat less than charming remnant of past eras of prior privilege, when universities were the exclusive province of the economic and cultural elite. The politics of the academy aside, the economic realities of North America were such that, for a very long period beginning in the mid-to-late 1970s and abating only now, good academic jobs were few and far between. The academic market recovered somewhat earlier in the United States than it did in Canada, but the circumstances in either case were bleak. Either there were no jobs at all to be had, or the number of qualified applicants for any given position numbered in the hundreds. The practical effect of a paralyzed job market upon academic fields and generations has been significant.

One straightforward effect was the loss of innumerable promising and qualified scholars to academic life. Some ended up eking out a living at the margins, teaching courses here and there, or else working in related capacities while trying to maintain some kind of research profile. It is not incidental that the hiring freeze occurred just as feminist scholarship was gathering considerable energy and profile. It is interesting to consider how the field might be different, had positions been open in sufficient numbers, and more feminist scholars hired. As noted previously, new approaches to scholarship need to be institutionalized if they are to fully develop and shape the field in foundational ways. For North American scholars of religion in the last two decades of the twentieth century, this meant facing a series of grim realities: cutbacks to post-secondary education funding from governments; a tiered employment system that exacerbated differences in opportunity and sheer quality of life between permanent and temporary faculty; a "lost generation" of scholars, leaving departments, and disciplines, with a considerable gap of scholars in mid-career range; and institutional vulnerability, as this destabilization allowed for new agendas to begin to shape academic life in the twenty-first century.

The remainder of this section will briefly consider two of these, one in Canada and one in the United States. While there are commonalities in North American life, as has been noted above, there are also important discontinuities. A useful resource in this regard is Michael Adams' *Fire and Ice: The United States, Canada and the Myth of Converging Values*. Adams' data on the different place of religion in each national culture is particularly important for our topic, and more will be said on this point below. Here, it is enough to say that each of these new agendas has the power to wreak considerable damage on the traditional academy, and the study of religion within it.

The Canadian Scene: Corporatization of the University?

What is a university *for*? At the end of the twentieth century in Canada, the answer to that question was increasingly framed in instrumental terms. For students, the purpose of a university education was to get a job at the end of it. For scholars and researchers, the purpose was to generate an intellectual product someone could use. Knowledge for its own sake, or even knowledge whose application is not immediately apparent, were seemingly considered luxuries of the past. There was a great deal of talk about "new realities" — the so-called "Information Highway" and/or "the Knowledge Economy" — with the continued exhortation that universities need to change in fundamental ways to keep up with these new realities. Instead of knowledge that produces an educated citizenry and a rich and vibrant culture, research needs to have direct application to "research users:" according to a pamphlet circulated in 2003 by the Social Sciences and Humanities Research Council (SSHRC), "knowledge utilization" is the order of the day.[50]

Some fear that the Canadian academic scene is in serious danger of becoming instrumentalized and corporatized under the rhetoric of "relevance" in research. Universities are now developing "business plans" in which Deans and other administrators are envisioned as CEOs whose task is to "grow their units." The government of Canada has implemented a program of what it calls "Canada Research Chairs," or CRCs. In accordance with size and mandate, universities are accorded a certain number of these positions, the purpose of which is it produce "excellence" in research, through supporting research programs that will be relevant and useful (it is claimed) to Canadians overall. Chairs are disproportionately granted in the sciences and professional programs, at large universities. To date only 18% of CRCs have been awarded to women.

The practical effect on the academic study of religion of initiatives like the CRC program, and the disposition it reflects, is serious. In the past, universities tended to allocate their resources along traditional disciplinary lines, filling positions as they became vacant, to maintain a diversity of disciplinary expertise. Under an instrumentalist agenda, resources are much more likely to be allocated to "bang for your buck" research, with its significance determined not by researchers within the academic community, but by "knowledge utilizers" outside of it. Scholars of religion fare poorly under this aegis. Merged departments are but one symptom of what some fear will be a gutting of the traditional academy in the service of commerce. Disciplinary integrity carries little cachet in this environment, particularly given the emphasis on inter- and multi-disciplinarity in research. While in itself, this latter concern might fairly be seen to bolster the study of religion, in fact its problematic status within the academy has yielded a different result.

The fact that within the first decade of the twenty-first century approximately one-third of the faculty at Canadian universities is set to retire is cause for further concern. University departments of religion/religious studies in

---

50 *From Granting Council to Knowledge Council: Renewing the Social Sciences and Humanities in Canada* (2003). Subsequent to a widespread consultation process with universities, SSHRC released its *Report on the Transformation of the Social Sciences and Humanities Research Council of Canada* on May 17, 2004, available on its website, which appears more congenial to the traditional academy in its affirmation of the importance of foundational research in knowledge development. Whether the recommendations of the *Report* will be supported by the government remains to be seen.

Canada have already been hit with the dearth of hirings in the 1980s and 1990s; when senior faculty retire, entire programs could be decimated. It remains to be seen how this reality will unfold.

The American Scene: "Homeland Security" and the Threat to Academic Freedom

The November-December 2003 issue (Vol. 89, 6) of the American Association of University Professors (AAUP) featured a Report of an AAUP Special Committee entitled "Academic Freedom and National Security in a Time of Crisis." The AAUP committee was formed on September 11, 2002, and had as its mandate "assessing risks to academic freedom and free inquiry posed by the nation's response to the attacks on the World Trade Center and the Pentagon."[51] According to the findings of the committee, these risks have been considerable. One vital area of concern has been the impact of the "hastily enacted" USA Patriot Act, namely "the ominous mingling of law-enforcement and intelligence-gathering activities, the impairment of public access to vital information, and the questionable efficacy of these measures in combating terrorism. Specific concerns include the loosening of standards under which the government authorities can compel disclosure of electronic communications."[52] Under the act, federal agents can obtain warrants to determine the books people buy or take out of libraries, with minimal reason; moreover, persons served with such warrants are prohibited from revealing that fact. Another concern treated centrally in the report is restriction on information, and the "elusive category of 'sensitive but unclassified' information."[53] In the view of the AAUP, treatment of unclassified information is the responsibility of the scientific community, not the government.

　　Further concerns have to do with the treatment of non-national/foreign scholars and students (increased restrictions on admission of such persons) and "the apparent expansion of academic subjects and foreign nations to which intensive surveillance applies."[54] Silencing of open debate on campus has been another product of the post 9/11 political climate in the United States. Incidents of suppression of free speech have occurred both with regard to university employed faculty, and with visiting speakers. While mindful of the importance of being sensitive to the situation, the committee's position is best summarized as follows:

51　"Academic Freedom and National Security in a Time of Crisis" (2003).
52　Ibid.: 34.
53　Ibid.: 35.
54　Ibid.

The report rests on the premise that freedom of inquiry and the open exchange of ideas are crucial to the nation's security, and that the nation's security and, ultimately its well-being are damaged by practices that discourage or impair freedom. Measures to ensure the nation's safety against terrorism should therefore be implemented with no greater constraint on our liberties than is necessary ... We contend that in these critical times the need is for more freedom, not less.[55]

The implications of the subject of the report on academic life in the United States are chilling; moreover, given the nature of the conflict and its construction(s), they are of particular import for scholars of religion. Will scholars of Islam—and scholars who are Muslim—have the freedom to express dissenting opinions, or even alternate interpretations of what may be happening in the United States' involvement in Iraq, or Afghanistan? Will such views be seen as "unpatriotic" and therefore worthy of censure (or worse)? Clearly, the AAUP considers these to be perilous times for academic life in the United States, a context that cannot help but shape the possibilities for the academic study of religion within it.

The situation is complicated by the religious makeup of the American population. As author Gertrude Himmelfarb has noted, religiosity in the United States is on the rise, and it is primarily conservative. She says of fundamentalism:

The movement as a whole—about 60 million people in 1988 ... about a fifth of the adult population—is dominated by the fundamentalist, pentecostal, and charismatic Protestant denominations (generally lumped together under the label 'evangelical'); but it also includes as many as 20 million members of the mainline Protestant churches, 6 million 'born-again' Catholics, and almost 5 million Mormons. [56]

In fact, "[a] 2002 Pew Research Center poll found religion to be important to 59 percent of Americans—the highest proportion in all the developed nations surveyed."[57] In contrast, Canadians logged in at around 30%, a percentage comparable to Great Britain and Italy.

Also unlike Canadians, who according to Adams are more like Europeans in their "postmodern" secularism, Americans are also increasingly deferential to and supportive of patriarchal authority. Adams claims:

In 1996, 26 per cent of Canadians told us that men are naturally superior to women, while 30 percent of Americans felt the same way ... By 2000, the proportion in Canada stood at 24 per cent while that in the U.S. shot up to 38 per cent. It only stands to reason, many Americans seem to be telling us, that if God-fearing men are the superior beings on this planet, then they should certainly be the bosses in their own homes.[58]

---

55 Ibid.: 34.
56 Himmelfarb, quoted in Adams 2003: 40.
57 Adams 2003: 50.
58 Ibid.: 51.

Adams' study on the differences between Canadian and American cultures is worthy of consideration for a variety of reasons. For our purposes here, his findings suggest that academic colleagues in the study of religion may be facing somewhat different challenges in the years to come. What must be acknowledged in both instances, however, is that academic debates on the legitimacy of, and acceptable approaches to, the study of religion cannot be assessed in isolation from the social, cultural, economic, and political contexts within which they are found.

Conclusion

As we have seen, the last two decades of the twentieth century have yielded creative and important debates about the academic study of religion. Once dominant schools of thought, like phenomenology, have become contested, with new approaches like feminism, postmodernism and the like staking out their turf. That no consensus has been reached on "the" best approach to the study of religion may be considered one of the field's greatest strengths. Some-times—perhaps always—the most creative and intellectually challenging work is that which is done when paradigms proliferate. It is in the interstices between theories that exciting new insights are sought and found, and in engaging contradictions that new concepts are generated. While undoubtedly, and seriously, challenged by the contexts of academic work in North America at the turn of the century, the vitality of the study of religion, and its promise for the future, is evident, and its support and engagement all the more required thereby.

Bibliography

"Academic Freedom and National Security in a Time of Crisis" (2003), reprinted from *Academe* 89 (6) November-December. Available at: www.aaup.org/statements/REPORTS/Post9-11.pdf.

Adams, Michael (2003), *Fire and Ice: The United States, Canada, and the Myth of Converging Values*. Toronto: Penguin.

Allen, Charlotte (1996), "Is Nothing Sacred? Casting Out the Gods from Religious Studies," in: *Lingua Franca*, November.

Badertscher, John et al., eds. (1993), *Religious Studies in Manitoba and Saskatchewan: A State-of-the-Art Review*. Waterloo: Wilfrid Laurier University Press.

Bowlby, Paul, with Faulkner, Tom (2001), *Religious Studies in Atlantic Canada: A State-of-the-Art Review*. Waterloo: Wilfrid Laurier University Press.

Braun, Willi/McCutcheon, Russell, eds. (2000), *Guide to the Study of Religion*. London/New York: Cassell.

Chidester, David (1996), *Savage Systems*. Charlottesville, Va.: University Press of Virginia Press.

Despland, Michel/Rousseau, Louis (1988), *The Study of Religion in Quebec: A State-of-the-Art Review*. Waterloo: Wilfrid Laurier University Press.

Donaldson, Laura E./Pui-lan, Kwok (2002), *Postcolonialism, Feminism and Religious Discourse*. New York/London: Routledge.

Downs, Laura Lee (1993), "If `Woman' is Just an Empty Category, Then Why Am I Afraid to Walk Alone at Night? Identity Politics Meets the Postmodern Subject," in: *Comparative Studies in Society and History* 35.

Fitzgerald, Timothy (2000), *The Ideology of Religious Studies*. New York: Oxford University Press.

Fraser, Brian (1995), *The Study of Religion in British Columbia: A State-of-the-Art Review*. Waterloo: Wilfrid Laurier University Press.

From Granting Council to Knowledge Council: Renewing the Social Sciences and Humanities in Canada (2003), SSHRC pamphlet, fall.

Garber, Marjorie/Walkowitz, Rebecca L., eds. (1999), *One Nation Under God? Religion and American Culture*. New York: Routledge.

González, Justo L. (2002), *The Changing Shape of Church History*. St. Louis, Mo.: Chalice Press.

Gray, Edward, "Highlights," in: *Religion and Theology Programs Census*: www.aarweb. org.

Haddad, Yvonne Yazbeck/Esposito, John, eds. (1998), *Islam, Gender, and Social Change*. New York: Oxford University Press.

Harding, Sandra (1991), *Whose Science? Whose Knowledge?* Ithaca, N.Y.: Cornell.

—— ed. (1993), *The "Racial" Economy of Science*. Bloomington, Ind.: Indiana University Press.

—— (1998), *Is Science Multicultural?* Bloomington, Ind.: Indiana University Press.

Hart, D.G. (1999), *The University Gets Religion* . Baltimore, Md.: Johns Hopkins.

Joy, Morny et al., eds. (2002), *French Feminists on Religion: A Reader*. London: Routledge.

Juschka, Darlene (1999), "The Category of Gender in the Study of Religion," in: *Method and Theory in the Study of Religion* 11 (1).

—— ed. (2001), *Feminism in the Study of Religion*. London: Continuum.

Klassen, Chris (2002), "Cybercoven: Being a Witch online," in: *Studies in Religion/ Sciences Religieuses* 31 (1).

Kramarae, Cheris/Spender, Dale, eds. (1992), *The Knowledge Explosion*. New York: Teachers College Press.

Larouche, Jean-Marc/Ménard, Guy, eds. (2001), *L'étude de la religion au Québec: Bilan et prospective*. St. Foy: Laval University Press.

Lincoln, Bruce (2003), *Holy Terrors*. Chicago: University of Chicago Press.

Linenthal, Edward T. (2003), *The Unfinished Bombing: Oklahoma City in American Memory*. New York: Oxford University Press.

Linenthal, Edward T./Chidester, David (1995), *American Sacred Space*. Bloomington, Ind.: Indiana University Press.

Linenthal, Edward T./Englehardt, Tom (1996), *History Wars*. New York: Metropolitan Books.

Longino, Helen (1990), *Science as Social Knowledge*. Princeton, N.J.: Princeton University Press.

Marks, Lynn (1996), *Revivals and Roller Rinks: Religion, Leisure, and Identity in Late-Nineteenth-Century Small-Town Ontario.* Toronto: University of Toronto Press.

Marsden, George (1994), *The Soul of the American University: From Protestant Establishment to Established Non-belief.* New York: Oxford University Press.

— (1997), *The Outrageous Idea of Christian Scholarship.* New York: Oxford University Press.

Marsden, George/Longfield, Bradley, eds. (1992), *The Secularization of the Academy.* New York: Oxford University Press.

Mazur, Eric/McCarthy, Kate, eds. (2001), *God in the Details.* New York: Routledge.

McCutcheon, Russell T. (1997), *Manufacturing Religion.* New York: Oxford University Press.

— ed. (1999), *The Insider/Outsider Debate in the Study of Religion.* London/New York: Cassell.

McDannell, Colleen (1995), *Material Christianity: Religion and Popular Culture in America.* New Haven, Conn.: Yale University Press.

Method and Theory in the Study of Religion (2004), vol. 16 (1).

Mizruchi, Susan, ed. (2001), *Religion and Cultural Studies.* Princeton, N.J./Oxford: Princeton University Press.

Neufeldt, Ronald W. (1983), *Religious Studies in Alberta: A State-of-the-Art Review.* The Study of Religion in Canada/Sciences Religieuses au Canada 1. Waterloo: Wilfrid Laurier University Press.

Olupona, Jacob, ed. (2004), *Beyond Primitivism: Indigenous Religious Traditions and Modernity.* New York/London: Routledge.

Religious Studies Review (2003), vol. 29 (3).

Remus, Harold et al., eds. (1992), *Religious Studies in Ontario: A State-of-the-Art Review.* Waterloo: Wilfrid Laurier University Press.

Rennie, Bryan (1996), *Reconstructing Eliade.* Albany, N.Y.: SUNY Press.

Rose, Hilary/Rose, Steven (1976), *The Political Economy of Science: Ideology of/in the Natural Sciences.* London: Macmillan.

— (1976), *The Radicalisation of Science: Ideology of/in the Natural Sciences.* London: Macmillan.

Sands, Kathleen (2002), "Tracking Religion: Religion through the Lens of Critical and Cultural Studies," in: *CSSR Bulletin* 31 (3) September.

Sardar, Ziauddin (1998), *Postmodernism and the Other: The New Imperialism of Western Culture.* London: Pluto Press.

Sardar, Ziauddin/Van Loon, Borin (2001), *Introducing Science.* Cambridge: Icon.

Smith, Jonathan Z. (1998), "Religion, Religions, Religious," in: *Critical Terms for Religious Studies,* ed. by Mark C. Taylor. Chicago: University of Chicago Press.

Taylor, Mark C., ed. (1998), *Critical Terms for Religious Studies.* Chicago: University of Chicago Press.

Tuana, Nancy, ed. (1989), *Feminism and Science.* Bloomington, Ind.: Indiana University Press.

Warne, Randi R. (1995), "Further Reflections on the Unacknowledged Quarantine: Feminism and Religious Studies," in: *Changing Methods: Feminists Transforming Practice,* ed. by Sandra Burt/Lorraine Code. Toronto: Broadview Press.

— (2000), "Gender," in: *Guide to the Study of Religion,* ed. by Willi Braun/Russell T. McCutcheon. London/New York: Cassell.

—— (2001), "(En)gendering Religious Studies," in: *Feminism in the Study of Religion*, ed. by Darlene Juschka. London: Continuum.

Wiebe, Donald (1999), *The Politics of Religious Studies*. New York: St. Martin's Press.

Williams, Peter W., ed. (1999), *Perspectives on American Religion and Culture*. Malden, Mass.: Routledge.

Wolfhart, Johannes (2000), "Postmodernism," in: *Guide to the Study of Religion*, ed. by Willi Braun/Russell T. McCutcheon. London: Cassell.

A Survey of New Approaches to the Study of Religion in Europe

by

PETER ANTES

To talk about new approaches in the study of religion in Europe is not an easy task, for newness is not a generally accepted classificatory category for research. It is, on the contrary, a highly contextual term. Consequently, before entering the subject and looking at the different eight contexts considered individually below, some preliminary remarks regarding these contexts are necessary.

1. The Diversity of Contexts in Europe

One of the most striking characteristics of Europe as a whole is its cultural diversity. This diversity finds its expression in both different languages and different academic traditions, and these have significant consequences for the study of religion.

1.1. Different Languages

From their inception up until the 1990s, the International Association for the History of Religions (IAHR) and its official organ *Numen* accepted four languages of scholarship, namely English, French, German, and Italian. These represented the main university traditions that contributed to the study of religion in Europe. European scholars from other areas such as the Netherlands, and northern or eastern European countries were required to adopt one of these four languages in order to join in academic debate. Fortunately, the school curricula of these countries guaranteed that all scholars were more or less able to cope with these linguistic requirements.

The situation has changed considerably in the meantime, in two different directions. On the one hand, knowledge of all four languages can no longer be supposed in the academic study of religion. Italian was the first loss, and is now widely unknown to many scholars in the field. But this is now increasingly true for French and German, such that, as is evident in more recent issues of *Numen*, English has become the predominant language of research. On the other hand, this general tendency towards a single academic language exists side by side with an increasing plurality of academic languages in use. This particularly applies to Spanish but it is also true for other languages less known in the academic world such as Catalan, Polish, Hungarian, or Modern Greek, in which valuable academic studies are published but which are usually beyond the linguistic capacities of the majority of scholars. As a consequence, the academic world is becoming more fragmented. Even with regard to French, Italian and German contexts, there are signs that insular academic worlds are developing. If so, this is a problem for the scholarly community as a whole, currently and even more so in future, if there are no ways to bridge these linguistic gaps effectively, either through more translations or through various kinds of information services in English such as the French *Bulletin Signalétique* or the English *Science of Religion Bulletin Abstracts*.

It may sound very pessimistic to speak of insular contexts but a close look at recent publications on theory in the study of religion shows that French books and articles rarely discuss German works that are not accessible in French or English translations. The same is true for German books and articles with regard to untranslated research work in French. In neither case are references usually made to publications in Italian. One is left with the impression that the only foreign publications that matter in the field are those published in English; all others may be ignored as parochial discussions without any relevance to the academic community as a whole. What has, until recently, been the case for lesser known languages like Polish, Hungarian, Finnish, or Modern Greek may soon also be the case for French and German.

The primary way to bridge the gap is through translations and to a lesser degree, through information services. In both cases, it is worth noting that the discussion of a book or article starts with the date of its being known to scholars. The publication of the original book/article and that of its translation may thus differ considerably. What is new in one context, may consequently not be so in another. Newness is thus context-specific, not a general standard in and of itself.

The study of religion in Europe is further context-specific as far as different academic traditions are concerned.

1.2. Different Academic Traditions

The study of religion is much more embedded in its respective contexts than most scholars tend to believe. This is so both for what is seen to constitute the study of religion and how that relates specifically to other disciplines, and to a more general understanding of religion and its contribution to education.

1.2.1. The Contents of the Study of Religion

A close look at the study of religion in Europe reveals two different conceptualizations of its appropriate content. There is a rather restrictive academic orientation found primarily in France and Italy, and a broader understanding of its tasks, found primarily in Germany, and in northern and eastern European countries.

The restrictive academic orientation concentrates solely on the "History of Religions," emphasizing the historical aspect in the study of religion to such a great extent that Sociology of Religion and Psychology of Religion are not considered subdisciplines within the study of religion. As a consequence, research parameters are circumscribed, leaving disciplines like Sociology of Religion and Psychology of Religion to establish themselves as independent disciplines with organizations of their own, seeking national and international representation outside the frame of IAHR. The practical effect of this circumscription is that, for the history of religions, only historical research methods are considered acceptable, and are presented as normatively constitutive of the discipline as such. Hence, new approaches do not emerge from interdisciplinary investigation but are mainly influenced by the methods used in history departments. These shape scholarship to the degree that broader approaches to studying single religious traditions or general theorizing about religion are not undertaken. As a result, new approaches to the study of religion are much less frequent in the restrictive orientation to the study of religion than where it is more broadly conceived.

A broader conceptualization of religion embraces all its forms of manifestation. It focuses on the history of religions as well as on sociology of religion and psychology of religion. It is indeed the German concept of "Religionswissenschaft" that has no disciplinary boundaries and welcomes all types of studies of religion across a range of university disciplines. Consequently, this approach to the study of religion is a multi-disciplinary enterprise, with obviously greater potential for new approaches than in the restrictive orientation described above.

1.2.2. The Specificity of the Study of Religion with Regard to Other Disciplines

European countries differ widely in how the study of religion relates to other university disciplines. A key problem is defining its relation to theology where faculties of theology coexist with the study of religion. In Germany tensions between the two have shaped the debate for a long time, and indeed have increased in more recent methodological discussion as theology and the study of religion have begun to cross boundaries to enter each other's field. Ongoing discussion shows that new approaches have an influence on both, and challenge both, in their attempts to define more concretely what they are doing, particularly in terms of methodology. In northern European countries the relationship between theology and the study of religion is less conflicted because of the strong influence of the study of religion on Christian theology in these regions. Similar observations can be made for the Netherlands and the Flemish speaking part of Belgium. In the United Kingdom, the study of religion and theology seem to coexist without conflict. As in most of the universities of the USA, in the United Kingdom (though much less frequently in Canada), we find departments of theology and religious studies that encompass both disciplines without making any clear distinction between the two, at least not in terms of methodology.

In France, Italy and Spain, the study of religion is conceived as independent from theology although the concrete forms of this independence vary from country to country. Here, the study of religion mainly concentrates on particular religions or denominations, and movements taking place within one religion. Consequently, linguistic preparation is strongly emphasized and combined with historical research while contemporary analyses of religion are often left for scholars of sociology and political science. The study of religion is therefore found in close relationship to languages (with a certain preference for classical and oriental languages) and history as a discipline. Socio-empirical research is less associated with the study of religion and relegated to other disciplines such as sociology of religion and psychology of religion.

1.2.3. The General Understanding of Religion

The proximity of the study of religion and Christian theology has led to a positive understanding of religion as the experience of the holy. Even where the historical record of various traditions gives evidence of cruelty, inhumanity, and other forms of violence, religion *as such* is rarely associated with predominantly negative characteristics. Consequently, the relation between religion and crime is not really taken as a topic of research in the study of religion. The discipline was thus ill-prepared to respond in the 1990s when more and more governments and political parties called for help to discuss allegations and challenges that society saw in so-called new religious movements.

The political debate about new religious movements has shown that there is no unanimity among scholars of the study of religion as to which movements should be studied (in particular within Christianity) and which criteria should be applied to assess them. As a consequence, debate on this issue is more determined by the context in which it is undertaken than by any overarching framing of the question by the study of religion in general.

1.2.4. The Contribution to Education

There are also differences in Europe with regard to educational requirements and the study of religion. In France, for example, religious education is completely excluded from the school curriculum. Many other countries include it however, and in most of these cases religious education is even compulsory. In these instances, the study of religion is undertaken as an alternative to or substitute for religious education organized by religious communities, and does not represent the commitments of any particular tradition. Where religious education is in the hands of religious communities, the study of religion in school curricula is extremely rare or is so circumscribed as to have no general significance for our discussion.

Involvement in school programs requires the study of religion to fulfill tasks that do not exist in other contexts. It has to select and provide appropriate material to meet the specific demands of the society it serves, something that is not required in countries where such an involvement does not take place. Obviously, such demands inform academic debate, leading in many cases to insights and results that would not have emerged without these context-specific challenges. The following eight context by context descriptions emphasize, therefore, not only what is being worked on and how that is done, but also the need to see this work within the framework of the debate that is typical of each of the contexts under consideration.

2. The French Context

France, together with the French speaking part of Belgium, is an area where, in spite of some other traditions in Alsace-Lorraine and in the French-speaking cantons of Switzerland, the restrictive orientation is predominant in the study of religion. Moreover, the whole concept of the study of religion is marked by a strong laicist tendency that strongly demarcates it from all types of Christian theology in both teaching and research. The restrictive understanding of the study of religion finds its most visible expression in the fifth section of the Ecole des Hautes Etudes in Paris and to some extent in the Collège de France of Paris, where the study of religion is combined with history and languages. Neither comparative nor socio-empirical approaches are found in this context, in spite of Meslin's call for multi-disciplinary studies in the field. The sixth section of the Ecole des Hautes Etudes in Paris, on the contrary, is dedicated to socio-empirical studies, including sociology of religion.

The consequence of this division of labor is that the study of religion in its historical perspective follows the rules of research as commonly adopted in oriental languages and history departments. This means that Islam, Hinduism, Buddhism, Taoism, Shintoism and so forth are studied as single religions in their respective linguistic and historical contexts. Often, however, studies are even more specialized, concentrating on specific movements within these religions. Because of the emphasis on language skills, comprehensive studies on Islam as such are relatively rare and if done, they exist primarily in form of collective works with specialist contributions from each contributor's field of research. If sufficient source material is available, these studies satisfy the interests of intellectual history. On the whole, the methods used are classical in the good sense of the term, not significantly different from those used in the past. The same is true for Judaism and Christianity with the difference that, in particular for the latter, studies are subdivided not only with regard to language but also according to chronological periods such as early Christianity, medieval Christianity and so forth.

The restrictive orientation of the study of religion is the reason why socio-empirical analyses of present-day Christianity in France, or the study of France as a multi-cultural society in which specific trends within Islam are represented, is mainly a subject for sociology of religion or political science, but rarely for the history of religions as such. It is therefore not surprising that the scholars of history of religions were practically absent from the debate of the so called "foulard" issue of 1989 (i.e. the debate about whether Muslim girls in French state owned schools would be prohibited from wearing headscarves, on the ground that they were a form of propagation of faith, thus violating the laicist principle of French schools). In contrast, sociologists of religion like Emile Poulat or specialists of political science like Gilles Kepel played an active role in the debate.

The restrictive orientation, with its emphasis on specific language skills and historic contexts, is also the reason why comparative studies are rarely undertaken in the study of religion if they go beyond the narrow boundaries set by this frame. For example, studies on Islam in general are rare, and even more so comparative studies that consider more than one religion. What is, for instance, very common in Germany, the Netherlands or the United Kingdom, namely comparative volumes on founders of religions, general surveys about the religions of the world, can hardly be found on the French book market (exemptions from the rule are books like Baladier's). Thematic studies, common in other countries, addressing the concept of evil, the afterlife, or God in different religions, are also extremely rare. Where they are found, they are generally not comprehensive overviews but rather a collection of highly specialized treatments by scholars working within their narrow areas of specialization. It seems that comparative studies on a broader scale are not taken as serious research work worthy of the discipline. Thus culturally defended self-limitations are responsible for the books and articles found in this context.

New approaches are found in the field of sociology, where a shift from ethnology to sociology has taken place. The shift as such is not new in France where ethnology and sociology have always had strong links with each other, thus—if we think of authors like Emile Durkheim or Claude Lévi-Strauss—distinguishing French sociology from that practiced in other West European contexts. What is new is the analysis of human behavior in everyday contemporary life situations in terms of rites and rituals. Hence, according to Claude Rivière, the rules of daily school life, of hygiene, eating, drinking, sports and so forth are nothing else but "profane rites" in a secularized society that fulfill the same functions and needs as religious rites in premodern African societies. This form of sacralization of profane existence parallels the forms of sacralization found in non-religious societies described by Albert Piette. His interest is to show that secular society has kept and sometimes recreated religious symbols for secular phenomena. One need only think of the former Soviet Union and its cult of the heroes of the Revolution, the veneration of the corpses of Lenin and Mao Tze Tung, the catechisms of atheism and many other signs of quasi-religious adoration in spite of an officially atheist doctrine of the state. Similar examples can be detected in all secular societies. Thanks to this new approach, secular and religious societies seem to have much more in common than might otherwise be expected. They resemble each other considerably in their rituals but they differ from each other with regard to belief and conceptual framework. The rediscovery of the importance of rites might, therefore, help to generate a new understanding of processes going on in society that are obscured or distorted in approaching non-religious and religious societies with an exclusive focus on differences in belief.

The study of religion in France has not made a significant contribution to the question of how to cope with new religious movements. Nor has France ever been forced to provide school material on religion(s) because of its clear stand in favor of a laicist school system that prohibits any religious education at all.

3. Italy

Like France, Italy also employs a restrictive orientation of the discipline. Sociology of religion is practiced independently, and phenomenology of religion is usually more related to theology than it is to the history of religions.

One of the most influential scholars in the field of the history of religions in Italy over several decades in the second half of the twentieth century was Ugo Bianchi. He formulated the difference between theology and the history of religions by saying,

> theology can be defined as the critical self-consciousness of the Church, and Biblical theology as well as ecclesiastical history can be defined as the scientific apparatus in which the living memory of the Church is clad; as for the history of religions, its main methodological tenet and presupposition consists in the use of critical-historical

methodology which implies the possibility of intersubjective scientific permeability
between all those who share that specific methodology (1989: 51).

Consequently, for Bianchi the understanding of the history of religions is, as in
France, laicist, and he insists on intersubjective scientific controllability as one
of its main characteristics. According to him, however,

> the history of religions is far from being a merely descriptive and philological
> discipline. It is comparative-historical and cultural-historical. As such, the history of
> religions fits in perfectly with the holistic treatment of religious data. We mean holistic
> in the sense that the cultural-historical treatment is most appropriate for the study not
> only of the different functions of religion in a culture or a society but also of the whole
> contents of religion in that particular culture and society, without being a priori
> selective and a priori reductive due to theoretical reasons. At the same time, the
> comparative-historical setting of the history of religions on a plenatory scale makes it
> impossible or difficult to neglect any real aspect and any possible motivation of religion
> in the vast scope of the cultures of the world, all the more so since we are prepared to
> consider the notion of religion as an analogical, not a univocal concept: I mean an
> analogical concept which covers realities, whose continuities and discontinuities can
> reach to the same depth. It is clear that the multiplicity and partial dyshomogeneity of
> the religious manifestations on our planet will discourage any overhasty and general
> explanatory endeavour concerning religion and religions (ibid.: 50).

Research work in the history of religions should therefore be based on
historical data but Bianchi understands this in a very broad sense, suggesting
that archeological and anthropological material should also be included in this
type of study. He thus is open, at least theoretically, to more perspectives than
most of his disciples who—with the exception of Giovanni Casadio—have
rarely gone beyond the frame of ancient history which is the main field for
most historians of religions in Italy. Though orientalists like Alessandro
Bausani were leading representatives of Italy's history of religions, the
discipline seems to be dominated by scholars who concentrate on ancient
History, focussing on the Roman Empire and its religious diversity of which
Christianity is a part, and hence worthy of being taken into consideration in
these studies in the manner Bianchi advocated. In this respect it might suffice to
consult the most prestigious encyclopedia published in Italian: *Enciclopedia delle
Religioni*.

In Italy, sociology of religion is undertaken within the discipline of Sociology. Here, the empirical research of scholars like Vincenzo Cesareo, Roberto
Cipriani et al. is of great value. The same is true for more historically oriented
studies of sociology of religion such as those of Arnaldo Nesti. Moreover, Enzo
Pace's work on the sociology of Islam and the review *Religioni e Società* provide
a good perspective on the studies being done in this field. The latter concentrates on themes of particular relevance to Italy during the last 200 years with
considerable emphasis on current developments. In all this it is less the methodological approach that is new than the results of the research, that show that

Italy is also highly affected by secularization and a slowly noticeable process of dechristianization as it is found more significantly in Germany and other central European countries.

In the field of phenomenology of religion, the works of Aldo Natale Terrin are noteworthy. In his book on rituals he tries to describe the forms of rites in music, dancing, theatre and games in order to demonstrate human reality in a holistic perspective. His aim is to thus find a new approach to religion through these phenomena that will open new ways for religious practice in the Church instead of insisting on dogma as the main reference for religiosity. It seems that in the Roman Catholic Church in Italy the distinction between theology and history of religions is not of great concern. On the contrary, there is a great readiness to take benefit from all types of research available regardless of the source, as widely documented in the bibliography of the collective work edited by Giuseppe Lorizio. There, studies on religions are integrated into fundamental theology to show human religious development either in the light of interreligious dialogue or with the perspective of the culmination of religious thought in Christian theology. The book also makes wide use of translations into Italian in the field of the history of religions. Thus, foreign contributions to the discipline meet with positive engagement if accessible in Italian.

What is not yet developed in Italy is alternative education to Church related religious education. In legal terms the alternative is already anticipated; its practical realization, however, is still to come. As a result, there is no demand as yet for school material on religions, so it remains nonexistent on the market as well as in the school material programs of publishers.

4. Spain

Spain has moved forward a great deal in the field of the history of religions in the 1990s through the foundation of the Spanish Association for the history of religions, the publications of its *Bulletin* (since 1993) and of *'Ilu (revista de ciencias de las religiones* [Madrid: Complutense] since 1995), as well as through the establishment of postgraduate courses in the University Complutense of Madrid and some other universities of the Peninsula and in Tenerifa (cf. Díez de Velasco 1995).

It is noteworthy that the first issues of the *Bulletin* of the Spanish Association were dedicated to problems of methods, by giving an overview of what was done in other countries. Both the restrictive and the broader orientations of the discipline were thus included in the debate. Through the influence of Latin American research in the fields of anthropology and ethnology there is also a great appreciation of these approaches as a legitimate part of the study of religions. The same applies to the academic study of popular religiosity. It is significant that the term *ciencias de las religiones* (sciences of religions) was chosen in Spain instead of the restrictive concept of the "history of religions."

A wide range of research topics is documented in the different issues of *'Ilu* and shows that most of the scholars, who are specialists either of ancient history or of oriental languages, engage new fields of research covering the history of religious thought of humankind as a whole, as in the very impressive handbooks on the history of religions by Carlos Díaz and Francisco Diez de Velasco (1998). As in Díaz' handbook, studies on new religious movements and sects are also part of the study of religions in Spain whereas in other parts of Europe those studies are rarely found in the discipline and often left to church related institutions. The range of specific subjects is remarkably wide, from ancient mythology, through religion on the internet, to problems of how to bring religion(s) into schools where an alternative to church related religious education (cf. Díez de Velasco 1999) has yet to be instituted.

Sociology of religion mainly concentrates on the situation of the Roman Catholic Church in Spain and the question of how strong religious practice and faith are in present-day Spain. Empirical studies are regularly published in this field, as shown in studies by Norberto Alcover, Juan González-Anleo, Pedro González Blasco, Andrés Tornos and many others. They all agree that there is a significant decline in knowledge about Christianity and the Christian creed as well as in religious practice and acceptance of church related moral teachings. Methodologically, these studies follow well established rules for empirical research; what is new, as in Italy, are the results, which contradict the stereotype of Spain as a Catholic country.

Phenomenological studies like those of Juan Martín Velasco and Xabier Pikaza tend to be done in circles close to the Church, with an emphasis on theological and psychological interests rather than on cataloguing or systematizing religious data. The question that motivates these studies is whether people today remain interested in religion or whether they are so secularized that the question of being religious no longer matters to them. This is also a question of philosophy of religion, which as a discipline is found in Spain within the study of religion as documented through the numerous works of Raimon Panikkar.

5. The Netherlands

In the Netherlands the history of religions has always played an important role, and was fully accepted alongside theology. Quarrels like those in Germany over the difference between the two did not occur. Moreover, the history of religions was always understood in the sense of a broader orientation of the discipline, combining all sorts of studies on religion(s), historical as well as empirical.

Studies of specific religions place a strong emphasis on contemporary problems, including those of migration with regard to Muslims in Surinam and Europe or of Hindus and African religions in the Netherlands. Systematic studies, on the other hand, pay particular attention to the history of the discipline (cf. Molendijk/Pels) as well as to terminology (cf., for instance, Platvoet/Molendijk). With books on classical subjects of the phenomenology of religion, such as the founders of religions (cf. Beck et al.), the Dutch contribution to international history of religions is a significant one, helping scholars to reengage fundamental disciplinary categories for the systematization of religious data.

6. The United Kingdom

The situation of religious studies in the United Kingdom (cf. King 1990: 21–141) is very different from the general debate on the continent. The distinction between theology and history of religions in the broader sense does not seem to be of any significant importance here. Most departments are called "Theology and Religious Studies," and their purpose includes contributing to the formation of the clergy as well as of teachers for religious education where people from both Christian denominations and other religions are welcome.

Studies on religion(s) include not only historical textual material but also the living practice of local religious communities. They embrace sociological empirical research as well as the psychology of religion. Religious studies in this context is a multi-disciplinary enterprise asking questions typical of each of its components. And since the idea of the society people in which live (modern, post-industrial, post-modern, late-capitalist, secular, multifaith etc.) has changed over the years in sociology, concepts of how to cope with it from the point of view of religion(s) have also changed with it. The same applies to fundamental social issues like feminism, sexual orientation, environmental protection, integration and so forth. They all have left their mark on theoretical debate and on the themes of the book market in religious studies. Thus they treat not only denominational positions within Christianity but also concentrate on the other religions of the world. It is obvious that, with reference to Christianity and even more so for all the other religions, new interpretations must be undertaken to address contemporary demands in an adequate way.

With regard to religious education, religions are studied in sequence, from the first school year onwards to graduation. All this is done in classrooms where learners from all these religious backgrounds are present and who expect to see their own religion(s) being treated with respect and competence. Religious studies is the adequate academic answer to religious pluralism in the country, and is generally accepted as the means to promote better understanding among people of different religious backgrounds. It is the intellectual basis for successful interreligious dialogue and thus an important support of all attempts to achieve integration in a multifaith society.

7. The Northern Countries

The northern countries have, in spite of undeniable differences, much in common that is reflected in their shared view of the history of religions. The discipline is well established in universities as an academic discipline, of which the broader orientation in the fields of research and teaching is characteristic. It either coexists with theology as in Denmark or has replaced theology as in Norway and Sweden.

Unlike Germany, Norway has a long tradition of teaching Christianity as a subject in the history of religions. It is therefore not surprising that Sigurd Hjelde undertook a discussion on methodological differences between history of religions and theology. He made wide use of the interpretive models available, successfully demonstrating their strengths and weaknesses. His argument is that the history of religions has not yet made sufficiently clear what its interest is in the study of Christianity, hence it has yet to work out the questions and goals that would constitute its appropriate study. This needs to be done if the history of religions wishes to have a distinct approach of its own, different from that of theology.

In most academic work, northern European countries follow the research profiles of other countries like the United Kingdom, the Netherlands, and Germany. Compared with the latter, interest in new religious movements and readiness to accept these as authentic religions is much more obvious than in Germany, where most studies are undertaken by church related institutions with missionary objectives, with less concern to describe these new movements favorably as a consequence. One way to achieve a more positive answer in this respect is to recognize that while religion that cannot be defined to everyone's satisfaction, it at least can be described with reference to different dimensions (of faith, practice, community, rituals etc.) so that if all these are present it is legitimate to consider the new group or movement as a religion.

The history of religions is strongly committed to education, making valuable contributions to school material of all kinds. In most of these countries there is an educational program independent from Church related instruction, to which the history of religions is one of the main contributors along with practical philosophy and ethics.

8. Germany

Methodological discussion in Germany concentrated for decades on the difference between theology as practiced in faculties of (Catholic and Protestant) theology and the history of religions as an independent academic discipline. From the inception of the latter, the broader orientation of the discipline's tasks was predominant. However, the discussion came to a standstill because a distribution of labor took place that sidetracked theoretical debate on methodological differences. The distribution of labor was that theology would deal with subjects of Christianity and to some extent Judaism, as well as the Ancient Orient and Hellenistic Mediterranean civilization, while the history of religions studied all the other religious traditions, particularly Islam, Hinduism, and Buddhism. Yet by the late 1960s theologians had given up this de facto distribution of labor, entering into the field of the world religions as a result of the theology of interreligious dialogue. Since the 1990s this distribution of labor has also finally been relinquished by historians of religions because of the undeniable lack of knowledge about Christianity among students of religion. The question of methodology has thus come back onto the agenda. According to Christoph Bizer there is only one alternative in this respect: Either theology will be absorbed by history of religions or it will find a new approach to its topics by developing a new kind of interreligious dialogue so that, for instance, holy scriptures would be taught by a Jew, a Muslim and a Christian who together might find a new understanding of holy books in dialogue with each other (Bizer 1998: 338). The basis for this alternative is the observation that most of the work done in faculties of theology is in fact history of religions, raising the question of what distinguishes theological research with regard to non-church related studies on religions. Moreover, the alternative is interesting because it reverses the previous situation where theologians used to challenge the history of religions to define its tasks as distinct from what de facto is done in theology. Here the real question is, what is typical of theology in comparison with history of religions as a discipline of the humanities, using all the methods there employed. Bizer's proposal makes an important point. What is needed is a new methodological understanding for theology, and not for the history of religions as a discipline. How this will be developed in the future is a task for the forthcoming decades, and its resolution will be most interesting to observe.

An important methodological consideration in the field of religion is how to write an introduction to Christianity that would correspond to the needs of the discipline and demonstrate a different approach from that usually undertaken in theology. One way to do this is to adopt the methods usually used to describe non-Christian religions and apply them to Christianity (cf. Antes 1985 and Antes 1999). Studies on feminism and gender as well as empirical research on female religiosity can be produced by both theologians and historians of religions, often without any difference in method, because a theological orientation in those areas is rare. The question may be extended to other religions as well. For example, Muslim imams or Buddhist monks and nuns living in Germany may come to the university and study history of religions. If they choose their own religion as their preferred subject then the distinction between history of religions and their religious interpretation of the subject is as relevant as in the case of Christianity with regard to the history of religions. The debate on the relationship between theology and history of religions should, therefore, include those cases as well, rather than assuming Christian theology is the only case of this kind.

Besides methodological questions with regard to theology, the history of religions has also had to defend its position and methodology in comparison with oriental languages and civilizations, as well as with political science, sociology, and psychology, if one thinks of particular case studies on Islam, Hinduism, and Buddhism, whether they concentrate on Asia, on Europe or in other global contexts. The German book series *Die Religionen der Menschheit* is a good example of those studies in which contributors from all relevant disciplines make their knowledge accessible to the reader and thus offer an insight into the ongoing research on specific topics in the history of religions.

Regarding the systematic categorization of religious data, the classical approach of phenomenology of religion was rejected during the 1970s and 1980s because of its strong emphasis on the *Wesensschau* (i.e. an attempt to define the essence or true nature of religion. The argument against it was that the philosophical approach could not fulfill the requirement of intersubjective control and was, moreover, a misunderstanding of the philosophical approach of phenomenology (cf. Becke 1999: 187–223). However, there is a new type of phenomenology of religion that combines facts in a new order (cf. Schimmel 1995 and Antes 1996) to help better understand what is going on in religions, and also addresses how classical topics in the phenomenology of religion such as religious founders, or ethics in religions, can be seen in fresh ways in light of recent research.

One area of research that is widely neglected by the history of religions in Germany is the study of new religious movements. Here, church related institutions, both Protestant and Catholic, have established a domain of their own and dominate the discussion to such an extent that they were successful enough to influence the public debate on the subject and to encourage the foundation of an inquiry group in which they were rather powerful and historians of religions had only a minor role to play.

The most significant new approach is that of sociology of religion. It started after the end of communist rule in the former "German Democratic Republic" (GDR) and has then confronted empirical data with theories about secularization, asking whether the GDR reality will, in the future, follow the model of secularized societies in the West or develop along a different course of its own (cf. Pollack et al. 1998: 29–49). The question cannot yet be answered. Consequently, continued attention must be paid to see what will transpire. It seems that, for the first time in history, we are confronted with an obviously nonreligious population, for the majority of which religious questions do not arise, even in extreme situations like death and incurable illness. It is an area in which not only religious practice is nonexistent but also cultural socialization in religion in general and Christianity in particular. As a consequence, there is a complete lack of knowledge in the field and an incapacity to understand religious thinking as such.

The nonexistence of cultural religious socialization is a specific challenge to education. Symbols and rites have to be introduced and their significance must be taught. It may therefore seem that teaching Christianity at school is similar to visiting a zoo, with Christians appearing to be a strange species that has no common ground with the majority of the population. Some similar phenomena in the Western part of Germany seem to indicate that this situation is not unlike that of the country in general. The challenge for schools is obvious and alternative teachings to church related religious education try to do their best in bringing a good range of the history of religions into schools. Collaboration with the history of religions is welcome in this field and many booklets and some school books are available as a result. The more the cultural socialization in religious matters is noticeably lacking, the greater is the need for basic information on a very simple level, and that, unlike so many books on religion written by theologians, cannot presuppose any knowledge or experience as a starting point.

9. The Eastern Countries

The situation of the former communist block countries differs considerably from country to country. This is due to different religious heritages (Orthodox, Protestant, Roman Catholic), to different political and economical situations, and to different reactions to the contemporary situation in the academic world. The history of religions is mainly concerned with the last of these.

The history of religions was taught in most of the former communist countries within the ideological framework of Marxism, which gave explicit guidelines as to how to study the world's religions. The frame was thus clear from the beginning and only changed over the years with regard to Islam because it did not fulfill the theoretical expectations of the ruling philosophy, with the result that investigations finally had to adjust to the reality that actually existed. This holds particularly true after the Shah's departure from Iran (1979) and the establishment of an Islamic Republic in Iran under the leadership of Ayatollah Khomeini. For many scholars, the only way to avoid

the official doctrine in research was to adopt a purely descriptive, ethnographical approach that eschewed ideological explanatory categories.

After the end of communism a new phase started and many scholars
widened their horizons by reading all kinds of theories and source books from
the West that were inaccessible to most of them for a long time or, if read, could
not be put into application. Consequently, the academic world of the eastern
countries looks like a fascinating laboratory with old and newly adapted
formulae. Thus Friedrich Heiler's and Rudolph Otto's understandings of religion are competing with those of Niklas Luhmann and Hjelmar Sundén. The
ongoing process does not allow a definite assessment of where this will eventually lead to, but it is certainly not an exaggeration to think that in all the
subdisciplines of the history of religions in its broader orientation, there will be
new ways of studying the phenomena, combining imported traditional theories
with local modifications due to new data taken from the respective countries
(cf. the different country profiles in Pollack et al.). Most of this discussion will
certainly take place in East European languages and thus is unlikely to be
immediately accessible to the Western reader. But it can be hoped that, thanks
to international exchange programs, the most important new approaches will
become known to the West so that others can also participate in this highly
promising debate of the future.

10. Conclusion

This survey of a representative number of contexts in Europe has shown how
decisive they are in determining what is being discussed and dealt with in
them (cf. Kippenberg 1997: 268–70 and Antes 1994b). Thus the history of
religions, though being an academic discipline with international horizons, is
concretely embodied in a variety of context-specific shapes. What is new in one
context may be less so in another and vice-versa.

In most of the contexts explored here, the distinction between history of
religions, in its restrictive as well as in its broader orientation, and Christian
theology is a major issue for methodology and its implementation. Another
point of difference is the extent and ways studies on Christianity are encompassed within the history of religions as a discipline. Moreover, context also
determines whether and to what extent the history of religions as a discipline is
asked to make contributions to school material and educational programs.

We have seen that, in most countries considered in this article, the history
of religions is absent from the debate about new religious movements. It often
limits itself to the statement that religion cannot be defined, without saying that
a general description of the dimensions of religion could be given and would
help, as in the case of the northern countries, to decide whether or not particular movements or groups ought be labeled as religions or religious. And if so,

there is still one question left unanswered, namely whether or not religions can and should be morally judged, as suggested by Kippenberg (1999), so that some might be properly described as pernicious, and others good.

As concerns the specific profile of the discipline, practice should be more emphasized than previously, where texts and in particular, religious dogma, were in the primary focus of academic attention. Through such a shift to practice, popular religion would garner greater attention instead of being relegated to the margins along with "superstition" and other forms of pejoratively labeled religiosity. Those labels betray dogmatic assumptions that are not acceptable in an ideologically neutral form of the study of religion. The same applies to polytheism which is often interpreted from a monotheistic perspective that assumes its own superiority as a worldview.

With regard to theories, the great number of unbelievers in Europe, in particular in eastern European countries, makes studies of the "homo religiosus" imperative in order to show his/her characteristics in comparison with the "homo saecularis" understood as an unbeliever with little or no sense of religiosity.

Scholars' attention must also be drawn to the role of religion in the formation of specific cultures and civilizations so that the cultural dimensions of religion(s) in particular societies become obvious, and a subject for further work that will distinguish the discipline within the context of academic studies of culture and society more generally. Similar phenomena could also be undertaken with a more individual focus within the context of the psychology of religion, with the potential to yield fascinating new approaches to and new insights into the rich variety of human experience including dreams, imagination, and religion, past, present and future.

Select Bibliography

Alcover, Norberto (1995), *España 1982–1995: De la Fascinación al Quebranto*, Prólogo de Javier Tusell. Madrid: PPC.

Antes, Peter (1985), *Christentum: Eine Einführung* (Urban 378). Stuttgart/Berlin/Köln/Mainz: Kohlhammer.

—— (1994a), "Struktur oder Strukturierung von Religion? Zur Zielsetzung religionssystematischer Forschung," in: Holger Preißler/Hubert Seiwert in cooperation with Heinz Mürmel, eds., *Gnosisforschung und Religionsgeschichte: Festschrift für Kurt Rudolph zum 65. Geburtstag*. Marburg: Diagonal: 357–65.

—— (1994b), "Approches et Traditions dans l'Histoire des Religions en Europe continentale," in: Ugo Bianchi in cooperation with Fabio Mora/Lorenzo Bianchi, eds.: *The Notion of 'Religion' in Comparative Research: Selected Proceedings of the XVIth Congress of the International Association for the History of Religions. Rome, 3rd–8th September, 1990*. Roma: L'Erma di Bretschneider: 641–44.

—— ed. (1996), *Die Religionen der Gegenwart: Geschichte und Glauben*. München: Beck.

—— (1999), *Mach's wie Gott, werde Mensch: Das Christentum*. Düsseldorf: Patmos.

Baladier, Charles, ed. (1988), *Le grand Atlas des Religions*. Paris: Encyclopaedia Universalis France.

Beck, H.L./de Jonge, M./van Koningsveld, P.S./van der Toorn, K./Vetter, T.E. (1997), *Grondleggers van het Geloof*. Amsterdam: Prometheus.

Becke, Andreas (1999), *Der Weg der Phänomenologie. Husserl, Heidegger, Rombach*. Boethiana, vol. 36. Hamburg: Kovać.

Bianchi, Ugo (1989), "The Study of Religion in the Context of Catholic Culture," in: Michael Pye, ed., *Marburg revisited: Institutions and Strategies in the Study of Religion*. Marburg: Diagonal: 49–53.

Bizer, Christoph (1998), "Flurgespräche in einer traditionsreichen Theologischen Fakultät," in: Bärbel Köhler, ed., *Religion und Wahrheit: Religionsgeschichtliche Studien: Festschrift für Gernot Wießner zum 65. Geburtstag*. Wiesbaden: Harrassowitz: 329–38.

Cesareo, Vincenzo/Cipriani, Roberto/Garelli, Franco/Lanzetti, Clemente/Rovati, Giancarlo (1995), *La Religiosità in Italia*. Milano: Arnoldo Mondadori.

Díaz, Carlos (²1998), *Manual de Historia de las Religiones*. Bilbao: Desclée de Brouwer

Díez de Velasco, Francisco (1995), "La Historia de las Religiones en España: Avatares de una Disciplina," in: *'Ilu* 0 51–61.

——(²1998), *Introducción a la Historia de las Religiones: Hombres, Ritos, Dioses*. Madrid: Trotta.

——(1999), "Enseñar Religiones de una Optica no confesional: Reflexiones sobre (y más allá de) una Alternativa a Religión en la Escuela," in: *'Ilu* 4: 83–101.

Garelli, Franco (1991), *Religione e Chiesa in Italia*. Bologna: Mulino.

González-Anleo, Juan/González de Cardedal, Olegario/Laboa, Juan María/Romero Maura, Joaquín/Rouco, Antonio María/Sebastián, Fernando/Uriario, Juan María/ Yanes, Elias (1999), *La Iglesia en España: 1950–2000*. Edición preparada por Olegario González de Cardedal. Madrid: PPC.

González Blasco, Pedro/González-Anleo, Juan (1992), *Religión y sociedad en la España de los 90*. Madrid: Fundación Santa María.

Hervieu-Léger, Danièle/Garelli, Franco/Giner, Salvador /Sarasa, Sebastián/Beckford, James E./Daiber, Karl-Fritz/Tomka, Miklós (1992), *La Religione degli Europei: Fede, Cultura religiosa e Modernità in Francia, Italia, Spagna, Gran Bretagna, Germania e Ungheria*. Torino: Edizioni della Fondazione Giovanni Agnelli.

Hjelde, Sigurd (1994), *Die Religionswissenschaft und das Christentum: Eine historische Untersuchung über das Verhältnis von Religionswissenschaft und Theologie*. Leiden/New York/Köln: Brill.

King, Ursula, ed. (1990), *Turning Points in Religious Studies: Essays in Honour of Geoffrey Parrinder*. Edinburgh: T&T Clark.

Kippenberg, Hans G. (1997), *Die Entdeckung der Religionsgeschichte. Religionswissenschaft und Moderne*. München: Beck.

—— (1999), "Kriminelle Religion: Religionswissenschaftliche Betrachtungen zu Vorgängen in Jugoslawien und im Libanon," in: *Zeitschrift für Religionswissenschaft* 7 (1): 95–110.

Lorizio, Giuseppe, ed. (1998), *Religione e Religioni: Metodologia e Prospettive ermeneutiche*. Padova: Ed. Messaggero.

Martín Velasco, Juan (1985), *Dios en la Historia de las Religiones*. Madrid: Fundación Santa María.

Meslin, Michel (1973), *Pour une Science des Religions*. Paris: Seuil.

Molendijk, Arie L./Pels, Peter, eds. (1998), *Religion in the Making: The Emergence of the Sciences of Religion*. Studies in the History of Religions. Numen Book Series, vol. 80. Leiden/Boston/Köln: Brill.

Montclos, Xavier de (²1990), *Histoire religieuse de la France*. Paris: P.U.F.

Nesti, Arnaldo (1997), *Il Catttolicesimo degli Italiani: Religione e Cultura dopo la secolarizzazione*. Milano: Ed. Angelo Guerini e Associati.

Pace, Enzo (1999), *Sociologia dell'Islamismo: Fenomeni religiosi e Logiche sociali*. Roma: Carocci.

Pikaza, Xabier (1999), *El Fenómeno religioso*. Madrid: Trotta.

Platvoet, Jan G./Molendijk, Arie L., eds. (1999), *The Pragmatics of Defining Religion: Contexts, Concepts and Contests*. Studies in the History of Religions: Numen Book Series, vol. 84. Leiden/Boston/Köln: Brill.

Pollack, Detlef/Borowik, Irena/Jagodzinski, Wolfgang, eds. (1998), *Religiöser Wandel in den postkommunistischen Ländern Ost- und Mitteleuropas*. Religion in der Gesellschaft, vol. 6. Würzburg: Ergon.

Poulat, Emile (1988), *Liberté, Laïcité: La Guerre des Deux France et le Principe de la Modernité*. Paris: Cerf.

Religioni e Società. Rivista di scienze sociali della religione 37, Anno XV, maggio-agosto 2000 [special issue on "L'insegnamento delle scienze religiose in Europa"].

Schimmel, Annemarie (1995), *Die Zeichen Gottes: Die religiöse Welt des Islams*. München: Beck [enlarged German translation of the English original of 1994: *Deciphering the Signs of God*. Edinburgh University Press].

Terrin, Aldo Natale (1999), *Il Rito: Antropologia e Fenomenologia della Ritualità*. Brescia: Morcelliana.

Tornos, Andrés/Aparicio, Rosa (1995), *Quién es Creyente en España hoy?* Madrid: PPC.

Tyloch, Witold, ed. (1990), *Studies on Religions in the Context of Social Sciences: Methodological and Theoretical Relations*. Warsaw: Polish Society for the Science of Religions.

The Study of Religion, the History of Religions and Islamic Studies in Turkey

Approaches from "Phenomenological Theology" to Contextualism

by

BÜLENT ŞENAY

In this age of globalization and transformation, and of an increase in religious commitments, academic viewpoints not only affect but also shape the future of the relationship between religious hermeneutics and the trio of modernity, secularism, and globalization. The academic study of religion in general, and of Islam in particular, can generate insight into globalization and "glocalization" alike.

This chapter presents a brief history of the study of religion and the history of religion as academic disciplines in the faculties of divinity in Turkish universities. It presents a descriptive survey of theoretical and critical approaches and trends in the study of religion and Islamic studies in Turkey, including reference to a few leading scholars alongside a selected leading bibliography on the topic. It is impossible to give a detailed picture of the many subjects, studies, and trends that are in some way related to the study of religions in the whole of Turkish faculties of divinity without locating the topic within a general religio-historical context.

In order to set the stage for the status of study of religion and the history of religion in Turkish universities, one must first understand the "present" of Turkey. Contemporary Turkish society emerged out of the context of the so-called westernization and secularization (laicism) project, and their impact on the intellectual, institutional and educational makeup of Turkish society. A brief look at the emergence of modern Turkey is therefore necessary to contextualize the concerns of the rest of this chapter.

1. The Context at the Juxtaposition of Turkish History, Culture and Religion

The past and the present of the study of religion in Turkey are construed here in the context of the intellectual and social-religious history of Turkey. The "present" of Turkey continues to be culturally, intellectually and politically an arena in which the relationship between laicism and Islam still has an impact on institutional and academic "making" and "thinking". As aptly put by Ahmet Davutoğlu, a respected professor of international relations and diplomacy, this is primarily due to the fact that:

> [t]he principle difference between Islamic and Western *Weltanschauung* is related to the contrast between the 'ontologically determined epistemology' of Islam and the 'epistemologically determined ontology' of the Western philosophical traditions. This difference is especially significant in understanding the axiological basis of political legitimacy and the process of justification (Davutoğlu 1994: 5).

Due to this epistemological contrast, the academic study of religion in Turkish universities has inevitably been influenced by the extensive clash that occurs between the Muslim's self-perception based on ontological presuppositions, and conjectural self-perceptions of modernizers in an age of the supremacy of the Western civilization. As Davutoğlu explains in his *Alternative Paradigms*, in Muslim societies this has much to do with attempts to transform the traditional self-perception of Islamic civilization to more closely resemble the self-perception of the West (*Selbstverständnis*), as formulated by Edmund Husserl as the basic reason for Western civilization's alleged superiority (Davutoğlu 1994; Husserl 1970; Uygur 1998). In terms of the transformation of traditional values, as Şerif Mardin explains, the modern Turkish experience of secularism does not appear to have succeeded since the Islamic self-image offers a very strong ontological consciousness for which modernizers failed to provide a substitute (Mardin 1983: 110–13).

On the other hand, Turkish-Muslim scholars aimed to rebuild the epistemological and methodological structures of Islamic intellectual tradition to overcome the challenge of the epistemologically formulated self-perception of the westernization-oriented elite in Turkey. The spread of periodicals and books for the verification of religious truths via scientific innovations might be explained through this perceived need. Although the academic orientation in the 1990s, in terms of both the quantity and the quality of publications in "religion-related" studies, reflects a relative independence from the effects of the secularization debate, we still have to be aware of the fact that Turkish society might be evaluated as a model for such an extensive contrast, which in turn makes an impact on the whole of academia (Davutoğlu 1994: 7).

A steady trend towards secularization in traditional institutions is a feature of Muslim societies facing the impact of modern civilization. Secularization as a sociological process is claimed to be universal, but the attitude towards the problems created by it differs from case to case. This idea of secularization can be traced back to the founders of modern social thought in the West: to Comte, Spencer, Durkheim, Marx, and Weber. Conventional academic wisdom has it that religion is dying out in the modern world. In the latter half of the twentieth century, however, sociological analyses, including works by Thomas Luckmann, Mary Douglas, Talcott Parsons, and Robert Bellah, are less sanguine about the alleged inevitability of the decline of religion. For scholars of this persuasion, the watchword of modern religious history is not decline but transformation. Peter Berger rightly says that this transformation is due to the fact that, in contrast to the general belief that modernity necessarily leads to a decline of religion, counter-secularization is at least as important a phenomenon in the contemporary world as secularization. According to Berger, one of the most important topics for the sociology of contemporary religion is precisely this interplay of secularizing and counter-secularizing forces (Berger 1997: 6). Nevertheless, as far as the manifestation of secularization is concerned, it was in Turkey among the Muslim countries that, prior to World War II, a secular concept of state, religion, law, education, and economy was first promoted, and a definite doctrine of secularism (*laicism*) implemented as a political, constitutional, educational, and cultural policy. Following World War I, the new state, under the political leadership of Mustafa Kemal, who later took the name of Atatürk—father of the Turks—was created from the ruins of the Ottoman Empire against great odds, both internal and external. Turkey was among the losers of World War I, but compared to Germany or Hungary, it emerged with dignity, keeping reasonable natural borders in a state of manageable size and expelling the various foreign armies hoping for control of a slice of Turkish territory.

When Mustafa Kemal Atatürk founded the modern Turkish Republic in 1923, neither he nor his compatriots had any nostalgia for the dead Ottoman Empire. On the contrary, they viewed the old order with disdain and contempt. Atatürk believed his plans to modernize the Turkish nation required the obliteration of all things Ottoman. This attitude was understandable. The Ottomans had been in decline for several centuries, and the final hundred years (ending with the Empire's destruction in World War I) were a nightmare of weakness, humiliation, and defeat. Beginning with the Greek Revolution in 1821, the Turks suffered a seemingly unending series of serious losses in both territory and human life. Over those last hundred years of slaughter in the Balkans, the Caucasus, the Crimea, and Anatolia, Turkish/Muslim dead (both military and civilian) amounted to, by conservative estimate, well over five million people, mostly at the hands of Czarist Russia and the various ethnic nationalist movements in Bulgaria, Yugoslavia, and so forth. Not only was the Ottoman Empire too weak to defend its territories and citizens against the invading armies and their domestic insurgent allies, it was too poor to accommodate the rivers of refugees that flowed ceaselessly from the lost lands into Turkish-held Anatolia. The Ottoman Empire became known as "the sick man of Europe" during this period for a reason. Atatürk's awareness of this almost unimaginable national and human catastrophe, spanning several generations throughout the nineteenth and early twentieth centuries, decisively shaped the social and state architecture he created for the new Republic. Atatürk saw the Ottomans and their society as backward and pathetic. He believed that unless the entire Ottoman imperial system was razed and replaced with a modern, Western-style social structure and national government, Turkey's future would be bleak at best, and perhaps nonexistent. For Atatürk, Islam was an integral part of the old, hated Ottoman system, and had no place in the public life of the new Turkey. Like everything Ottoman, Islam was considered to be a source of national rot and weakness that had to be quarantined for the Republic to thrive. In those early days, Atatürk's word was law, and so an impermeable partition arose between religion and public life.

In quick succession Mustafa Kemal abolished the Sultanate in November 1922. The capital was moved from İstanbul to the central Anatolian town of Ankara in 1923. The Caliphate was abolished in March 1924 and Mustafa Kemal was designated head of state. He closed the *madrasas* (religious schools, secondary and higher) and religious courts, and a new Ministry of Religious Affairs supervised the assets of the *waqfs* (religious endowments). The *sûfî* orders were banned in 1925 and this was followed by the substitution of Western-based legal codes for the *shar'iah* in a year later. The old Ottoman script, consisting of Turkish words written in Arabic characters, was replaced with the Latin alphabet. The emendation of the constitution was the next step. In 1928 the clause that read "the religion of the Turkish state is Islam" was deleted, "laicism" was established as one of the six Kemalist principles (Republicanism, Nationalism, Popularism, Etatism, Laicism, Revolutionism) of that state. Altogether the role of Islam's traditional representatives and symbols in the country's life was circumscribed generally and firmly by law (Smith 1959: 165–208; Mortimer 1982: 134–58). Mustafa Kemal maintained that "the new Turkey has no relationship to the old." The Ottoman government passed into history. An arch-westernizer, he was determined to "drag Turkey into the twentieth century." A new Turkey was now born. A new history and new traditions were invented to compensate for the ones that were being abandoned. The origins of the burgeoning nation were located in Sumerian and Hittite societies; principles of Turkism were elaborated, with all the appropriate paraphernalia and customs. After Atatürk died in 1938, his word became more than law. It became Kemalism, a system of national rhetoric and dogma that continues to guide Turkish debate and public policy to this day, a system in which the separation of politics and religion is axiomatic (Robins 1996: 68–72).

According to Niyazi Berkes, author of *The Development of Secularism in Modern Turkey*, the transformation of Turkey from a traditional to a secular/

laicist state illustrates the complex relations amongst economic, technical changes, political and religious changes. Turkey was geographically closer to the centres of change than any other non-Western society and was the first to feel their influence. When, from the about the middle of the nineteenth century, the state was forced by external pressures to promote change, it appeared to be the instrument of those pressures, and found itself stripped of its traditional religious legitimization. Mounting tension contributed to the separation of the two intertwined elements of the traditional order, in spite of all efforts to keep state and religion side by side in a new dual relationship. Attempts to delineate the respective areas of the two produced, not a secular state with a religious organization outside it, but rather a series of divisions in the political, legal, and educational institutions, each of which manifested a religious-secular duality. Especially since World War II, the national state could no longer maintain the traditional association between state and religion characteristic of the traditional polity. In the resultant secular state, a new arrangement was found for what was taken as national, religious, and modern; this was worked out within the framework of a policy of secularism which, though pursuing the same aim, differed from the varieties of Western secular regimes in its means and priorities. The manner in which religion had become institutionalized in Turkey made it appear as though the question of religion in secular state had implications for its whole social existence, hence the two facets (Turkish Nationalism and Turkish Islam) of Turkish secularism, each inviting a different approach. Under the regime of popular sovereignty the religious question became one of religious enlightenment on the one hand, and, in terms of a national existence, one of moral reintegration on the other. Turkish secularism within the Kemalist rhetoric mentioned above took final shape with the interaction of these two approaches (Berkes 1998: 479–510; also Ahmad 1993). State secularism was thus an identity-building project in Turkey, with the assumption that Islam was to be limited to the private sphere. The disjuncture of an Islamic past and present had already begun.

As much as it has been shaped by the assimilation of Western culture, modern Turkish identity is a product of various negations. The Ottoman Empire had been characterized by a spirit of cosmopolitanism, by ethnic, linguistic and religious mixture and interchange. The Turkish state that emerged out of its collapse was fundamentally opposed to such pluralism of identity. The new state aimed to transform Turkish identity "through uniform incorporation, connecting the concept of citizenship with that of social-cultural-linguistic assimilation" (Robins 1996: 61–86). Religious attachment was seen as a subversive force, also posing a threat to the modernization and nationalization process in Turkey. According to Richard Tapper, the secular alternative, however, was no alternative to Islam in providing identity and organizing principles of life. At the public level, it was no substitute for the divine laws of

Islam; at the individual level, it could not meet intellectual needs for an ethics and eschatology, and its values were inadequate and thin (Tapper 1991: 7).

2. Faculties of Divinity in Post-Ottoman Turkish Universities

The crux of experiments in laicism in Turkey was not to turkify Islam just for the sake of nationalism, but to turkify Islam for the sake of religious enlightenment. The triumph of the idea of a secular state over the idea of an Islamic state produced a series of secularizing reforms within legal, educational, and cultural institutions. The first phase of these reforms began with the abolition of the Caliphate. Two more bills were passed, one abolishing the Ministries of *Shar'iah* and *Awqaf*, the other closing the *madrasahs*, unifying education under the Ministry of Education. Bills abolishing the religious orders and their cloisters were passed shortly thereafter. This phase ended with the secularization of the Constitution on November 3, 1928. The second phase, from 1928 to 1938 was one in which the previous changes were supplemented, extended, and consolidated. Article 9 of the Law of Associations promulgated in 1938, prohibited the "formation societies based on religion, sect, and *tarîqa*." Propaganda against the principles of laicism was prohibited by Article 163 of the Penal Code adopted in 1926 (Berkes 1998: 461–78). Each of these experiments in laicism in political, legal, and educational institutions manifested a religious-secular duality.

Although the Turkish state had renounced its connection with Islam, in practice it considered religion far too important and dangerous a force to be left in the hands of the religiously minded. While non-Muslim communities retained their autonomy in religious matters, the mosques, the Islamic endowments (*awqaf*), the education, appointment, and payment of *imams* and *khatibs* all remained firmly under government control (Mortimer 1982: 146).

In any case, religion has clearly been central in the developments that have occurred throughout the last century of modern Turkish history. Islam has emerged again as a dynamic element in the culture, and has increasingly developed a strong presence in civil society. By 1924, the new post-Ottoman Turkish Republican Regime had already constituted a Directorate of Religious Affairs (*Diyanet İşleri Başkanlığı*) to manage the administrative affairs of religion. The approach was predominantly pragmatic. It did not aim at a religious doctrine, a dogma, or a theology; it remained experimental with respect to religious reform and led progressively to the further secularist facilitation of religious services and reform. The new organizational apparatus was not designed to be a spiritual organization. It was from this pragmatic ground that a Faculty of Divinity was also established in the University of İstanbul in 1924 (Berkes 1998: 490).

Secularization trends in Ottoman higher education played the crucial role in the rise of general, non-theological study of religion in nineteenth century. Similar to the Dutch experience of secularization, the secularization trend on Ottoman soil was also strengthened by the rise of a secular intellectual life after the *Tanzimat* (literally meaning "new regulations"), which brought a policy of secularism in the sense of bringing forth a differentiation between the "temporal" and "religious" in the Turkish-Islamic context. *Tanzimat* was the period of government reforms in the Ottoman Turkey, which began in 1839 with the reign of Abdulmajid I, the first reform being the edict known as the *Hatt-ı Sharif* of Gülhane. It promised all subjects in the Empire, regardless of nationality and religion, security of life, honor, and property: regular military service for Muslims, the lifting of oppressive monopolies, the abolition of confiscations, the end to the leasing of the right to taxation of the provinces to the highest bidder. A series of other laws followed. The doors to the West were thrown wide open in 1839 with *Tanzimat*. Turkish economic, political, legal, and educational institutions began to change in a way that involved basic values without any particular reference to Islam. *Tanzimat* came into existence through the political impact of the West upon the policies of reform that began in the form of diplomatic intervention by the European powers (MacFarlane 1850, I: 25). Throughout the conflicts over the so-called Eastern Question, religion was used as a cover for power politics. Russia, France, and Great Britain pursued their policies on the basis of claims to the right of protection over the Orthodox, Catholic, and Protestant communities of the Ottoman Empire. Russia as a foe, and England and France as friends, demanded reforms with respect to the conditions of these communities which were already protected under the Ottoman-Islamic *Dhimmî* law. The demands inevitably had implications for reform policies. This led to diverse interpretations of the reforms, and finally, caused further complications of the principles enunciated in a charter known as the *Tanzimat* Charter. The experiments of the Tanzimat reformers gave shape to a policy of secularism in the sense of bringing forth a differentiation between the "temporal" and "religious" in the Turkish-Islamic context (Berkes 1998: 137–200).

It was during the post-*Tanzimat* period that a secular intellectual life began to emerge. The very rise of a secular intellectual life was also the beginning of the emergence of two mentalities that arose and began to diverge from one another. A close look at the educated elite of the post-*Tanzimat* era would allow us to see the implications of the split between the worldviews regnant in the "religious" and in the "secular" areas of intellectual and educational life. In order to work out an integration between the "new" and the "traditional," an institution, called *Encümen-i Dâniş* (Society of the Learned), was established within the educational field under the lead of Ahmet Cevdet Pasha, a well known historian and intellectual. Cevdet's stance was that success in renovating Turkey lay neither in stubborn resistance to change, nor in automatic imitation of the West, but in the intelligent revival of traditional and Islamic institutions by the infusion of Western scientific and technological inventions (Berkes 1998: 178; Ülken 1979). This has been the essential ethos with regard to the nature of and direction of "change" advocated and still being maintained by the Islamicists then and now. From the idea of *Encümen-i Dâniş* emerged the idea of establishing the *Dâr al-Funoon* (a House of Sciences). This was the first attempt in a Muslim country to establish a modern university in contrast to the traditional medieval academy. It constitutes an interesting case. Courses were first offered in the 1870s and varied over time. Eventually the general idea of "the study of religion" found its way into the Turkish university system as part of Islamic studies. The rise of a secular intellectual life coincided with the introduction of "general history of religions" in the *Dâr al-Funoon* curriculum.

"Religious studies" in a modern university format had been attempted in 1900 in İstanbul University, the then called *Dâr al-Funoon*. It was in this university that the first faculty of divinity (then called the Department of *al-uloom al-shar`iyyah*) was founded, along with several other departments. İstanbul University was transformed from the old *madrasa* model into a modern institution of higher education. Originally initiated in 1863, in 1870 it was enlarged to unite different separate higher education *Madrasas* within one university structure. This aim finally was accomplished in 1900 (Akyüz 1999: 146–49). Nevertheless, the faculty of divinity within this *Dâr al-Funoon* was closed down in 1914 and the students were transferred instead to a separate traditional *Mutahassısîn Madrasah* (a higher education college for specialization in religious studies) which later in 1918 was named *Sulaymânıyya Madrasah*, where courses on the history of religions were taught in the Department of *Kalâm* and *Hıkmah*. The closure of the first Faculty of Divinity within the *Dâr al-Funoon* in 1914 meant that there would be no study of religion at university level until 1924, when a new Unification of Education Act (*Tevhid-i Tedrisat*) brought structural transformation of the traditional educational system to the modern norm. With this transformation in 1924, the *Department of Kalâm and Hıkmah in Sulaymânıyya Madrasah* was renamed the faculty of divinity which continued until 1933 (Usta 2001; Atay 1993; İhsanoğlu 1990; Ergin 1977: Ayhan 1999: 38–39).

From 1900 to 1924 when the new republican state set its education policy with the new Unification of Education Act (*Tevhid-i Tedrisat*), there were a number of *madrasas* which offered higher religious education (Usta 2001: 34–35). In 1924, the new Unification of Education Act (*Tevhid-i Tedrisat*) was passed and a new faculty of divinity was established in Istanbul University. However, this faculty was closed down in 1933 and no theological and religious studies were available from 1933 to 1949 due to political reasons. The Kemalist program as noted above utilized a program of reforms that effectively removed Islam from political life and secularized society. The question of how to assess the success of a program based on the idea that Islam was the cause of the country's "backwardness" needs to be answered carefully. The Islamic tradition had developed very deep roots among Turkish Muslims. Therefore, despite legal and political reforms attempting to minimize the role of Islam in public and intellectual life, academic study of Islam did not cease and the scholars such as İzmirli İsmail Hakkı (*Kalâm* and Islamic Thought), Mehmet Ali Aynî (Islamic History and Mysticism), Hilmi Ömer Budda (History of Religions), Şemseddin Günaltay (History of Religions) and others continued to contribute to this Faculty until 1933. After a period of silence, in 1949, following lengthy discussions, the re-establishment of a faculty of divinity was approved by the Parliament with full support of its members. Since then, despite numerous political debates surrounding the future of religious education in the country, faculties of divinity continue their missions under the Turkish Higher Education Law, increasingly establishing their status in the academic and educational life of Turkish society. By 2001 there were 23 faculties of divinity providing theological and religious studies at both undergraduate and postgraduate level in Turkey (Usta 2001). Graduates from these faculties are eligible for becoming either *RE* (religious studies) teachers in primary, secondary and further education schools, or working in various areas of religious services (*mufti, imam,* and preacher) under the Turkish Directorate of Religious Affairs, or if they wish, can continue to postgraduate studies.

One has to remember that Turks today are Muslims in the same way that most Europeans and Americans are Christians. Their religion is an integral part of their culture and significant in an individual's life primarily as a framework for rites of passage. Turkish studies of religion are part of this overall reality in Turkey.

3. The History of Religions, the Phenomenology of Religion and "Phenomenological Theology" in Turkish Universities

There has been a long tradition of the study of religion in Muslim culture developed from famous Muslim scholars in the past who provided a basis for religious studies as understood in the International Association for the History of Religions (IAHR) today. Contemporary Turkish scholarship in the field, with its long heritage transformed from the Ottoman *madrasa* institution (as an extension from the *Nizamiyyah madrasa* model of the Abbasids) is significant in terms of an empirical and historical study of religions other than Islam. A survey of the study of religion in twenty-three faculties of divinity in Turkish universities shows that alongside the ongoing transformation of higher education in the country, the "phenomenological/secular" type of the study of religion has found its way into the traditional pattern of institutional self-understanding with relative ease. In part, this is due to the fact that the

Turkish-Muslim experience (quite a different one compared to the Arab-Muslim experience) of overcoming the tension between modernity/secular-ization and Islam has led to a wider tendency towards intellectual freedom and a "value-free" study of religion despite criticism of the idea of "value-free" study itself. There is also a general positive attitude toward "interdisciplin-arity". The study of religion has a special meaning in a country like Turkey with its secular democracy and with a population following Islam in general. The study of religion in Turkey classically meant the study of religion within Islamic disciplines. It did not exclude, of course, a study of other religious traditions. However, during the formative period and early history of the Ottoman state the discipline of the history of religions was not to be found in the curricula of the *madrasas*, institutions that served as the basic and perhaps the most advanced teaching organizations throughout the empire. Nor was the subject taught in other schools. The history of religions that came into being in the nineteenth-century Europe had a considerable influence in the Ottoman state. In 1874, the program of the faculty of literature in İstanbul University included a course entitled "General History and Science of the Religions of Ancient People" (*Tarih-i Umumi ve İlm-i Esâtiri'l-Evvelîn*). However, since the very first department of religious studies in *Dâr al-Funoon* a hundred years ago, the study of religions other than Islam has not essentially been an academic discipline in an independent department as in, for example, departments of religious studies in Lancaster, Marburg or Santa Barbara. Individual courses in what we now call religious studies are taught as part of the general field of Islamic studies in faculties of divinity. One should also remember that faculties of divinity in Turkey were essentially established to train both religious educa-tion teachers and religious services specialists (*imams*, preachers and profes-sionals to work under the Turkish Directorate of Religious Affairs).

The history of religions and the study of religions in the context of human-ities and social sciences have eventually been incorporated within the teaching programs of the faculties of divinity in Turkey. It seems appropriate—indeed, imperative—if one is to progress far, or ever to speak with any authority, to equip oneself with the tools, methods, and content of technical scholarship in one special field, but the concern for greater depth of study and knowledge of one historical religious tradition is in no sense a renunciation of the broader aims of history of religions. However, it has proven difficult to see a direct and fruitful relationship between the activities of Islamicists and those of historians of religions.

One of the reasons for this difficulty can be said to have been the ever-increasing adherence to the so-called phenomenological approach. Although a wide variety of scholars employ the word "phenomenology" to describe their methodological intentions, they do not always agree on what the label means. Nor do they always share a clear sense of the intellectual traditions without which phenomenology of religion has arisen. The reason for this lack of agreement is that there are at least two strands of thought—two intellectual points of departure—which can produce a phenomenology of religion. The most obvious is the one that stems directly from post-Kantian and post-Hegelian continental philosophy. Regardless of whatever else it includes, this strand always lists Edmund Husserl (1859–1938) as its primary inspiration and founding father. Thus, to this day, the phrase "phenomenology of religion" tends to evoke Husserlian interest, Husserlian techniques, and Husserlian conceptual terminology. Religious studies has taken more from examples of the ways Husserl approached things than from the substance of his philosophy. The second strand of phenomenology has been nurtured from within the history of religions. Many Western scholars, recognized to be phenomenologists of religion, have been trained first as historians of religion and not as philosophers. Many would also understand history of religions and phenomenology of religion to be complementary and interchangeable undertakings. Such phenomenologists of religion frequently admit to having no more than a surface understanding of Husserl's fundamental contentions (see, Bettis 1969; Sharpe 1992). When they trace their intellectual roots, the genealogy they offer tends to reach back not to Husserl (who, nevertheless, is usually mentioned), but to such figures as Cornelius Petrus Tiele (1830–1902), and Chantepie de la Saussaye (1848–1920) in Holland. It was around this time that the Dutch Universities Act, passed on 1 October 1877, separated the theological faculties at the four state universities (Amsterdam, Groningen, Leiden, Utrecht) from the Dutch Reformed Church. The original draft of the Bill had referred to the establishment of "Faculties of Religious Sciences", but in the event, the title "Faculty of Theology" was retained. However, dogmatics and practical theology were removed from the curriculum, their place being taken by the history of religions, which was assumed to be neutral and scientific (Sharpe 1992: 121). In the nineteenth century, there were powerful secularizing influences at work in this development, and in this sense the Dutch university served as a paradigm for the kind of situation which was to arise in other countries in Europe. It should not be surprising therefore to see that in Turkey, which was experiencing a transformation period from an empire to a nation-state, similar developments were occurring. In parallel to various reformative developments in Turkish higher education during those years, the General Education Act, passed in 1869, a year before the Dutch Universities Act, made provision for the permanent establishment of the *Dâr al-Funoon* which was to consist of three faculties: Philosophy and Literature; Law; and Mathematical and Physical Sciences (Aynî 1927; Akyüz 1999). It was in the department Philosophy and Literature that a subject course on the history of religions called "Introduction to History and the Study of Ancient Religions and Mythology" was introduced. After the declaration of the *Meşrutiyet II* in 1908 (the new constitutional era addressing major political-social issues), the course became "The History of Islam and the History of

Religions" (*Tarih-i Din-i İslam ve Tarih-i Edyan*) and was 6 credit hours a week (Tanyu 1960).

At the same time that Chantepie de la Saussaye was a professor of the history of religions at Amsterdam, a leading Turkish scholar in Istanbul, Ahmet Midhat Efendi was writing his lecture notes for *History of Religions*, the very first systematic textbook on the history of religions written in Ottoman Turkish. The book was published in 1912, the same year of the publication of Durkheim's *Les Formes Elémentaries de la Vie Religieuse*. In his *History of Religions*, Midhat mentioned Chantepie de la Saussaye as one of the few leading European scholars of the history of religions. He also pointed out that the history of religions (*Tarih al-Adyaan*) was relatively a new discipline and that Muslim scholars since the tenth century classical writings on "other religions" (for example, *Kitâb al-Milal wa'n-Nıhal* by *ash-Shahrastânî*) had not produced a systematic "history of religions" except for theological reasons, and that recently European scholars had started to write systematic books on the subject (Midhat 1912). What makes Midhat's work significant is the fact that he understood and explained in a very articulate way the difference between "making normative theology" and the "descriptive study of religion." In Ottoman higher education, he was the first scholar to teach the subject of history of religion within the department of divinity. While he tried to convince his reader of both the importance of history of religions and its compatibility of Islamic studies, he also emphasized the importance of objectivity: "The purpose of the History of Religion is not to bring evidence in favour of or against any religion. Therefore it is essential that the historian of religion study the 'religious phenomenon' with an objective approach" (Midhat 1912: 15).

Midhat supported his point about the need to be objective to the point of agnosticism by referring to Descartes's assertion that to do philosophy one must forget all that one has learned and look at things without bias. According to Midhat, this approach should be fundamental for the historian of religion. His emphasis on the necessity of studying religions in terms of their own beliefs, rituals and institutions allows him to be called an early defender of phenomenology of religion in Turkish academia. He also encouraged an interdisciplinary approach for the historian of religion. As early as 1912, by referring to "geography of religions," "sociology of religion" and "psychology of religion" (without neglecting ethnology, philology and archaeology), his work suggested that the history of religions needed to move towards a systematic and interdisciplinary study of religion as an academic discipline (Midhat 1912: 2–17).

In Holland, another contemporary of Midhat, Cornelius Petrus Tiele, was perhaps the continental equivalent of F. M. Müller in England. Tiele and Chantepie are credited as being the first phenomenologists of religion, if only because they employed a descriptive system of classification in coming to terms with the particulars of religion. This strain of phenomenology of religion in the continental Europe has moved from Tiele and Chantepie into the twentieth century through the influence of W. Brede Kristensen, Gerardus van der Leeuw, C.J. Bleeker, Mircea Eliade, their students and a host of others from Jacques Waardenburg to Eric Sharpe. The two phenomenologies share terminology, method, and conviction, yet their intentions can be remarkably different. The course of developments of the history of religion and the phenomenology of religion in the West are well known to Turkish scholars of religious studies. However, what is needed by the latter is a broad approach to the study of religion that balances philosophical-epistemological concerns with phenomenological-historical modes of approach.

Ahmed Midhat's work allows us to say that the history of religions was the first discipline of religious studies that entered into the academic curriculum in Turkish universities in nineteenth century. In line with what has been said about the origins of the discipline there have been subsequent developments in the area. As noted above, following lengthy discussions the first faculty of Divinity, closed down in 1933, was re-established in 1949. Various scholars have taught history of religions since then. Ömer Hilmi Budda (1949–1952) was the first historian of religion who taught in this faculty. The following scholars were the pioneers of the history of religion in this first faculty of divinity in Turkey: Mehmet Karasan (1952–1954), Annemarie Schimmel (1954–1959), Hikmet Tanyu (1959–1960; 1962–1972; 1973–1982), Kemal Balkan (1960–1962), Mehmet Taplamacıoğlu (1972–1973), and the late Günay Tümer (1980–1985; he taught in and retired from the faculty of divinity in Uludağ University). From this line of scholarship the discipline gradually spread to other faculties of divinity.

One contemporary example is Ömer Faruk Harman (1950–), a professor of history of religions. Harman currently teaches history of religions at the Faculty of Divinity at Marmara University, İstanbul. His doctoral study was on al-Shahrastânî, and after his work on text and context in Jewish sacred writings (*Metin ve Muhtevâ Açısından Yahudi Kutsal Kitapları*), he presented his qualifying thesis for full professorship on the value of the Gospel of Barnabas in the context of Biblical studies. Harman's other major contributions in the field of history of religions were made through the articles[1] he wrote for the new *Encyclopaedia of Islam*, like many other scholars of religious studies in Turkey. This *Encyclopaedia of Islam* in itself is an indicator of developments in Islamic Studies and religious studies in Turkey. Harman, one of the few students of late Hikmet Tanyu (1918–1992) who devoted himself to the history of "Turkish religion" amongst several other subjects, is a typical example of a Turkish-Muslim

---

1   Harman's work covers a range of topics, both specific to Christian, Jewish, and Islamic traditions (such as the Bible, Christian Councils, Mary the mother of Jesus, missionaries, Christians, and Nazareth) to more general comparative treatments of topics like religion, sin, pilgrimage, saints, mountains, and women.

scholar caught in between the Western secular-oriented religious studies tradition and the Islamic studies tradition in Turkish faculties of divinity. He believes that there is no reason why the study of religion and the history of religions as an academic enterprise cannot be methodologically secular, and that Islamic studies can certainly benefit from the findings of the Western history of religion.[2] Another scholar in this category is Günay Tümer (1937–1995), the late professor of history of religions. In addition to his general contribution to the history of religions in Turkey, one of his major works is *Bîrûnî'ye Göre Dinler ve İslam Dîni* (Islam and Other Religions According to al-Bîrûnî). Al-Bîrûnî (d. 1048) is one of the most significant classical scholars of comparative religion in Islamic scholarly tradition. Tümer's work provides an analytical evaluation of al-Bîrûnî's works (*Kitabu`t-Tahqîq ma lil-Hind min maqûla maqbûla fi l-`aql aw mardhûla*) on Hinduism and Indian civilization.

Today in the field of history of religions, a disciplinary tradition has already emerged in Turkish faculties of divinity in which non-confessional studies are conducted on various aspects of non-Islamic religions.[3] There is also currently a Turkish Association for the History of Religion, not yet affiliated to the IAHR, that has already organized its third symposium in different subjects and published the papers as the *Proceedings of History of Religions*. The third conference was held as an international symposium on "The Past, Present and Future of Christianity in its 2000th year" in June 2001. This symposium was attended by scholars from outside Turkey such as Peter Antes, the president of IAHR. The author of this article also attended this symposium, delivering a paper on "Contemporary Jewish Christians in Britain as a case of Religious Hybridity." The *Proceedings* of this symposium were published in Turkish.

Returning to the phenomenology of religion and its relevance for the study of Islam, the contribution that the phenomenology of religion has made and may make to the ongoing enquiry into the significance of religion in human life must be acknowledged. The problem, however, in integrating "Western" approaches to the study of religion with Islamic studies arises precisely where the "phenomenology of religion" meets with questions of truth and meaning. Despite its significance for the study of religion, phenomenology can be criticized for evading the responsibility of identifying the epistemological ground on which knowledge is founded. It can be claimed that the phenomenological enterprise, as a descriptive endeavor with a focus on objective enquiry, defeats itself precisely because of its tendency to circumnavigate this question. In attempting a typology of manifestations of a comparative nature any data from

---

2   An Interview with Ömer Faruk Harman on the study of religion and the history of religion in Turkey, 23 July 2001, İstanbul.

3   These subjects range from Jewish Christianity to Maimonides, and from Mandeans to Hindû Scriptures.

the history of religious traditions it distorts the study of religion's aim to understand its subject, by implicitly taking up an agnostic stance in relation to the nature of knowledge or reality. The apparent objectivity or neutrality of this phenomenological approach is, on closer scrutiny, a judgment *against* religious worldviews. Despite Max Müller and his associates' belief that they could explain not just aspects of religion but *all* of religion through an investigation that was mainly historical (Pals 1996: 7), an alternative paradigm for the study of religion, as Donald Wiebe argues, is required. Wiebe criticizes the phenomenological approach for its relativism. It fails because it is uncritical in the way it determines its subject of study and in the way in which it is content to allow different "truths" to be possible. According to him, addressing the question of truth in a more direct way would be a contribution to methodology in the study of religion (Wiebe 1981: 228). This might even mean that we will need to reevaluate the status of sociology of religion, psychology of religion and practical theology as well as philosophy of religion and the history of religions (Ward 2000: 170).

In relation to the question of truth and the phenomenological approach, it is true that by means of *epoche*, a scholar of religion attempts to bracket his/her subjective position (Platvoet 1982: 5). Nevertheless, here theology, which is assumed to tackle the question of "truth," can be helpful, as it is not necessarily confined to doctrinal formulation. As Frank Whaling aptly argues, "there is the descriptive, historical, positivistic type of theology beloved of historians in each tradition who attempt to describe what the case is doctrinally in a functional way without passing over into value judgments." Such value judgments cannot be totally avoided for the contexts themselves contain presuppositions that are not value-free. Nevertheless, this is the nearest thing to a "phenomenological theology" and it focuses upon description rather than confessing the faith. On the other hand, systematic theology takes a confessional approach with no attempt to be value-free, in order to enhance the tradition. All religious traditions contain this type of theology. In line with this type of theology there is also the philosophical type of theology that engages other positions at a philosophical level by taking them seriously and reacting to them. In this stance, there is room for argument and divergence. Another type of theology is what might be broadly called the theology of dialogue that implies an open attitude towards learning from others (Whaling 1999: 239–40). We need to remember the fact that contemporary "religious studies" as a separate field of the study of religion arose out of the matrix of Christian theology (Whaling 1999: 239–40). In other words, there is a discernible process in the development of religious studies — on the one hand rejecting theology (while at the same time ironically drawing on Protestant theological tradition in the use of Otto, and beyond him, Schleiermacher), and on the other hand embracing Müller's idea that there can be a science of religion (Flood 1999: 18). Islamic studies in Turkey, against this backdrop, falls closest to what Whaling calls "phenomenological theology." (For a further analysis of phenomenological theology, see Laycock, ed., 1986: 1–22). However, there are still problems with regard to "phenomenology" itself.

As the phenomenological approach, or some variation of it, whatever it may be called, has gained ever more adherents—until recently, almost every historian of religions has been a phenomenologist at one point or another—the tendency has been for scholars to seize upon certain results of phenomenological analysis. There is no doubt that, as a result of the phenomenological method and the scholarly emphases it has established, our awareness of many areas of human religiousness has been vastly expanded; similarly the phenomenological mode of thinking has served to clarify and facilitate the task of the historian of religions. For the student of Islam, however, the succession of emphases and the direction of development in the history of religions have had little direct significance. Not all of these emphases evoke an immediate and enthusiastic response as offering resources to probe more deeper into the Islamic tradition and to forge more adequate understandings of it. Although phenomenology of religion can still be described as the systematic treatment of history of religion, as did W. Brede Kristensen in 1950s (Kristensen 1960), the study of Islam as a purely religious phenomenon results in major gaps and neglected areas, which are all the more unforgivable for being nonexistent in the study of Christianity and Judaism.

4. Islamic Studies in between Religious Studies and Theology

In the West, many universities, especially in England and Germany, no less than in the United States, have kept their old departments of theology or opened new ones. The situation has been similar in Turkey. However, a problem that is presenting itself more and more in faculties of divinity is the extent to which it is possible today to continue a course of Islamic studies that starts from the point of committed faith. Therefore, there is a tendency to substitute religious studies, where the phenomenon of "religion" is studied in a more detached, historical and interdisciplinary manner, although with sufficient attention paid to aspects of religious experience usually described as "spiritual" or "mystical." Despite this interdisciplinary tendency, however, the dominant orientation of study of religion in Turkey remains Islamic in character and approach. Other disciplines such as history of religions, sociology of religion, psychology of religion and philosophy of religion come in as complementary studies at undergraduate and postgraduate levels.

After all that has been said thus far, first and foremost it must be both acknowledged and emphasized that *Religionswissenschaft* is an Islamic discipline, in the sense that it first emerged as a scientific endeavor in the Muslim world. The honor of writing the first history of religion in world literature seems in fact to belong to the Muslim Shahrastanî (d. 1153), whose *Religious Groups and Schools of Philosophy* described and systematized all the religions of the then known world, as far as the boundaries of China (Sharpe 1986: 11). Therefore it can rightly be claimed to be a special legacy of Islam to humanity's intellectual history. But this discipline, like many other disciplines, suffered neglect in those centuries when Muslim attention was taken up with the struggle for independence from economic and political colonization. Where the Muslims left off, the West picked up, and thus the discipline was subsequently developed under a different worldview (Smart: 1991) and academic tradition, for different needs and purposes. The Enlightenment influence, and the evolutionary and anti-religious sentiments that have dominated the Western intellectual milieu over the last few centuries, led to a certain trend of thought that found its way into almost every aspect of disciplinary scholarship, including the study of religion. Henceforth grew numerous approaches, or methodologies, in the science of religion such as the anthropology of religion, the sociology of religion, the psychology of religion and the phenomenology of religion (from Chantepie de la Saussaye to Ninian Smart). It is amongst these patterns of thought that contemporary *Religionswissenschaft* stands (Kamaruzaman 1998: 31) and develops its "self-analysis." The roots of contemporary academia, institutionalized in the modern Western university system, are established in the soil of the Enlightenment. Religious Studies in the West, of course, is a relatively modern academic discipline that has tended to have a particularly uneasy relationship its older sibling, theology. The distinction often made between the two runs along the following lines: theology is the traditional study of the "Judaeo-Christian" religions, usually with some presumption of Christian allegiance. Religious studies, on the other hand, is a secular discipline that neither presumes nor precludes allegiance to any particular religious system or worldview. Within a secular academic institution, the conception of religious studies as an avowedly non-confessional, secular and "open-ended" academic discipline has clear advantages in terms of the prevailing attitude towards the academic work of that department. It also has implications for the perception of religious studies in the wider academic and non-academic communities in which scholars live and work. The very fact that the modern study of religion is not unaffected by the Christian heritage of Western culture and by the development of theology as an academic discipline in the West, in the sense that even humanistic and atheistic forms of secularism in the post-Enlightenment West continue to define themselves in opposition to the Christian theological categories that they claim to have superseded (King 1999: 41–42), is precisely the reason why Islamic scholars subsequently tend to think of religious studies as a Western discipline, with its methods and approaches being of little interest to them. Thus there is an urgent need to reactivate Muslim scholars' interest in this field in order to create a productive cooperation with non-Muslim scholarship, despite the fact that there are a number of theoretical presuppositions that condition the manner in which religions come to be understood by the modern Western academic. These factors are the success and development of natural sciences and the rise of scientific rationalism as a potent worldview in the modern Western world, the rise of secular humanism, a progressive view of history, and eurocentrism.

One major issue that allows us to better understand the question of "approaches" in the study of religion in Turkey is the relationship of social sciences to "religion." In other words, the relationship between the study of religion and the secular social sciences is a crucial topic to understand the question of "approaches" in the study of religion in Turkish academia. Social sciences in the modern sense entered Turkey through continental European studies of the social sciences and humanities. Nevertheless, they have been used in a selective way in order to appropriate whatever the researcher has in his/her academic agenda. This sometimes extends to using social sciences to develop an apologetic stance in favor of Islam. One also has to remember that the study of religions in general has no methods of its own. The methods that are appropriate to its very diverse materials and research goals are borrowed from the humanities and social sciences (Platvoet 1982: 225 n. 35). Therefore, they can also be seen as inadequate for the study of religion. There is of course a tendency to see the critical, reductionist approach to the interpretation of religion in the social sciences as "ill-defined." But one should remember that Muslim academics in Turkey read and know what is written and thought in distant places. Scholarly work elsewhere is taken up by Muslim scholars as part of the equipment with which they approach and appropriate their own heritage. That is to say, not only do Muslim scholars respond externally to the views of other scholars; they also incorporate new advances in understanding so that their own views of themselves and their tradition is changed and reformed by these new elements. On the other end of the scholarship, however, Islam continues to be excluded from the fields of sociology, social psychology, discourse analysis and cultural anthropology; it can even be said that since Ibn Rushd, Islam has been ignored by Western philosophers in their discussions of truth and its theory and practice (Arkoun 1987: 339). This is so, for example, in spite of the very significant contribution of the school of perennial philosophy (*philosophia perennis*), including scholars from different faith communities such as Seyyed Hossein Nasr, Huston Smith, A.K. Coomaraswamy, R. Guenon, T. Burckhardt, M. Lings and F. Schuon, that has articulately advanced the thesis that religions are different externally (in a formal and not in a judgmental way) but internally they converge at the level of spirituality (Whaling 1999: 239; Nasr 1982; Needleman 1986). One wonders here whether Edward Said is not correct in his analysis that the "area specialist" (Islamicists) or the social scientists who write on Islam continue to maintain an academic attitude—a learned perspective— towards the Islamic phenomenon with a well-informed Orientalist approach in the sense that their "… learned perspective can support the caricatures propagated in the popular culture ... the most current transformation overtaking Orientalism: its conversion from fundamentally philological discipline and a vaguely general apprehension of the Orient into a social science specialty" (Said 1995: 290). According to Said, the new Orientalist took over the attitudes of "traditional" Orientalism.

In terms of the present-day trends in the study of religion within Islamic studies in Turkish faculties of divinity, while there is an effort to integrate Islamic studies and the general study of religion more fully, there is also a greater openness to the study of other religious traditions. However, in comparison to the general study of religion, so far as understanding in the field of Islamics is concerned, proceeding from the preoccupations of the leading Western scholars of religion seems to have produced little gain. There are several reasons for this. At the points where the history of religions has had some of its greatest successes, it has been irrelevant to the work of Islamicists, and Islamicists have in consequence exhibited very little interest in what historians of religions have to say (Adams 1967: 182). According to Adams, this problem has emerged due to "an apparent lack of meaningful relationship between the systematic scientific study of religion on the one hand and the work done by Islamists on the other" (Adams 1985: vii). Muslim scholars, however, have described the problem somewhat differently. The late Fazlur Rahman, for example, believed that the study of Islam suffered a great deal in the West, not specifically because of the gap between historians and Islamists, but mainly because of the lack of scientific objectivity on the part of Western scholars. Citing the problems of prejudice, he explained that:

> pre-nineteenth century Western treatments of Islam suffered from ... [religious prejudice], while nineteenth and early twentieth century scholarship suffered particularly from ... [cultural and intellectual prejudice] (Fazlur Rahman 1985: 193).

This criticism has not gone without response. In an attempt to minimize possible prejudices, and to achieve a greater degree of scientific objectivity, Wilfred Cantwell Smith suggested that scholarly research which concerns a religious community should be verified by members of that community itself. Thus for a statement to be valid about a religion, it must be true or valid for those "inside" that religious tradition, not just according to the evidence drawn by "outside" scholars (Smith 1959: 18). Smith's suggestion seems to be a good starting point for overcoming past prejudices in regard to the study of Islam. Yet it is still not a complete answer to the problem of scholarly objectivity. Rahman has pointed out the problems in applying this principle by referring to the fact that there is no consensus amongst believers of any religion, including Islam. He has remarked that there are many statements made all the time by some insiders that are repudiated by other insiders (Fazlur Rahman 1985: 193–94). Rahman's criticism has been further strengthened by William Roff's question: "How many—or how few—Muslims may in such circumstances constitute a court?"

(Roff 1985: 78). Thus the problem of developing an objective or at least an unprejudiced methodology runs into the more basic problem of defining what is properly considered to be Islam or Islamic. Is it, as Wilfred Cantwell Smith argues, what Muslims believe? Is it something judged acceptable to the Muslim community? Or should one follow other tests of validity such as referring to the tenets of the religion itself, to the Qur'an as the revealed and infallible word of God and to historical accounts of the words and the conduct of Prophet Muhammad?

While all these questions remain to be addressed, one must nevertheless say that Muslim students of the history of religions recognize the positive contribution of the Western history of religions as a discipline and the phenomenological approach within an interdisciplinary context to the field of Islamic studies itself. Also, the interrelationship of several disciplinary approaches, namely ontological, epistemological, axiological, historical and sociological, might be a meaningful "anchor point" to understand the so-called differences between the Western and Islamic *Weltanschauung* in relation to the academic study of religion, notwithstanding the semantic differences of the key-concepts such as *dîn* (religion). Even the category of "religion" clearly has a history that is bound up with the cultural and intellectual history of the West and deserves some attention in any discussion on the nature of religious studies as a discipline in Muslim academia. The modern Western use of the concept of "religion" is the product of the culturally specific discursive processes of Christian history in the West and has been forged in the crucible of inter-religious conflict and interaction. Christianity has generally served as the prototypical example of a religion and thus, as the fundamental yardstick or paradigm-case for the study of "other religions." One of the central tasks for the scholar of non-Christian religions is, therefore, precisely to work towards untangling some of these presuppositions that have framed the discussions in the study of religion thus far (King 1999: 35).

In order to achieve this above-mentioned anchor point in Turkish Faculties of Divinity, a greater variety of compulsory and optional courses have been introduced in Divinity curricula. Courses in the fields of Qur'anic studies, Islamic legal studies, the Prophetic tradition and Islamic theology, are accompanied by courses on the history of religions, the sociology of religion, the psychology of religion, and so on. However, the latter, namely, general religious studies subjects, are predominantly Western-oriented in their theoretical and methodological approaches, with only occasional adaptation to Islamic cases and phenomena. There are, however, a few exceptions to this orientation. One such example is İzzet Er (1949–), a professor of sociology of religion, whose works address the compatibility of applying the methods and approaches of Western sociology of religion to Islamic phenomena, as a primary issue for the sociology of religion in relation to both Islamic and Turkish-Muslim phenomena. In *Sosyal Gelişme ve İslam* (Social Development and Islam),

Er constructs a sociological analysis of certain Islamic categories (such as the role of zakat—alms-giving as an economic institution in social stratification, mobility and integration) that helps us to understand Muslim societies both in historical and contemporary contexts. While he essentially does not see any difficulty in holding the social sciences idea of "objectivity" in his analysis, he also presents us an example of study that deals with its subject through the lines of an inevitable contextualization of culturally constructed scholarship. According to Er, this does not and should not contradict with the general ethos of the sociology of religion (Er 1999: xii).

Er's other contributions to Turkish sociology of religion can be found in his *Din Sosyolojisi* (Sociology of Religion), a collection of his articles on various subjects from the history of sociology of religion in Turkish academia to a sociology of "*hijrah*-migration" in the Islamic context. Er's work reveals a disciplinary stance that questions how Muslim social scientists do their work of sociological theorizing, how Muslim social and cultural systems are to be defined and ordered, and what relationship they will have with the modern world. In his writings, Er draws his readers' attention to the distinctions between the culturally and historically constructed, secular development of Western sociology of religion, and sociological studies of religion on Muslim societies. One of Er's central emphases is that the experience of modernity should not be taken as equal to Westernization, and that Muslims can experience modernity within an Islamic civilizational and cultural context. His analyses of migration, modernization, religion and the social environment, Islamic sociology, and Ibn Khaldûn's founding position in the history of Islamic social science are all valuable contributions to the sociology of religion in the Turkish-Muslim context (Er 1998).

Er's work will prompt a careful reader to think that timeless (eternal), non-spatial (universal), and non-social (abstract) concepts alone will not help us construct a social theory relevant to a contemporaneously, empirically and materially existent Muslim society. What Muslim social scientists need is an empirical-theoretical paradigm of Muslim society that can serve the needs of Muslims practically, empirically, and reconstructively, not a paradigm within which real social problems and puzzles are only solved in the abstract. Muslim scholarship needs to develop a social science of societal change—of reformation and transformation. The "social, economic, and political in institutional relation with the religious" should be the framework for theorizing and social action within which Islamic social science theories have to be constructed and their conclusions and findings recommended for implementation. Considering the fact that Western social science assumes that humans are rational beings and constructs its theories on the basis of this assumption, what meta-theory with regard to philosophical anthropology can an Islamic social science set for itself? How can this social science work out a micro-macro integration or the agency-structure linkage either in theory or practice? In working out this kind of social science, one has to be aware of the fact that all sorts of historical, sociological, and political factors, indeed, politics itself, enter into the choice of a paradigm of any science. The Kuhnian definition of a paradigm reveals the significance of this integration of dimensions: "the entire constellation of beliefs, values, techniques, and so on shared by the members of a given community" (Kuhn 1970: 175). What the paradigm for Islamic social science will be is an all-important question facing Muslim scholars of religion. It is from this form of the study of religion that religious studies in Turkey might come closer to an approach that recognizes that theology in future, a theology within a re-enchanted world, will be more aware of the place it occupies in discursive borderlands, and that theology is profoundly interdisciplinary, drawing upon the work done in both natural and cultural sciences (Ward 2000: 171).

5. Islamic Studies from Contextualization to Contextualism

In Turkish academia, the study of religion within the framework of theologically-oriented studies is traditionally represented by Islamic studies. This is due to the fact that we are the history makers: we perceive a chain of events and see progress in that chain. Theology's concern with the question of history and "tradition" is profound. The Islamic faith is rooted in historical, sometimes "meta-historical," events. The various disciplines of Islamic studies are deeply concerned with historical texts and events. Where do the facts end and their interpretations begin? What do the facts about the life of Muhammad the Prophet of Islam mean for the contemporary person and how are they determined? Islamic theology's concern with history does not stop at its meditation upon the founding events of the Islamic religion and their interpretation. The changes and transformations in the Islamic tradition of interpretations itself is a history—a history of dissemination and traditions (for example, in Islamic jurisprudence, *Hadith*, and *Kalâm*). It is a history given particular theological validation in terms of the origins of the Islamic ethos, and how it remains relevant and effective today. On the one hand, Islamic studies from Islamic Law (*Fıqh*) to Islamic Theology (*Kalâm*) and from Qur'anic studies to the *Hadith* deal with the essential question of how Islam as a historical and prophetic tradition remains relevant for contemporary mind and heart. On the other hand, the very secularist experience in Turkey where the West and Islam meet in a unique way inevitably draws scholars of Islamic studies to tackle this question in an interdisciplinary context in order to maintain the sense of continuity of Islam on Turkish soil, or whatever remained from the "last of the caliphates."

In terms of how Islamic studies from Islamic Law (*Fıqh*) to Islamic Theology (*Kalâm*) and from the Qur'anic studies to the Hadith deal with the essential question of Islamic origins and its relevance for contemporary life, the most significant area of theoretical debate within Islamic scholarship and the study of religion in Turkey today is the methodological debate over the question of contextualization. As far as Islamic studies are concerned, "theology/religious studies" scholars in Turkey are deeply engaged in this task of contextualization. The notion of context is a way of both comprehending past plenitude and portraying it through "thick description," to borrow a term from Clifford Geertz (Geertz 1973: 14). For the Islamic studies tradition in Turkish academia, the question of contextualization is of central importance for the ways and methods Islamic sources and origins are interpreted. Through contextualization, words and sentences must be read in the context of the document, and the document itself read as part of its community of discourse of the belief system that gave it meaning at the time. Discourses, worldviews, and beliefs in turn must be understood in the context of their times and cultures. Likewise, human activities and institutions are to be understood in relation to the larger network of behavior or social organization and structure of which they are said to be part. Social, political, religious, economic, family, and other institutional practices make sense only when placed in their social and cultural contexts (Berkhofer 1995: 31). Although they do not question the desirability of finding "proper context" as the appropriate background for understanding the Islamic past, behaviors, and institutions, scholars in various disciplines of Islamic studies and the study of religion in Turkish universities differ among themselves about what constitutes a proper context in any given case. Contextualization in Islamic studies predominantly operates as a "modernist" methodology and in the end tend to turn into contextualism. This is exactly what "non-modernist" scholars of Islamics criticize. According to them, contextualization is also a question of "position." The study of religion itself becomes a question of position. A position, such as phenomenology, which seems to deny the link between "religious phenomena" and "meaning" is, for example, necessarily a critical position regarding religion. Overtly antireligious perspectives like secularism or Marxism likewise view the history of Islam in a negative light. From a religious perspective, the representations of a religion contain or refer to a tradition-specific reality, whereas from a phenomenological perspective, because of the separation of meaning from phenomena, this link is broken. This is not to say that religious discourse such as Islamic Theology is irrational, but rather that the legitimacy of a discourse is governed by the wider historical context in which it is embedded, as opposed to some notional, independent rationality. Certainly, rational process is a property of most discourse, based upon sometimes unreflexive, unquestioned presuppositions. An Islamic discourse about Qur'anic Law clearly operates according to processes which are rational (such as the method and approach of *İjtihâd*), but within the boundary of the presuppositions of the Qur'an as revelation, while phenomenological discourse about Islamic law and origins operates according to secular rationality, itself founded upon the ontological presuppositions of modernity.

It is exactly at this point that, Hayreddin Karaman (1934–),[4] professor of Islamic Law and a leading scholar in Turkey, observes that in terms of the study of religion, Islamic Law with its "methodological philosophy" (*Usûl al-Fıqh*) is not just any discipline but a discipline reflecting the whole Islamic *Weltanschauung*; consequently, Islamic studies cannot follow the phenomenological approach, through which the discourse/study is separated from the subject and the "truth" is bracketed. According to Karaman, the recent trends in Turkish academic circles that claim to "reread" and "reinterpret" Islamic origins are essentially confused methodologically and epistemologically. He believes that these "re-readings" are just new attempts to rewrite Islamic thought and history overall in the name of a new hermeneutical approach. This approach is no more than a reductionist and simplistic way of incorporating the ontological presuppositions of modernity into the Islamic framework under the pressure of the Turkish experience of secularism. In doing so, these modernist interpreters of Islamic sources (the Qur'an and the *Hadith*), origins (the Early Islamic History) and traditions (*Fıqh*, *Kalâm*, etc.) simply take the easy road to arrive at both modern and at the same time Islamic solutions, bypassing the challenging and more systematized method and approach of *Ijtihad*[5] as an

---

4   Hayreddin Karaman is currently the most well known scholar of Islamic law in Turkey; he retired from his chair at the Faculty of Divinity at Marmara University in 2001. After many years spent in the service of academia at both undergraduate and postgraduate levels, with both his classical and modern knowledge he still continues to contribute to various debates ranging from academic topics to questions like 'how to live as a Muslim in a secular society' such as the Turkish society through his writings and once-a-week column in a daily newspaper (Yeni Şafak). Karaman's views on the subject quoted in this article were taken from a personal interview with him on July 30, 2001.

5   *Ijtihâd* literally means hard striving, but technically it means exercising independent juristic reasoning to provide answers when the Qur'an and Sunnah are silent. Islamic jurisprudence dealt with questions of religion and acts of worship, and with legal transactions, along with all provisions, rules, and particulars derived from them. That is why jurists in Islam were at once men of religion and jurisprudence. They were called "scholars" (`ulamâ) because their field of study included all departments of ancient knowledge. As a result, Islamic jurisprudence played such a significant role in the history of Islamic thought as well as in all aspects of Muslim life. It is known that Islamic jurisprudence is based on two sources: the Qur'an and the Sunnah (The Prophetic Tradition). There are various methods accepted by the majority of the jurists to derive rules from these two sources. *Ijmâ*` (consensus of opinion) and *qıyâs* (analogy) are the two major ones. There are other methods acknowledged by some schools but refuted by others. These are based on necessity, custom and equity; such as *istihsân* (appropriateness) in the Hanafi school, *al-masâleh al-mursalah* (excepted interests) in the Mâlikî school, and the like. The jurists took up all these sources and methods, known as evidence (*adillâh*) of the law, in a special branch of knowledge called `ilm al-usûl

internal interpretative dynamic in Islamic scholarly tradition, thereby producing hybrid and at best superficial answers. Karaman suggests that the method and approach of *Ijtihâd* is certainly worth taking seriously in religious studies discourse in relation to Islamic studies. He strongly believes that the Islamic tradition of scholarship needs only to revitalize and reformat its methods, approaches and meta-theories in the light of modernity's (and post-modernity's) ontological and sociological challenge. *Ijtihad*, from this perspective, is the premier theoretical approach and method for recasting the Islamic studies tradition, rather than "putting everything into the basket of historicism," since historicism is essentially a secular-modernist stance in relation to religion and society.

In the view of non-modernist Muslim scholars, historicism is a principle underlying the contextualist approach. Contextualism is not necessarily the same as contextualization. Contextualism as a methodology in religious studies presupposes that events and ideas can be explained only by being set within the context of their occurrence. Why they occurred as they did is to be explained by the revelation of the specific relationships they bore to other events occurring in their circumambient historical space. The contextualist insists that

---

(science of basic sources and methods). They began to work at discovering legal solutions from such sources and evidences. This sort of activity was and is referred to as *ijtihâd* (endeavor or interpretation). It was a cause and approach at the same time for expanding legal provisions to comprise new cases, as well as strong factor in the development of Islamic law according to the needs of countries and the conditions of changing times. If questions arose about the meaning of a Qur'anic text or tradition or revelation, and early Muslim practice were silent, jurists applied their own reasoning through these methods to interpret the sources. *İjtihâd* essentially consists of an inference (*istinbât*) that amounts to a probability (*zann*), thereby excluding the extraction of a ruling from a clear text. The laws or rulings are provided by clear texts from a specific framework called *al-ma'lûm min ad-dîn bid-darûra*, meaning that they partake of the fundamental essence of Islamic jurisprudence and that they lead, if rejected, to the negation of Islam. Nevertheless the great majority of the Qur'anic verses and the Prophet's traditions are not of this very strict nature. The Qur'an is authenticated per se (*qat'î ath-thubut*) but the majority of verses containing legal rulings (*âyât al-ahkâm*) are subject to analysis, commentaries and interpretations (*zannî*) as is the case for the Prophet's traditions (*ahâdith*) which are for the most part open to speculation regarding both their authenticity (*thubût*) and their meaning (*daleel*). *İjtihâd* as a whole (as both a source and approach), has in fact been considered by many 'ulamâ (scholars of Islam) as the third chief source of the Islamic Law in which one will *find ijmâ'*, *qıyâs, istislâh, istihsân* along with all the known subdivisions among the so-called supplementary sources of the Islamic law. The various methods of Islamic law that feature next to the Qur'an and Sunnah are all manifestations of *ijtihâd*, albeit with differences that are largely procedural in character. In this way, consensus of opinion, analogy, juristic preference, considerations of public interest, etc., are all inter-related under the heading of *ijtihâd*. For further details, see Kamalî 1991.

"what happened" in the field can be accounted for by the specification of the functional interrelationships existing among the agents and agencies occupying the field at a given time (Ritter 1986: 183–88; also, D'Amico 1989). Whether or not contextualism produces accurate explanation with regard to religious phenomena according to social scientific standards, its exponents, whether in Islamic studies or Christian studies, believe that historicism is the principle approach for contextualism. Historicism, therefore, means that what happened is described and thereby explained in terms of when it happened (such as referring certain Islamic traditions back to the Arab *jaahiliyyah*/pre-Islamic culture) and what happened around it at the same time or over time, depending upon emphasis is put on synchronous or diachronous interpretations. This is not to argue whether historians do or do not abstract, generalize, select, and organize data as they contextualize, for they do. As a consequence of contextualism's presuming and producing uniqueness as its chief explanatory or interpretive mode, modernist scholars in the area of Islamic studies tend to describe past ideas, activities, events, and institutions as more and more self-contained and distant from the present day as they are increasingly contextualized to their times. This contextualism through historicism results in various degrees of cultural and historical relativism. This is a major challenge facing Muslim scholarship in theology and religious studies.

One of the essential tasks of theology and religious studies in Turkish universities, therefore, seems to be to develop a meaningful, stronger but contemporary discourse, over the "old" question of whether "religion" (interpreted through metaphysics, theology, and general religious studies) can be taken as a source for the genuine knowledge achieved through the methods of science. A contemporary discourse within Islamic studies tradition will help to develop a reflexive contextualization of the religious phenomenon without going to the extreme of contextualism.

In Turkey, contextualization, and the historicist position of contextualism, are currently major areas of debate in the field of Qur`anic studies and exegesis. This can be seen, for example, in a recent series of publications such as the proceedings of *A Symposium on the Question of 'Historicism' in Understanding the Qur`an—November 1996*. The discussions presented here clearly suggest that contemporary Turkish scholars of religion and Islamic studies are aware of where current debates in hermeneutics, philosophy of history, and religious studies are heading in general. But the problem lies in the central question of the extent to which historical and textual criticism under the methodological approach of historicism ought be applied to Islamic origins. This book from the Symposium provides us an opportunity to read and engage in this critical debate through the opinions of a group of leading Turkish scholars of Islamic studies. Another significant text is *İslam Düşüncesinde Yeni Arayışlar* (New Perspectives in Islamic Thought, I–III), a collection of writings and papers presented in various conferences and symposia in Turkey. This series of books contains the views of Turkish-Muslim scholars on various subjects ranging from the familiar question of historicism to the question of whether the Qur'an is a "word," "text" or "logos," whether "the purposes of *sharia*" can be a methodological base for interpreting the Islamic origins in a historicist approach, to the question of Qur'anic hermeneutics.

This debate around historicism and contextualism with regard to Islamic origins takes a different turn when one looks at Islamic philosophy. According to Mehmet Aydın (1943–), now a leading scholar in the field as a professor of philosophy of religion, it seems that the traditional Turkish attitude to philosophy in general and to Islamic philosophy in particular never freed itself from the influence of Islam's classical writings, especially al-Ghazzâlî's well-known criticism of the *falâsifah*. Aydın points out that it was due to this influence that one can see a theologico-philosophical endeavor which one might loosely name as "the *tahâfut* tradition" — a tradition which was largely based on *Tahâfut al-Falâsifah* ("The Incoherence of the Philosophers") and which took little notice of the *Tahâfut al-Tahâfut* of Ibn Rushd. This does not mean, however, that al-Ghazzâlî's criticism of the *falâsifah* was accepted uncritically. Aydın believes that in spite of the classical and modern interest in some major theological and philosophical problems, Islamic philosophy, especially its metaphysical dimension, never became popular in the Ottoman educational system (Aydın 1996: 113). The situation is quite different in Turkish Faculties of Divinity today. There are many works, published and unpublished, in the field of Islamic Philosophy. Aydın, a leading scholar who has contributed to Islamic philosophy through his writings, currently teaches at postgraduate level at Faculty of Divinity in İzmir. One of Aydın's works is his *Din* Felsefesi (Philosophy of Religion) in which he explores Islamic theological discussions at the juxtaposition of *Kalâm* and contemporary philosophy of religion. A collection of his philosophical writings on various subjects, from the idea of *Al-Madîna Al-Fâdıla* (*The Virtuous City* by Al-Fârabî) to Ibn Sîna's understanding of happiness, and from al-Ghazzâlî's Approach to the question of '*Ta'wîl*' (method of interpretation, an important subject for Islamic scholars) to *Mawlânâ's* understanding of freedom of the will, and to Muhammad Iqbâl's analysis of religious experience can be found in another work, *İslam* Felsefesi Yazıları (Essays on Islamic Philosophy) (Aydın 2000). Aydın's essential focus has been to emphasize the need to first rediscover the Islamic philosophical tradition and then reflect upon it from a contemporary perspective.

As for the specific theological discipline *Kalâm* (Islamic theology) in Islamic scholarship, the medieval Christian use of the expression of "theology as the queen of the sciences" reminds us that it would not possibly be surprising to know that Kalâm used to be treated as the highest of the disciplines (*ashraf al-'uloom*) in classical Islamic tradition. In fact, Islamic systematic theology arguably pre-dates Christian "systematic" theology, with tenth century Asharite and Maturidite scholars producing comprehensive philosophical and theological accounts of Islamic belief two centuries before Thomas Aquinas (1226–1274) produced a similar account for Christianity.

Regarding contemporary studies in the field of Islamic theology, relatively new and "non-confessional" works have already become available for the academic and general reader in Turkey. A leading scholar in the field of Islamic theology is Bekir Topaloğlu (1936–) whose works (Topaloğlu 1985) have provided a valuable foundation for the new generation of theologians in Turkish faculties of divinity. For example, Ahmet S. Kılavuz (1954–), one of his students, focused on the question of "the borderline between blasphemy and faith" in his doctoral study which is an example of new interdisciplinary trends in theological studies in Turkey. Kılavuz is currently a professor of *Kalâm* and teaches Islamic theology/*Kalâm* in the faculty of theology of Uludağ University. In this work, he presents his subject in an interdisciplinary context of theology and Islamic law. Following a descriptive analysis of the views of various Sunnî theological schools on the question of blasphemy, he connects his theological analysis of blasphemy with the question of apostasy in Sunnî-Hanafî legal tradition. In doing so, Kılavuz takes a non-confessional stance (Kılavuz 1994). Kılavuz's *İslam Akâidi ve Kelâm'a Giriş* (Introduction to Islamic Theology) is also a very concise but analytical textbook for those who are interested in the concepts, debates, schools and history of *Kalâm*, a book that needs to be made available for the international academia in Islamic studies (Kılavuz 1987). It provides a systematic, descriptive analysis of Muslim theological schools and trends with an extended bibliography. A similar work in terms of approach is by Cağfer Karadaş (1964–), who, in his recently published doctoral work, deals with Ibn Arabî's theological views in an interdisciplinary way, taking a non-confessional approach, an uncommon stance in the field of Islamic mysticism and theology. Karadaş presents Ibn Arabî as a scholar of multiple disciplines — from philosophy to theology — who brought together the various threads of rich Islamic disciplines with a new *sûfî* terminology (Karadaş 1998).

Scholars of Islamic theology in Turkey frequently refer to *İzmirli İsmail Hakkı* (1868–1949), an early twentieth century Turkish scholar of *Kalâm*, whose so-called *New Kalâm* is seen as a fresh attempt to revitalize Islamic theological discussion. With his bridging approach to al-Ghazzâlî and Ibn Taymiyyah, the two opposite ends of Islamic theology and interpretation, İzmirli is recognized as one of the few contemporary Turkish Muslim scholars of *Kalâm* to relate his theological views to philosophy and Islamic law. İzmirli attempted to synthesize *Kalâm* and *Falsafah* under the name of *Yeni İlm-i Kelâm* ("new theology"). He also made comparisons between the *Mutasawwıfs* (Islamic Sûfî masters) and Western mystics. His reply to a letter about Islamic religion sent by the Anglican Church in 1916 to *Dâr al-Hikmah* (then the highest religious institution in İstanbul) was later summarized by Abdulaziz Çaviş and translated into Turkish by Mehmet Akif (İzmirli 1946: 249–51). In various areas of Islamic studies, there are certainly others who ought be mentioned for their contributions to Islamic studies in contemporary Turkish intellectual history. There is a need for individual works by scholars like Ahmed Hilmi, Musa Kazım, Said Halim Pasha, Hamdi Yazır, Ferid Kam, İsmail Fennî and Said Nursî to be made available in Western languages. One valuable source to learn more generally about the contributions of these Turkish scholars to Islamic studies is *Türkiye'de İslamcılık Düşüncesi—Metinler ve Kişiler* (Islamicist Thought in Turkey—Texts and Authors) by İsmail Kara (Kara 1987).

Another interesting disciplinary area in Islamic studies in Turkey is *Tasawwof* (Islamic Mysticism). The history of the subject of, and discourses about *Tasawwof* is not much different from the history of other Islamic disciplines in faculties of divinity in Turkey. However, it is perhaps due to the problematic history of popular *Tasawwof* in the Turkish experience of republican secularism that the subject was integrated into undergraduate and graduate teaching at a relatively late stage. Virtually until the 1950s, Islamic mysticism was not a subject of academic study in Turkish studies of religion aside from a few individual but important works. This was a period of silence in the area of academic *Tasawwof* in Turkey due to the political pressure placed on *sûfi* groups, a consequence of the policy of radical secularization that abolished religious orders and their cloisters.

This silencing notwithstanding, there were individual works on *Sûfism* in Turkey in the first quarter of the twentieth century. The earliest known academic study in the field of *Tasawwof* is considered to be *Malâmiyyah and the Malamites* by A.B. Gölpınarlı (1900–1982) which appeared in 1930. Gölpınarlı was an outstanding writer who authored approximately 100 books and 400 articles in the field of Islamic mysticism. The first faculty of divinity in 1949 did not include *Tasawwof* in its academic courses. However, following *Jareeda-i Sûfiyyah* (1909–1919), the first known journal on *Sûfism*, another journal called *Tasawwof* appeared in 1949 that discussed various subjects in philosophy and mysticism. According to Mustafa Kara (1951–), a professor of Islamic mysticism, what one can call an "academic study of *Tasawwof*" emerged in the 1970s through major translations of *Sûfi* classical writings into Turkish. One such example is the 1976 translation of *Shifâu's Sâeel* of Ibn Khaldûn by Süleyman Uludağ (1940–), a professor of Islamic thought and mysticism. Kara, who was a student of Uludağ's, continued his work in topics related to various local histories of Turkish *sûfism* (Kara 1993), whereas Uludağ's contributions in the field of Islamic thought and mysticism came through his very informative academic introductions to his translations of classical *Sûfi* literature, and later on his widely read book entitled *The Structure of Islamic Thought*.[6] This book looks at the three major trends and schools in the history of Islamic scholarly

---

6   Süleyman Uludağ and Mustafa Kara are currently professors of Islamic thought and *Sûfism* at the faculty of divinity in Uludağ University, Bursa.

tradition: *Salafiyyah* (the traditionist), *Kalâm* (Islamic theology), and *Tasawwof* (Islamic mysticism), with general mention of the place of *Falsafah* (philosophy) in relation to these three schools. Uludağ essentially attempts to remind his readers that these various schools of interpretation are all parts of the wider circle of Islamic tradition of interpretation, each emphasizing different dimensions of the same discourse, namely *Salafiyyah* with its preoccupation with the *nass* (revealed text), and *naql* (narrative), *Kalâm* with its emphasis on `aql (reason) and *istidlâl* (drawing rational analysis from the rule), and *Tasawwof* with its priority of *kashf* (experimental/inspired knowledge) and *ilhâm* (inspirational knowledge). According to Uludağ, these three lines of interpretation are complementary epistemological approaches to each other, with various types of standpoints within them. The most liberal position is *Tasawwof* and the strictest one is *Salafiyyah*. Uludağ describes the *falsafah* in historical Islamic tradition as always struggling for recognition, especially due to the Ghazzalian influence (Uludağ 1985). Uludağ's other contributions include his Turkish translation of *Fasl al-Maqâl*, a philosophical treatise, and *al-Kashf `an Minhaj al-udellah*, a theological treatise, both by the famous classical scholar Ibn Rushd. In addition to his informative introduction to these translations, Uludağ tells us that the importance of these two treatises comes from the fact that in *Fasl* Ibn Rushd basically argues for, and in fact defends the *falsafah*, without denying the place of revelation, whereas in *al-Kashf* he directs his criticism from philosophical and theological perspectives against the then and to some extent still dominant theological (*Kalâm*) school of *al-Ash`ariyyah*, including the question of *Ta`wîl* (Uludağ 1985: 61–73).

In Turkish theological circles there is a significant interest in studying Ibn Arâbî, as seen in both through published and unpublished academic work. *Diyânet*, the Directorate of Religious Affairs in the Turkish government, has generally kept silent on the question of Islamic mysticism, probably due to the Turkish legal ban on the *Sûfî* orders in effect in Turkey since 1925. It nevertheless published a few works on the subject, one of which is a major work entitled *the First Sûfîs in Turkish Literature* by Fuad Köprülü (1890–1966) who was a well-known scholar in the field.

Any reference to academic and intellectual work in the field of *Tasawwof* in Turkey would be incomplete without making mention of Erol Güngör's (1938–1983) major intellectual work, *İslam Tasavvufunun Meseleleri* (Issues on Islamic Mysticism, 1980). Although the late Güngör was a professor of social psychology, his two major works are considered intellectual masterpieces on the subjects with which each deals. The first, *İslam Tasavvufunun Meseleleri*, engages its subject from both comparative and social psychological perspectives. With his valuable assessments of topics varying from the origins of *Sûfism* to the concept of *Ma`rifah* (knowledge), from the psychology of *Wajd* (spiritual ecstasy) to contemporary problems facing *Sûfism*, the quality of his scholarship is outstanding (Güngör 1987). *İslam'ın Bugünkü Meseleleri* (Contemporary

Problems of Islam) is another masterpiece in which Güngör eloquently and deeply engages in analytical debates surrounding Islamic history, philosophy, worldview, modernity and Muslim society, Islamic law, and politics (Güngör 1987). Today, these books are included in the lists of required readings for students of faculties of divinity.

Perhaps it is best to conclude this section with a brief but necessary mention of *The TDV Encyclopaedia of Islam*, one of the most important publications financed by the Turkish Religious Foundation (*Türkiye Diyanet Vakfı, TDV*). Ten years after it was initiated in 1983 under the Directorate of Encyclopaedia, the work was administratively transferred to the Centre for Islamic Studies (*İslam Araştırmaları Merkezi, TDV*) in 1993. This Centre for Islamic Studies[7] continues with this work of the publication of the *Encyclopaedia of Islam* which currently has published its 22nd volume, and is expected to comprise 35 to 40 volumes in total. *The TDV Encyclopaedia of Islam* is in Turkish and consists of completely original articles, of which there will be at least 18,000 when completed. Under the supervision of various committees in specialist areas from *Tafsîr* (Exegesis) to *Fıqh* (Islamic Jurisprudence), from Islamic history and civilization to the history of religions, and from Islamic arts to Arabic literature, the *Encyclopaedia* provides rich academic articles with reliable up-to-date sources. So far contributions have been received from over 900 Turkish and foreign scholars. Faculties of divinity have always been the main source of academic support to this project in Turkey. It is expected that the *TDV Encyclopaedia of Islam* will be a most significant contribution of Turkish scholarship in Islamic and religious studies, when completed and (it is hoped) translated into various languages.

6. Conclusion

Cultural experience is always experience of the others: the others, the real others, are the indispensable transformational objects in historical change. History is created out of cultures in relation and reaction. This, it is hoped, means that a non-European contribution to the study of religion, as well as in other areas, can play a critical-constructive role in "re-historicizing" European academic and social culture. It affords the possibility to expose the whole range of European experiences, in depth, to other norms, other values, and perhaps other categories. It is from the perspective of this vision that this article has surveyed the academic history and context of the study of religion in Turkey.

---

7   The author worked in this Centre as a research fellow in his subject area of history of religions from 1990 to 1993.

There is considerable hope that general Islamic studies in faculties of divinity in Turkish universities will be more open to recognizing that the broad objectives of history of religions, i.e., arriving at an understanding of religious phenomena qua "religious," dovetails with the concerns of those studying the tradition and forms of Islamic religiousness. Perspectives should be freed from the limitation of two ways of looking at and thinking about the world, namely, the effects of the "post-modern condition" on the one hand, and the use of criteria, definitions, and values inherited from the Enlightenment tradition to analyze all other cultures and societies on the other (Arkoun 1987: 340). What needs to be done is to work towards reflexive and multicultural (con)textualizations in religious studies. Only openness to such an orientation will allow for the generation of comprehensive answers that also derive dynamically from within the methodological approaches of religious traditions themselves.

As Russell McCutcheon has argued, the role of the scholar of religion involves giving up the claim that "religion" has an autonomous essence and "developing interdisciplinary connections with their colleagues in the social sciences, investigating the theoretical basis for their scholarly interests, and communicating to their undergraduate and graduate students the situated, polymethodic, polytheoretical nature of scholarly discourses" (McCutcheon 1997: 210). This approach, however, should provide a suitable perspective through which Islamic phenomena could be studied, not only as a set of abstract categories but a tradition that lives in history and society, and is espoused, in one way or another, by nearly a billion people on the face of the earth.

In terms of the relation between religious studies and Islamic studies, the ground has now shifted, and old debates and antagonisms between religious studies and theology as such have been or, in fact, should be superseded by fresh debates in the wider academy. Although they have different histories and approaches, both religious studies and Islamic studies are kinds of "writings about religion," with convergence and divergence, and both arise from the practice of "rational" methods. If there is an essential difference between the two, this is the difference of language. Whereas religious studies is a kind of writing about religion in which there is a clear separation between the discourse and the object of the discourse, Islamic studies, on this view, is a kind of writing about religion in which there is no separation between the discourse and its object. The language of Islamic studies is a language which expresses religion whereas the language of religious studies is a language about religion. The issue of the distinction between religious studies and Islamic studies as a category of "theological" studies is, therefore, about different kinds of discourse and about the kind of the language they employ. This point allows us to conclude that there is no reason why Islamic studies in general cannot use or incorporate the data as well as methodological approaches of religious studies in a reflexive way.

Today it is difficult for Islamic scholars to ignore the work of religious studies scholars. In this article it has been possible to consider only a few figures and works in the Turkish tradition of the study of religion. Islamic studies in Turkey can scarcely function without some awareness of the contribution of the study of religion outside the Islamic circle. It would be misleading to give the impression that the contemporary enterprise of religious studies is nothing other than old-style history of religions (historical, philological, philosophical) forced into an administrative (and secular) marriage of convenience with the social sciences. What is suggested here is that the re-entry of theology into contemporary discourse can bring new intellectual opportunities. Theology (and here it is worth noting that there are Jewish, Muslim, and Hindû theologies as well as the Christian varieties dominant in Europe and North America) in principle elucidates, not human behavior, but divine revelation as mediated by figures like prophets, lawgivers, seers or saviors, communicated along a line of authoritative tradition. What has been attempted here is to remind ourselves that knowledge of where we have been may at least convey a sense of proportion, and can communicate a sense of the lasting importance of a broad approach to the study of religion and religions. In our view, as long as "theology" can become and remain pluralistic (acknowledging a diversity of contexts), applied, rooted, critical, constructive and imaginative (as its object, belief in God cannot be objectified), then the study of religion in general is still in need of it. It must approach its tasks and responsibilities with sensitivity and openness, not prejudice and presumption.

In ending this overview of the study of religion, the history of religions and Islamic studies in Turkey, I would like to summarize my point in Frank Whaling's words:

> [t]here is the potential problem of religious studies being reduced to theology, just as there is the potential problem of religious studies being reduced to psychology, sociology, history, and so on ... The developing global situation, with its ecological, humane, and moral/transcendental problems and opportunities, demands an input from religious studies and theology that neither can offer separately (Whaling 1999: 256–57).

Study is something we do on a basis of the images and impressions we have formed in interplay with the values we hold. By the time these reach us, they will have passed through many minds and along chains of tradition, some of them shaped by the sanctuary and others by the academy, while others remain practically unclassifiable. Whether we call the enterprise "religious studies," "the history of religions" or "the study of religion," has little bearing on these conditions. In every case we are confronted both by our presuppositions and those of the societies, communities and cultures to which we belong. We need to be modest enough to acknowledge that to listen others is an art; to grasp what they are saying involves both a craft and a science.

In conclusion, one might quote a beautiful illustration from Ibn Arabî, one of the famous *Sûfî* masters. He says that:

[w]hen we look at a jewel which has been set in a ring, we first think that this jewel was made for the ring. But if we think deeply in the matter we realize that it is the ring which has been made in such a way as to enable us to set the jewel in it and was made for the jewel, not the jewel for the ring. Similar is the case with the human receptacle and divine revelation (S.H. Nasr 1997: 101).

If the subject matter of religious studies is, in this sense, the relationship between the human receptacle and divine revelation, then the final point may be that a universal approach of religious studies is still in the making with the contribution of the Other. From this perspective, religion is not fully translatable into religious studies, and this is an analytical and interpretative truth. Within the borders of intellectual standards and academic rigor, the study of religion can even be a critique of everything in the light of the sharpened awareness of the Real. This is a critical awareness to which Turkish scholarship in the field of the study of religion and Islamic studies in Turkey is open.

Bibliography

Adams, Charles J. (1967), "The History of Religions and the Study of Islam," in: Joseph M. Kitagawa/Mircea Eliade/Charles H. Long, eds., *The History of Religions—Essays on the Problem of Understanding*. Chicago/London: The University of Chicago Press.

—— (1985), "Foreword," in: *Approaches to Islam in Religious Studies*, ed. by Richard Martin. Tucson, Ariz.: University of Arizona Press.

Ahmad, Feroz (1993), *The Making of Modern Turkey*. London: Routledge.

Akyüz, Yahya (1999), *Türk Eğitim Tarihi* [History of Turkish Education—from the Beginning to 1999]. İstanbul: Alfa.

Arkoun, Muhammad (1987), "Islamic Studies: Methodologies," in: M. Eliade, ed., *The Encyclopedia of Religion*, vol. 7: 332–40.

Atay, Hüseyin (1983), *Osmanlılarda Yüksek Din Eğitimi* [Religious Studies in Ottoman Higher Education]. İstanbul: Dergâh Yayınları.

Aydın, Mehmet (1985), *Turkish Contribution to Philosophy*. Ankara: Atatürk Kültür Merkezi.

—— (1990), *Din Felsefesi* [Philosophy of Religion]. İzmir: D.E.Ü. Matbaası.

—— (1996), "History of Islamic Philosophy in Turkey," in: S.H. Nasr/O. Leeman, *History of Islamic Philosphy*. Part I-II. London: Routledge.

—— (2000), *İslam Felsefesi Yazıları* [Writings on Islamic Philosophy]. İstanbul: Ufuk Yayınları.

Aydın, Mehmet Şevki (2000), *Cumhuriyet Döneminde Din Eğitimi Öğretmeni Yetiştirme ve İstihdamı* [The Training and Employment of Religious Education Teachers in Republican Education System]. Kayseri: İBAV.

Ayhan, Halis (1999), *Türkiye'de Din Eğitimi* [The Religious Education in Turkey]. İstanbul: İFAV.

Aynî, M. Ali (1927), *Darülfününun Tarihi* [The History of Dar al-Funûn]. İstanbul: Yeni Matbaa.

Berger, Peter (1997), "Secularism in Retreat," in: *The National Interest*, 1996/1997.

Berkes, Niyazi (1998), *The Development of Secularism in Turkey*. New York: Routledge.

Berkhofer, Robert (1997), *Beyond the Great Story. History as Text and Discourse*. Cambridge, Mass.: Harvard University Press.

Bettis, Joseph Dabney, ed. (1969), *Phenomenology of Religion*. London: SCM Press.

Çaviş, Abdülaziz ([1918] 1974), *Anglikan Kilisesine Cevaplar* [Answers to the Anglican Church]. Turkish Translation by Mehmet Akif. Ankara: Turkish Directorate of Religious Affairs.

D'Amico, Robert (1989), *Historicism and Knowledge*. London: Routledge.

Davutoğlu, Ahmet (1994), *Alternative Paradigms: The Impact of Islamic and Western Weltanschauungs on Political Theory*. Lanham, Md.: University Press of America.

Dinler Tarihi Araştırmaları I–III [Researches in History of Religions]. I. November 1996; II. November 1998; III. June 2001. Ankara: Dinler Tarihi Derneği [The Turkish Association of the History of Religions].

Er, İzzet (1998), *Din Sosyolojisi* [Sociology of Religion]. Ankara: Akçağ Yayınları.

— (1999), *Sosyal Gelişme ve İslam* [Social Development of Islam]. İstanbul: Rağbet Yayınları.

Erdoğan, Mehmet (1990), *İslam Hukunda Ahkamın Değişmesi* [The Change of the Rules in Islamic Law]. İstanbul: İFAV Yayınları.

Ergin, Osman (1977), *Türkiye Maarif Tarihi* [History of Turkish Education]. Vols. I-V. İstanbul.

Fakhry, Majid (1998), *An Introduction to Islamic Philosophy, Theology and Mysticism*. Oxford: Oneworld.

Fazlur Rahman (1985), "Approaches to Islam in Religious Studies: An Introductory Essay," in: *Approaches to Islam in Religious Studies*, ed. by Richard Martin. Tucson, Ariz.: University of Arizona Press.

Flood, Gavin (1999), *Beyond Phenomenology: Rethinking the Study of Religion*. London: Cassell.

Geertz, Clifford (1973), *The Interpretation of Cultures*. New York: Basic Books.

Goodwin, Jason (1999), *Lords of the Horizons. A History of the Ottoman Empire*. London: Vintage.

Güngör, Erol (1987), *İslam'ın Bugünkü Meseleleri* [Contemporary Challenges to Islam]. İstanbul: Ötüken.

— (1987), *İslam Tasavvufunun Meseleleri* [Issues on Islamic Mysticism]. İstanbul: Ötüken.

Husserl, Edmund (1970), *The Crisis of European Sciences and Transcendental Phenomenology*, translated from German by David Carr. Evanston, Ill.: Northwestern University Press.

Ibn Khaldûn (1977), *Shifa' al-Sa'il li-Tahdhib al-Masâ'il*, Turkish translation (*Tasavvufun Mahiyeti*), by Süleyman Uludağ with an Introduction. İstanbul: Dergah.

Ibn Rushd, *Fasl al-Maqâl* (1985), Turkish translation (*Din-Felsefe İlişkileri*) by Süleyman Uludağ with an Introduction on the Relations between Philosophy and Religion. İstanbul: Dergah.

İhsanoğlu, Ekmeleddin "Darülfünun Tarihçesine Giriş" [Introduction to the History of Dar al-Funûn], in: *Belleten*, Ağustos 1990, v. LIV, no. 210: 699–738.

İslam Düşüncesinde Yeni Arayışlar [A Collection of Writings] (1998). New Perspectives in Islamic Thought I-III. İstanbul: Rağbet.

İzmirli, Celaleddin (1946*)*, "İzmirli İsmail Hakkı: Hayatı, Eserleri, Dînî ve Felsefî İlimlerdeki Mevkii" [The Life, Works of İzmirli İsmail Hakkı and His Place in Religious and Philosophical Studies]. İstanbul: Hilmi Kitabevi. [Also in: M. Şeker/ A.B. Baloğlu, eds., (1996), *İzmirli İsmail Hakkı. Vefatının 50. Yılı Anısına* (İzmirli İsmail Hakkı. In the Memory of His 50th Anniversary. İstanbul: TDV yayınları)].

Kamalî, M. Hashim (1991), *Principles of Islamic Jurisprudence*. Cambridge: The Islamic Texts Society.

Kamaruzaman, Kamar Oniah (1998), "Towards Forming an Islamic Methodology of Religionswissenschaft: the Case of al-Bîrûnî," in: *al-Shajarah* 3 (2). Kualalumpur, Malasia: International Institute of Islamic Thought and Civilisation (ISTAC): 19–44.

Kara, İsmail (1987), *Türkiye'de İslamcılık Düşüncesi—Metinler ve Kişiler* [The Islamicist Thought in Turkey—Texts and Authors]. İstanbul: Risâle yayınları.

Kara, Mustafa (1980), *Tekkeler ve Zaviyeler* [Sûfî Training Houses and Centers]. İstanbul: Dergah Yayınları.

— (1990-1993), *Bursa'da Tarikatlar ve Tekkeler* [Sûfî Orders and Centres in Bursa]. 2 vols. Bursa: Uludağ yayınları.

— (1999), "Tarikatlar Dünyasına Genel Bir Bakış" [A General Look at the World of Sûfî Orders], in: *İslamiyat*, no: 3, Ankara.

— (2000), "Tasavvufî Şiirin Gücü" [The Power of the Sûfî Poetry], in: *U.Ü.İ.F.D.* (*The Journal of the Faculty of Divinity, Uludağ University*) 9. Bursa.

Karadaş, Cağfer (1997), *İbn Arabî's İtikâdî Görüşleri* [Ibn Arabî's Theological Views]. İstanbul: Beyan.

Karaman, Hayreddin (1991), *Mukayeseli İslam Hukuku* [Comparative Islamic Law]. 3 vols. İstanbul: Nesil yayınları.

— (1996), *İslam Hukukunda İçtihad* [İjtihad in Islamic Law; first published in 1975 by DİB]. İstanbul: İFAV yayınları.

Kılavuz, Ahmet S. (1987), *Anahatlarıyla İslam Akaidi ve Kelam'a Giriş* [Introduction to Islamic Theology]. İstanbul: Ensar Yayınları.

— (1994), *İman-Küfür Sınırı* [The Borderline between Faith and Blasphemy—A Theological Treatise]. 4th ed. İstanbul: Marifet Yayınları.

Kılıç, Sadık (1999), *Tarihselcilik ve Akılcılık Bağlamında Kur'ân'ı Anlama Sorunu* [The Problem of Understanding the Qur'an in the Context of Historicism and Rationalism]. İstanbul: İhtar Yayıncılık.

King, Richard (1999), *Orientalism and Religion. Postcolonial Theory, India and 'The Mystic East'*. London: Routledge.

Köprülü, Fuad ([1919] 1991), *Türk Edebiyatında İlk Mutasavvıflar* [The Early Sûfîs in Turkish Literature]. Ankara: D.İ.B. yayınları.

Kristensen, W. Brede (1960), *The Meaning of Religion*. The Hague: Martinus Nijhoff.

Kuhn, Thomas (1970), *The Structure of Scientific Revolutions*. Chicago: Chicago University Press.

Kur'an'ı Anlamada Tarihsellik Sorunu Sempozyumu [Symposium Proceedings on the Question of 'Historicism' in Understanding the Qur'an]. 8-10 November 1996. KURAV (Bursa) publications. İstanbul: Bayrak Yayınları.

Laycock, Steven W., ed. (1986), *Essays in Phenomenological Theology*. New York: State University of New York.

MacFarlane, Charles (1850), *Turkey and Its Destiny*. London: John Murray.

Mardin, Şerif (1983), *Din ve İdeoloji* [Religion and Ideology]. İstanbul: İletişim.

—— (2003), *Religion, Society and Modernity in Turkey*. Syracuse, N.Y.: Syracuse University Press.

McCutcheon, Russell (1997), *Manufacturing Religion: The Discourse on Sui Generis Religion and the Politics of Nostalgia*. New York/Oxford: Oxford University Press.

Midhat Efendi, Ahmet (1912), *Tarihu`l-Edyan* [The History of Religions]. İstanbul: Hukuk Matbaası.

Nasr, Sayyed Hussain (1982), *Knowledge and the Sacred*. New York: Crossroad.

—— (1997), "Summary of Remarks by S.H. Nasr," in: "The Subjective and Objective Dimensions of the Study of Religion" [a Panel Discussion by John Hick, Robert Segal, S.H. Nasr, Arvind Sharma], in: *Religious Traditions. A Journal in the Study of Religion*, vol. 18 (1995) 19 (1996) 20 (1997).

Needleman, Jacob, ed. (1986), *The Sword of Gnosis: Metaphysics, Cosmology, Tradition, Symbolism*. London: Arkana.

Öcal, Mustafa (1998), "Cumhuriyet Türkiyesi'nde Din Eğitimi" [Religious Education in Republican Turkey]. U.Ü.İ.F.D. (*The Journal of the Faculty of Divinity, Uludağ University*) 7. Bursa.

Pals, Daniel L. (1996), *Seven Theories of Religion*. Oxford: Oxford University Press.

Platvoet, J.G. (1982), *Comparing Religions: A Limitative Approach*. New York: Mouton Publishers.

Qushayrî, *Al-Risâlah* (1979), Turkish translation by Süleyman Uludağ with an Introduction. İstanbul: Dergah.

Ritter, Harry (1986), *Dictionary of Concepts in History*. Westport, Conn.: Greenwood Press.

Robins, Kevin (1996), "Interrupting Identities: Turkey/Europe," in: Stuart Hall/Paul du Gay, *Questions of Cultural Identity*. London: Sage Publications.

Roff, William (1985), "Pilgrimage and the History of Religions: Theoretical Approaches to the Hajj," in: *Approaches to Islam in Religious Studies*, ed. by Richard Martin. Tucson, Ariz.: University of Arizona Press.

Said, Edward (1978/1995), *Orientalism: Western Conceptions of the Orient*. Harmondsworth: Penguin.

Sayar, Kemal (2000), *Sûfî Psikolojisi* [Sûfî Psychology]. İstanbul: İnsan Yayınları.

Şenay, Bülent (1998), *The Making of Jewish Christianity: Hybridity, Identity and Tradition*, Unpublished PhD thesis. Lancaster, UK: Lancaster University.

—— (1998), "Revelation, Diversity, and Living Together: an Islamic Approach," in: *Discernment* 5 (1). Oxford: Westminster College.

—— (1998), "Another Introduction to Islam: Myth of the Value-Free Study of Religion," in: *American Journal of Islamic Social Sciences* 15 (2) Summer 1998. Herndon, Va.

—— An Interview with Hayreddin Karaman on Islamic Studies and the Study of Religion in Turkey, 30 July 2001, İstanbul.

—— An Interview with Ömer Faruk Harman on the Study of Religion and the History of Religion in Turkey, 23 July 2001, İstanbul.

Sharpe, Eric (1992), *Comparative Religion—A History*. 2nd impression. London: Duckworth.

Smart, Ninian//Konstantine, Steven (1991), *Christian Systematic Theology in a World Context*. London: HarperCollins.

Smith, Wilfred Cantwell (1959), *Islam in Modern History*. New York: Mentor Books.

Tanyu, Hikmet (1960), "Türkiye'de Dinler Tarihi'nin Tarihçesi" [History of the History of Religion in Turkey], in: *A.Ü.İ.F. Dergisi* (*The Journal of the Faculty of Divinity, Ankara*) 8: 109–24.

Tapper, Richard, ed. (1991), "Introduction," in: Richard Tapper, ed., *Islam in Modern Turkey: Religion, Politics and Literature in a Secular State*. London: I.B. Tauris

The TDV Encyclopaedia of Islam (1983-still continues), vols. 1-22 (continues). İstanbul: İSAM.

Topaloğlu, Bekir (1985), *Kelâm İlmi* [The Science of Kalâm]. İstanbul: Damla.

Tümer, Günay (1986), *Bîrûnî'ye Göre Dinler ve İslam Dîni* [Islam and Other Religions According to al-Bîrûnî]. Ankara: D.İ.B.

Ülken, Hilmi Ziya (1979), *Türkiye'de Çağdaş Düşünce Tarihi* [History of Contemporary Turkish Thought]. İstanbul: Ülken Yayınları.

Uludağ, Süleyman (1985), *İslam Düşüncesinin Yapısı* [The Structure of Islamic Thought]. İstanbul: Dergâh Yayınları.

Usta, Mustafa (2001), *Türkiye'de Yüksek Din Eğitiminin Kurumlaşma ve Ekolleşme Sorunları* [The Institutional Problems of Religious Studies in Turkish Higher Education]. İstanbul: M.Ü.İ.F.

Uygur, Nermi (1998), *Edmund Husserl'de Başkasının Ben'i Sorunu- Transzendental Fenomenoloji ile Transzendental Felsefenin Özüne Giriş* [The Question of the 'Other-Self' in Edmund Husserl: Introduction to the Essence of Transcendental Phenomenology and Philosophy]. 2nd ed. İstanbul: YKY.

Walsh, W.H. (1967), *An Introduction to Philosophy of History*. London: Hutchinson.

Ward, Graham (2000), *Theology and Contemporary Critical Theory*. 2nd ed. London: Macmillan.

Watt, W. Montgomery (1996), *A Short History of Islam*. Oxford: Oneworld.

Whaling, Frank (1999), "Theological Approaches," in: Peter Connolly, ed., *Approaches to the Study of Religion*. London: Cassell.

Wiebe, Donald (1981), *Religion and Truth*. The Hague: Mouton Publishers.

The Study of Religion and Social Crises

Arab-Islamic Discourse in Late Twentieth Century[1]

by

ABDULKADER TAYOB

The study of religions in the second half of the twentieth century cannot ignore seminal developments in Europe. However, the political contexts of other regions have to be taken into consideration when making assessments and predictions of the nature of the discipline as a whole. This paper argues that there are some significant developments in the Arab discourse on religion since 1967 that has eluded observers. Part of the problem arises from the fact that proponents of the study of religion use more recent institutional and theoretical developments in Europe and North America as norms and criteria for evaluating trends in other areas. While theories and methodological debates in international contexts cannot be ignored, this paper suggests a different approach to appreciate developments in the Arab discourse on religion in general, and Islam in particular. It argues that an appreciation of the crisis context of Arab scholarship sets the ground for a critical approach to the study of religion and Islam. Some of this scholarship does not aspire to meet the demands of objectivity, but engages in the critical study of religions even when it engages in the critical re-definition of religion.

The study of religion in mainly European contexts has changed dramatically since Enlightenment intellectuals identified religion as a unique category for analysis. On the basis of such identification, religion played a significant role in the analysis of social and individual human conditions. David Hume linked types of belief (monotheism and polytheism) to social organisation while Weber found the driving force of modernity in religious practices and systems. For Durkheim, religion was the key projection of social awareness while Freud regarded it as a form of neurosis. Secularisation theory declared the end of religion in the seventies, but more recent scholars of religion bestowed for it a

---

1   This research has been supported by the National Research Foundation, formerly the Centre for Science Development, in South Africa. My gratitude extends to the Foundation for making funds available to travel to the Middle East, but I take full responsibility for the contents and views expressed herein.

place in a revamped neo-secularisation paradigm. Post-modernism has also suggested unique ways of making sense of religion in society. The purpose of this paper is to turn attention from this rich tradition of the study of religion, and focus on developments in the study of religion (particularly Islam) in Islamic contexts.

In the second half of the twentieth century a small number of studies have been published that catalogue and analyse the study of religion in non-Western contexts. The formation of the African Association for the Study of Religions has placed the spotlight on developments in Africa while some have played attention to developments in Asia (Platvoet/Cox/Olupona 1996; Westerlund 1991; Cox 1994; Platvoet 1993a; Olupona 1991; Illesanmi 1995; Pye 1990; Whaling 1995). Waardenburg has paid specific attention to developments in Muslim societies, followed by Herman Beck and Sjoerd van Koningsveld on the study of religions in Indonesia and Morocco respectively (Waardenburg 1998; Koningsveld 1997; Beck 1997).

Ideological Obstacles in the Study of Religion

These studies have played an important role in identifying trends towards the development of a disciplined study of religion (*Wissenschaft*). Generally, the conclusions, particularly of those concerned with the studies of religion in Islamic contexts, are gloomy as far as the prospects for the independent study of religions are concerned.

Waardenburg recognised some interesting development in Muslim contexts, but suggests that certain theological, political and financial obstacles stood in the way of the full development of an independent, critical discipline. In particular, he argued that Islamic theology presents a major obstacle in that "the adage that Islam is the final and true religion" has an "an unfortunate impact" on the development of a neutral and objective approach to other religions (Waardenburg 1998: 246). According to Waardenburg, another obstacle to the study of religion is the politicisation of Islam where "an empirical and potentially critical interest in interpretations of Islam may thus become politically suspect" (Waardenburg 1998: 247).

Waardenburg presents two problems, one theological and the other political. Both may be regarded as emanating from the religion itself since religion and politics are considered inseparable in Islam. More detailed reviews of the study of religions in Muslim contexts show that the problems are directly related to contemporary experiences of politics and state. The theological obstacles may play a role, but they are made worse by the particular political conditions in some countries. Van Koningsveld's review of religion in Morocco refers to the political problems in the study of religion in Morocco. According to him, the monopoly of religious legitimisation by the monarchy prevents the emergence of a critical approach to contemporary religious developments. Some studies on the history of Islam are tolerated, but more critical approaches are published outside the country:

> The political situation in Morocco is a serious obstacle for the scientific, comprehensive study of Islam as a living force in Moroccan society. Moroccan historians hardly occupy themselves with religious aspects of contemporary history. The publications of Moroccan social scientists tend to be limited to subjects that are acceptable within the prevailing political climate. Comprehensive studies of contemporary Islam within the context of Moroccan society and politics are rare, and they are usually published outside Morocco (Koningsveld 2002: 281).

Herman Beck's review of the dominant discourse of comparative religions in Indonesia also suggests a political entanglement. While van Koningsveld pointed to the oppressive and monopolistic role of the state, Beck shows how the study of religion serves the state. Using Hasbullah Bakry and Mukti Ali as prime examples, Beck shows the transformation of the study of religions from a theological enterprise to one that favours dialogue and good neighbourliness. Hasbullah Bakry promoted the study of other religions as a natural expansion of Qur'anic exegesis. In this paradigm, the study of other religions "plays an important part in revealing the inadequacy of Christianity and in showing the superiority of Islam" (Beck 2002: 333). Beck argued that this approach coincided with the Muslim fear of Christian missionary work after the declaration of independence in 1945. Later, Mukti Ali took the study of religion in Indonesia one step further when he promoted comparative religion for national purposes. The study of religions promoted religious tolerance, while it also served to assert that Islamic theology alone was compatible with the official ideology of Pancascila (Beck 2002: 334).

Clearly, the difficulties experienced in the study of religion arise from the presuppositions of Islamic theology as well as the particular problems of the day in a variety of social and political contexts. Both the political and theological obstacles are also emphasised in the international debates on the nature of religious studies. Protagonists for a disciplined science of religion like Donald Wiebe, Armin Geertz, Jan Platvoet and others, argue that such theological and ideological constrictions hamper the development of the discipline. According to Wiebe, the academic study of religion is "undermined by a conflict of loyalties and aspirations of many of its practitioners who were committed both to the scientific study of religion and the maintenance of religious faith" (Wiebe 1997: 167). Similarly, Platvoet decries South African scholars of religion who espouse "non-denominational, inter-axial faiths, natural theology, or philosophical anthropology" which "prevent the study of religions in Religious Studies from being a fully secular, fully neutral discipline" (Platvoet 1993b: 13). Such an approach, continues Platvoet, keeps the study of religions "in competition and contest with other ideologically motivated approaches, the positivist and the orthodox-theological ones" and "causes it to engage, in

Eliadean fashion, is (sic) creative and total hermeneutics which has reformative, therapeutic and even totalitarian intentions" (Platvoet 1993b: 14). Armin Geertz also focuses on the obstacles to objectivity and a value-neutral tradition, and suggests a partnership between (Western?) students of religion and indigenous students of religion in order to overcome or minimise mistranslation and errors of judgement (Geertz 2000). In summary, then, the study of religion should be a disciplined activity that strives to attain objectivity in the description and analysis of religion in society. Both theological and political prejudices and projects clash with this approach, and hamper analysis of the role and meaning of religion in society.

The Study of Religion in Context

The study of religion is part of a greater project of the critical study of society. And the strength of the latter will be reflected in the strength of the former. In my view, a critical assessment of the study of religions in Muslim contexts should not begin and end with the degree of objectivity in the description and analysis. Political and theological biases, of course, hamper the development of a scholarly discipline, and ought to be treated with caution and circumspection. But an appreciation for the prospects of the discipline must also be concerned with the motivation for such a scholarly approach. Disciplinary rigour and neutrality are the end-products of the discipline, but they do not explain the choice of subjects, the social value of these studies, and the resources that find their way into research projects. Each of these highly subjective issues guides the theoretical development of the discipline, as much as the scientific demands of method. Lack of appreciation of such contextual issues ignores the history of the discipline in the eighteenth and nineteenth centuries, and ignores evidence of such a discipline in Muslim contexts. This paper proposes to underscore the emergence of a critical discourse on religion that has developed in Arabic since 1967, and that has been ignored in the reviews of religious studies. But first a brief detour on the development of the discipline at the end of the nineteenth century will place the development of the Arab discourse in perspective.

The history of the discipline has received extensive attention in the work of Hans Kippenberg that suggests that the focus on objectivity alone is flawed. Instead of probing only for the relative degree of objectivity between scholars in different cultural contexts, Kippenberg's analysis suggests that it would be more interesting to explore the motivations for studying religion. In a series of articles, Kippenberg has argued that the study of religion was inextricably linked with the philosophical discourse on the role of religion. Theories of religion were not only developed on the basis of empirical data, but on assumptions of a good state and society:

When European philosophers recognised this contradiction between reason and history, they faced the task of explaining historical religions by additional means, mainly by the functions which religions performed. First, historical religions could be interpreted as crude explanations of natural events. Second, others regarded morals as the place in which historical religions fulfilled useful and necessary functions. Third, some philosophers pointed to human emotions as an area of contribution by historical religions. Finally, some philosophers regarded world-rejection as a peculiar achievement of religions, since it was constitutive for human subjectivity. These four positions developed one after the other. But their relationship was not part of a process of falsification. The succession of position had nothing to do with a superior explanation of anomalies. They were inspired by an awareness of the limitations of Enlightenment philosophy. (Kippenberg 1997: 163)

The quotation clearly indicates the dominant assumptions of religions in Kant, Tylor, Durkheim, Weber, and others. A critical review of religion and society suggested that religion was essentially moral, or that religious institutions played a part in the rationalisation of society, or that religion was a primitive form of scientific explanation. Furthermore, the debate was not only descriptive of religions on an empirical level, but also prescriptive. The theories espoused the dominant assumptions of what religions ought to be in a modern society. Kippenberg's analysis points to the strong link between scholarly discourse on the development of society, and the analysis of religious data. Beyond philosophical reflection, Kippenberg also explored the study of religion as a response to the nature and development of the European state. In the first half of the nineteenth century, the idea of an unfolding history was a sufficient basis for the nation state to think of itself and its history. But an appreciation of history from a critical perspective was bound to turn against the idea of a nation state itself. History tended to relativise the very values the nation state glorified. In place of history, then, the threat of relativity and the absence of core values for the nation state could be addressed by the study of religion. The study of religion, in both France and Germany, was regarded as a possible source of such secure and stable foundations. At the core of religion lay perhaps the human capacity to overcome the ill effects of modernity (Kippenberg 1996: 90, 95; Kippenberg 1994: 387). The enlightenment project, then, was threatened by its own success, which only the study of religion could save.

In the context of such debates, scholars of religion were divided between those who tended to see religion as essentially a feeling of awe and emotion (Schleiermacher, Dilthey, etc.), and those who argued for the place of religion at the head of modernity (asceticism) or within society (civil religion) like Weber and Durkheim (Kippenberg 1996: 101). The brief summary of Kippenberg's analysis suggests that the study of religion emerged in contested political and philosophical circles. While theories of religion could in principle be tested against empirical data, they were forged in deep political and philosophical debates.

Kippenberg's analysis may be supplemented by the insights of Chidester who has shown us how the actual material was collected, and then analysed. Looking at this material from the colonial periphery, he has argued that the study of religion cannot be extricated from the experiences of empire building. In his brilliant book *Savage Systems*, Chidester points out that definitions and denial of religions had disastrous consequences on the actual existence of peoples. Denial of religions was the prerequisite for genocide and occupation, while the definition of religious systems implied subjugation and control: "Knowledge about religion ... reinforced a global control over the entire expanse of human geography and history" (Chidester 1996: 3). Initially, the collusion was quite explicit, but later the involvement between science and colonialism was obscured. The analysis was stripped of any contextual conflict, and "all that remained for analysis in the disembodied evidence accumulated by imperial comparative religion was a mentality, whether that mentality was designated as religious, magical, superstitious, or primitive" (Chidester 1996: 3). At home in Europe, colonised people were compared with women, children and the mentally deranged. The study of religion, then, produced a "universal discourse about otherness" which "established a discursive regime of sameness that served the interests of global control over 'primitives' at home and abroad" (Chidester 1996: 3–4). Chidester laments the fact that "academic debates about the definition of religion have usually ignored the real issues of denial and recognition that are inevitably at stake in situations of intercultural contact and conflict" (Chidester 1996: 254). In another article on Max Müller, Chidester argued that notions of the systematic development of religions which dominated the study of religion in the nineteenth century were invented by colonial authorities, or local experts:

> Where indigenous informants recorded religious arguments and tensions, changes and innovations, confusions and contradictions, or often their own Christian critiques of indigenous religion, the local experts on the periphery distilled a system, a distinct, coherent, and functional religious system. (Chidester 2004: 72–73)

Such systematic descriptions fitted into neat theories of the evolution of religious systems but ignored the complexity of religious practices and beliefs.

The damning history of religious studies reconfirms my view that the search for objectivity was not the only motivation and guide for the development of the discipline. Clearly, theoretical paradigms were and continue to be driven by concerns other than scientific demands. In principle, then, a review of studies on religion should not begin and end with questions of objectivity and bias, but with the general social motivation driving a particular discourse. I do not for a moment suggest that questions of objectivity should be ignored. All I am saying is that the location of a discourse is as important as the mechanics of methodology, and should form an integral part of review, comparison and analysis.

Arab Discourse on Religion

As in Europe, the Arab discourse on religion originates from a social and intellectual predicament. The first Arab-wide discussion on this topic was convened by the Arab League Educational, Cultural and Scientific Organisation (ALESCO) in October 1971, followed by other meetings and discussions in various Arab capitals. The conference met to discuss "Authenticity and Renewal in Contemporary Arab Culture" and situated the turn to religion in the context of a search for authenticity. The general debate in this conference and other subsequent publications and meetings did not exclusively deal with religion, but addressed the significance and relevance of the Arab heritage to the development of contemporary Arab society. However, since Islam was a significant part of that culture and heritage, discussions about Islam dominated the discourse. A significant part of the debate revolved around how to approach the texts, values and symbols of Islam in contemporary society. Moreover, the discussions acknowledged and addressed the turn to religion in Arab countries after the defeat of the Arab armies in the 1967 Arab-Israeli War. It is this discourse that provides the material for appreciating the development of the study of religion in Arab academic circles.

The turn to religion after 1967 is well attested in the general literature, and is evident in the establishment of religious organisations, the emergence of political ideologies and parties, the increasing adherence to religious rules, and greater visibility of Islamic codes in public life (Faris 1986; Floors 1989). But the emergence of a critical discourse of Islam has received scant attention. Boullata has introduced English readers to these discussions, and a number of German academics have paid attention to individuals and themes (Boullata 1990; Gaebel 1995; Hüpp 1988; Salvatore 1995; Steppat 1991; Termeulen 1995; Von Kügelgen 1994; Wielandt 1971; Wild 1986; Ziyadah 1989; Kermani 1996). To my knowledge, none of these studies have reflected on the discourse as a critical study of religion. And yet, they have reflected on some categories in the study of religion: the appropriation of symbols in Islamic history (Von Kügelgen 1994), historical criticism of the Qur'an (Wielandt 1971), and alternative development of subjectivity (Salvatore 1997). In spite of these important questions, a systematic study of how religion is the focus of cultural and social renewal will shed light on some important assumptions and insights that Arab scholars bring to the debate.

My attention is focused on the critical discourse on Islam, and not on the discourse of the Islamists who propose that Islam has the solution for all the challenges of modern society. Some scholars have seen Islamism as a kind of postmodernism. Perhaps it has something to do with the rejection of modern society and the rise of postmodernism in Europe and America in the 1960s. The coincidence between European postmodernism and Islamic revival has led to the conclusion that Islamic fundamentalism and its rejection of modernity may be compared with the rejection of modernity by postmodernists (Gülalp 1995; Euben 1997). There is probably some truth in this thesis because of the global experience of modernity, but I have doubts about this trend of analysis. In my view, the experience of modernity is very different in these contexts, and reactions are deceptively similar. More importantly, however, such comparisons ignore the wealth of Arab discourse that attempts to critique and deconstruct the turn to Islam. What is less well known and recognised than the rise of Islamic fundamentalism, is the intense intellectual debate about the nature of Islam and religion in society. The focus of this paper lies precisely on the intellectual discourse in Arab society that has accompanied the turn to religion. Taking into consideration the origins and motivations of the sociology of religion in Europe, we can better understand and appreciate the achievements and shortcomings of the Arab discourse on Islam/religion.

For this paper, I propose to present the approaches to religion of three individuals that have made a significant contribution to the heritage discourse. I have chosen three scholars who have written almost exclusivity in Arabic, and whose books and articles have made a significant impact. As mentioned before, they have also received some attention in non-Arab scholarly studies. Each of the three takes a slight different approach to Islamic texts, which illustrates the richness of the intellectual discourse on religion. At the same time, my choice for the three is fairly arbitrary, and no claim to be comprehensive is made. I could have presented a different set of scholars to achieve the same purpose of providing a glimpse into the development of critical thought on religion in an Arab Muslim context. I have deliberately left out those who advocate a return to religion in an uncritical fashion.

Before providing a brief outline of their major approaches and theories, I want to say something about the context of this discourse. Firstly, as in many societies in Africa, Arab intellectuals engage in both scholarly and non-scholarly activities, according to their own admission. Thus, many of their writings are deliberately addressed to lay readers, many of them write for newspapers, and some of them engage in polemical debates with their opponents. This is probably the first impression of many observers, which tends to cast Arab scholars as engaged, and thus less worthy of being called serious intellectuals. Any assessment and appreciation of this work must take into consideration the multiple roles of the intellectual in a particular society. And this raises a number of related issues of theory and methodology.

In particular, Weber and more lately Paul Rabinow depict the scholar as the ideal inwardly ascetic person in a society, genuinely estranged from any direct involvement in the development of the society. As scientists, they have taken the option not to become entrapped in their own labels and categories (Gerth/Mills 1970: 145). As Rabinow so eloquently states, the social scientists,

> while acting in terms of their sociologically structured self-interest, can never know what that self-interest is precisely because they must believe in the illusion that they are

pursuing something genuinely meaningful in order to act. Only the sociologist is capable of understanding what is really and truly going on: the reason for that success stems from the sacrifice on the altar of truth that the sociologist makes of his own social interests. (Rabinow 1996: 8)

Rabinow is clear that the success of the social science project rests on its non-committal nature. A review of the Arab discourse will shed light on the veracity of this claim, and its relevance in Arab societies. It raises the question of the role of the intellectual in relation to the society and the state, which was raised by the founders of the discipline in Europe at the nineteenth century.[2] By extension, the question must shed light on the global nature of social science, and role and place of intellectuals and social scientists in this project.

The second complication of this "engaged" scholarship is its repercussions on the social and political fronts. Since many of the intellectuals are engaged in social projects, and openly express themselves, they often have opponents and antagonists in the media, politics and sometimes, other civil society structures (Floors 1992). This means that, apart from the intellectual discourse that I am focussing on, there is a public discourse on religion/Islam that supports and categorises, but sometimes also caricatures, the theories and ideas of the debate. My analysis cannot ignore this dimension of the debate, but it focuses on the theoretical and methodological tools developed in the intellectual debate.

On the other hand, as a result of this public discourse, many or most of the intellectuals seem to see themselves as a distinct group, sharing some key ideas and approaches. I am referring to this self-characterisation at a popular level. In brief, it involves a commitment to rationalism against traditionalism; a desire to reform Islamic law and practice through intellectual exertion (*ijtihad*); an awareness of the abuse of religion in politics; and a search for the true meaning of Islam by way of a critical, historical reading of texts. This particular approach might immediately sound too theological and/or ideological, and deserves the censure of a neutral, uncommitted approach to religion. More detailed analysis reveals that this common agenda on a popular level cannot be sustained on the intellectual level. There are significant differences among scholars of religion, but the common agenda serves as a useful pillar of identity in public discourse. Probably because of this populist dimension, there is a lack of mutual scholarly critique among the intellectuals. There are many exceptions to this rule, which I will point out. However, there seems to be an overdue caution among the intellectuals, directly affected by the presumably common front on the popular level. This does not detract from the level of the discourse, but points to some of its weaknesses. With these brief remarks, I am now ready

---

2   Several such studies deal with the role of the intellectual in Arab societies, which has a direct impact on the nature of religious studies, but which cannot be reviewed in this article (al-Ramihi 1996; Barakat 1987; Eickelman 1985; Floors 1992; Sagiv 1995).

to present a short outline of the three scholars and their approach to Islam/ religion.

Hasan Hanafi

Hasan Hanafi is professor emeritus of philosophy at the University of Cairo. He obtained his doctorate from the Sorbonne, and has extensive international teaching experience. Prof. Hanafi has been the subject of a number of studies, particularly in Germany. However, none of these has focused on his contribution to the discourse on religion in Arab society. Hanafi's main expertise lies in philosophy, particularly phenomenology, which he brings to bear upon his analysis of contemporary Islam, and Islamic texts. He is a prolific commentator on contemporary Egyptian society, and the author of *Religion and Revolution in Egypt 1952–1981* (8 volumes). By his own account, his substantial contribution lies in his appraisal of the Arab-Islamic heritage, entitled *Heritage and Renewal* (5 multi-volume works) on philosophy, theology, history, jurisprudence and mysticism. He has completed the volumes on all but the last-mentioned. Hanafi is also the author of a few other works, some popular simplifications, some of which I will mention below.

Hanafi's approach may be reduced to two major components: the one philosophical, and the other historical. In the former, he asserts that the Arab is faced with a triad within which s/he negotiates the past, present and future. The triad is ridden with tension and angst, and consists of the following sides: heritage (mainly textual heritage in Arabic), Europe (including colonialism, science and modernity), and the self (including contemporary social and political conditions). From a philosophical point of view, the modern Arab is caught in the tensions and contradictory demands of the three dimensions of the triad. Hanafi argues that none of the constituent parts of the triad can be ignored. The Arab-Islamic past continues to affect attitudes and institutions. Neither can the West be ignored with both its successes, its intrusions and challenges. The role of religion, particularly Islam, has clearly been identified as a source of heritage invoked against the other (Europe). At the level of consciousness, the heritage must be approached with respect and the desire for transformation: "The past is not a place for defence or attack, but to restore, and the future also is not a subject of defending or attacking, but preparation and planning, and the present cannot be returned to the past (as proposed by Islamists) or pushed towards the future (as proposed by the secularists), but it is a place where the three sides interact with each other" (Hanafi 1991a: 79). Hanafi discusses this predicament mainly in *Religion and Revolution in Egypt 1952–1981*.

His approach contains an analysis and assumption of the predicament faced by Arab societies. His conception of the contemporary Arab self is rooted in both a phenomenological and existential sense of being. This rootedness of the self establishes a guide and rationale for Hanafi's solution of how to read the past in general and Islamic texts in particular. Islam (or the heritage) cannot be read from texts, but issues forth from reality: "In the first principle, I do not interpret the heritage from the text, because the text in my view is reality—and the noble Qur'an developed from occasions of revelation, that is, the priority of reality over thought" (Hanafi 1996b: 47).

Hanafi's approach to Islam at the level of consciousness may be compared with the questions that plagued European intellectuals about the value of religion in a modern state. Hanafi is faced with a different predicament, but the philosophical search and deliberation to solve the problem remains comparable. For Hanafi, the revival and the demand for Islamic politics were reactions to the failure of modern Arab states to deliver freedom and prosperity. Having dabbled with liberalism and socialism, Arab society now yearns for an idealised heritage. This particular predicament cannot be ignored by the Arab intellectual who has to read the classic texts of the past. That reading has to be faithful to the past, as well as respond to the demands made in contemporary society. From this vantage point, it is clear why Hanafi's work explores a reading of Islamic texts.

Hanafi's philosophical analysis is complemented by a critical view of the texts and values that dominated the Islamic tradition in the past. Hanafi advocates, and himself applies, a critical historical reading of the texts of Islam (and the West) in order to liberate the Muslim from the text and find him or herself: "historical consciousness demands that one takes a critical approach to the heritage, neither attacking it nor protecting it" (Hanafi 1991a: 78). A critical reading relativises the text so that one can accept or reject it. But there is no doubt that he demands a desacralisation of the heritage. One has to, he argues, "remove the sacredness of the heritage and return it to its history" and to know that historical traditions have changed. Recognition of historical change opens the way to read "the classicists, philosophers, jurists, Sufis and legal philosophers" (Hanafi 1996b: 45–46).

According to Hanafi, the questions concerning the attributes of God raised in Islamic theology were questions of power and wealth. Sometimes, he seems to argue that religious debates were essentially political and social confrontations. Religious questions served to mask issues of power and ownership, and a clearly materialist reading and critique of the religious history of Islam may be noted. On a popular level, its particular association with Marxism has earned Hasan Hanafi much reproach from religious circles. However, Hanafi does not commit himself to materialism as a reader of texts to an extent that is common to scholars like the Syrian Sadiq Jalal al-Azm or the Lebanese Husayn Muruwwah. In his view, he steers between those who failed to see that the heritage was produced by people, and those who simply followed Western fads: "In my opinions such (approaches) remove the heritage from its historicity, while others [imply] that the West with its tools and methods is the only road to renewal" (Hanafi 1996b: 45). Ignoring his own entanglement with contemporary philosophical trends, Hanafi focuses his attention on the philosophical and existential questions that he is addressing.

Parallel to his historical reading, Hanafi sometimes says that the questions of metaphysics and belief are no longer threatening the Arab self. Here, he seems to be arguing for a perspective of human society where religious questions in themselves are not as important in modern times as they were in medieval times: "Is it not allowed for a new theology to turn to the source of danger as the source of the old danger centred around the concept of the unity of God and speculative belief? The essential danger today is of a practical nature. So nobody is attacking me concerning God but I am being attacked in Jerusalem, Palestine and for my precious resources, in the honour of the *ummah* (religious community), on its future and its role in history" (Hanafi 1998c: 62–63). In summary, then, taking into consideration the predicament of the Arab today, Hanafi suggests that the texts of Islam should be read in their materialist context and as the responses to the political and social issues of the day.

In addition to the critical reading of Islamic texts, Hanafi also proposes a critical reading of the West. He is the author of *Introduction to the Science of Occidentalism* where he attempts a critique of the West. Such a project, he believes, will enable the Arab to historicise and relativise the West. For Hanafi, Western philosophy is basically a rejection of the past and a rejection of foundations. Its analytical and deconstructivist nature robs it of any meaningful centre.

For Hanafi, the critiques of both the Islamic historical texts and Western tradition will help to focus on the Arab in both the present reality and his or her own self. He thinks that the religious trends in society are committed to sacralising the past, and keeping Arabs imprisoned in the texts. On the other hand, secularists have a morbid sense of their own worth, and are prepared to sacrifice their true selves in order to gain recognition and praise from the West. His solution is to read the past historically to escape the deleterious effect of the religious trends, and to be committed to the reality of the here and now to escape the clutches of the West. It is clear how such a philosophical and political project advances a critical reading of religious texts.

Muhammad Abid Jabiri

Muhammad Abid Jabiri is the second author that I wish to bring into a review of Arab scholarship on religion. He is a Moroccan philosopher who has written widely and extensively on a number of topics, including philosophy, contemporary Islam, and European philosophy. Jabiri is also concerned about contemporary Arab discourse of the heritage, in which religion plays a decisive role.

Where Hanafi began with existential questions, Jabiri begins with the epistemological underpinnings of early Islamic society and of contemporary debates about the reconstruction of society. He proclaims that his project seeks to uncover the structural foundations of the Arab mind (al-aql al-arabi) which dominates contemporary discourse, and hampers progress of Arab society. Jabiri is careful not to limit his study to religion, and thus argues that he is not studying the foundations of the "Muslim mind". He believes that such a project would have to include a great deal of anthropological analysis, which he chooses not to engage. Furthermore, he also argues that the religious discourse of the past was a veiled discourse of politics. Where Hanafi saw some justification for theological debates in the past, Jabiri thinks that political conditions forced the discourse in a religious direction:

> ... when oppressive and imperial rule was established by the Umayyads and Abbasids, no political terms existed which the people could use to express political matters. The theologians then slipped and were forced to talk of political matters using religious concepts, and argued about the divine qualities meaning thereby human matters. Today we are free and able to talk directly of human matters, and on politics directly, and we do not need to use religious discourse for politics by using theology. (al-Jabiri 1998: 42)

Jabiri, like Hanafi, but a with a different justification, urges his readers to read religious texts beyond their literal import. Religious texts do not signify theological truths, but the socio-political struggles of the day. Not surprisingly, in spite of eschewing the Islamic questions, Jabiri's analysis of Arab discourse includes a great deal of religious texts, and his subsequent analysis of contemporary discourse presents significant insights on the meaning and significance of contemporary Islam.

Jabiri is keen for Arab scholars to develop a distinctive, critical approach to the past. His study of Ibn Khaldun argued that this well-known historian should be contextualised in the history of Arab/Islamic thought, and not simply as a precursor to modern sociology or philosophy of history, as is the case among modern apologists. According to Jabiri, contemporary modernist thought tries to prove the modernity of Islam by showing the confluence between some thinkers and ideas in the Arab-Islamic tradition with current developments in Europe. Such an analysis serves to confirm the peripheral nature of Arab-Islamic traditions. Rather, Jabiri proposes that the objectivity of texts should be uncovered by a structuralist analysis of the language of texts, their historical imbeddedness and their ideological function. Furthermore, Jabiri recognises the continued dominance of the past in Arab consciousness which calls for an objective look at the self, and not an anthropological gaze from the outside (al-Jabiri 1991: 32–33). The objective for this analysis should be "to transform the constant to changing, the absolute to the relative, the ahistorical to historical, and atemporal to temporal" (al-Jabiri 1991: 47).

It is clear that Jabiri displays a systematic approach to the texts produced in Islam. This approach rests fundamentally on epistemic foundations of such texts. In 1982, Jabiri published a book *Contemporary Arab Discourse: A Critical, Analytical Study* in which he argued that Arab discourse was trapped in history. Both religious and non-religious discourse could not directly understand and address the contemporary challenges and predicaments of Arab society. In this book, he suggested that the first thing that needed to be done was to systematically study the epistemological foundations of Arab thought as developed in history. In the next few years, Jabiri produced a three-volume book entitled *The Arab Mind* in which he presented a structural analysis of such foundations.

Jabiri argued that Arab discourse had three clear epistemological trajectories, all of which emerged during the age of compilation (*asr al-tadwin*). This period began at the end of the eighth century through the thirteenth century when the major classics of linguistics, grammar, jurisprudence, philosophy, theology and mysticism were composed. These disciplines constituted the key components of the general discourse of Islam. The tools and methods used were directly or indirectly related to reading the sacred texts of Islam, through the development of methods and instruments. A careful analysis of this heritage reveals three conflicting trajectories in epistemology. Jabiri calls the first *bayan*, meaning clarity. Essentially, this particular approach is clearly evident in linguistics and jurisprudence, and may be traced to the centrality of language and the sacred text in Islam. Jabiri follows this trajectory in some seminal works of great jurists and linguists and shows the search for clarity, perspicacity and exactness in the spoken and written word. Jurisprudence, then, was founded on the linguistic and semantic analysis of the Qur'an and the prophetic traditions handed down from one generation to the next. God revealed the word, and it was the responsibility of jurists and grammarians to know this clarity (*bayan*) and extend its significance to new contexts.

Jabiri's major insight into the epistemology of clarity (*bayan*) lies in his assessment that Arab discourse is trapped in its linguistic signification:

> The Arab mind works with words more than it works with concepts ... It only thinks from the standpoint of a principle or foundational (text) (*asl*), and guided by it. The principle or foundation has the authority of the past either in the form of a word or its meaning, and its principle tool to attain (or come to) knowledge—and not its production—is approximation (or *bayan* analogy) or metaphor (or philosophical analogy). In all this (the mind) depends on probability as a first principle and a general law that determines its method in thinking and its view of the world. (al-Jabiri 1992b: 564)

The foundational text is the starting point from which all new meanings are generated. But beyond the foundation, Arab discourse realises the probable nature of new meanings. As a result, the foundational text also becomes the end-point of the epistemological search. Arab scholars were aware that the linguistic sign can never be completely known, but they could not conceive an escape from the sign. The foundational sign was the only clue available to both the world and the will of God.

The frustration of language led to the development of a second trajectory. Clarity in language (*bayan*) was supplemented by a trajectory that sought knowledge through gnostic illumination (*irfan*). Mysticism, both speculative and practical, in Arab discourse argued against the adequacy of linguistic systems, and suggested that only divine revelation (*kashf*) was able to reveal the truth to its seekers. The epistemological trajectory of *irfan* in Arab discourse argues for the hidden and esoteric (*batin*) dimension of the linguistic sign. For those who embrace *irfan*, the outward aspect of the sign revealed only the exoteric dimension (*zahir*). Proper mystical training and divine assistance may lead one to its hidden, true dimension.

The third trajectory of Arab epistemology was that of demonstrative reason (*burhan*) which was pursued, partially by theologians, but more systematically by philosophers. Jabiri is keen to point out that not all philosophers were consistent in their application of the principles of reason to their logical conclusion. The path of illumination (*irfan*) was an attraction that many of these philosophers could not resist. For Jabiri, such mystical tendencies were not helpful for the development of philosophy in Arab societies. Only the true philosophers, like Averroes, sought knowledge and truth by demonstrative reasoning, undeterred by the conventions and demands of ideology, religion or tradition. More importantly, these philosophers realised they should not get lost in the complexities of the sacred book that trapped those who thought that the ultimate symbol was the linguistic sign. They also avoided the speculation of mystics who claimed a privilege based on personal gnostic illumination. The champions of demonstrative reasoning also straddle across disciplines. According to Jabiri, they "liberated the mind from the authority of the phrase and foundationalism" as they privileged "reading, production, generalities and goals" that accorded with causal thinking. There is no doubt that Jabiri favours this third trajectory which conforms with "structures on which modern thought in Europe has been built and which continues to found scientific knowledge today" (al-Jabiri 1992b: 564).

Having established the epistemic foundations of the Arab mind, Jabiri proceeds to show how the first two trajectories dominate contemporary Arab discourse. Jabiri points out that Arab discourse is guided by a maxim first articulated by Malik b. Anas, one of the founders of Islamic legal thinking: "The affairs of this nation will only be set right by the same means used in the past" (al-Jabiri 1992a (1982): 33–35). Malik meant by it that Muslim thinking must return to the example of the Prophet Muhammad. For Jabiri, however, this maxim is translated into two tendencies that underscore the problems of Arab societies. Firstly, it means that Arab approaches to contemporary problems are dominated by importing models from others. The original text (or condition) exists in early Islam, or in Europe. Thus, both Islamists and liberal secularists

constantly search for foundation texts in their respective domains. The discourse ignores a systemic evaluation of the present condition. Solutions are
imported from a glorious Islamic past, or a powerful and ascendant Europe. In
both cases, an original text must be found that could directly or indirectly
account for a new discovery or a new political solution.

Entrapment within a closed linguistic sign and speculative theology
thwarts any attempt at reform. In particular, the return to religion means a
return to the epistemological trajectory of clarity (*bayan*) or divine illumination
(*irfan*). As mentioned, this preference for clarity revolves around the original
texts. Clarity is not sought of the existing conditions of society, but of the
original foundational texts as such. New scientific discoveries, social and historical insights, and ethical paths cannot be conceived. At best, they must be
found retrospectively in the limitless probabilities of the foundational texts. At
worst, they can be kept at a distance and blocked from critical evaluation.

Furthermore, Jabiri argues that because of this dominating maxim and the
conflicting epistemological trajectories of the Arab mind, problems and
challenges are not addressed in a fruitful manner. Conflicting solutions are invoked from the past or from Europe, often without consideration of their suita-
bility for the present. Taking the example of religion and politics, Jabiri argues
that the question of religion and politics has been imported with disastrous
consequences for contemporary Arab discourse. Some argue for complete
separation of religion and state, while others argue for its complete amalga-
mation. Parties take conflicting approaches without a critical regard for the real
questions facing Arab societies.

Jabiri's own reading of the problem does not begin with the separation of
religion and politics. Using Ibn Khaldun, he argues that Arab politics must be
read from the perspective of belief (*aqidah*), group affiliation (*qabilah*) and spoils
of war (*ghanimah*). Using these terms for reading the life of Muhammad, Jabiri
argues that the earliest phase of the community was focused on its beliefs even
if the opposition was concerned about the political impact of the new religion.
The Prophet's opposition was focussed on its group cohesion and its privileged
access to the material benefits of the sanctuary. When the Prophet, however,
attacked the gods worshipped by Arab society, he attacked the economic and
social foundations of this society. As a religious belief, Islam was tolerated in
Arab society. But as a religious system that undermined the foundation of the
society, it met with vehement opposition. Henceforth, the responses of Muhammad and his close companions reflected the contingencies of the Arabian
context (al-Jabiri 1991: 61 passim). Jabiri's reading of the life of Muhammad
reveals a commitment to the historical unfolding of the Prophetic message. The
place of politics in the religion does not reveal an essentialist binding of the
two. Consequently, he suggests that even the life of the Prophet Muhammad
reveals a complex historical condition that includes religion, politics and econo-

mics. Against the Islamists, however, Jabiri seems to be saying that religious and materialist interests are identifiable, and can be de-linked from each other.

In 1991, Jabiri wrote what may be characterised as a postscript. In *Heritage and Modernity: Studies and Debates*, the author deals with major criticisms of his work. Most importantly, however, he clarifies the implication of his work for Arab societies. Here he argues very clearly that a critical historical awareness of the past and the present would catapult Arab societies to address the problems facing them. In this regard, he seems to be echoing the concerns of Hanafi to return to the past in order to liberate the present.

Jabiri's approach to religious texts is guided by a concern for the development of Arab society and Arabic philosophy. His reading of religious texts leads him to epistemology and structuralism with which he analyses the concerns of early Islam, and those of present debates in the society. Like Hanafi, he does not engage religious debate in order to posit a religious essence (as evident in Eliade) or an apologetic for religion or Islam. He uses philosophy and anthropological categories to critically understand the religious discourse, and suggests a method of deconstruction, a way for rebuilding Arab society.

Nasr Abu Zayd

My third choice for an Arab intellectual is Nasr Abu Zayd, a Cairene intellectual who now lives in Leiden, the Netherlands. Abu Zayd catapulted into fame when University of Cairo professors tried to block his promotion in 1994. The matter became an issue of public debate when Abu Zayd was accused of insulting the Qur'an. Eventually he did earn his promotion to professorship, but his opponents took the matter to a state court which found that his writings were heretical. In terms of Islamic law of apostasy, then, his opponents requested the court to annul the marriage to his wife, Ibtihal Younis, since Abu Zayd himself was no longer a Muslim. Fearing for the safety of his life, Abu Zayd and his wife were forced to leave the country.

Abu Zayd is also a philosopher, but his work deals more directly with religion than Hanafi and Jabiri. His work may be divided into three interconnected parts. In the first instance, he is engaged in an analysis of the Qur'an and other religious texts. This part of his work covers his analysis of the Qur'an as a literary text (Abu Zayd 1996b). Secondly, Abu Zayd critically discusses the ideological use and abuse of religion in early Islam as well as in contemporary Arab society (Abu Zayd 1996a, 1994, 1995b). And thirdly, Abu Zayd presents a reformed approach to religion by recovering marginal voices in early Islam. A brief summary of his approach in each part follows.

For Abu Zayd, semiotics provides the key to understanding the universe of the text. In this regard, he brings together the classical Islamic disciplines of language and textual hermeneutics, and contemporary approaches in literary theory. Reviewing the complex notions of texts (*nass*), Abu Zayd paints a picture of a culture which clearly understood the complexity of reading texts. He argues that the direct, literal reading of the text promoted by some revivalist groups is a recent innovation that echoes religious fundamentalists in general. The unequivocal texts of Islam consist of a small number of texts, and classical Islamic disciplines proposed a complex approach to the rest (Abu Zayd 1994: 121–23). Contemporary revivalists want to destroy this complexity in the name of religion. In the first instance, Abu Zayd proposed a more nuanced reading of hermeneutics in Islamic history. It is a reading that is bold, and does not flinch at the icons of that history

Abu Zayd's analysis recalls the assertion of Jabiri that clarity (*bayan*), revealed clearly in language, forms one of the epistemological trajectories of Arab discourse. Similarly, Abu Zayd's main contribution lies in showing how that classical discourse was trapped within the semiotic universe of the religious texts. At the outset, the religious text was an adequate signifier of the world and the Divine. The Qur'an was "directed to addressees as a text signifying the speaker" (Abu Zayd 1996b: 59). Coming from God, it had a very specific message addressed to its audience. However, Abu Zayd then argues that this Qur'anic discourse was transformed into a semiotic system serving certain theological and political interests. This was the ultimate process of legitimisation that I will shortly discuss.

Where Jabiri saw a fairly complete epistemic system, Abu Zayd sees a semiotic system turn upon itself. The influence of the *langue*, the system of meaning in the Qur'an as a unity, was to reduce all events, all of history, to the principle of the unity of God. God as unity (*tawhid*) obliterated the distinctiveness and uniqueness of creation. Under the influence of the unity of God in the sacred book, the language of the sacred book signified (pointed to) the true reality of God. Under the influence of such a semiotic system, then, theologians developed the notion that only God was truly real. More tellingly, the semiotic system was eventually deemed to be an ineffective signification of God (Abu Zayd 1995b: 219). The mainstream theological school posited the Divine as the only real, and assigned all else to allegory (Abu Zayd 1995b: 176–83). Mystical schools joined in, and showed adepts how to reach the truly divine. Eventually, in a twist of irony, texts as words were insufficient to signify the essence of the Divine. The texts, while sufficient in themselves as part of a semiotic system, were unable to decisively signify God or the world. In the semiotic system of the Qur'an, only God was real. For Jabiri, the epistemological tradition of *bayan* (clarity) was vigorously pursued in a number of disciplines. Abu Zayd argued that its product was a recognition that signification could only be accommodated in mystical discourse. Illumination (*irfan*) provided a means for turning the text into allegory (*majaz*), unable to contain the vast knowledge of God. The word of God was then left to the vagaries of mystical speculation. All was allegorical, approximate in the face of the absolute God. The Qur'an, revealed to the Prophet to disclose God and His acts, became a system that could not adequately signify God.

The reason for this, according to Abu Zayd, lay in the closure imposed upon the text for political and theological purposes. Recognising this dilemma, Abu Zayd suggests another way of reading the texts. By focusing on the techniques of analysing the opaque dimensions of the texts, Abu Zayd reveals a discourse that was sufficiently open to reading signs in contexts. It is this particular tradition that he suggests should be pursued. He argues for a contextual approach to texts where the context was signified (clearly or opaquely) in the text. Those who decontextualised the meaning of the text invited a mystical, speculative reading of the text. The latter becomes possible when the text floated freely, ready to be invoked by interest groups in politics or theology. A similar strategy operated in the ideological (mis)use of the text.

Abu Zayd's careful work examines the ideological use of religion in both classical Arab-Islamic and contemporary society. In a well-known book, *Naqd al-khitab al-dini* (The Critique of Religious Discourse), Abu Zayd shows how the linguistic and juridical ideas of al-Shafi'i, the leading jurist in Sunnism who influenced subsequent Islamic thought, was an ideological discourse of moderation. Using literary analysis, Abu Zayd demonstrates how the interpretative strategy of this great jurist served the hegemony of Arabs against the newly converted non-Arab Muslims, particularly the Persians. The main thrust of his argument is that al-Shafi'i posited an approach that clearly privileged the Arabs over non-Arabs. Firstly, the Qu'ran provided the solutions to all problems encountered by human beings in the past, present, and possible future. Secondly, this was only possible because of the special, Divine nature of the language (Arabic) whose extensiveness and richness was proverbial. Finally, the full extent of the language could be fully mastered only by an Arab, preferably a Prophet:

> The idea that the Book contains the solutions to all the problems, past, present and future, is established from Shafi'is view of the Arabicity of the Book. That is, on the basis of the language in which it was revealed, which is so extensive that only a Prophet is able to master it ... And this link between completeness of the book of all realities and the extensiveness of the Arabic language, makes the exegesis of the Book and its understanding a difficult task which only a pure Arab can accomplish. Who else but an Arab can achieve such a standard of Arabic however much he delves into the acquisition of the language and its learning. (Abu Zayd 1996b: 68)

Such an interpretive strategy privileged Arabs, and basically supported the status quo of the Arab caliphate. The support for the dominance of the Quraysh was reflected in this excessive reliance on their language. According to Abu Zayd, then, the juristic strategy of reading the sacred text became an ideological reading in favour of the ruling authorities. He argues that an ideological reading takes place when the context of a text has been separated from the text. In fact, Abu Zayd also argues in the same book that the project of Hasan

Hanafi's socially engaged Islam is flawed precisely on the same basis. Like al-Shafi'i before him, Hanafi has to destroy or ignore the context of the past and the present in order to seek solutions in the past (Abu Zayd 1994a: 160). Even a progressive reading of a text is problematic as it "plants the focus of fabulous, clandestine thinking at the moment of raising the flag of science, and that is because it confirmed a priori a program by mathematical means for reading a religious texts—or part thereof—in the preserved tablet [of the original Divine text]" (Abu Zayd 1995b: 140–41). Ideological readings read their programmes into Divine script. The systematic dismantling of the context, demonstrated brilliantly by al-Shafi'i in his emphasis on the richness of the Arabic language, was an ideological method followed by many in contemporary Islamic discourse. This dismantling opened the way for ideological readings.

The third part of Abu Zayd's work focuses on the recovery of some trajectories in heritage for contemporary Arab society. He argues that the Mu`tazilite school of theology provides some insights into how a modern approach to Islam may lead to a more progressive and enlightened approach to religion. Abu Zayd makes a distinction between religion (din) and religious thought (al-fikr al-dini), the latter being guilty of imprisoning Muslims in the past. On the other hand, religion (din) had its proper place in "life and society, in the characters of individuals, their customs, and their ethical behaviour, and not as simply fuel for political, social and economic war." And he concludes that a secular approach to problems is the "true interpretation and scientific conception of religion" (Abu Zayd 1995a: 72). This is not the place to explore in detail the alternative approach to religion proposed by Abu Zayd. Suffice to say that his critique of the ideological reading of religious texts, in which the context is destroyed, provides the clue for a new reading of Islam. In principle, it conveys a meaning of Islam which is open to non-religious, secular, approaches to the challenges of contemporary society. Secondly, it guards vigilantly against ideological abuse of religion by paying attention to the semiotic systems created around religious texts.

Evaluation and Conclusion

I have demonstrated the presence of a critical discourse on religion in Arab scholarship. The discourse does not develop a clearly demarcated category of religion, but is overly concerned about the meaning and role of religion in the re-construction of modern society. The particular relevance of religious solutions is then subjected to scrutiny in two important dimensions. In the first place, the meaning of religious thought and religious texts are deconstructed in their original meaning and reference. Secondly, the meaning of such discourse in contemporary discourse is similarly analysed and deconstructed. I think that the political and ideological critique can be compared with similar critiques in scholarly debates outside Arab contexts.

Among the three thinkers examined here, we find that the critical method is applied to texts in order to uncover the particular ideological (mis)use of texts. Hanafi may be seen as the person who raises the general possibility of reading texts in their historical context. Abu Zayd uses the tools and concepts of linguistics to show how the *langue* of the Qur'an erases the context, and thereby the possibility of meaning. In a similar way, Jabiri uses the notion of *epistemes* to define the structure of Arab thought and discourse. Both suggest that Arab religious texts have been and continue to be mobilised for ideological readings in support of particular authorities. Jabiri focuses on the imprisonment of the epistemic foundations, while Abu Zayd is more specific in the semiotic mechanism at play. Both lament the religious (theological) stranglehold of the textual and epistemological systems.

On the other hand, all three suggest ways in which the religious discourse can be harnessed for progress and development. Hanafi's assertion of the triad seems to be echoed in Abu Zayd and Jabiri's desire to recover something of value from the tradition. For Abu Zayd, progressive readings buried in Islamic history may be recovered. Jabiri is equally committed to an enlightened reading of the texts. According to Gaebel, Arab scholars cite the work of Antonio Gramsci to show how independent intellectuals can play an important role in civil society (Gaebel 1995: 74; Fulton 1987). Jabiri and Hanafi use Gramsci to appeal for a grasp of history through which one is freed of its oppressive hold over the present:

> Freedom of the heritage does not mean throwing the museums into the waste bins. This is not possible. Freedom from the heritage means owning it, ascertaining it and overcoming it. This will not happen unless we rebuild it by examining the arrangement of its parts on the one hand, and by examining the arrangement between us and it on the other, in a manner which returns us to understanding its historicity and the relative understanding and statements. (al-Jabiri 1992a [1982]: 205)

Similarly, Hanafi also believes that a thorough grasp of history will deliver the Arab people.

It is clear from the example of Gramsci that Arab scholars are not an island unto themselves. General linguistic and philosophical debates echo in the discourse. Arab scholars were also fully aware of European theorists of religion such as Karl Marx, Max Weber, Émile Durkheim, as well as some of the earliest Enlightenment critics of religion such as David Hume. However, very little mention is made of the value and significance of the study of religion as a category. Consequently, the insights on myths, rituals and symbols do not seem to find echo in the debates and discussion. There is tremendous scope for entering into some form of debate and discussion about the validity and usefulness of such concepts developed in the critical study of religion.

Arab discourse on religion relies excessively on textual analyses. In many Arab societies literacy rates are still very low, and religious texts are largely the preserve of intellectuals and a small middle class. In this regard, hardly any studies focus on the iconic, symbolic nature of texts explored by students or religion and anthropologists. Mohammed Arkoun, a North African intellectual based in Paris whose writings are translated into Arabic, must be mentioned for attempting to address this problem. He uses the concept of *social imaginaire* to describe the unspoken structure of social life. The *social imaginaire* "of an individual, a social group, or a nation is the collection of images carried by that culture about itself or another culture—once a product of epics, poetry, and religious discourse, today a product primarily of the media and secondarily of the schools" (Arkoun 1994: 6; Arkoun 1987: 9). Even Arkoun, however, relies mainly on texts to discover the spoken and unspoken assumptions of the Arab world. The oral nature of the debates, the role of sermons, and popular religion, are ignored by such emphases on the literary heritage of classical Islam. The study of religion could be fruitfully applied here.

The solutions offered through a critical reading of texts are insightful in themselves and a contribution to the ideological use of texts in general. However, they expose the clearly circumscribed nature of the debate between the Islamists and the progressives in contemporary Arab societies. The Islamists pose the religious heritage as a source of authenticity and values for social and political problems. The critical discourse attempts a deconstruction of this discourse, and the historical legacy it invokes. Between the thesis and counterthesis, much more needs to be done. A critical analysis of how exactly Muslims and Arabs appropriate the sacred texts as literary document, identity marker and cultural artifact must accompany such critical readings. The scholars discussed in this paper have suggested that Islamists study the texts, but they have not dealt with the rest (the majority) who do not belong to this camp.

Since Arab scholars almost exclusively assume that Muslims read texts in their cognitive dimensions, they also posit some or the other form of rationality as the panacea. Again, there is some recognition of the problem posed by an essentialist approach to rationality. Most fundamentally, however, it seems that not sufficient attention is paid to the transformation of religion in modernity. The role of religion in modern society or in the information age is a missing element in the analysis of religious texts. Religion, as a category, is not sufficiently problematised even though religious texts are subjected to careful and minute scrutiny. In general, an enlightened approach to religion is regarded as the desire goal. But the role of religion in providing a sense of meaning and stability, or the most effective means of protest, are neither acknowledged nor carefully analysed.

Finally, one additional and significant structural criticism needs mention. The Arab discourse is shared at conferences, in a number of journals and edited collections. And as illustrated in this paper, there is much that can be shared about a common discourse. However, apart from minor exceptions, the scholars themselves do not acknowledge or challenge each other's work. Every scholar has a project and rarely addresses the theories of the other. The blame for the lack of such a debate may be laid at the door of the political nature of the debate. The development of a disciplinary approach to religion can address this lack of dialogue, challenge and counter-challenge. I have no doubt that the insights produced in the discourse will be richer for a more robust debate.

Bibliography

Abu Zayd, Nasr Hamid (1994 [1990]), *Naqd al-Khitab al-Dini* [The critique of religious discourse]. Cairo: Dar Sina.

—— (1995a), *Al-Tafkir fi zaman al-takfir: didd al-jahl wa 'l-zayf wa 'l-khurafah* [Thinking in an era of apostasy: against ignorance, falsehood and legends]. Cairo: Dar Sina.

—— (1995b), *Al-Nass, al-sultah, al-haqiqah: al-fikr al-dini bayn iradah al-ma`rifah wa iradah al-haymanah* [Text, authority, reality: religious thought between the will to knowledge and the will to hegemony]. Beirut: Al-Markaz al-thaqafi al-`Arabi.

—— (1996a), *Al-Imam al-Shafi`i wa ta'sis al-aydiyulujiyyah al-wasatiyyah* [al-Imam al-Shafi`i and the establishment of the median ideology]. Cairo: Maktabah Madbuli.

—— (1996b), "Khitab Ibn Rushd bayn haqq al-ma`rifah wa dughut al-naqid" [The discourse of Averroes between the right to knowledge and the suppression of the critic], in: *Alif*: 6–35.

al-Jabiri, Muhammad Abid (1991), *Al-Turath wa 'l-hadathah: dirasat wa munaqashat* [Heritage and modernity: studies and discussions]. Beirut: Markaz dirasat al-wahdah al-`arabiyyah.

—— (1992a [1982]), *Al-Khitab al-`arabi al-mu`asir: dirasah tahliliyyah naqdiyyah* [Contemporary Arab discourse: a critical, analytical study]. 4th ed. Beirut: Al-Markaz al-Thaqafi al-`Arabi.

—— (1992b), *Naqd al-`aql al-`arabi*. Vol. 2, *Bunyat al-`aql al-`arabi* [The critique of the Arab mind. The structure of the Arab mind]. 4th ed. Beirut: Markaz Dirasat al-wahdah al-`arabiyyah.

—— (1998), "Su'al al-ma`na al-mutabiq: madkhal ila al-mustaqbal" [The Question of the appropriate meaning: door to the future], in: *Al-Muntalaq* 121 (Autumn 1998): 39–46.

al-Ramihi, Muhammad (1996), "Hadith al-shahr: azmah al-muthaqqaf al-`arabi" [The discussion of the month: crisis of the Arab intellectual], in: *Al-`Arabi* 457 (December 1996): 14–23.

Arkoun, Mohammed (1987), *Rethinking Islam Today*. Occasional Papers Series. Center for Contemporary Arab Studies.

—— (1994), *Rethinking Islam: Common Questions, Uncommon Answers*. Translated by Robert D. Lee. Boulder: Westview Press.

Barakat, Halim (1987), "Al-Muthaqqafun fi '-mujtama` al-`Arabi al-mu`asir: Mulahazat hawl usulihim wa 'intima'atihim al-tabaqiyyah" [Intellectuals in contemporary Arab society: observations on their principles and their class affiliation], in: *Al-*

Antalagentsiya al-ʾArabiyyah, edited by al-Tahir Labib. Tunis: Al-Dar al-ʾArabiyyah li 'l-kitab: 45–52.

Beck, Herman L. (2002), "A Pillar of Social Harmony: The Study of Comparative Religion in Contemporary Indonesia," in: *Modern Societies and the Science of Religions. Studies in Honour of Lammert Leertouwer*, ed. by G.A. Wiegers in association with Jan Platvoet. Leiden: Brill: 331–49.

Boullata, Issa J. (1990), *Trends and Issues in Contemporary Arab Thought*. Albany, N.Y.: SUNY Press.

Chidester, David (1996), *Savage Systems: Colonialism and Comparative Religion in Southern Africa*. Studies in Religion and Culture. Charlottesville, Va./London: University Press of Virginia.

— (2004), "'Classify and Conquer': Friedrich Max Müller, Indigenous Religious Traditions, and Imperial Comparative Religion," in: *Beyond Primitivism: Indigenous Religious Traditions and Modernity*, ed. by J. Olupona. London/New York: Routledge: 71–88.

Cox, James L. (1994), "Religious Studies by the Religious: A Discussion of the Relationship Between Theology and the Science of Religion," in: *Journal for the Study of Religion* 7 (2) September 1994: 3–32.

Eickelman, Dale F. (1985), *Knowledge and Power in Morocco: The Education of a Twentieth Century Noble*. Princeton, N.J.: Princeton University Press.

Euben, Roxanne L. (1997), "Comparative Political Theory: An Islamic Fundamentalist Critique of Rationalism," in: *The Journal of Politics* 99 (1) February 1997: 28–55.

Faris, Hani A. (1986), "Heritage and Ideologies in Contemporary Arab Thought: Constrasting Views of Change and Development," in: *Journal of Asian and African Affairs* 21 (1–2) : 89–103.

Floors, Alexander (1989), "Fu'ad Zakariyya wa jadaliyyatuh li 'l-zahirah al-islamiyyah al-muʾasirah" [Fu'ad Zakariyya his argument of the contemporary Islamic phenomenon], in: *Al-Ijtihad* 1: 189-202.

— (1992), "Al-Muthaqqafun al-misriyyun: Al-Islam al-siyasi wa 'l-dawlah" [Egyptian intellectuals: Political Islam and the state], in: *Al-Ijtihad* 4 (14) Winter 1992: 189–99.

Fulton, John (1987), "Religion and Politics in Gramsci: An Introduction," in: *Sociological Analysis* 48 (Fall 1987): 197–216.

Gaebel, Michael (1995), *Von der Kritik Des Arabischen Denkens Zum Panarabischen Aufbruch: Das Philosophische und Politische Denken Muhammad Abid al-Gabiris* (Islamkunde Untersuchungen Band 189). Berlin: Klaus Schwarz Verlag.

Geertz, Armin W. (2000), "Global Perspectives on Methodology in the Study of Religion," in: *Perspectives on Method and Theory in the Study of Religion: Adjunct Proceedings of the 17th Congress of the International Association for the History of Religions, Mexico City 1995*, ed. by Armin W. Geertz/Russell T. McCutcheon. Leiden: Brill: 49–73.

Gerth, H.H./Wright Mills, C. (1970), translators and editors. *From Max Weber: Essays in Sociology*. London: Routledge and Kegan Paul.

Gülalp, Haldun (1995), "Islamism and Postmodernism," in: *Contention: Debates in Society, Culture, and Science* 4 (2) Winter 1995: 59–73.

Hanafi, Hasan (1991), *Muqaddimah fi ʾilm al-istighrab: al-turath wa 'l-tajdid: mawqifuna min al-turath al-gharbi* [Introduction to the science of occidentalism: heritage and renewal: our position with respect]. Cairo: Al-Dar al-Fanniyyah li 'l-Nashr wa 'l-tawzi'.

— (1996), "Qadaya al-turath wa l-tajdid wa ishkaliyyat al-naql wa 'l-ibda'" [Issues of heritage, renewal and the problematic of transmission and creativity], in: *Al-Muntalaq* 114 (Winter 1996): 41–57.

— (1998), "Tajdid 'ilm al-kalam: al-usas, al-dawafi' wa 'l-ghayat" [Renewal of theology: foundations, motivations and goals], *Al-Muntalaq* 120 (Spring 1998): 57–79.

Hüpp, Gerhard (1988), "Unterentwicklungung und Islam. Zum Problem der Erbe-rezeption in Arabischen Ländern unter den Bedingungen des Kolonialismus," in: *Afrika Asien Lateinamerika* 3: 440–52.

Illesanmi, Simeon O. (1995), "The Civil Religion Thesis in Nigeria: A Critical Examination of Jacob Olupona's Theory of Religion and the State," in: *The Council of Societies for the Study of Religions Bulletin* 24 (3–4) September–November 1995: 59–64.

Kermani, Navid (1996), *Offenbarung als Kommunikation: Das Konzept Wahy in Nasr Abu Zayds Mafhum al-Nass*. Frankfurt: Peter Lang.

Kippenberg, Hans G. (1994), "Rivalry Among Scholars of Religions: The Crisis of Historicism and the Formation of Paradigms in the History of Religions," in: *Historical Reflections* 20 (3): 377–402.

— (1996), "Die Krise der Religionen und die Genese der Religionswissenschaften," in: *Vom Weltbildwandel zur Weltanschauungsanalyse: Krisenwahrnehmung und Krisenbewältigung um 1900*, ed. by Volker Drehsen/Walter Sparn. Berlin: Akademie Verlag: 89–102.

— (1997), "Rationality in Studying Historical Religions," in: *Rationality and the Study of Religion*, ed. by Jeppe S. Jensen/Luther H. Martin. Aarhus, Denmark: Aarhus University Press: 157–66.

Koningsveld, P.S. van (2002), "The Study of Contemporary Islam in Morocco," in: *Modern Societies and the Science of Religions. Studies in Honour of Lammert Leertouwer*, ed. by G.A. Wiegers in association with Jan Platvoet. Leiden: Brill: 272–82.

Olupona, Jacob K. (1991), "Major Issues in the Study of African Traditional Religion," in: *African Traditional Religions in Contemporary Society*, ed. by Jacob K. Olupona. New York: Paragon House: 25–34.

Platvoet, Jan (1993a), "Eliade at Unisa: A Critical Review of Shirley Thorpe's 'African Traditional Religions' and 'Primal Religions Worldwide,'" in: *Journal for the Study of Religion* 6 (2) September 1993: 103–12.

— (1993b), "Hawk Says/Osansa Se: Ade a Onyame Aye Nhina Ye: An Observer's View of the Development of the Study of Religion in South Africa." Conference presentation, Association for the Study of Religion Congress. Swaziland.

Platvoet, Jan/Cox, James/Olupona, Jacob, eds. (1996), *The Study of Religions in Africa: Past, Present and Prospects*. Religions of Africa 1. Cambridge: Roots and Branches.

Pye, Michael (1990), "Introduction," in: *Emerging from Meditation*, ed. by Michael Pye. London: Gerald Duckworth & Company: 1–47.

Rabinow, Paul (1996), *Essays on the Anthropology of Reason*. Princeton, N.J.: Princeton University Press.

Sagiv, David (1995), *Fundamentalism and Intellectuals in Egypt, 1973–1993*. London: Cass.

Salvatore, Armando (1995), "The Rational Authentication of Turath in Contemporary Arab Thought: Muhammad al-Jabiri and Hasan Hanafi," in: *The Muslim World* 85 (3-4) July-October 1995: 195–214.

Steppat, Fritz (1991), "Al-Muslim Wa 'l-Sultah," in: *Al-Ijtihad* 3 (12) Summer 1991: 65–87.

Termeulen, Arend Jan (1995), "Metanarratives and Local Challenges: Islamist and Modernist Discourses in Contemporary Tunisia," in: *Changing Stories: Postmodernism and the Arab-Islamic World*, ed. by Inge E. Boer/Annelies Moor/Toine van Toefellen. Amsterdam/Atlanta, Ga.: Rodopi: 53–68.

von Kügelgen, Anke (1994), *Averroes und die Arabische Moderne: Ansätze zu einer Neubegründung des Rationalismus im Islam*. Leiden: E.J. Brill.

Waardenburg, Jacques (1998), "Observations on the Scholarly Study of Religions as Pursued in Some Muslim Countries," in: *Numen* 45 (3): 235–57.

Westerlund, David (1991), "*Insiders* and *Outsiders* in the Study of African Religions: Notes on Some Problems of Theory and Method," in: *African Traditional Religions in Contemporary Society*, ed. by Jacob K. Olupona. New York: Paragon House: 15–24.

Whaling, Frank (1995), "The Study of Religion in a Global Context," in: *Theory and Method in Religious Studies: Contemporary Approaches to the Study of Religion*, ed. by Frank Whaling. Berlin: Mouton de Gruyter: 191–251.

Wiebe, Donald (1997), "Dissolving Rationality: The Anti-Science Phenomenon and Its Implications for the Study of Religion," in: *Rationality and the Study of Religion*, ed. by Jeppe S. Jensen/Luther H. Martin. Aarhus, Denmark: Aarhus University Press: 167–83.

Wielandt, Rotraud (1971), *Offenbarung und Geschichte im Denken moderner Muslime*. Wiesbaden.

Wild, Stefan (1986), "Eine Kritik der Islamischen Vernunft. Zu den gesammelten Schriften Mohammed Arkouns," in: *Die Welt des Islams* 26: 163–66.

Ziyadah, Khalid (1989), "Zuhur al-muthaqqaf al-`arabi: qira'ah fi a`mal Sharabi wa 'l-`Arawi wa 'l-Jabiri [The emergence of the Arab intellectual: reading the works of Sharabi, Laroui and Jabiri], in: *Al-Ijtihad* 2 (6) Autumn 1989: 149–87.

A Survey of New Approaches to the Study of Religion in India

by

PRATAP KUMAR

Abstract

This essay focuses on the methodological and theoretical approaches in the study of religion in the last two decades of the twentieth century. While it takes stock of the past studies in a cursory way, it raises a fundamental question as to why comparative religion/history of religion as a discipline did not emerge in the Indian academic scene in spite of the several thousands of books and papers written on Indian religions and despite religion being a major social phenomenon in India. In attempting to answer this question, it raises other more fundamental issues, such as the notion of rationality and religion, religion as a personal matter, colonialism and so on. These issues are often beneath the reasons ascribed by the Indian academics for the absence of comparative religion/history of religion as a discipline in the Indian universities. The paper also attempts to look at some of the real concerns behind these objections. Finally, the paper identifies some of the main types of studies that have emerged in the last two decades of the twentieth century and the methodological approaches that have become part of those studies.

Several thousands of books have been written on Indian religions in the last three hundred years or so both by Western scholars as well as Indian scholars. Most of the world's religions have found a home on the Indian soil. Naturally, religion is a major phenomenon in India both at the national level as well as at the village level and pervades virtually all sectors of society, not to mention that it has been a constant source of irritation at the level of politics. India has agonised over religion in the last many centuries,[1] most certainly beginning from the Moghul rule. The hijacking of the Indian Airlines plane in Amritsar on Christmas eve in 1999 by pro-Islamic fighters over Kashmir illustrates the

---

1   G.J. Larson in his book *India's Agony Over Religion* (Larson 1997) discusses the religious conflict in India.

extent to which religion has become important in South Asian politics. Notwithstanding all the above facts, study of religion has not yet become a discipline in the Indian universities and comparative religion/history of religion as a discipline is yet to emerge in the Indian academic world.

On the one hand, Hinduism, Islam, Sikhism and Christianity are studied within their respective theological frameworks: Hinduism is studied in places like Benares Hindu University and in some universities as part of the Indian philosophy departments; Islam is studied in places like the Alighar Muslim University and Osmania University; Sikhism is studied in places like Patiala University, and Christianity is studied within Christian seminaries and theological institutions, with the exception of a chair in Christianity established in Mysore University couple of decades ago. Many of the smaller religions, such as Buddhism and Jainism, on the other hand, are studied either in the Sanskrit departments or in the Indian philosophy departments more as part of philosophy and logic than as religion. Zoroastrianism is perhaps one of the most neglected ones. The many hundreds of what anthropologists called folk traditions or tribal religions classified under the broad category of "Little Traditions" are by and large studied within the departments of anthropology and sociology. Generally, the major religions that I have cited above are studied and taught by their adherents and primarily within the context of promoting and training their own future theologians and religious functionaries, whereas the so called "Little Traditions" are not necessarily studied by their adherents. Only recently in regions, such as Bihar and Orissa and the North East Indian states, the new intelligentsia among the tribal population are beginning to study their own religions within social/cultural anthropology discipline.

While such is the more conventional scene in the study of religion in India, in the last two decades of the twentieth century study of religion has entered other disciplines such as journalism, political science, economics, business administration and has also become subject matter in the hands of a host of feminist scholars located in various disciplines, such as literature, media and film studies.

Before we ask the more obvious question of what new approaches have become part of the study of religion in India, we need to ask why serious comparative study of religion/history of religion as a discipline has not developed in India despite religion being a subject matter in the academic and nonacademic discourse for so long. Is it because such a discipline is rooted in the Western rationality which generally guides the social scientific inquiry? Is it simply because it is developed in the Western academic institutions where religion is not necessarily a personal matter but something too intellectual and hence distanced from ones personal life? Is it because it is a by-product of colonialism? Or is it because, within the context of India, religion is more about practising it than intellectually comprehending its various not too direct or obvious implications? Any one of these or all of these could be either valid reasons or lame excuses for the lack of the kind of study of religion that has emerged mainly in the Western world. If these were to be lame excuses, then, is there a scope for comparative/history of religion as a discipline within the academic world in India. Now that globalisation is taking place in every facet of our lives, will globalisation[2] of the study of religion also occur? (I shall return to the prospect of globalisation of the study of religion and its impact on India later in this essay). Given the criticism that globalisation is a Western economic expansionistic programme, will such criticism stand in the way of a *serious* attempt by international scholars to establish a *genuine* discipline in the study of religion? Is comparative/history of religion a genuine discipline, in the first place? Or is it another method of pushing Western ways of constructing knowledge? I certainly cannot do justice to answer all of these questions that I have raised so far within the scope of this essay. But let us see if we can unpack some of them, at least, even if it has to be cursorily.

Is the Study of Religion Rooted in Western Rationality?

The obvious answer to this question is perhaps yes. In other words, there is some truth in that the modern scientific discoveries and knowledge by and large emanated out of a particular empirical rational discourse that has Western roots. But then, is rationality an exclusive domain of the Western discourse any more? Isn't all scientific inquiry based on rationality, no matter in which society and culture it exists? If rationality is the basis of any scientific inquiry, no matter where it is pursued, then, why should the study of religion be seen differently? That is to say, we do not see the study of modern physics or chemistry as particularly Western any more, even though the bulk of those studies may have emanated in the Western institutions. If that is the case, either to make religion a case of exception to the rule or to invent another kind of ratio-

---

2   I hesitate to use the expression which has been used by some scholars, viz., "internationalising" the study of religion (David Chidester [1998], "Embracing South Africa, Internationalizing the Study of Religion," in: *Journal for the Study of Religion* 11 [1]: 5–33). The concept of "internationalisation" has been used in many different contexts and mainly in the context of economics, business and trade where it has been criticised by the developing countries as a negative force which gave an advantage to the first world due to its superior technological and other infra-structural facilities. In essence, the concept has been criticised as an indirect move by the so called first world to dominate the emerging markets in the developing world. Using such a concept that has raised so much criticism and negative sense for the study of religion can only lead to further misunderstanding that the Western academic associations for the study of religion are attempting to expand their dominance over the third world institutions. Therefore, I use a little softer concept of "globalisation," although it also is not totally devoid of criticism.

nality for the study of religion is not justified. Furthermore, there are a host of cultural protagonists in India, who make repeated claims to the rightful contribution that the ancient Indian intellectual tradition (which is deeply rooted in religious worldview) made to scientific and rational inquiries in the areas of mathematics, medicine and a host of other scientific disciplines. That is, they do not see rationality as an exclusive Western category but rather integral to Indian culture. If rationality is a common category shared by all cultures, why then is a discrepancy in the way that some disciplines are not seen alien to the Indian culture even though they have been constructed in Western institutions (e.g., modern physics, space technology and so on) while disciplines that have religious and cultural overtones are seen with suspicion if they have been established in the Western academia? So, even if one were to argue that the idea that rationality is a Western category and, therefore, is not useful or meaningful in the study of religion in the particular cultural milieu of India, the argument would lack credibility in the sense that we cannot on the one hand claim that rationality is integral to the construction of knowledge in India and yet not allow it in the context of the study of religion. Furthermore, the argument that the realm of religious knowledge is of a different kind from those of the natural/empirical sciences does not hold water as anyone who has pursued a substantial study of the ancient Indian materials, such as the Vedic literature, would know that the very sciences of medicine, mathematics and so on were all pursued within the context of religious pursuit. Thus, there is no substantive evidence within the Indian cultural sources to distinguish between rational knowledge and non-rational knowledge. In fact, the Indian tradition has always prided itself on being the first to have developed the most rational principles of epistemology, namely perception, inference, comparison and analogical reasoning. And, what is interesting is that it had no problem placing them alongside the principle of revelation or scriptural testimony.

Another important factor in this context is that a generic notion of religion in India is absent in its vocabulary. So, in the absence of a generic notion either a general comparativism or a historical treatment of religion as a general phenomenon could not take place. One observes that while in many Western societies there has been a serious secular critique of religion, such a critique is markedly less common in the Indian scene in spite of the fact that the post-independent Indian constitution provided for a socialist, secular, democratic constitution. In the context of India, the secular state is usually understood in the sense that the state embraces all religious groups and provides for all of them, even if that meant special holidays, a place for rituals in public institutions and so on. This is markedly different from the way it is understood in many Western societies. In countries such as the U.S., for instance, the church and state are radically separated. This separation of religion and state in Western societies by and large gave scope for a meaningful critique of religion without the religious institutional interference. But in India, religious institutional interference in matters of religion is often alarmingly high. Therefore, the state has to be always on the look out for problems that might arise when a particular religious issue confronts the national attention. A case in point is to consider Salman Rushdie's book *Satanic Verses* which was freely available in most Western countries while India banned the book even before Iran and other Islamic states did. Another case would be the Babri mosque episode of 1992 when some right-wing Hindus went about destroying it and the state was caught in between. Even though, India had never had a very clear-cut situation where a particular religion was a state religion, during its thousands of years of history, one or another religion from time to time did enjoy state patronage. For instance, during the rule of the Gupta dynasty what we today call Hinduism did enjoy the patronage of the rulers; during the reign of the emperor Asoka, Buddhism did enjoy almost the status of being the state religion, and during the Moghul rule, Islam did enjoy greater patronage than its counterpart, Hinduism and its many sectarian branches. Although the policies of both the British East India Company and the British Empire expressly discouraged the Christian missionary activities, generally during the British raj Christianity did enjoy greater patronage in India.[3] However, it is during the British raj that India began to experience greater distance between religion and the state for mainly political reasons. It is during the same period that we begin to see greater awareness of the diversity of religious worlds that existed for centuries in India. Whether religion enjoyed state patronage or not, for centuries organised religion (be that Hinduism, Islam, Jainism, Parseeism/Zoroastrianism, Christianity and others) in India has been so strong and conspicuous through ritual and other public manifestations that public discourse on religion always bordered on confessionalism and in defence of it rather than being a neutral and general debate. Even in the context of a dialogue with other religions which is a more recent phenomenon (with the exception of a few examples in the past history e.g., Akbar's engagement with what he called Dīn-i-ilāhī), either it is the defence of ones position which is more critically pursued or some selective assimilations between religions than a serious understanding of religion in general. In this sense, even philosophy of religion in India is of a different kind than its counterpart in the West. In other words, a social and secular critique would have been made possible in India, if there was a generic notion of religion in its religious vocabulary. Such a notion was alien to Indian culture until the Western discourse imposed it on the Indian intellectual consciousness. Nonetheless, in more recent years one should recognise the social and secular critique of religion in various other forms, such as art, literature, especially

---

3   For instance, when the famous missionary trio, Carey, Marshman and Ward, first arrived, the British East India Company denied them the entry and they had to come through the Dutch East India Company patronage.

Indian novels written in English, and various feminist journals. For a sustained academic discourse on religion along the lines of critical and social scientific theories, such passing critiques found in other literature need to be brought into the mainstream scholarship in religion studies in India. One of the stumbling blocks a scholar faces in doing this is that often dispassionate secular critiques emanate from Western scholars and Indian scholars respond invariably in defensive mode. A case in point is the recent debate on the study and interpretation of the Bhagavadgita which was sparked off by Wendy Doniger's alleged remark on the Gita as a text that promoted war, and another study by Jeffrey Kripal on *Kali's Child*.[4] Both happen to come from Western scholars, and the Indian scholarly and non-scholarly response has been mixed. The responses ranged from serious objections to both views to moderate acknowledgement of the critiques but with an attempt to reinterpret the Indian religious texts. Responding to Doniger's interpretation of the Gita, V.V. Raman says,

> Bookish academics need to remember that when it comes to analyzing works regarded as sacred by vast numbers of people, sound scholarship is like the firmness of bones, while appreciation and sensitivity are like flesh and blood. Without the latter, the former is merely an ugly skeleton: morbid and monstrous, lifeless and lamentable. With the latter, scholarship becomes robust and living. Ignoring this fact has led to many otherwise meaningful commentaries.[5]

Another Indian response on the same topic but related to Rushdie's book is by Bhadraiah Mallampalli who justifies censorship in India saying,

> [A]s for censorship, government of any society has its reason to limit social unrest. Just because Rushdie and some book distributors want to make a quick buck, India doesn't have to suffer damage to life and property.[6]

Contrasting the above two is the view of Lars Martin Fosse, a Western scholar, when he comments on the book *Kali's Child* by Jeffrey Kripal,[7]

---

4   Jeffrey J. Kripal (1998), *Kali's Child: The Mystical and the Erotic in the Life and Teachings of Ramakrishna*. Chicago: University of Chicago Press [first published in 1995].

5   Quoted from the daily discussion on Indology@Listserve.liv.ac.uk, posted on Wed, 14 Mar 2001 11:27:42 -0500; Sender: Indology <INDOLOGY@LISTSERV.LIV.AC.UK> From: "V.V. Raman" <VVRSPS@RITVAX.ISC.RIT.EDU> Subject: Re: SV: "Bagger Vance" & Doniger on the Gita.

6   Quoted from the daily discussion on Indology@Listserve.liv.ac.uk, posted on Wed, 14 Mar 2001 12:04:36 -0500 Reply-To: Indology <INDOLOGY@LISTSERV.LIV.AC.UK> Sender: Indology <INDOLOGY@LISTSERV.LIV.AC.UK> From: Bhadraiah Mallampalli <vaidix@HOTMAIL.COM> Subject: Re: "Bagger Vance" & Doniger on the Gita.

7   Jeffrey J. Kripal (1998), *Kali's Child: The Mystical and the Erotic in the Life and Teachings of Ramakrishna*. Chicago: University of Chicago Press [first published in 1995].

I would like to point out, that although the contents of the book may be offensive to many Hindus, it is only fair to say that critique of Christianity by many secularized people (agnostics/atheists) in the West is just as, or even more, offensive. Thus Hindus should not feel that they are being treated differently from others. They are just facing the brunt of free speech in a society that values free speech higher than religion (one of the reasons why the Rushdie affair had such devastating consequences in many places and brought Muslims into such disrepute. The fact that the book was insensitive to Muslim beliefs is of no consequence to the Western person, who simply believes that people shouldn't be too sensitive about their views and beliefs).[8]

The above comments demonstrate the typical ways in which Indian or South Asian scholars on the one end of the spectrum and the Western scholars on the other end of the spectrum view matters of religious nature. While South Asian scholars tend to pitch from an assumed religious background and are more concerned about hurting religious feelings of communities in which they live, the Western scholarly tendency is to assume the secular nature of a democratic society. Herein lies the difference. That is to say, the Western scholar is able to distance himself/herself from personal religious background and engage in a secular discourse on religion, South Asian scholars, let alone ordinary people, are seemingly unable to distinguish from the practice of religion and an academic debate on religion. This raises the question whether it is because the fundamental thing in India is that religion is more about one's personal life (hence experiencing it) than serious intellectual discussion on religion.

Is Religion a Personal Matter?

The other possible objection for comparative/history of religion to emerge in India is that such a study of religion is far removed from ones personal life, whereas religion in Indian culture is more about ones personal goals than mere intellectual understanding of it. While this perception is generally prevalent among many average Indians, there has been a sustained intellectual legacy that was left by Indian religious reformers, leaders, gurus and intellectuals like, e.g., Aurobindo[9] and Radhakrishnan.[10] Even when Indian social scientists dealt with Indian culture, society and religion, it is largely from the standpoint of religion as a "way of life" utilising traditional concepts such as caste, *varna*, *jati* and so on rather than how religion and society are constructed *via* these con-

---

8   Quoted from the daily discussion on Indology@Listserve.liv.ac.uk, posted on Date: Tue, 20 Mar 2001 16:03:29 +0100 Sender: Indology <INDOLOGY@LISTSERV.LIV.AC.UK> From: Lars Martin Fosse <lmfosse@ONLINE.NO> Subject: SV: reviews and comments (Freud, Vishnu, Kali, Indus Samskrut).

9   Sri Aurobindo (1970), *The Life Divine*. Pondichery: Sri Aurobindo Ashram.

10   S. Radhakrishnan (1927), *The Hindu View of Life*. London: Allen & Unwin.

ventional concepts and what ideological underpinnings have been at the base
of these constructions and what changes and assimilations have occurred in the
course of a long history of Indian society. Writing in the essays in honor of
Louis Dumont, T.N. Madan expresses this very restlessness about the way sociological studies on India have gone on prior to Dumont making a difference by
bringing in empiricism and rationality as methodological tools to understand
and explain the Hindu society and culture. Madan says,

> An overwhelming preoccupation with caste and the understanding of it in terms of
> systematic models of interaction was, then, the distinctive contribution of sociologists
> to the understanding of Indian society during the first two decades of the present half
> of the century [that is, the twentieth century]. Indian society and culture had been,
> however, reflected upon and written about earlier in the century, and for longer than
> that, by scholars trained in Western methods of research and study. These earlier
> scholars had retained the traditional comprehensive viewpoint of the sociocultural
> reality which looked upon caste or *varna* as an element in a complex whole called the
> *varnasrama dharma*, or the appropriate *way of life*, based on the organisation of society in
> terms of the four social divisions called *varna* and the ordering of individual lives in
> terms of the four life-stages called *asrama*. An overarching ideological framework for
> the individual and social dimensions of life was provided by the concept of the four
> goals of life called the *pursarthas* and the notion of moral obligations entailing the five
> sacrifices or the *pancamahayajna*. Thus, one finds this comprehensive theory of society
> not only in the *Manusmrti* (see Bühler 1886) but also in such widely read and influential
> contemporary expositions as Radhakrishnan's *The Hindu view of life* (1927). I am not
> concerned in this essay with the criticism that this and similar expositions were written
> for Western audiences and contained oversimplifications and even distortions to
> present Hinduism in a form in which it would appear respectable in the West. The
> criticism is, perhaps, fair but Indian sociologists have been worse sinners in this regard
> and that is what is relevant here.[11]

In other words, even in the context of social scientific studies, the traditional
concepts that were utilised to explain Indian society were predominantly those
that have reinforced the view that it is ones personal life and hence the "way of
life" that is more relevant even in explaining the social ramifications of it. Prior
to Dumont social scientific studies in India focused on societal issues such as
caste and social organisation without taking into account the cultural and
religious values that impact on society. Thus, Dumont's contribution lies in
bring together hither to separately approached fields, namely sociology and
indology. Madan rightly points out,

> The recognition of the crucial significance of the dual viewpoint led Dumont to con-
> sider the dialectics of Hindu social life: alongside of caste, anti-caste or sect would have
> to be studied; alongside of kinship and worldly obligations renunciation would have to

---

11   T.N. Madan (1988), "For a Sociology of India," in: *Way of Life: King, Householder,
     Renouncer, Essays in Honour of Louis Dumont*, ed. by T.N. Madan. Delhi: Motilal
     Banarsidass Publishers: 407 (text in paranthesis is mine).

be accorded its due place of importance; alongside of the status of the Brahman the power of the king would have to be recognised as an element within the social system; and so on.[12]

This bringing together of the elements of the social and the religious, trans-cendental and the empirical inevitably involves an approach of holism and comparison as reflected in Dumont's work. Nevertheless, as far as India is concerned, such efforts to combine the social and the religious have predomi-nantly remained in the social sciences and have not yet become part of the study of religion in general. Scholars of religion in India continue to be caught up in the practice and the experience of religion and hence theological treat-ment of it rather than looking at religion as part of a totality that includes religion as a social phenomenon.

Generally speaking, in all cultures where religion is practised, it is indeed a personal matter in the first place. Indian culture is no exception to it. It is not as if intellectual pursuit of religion is alien to Indian culture. Most of what is known as Indian philosophy is about abstract and intellectual understanding of religion, in any case. In all those of Indian philosophical debates comparing Buddhism, Hinduism, Jainism and other religio-philosophical positions is quite common, albeit for purposes of disputing the other's claims. In fact, compari-son is a fundamentally important epistemological category within the context of Indian religio-philosophical discourse. In other words, comparative study did take place in the older religious debates for theological reasons. However, such attempts were not made within the modern religious context of India in dealing with religions, such as Islam and Christianity. This is not to say that there were no writers who did some work on such comparative study, either from Islamic perspective looking at Hinduism, or the other way around. Cer-tainly there are some reasonably good works which were done from the standpoint of Christianity and comparing its ideas with those of Hinduism, of course, from the point of view of either wanting to establish ones theological supremacy or desiring to enter into dialogue.[13] So the argument that religion in the Indian milieu is more personal and, therefore, a serious scholarly study of religion which is distanced from ones theological convictions has not taken

---

12   Ibid.: 410.

13   See a Muslim scholar's attempt in: Muhammed Jawed Zafar (1994), *Christo-Islamic Theologies*. Delhi: Adam Publishers & Distributors; for a Christian theologian's attempt see A.J. Appasamy (1970), *The Theology of Hindu Bhakti*. Bangalore: The Christian Literature Society Press; for a neo-Hindu Guru's attempt see Maharaj Charan Singh (1985), *Light on Saint John*. New Delhi: Radha Soami Satsang Beas, Punjab, India. To these one might add more scholarly ones like Raimundo Panikkar (1964), *The Unknown Christ of Hinduism*. London: Darton, Longman & Todd; John Nicol Farquhar (1913), *The Crown of Hinduism*. London: Oxford University Press; and many more from a Christian point of view.

deeper roots in Indian academia does not hold water. Neither is it right to argue that religion being personal is something exclusive to India nor is it appropriate to dismiss that comparative study is something alien to Indian culture. The real reasons must be sought elsewhere.

Is the Contemporary Academic Study of Religion a By-product of Colonialism?

A convenient way of dismissing something is to attribute it to the colonial history. There is no denying the fact that the modern study of religion within the discipline of comparative/history of religion emerged in the context of colonial interaction with Asian and other cultures. I noted elsewhere that

> [t]he study of non-Christian religions began as a result of the emergence of Western colonies in the East. Although many pietistic missionaries denounced the non-Christian religions, some did venture into those prohibited avenues of human culture. We have number of examples of missionaries that seriously undertook, not only the study of those religions, but even becoming influenced by those religious and cultural values (Robert de Nobili in India during the seventeenth century is a case in point). During the eighteenth century and the early nineteenth century many missionaries and secular Western scholars dug out the treasures of the ancient literatures of India and China. The results of those efforts is perhaps manifold. Certainly the Christian attitude toward other religions has never been the same.[14]

Aside from the change of Christian attitude, there was the gradual emergence of a new field called the study of religion. Max Müller's grand project of translations of Sanskrit texts into English during the early part of the nineteenth century has certainly made available materials that the European scholars were so fondly waiting for. The study of religion was undertaken during this time largely as part of philology. European indologists were mostly interested in Indo-European philology, and Sanskrit provided the most fascinating materials on it. Nonetheless, since virtually all the Sanskrit material was of religious nature, study of religion became inevitable. To those who were looking for materials on religious myths, symbols, rituals, etc., it was certainly a golden opportunity. Slowly the Indic materials went from the hands of philologists (Rudolph Roth, Otto Böhtlingk, A. Weber and others) to the comparative religionists. A serious and scientific comparative study of religions began taking shape gradually. Even philologically oriented scholars began indulging themselves in the study of Indian philosophies and religions, such as Monier-

---

14 P. Kumar (2003), *Methodological and Theoretical Issues: Perspectives from the Study of Hinduism and Indian Religions.* Durban: University of Durban-Westville.

Williams, who was appointed as the Boden Professor at Oxford and gave a series of public lectures there.[15]

The early attempts at studying non-Christian religions and cultures were clearly guided by the principles of Christian mission to the non-Christian lands. For instance, Monier-Williams points out that the founder of the Boden Chair at Oxford clearly stated in his will "that the special object of his munificent bequest was to promote the translation of the Scriptures into Sanskrit, so as 'to enable his countrymen to proceed in the conversion of the natives of India to the Christian Religion.'"[16] This very aim has guided not only the work of Professor H.H. Wilson but also the work of Monier-Williams.[17] Monier-Williams, however, adds more to his agenda when he states that part of the purpose of his work in Sanskrit language is "the promotion of a better knowledge of the religion and customs of India, as the best key to a knowledge of the religious needs for our great Eastern Dependency."[18] This clearly shows that the initial attempts to study the non-Christian religions and cultures was to inform the Christian Missions abroad on the one hand, and the colonial governments on the other. Whatever might have occasioned the study of other religions and cultures, surely a new discipline and a new field of study was emerging.[19]

Having stated the above, it must also be remembered that a host of other disciplines in the field of natural sciences as well as in social sciences (e.g., anthropology, sociology, psychology, etc.) also emerged during the same period. Nevertheless, those disciplines were not necessarily rejected by the Indian intelligentsia as being colonial by-products. Is it then practical realism that led India to choose certain disciplines and not some as part of its academia?

What Are the Real Reasons for a Serious Absence of Comparative/History of Religions in India?

First, one has to admit that there is a general lack of scholars who could produce sound scholarship in the discipline of comparative/history of religions. Generally speaking, the field of humanities and social sciences is a grossly neglected area in Indian universities. This is, perhaps, largely due to funding problems. The universities in India put more money into the disciplines that are seen as more practical and that can provide the country with the necessary

---

15 Monier Monier-Williams (1979), *A Sanskrit-English Dictionary*. Delhi: Motilal Banarsidass: vi.

16 Ibid.: ix.

17 Ibid.: ix.

18 Ibid.: x.

19 P. Kumar (1996), *Category Formation in Religious Studies: Methodological Dilemmas*: 1.

technological edge. As a result, most universities do not have strong departments in the field of humanities and social sciences.

Second, if there is a place for the study of religion it has to be in the humanities and social sciences. But, if there is a lack of a pool of good scholars who could provide foundation for such studies in the humanities and social sciences, how can such study of religion, which could have led to a discipline, emerge?

Third, whatever little that exists as part of the study of religion within the departments of philosophy, language, literature and so on, is dominated by descriptive and theological/phenomenological expositions. In this respect, the older philological methods still dominate in the study of religion in India. Finally, the whole area of religion is generally perceived with a great deal of suspicion both within the academic world as well as in society at large because of its historical role in the conflict ridden Indian society. In other words, any attempt at comparative study of religion has to be very sensitive to the emotional outbursts that it can generate in the context of politics and economics. Subsumed under the talk of tolerance toward other faiths, the Indian populace generally are not comfortable with critical comments made about their religions. Even an artist's innovative depiction of the goddess in modern terms can send political heat waves throughout the country and the artist can be subjected to almost excommunication. But, in so far as comparative/history of religion with its roots in critical social scientific methods cannot guarantee that it would not make critical comments on any religion or religion in general, it needs to be seen as a serious limiting condition for the development of critical scholarship on religion in India. As such, although hundreds and hundreds of books are published every year via Indian publishers (a good deal of them are by Western scholars), most of them are mere (good) descriptive studies and do not engage in critical reflection on the nature of religion, its construction in human society, and its various empirical aspects. One only needs to look at the titles that come out in the book publishers lists to make out the kind of studies that are done on religion. The above are some of the limiting conditions for the emergence of the study of religion in India along the lines of comparative/ history of religion.

What Are the Trends in the Last Two Decades of the Twentieth Century?

The proliferation of books on individual religions mainly from a descriptive methodological slant continue to dominate the study of religion in India. Although a substantial number of these books are produced by Western scholars, there is a growing number of Indian scholars writing on religion. Most of these scholars come from within the tradition although there are many exceptions. Another characteristic of the books that have been produced in the last couple of decades of the twentieth century is that most of them are issue related (e.g., women, identity, politics, violence, conversion, secularism, and so on (Khan 1997; Copley 1997; A. Sharma 1997a, 1997b; Ramaswamy 1997; J. McGuire et al. 1996). The new books of the last couple of decades have made a major departure from the more conventional studies which were based on philological, textual and philosophical methods. Many of these new books have drawn from ethnography, anthropology, art, literature and even economics and management studies (e.g., Religious Pursuit and Material Growth[20]). This issue-relatedness in the study of religion in India will perhaps dominate the scene for some decades to come as these issues deal with the day-to-day lives of people. One significant factor that seems to be important in the contemporary study of religion is that more and more women have begun to write and thereby enabled a new perspective to emerge. While the conventional philological and textual studies remained still in the hands of the male scholars (be they Western or Indian), women scholars have begun to utilise a whole variety of sources that were never used by the older generation of scholars. These sources include folklore, popular stories, myths, legends, conversations, cinema, media, art, literature and so on. The issue relatedness and the search for new sources seem to have occurred about the same time that it is no accident but rather conscious on the part of the new stream of scholars (mainly women) to deal with religion and its many facets on the ground (Doniger 1980; Winslow 1980; Douglas 1970; Leslie 1994; Ramaswamy 1996, 1997; Caldwell 1999; Sikri 1999). In this sense, study of religion in India has for the first time begun, quite unwittingly, a new chapter which focuses on the empirical and historical side of religion more than the metaphysical/transcendental dimension. In other words, the study of religion in the contemporary Indian society is more about how people have constructed their religious worlds and what issues of social significance have emanated out of such constructions than about the soteriological motifs of religion. Scholars are more interested, for instance, in how women have been treated in the temples than what Sanskrit texts have informed the construction of the temple; how women used devotional cults to escape male dominant prejudices; what influences have shaped both Hinduism and Islam in the last few centuries; how religion has been used as means to achieve political goals; why, for instance, Sikh fundamentalism became a major factor in the Sikh politics; how temples and mosques have become sources of conflicts;—and one can enumerate more, but suffice to indicate the shifting trends.

---

20 Ranjit Gupta/B.L. Tripathi (1997), *Religious Pursuit and Material Growth: A Study of Sri Dharmasthala Manjunatheswara Kshetra*. Ahmedabad: Indian Institute of Management, Centre for Management in Agriculture.

Another important trend that is emerging in relation to the study of Indian religions is driven by a compelling sense, both on the part of the Indian scholars as well as the Western scholars, that there exists many inadequacies in the translations of Indian textual materials on different religions which were produced, especially, during the eighteenth and the nineteenth centuries. Notwithstanding the fact that many Indian scholars and traditional pundits were in fact involved in the massive translation works of the last two hundred years, the very fact that most of these translations were either edited or overseen by Western scholars gave rise to important hermeneutical problems. Some of these problems were directly related to how Indian religions have been studied in the last several decades. W.C. Smith's critique of giving names to religious traditions and treating them as though they are some reified/finished products, which can be independently accessed for studying and interpreting by Western scholars, has some relevance to the study of Indian religions (W.C. Smith 1964).[21] In recent years, there has been a substantial discussion around the name Hinduism and the problems associated with it (R. Baort 1994; Frykenberg 1997; Malik 1997; B.K. Smith 1996; R. Thapar 1997; R. King 1999). Scholars on Indian religions, both the Indian as well as the Western, have begun to look at Euro-centred translations and their implications for the study of Indian religions. For instance, Sweetman in his recent doctoral thesis looks at the issue of how Hinduism has been created by European scholars in the seventeenth and the eighteenth centuries. He says,

> [t]he historical importance of the study of Indian religion lies in the fact that the early study of these religions was coincident with a change in the meaning and range of applications of the term *religion* itself and the emergence of a tradition of study of the religions which lies at the root of the contemporary academic study of religions. One of the most influential achievements of this early study was the formation of the concept 'Hinduism' itself; ...[22]

He argues that the very early writers on Hinduism, such as de Nobili, Ziegenbalg and others in the seventeenth century were indeed aware of the religious diversity and were cautious in using the concept of Hinduism as a monolithic term. This view of Sweetman is in contrast to the one presented by many other scholars such as R. King (1999), Inden (1990), and Marshall (1970) who located

---

21 I have looked at the relevance of Smith's critique to the study of Indian religions elsewhere in an article. See P. Kumar (1983), "Religion and Theology: Issues in W.C. Smith's *Towards a World Theology*," in: *Bangalore Theological Forum*, India 15 (2): 151–62.

22 B.W.H. Sweetman (1999), *Mapping Hinduism: 'Hinduism' and the Study of Indian Religions, 1630–1776* (unpublished thesis submitted to the University of Cambridge): 1. (Emphasis in the quote is mine).

the origins of the term Hinduism as a unified concept in the Western Christian and imperialist perceptions.[23]

Thus, there is a new thrust towards looking at writings on Hinduism in the last two hundred or more years. This new thrust on studying the writings on Hinduism, for instance, is an example of studying a given religious tradition not merely through its texts, but also through the history and the discourse of its study. The attempt of how the classical texts (and the very understanding of Indian religions which emanated from them) have been translated into modern conceptual categories will certainly yield a very fruitful data which will enable us to revisit not only those very classical texts from a different point of view, but also to revisit our engagement and the construction of images of Indian religions. A reviewing process of the literature on these Indian religions will also have socio-political implications for the sub-continent, in the sense of challenging the very views that the adherents of those religions have about their own traditions. In other words, as new and challenging materials come to light, it is bound to affect the very worldview of the people of the sub-continent as a whole.

Globalisation of the Study of Religion and India

As I noted earlier, Indian religions have contributed immensely to the academic study of religion both by providing the materials as well as the pluralistic context to study and understand those materials comparatively. Long before the Western world experienced the need for comparative understanding of religion, India provided a natural home for such comparative context by virtue of the pluralistic nature of its society. Nevertheless, a systematic academic study of religion along comparative lines developed and flourished in the Western academic institutions and not so much in the Indian ones. European scholars who made visits to India and collected materials on Indian religions took them back home and engaged in the systematic analysis of those religions using philological, historical and comparative methods. The extent to which those academic investigations illuminated the understanding of their own religions and cultures cannot, however, be underestimated. Nonetheless, those Western engagements of the earlier times did have a profound effect as to how Indian society understands its religions in the contemporary times. Many books that emanated out of those Western engagements with Indian religions have not only become basic source materials for Indians regarding their own religions, but also the concepts and categories introduced by those books became part and parcel of the modern Indian's religious vocabulary. As a result a great deal

---

23   Ibid.: 155ff.

of cross fertilisation has occurred between India and the West with religion being the main medium of such social transformation.

As such, the roots of contemporary globalisation process are traceable to the initial beginnings that religion had provided in the context of India and the West. In other words, religion was perhaps one of the first products that has exchanged in the international social markets. Today we speak of globalisation primarily in economic terms. However, such globalisation process cannot either ignore or obscure the social significance that religions of India have had across many cultures. Today not only are we talking about economic globalisation but there is also an attempt by Western associations for the study of religion to extend such endeavours to the Indian academic scene. That is, the study of religion which has evolved in the West in the last two hundred years in interaction with the materials drawn from Indian religions is now beginning to make an impact on how scholars in India study religions. The materials that were taken from India have been worked on through Western methods and theoretical tools and now having sharpened those tools, the West seems poised to offer them to Indian society and the academia, perhaps, in exchange for the materials that they have borrowed from India to develop their methodological and theoretical knowledge. Those of us who originated from India and now located ourselves outside India have already become recipients of such Western methodological and theoretical tools in the study of religion. Whether such an exchange between Western theoretical knowledge in the study of religion and the many Indian academic institutions on a large scale is possible without much social discomfort is yet to be seen. Furthermore, whether the methodological and theoretical tools developed in the West can be suitable in the social context of India is also something that needs to be tested. Perhaps, this is where the major difference lies between the way the natural sciences, with their methodologies and theories developed in the modern West, which have been quite easily assimilated into the Indian institutions, and the way in which the human sciences such as the study of religion have been able to become part of the Indian institutions. That is to say that the natural sciences have been accepted quite easily into the Indian institutions in large measure due to the fact that the economic globalisation process made it increasingly necessary to exchange such technological tools. However, in the context of religious and cultural institutions, many countries like India have insulated themselves from overseas influences in their quest for self identity. Religion and culture have provided effective tools to remain unique and different in the increasing possibility of becoming obscured by the globalisation process. Countries such as India have prided themselves to be traditional societies while in the thick of the modernisation process due to the massive globalisation impact. It is precisely because of such a need of India to remain a traditional society or rather desiring to preserve their traditional systems of thought intact that will pose the greatest challenge to the Western methodological and theoretical tools in the study of religion. Nevertheless, just as the West had to come to terms with the mass of materials that India had provided in the study of religion, India has to come to terms with the mass of materials now being provided through Western discourse on the study of religion. Perhaps in the course of this interaction, new methodological and theoretical tools might become a reality both for the Indian scholars as well as the Western scholars.

Suggested Bibliography

Amaladass, Anand (1997), *The Problem of Evil: Essays on Cross-cultural Perspectives*. Chennai: Satya Nilayam Publications.

Bajracharya, Naresh Man (1998), *Buddhism in Nepal: 465 B.C. to 1199 A.D.*. Delhi: Eastern Book Links.

Baort, R. (1994), "Hinduism and Hindus in Europe," in: *Religion in Europe: Contemporary Perspectives*. Kampen: Pharos.

Bloss, Lowel W. (1996), *Theories of Religion*. Patiala: Publications Bureau, Punjabi University.

Caldwell, Sara (1999), *Oh Terryfying Mother: Sexuality, Violence and Worship of the Goddess Kali*. Oxford: Oxford University Press.

Choudhary, Shahid A. (1998), *Sufism Is Not Islam: A Comparative Study*. New Delhi: Regency Publications.

Copley, Antony (1997), *Religions in Conflict: Ideology, Cultural Contact and Conversion in Late-Colonial India*. Delhi: Oxford University Press.

Dash, G.N. (1998), *Hindus and Tribals: Quest for a Co-existence: Social Dynamics in Medieval Orissa*. New Delhi: Decent Books.

Doniger, Wendy (1980), *Women, Androgynes and Other Mythical Beasts*. Chicago: The University of Chicago Press.

Douglas, Mary (1970), *Purity and Danger. An Analysis of Concepts of Pollution and Taboo*. Harmondsworth: Penguin.

Engineer, A.A./Mehta, Uday, eds. (1998), *State Secularism and Religion: Western and Indian Experience*. Delhi: Ajanta Publications.

Frykenberg, Robert E. (1997), "The Emergence of Modern 'Hinduism' as a Concept and as an Institution: A Reappraisal with Special Reference to South India," in: *Hinduism Reconsidered*, ed. by Günther-Dietz Sontheimer/Hermann Kulke. Delhi: Manohar.

Gopal, Ram (1998), *Islam, Hindutva and Congress Quest: A Study in Conflicting Ideologies*. New Delhi: Reliance Publishing House.

Grewal, J.S. (1997), *Historical Perspectives on Sikh Identity*. Patiala: Publication Bureau, Punjabi University.

— (1998), *Contesting Interpretations of the Sikh Tradition*. New Delhi: Manohar Publishers.

Hasan, Mushirul, ed. (1998), *Islam, Communities and the Nation: Muslim Identities in South Asia and Beyond*. New Delhi: Manohar Publishers & Distributors.

Inden, Ronald (1990), *Imagining India*. Oxford: Blackwell.

Jatava, D.R. (1998), *Indian Society: Culture and Ideologies*. Jaipur, India: Surabhi.

Khan, Dominique-Sila (1997), *Conversions and Shifting Identities: Ramdev Pir and the Ismailis in Rajasthan*. New Delhi: Manohar Publishers & Distributors.

King, R. (1999), *Orientalism and Religion: Postcolonial Theory, India and 'the Mystic East.'* London: Routledge.

Kishwar, Madhu (1998), *Religion at the Service of Nationalism and Other Essays.* Delhi: Oxford University Press.

Kumar, Stanley J./Muralidhar, B.V., eds. (1997), *Achieving Communal Harmony and National Integration: A Dream for Every Indian.* New Delhi: M.D. Publication.

Larson, Gerald James (1997), *India's Agony Over Religion.* Delhi: Oxford University Press.

Leslie, J. (1994), "Some Traditional Indian Views on Menstruation and Female Sexuality," in: *Sexual Knowledge, Sexual Science: The History of Attitudes to Sexuality,* ed. by Roy Porter/Mikula Teich. Cambridge: Cambridge University Press: 63–81.

Liebeskind, Claudia (1998), *Piety on Its Knees: Three Sufi Traditions in South Asia in Modern Times.* Delhi: Oxford University Press.

Mahajan, Gurpeet (1998), *Identities and Rights: Aspects of Liberal Democracy in India.* Delhi: Oxford Univesity Press.

Malik, A. (1997), "Hinduism or 3306 Ways to Invoke a Construct," in: *Hinduism Reconsidered,* ed. by Günther-Dietz Sontheimer/Hermann Kulke. Delhi: Manohar.

Maneck Stiles, Susan (1997), *The Death of Ahirman: Culture, Identity and Theological Change among the Parsis of India.* Mumbai: K.R. Cama Oriental Institute.

Marshall, Peter J. (1970), *The British Discovery of Hinduism in the Eighteenth Century.* Cambridge: University Press.

McGuire, John/Reeves, Peter/Brasted, Howard, eds. (1996), *Politics of Violence from Ayodhya to Behrampada.* New Delhi: Sage Publications.

Parratt, S.N.A./Parratt, John (1997), *The Pleasing of the Gods: Meitei Lai Haraoba.* New Delhi: Vikas Publishing House.

Ramaswamy, Vijaya (1996), *Divinity and Diviance: Women in Virasaivism.* Delhi: Oxford University Press.

— (1997), *Walking Naked: Women, Society, Spirituality in South India.* Shimla: Indian Institute of Advanced Study.

Robinson, Rowena (1998), *Conversion, Continuity and Change: Lived Christianity in Southern Goa.* New Delhi: Sage Publications.

Schuon, Frithjof (1996), *Christianity/Islam: Essays on Esoteric Ecumenism.* Bangalore: Select Books.

Sharma, A., ed. (1997a), *Today's Women in World Religions.* Delhi: Sri Satguru Publications.

— (1997b), *Religion and Women.* Delhi: Sri Satguru Publications.

Sharma, Sita Ram (1998), *Anatomy of Communalism.* New Delhi: A.P.H. Publication Corp.

Sikri, Rehana (1999), *Women in Islamic Culture and Society: A Study of Family, Feminism and Franchise.* New Delhi: Kanishka Publishers & Distributors.

Singh, Dhirendra (1998), *Indian Heritage & Culture.* New Delhi: A.P.H. Publishing Corporation.

Singh, Jagdev Brigadier (1998), *Hindus of India.* New Delhi: Gyan Publishing House.

Singh, Jodh (1997), *Multifaith Society: Issues and Concerns.* Patiala: Publication Bureau, Punjabi University.

Smith, B.K. (1996), "Re-envisioning Hinduism and Evaluating the Hindutva Movement," in: *Religion* 26: 119–28.

Smith, W.C. (1964), *The Meaning and End of Religion: A New Approach to the Religious Traditions of Mankind.* New York: New American Library.

Srinivas, S. (1998), *The Mouth of People, the Voice of God: Buddhists and Muslims in a Frontier Community of Ladakh*. Delhi: Oxford University Press.

Straddet-Kennedy, Gerald (1998), *Providence and the Raj: Imperial Mission and Missionary Imperialism*. New Delhi: Sage Publications.

Thakur, M.R. (1997), *Myths, Rituals & Beliefs in Himachal Pradesh*. New Delhi: Indus Publishing Co.

Thapar, R. (1997), "Syndicated Hinduism," in: *Hinduism Reconsidered*, ed. by Günther-Dietz Sontheimer/Hermann Kulke. Delhi: Manohar.

Tyagi, Anil Kumar (1997), *Communalism and Ramakatha in Historical Perspective*. New Delhi: Institute of Objective Studies.

Vineeth, V.F. (1997), *Self and Salvation in Hinduism and Christianity: An Inter-religious Approach*. New Delhi: Intercultural Publications.

Winslow, D. (1980), "Rituals of First Menstruation in Sri Lanka," in: *Man* 15 (4): December 1980: 603–25.

A Survey of New Approaches to the Study of Religion in Australia and the Pacific

by

GARRY W. TROMPF

I am privileged here to be personally retrospective about scholarly studies in religion in my part of the world. Since I have been researching the world of religion for over forty years, it is inevitable that I will reflect, not only on my own place in the ongoing history of investigations in Australasia and Oceania, but also on the labors of many fine scholars whom I count as mentors, friends, and collaborators (among them many of my former students).

1. Background

The seeds of contemporary intellectual achievements in the Pacific region were sown in theological colleges and university divinity schools. Insofar as theology has entailed theoretical, methodological and hermeneutical considerations, its better practitioners in Australia and New Zealand have made a solid contribution to the critical study of religion throughout the twentieth century. Australia, admittedly, has not produced any great systematic theologian: neurologist Sir John Eccles and biologist Charles Birch would be the only theologically engaged *savants* with genuine international acclaim, but this because of their work on synaptic theory and process thought respectively (e.g., Eccles 1980; Birch 1990) rather than on "mainstream" matters. The controversial New Zealander Lloyd Geering (e.g., 1980) has been the only memorable "classic-looking" theologian born and bred in the whole South Pacific region, although that may have been because such an impressive figure as Colin Williams was lost to the northern hemisphere (Yale), while others have yet to make their mark internationally.[1] Yet a fair crop of well-known experts in the

---

1   Note for consideration an earlier generation of theologians that included Leon Morris, Norman Young, and Harry Wardlaw, aside from various theological "expatriates" in the region, such as the Scots John McIntyre and George Knight, Northern Irishmen

Bible and Patristic thought has sprung up out of the Antipodean intellectual environment, with New Zealand being noted in the 1970s for a small export industry in Biblical theologians.[2]

Looking back at the turn into the twenty-first century, some features of this inheritance stand out as backcloth to the present assessment, as do some names. It may have been a venturesome thing to involve the comparative study of religions in theological studies, yet we can detect a quiet pattern of ex-panding research into "extra-Biblical" materials over the years. In the 1920s, Samuel Angus, a pupil of Adolf Deissmann at Berlin, put University of Sydney theological studies on the map with some remarkable studies of the Hellenistic mystery religions in relation to early Christianity (1925, 1929). Writing in the temper of the *Religionsgeschichtliche Schule* of Wilhelm Bousset and Richard Reitzenstein, Angus also gave Sydney notoriety when his liberal version of Christology drew a heresy charge, which he skillfully thwarted (cf. S. Emilsen 1991). Interests in the interface between Christianity and the religions of its Romano-Hellenistic setting have intriguingly remained a crucial component in the Sydney intellectual scene over the long term. During the post-War years, to cite a key enterprise in point, New Zealander Edwin Judge dedicated his life's work to building up one of the most impressive schools of Ancient History in the world, at Sydney's Macquarie University. Starting with his little book on *The Social Pattern of Christian Groups* (1960), historically-oriented New Testa-ment studies came to be given a credible place there, and the religious history of Later Antiquity granted a very high profile. Aside from the presence of "classical Egyptology," Macquarie stands at the forefront of papyrological research, with its Ancient History Documentary Research Centre a kind of sister outfit to the *Corpus Hellenisticum* at Holland's Universiteit te Utrecht (e.g., Horsley 1981–1987).

The University of Melbourne made the earliest inroads into ancient Meso-potamian archaeology and traditions, in a department of Semitic (later Middle Eastern) studies (1957–1993), for twenty years under the Scots professor John Bowman.[3] The University of Sydney, with its own Department of Semitic

---

Davis McCaughey and (the latercoming) Richard McKinney; Swiss-German Thorwald Lorenzen; and Japanese Kosuke Koyama.

2   Including Graham Stanton (Cambridge) and Ruth Page (Edinburgh). For Australia note the Biblical scholarship of Gerald O'Collins (working from the Vatican).

3   The first long-lasting journal of comparative religion, *Milla wa-Milla: The Australian Bulletin of Comparative Religion* (1961–1979) was founded from this department, and the first Charles Strong Memorial Trust Lecture (requiring attention to religions other than Christianity) was published within it (Vol. 1, 1961). Related to the first-named journal was the first edited collection of articles into the small book *Essays on the Religious Traditions of the World* (1972, ostensibly edited by V. Yogendra, but actually produced

Studies formalized by 1978, strengthened in its cultural studies of Judaism, Islam and related traditions upon the Melbourne experiment's gradual demise. In 1962 the Faculty for Asian Studies was established at the Australian National University, its prestige immediately enhanced by the great English historian of South Asia A.L. Basham (e.g., 1967), not to mention Buddhologist Jan De Jong (e.g., 1979), Islamicist Antony Johns (e.g., 1982), and others (cf. Rizvi, e.g., 1983) (though the whole operation dwindled badly in 1990s after their retirements). Looking elsewhere history departments in the Australasian region were quickest off the mark among others to appoint teachers covering Indian, Chinese and Southeast Asian materials. Anthropologists in these fields came in a close second, and both linguists[4] and philosophers had their special role to play.

Such were important conditions making for the acceptance of religious studies when they presented an attractive possibility for most university arts faculties in the 1970s. During the second half of the century some eminent individuals whose major work preceded yet heralded the entrance of the apparently "new" discipline deserve mention. I discuss them here because some are known to have sought chairs when programs in the study of religion were being established, or would have if they had arisen earlier. Eric Osborn, for the most part marginalized from the Melbourne campus at Queen's College, has been and remains a veritable Australian *magister* of patristics, eventually taking an honorary professorship by 1996 at Latrobe University (also in Melbourne). His researches on Clement of Alexandria (1957) drew him early into the wider Hellenistic religious scene that had so interested Angus (cf. also 1997). Since so many Australian Biblical scholars have specialized on Luke-Acts, that Biblical text which most opens itself on to Hellenistic religious crosscurrents, reference has to be made to their greatest inspirers Robert Maddox (mainly at Sydney, but for a time in Perth) (e.g., 1982) who maintained strong ties with Munich, and John O'Neill (Melbourne) (e.g., 1961) soon lost to Cambridge and Edinburgh (cf. also Wilcox 1956).

Well known historians specializing in religious themes also bear mention here, especially since the famous *Journal of Religious History* (1960–) was founded in Sydney by Reformation specialist (and Australian) Bruce Mansfield. He, along with an impressive cluster of ecclesiastical historians, showed interest in theories about religion more generally. Among his more significant contemporaries were Melbournian George Yule, expert on Puritan affairs (who, though taking a chair at Aberdeen, worked most of his life in Melbourne), and

---

under the direction of G. Mullins), while the Strong lectures for the years 1961–1970 were edited by J. Bowman in the book *Comparative Religion* (1972).

4   Note the founding of *The Journal of the Oriental Society of Australia* (1963–) from the University of Sydney Department of Oriental Studies (now part of Asian Studies within the School of Languages).

English *émigré*-cum-Sydneysider Robert Pretty, whose fine translation and commentary on the ancient *Adamantius Dialogue* between an orthodox and five Gnostics (published posthumously, 1997), reveals a remarkable combination of philological and historical acumen. Over in New Zealand one finds Austrian-born Peter Munz accrediting himself as an historian at Victoria University. He learnt much as a student from philosopher Karl Popper during their shared years at Otago, and came to write insightfully about Western mediaeval ideologies, if later more abstrusely about myth typologies and fault-lines in the theories of James George Frazer and Claude Lévi-Strauss (1973).

Among more rationalistic yet brilliant philosophical minds in prominence during the 1960s and 1970s, furthermore, some saw the point of religion being studied objectively within a non-confessional discipline. At the Australian National University the history of Western religious ideas was being tackled: thus *inter alia* John Passmore addressed the idea of human perfectibility (1977), and Russian-born Eugene Kamenka the theology of Feuerbach (1970) (with Evan Burge, Plato specialist, also being with them for a time, even if of a mind with a quite different disposition towards faith). Another eminent historian of ideas, John Pocock (who emigrated from Poland as a child) grounded his life's work in New Zealand and developed strong Australian connections before ending up at the Johns Hopkins University, Baltimore. Others could be added here, yet either they overlap with the new period, or they can be brought into the story in another way.

The earlier appointments in religious studies in Australasia, curiously, were made from the margins, first in New Zealand from 1966, and at the infant University of Papua New Guinea from 1972, three years before the Territory of Papua/New Guinea was to become a new state independent from Australia. Quite a few pioneering developments occurred in New Zealand. A religious studies program emerged out of philosophy at the University of Canterbury in 1966 (with James Thornton in philosophical theology and James Wilson in Asian philosophy and religions). Within the same year Albert Moore was appointed to teach the history and phenomenology of religions at the University of Otago, Dunedin, the first "generically significant" appointment in the comparative study of religions for the whole region. By 1970 Australian Brian Colless was to be appointed to the new Massey University, Palmerston North, under the rubric of religious studies, and the first professorial chair of religious studies fell to Geering at Victoria University in 1971, with Munz being influential in setting up the new department.

As for Australia, the first two lectureships in religious studies were placed in the history department at the University of Papua New Guinea (UPNG) from 1972, and this umbrella arrangement never altered. In this context my own involvement intensified. As one of two appointees (away from the rationalistic supervisions of Kamenka and Passmore) I veered increasingly towards comparative religion and the study of the complex Melanesian religious world;

while the other lecturer, Carl Loeliger, who was a Syriac specialist (and product of Melbourne's Middle Eastern outfit), developed Biblical studies for a Pacific island context. Three years after, in 1975, studies in religion were to be implanted into the arts faculty of the University of Queensland, under the readership of English scholar Eric Pyle (cf., e.g., 1961) and the first Chair in religious studies in Australia came with the appointment in 1977 of Eric Sharpe, formerly from Manchester and Lancaster in the United Kingdom. Subsequent developments in the region make for an increasingly complex story, with leading Australian scholars playing key roles in the transition from "the old to the new order." In Victoria we find Sinologist Paul Rule at LaTrobe University, philosophers Max Charlesworth and (the latercoming) Ian Weeks at Deakin (both the named Victorian institutions starting their programs in the 1970s). Semantics theorist Francis Andersen occupied the first Queensland chair of studies in religion by 1981; commentator on the Book of Job, Norman Habel, a key figure in the emergent University of South Australia, eventually held a professorship there. Charlesworth, in fact, had already made "a head start" in teaching a religious studies course—basically the philosophy of religion—at Melbourne as early as 1970, but he was to institutionalize his dreams as a professor at Deakin (in Geelong, just outside the city where he had taught for so long).

As for the further history of New Zealand affairs, Paul Morris, who is especially acclaimed for his work on Judaism (e.g., Morris/Sawyer 1992), arrived back in Wellington from Britain in 1993 to take over the chair from Geering (his old teacher, yet against whom he had reacted). Africanist and Yoruba specialist Elizabeth Isichei (e.g., 1982), a New Zealander, had been established there for over half a decade earlier, bringing high quality European scholarship as a reader (and then moving on to Otago in 1992). These two consolidated the field across the Tasman Sea with such Australasians of prior esteem as Moore (by then an authority on religious art, e.g. 1977), Colless (acquitting himself ably in Syriac Patristics, e.g., 1975), James Veitch (a Geering-inspired Biblical theologian, e.g., 1996), and Peter Donovan (an instructive philosopher of religion (1976, 1979).

With this background, what have developed as distinctive Australian and New Zealand (or Southwest Pacific) approaches to the study of religion over the last quarter of a century or so? It is very hard to be exhaustive, and generalities do not come easily, but we shall essay an answer under a series of generic headings. In the following pages somewhat more space will be given to scholars born in Australia and New Zealand, but the pursuit of a whole picture will not be forgotten, and I myself have to live with the embarrassment of being a somewhat obtrusive part of the scenery.

2. Methodological Research and the Issue of Religious *vis-à-vis* Theological Studies

Publishable reflection on method in the study of religion more generally really only begins in Australasia with the presence of Professor Eric Sharpe. Before his arrival there were attempts to establish what religious studies covered as a field, and how far Australian scholarship had gone towards broaching its possibilities (e.g., Osborn 1978). But Sharpe arrived in the wake of his monumental study *Comparative Religion: a History* (first ed. 1975), and his reputation as one of the world's leading methodologists in the comparative and historical study of religions was made through that work—and thus mostly from Australia. In fact, if one might have said that there was competition between Sharpe and other *doyens*—Eliade, Smart and Waardenburg, for three—over who was the greatest living methodologist in the field by the 1980s, Sharpe certainly established himself from Australia as "the world's foremost authority on how you would go about orienting yourself for understanding 'other religions.'"[5] Books confirming this status were *Understanding Religion* (1983) and *Nathan Söderblom and the Study of Religion* (1990), even if both were to expose his flanks to theorists of a different bent.

While honored as the preeminent historian of the discipline's founders and protagonists, in the last stages of his career Sharpe was subjected to strong criticisms by younger methodologists that his work carried a hidden theological agenda. He had perhaps protested too much in *Understanding* that religious studies was quite different from divinity, because at Sydney, just before religious studies was located in the arts faculty in a separate geographical location, he had to face the fact that the new project he was to manage had been negotiated into place by the divinity board. He also had to engage the forceful style of Dr Barbara Thiering, an insightful Australian feminist theologian (1976, 1977) who later wrote as a Qumran specialist (1979, 1983). But however much he sought to draw a line between divinity/theology and the historical and phenomenological study of religion, he looked in critics' eyes to be a man with theological proclivities himself—given his Doctorate in theology from Uppsala under the great missiologist Bengt Sundkler (cf. Sharpe 2001) and the arguable missiological slant of many of his later writings.

Some of these associations, even if in curiously contradictory ways, came up in the so-called "Sharpe Symposium" in the November 1988 meeting of The American Academy of Religion in Chicago (published soon after in the first number of *Method and Theory in the Study of Religion*, 1989). Among the critics, Canadian Donald Wiebe, though respectful, was perhaps the most penetrating-

---

5   See Trompf, Eulogy: Eric John Sharpe, St. Alban's Anglican Church, Epping, Sydney 25
     Oct. 2000; and idem, Obituary, in: *Sydney Morning Herald* 27 Oct. 2000: 29.

looking (and it was not without significance that Wiebe edited the Ninian Smart Festschrift with Peter Masefield [1994], a highly accomplished Buddholo-gist who emigrated to Australia but, through lack of funds, did not last long in the Sydney department). The intellectual clash calls for comment, in that, while Wiebe suspected Sharpe of "closet theology," Sharpe always maintained that only a distorted methodological orientation could arise if a theorist had rejected his own tradition (as when one might abandon a conservative version of it, to take Wiebe's case). This was later to bolster an important feature in my own methodological repertoire (Trompf/Hamel 2002), and my suspicion that many Western theoreticians of religion who had abandoned Christianity for another position were never able to treat their natal tradition with equanimity (perhaps even creating Enlightenment or post-modernist "methodological ideologies" as alternatives to their protagonists' original "spiritual home"). In any case, Sharpe's approach to theology was much more subtly nuanced than his pub-lished work suggested. It is true that he denied the possibility of escaping theological values (1989, 1997a). Phenomenology could never be an act of pure objectivism *per se*; it inevitably involved "charity," or the concession of good-will to give someone the chance to voice their commitments. He appeared to hold that studies in religion cannot and should not be willfully secularized (1987a: esp. 269) and that the scholar of religion did best with a "dual citizen-ship" of his/her own or another's tradition (forthcoming). In some private notes, however, he wrote perceptively that "humanly speaking, theology is the widest of all concerns," yet "professionally speaking, it may be one of the narrowest and most inbred" (1998a). When broadened, "Faith can meet Faith" in generous inter-religious dialogue, and willing theologians should be welcomed in the dialogical process (1977). When narrow in focus, though, theologians might shut themselves up in their own dogmatic attics. Few have been as keenly perceptive of this problematic as Sharpe was, and yet, for all his special hesitations, he always wrote as someone wanting to retain an openness to the challenges of theology, which in any case had left an indelible impression on the course of his own chosen discipline.

As studies in religion consolidated in the Australian and New Zealand scene, expectedly, pre-existing boards of divinity (serving professional training in ministry) were to be dismantled, as at the Universities of Queensland (in 1975), and Sydney (1991). Yet in both institutions Biblical studies retained a strength, perhaps less so at Sydney after the death of William Jobling, an authority on Semitic languages and the Northwest Arabian region,[6] and more so in Queensland, with a string of scholars making their impact in turn. Among these have been Hebraists Francis Andersen (brilliant at Biblical languages) and

---

6   Though Semitic Studies had its own specialists in aspects of religion, e.g. Crown (1989); Shboul (1979); and Ebied (1986–).

Edgar Conrad (American Old Testament commentator, cf. Conrad/Newing on
Andersen, 1987); along with Irishman Seán Freyne (e.g., 1980) and German
Australian Michael Lattke (e.g., 1992) on New Testament and early Christianity.
The University of South Australia also made a significant dent here, through
such scholars as Habel, the constructor of the environmental or Earth Bible
commentary (e.g., 1995, 2000–2002), and expert on Jesus studies Robert Crotty
(e.g., 1996). Sydney scholarship, to be sure, has been particularly strong in the
study of Luke-Acts and its historiographical character (e.g., Trompf 1979,
2000a; Maddox 1982; Esler 1989; Squires 1993 [even if Esler was lost to St
Andrews, Scotland]), yet in most cases scholars addressing Biblical matters
were working at universities in part-time teaching roles (as also Pryor 1992) or
as doctoral students (e.g., Lee 1994; Paddison 2001, these all working on John),
and came to take positions in theological colleges, mainly in Sydney itself or
Melbourne (Barnes 1999; cf. also Barnett, e.g., 1997). Elsewhere Biblical and
Patristic scholars have been more isolated in universities, if nonetheless
outstanding (Graeme Clarke [Clarke et al. 1990] and Robert Barnes [Barnes/
Prickett 1991] at the Australian National University, for instance, and John
Painter [1975] at LaTrobe) (cf. also Carnley, e.g., 1987). In New Zealand there
has been greater durability for divinity or theology as fixtures within university
programs, and a strong tradition of Biblical scholarship pertains there, despite
the amount of "exporting" overseas (cf., e.g., Carley 1975 as a returnee). Occasionally the yielding of brilliant minds in Australian theological colleges has
meant their ready welcome into the university scene. Melbournians Andersen
(to Queensland) and Osborn (to LaTrobe) are obvious cases in point, and more
recently Roland Boer, an outstanding Old Testament expert and exponent of
Jamesonian post-modernist thought (1996) (to Monash University, Victoria).

   Much of the work by the scholars just mentioned sits easily with university
syllabi in comparative religion, though there is often a choice presented to
scholars about annual regional conferences—between the Australian Association for the Study of Religions and the Australian and New Zealand
Association for Theological Studies, if and when the organizations do not put
on their conferences together. The latter body will tend to attract thinkers
working more directly on theology, as with those in the relevant New Zealand
faculties, or those teaching theology at Monash, Victoria (e.g., Hart 1985) or
Flinders, South Australia (e.g., Dutney 1993), or in and around the new Australian Catholic University (esp. Newman 1990; Gascoigne 2001; noting also such
other authors as Neil Omerod, David Coffey, Peter Malone and Gideon
Goosen) or theological colleges. Apart from Sharpe in his *Understanding
Religion*, however, no one has yet tried a hand formulating the relationships
between religious studies and fideistic or confessional writing, and very little
has been done even on the hermeneutical interface between comparativist and
"scripturally-oriented" scholarship (yet cf. White 1986; Prickett 1986). A good
deal of bridge-building between the two "zones," however, has been provided

by workshops published by the New Zealand organ *Prudentia*, spearheaded by philosopher David Dockrill, with both classicist Godfrey Tanner from the University of Newcastle (New South Wales), who combined expertise in classical Graeco-Roman thought and New Testament textual studies (e.g., Dockrill/ Tanner 1988) and Raoul Mortley (Macquarie; and then Bond University), highly acclaimed in Romano-Hellenistic and Patristic currents of thought (e.g., Dockrill/Mortley 1981, cf. Mortley 1973, 1981, 1996). There is perhaps something specially Australian in the way the divide between traditional and newer interests of scholarship are being creatively addressed, yet (apart from minor excurses into general theory, e.g., Crotty 1995), no peculiarly Australian summary of the methodological issues and tensions involved has yet been forthcoming (cf. Sharpe 1981, 1998b; Forrest 1996).

Who should actually do this is a sensitive matter, because, a problem for some, gender issues have gotten bound up in religious/theological studies relations. For example, a major work from the comparativist side, *Reclaiming our Rites*, edited by Morny Joy and the late Penny Magee (1994, cf. Sharma 1999), bears with it an evaluative agenda to do with social justice, something it shares with feminist theology, from whence the majority of women's "religious writing" has been forthcoming. Of great interest is the ethos of the Women-Church grouping, in which one finds everything from a quest for the reappropriation of the Divinity as Goddess (e.g., White/Tulip 1991) to a studied Euro-feminist deconstruction of male structures in religious life (e.g. Confoy/ Lee 1995). *Prima facie* these developments belong to Western feminist discourse in general and bear little that is distinctively Australian about them, yet the range and intensity of Australian women's writing is already of international consequence (as, for example, in the lobbying the Vatican over women priests), and there have been some important new engagements with post-modernist implications for feminism (e.g., Barker 1995).

Most important among Australian female voices, however, are the new penetrating black ones, Aboriginal scholars have started to invoke womanist (or "black feminist") positions against white perspectives. Muri (or Queensland) academic Anne Pattel-Gray has already accused white feminists of being middle class in orientation, and far from "color blind" (1995), and charged the Australian churches in general of a Christological heresy for not properly recognizing a whole branch of people—the Aborigines—as part of the human species (1998). Aboriginal Tasmanian Lee Skye has introduced *Tidis* or Aboriginal womanist theology as distinctive, and more attuned to the new creation theology than "sin and salvation" modes of church discourse (e.g., 1998). It remains to be seen how all the new methodological critiques and insights raised by women's publications can be gathered up into an integrated Australian contribution to methodological refinement. Perhaps queer theory would have to be included in the integration, and body theory more generally, however, no ambitious scholar has yet come forward to do this job. Certainly, as paramount methodologist of religion in Australia, Sharpe paid little attention in his work to gender issues (though he educated many women who became prominent in feminist scholarship), and he also tended to eschew discussion of "political" topics (such as environmentalism, yet cf. 2002) or left wing (e.g., Marxist) interpretations of religion (cf. Trompf 1990a: 46–61; Weeks 1999)—except to criticize liberationist politicizations of the Kingdom of God in his last and posthumous opus (2004). Thus there is important work to be done. Whoever would be able to bind trajectories of comparativism, critical theology, gender issues and indigenous concerns together would certainly be accomplishing an act of methodological clarification for distinctively Australasian needs, coming close to the cutting-edge of Antipodean debates.

3. The History of Scholarship behind Comparative Religion

Over and above his more straightforward excursions into methodological issues, Eric Sharpe produced a number of important studies on individual researchers, whose works, whether conceived to be comparativist, theological or missiological, contributed to the discipline. These figures first included Nathan Söderblom (1990, 1997b), in whose personal study-room Sharpe labored for a year (1980–1981) when "testing" the Arts Faculty Chair of comparative religion in the University of Uppsala—to see whether he preferred Sweden to Australia. Some other figures he researched were Karl Ludwig Reichelt (1984), Tor Andrae (1987b), and Alfred George Hogg (1999, cf. 1971). His final work—the posthumously published one alluded to at the end of the last section—is entitled *The Quest for the Kingdom of God: A Study in the History of a Vision*, in which he explored connections between theology and the study of religion and treated the history of certain theological ideas for their own sake (2004).

To avoid the later stings of criticism, Sharpe was only too happy to call himself an historian of religious ideas and sometimes an historian of missionary approaches, and to deny being either theologian or missiologist.[7] But the fact that he was open to the challenge of ideas from those scholars fitting these last-mentioned categories does say something about one distinctive aspect of Australasian religion studies, that there have been researchers wanting to make a point of this openness in one way or another. In his work on the Kingdom of God, for example, Sharpe was bound to say a good deal about Rudolf Otto, who integrated his epistemology of the holy into his theological vision of how

---

7   Statement 1 Nov., 1999 at the conference in his honor that led to the Festschrift edited by Cusack and Oldmeadow (1999).

this Kingdom encompassed the world's religions (as in his *Reich Gottes und Menschensohn* of 1934). Philip Almond, an Australian student of Ninian Smart's, made a notable defense of Otto's position, especially his 1926 *West-östliche Mystik*, as a necessary reminder that to remain with purely etic apprehensions of religion amounted to willful reductionism (1984, 1994). From the University of Queensland, he has pursued this theme further through examining scholarly approaches to mysticism, and how it demanded from its students a more than objective treatment (1982). Professor Almond, currently head of the School of History, Philosophy, Religion and Classics at Queensland, is interesting for taking older theological minds, many of those in the seventeenth century, with utmost seriousness, not just to get their ideas straight but to address their philosophical and theological "bite" as well (1999), and in this he has had some Australian companions—David Dockrill (Newcastle) (e.g., 1982) and Peter Harrison (Bond) (1990, esp. 174–75) for two. Almond shares with these scholars an agenda to put European intellectual history in a proper perspective: for too long religion has been written out of the history of ideas, but proper culturo-contextual work should put it right back in the center—as the major factor making sense of Western thought.[8]

At both Brisbane and Sydney, related or complementary work shows up in studies by Patrick Burke and Arvind Sharma, and to some extent in my own research. The major excurses into methods of comparing religions by the first two were however published only after they moved to North America (Burke 1979, 1996; Sharma 1995 [yet cf. 1976[9]]), with the latter editing a Festschrift for Sharpe there (1996). As for my own work from Australia, in terms of mainstream theory I have thus far tended to limit my work to the history and critical analysis of European ideas about the origin and nature of religion (e.g., 1978, 1990a). As Professor in the History of Ideas at Sydney from 1995, in any case, a good deal of my scholarship sits tangentially to religious studies, in that I am as much interested in formulations about science, history and civilizations macroscopically conceived, and also political economy, as about religion (e.g., 1979; forthcoming). Most of my work takes the history of ideas as "the queen of the sciences," since all attempts at methodological formulation eventually fall into contexts within ideational trajectories (1994b; cf. also Swain 1985, 1999). Burke and Sharma, who have also shown their interest in socio-political questions (e.g., 1987, 1994 respectively), both established their methodological positions earlier: the former mixing phenomenological theory with a certain Catholic formalism, and expatriate Brahmin Sharma showing himself very sup-

---

8   Cf. also R. Gascoigne 1985. I hold that this was a paramount principle of my earlier teacher R. Max Crawford, but one really rather neglected for social history by those in his wake.

9   Sharma founded the journal *Religious Traditions* from 1978 (soon after to be a 'Commonwealth' journal with McGill University, Canada).

portive of the special "traditionalism" of Huston Smith (esp. 1991, cf. also the late Kesarcodi-Watson 1976).[10] My own methodology, even if I have recently dabbled in theological and aesthetic issues, is latecoming in its clear "positioning." The only theory I have proffered to complement the agendas of Sharpe as my senior colleague, for example, concerns the paradigm of a basic, fundamental and in this sense perennial religion—that celebrates fecundity and victory above all—and a configuration that never gets eliminated in spite of the efforts to transcend it through "salvation religions" (1988a, yet see below on a quite different angle).

Signs that others are restless over "taking more of a stance" theoretically and methodologically, however, have recently come from the south, where Kenneth ("Harry") Oldmeadow has recently published a remarkable defense of the traditionalist views or perennialist philosophy associated with Frithjof Schuon, Seyyed Hossein Nasr and their like (see below). Late in his career, moreover, the great Melbournian philosopher of religion Charlesworth put together an important text on "inventing" religion (1997). He had long explored the relationship between religious claims and the culture of trust in science (scientism), and found the latter more wanting and dangerous to social health than the former (e.g., 1992). In this work on *Religious Inventions* he went further in exploring the ideological tendencies to multiply revelations, construct an Aboriginal spirituality (cf. Hume 2000), and "make" Christian ethics. This work connects back, perhaps unwittingly, to Berger-influenced "constructionist" theory in Australia (e.g., Blaikie 1993), but is more important for anticipating the need to clarify the dimensions of religion *vis-à-vis* the proclivities of post-modernist analyses to "read the world" with new licenses (see esp. Hart 1985; cf. Sadler, e.g., 1995).

4. The Construction of Eastern Traditions

Apropos "inventing religion," recent processes of methodological reappraisal in the study of religion have had to do with the reification of huge (clusters of) traditions (such as "Hinduism," "Buddhism," etc.), and with deconstructing Western scholarly and popular representations of them over the last two or more centuries. Philip Almond is easily the most important Australian contributor to such revisionist work, with his well reasoned case for concluding that "Buddhism" as we find it in most textbooks is a Western invention. As Almond himself astutely states it,

---

10   A translator of Guénon, Kesarcodi-Watson was a still stauncher traditionalist, until falling quite disillusioned.

... from the later part of the eighteenth century [Buddhism] *becomes* an object ... it takes the form of an entity that 'exists' over against the various cultures [around it; and] during the first four decades of the nineteenth century, we see the halting yet progressive emergence of a taxonomic object ... Buddhism, by 1860, had come to exist not in the Orient, but in the Oriental libraries and institutions of the West, in its texts and manuscripts ...

so that the West came to "control" the Buddhist past, those involved during the Victorian era even doing it for the sake of the East itself (Almond 1988: 12–13, 140, cf. 37, 73–74). At a slightly later stage, when he went on to ponder the Victorians' invention of Islam (1989), Almond's work quite naturally linked with Edward Said's deconstruction of "Orientalism."

Other researches in Australia on Western scholarly constructions of religions have involved "Hinduism" (e.g. Mukherjee 1968), Chinese traditions (Rule, e.g., 1986; cf. Swain [forthcoming]); Persia (Trompf 1998), and Manichaeism as a remarkable transcultural gnosticism (e.g., Gardner 1996–; Franzmann 1996; S. Lieu 1998). A good deal of solid textual work on Eastern materials, of course, goes on in Australasia that is similar to the exposition (and translation) known in good international scholarship (e.g., Bailey 1983; Comans 1988; Bilimoria[11]/Fenner 1988; P. Oldmeadow 1994; cf. Masefield 1986; and on more icono-architectural matters, Snodgrass, e.g., 1985). Perhaps distinctive Australasian approaches to the East, however, over and above Almond's work, have to do with exploring the various dimensions of meditation studies (Bucknell and Kang 1997; Crangle 1994), taking their content seriously as more than intellectual but still as a "cognitive mode" (e.g., Crangle 1995), or assessing countervailing defenses of renunciation and activism (e.g., Bailey, 1985). We wait to see, however, whether a peculiarly Antipodean school of traditionalism, with a special orientation toward Eastern verities, will arise from Kenneth Oldmeadow's syntheses (cf. also Sworder 1995), that will rekindle earlier attempts in Australia to bring Eastern and Western philosophies into a more fruitful and lasting dialogue.

5. The Theory of Retributive Logic

Thus far we have considered Australasian theory that either relates to opening up of methodological horizons in international scholarship or to particular (sets of) traditions. The only "home-grown" development of a *general* theory about religion has come through the exposition of "retributive logic" (esp. Trompf 1975, 1979: 85–106, 176–205, 283–95, 1994a, 2000a: 1–46). Otherwise known as

---

11 Note that Bilimoria also founded the Australian Society for Asian and Comparative Philosophy during the 1980s, and currently edits the journal *Sophia*.

"payback theory," here I have interpreted human behavior and thought within the frames or apparent "universal structures" of concession and revenge and the explanations of events in terms of praise and blame. Lineaments of this approach go back to Giambattista Vico, Friedrich Nietzsche and S.R. Steinmetz, but the theory of retributive logic involves a systematic analysis of the socio-psychological dynamics of "helping friends and harming enemies" (as Mary Blundell puts it of ancient Greek religion), and how this is legitimated, trans-formed and modified in various culturo-religious contexts. Within or alongside complexes of gift-giving, and of exchanges with those from whom a given group expects mutual benefit, lie offerings to spirit beings and ritual ex-pressions of desire for some "divine blessing." In wanting to get fitting deserts to befall enemies or people who flout taboos or laws, there arise hopes in the support of "higher" punitive powers or "preternatural" techniques (like sor-cery, imprecations, etc.) to heighten the likelihood of blood being assuaged, bad deeds requited, or order secured over chaos. Thus each culture inherits over time a received "assumptive world" about how positive and negative relations are to be expressed, and how life's circumstances are to be explained in terms of praise or blame, reward and punition (Trompf 1997a–b).

As a structure of consciousness, retributive logic can subsist without reli-gion—a modern, secularizing Machiavellian, for instance, can justifiably assert that cunning persons will win out and careless ones pay adversely for their own folly—but through the history of most societies retributive logic has been integrally tied up with "religion" *qua* "dealing with spirits, deities, etc." It provides a lens, though, by which religion need no longer be treated only as distinctively concerned with what it has been conventionally associated with: for retributive logic encompasses economic, political and military life—and the "hard," often "negative" edges of cultures as well—and allows religion's rela-tion to these dimensions of life to be clarified, instead of always steering religiosity in the direction of the ritualistic, the high conceptual, the spiritual, or the mystical. This approach challenges the customary sacred/profane dichoto-my and invites its serious qualification (cf., e.g., Trompf 2000b).

I have thus far grounded this theory in extensively researched anthropol-ogical materials (thus on Melanesia, see below); explored the historicization of retributive logic, from classical Hebrew and Graeco-Roman historiography (esp. 1979), through Patristic developments (2000a), on to modern times (forth-coming); and attempted to plot its secularization and to define modernity (and certain threads of post-modernism) as an avoidance of traditional retributive challenges (e.g., 1979: 285–87, 1991: 248–51, 1999a: 95–96).

6. The Study of Religion and Social Research

The sociological study of religion has established a solid tradition for itself in Australasia. The Dutch émigré scholar Hans Mol was one of the first to put "research into religion" on the map in the region, and as a social scientific enterprise. Moving from rather quantitative studies of Australians' formal connections with religious institutions (1971; cf. also 1985), Mol eventually went on to do important theoretical work on religion as socio-existential anchorage (esp. 1976). Following in his train are Australians Alan Black (e.g., 1983) and two collaborators for the Christian Research Association, Tricia Blombery (1989) and Philip Hughes (1989), followed by North American scholar Gary Bouma (1997, 1999). Work on census material and religious life surveys by these scholars has produced a cooperative body of social research hard to match for "the national benefit" anywhere in the world. Hughes has recently launched a significant CD-Rom on as many Australian religious groups as he could detect (2001), and, although engaged in hard-nosed statistical work, he has adapted Anthony Giddens' sociological insights to Australia to show how traditions are being left behind for a post-traditional world. People are now beginning to construct their own spiritualities; for example, by 1997–1998 10% of Australians had engaged in multi-religious exploration. Bouma has been very insightful on immigration as adding to this Australian religious plurality (cf. also Bilimoria 1996), and we await the findings of Michael Mason on shifting balances in Australian Catholicism—on Anglo-Celtic elements leaving its institutional life in protest and immigrants shoring up its numbers.

The psychology of religion has received special attention in Australia. Empirical and clinical work has been dominant methodologically, with the first *International Journal of the Psychology of Religion* (1991–) being established by New Zealander Lawrence Brown at the University of New South Wales (and one of his protégés, Kathleen O'Connor teaching religious studies for a while in Sydney). American Richard Hutch has made an international reputation for himself by developing the personal biographical approach to the psychology of religion, using Australian materials (e.g., 1983). Others have broken new ground on such issues as personal/bodily stress and spiritual needs among women (McPhillips 2000; Franzmann 2000), men (Byrne 2001) and also clergy (R. Pryor 1982). Expatriate Australians' inability to adjust spiritually to the landscape has been a matter of continuing concern (e.g., Millikan 1981; Tacey 1995; Ferguson/Cryssavgis 1990; Haynes 2000).

Applying the (multi-)discipline of studies in religion to social history and traditional world views in their social and civilizational contexts in history has been another feature of Australian work. Seventeenth century England has been of special attention to Almond and others, for example (see above); and one of my own major projects (1979; forthcoming) has been to trace ideas about historical recurrence during various "phases" in the history of Western civilization. Religious history and especially the religious impetuses in Western history, including that of Australia, has long been a significant scholarly field in Australian scholarship, with such key British figures as John McManners and Patrick Collinson coming into the story as long-term "visitors," and Bruce Mansfield, internationally significant in Erasmian studies himself (e.g., 1979) founding *The Journal of Religious History* from the Sydney History Department.[12] Macquarie University has obviously played an enriching role here in stressing religious dimensions of ancient history, and raising the study of Late Antiquity as one of the most exciting "new industries" in historical research (e.g., Croke/Emmett[-Nobbs] 1983; Clarke et al. 1990; Mortley 1996)—including New Testament studies (e.g., Banks 1979; J. Lieu 1996). But a variety of other historians coming from history departments or theological colleges have contributed to the social study of religion, especially over the post-War years (e.g., Barnes 1999; W. Emilsen 1994; Hilliard 1978; Oddie 1991; and for a survey on Australian topics, Carey et al. 2001). Scholars of religion have been intensely involved in historical questions as well. Among the recent clusters of interests, conversion in late antique and early mediaeval times has enticed theoretically interesting work (e.g., Olson 1996; Cusack 1998). The history of esoteric and recent theosophic currents have received increasing attention (e.g., Tillett 1982; French 2000); and two Australians, myself and John Cooper, were involved in the founding of the international monograph series *Gnostica* (out of Louvain, 1997–), the series in which a methodological defense for the placement of esotericism in the broader discipline of religious studies has been most systematically formulated.

As for more recent and contemporary developments, new religious movements have been assessed in some interesting ways. With Theosophy having its capital for a time in Sydney, a small industry surrounds it (thus above). Canadian-born Rachael Kohn has attended to what she calls "Self religions" (those fostering confident autonomy rather than dependence on the divine) (e.g., 1991; cf. also 1989), and Melbournian theorist of Arab nationalisms Dennis Walker has tested the paradigm of micro-nationalism for Black Islam in the United States (e.g., 1993). Rowan Ireland is internationally acclaimed for work on the sociology of Brazilian religious life and change, especially grassroots "spiritistic" movements among black populations (e.g., 1991); interesting recent theoretical work has also been done on syncretism in newer religions as reflective of globalizing tendencies (Hartney 2001, 2003). In my own work I have sought to compare Melanesian villagers' hopes for European-style goods with Western UFO dreams of "miraculously injected" new technologies as different expressions of "cargoism" (1990b, 2003). I have also formulated a theoretical

---

12 See *supra*. Editorship has recently been in the hands of J. Gascoigne, with Trompf as Chairman and W. Emilsen as Secretary of the journal's Association.

framework for interpreting millenarism (2000c), with a concern to clarify both retributive elements in apocalyptic stances and the "invention of macrohistory" in times of crisis or dramatic change (cf. 1989). The first general text on Australian Wiccan and Pagan movements has also appeared (Hume 1997). Furthermore, Australian popular culture and civil religion are beginning to receive more sophisticated treatment (e.g., M. Maddox 2000), and a large Australian industry on religion and literature has been developing (e.g., Griffith et al., 1994–1995).

7. Aboriginal Religions

The Australian continent is of course home to much-studied indigenous peoples, and, however much publication on the Aborigines has been dominated over the generations by overseas specialists, research eventually came to be commanded by those born and bred within the region (starting with Elkin, e.g., 1943, 1945, and as later indicated by such interpreters as Stanner, e.g., 1959–1961; Berndt 1974; and Strehlow 1978). Of late, on the heels of a younger generation of "Euro-Australian" researchers (cf. Charlesworth 1984, 1998), Aboriginal scholars are beginning to make their mark (cf. Swain 1991 for a survey of the processes).

Among the "newer Australians" Swain's work is particularly interesting because, after publishing on Western theories about Aboriginal religion (1985; his first book actually came out of his Honors thesis), he went on to essay a history of what he called "Aboriginal being" (1993). It was the first such history ever attempted. He decided that very little could be reconstructed from precontact times, and thus began with the key, underlying themes that show up everywhere across the Australian board—especially those of the "ghost of space" (i.e., the sacrality and connectedness arising from the place where a mother becomes fertile) and the "Dreaming" as that which endures in and behind the important doings, group movements and excitements of the day (or "present"). He rightly questioned Eliade's applications of his principle of cosmic centre (*axis mundi*) in his *Australian Religions* (of 1973), because there was simply no one center, with diffuseness of sacred spatial associations dictated by birth connections (Swain 1993: 31–36). What he strongly maintained, moreover, was that some of the features of Aboriginal religion thought by many scholars (including Eliade) to be "archaic" were not. Beliefs about the so-called All-Mother in the north and the All-Father in the southeast were put down to contact, and were not taken as examples of autochthonous monotheisms. The Macassans, Torres Strait Melanesians, and finally the Christian talk of the latercoming Europeans, induced different responses that amounted to adjustment movements, and documented evidence of these group responses belonged to historical times (Swain 1993: 69–211). Comparably, the Aboriginal appeal to Mother Earth Swain claimed as very recent (1992), affected in the long run by the dissemination of Western theory (particularly that of Albrecht Dietrich) yet picked up in the more recent environmentally-oriented discourse of indigenous Christian theology. Thus it was expected, yet again, that such indigenous peoples as the Aboriginal Australians would express their closeness to the land in terms of mothering.

Swain took it as inevitable that Westerners would write their own agendas into reading the Aboriginal story, and for this he received some negativity from various anthropologists, whose orientations were challenged by his reapprais-als (Pecotic 2001). But, as might be expected in a changing intellectual climate, he also has come under criticism from an emergent cluster of black scholars suspicious of white experts. One substantive issue, intriguingly, concerns his claims about mother earth. One hears a great deal about "father's country" in Aboriginal discourse, but is the mother/earth connection really not there traditionally? The prophetic-sounding stances of Pattel-Gray (see above, and cf., e.g. 1991: 10–11) insisted they were, though without much investigative re-search. Scholar Graham Paulson has noted remembering his mother talk about the earth as mother as he sat on her knee out in the Western Desert (2000; cf. Dodson 1988). One suspects this debate has only just begun, as one among others. Aboriginal spiritual writing, in any case, has quickened in pace and spread (e.g., Pattel-Gray 1998; Rosendale et al. 1997) and the time is ripe for indigenous authors to present their religious outlooks in their own way.

8. Melanesian Religion and the Wider Pacific Scene

With early appointments to religious studies at the University of Papua New Guinea, a great deal of groundwork was carried out during the 1970s and 1980s to put the critical study of Melanesian religions on the map. The two lecturers involved, Carl Loeliger and myself, worked alongside competent ethno-historians in the UPNG History Department (the journal *Oral History* [1974–1993] being founded in that context). The atmosphere was exhilarating, and conducive to a disciplinary independence in a world attracting very many anthropological researchers. My own training had been in Pacific prehistory and ethnohistory at the University of Melbourne, where there had as yet been no Anthropology department,[13] and I had developed a distinct (now somewhat tempered) distaste for much anthropology as unhistorical and voyeurist.

---

13   Some prior University of Melbourne research in Melanesia had been significant, as by the Anglican missionary anthropologist Walter Ivens, who was a Research Fellow there between the Wars and wrote a number of works on the Solomon Islands, e.g., *Island Builders of the Pacific*, published 1930.

Loeliger and I also took a non-confessional, yet "broad ecumenist" and sympathetic approach to religious change in the region, and found ourselves sharing common research orientations with leading members of the Melanesian Institute (e.g., German Theo Ahrens, Italian Ennio Mantovani, and North American Darrell Whiteman, all earlier inspired by the work of well known Australian missiologist Alan Tippett, esp. 1967), and with Belgian Father Theo Aerts (of the Holy Spirit [Catholic] Seminary at Bomana, near Port Moresby), who was one of our successors (cf. Aerts, e.g., 1998). The field before us was vast: Melanesia was the most complex ethnic scene on earth, with the highest destiny of different languages, and with dramatic religious changes having occurred there over the last 150 years.

The major challenges presented to religious studies scholarship in the Melanesian region were as follows: 1. Domination of the traditional materials by anthropologists, usually unsympathetic to religious change, and with most investigators just specializing on "their" chosen culture.[14] 2. A narrowing of focus on cargo cults as the only Melanesian new religious movements worth social scientific attention, when there were so many other types (cf. Loeliger/ Trompf 1985: xi–xvii). 3. Studies in the developing "Christianization" of Melanesia were overly confined to mission history (more focussed on expatriate figures) and injured by competing, confessionalist-oriented writing. 4. Indigenous reflection on religious life had been barely published. 5. The grasp of Melanesian religion "in all its aspects" (Trompf 1988b) was badly needed, so that Melanesians themselves could get a general picture and frame of reference to grasp what had been going on in their parts of the world, rather than numerous disconnected ethnographies and many separate denominational stories. 6. Related to this last problem, there were books on religion across smaller regions of the vast cultural zone (e.g., Parratt 1976)—along with some books of collected articles (e.g., Lawrence/Meggitt 1965; Habel 1979; Mantovani 1984), and some Oceania-wide studies (e.g. Nevermann/Petri 1968)—but a detailed, critical and yet all too necessary grasp of Melanesia's geographical whole was still lacking. 7. Melanesian religions were badly known in the whole world of comparative religion.[15] No single discipline had equipped scholars to do the "proper and complete" study of religion even locally, let alone

---

14 Important exceptions here include Margaret Mead, Dutchman Anton Ploeg, Briton Andrew Strathern and German Friedegard Tomasetti, the latter emigrating to Australia (thus 1976).

15 E.g., even Eliade could be scattered and superficial in his references to Melanesia, as in his *Patterns in Comparative Religion* of 1958; yet his *Birth and Rebirth* (published 1958) and *The Two and the One* (published 1962) do better justice. Note, however, that a leading Dutch scholar of comparative religion, Theodorus van Baaren, made some efforts at active research (as in his *Korwars and Korwars Style: Art and Ancestor Worship in North-West New Guinea* (published 1968).

regionally. Religious studies was both polymethodic and multidisciplinary, and while it carried the disadvantage of being at one level too broad for purists in other disciplines, it bore the advantage of making up for prior theoretic deficiencies if working expertise in the social sciences, historical and legal studies, missiology and comparative theology was achieved.

By 1991 I had produced the first monographic overview of *Melanesian Religion*, and followed it up with the first grand-scale monograph on a major set of themes in Melanesian religions with the book *Payback* in 1994 (although before it lay James George Frazer's early "armchair" study on *The Belief in Immortality and the Worship of the Dead* in the Southwest Pacific and a few other thematic works). Region-wide surveys of cargo movements were already available (Englishman Peter Worsley's well-known *The Trumpet Shall Sound* of 1957 being a case in point, cf. Strelan 1977: 13–50), but detailed cross-denominational mission history came very late, even then not doing justice by Irian Jaya (Garrett 1982–1997), and work was to be done connecting both the sociology of protest movements and mission histories to religious studies. Out of the program of religious studies at UPNG, moreover, indigenous scholars cut their teeth academically and they were also encouraged to do so in such church-financed publications as *Catalyst* (1971–), and *Point* (1972–) (organs of the Melanesian Institute).

By the turn of the millennium I had the privilege of having sponsor-published perhaps the lion's share of black writers' academic studies on religious topics (cf. Trompf 2004). From both UPNG and the University of Sydney, beneficial interactions between studies in religion and those researching Melanesia from the social scientific disciplines were built up, with sponsorships, exchange activity and a culture of support (cf. e.g., Ahrens, 1992). Out of a religious studies context in Australia came the first detailed monograph study of a single (and major) cargo cult (Queenslander Gesch 1985);[16] the first Melanesian-authored full-scale study of the relationship between traditional religion and customary medicine (Papuan Kopi 1997) and concepts of time (Australian Martin 2001); and the first mission history of West Papua/Irian Jaya (New Zealander Neilson 2000).

Despite these developments, points of contact and opportunities for scholarly exchange, academics in other fields have been arguably overcautious about deferring to books outside their disciplines. Innovative black authors have been unfairly overlooked, perhaps the most obvious one being Willington Jojoga Opeba, who was first to stress the importance of dreams in generating religion (1977, yet cf. Stephen 1980), and first to deconstruct F.E. Willams' paternalist

---

16 Admittedly with the pre-existing inspiration provided through work on various Madang cargo cults by Peter Lawrence (1964), the Sydney anthropologist who examined Gesch's doctoral thesis.

imaging of the renowned Vailala response to Western interferences as a "Madness" (1987, yet cf. Lattas 1992). Part of the intellectual agenda of Melanesianists in religious studies has had to be a campaign against neo-colonial academicism. Part of it also has to involve just plain encouragement of indigenous research and writing. The current situation, with less stability in Melanesia as a political region, has seen a weakening of indigenous academic achievement in the field (except in contextual and pastoral theology, as in *The Melanesian Journal of Theology* [1985–], for applied theology has a tendency to outlast all other studies during serious socio-political vicissitudes).

With this background, what have been the significant methodological innovations in and through the study of Melanesian religions? Apart from addressing the listed points above—especially insisting on the widening of the scholarly scope of attention to encompass "traditional," "transitional" and "modernizing" aspects—other more specialist developments come to mind. These include opening up the systematic study of the payback complexes in Melanesian religions (Trompf, esp. 1974, 1994a; cf. May 2003: 25–60); participant observation of initiation ceremonies (Gesch e.g., 2001); the detailed historical analysis of cargo cults (e.g., Lawrence 1964; Gesch 1985; Trompf 1990b–c; Lattas 1998) and comparable movements (e.g., Jojoga 1977; Trompf 1990c); the study of Black Independent Churches of Melanesia ([the Solomonese] Tuza 1977, 1987; Trompf 1983), spiritistic or Holy Spirit movements (Stephen 1977; Barr 1983; Flannery 1983; Hume 1986), Melanesian indigenous theology (Trompf 1989; May 1985; 1990; cf. Knight 1977); along with the phenomenology of "magic," sorcery and altered states, the introduction to traditional dream interpretation; explorations of traditional "eco-sensitivities" (e.g., Stephen 1987; Trompf 1991: 78–136, 2000b), and attempts to elucidate Melanesian materials within the relationship between 'religion' and 'aesthetics' (Herdt/Stephen 1989; Trompf 1997c).

The wider world of the Pacific Islands has of course attracted New Zealand scholars. Prehistoric issues, which are of background importance in explaining how different culturo-religious complexes arose in the Pacific region, have attracted many. In my view the most intrepid archaeologist of our time is Jack Golson, who has well-nigh single-handedly established that the world's first horticultural revolution occurred in the New Guinea highlands (ca. 8,000 BCE) before developments in the ancient Near East.

Most other New Zealand scholars have sorted out more micro problems— oral historical materials about expeditions (Buck 1959), the nature and history of particular indigenous belief-systems, prophet movements, new churches, and so on (e.g., Irwin 1984; Webster 1979; Mol 1982: 26–54; Elsemore 1985), and general conceptualizations of the religious life of Pacific culture areas has generally been left to European or American scholars (yet cf. Donovan 1990; Moore 1997).

There was bound to be an eventual reaction to the old characterization of Melanesian religion as "magically-oriented" and both Polynesia and Micronesia as "distinctly more religious" scenes (as maintained, for example, by anthropologist Raymond Firth, who was at Sydney for a time). There seemed to be support for placing Melanesia on a lower cultural rung this way when the contrast was made between the region's more egalitarian "big-man" systems of leadership and the hierarchies, even kingships, of Polynesia (cf. Americans Marshall Sahlins and Irving Goldman). While warning against such generalizations, I have recently argued the case that, on balance, Melanesian cosmologies tend to be "horizontal" in focus (following the cue provided by Lawrence, esp. 1984), while Polynesian and Micronesian proclivities are more "vertical" (sky-earth-underworld), consequently legitimating the socio-structural hierarchies found in the wider Oceania islands (Swain/Trompf 1995), and also explaining distinctive features of religious change there (as also the researches by the Fin Jukka Siikala make clear). Swain and Trompf have attempted in the same breath to draw comparisons and contrasts between Australian Aboriginal and Pacific Island *Weltanschauungen*, but without going so far as to say that Aboriginal Australia has to be classified as a quite distinct religious stratum (à la Robert Bellah on religious evolutionism), or as somehow yielding a "world religion" in its own right (following David Turner).

Arising from the study of the religious scene various missiological issues have presented themselves. Christian missionary activity is very strong in Oceania, and scholars in the religious studies field find themselves in a kind of "proving ground" that tests their individual judgment. Are they to go the way of many anthropologists who criticize missionaries as culture-destroyers or as interfering with cultures they would like to see in a pristine state? In response to such attitudes they have tended to stress the positive role of missionary anthropologists, to share common ground in criticizing insensitive mission activity, and to remind social scientists that, in the field, they themselves are inevitably missionary in various, if sometimes subterranean ways. The present realities have to be faced, what is more, as against succumbing to pressures of a certain romantic nostalgia, and research work often has to begin within a new Christian context, working back to what can be recovered of "the old time" (Tomasetti 1976). Finding an even keel does not mean evaluations about agents of religious change can be avoided, nor should they be. Scholars in studies in religion in any case ought to be confident about their advantageous positions for making useful judgments. They usually have a better sense of missiology as a developing field and can facilitate assessments of what is healthy or worrying—as with the "mixed bag" found with Australian mission experiences (Swain/Rose 1988)—or encourage scholars to realize that powerful, arresting events, agents and developments in religious life do arise out of missionization processes, and require balanced academic assessment (e.g., Trompf 1999b). The founding of the *South Pacific Journal of Mission Studies* (Sydney, 1989–) by famous Columban Father Cyril Hally has provided a useful forum for sorting out the above issues (cf. Hally 1999).

Australian scholarship in religious studies faces interesting prospects. Its protagonists are fortunate to reside where over a quarter of the world's known, discrete religions have existed, but it is a fact of life that the foreign (especially North American) industry in field anthropology will be producing the great bulk of newly published data, while in the tertiary institutions of the Oceanic region itself there will be pressures for indigenous researchers to take over field research or collaborate with "expatriates," and for the European- (or other-) originated scholars to act as facilitators or "helpful generalizers."

As for work on the wider world of religions, intellectuals in the Antipodean and Pacific zones have the problems of "vestigial cultural cringe" to contend with, and the apparent threat of being neglected simply because of being far distant from metropoles such as New York, London or Paris. But sitting far away can provide a special vantage point whereby one may gauge what is going on in the rest of the world with macroscopic perspectives more difficult to attain from within the major *mêlées*. Certainly, even if helped by the stimulation provided through appointees from overseas, or by overseas experience, important developments in method and hermeneutics of religion have emerged out of academic forums in the Southwest Pacific.

Thanks to Philip Almond, Albert Moore, Peter Oldmeadow, Birgitta Sharpe and Ian Weeks for some fine details.

Bibliography

Aerts, Theo (1998), *Traditional Religion in Melanesia*. Port Moresby: University of Papua New Guinea Press.

Ahrens, Theodor (1992), "Die theologische Szene in Ozeanien," in: *Verkündigung und Forschung* 37 (2): 67–91.

Almond, Philip C. (1982), *Mystical Experience and Religious Doctrine: An Investigation of the Study of Mysticism in World Religions*. Religion and Reason 26. Berlin: Mouton.

—— (1984), *Rudolf Otto*. Chapel Hill, N.C.: University of North Carolina Press.

—— (1988), *The British Discovery of Buddhism*. Cambridge: Cambridge University Press.

—— (1989), *Heretic and Hero: Muhammed and the Victorians*. Wiesbaden: Harrassowitz.

—— (1994), "Rudolf Otto and Buddhism," in: Peter Masefield/Donald Wiebe, eds., *Aspects of Religion: Essays in Honour of Ninian Smart*. Toronto Studies in Religion 18. New York: Peter Lang: 59–72.

—— (1999), *Adam and Eve in Seventeenth Century Thought*. Cambridge: Cambridge University Press.

Angus, Samuel (1925), *The Mystery Religions and Christianity: A Study in the Religious Background of Early Christianity*. London: John Murray.

—— (1929), *The Religious Quests of the Graeco-Roman World: A Study in the Historical Background of Early Christianity*. London: John Murray.

Bailey, Gregory (1983), *The Mythology of Brahma*. Delhi: Oxford University Press.

—— (1985), *Materials for the Study of Ancient Indian Ideologies: Pravritti and Nivrtti*. Pubblicazioni di "Indologica Taurinensia" 19. Torino: Collana di Letture diretta da Oscar Botto.

Banks, Robert (1979), *Paul's Idea of Community: The Early House Churches in Their Historical Setting*. Sydney: ANZEA.

Barker, Victoria (1995), "Languages of the Other: Contemporary Feminist and Theological Discourses of the Other," in: Michael Griffith/James Tulip, eds., *Religion, Literature and the Arts: Conference Proceedings 1995*. Sydney: RLA: 97–106.

Barnes, Geoffrey (1999), *Doing Theology in Sydney: A History of the United Theological College 1974–1999*. Sydney: Openbook.

Barnes, Robert/Prickett, Stephen (1991), *The Bible*. Cambridge: Cambridge University Press.

Barnett, Paul (1997), *Jesus and the Logic of History*. New Studies in Biblical Theology 3. Leicester: Apollos.

Barr, John (1983), "A Survey of Ecstatic Phenomena and 'Holy Spirit Movements' in Melanesia," in: *Oceania* 54 (2): 109–32.

Basham, A.L. ([1954] 1967), *The Wonder That Was India*. London: Collins.

Berndt, Ronald M. (1974), *Australian Aboriginal Religion*. Iconography of Religions 5 (4), 4 fasc. Leiden: Brill.

Bilimoria, Purusottama (1996), *The Hindus and Sikhs in Australia*. Canberra: Australian Government Printing Service.

Bilimoria, Purusottama/Fenner, Peter (1986), *Religions and Comparative Thought: Essays in Honour of the late Dr Ian Kesarcodi-Watson*. Delhi: Sri Satguru.

Birch, Charles (1990), *On Purpose*. Sydney: University of New South Wales Press.

Black, Alan/Glasner, Peter (1983), *Practice and Belief: Studies in the Sociology of Australian Religion*. Studies in Society. London: George Allen & Unwin.

Blaikie, Norman W.H. (1993), *Approaches to Social Enquiry*. Cambridge: Polity.

Blombery, Tricia (1989), *God through Human Eyes*. Melbourne: Christian Research Association.

Boer, Roland (1996), *Jameson and Jeroboam*. Society of Biblical Literature, Semeia Studies. Atlanta, Ga.: Scholars Press.

Bouma, Gary, ed. (1997), *Many Religions, All Australian*. Melbourne: Christian Research Association.

—— ed. (1999), *Managing Religious Diversity: From Threat to Promise*. Adelaide: Australian Association for the Study of Religion.

Buck, Peter H. (1959), *Vikings of the Pacific*. Chicago: University of Chicago Press.

Bucknell, Rod/Kang, Chris, compil. (1995), *The Meditative Way: Readings in the Theory and Practice of Buddhism*. Richmond, UK: Curzon.

Burke, Patrick (1979), *The Fragile Universe: An Essay in the Philosophy of Religions*. Library of Philosophy and Religion. London: Macmillan.

—— (1994), *No Harm. Ethical Principles for a Free Market*. New York: Paragon House.

—— (1996), *The Major Religions: An Introduction with Texts*. Cambridge, Mass.: Blackwell.

Byrne, Mark L. (2001), *Myths of Manhood*. Sydney Studies in Religion 3. Sydney: RLA.

Carey, Hilary M./Breward, Ian/O'Brien, Anne/Rutland, Suzanne D./Thompson, Roger (2000), "Australian Religion Review, 1980–2000," in: *Journal of Religious History* 24 (3): 296–313.

Carley, Keith (1975), *Ezekiel among the Prophets*. Studies in Biblical Theology, New Series 31. London: SCM.

Carnley, Peter (1987), *The Structure of Resurrection Belief*. Oxford: Clarendon.

Charlesworth, Max, ed. (1984), *Religion in Aboriginal Australia: An Anthology*. Brisbane: University of Queensland Press.

—— ed. (1987), *Religious Business: Essays in Australian Aboriginal Spirituality*. Cambridge: Cambridge University Press.

—— (1992), *Life among the Scientists: An Anthropological Study of an Australian Scientific Community*. Geelong: Deakin University Press.

—— (1997), *Religious Inventions: Four Essays*. Cambridge: Cambridge University Press.

Clarke, Graeme/Croke, Brian/Mortley, Raoul/Emmett Nobbs, Alanna, eds. (1990), *Reading the Past in Late Antiquity*. Oxford: Pergamon.

Colless, Brian (1975), "The Pearl and Grail Quests," in: *Milla wa-Milla: The Australian Bulletin of Comparative Religion* 15: 27–35.

Comans, Michael (1988), *Advaitamoda: A Study of Advaita and Visistadvaita*. Delhi: Satguru.

Confoy, Maryanne/Lee, Dorothy A. (1995), *Freedom and Entrapment: Women Thinking Theology*. Melbourne: Harper-Collins.

Conrad, Edgar/Newing, Edward G., eds. (1987), *Perspectives on Language and Text: Essays and Poems in Honor of Francis I. Andersen's Sixtieth Birthday*. Winona Lake, Ind.: Eisenbrauns.

Crangle, Edward (1994), *The Origin and Development of Early Indian Contemplative Practices*. Studies in Oriental Religions 19. Wiesbaden: Harrassowitz.

—— (1995), "Cognitive Styles and the Study of Religion," in: *Australian Religion Studies Review* 8 (1): 22–26.

Croke, Brian/Emmett [Nobbs], Alanna, eds. (1983), *History and Historians in Late Antiquity*. Oxford: Pergamon.

Crotty, Robert (1995), "Towards Classifying Religious Phenomena," in: *Australian Religion Studies Review* 8 (1): 34–40.

—— (1996), *The Jew Called Jesus*. Sydney: E.J. Dwyer.

Crown, Alan, ed. (1989), *The Samaritans*. Tübingen: J.C.B. Mohr.

Cusack, Carole (1998), *Conversion among the Germanic Peoples*. Cassell Studies in Religion. London: Cassell.

Cusack, Carole/Oldmeadow, Peter, eds. (1999), *This Immense Panorama: Studies in Honour of Eric J. Sharpe*. Sydney Studies in Religion 2. Sydney: School of Studies in Religion, University of Sydney.

De Jong, J. (1979), *Buddhist Studies*, ed. by Gregory Shopen. Berkeley, Calif.: Asia Humanities Press.

Dockrill, David (1982), "The Fathers and the Theology of the Cambridge Platonists," in: *Studia Patristica* 17 (1): 427–39.

Dockrill, David/Mortley, Raoul, eds. (1981), *The Via Negativa*. Prudentia Supplementary Number. Auckland: University of Auckland.

Dockrill, David/Tanner, R. Godrey, eds. (1988), *The Idea of Salvation*. Prudentia Supplementary Number. Auckland: University of Auckland.

Dodson, Pat (1988), "The Land My Mother, the Church My Mother," in: *Compass Theology Review* 22: 1–3.

Donovan, Peter (1976), *Religious Language*. London: Sheldon.

— (1979), *Religious Experience*. London: Sheldon.

— ed. (1990), *The Religion of New Zealanders*. Palmerston North: Dunmore Press.

Dutney, Andrew (1993), *Food, Sex and Death*. Melbourne: Uniting Church of Australia.

Ebied, Rifaat, with van Roey, A./Wickham, L.R., eds. and trans. (1981–), *Peter of Callinicum, Anti-Tritheist Dossier*. Orientalia Lovaniensa Analecta 10. Louvain: Department Oriëntalisk, [8] Vols.

Eccles, John (1980), *The Human Psyche*. New York: Springer International.

Elkin, Adolphus P. ([1943] 1974), *The Australian Aborigines*. Sydney: Angus and Robertson.

— ([1945] 1977), *Aboriginal Men of High Degree*. Brisbane: University of Queensland Press.

Elsemore, Bronwyn (1985), *Like Them That Dream: The Maori and the Old Testament*. Tauranga: Tauranga Moana Press:

Emilsen, Susan (1991), *A Whiff of Heresy: Samuel Angus and the Presbyterian Church in Australia 1977–1997*. Sydney: University of New South Wales Press.

Emilsen, William W. (1994), *Violence and Atonement. The Missionary Experiences of Mohandas Gandhi, Samuel Stokes and Verrier Elwin in India before 1935*. Studien zur interkulturellen Geschichte des Christentums 89. Frankfurt am Main: P. Lang.

Esler, Philip (1989), *Community and Gospel in Luke-Acts: The Social and Political Motivations of Lucan Theology*. Cambridge: Cambridge University Press.

Ferguson, Graeme/Cryssavgis, John, eds. (1990), *The Desert Is Alive: Dimensions of Australian Spirituality*. Sydney: JBCE.

Flannery, Wendy, ed. (1983), *Religious Movements in Melanesia: A Selection of Case Studies and Reports*. Goroka: Melanesian Institute.

Forrest, Peter (1996), *God without the Supernatural. A Defense of Scientific Theism*. Ithaca, N.Y.: Cornell University Press.

Franzmann, Majella (1996), *Jesus in the Nag Hammadi Writings*. Edinburgh: T. &. T. Clark.

— (2000), *Women and Religion*. New York: Oxford University Press.

French, Brendan (2000), The Theosophical Masters: An Investigation into the Conceptual Domains of H.P. Blavatsky and C.W. Leadbeater (Doctoral dissertation, University of Sydney). Sydney, 2 Vols.

Freyne, Seán ([1980] 1998), *Galilee from Alexander the Great to Hadrian, 321 BCE to 135 CE: A Study of Second Temple Judaism*. Edinburgh: T. &. T. Clark.

Gardner, Iain, trans., ed. (1996–), *Kellis Literary Texts*. Oxbow Monographs 69– , Dakhleh Oasis Project Monograph 4– . Oxford: Oxbow Press Vols. 1– .

Garrett, John (1982–1997), [3 volume study:] To Live among the Stars: Christian Origins in Oceania; Footsteps in the Sea: Christianity in Oceania to World War II; Where Nets Were Cast: Christianity in Oceania Since World War II. Geneva/Suva: World Council of Churches and Institute of Pacific Studies.

Gascoigne, Robert (1985), *Religion, Rationality and Community: Sacred and Secular in the Thought of Hegel and His Critics*. Archives internationales d' histoire des idées 105. Dordrecht: Martinus Nijhoff.

—— (2001), *The Public Forum and Christian Ethics*. Cambridge: Cambridge University Press.

Geering, Lloyd (1980), *Faith's New Age: A Perspective on Contemporary Religious Change*. London: Collins.

Gesch, Patrick F. (1985), *Initiative and Initiation: A Cargo Cult-Type Movement in the Sepik against Its Background in Traditional Village Religion*. Studia Instituti Anthropos 33. St. Augustin: Anthropos-Institut.

—— (2001), "On Conversion from the Global to the Local: Going Beyond One's Best Understanding in Sepik Initiation," in: Carole Cusack/Peter Oldmeadow, eds., *The End of Religion?* Sydney Studies in Religion 4. Sydney: Department of Studies in Religion.

Griffith, Michael/Keating, Ross/Tulip, James, eds. (1994–1996), *Religion, Literature and the Arts: Conference Proceedings: Australian International Conference[s], Sydney, 1994; 1995, 1996*. Sydney: RLA.

Habel, Norman C., ed. (1979), *Powers, Plumes and Piglets: Phenomena of Melanesian Religion*. Adelaide: Australian Association for the Study of Religions.

—— (1995), *The Land Is Mine: Six Biblical Land Ideologies*. Minneapolis, Minn.: Fortress.

Habel, Norman C./Wurst, Shirley/Babalanski, Vicky (2000–2002), *The Earth Bible*. Sheffield: Sheffield University Press. 5 Vols. [thus far].

Hally, Cyril (1999), "The Story of the Universe: A Challenge to Missiologists," in: Carole M. Cusack/Peter Oldmeadow, eds., *This Immense Panorama: Studies in Honour of Eric J. Sharpe*. Sydney Studies in Religion 2. Sydney: University of Sydney: 171–95.

Harrison, Peter (1990), *'Religion' and the Religions in the English Enlightenment*. Cambridge: Cambridge University Press.

Hart, Kevin (1985), *The Trespass of the Sign: Deconstruction, Theology and Philosophy*. Cambridge: Cambridge University Press.

Hartney, Christopher (2001), "Syncretism and the End of Religion(s)," in: Carole Cusack/Peter Oldmeadow, eds., *The End of Religion? Religion in an Age of Globalisation*. Sydney Studies in Religion 4. Sydney: University of Sydney: 233–48.

—— (2003), A Strange Peace: Dao Cao Dai and Its Manifestation in Sydney (Doctoral dissertation, University of Sydney), Sydney. 2 Vols.

Haynes, Roslynn (1998), *Seeking the Centre: The Australian Desert in Literature, Art and Film*. Cambridge: Cambridge University Press.

Herdt, Gilbert H./Stephen, Michele, eds. (1989), *The Religious Imagination in New Guinea*. New Brunswick, N.J.: Rutgers University Press.

Hilliard, David, L. (1978), *God's Gentlemen: A History of the Melanesian Mission, 1849–1942*. Brisbane: University of Queensland Press.

Horsley, Gregory H.R., ed. (1981–1987), *New Documents Illustrating Early Chriistianity*, Vols. 1–4. Sydney: Macquarie University Ancient History Documentary Centre.

Hughes, Philip (1989), *The Australian Clergy*. Melbourne: Christian Research Association.

Hughes, Philip (2001), *Australia's Religious Communities: A Multi-Media Exploration* (CD-Rom). Sydney: Christian Research Association.

Hume, Lynne (1986), "Church and Custom on Maewo, Vanuatu," in: *Oceania* 56 (4): 304–13.

—— (1997), *Witchcraft and Paganism in Australia*. Melbourne: Melbourne University Press.

—— (2000), "The Dreaming in Contemporary Aboriginal Australia," in: Graham Harvey, ed., *Indigenous Religions: A Companion*. London: Cassell: 25–38.

Hutch, Richard (1983), *Emerson's Optics: Biographical Process and the Dawn of Religious Leadership*. Washington, D.C.: University Press of America.

Ireland, Rowan (1991), *Kingdoms Come: Religion and Politics in Brazil*. Pittsburgh, Pa.: University of Pittsburgh Press.

Irwin, James (1984), *An Introduction to Maori Religion*. Adelaide: Australian Association for the Study of Religions.

Isichei, Elizabeth (1982), *Varieties of Christian Experience in Nigeria*. London: Macmillan.

Johns, Antony H. (1982), *Moses in the Qur'an: Finite and Infinite Dimensions of Prophecy*. The Charles Strong Memorial Lecture 1982. Adelaide: Charles Strong Memorial Trust.

Jojoga Opeba, Willington ([1977] 1981), "The *Peroveta* of Buna," in: Garry W. Trompf, ed., *Prophets of Melanesia: Six Essays*. Port Moresby/Suva: Institute of Papua New Guinea Studies and Institute of Pacific Studies, University of the South Pacific: 127–42.

—— (1987) "Melanesian Cult Movements as Traditional Religious and Ritual Responses to Change," in: Garry W. Trompf, ed., *The Gospel is Not Western: Black Theologies from the Southwest Pacific*. Maryknoll, N.Y.: Orbis Books: 49–66.

Joy, Morny/Magee, Penelope, eds. (1994), *Claiming Our Rites: Studies in Religion by Australian Women Scholars*. Adelaide: Australian Association for the Study of Religions.

Judge, Edwin A. (1960), *The Social Pattern of Christian Groups: Some Prolegomena to the Study of New Testament Ideas of Social Obligation*. London: Tyndale.

Kamenka, Eugene (1970), *The Philosophy of Ludwig Feuerbach*. London: Routledge & Kegan Paul.

Kesarcodi-Watson, Ian (1976), *Eastern Spirituality*. Delhi: Agam Prakashan.

Knight, James, ed. (1977), *Christ in Melanesia: Exploring Theological Issues*. Special Issue of *Point* (1), Goroka: Melanesian Institute.

Kohn, Rachael (1989), "The Return of Religious Sociology," in: *Method and Theory in the Study of Religion* 1 (2): 135–59.

—— (1991), "Cults and the New Age in Australia," in: Gary Bouma, ed., *Many Religions, All Australian*. Melbourne: Christian Research Association: 149–62.

Kopi, Sibona (1997), *Traditional Beliefs, Illness and Health among the Motuan People of Papua New Guinea* (Doctoral dissertation, University of Sydney), Sydney.

Lattas, Andrew, ed. (1992), *Alienating Mirrors: Christianity, Cargo Cults and Colonialism in Melanesia*. Special Number of *Oceania* 63 (1): 1–96.

—— (1998), *Cultures of Secrecy: Reinventing Race in Bush Kaliai Cargo Cults*. Madison, Wis.: University of Wisconsin Press.

Lattke, Michael (1992), *Collected Studies in Early Judaism, the New Testament and Three Odes of Solomon*. Brisbane: University of Queensland.

Lawrence, Peter (1964), *Road Belong Cargo: A Study of the Cargo Movement in the Southern Madang District New Guinea*. Manchester/Melbourne: Manchester University Press/Melbourne University Press.

—— (1984), *The Garia: An Ethnography of a Traditional Cosmic System in Papua New Guinea*. Melbourne: Melbourne University Press.

Lawrence, Peter/Meggitt, Mervyn, eds. (1965), *Gods, Ghosts and Men in Melanesia: Some Religions of Australian New Guinea and the New Hebrides*. Melbourne: Oxford University Press.

Lee, Dorothy A. (1994), *The Symbolic Narratives of the Fourth Gospel: The Interplay of Form and Meaning*. Journal for the Study of the New Testament Supplement Series 95. Sheffield: JSOT Press.

Lieu, Judith (1996), *Image and Reality: Jews in the World of the Christians in the Second Century*. Edinburgh: T. & T. Clark.

Lieu, Samuel (1998), *Manichaeism in Central Asia and China*. Nag Hammadi and Manichaean Studies 45. Leiden: Brill.

Loeliger, Carl/Trompf, Garry W., eds. (1985), *New Religious Movements in Melanesia*. Port Moresby/Suva: University of the South Pacific/University of Papua New Guinea.

McPhillips, Kathleen (2000), "Hidden Histories of the Menstrual Body," in: *Australian Religion Studies Review* 13 (2): 23–44.

Maddox, Marion (2000), "'With Hope in God'—Religion, the Preamble Debate and Public Values in Australia," in: *Australian Religion Studies Review* 13 (2): 5–22.

Maddox, Robert J. (1982), *The Purpose of Luke-Acts*. Forschungen zur Religion und Literatur des Alten und Neuen Testaments 126. Göttingen: Vandenhoeck und Ruprecht.

Mansfield, Bruce (1979), *Phoenix of His Age: Interpretations of Erasmus c. 1550–1750*. Erasmus Studies 4. Toronto: University of Toronto Press.

Mantovani, Ennio (1984), *An Introduction to Melanesian Religions: A Handbook for Church Workers*. Point Series 6. Goroka: Melanesian Institute for Pastoral and Socio-Economic Service.

Martin, Graeme (2001), A Comparative Study of Time as Being among the Keraakie People of South-West Papua New Guinea (Doctoral dissertation, University of Sydney), Sydney.

Masefield, Peter (1986), *Divine Revelation in Pali Buddhism*. Colombo: Sri Lankan Institute of Traditional Studies.

Masefield, Peter/Wiebe, Donald, eds. (1994), *Aspects of Religion: Essays in Honour of Ninian Smart*. Toronto Studies in Religion 18. New York: Peter Lang.

May, John D'Arcy, ed. (1985), *Living Theology in Melanesia: A Reader*. Point Series 8. Goroka: Melanesian Institute.

—— (1990), *Christus Initiator: Theologie im Pazifik*. Theologie interkulturell 4. Düsseldorf: Patmos.

—— (2003), *Transcendence and Violence*. New York: Continuum.

Millikan, David (1981), *The Sunburnt Soul: Christianity in Search of an Australian Identity*. Sydney: Anzeas.

Mol, Hans (1971), *Religion in Australia: A Sociological Investigation*. Melbourne: Thomas Nelson.

—— (1976), *Identity and the Sacred: A Sketch for a New Social-Scientific Theory of Religion*. Oxford: Basil Blackwell.

—— (1982), *The Fixed and the Fickle: Religion and Identity in New Zealand*. Waterloo, Ont.: Wilfred Laurier University Press.

—— (1985), *The Faith of Australians*. Studies in Society. London: George Allen & Unwin.

Moore, Albert (1977), *Iconography of Religions: An Introduction*. London: SCM.

— (1997), *Arts in the Religions of the Pacific*. Religion and the Arts Series. London: Cassell.

Morris, Paul/Sawyer, Deborah (1992), *A Walk in the Garden: Biblical, Iconographical and Literary Images of Eden*. Journal of the Study of the Old Testament Supplement Series 136. Sheffield: JSOT Press.

Mortley, Raoul (1973), *Connaissance religieuse et herméneutique chez Clément d'Alexandrie*. Leiden: Brill.

— (1981), *Womanhood: The Feminine in Ancient Hellenism, Gnosticism, Christianity and Islam*. Sydney: Delacroix.

— (1996), *The Idea of Universal History from Hellenistic Philosophy to Early Greek Historiography*. Lewiston: Edward Mellen Press.

Mukherjee, Soymyen N. (1968), *Sir William Jones: A Study in Eighteenth Century British Attitudes to India*. Cambridge South Asian Studies 6. Cambridge: Cambridge University Press.

Munz, Peter (1973), *When the Golden Bough Breaks: Structuralism or Typology?* London: Routledge & Kegan Paul.

Neilson, David (2000), *A History of Christian Missions in Irian Jaya*. (Doctoral dissertation, University of Sydney), Sydney.

Nevermann, Hans/Worms, Ernest A./Petri, Helmut (1968), *Die Religionen der Südsee und Australiens*. Religionen der Menschheit 5,2. Stuttgart: Kohlhammer.

Newman, Martyn (1990), *Liberation Theology Is Evangelical*. Melbourne: Mallorn.

Oddie, Geoffrey, ed. ([1977] 1991), *Religion in South Asia: Religious Conversion and Revival Movements in South Asia in Medieval and Modern Times*. Delhi: South Asia Publications.

Oldmeadow, Kenneth S. (2000), *Traditionalism: Religion in the Light of the Perennial Philosophy*. Sri Lankan Institute of Traditional Studies.

Oldmeadow, Peter (1994), *A Study of the Wisdom Chapter (Prajnamaramita Pariccheda) of the Bodhicaryavatarapanjika* of Prajnakaranati (Doctoral dissertation, Australian National University), Canberra.

Olson, Lynette, ed. (1996), *Religious Change, Conversion and Culture*. Sydney Studies in Society and Culture 12. Sydney: Sydney Association for Studies in Society and Culture.

O'Neill, John C. (1961), *The Theology of Acts in Its Historical Setting*. London: SPCK.

Osborn, Eric (1957), *The Philosophy of Clement of Alexandria*. Texts and Studies 3. Cambridge: Cambridge University Press.

— (1978), *Religious Studies in Australia since 1958*. Sydney: University of Sydney Press.

— (1997), *Tertullian: First Theologian of the West*. Cambridge: Cambridge University Press.

Paddison, Evonne A. (2001), The Quest for Authorial Intent in the Fourth Gospel Story (Unpublished doctoral dissertation), Sydney: University of Sydney.

Painter, John (1975), *John: Witness and Theologian*. New York: Knox.

Parratt, John A. (1976), *Papuan Belief and Ritual*. New York: Vantage Press.

Passmore, John (1970), *The Perfectibility of Man*. London: Duckworth.

Pattel-Gray, Anne (1991), *Through Aboriginal Eyes: The Cry from the Wilderness*. Geneva: WCC Publications.

—— (1995), "Not yet Tiddas: An Aboriginal Womanist Critique of Australian Church Feminism," in: Maryanne Confoy/Dorothy A. Lee, eds., *Freedom and Entrapment: Women Thinking Theology*. Melbourne: Harper-Collins: 165–92.

—— (1998), *The Great White Flood: Racism in Australia*. American Academy of Religion Cultural Criticism Series 2. Atlanta, Ga.: Scholars Press.

Paulson, Graham (2000), The Impact of Modernisation on Aboriginal Spirituality (Masters of Philosophy dissertation prospectus). Cootamundra (NSW).

Pecotic, David (2001), "Three Aboriginal Responses to New Age Religion," in: *Australian Religion Studies Review* 14 (1): 3–9.

Pretty, Robert A. (1997), Adamantius, *Dialogue on the True Faith in God (de Recta in Deum Fide)*, ed. by Garry W. Trompf. Gnostica 1. Louvain: Peeters.

Prickett, Stephen (1986), *Words and the Word: Language, Poetics, and Biblical Interpretation*. Cambridge: Cambridge University Press.

Pryor, John W. (1992), *John, Evangelist of the Covenant People: Narrative and Themes of the Fourth Gospel*. London: Darton, Longman & Todd.

Pryor, Robin J. (1982), *High Calling, High Stress: The Vocation Needs of Ministers*. Adelaide: Australian Association for the Study of Religions.

Pyle, Eric (1961), *Introducing Christianity*. Harmondsworth: Penguin.

Rizvi, Saiyid A.A. (1983), *Landmarks of South Asian Civilizations*. Delhi: Munshiram Manoharlal.

Rosendale, George/The Rainbow Spirit Elders (1997), *Rainbow Spirit Theology: Towards an Aboriginal Theology*. Melbourne: Harper Collins.

Rule, Paul (1986), *Kung-tse or Confucius? The Jesuit Interpretation of Confucianism*. Sydney: Allen & Unwin.

Sadler, Ted (1995), *Nietzsche: Truth and Redemption*. London: Athlone.

Sharma, Arvind (1976), "Towards a Definition of the Phenomenology of Religion," in: *Milla wa-Milla: The Australian Bulletin of Comparative Religion* 16: 8–21.

—— (1980), *Hindu Scriptural Value System and the Economic Development of India*. Delhi: Heritage.

—— ed. (1991), *Fragments of Infinity: Essays in Religion and Philosophy: A Festschrift in Honour of Professor Huston Smith*. Sydney: Prism.

—— ed. (1995), *Our Religions*. San Francisco, Calif.: Harper & Row.

—— ed. (1996), *The Sum of Our Choices: Essays in Honour of Eric J. Sharpe*. McGill Studies in Religion 4. Atlanta, Ga.: Scholars Press.

—— ed. (1999), *Feminism and the World Religions*. Albany, N.Y.: SUNY Press.

Sharpe, Eric J. (1971), *The Theology of A.G. Hogg*. Bangalore: CISRS/Madras: CLS.

—— ([1975] 1986), *Comparative Religion: A History*. London: Duckworth.

—— (1977), *Faith Meets Faith: Some Christian Attitudes to Hinduism in the Nineteenth and Twentieth Centuries*. London: SCM.

—— (1981), "Religion in an Australian Context," in: *St. Mark's Review* 107: 20–26.

—— (1983), *Understanding Religion*. London: Duckworth.

—— (1984), *Karl Ludwig Reichelt*. Hong Kong: Tao Fong Shan.

—— (1987a), "The Secularization of the History of Religions," in: S. Shaked/D. Shulman/ G.G. Stroumsa, eds., *Gilgul: Essays on Transformation, Revolution and Permanence in the History of Religions: Dedicated to Zwi J. Werblowsky*. Leiden: Brill: 257–69.

—— (1987b), "Tor Andrae," in: Tor Andrae, *In the Garden of Myrtles*, trans. Birgitta Sharpe. Albany, N.Y.: SUNY.

—— (1989), "Sharpe on the Sharpe Symposium," in: *Method and Theory in the Study of Religion* 1 (2): 213–20.

—— (1990), *Nathan Söderblom and the Study of Religion*. Chapel Hill, N.C.: University of North Carolina Press.

—— (1997a), "The Compatibility of Theological and Religious Studies: Historical, Theoretical, and Contemporary Perspectives," in: *The Council of Societies for the Study of Religion* 66 (3): 52–60.

—— (1997b), "Nathan Söderblom (1866–1931)," in: Axel Michaels, ed., *Klassiker der Religionswissenschaft: Von Friedrich Schleiermacher bis Mircea Eliade*. Munich: C.H. Beck: 157–70.

—— (1998a), "Preface" [Unpublished, apparently for a second edition of *Not to Destroy but Fulfil*, in the possession of Birgitta Sharpe. Kindly made available].

—— (1998b), "Twenty Years On: Some Reflections on the Study of Religion," in: *Australian Religion Studies Review* 2 (2): 126–33.

—— (1999), *Alfred George Hogg*. Chennai: Christian Literature Society.

—— (2001), "The Legacy of Bengt Sundkler," in: *International Bulletin of Missionary Research* 25 (2): 58–63.

—— (2002), "The Secularization of Sanctity: the Case and Example of Francis of Assisi," in: Garry W. Trompf/Gildas Hamel, eds., *The World of Religions: Essays on Historical and Contemporary Issues in Honour of Professor Noel Quentin King for His Eightieth Birthday*. Religion, Politics and Society 1. Delhi: ISPCK: 155–67.

—— (2004), *The Quest for the Kingdom of God: A Study in the History of a Vision*. Sydney Studies in Religion 6. Sydney/Uppsala: Svenka Missionrådet.

—— (forthcoming), *Investigating Religion, or Dual Citizenship: Essays and Papers on Method in the Study of Religion*. Sydney: University of Sydney.

Shboul, Ahmad (1979), *Al Masudi and His World*. London: Ithaca.

Skye, Lee (1998), Kerygmatics (Messengers) of the New Millennium: A Study of Australian Aboriginal Women's Christology (Masters dissertation, University of South Australia), Adelaide.

Snodgrass, Adrian (1985), *The Symbolism of the Stupa*. Studies in Southeast Asia. Ithaca, N.Y.: Cornell University Press.

Squires, John (1993), *The Plan of God in Luke-Acts*. Society for New Testament Studies Monograph Series 76. Cambridge: Cambridge University Press.

Stanner, W.E.H. (1959–1961), *On Aboriginal Religion*. Oceania Monographs 11. Sydney: University of Sydney.

Stephen, Michele J. (1977), *Cargo Cult Hysteria: Symptom of Despair or Technique of Ecstasy?* Research Centre for South-West Pacific Studies Occasional Paper 1. Melbourne: La Trobe University.

—— (1980), "Dream, Trance and Spirit Possession: Traditional Religious Experience in Melanesia," in: Victor C. Hayes, ed., *Religious Experience in World Religions*. Selected Papers 3. Adelaide: Australian Association for the Study of Religions: 25–49.

—— ed. (1987), *Sorcerer and Witch in Melanesia*. Melbourne: Melbourne University Press.

Strehlow, T.G.H. (1978), *Central Australian Religion: Personal Monototemism in a Polytotemic Society*. Special Studies in Religion 2. Adelaide: Australian Association for the Study of Religions.

Strelan, John G. (1977), *Search for Salvation: Studies in the History and Theology of Cargo Cults*. Adelaide: Lutheran Publishing House.

Swain, Tony (1985), *Interpreting Aboriginal Religion: An Historical Account*. Special Studies in Religions 5. Adelaide: Australian Association for the Study of Religions.

— (1991), *Aboriginal Religions in Australia: A Bibliographical Survey*. Bibliographies and Indexes in Religious Studies 18. New York: Greenwood.

— (1992), "The Mother Earth Conspiracy: An Australian Episode," in: *Numen* 38 (1): 3–26.

— (1993), *A Place for Strangers: Towards a History of Australian Aboriginal Being*. Cambridge: Cambridge University Press.

— (1999), "D.H. Lawrence as a Theorist of Religion," in: Carole M. Cusack/Peter Oldmeadow, eds., *This Immense Panorama: Studies in Honour of Eric J. Sharpe*. Sydney Studies in Religion 2. Sydney: University of Sydney: 291–301.

— (forthcoming), *Chinese Religions*. Studies in World Religions 2–4. Delhi: Sterling, 3 Vols.

Swain, Tony/Rose, Deborah B., eds. (1988), *Aboriginal Australians and Christian Missions*. Adelaide: Australian Association for the Study of Religions.

Swain, Tony/Trompf, Garry W. (1995), *Religions of Oceania*. Library of Beliefs and Practices. London: Routledge.

Sworder, Roger (1995), *Mining, Metallurgy and the Meaning of Life*. Sydney: Quakers Hill Press.

Tacey, David (1995), *Edge of the Sacred: Transformation in Australia*. Melbourne: Harper Collins.

Thiering, Barbara (1976), "Liberation Theology," in: Gordon Dicker et al., *O Freedom! O Freedom!* Sydney: Australian Broadcasting Commission: 59–69.

— ed. (1977), *Deliver Us from Eve: Essays on Australian Women and Religion*. Sydney: Australian Council of Churches.

— (1979), *Redating the Teacher of Righteousness*. Australian and New Zealand Studies in Theology and Religion 1. Sydney: Theological Explorations.

— (1983), *Qumran Origins and the Christian Church*. Australian and New Zealand Studies in Theology and Religion. Sydney: Theological Explorations.

Tillett, Gregory (1982), *The Elder Brother: A Biography of Charles Webster Leadbeater*. London: Routledge.

Tippett, Alan R. (1967), *Solomon Islands Christianity: A Study in Growth and Obstruction*. London: Lutterworth Press/South Pasadena, Calif.: William Carey Library.

Tomasetti, Friedegard (1976), *Traditionen und Christentum im Chimbu-Gebiet Neuguineas: Beobachtungen in der lutherischen Gemeinde Pare*. Arbeiten aus dem Seminar für Völkerkunde der Johann Wolfgang Goethe-Universität Frankfurt am Main 6. Wiesbaden: Franz Steiner.

Trompf, Garry W. (1975), "Retributive Logic in Melanesian Belief," in: G. Trompf, ed., *Melanesian and Judaeo-Christian Religious Traditions*, Book 3,1. Port Moresby: Extension Studies, University of Papua New Guinea: 76–87.

— (1978), *Max Müller as a Theorist of Comparative Religion*. Bombay: Shakuntala.

— (1979), *The Idea of Historical Recurrence in Western Thought*. Vol. 1: *From Antiquity to the Reformation*. Berkeley, Calif.: University of California Press.

— (1983), "Independent Churches in Melanesia," in: *Oceania* 54 (1): 51–72; 54 (2): 122–32.

—— (1988a), "Salvation and Primal Religion," in: David Dockrill/R. Godrey Tanner, eds., *The Idea of Salvation. Prudentia* Supplementary Number. Auckland: University of Auckland: 207–31.

—— (1988b), "Melanesian Religion in All Its Aspects," in: *Catalyst* 18 (2): 155–62.

—— (1989), "Macrohistory and Acculturation: Between Myth and History in Modern Melanesian Adjustments and Ancient Gnosticism," in: *Comparative Studies in Society and History* 31 (4): 619–48.

—— (1990a), *In Search of Origins.* Studies in World Religions 1. London/New Delhi: Oriental University Press and Sterling.

—— ed. (1990b), *Cargo Cults and Millenarian Movements: Transoceanic Comparisons of New Religious Movements.* Religion and Society 29. Berlin: Mouton de Gruyter.

—— (1990c), "Keeping the *Lo* under a Melanesian Messiah: An Analysis of the Pomio *Kivung*, East New Britain," in: John Barker, ed., *Christianity in Oceania: Ethnographic Perspectives.* ASAO Monograph 12. Lanham: University Press of America: 59–80.

—— (1991), *Melanesian Religion.* Cambridge: Cambridge University Press.

—— (1994a), *Payback: The Logic of Retribution in Melanesian Religions.* Cambridge: Cambridge University Press.

—— (1994b), "Vico's Universe," in: *British Journal for the History of Philosophy* 2 (1): 55–86.

—— (1996), "The Power of Nature," in: James Veitch, ed., *Can Humanity Survive? The World's Religions and the Environment.* Auckland: Awareness Book Co.: 167–84.

—— (1997a–b), "La logica della ritorsione e lo studio delle religioni della Melanesia," in: *Religioni e Società* 12,28: 48–77. English trans.: "The Logic of Retribution and the Study of Melanesian Religions," in: Garnik Asatrian, ed., *Iran and Caucasus* I. Yerevan/Tehran: Caucasian Centre for Iranian Studies/International Publications of Iranian Studies: 125–46.

—— (1997c), "Croce and Collingwood on 'Primitive' and 'Classical' Aesthetics," in: *Literature and Aesthetics* 7: 125–40.

—— (1998), "An Agenda for Persian Studies," in: G. Trompf/Morteza Honari, eds., *Mehregan in Sydney: Proceedings of the Seminar in Persian Studies, Sydney, Australia, 1994,* 1–6. Sydney Studies in Religion 1. Sydney: Persian Cultural Foundation of Australia.

—— (1999a), "Religion, Politics and the University," in: *Arts* (Sydney) 21: 93–110.

—— (1999b), "Ethnicity, Missiology and Indigenous Theology," in: Carole M. Cusack/ Peter Oldmeadow, eds., *This Immense Panorama: Studies in Honour of Eric J. Sharpe.* Sydney Studies in Religion 2. Sydney: University of Sydney: 171–95.

—— (2000a), *Early Christian Historiography: Narratives of Retributive Justice.* London: Continuum.

—— (2000b), "Melanesians and the Sacred," in: Frédéric Angleviel, ed., *Religion et sacré en Océanie.* Paris: l'Harmattan: 49–66.

—— (2000c), Millenarism: "History, Sociology and Cross-Cultural Analysis," in: *Journal of Religious History* 24 (1): 103–24.

—— (2003), "UFO Religions and Cargo Cults," in: Christopher Partridge, ed., *UFO Religions.* London: Routledge: 221–38.

—— (2004), *Religions of Melanesia: A Bibliographical Survey.* Bibliographies and Indexes in Religious Studies. New York: Greenwood.

— (forthcoming), *The Idea of Historical Recurrence in Western Thought*. Vol. 2: *From the Later Renaissance to the Dawn of the Third Millennium*. Berkeley, Calif.: University of Califiornia Press.

Trompf, Garry W./Hamel, Gildas, eds. (2002), "N.Q. King as Wise Polymath," in: G. Trompf/G. Hamel, eds., *The World of Religions: Essays on Historical and Contemporary Issues in Honour of Professor Noel Quentin King for His Eightieth Birthday*. Religion, Politics and Society 1. Delhi: ISPCK: 1–8.

Tuza, Esau ([1977] 1981), "Silas Eto of New Georgia," in: Garry W. Trompf, ed., *Prophets of Melanesia: Six Essays*. Port Moresby/Suva: Institute of Papua New Guinea Studies/Institute of Pacific Studies, University of the South Pacific: 65–88.

— (1987), "The Demolition of Church Buildings by the Ancestors," in: Garry W. Trompf, ed., *The Gospel Is Not Western: Black Theologies from the Southwest Pacific*. Maryknoll, N.Y.: Orbis: 67–89.

Veitch, James, ed. (1996), *Can Humanity Survive? The World's Religions and the Environment*. Auckland: Awareness Book Co.

Walker, Dennis (1993), "Louis Farrakhan and America's 'Nation of Islam.'" in: Garry W. Trompf, ed., *Islands and Enclaves: Nationalisms and Separatist Pressures in Island and Littoral Contexts*. Delhi: Sterling: 71–100.

Webster, Peter (1979), *Rua and the Maori Millennium*. Wellington: Victoria University Press.

Weeks, Ian (1999), "The Disappearance of the Political in Comparative Religion: An Essay in Honour of Eric Sharpe," in: Carole M. Cusack/Peter Oldmeadow, eds., *This Immense Panorama: Studies in Honour of Eric J. Sharpe*. Sydney Studies in Religion 2. Sydney: University of Sydney: 1–9.

White, Erin (1986), *Ricoeur's Hermeneutic of the Sacred*. (Doctoral dissertation, Department of Religious Studies, University of Sydney), Sydney.

White, Erin/Tulip, Marie (1991), *Knowing Otherwise: Feminism, Women and Religion*. Melbourne: David Lovell.

Wilcox, Max (1956), *The Semitisms of Acts*. Oxford: Clarendon Press.

Section 2

Critical Approaches

Philosophy and Religion[1]

by

MORNY M. JOY

This chapter will not, nor could it, be an extensive coverage of the relationship between philosophy and religion which has a long and complex history. Instead, I wish to position myself within the contemporary context, and undertake a selective survey of a number of developments that are occurring there between philosophy and religion. I will also offer some suggestions toward ways of ameliorating some of the problems I discern. From a general perspective, it is obvious that there are definite forms of philosophy at work—be they of an epistemological and/or ontological nature[2]—at the basis of the different approaches to the study of religion that are currently employed. I am aware that there are clashes between the proponents of certain of these approaches— appearing like one more round in the interminable, simplistic and stereotypical debate of a classical Apollonian with an emotional Dionysian approach, or of Enlightenment rationalism with Romantic idealism. Yet, I believe that there are other scholars in the humanities, such as myself, who are of no particular religious affiliation, and who do not find any resonance or inspiration in these debates, particularly when it results as a stand-off between those who favor a strictly scientific method and those who defend a theology as an integral part of religious studies.[3] Both sides often seem so preoccupied with defending their

---

1   Certain small sections of this paper were published in "After Essence and Intuition: A Reconsideration of Understanding in Religious Studies," in: *Secular Theories in Religion,* ed. T. Jensen/M. Rothstein, Copenhagen: Museum Tusculum Press (2000: 69–86). Used with permission.
2   I believe that the term "ontology" (theory of being) need no longer imply traditional metaphysical ideals. I would argue that this is a perfectly acceptable term within a setting that does not necessarily entail any implication of religious foundations or paraphernalia. Yet because of its past metaphysical associations, there will be those— either for reasons of faith, or because of professional or personal distaste of mixing faith and scholarship—who will automatically take ontology as confirming their preference—be it for or against such a term.
3   From the beginning, there have been exchanges about what constitutes the subject matter and methods of the discipline—particularly with regard to the role of theology. See Wiebe 1984 and Davis 1984 and more recently Wiebe 1994 and Schüssler Fiorenza

positions that they fail to account for the fact that there are historical reasons for the philosophical presuppositions that inform their respective arguments and their method, which put into question the automatic assumption that their method and theory are superior. My intention is not to enter into these polarized arguments but to investigate the creative possibilities that are available within a spectrum of philosophical approaches to religion(s). I undertake this in the spirit of David Tracy who has remarked: "[T]he entire narrative of philosophy of religion in the modern West needs rethinking and retelling if both the 'roots' and 'fruits' of that curious modern invention, philosophy of religion, is one day to play a properly interdisciplinary and intercultural role" (1990: 29).

I intend to focus initially on two aspects in the area of philosophy and religion: 1. Philosophy of religion, especially as it has developed in Anglo-American philosophy, and 2. Phenomenology and its off-shoot hermeneutic phenomenology, particularly with reference to its use within a Continental philosophical approach to religion. I will examine separately each of these areas, and the criticisms that have been respectively raised against each. I then propose to evaluate the resultant resources that could be available within a hermeneutic phenomenological mode for a new *rapprochement* with history of religions/*Religionswissenschaft*.[4]

More specifically, with regard to philosophy of religion, I would like to examine the way in which the universal presumptions of an abstract reason, especially with reference to matters of faith and its justification, have dominated the field in the past century, at the expense of more concrete contemporary concerns, such as those that have been raised by feminist and postcolonial thinkers. With regard to phenomenology, my intent is to analyze the problem of why phenomenology, and the term most often associated with it—"understanding"—has had less than cordial reception in religious studies, especially in history of religions. For help in this undertaking, I will look particularly to hermeneutic phenomenology, as providing a model of interaction between explanation with understanding, where both of these aspects function as two

---

1993, 1994. This debate continues in more recent issues of the *Bulletin: The Council of Societies for the Study of Religion*. Other recent books: Kippenberg 2002; Capps 1995; McCutcheon 1999; Cady/Brown 2002.

4   The translation of the term *Religionswissenschaft* has been a definitional minefield. This was the term first used by the earliest thinkers in the discipline to distinguish the study of religion from theology. In North America the translation of this term that has generally been accepted is that of "history of religions". For purposes of this paper, I will use this term. This describes basically the study of religions other than Christianity, and the methodologies involved. However, in many places in North America, the term now functions as one area of study under the broader designation of *Religious Studies*. Debates still continue regarding the definition, methods and content of this area of study.

complementary rather than exclusionary modes of knowing.[5] I do this because I believe that ultimately this model can be of help in responding to the problems inherent in certain aspects of both philosophy of religion and phenomenology. This is because I also believe that, in both of these areas, what is necessary is the addition of a critical perspective that pays attention to the particular historical context, rather than automatically accepting the claims of an absolute/universal/objective mode of philosophizing.

Before starting the discussion on philosophy of religion and phenomenology, however, I would like to state that my own approach has been informed by Paul Ricoeur's hermeneutic phenomenology, and by feminist and postcolonial thought. These have had a decisive influence on my work since my original grounding both in philosophy of religion and history of religions. I would like to think, however, that these critical and self-reflexive influences have not turned me into an ill-disposed critic of a relativist, postmodernist persuasion. My own views are not of a negative nature, as postmodernism is often simplistically portrayed. Instead, I would hope that I am undertaking both a critical and constructive venture that is not involved in a dismantling of the Western intellectual heritage, but one that questions certain of its unacknowledged presumptions.

On a preliminary overview, it becomes apparent that in English-speaking countries twentieth century philosophy of religion has been largely confined to

---

5   The meaning of the term "understanding" (*Verstand*) has had an erratic history in German philosophy, especially since Kant. Unfortunately, there is not the space to develop a detailed overview of these different developments. However, with each important figure I discuss in this essay, I will outline their use of the term "understanding." In the development of hermeneutics from Schleiermacher to Gadamer, understanding has been identified with interpretation of both texts and works of art, and has come to be associated with a poetico-aesthetic form of knowing. I will look for an alternative to the contemporary hermeneutic thinker, Paul Ricoeur, who wishes to revise hermeneutics. He wishes to move beyond the split, attributed to Dilthey, between understanding and explanation, whereby understanding was defined as a mode of knowing that was unique to Humanities (*Geisteswissenschaften*), as distinct from explanation, that was specific to the natural sciences (*Naturwissenschaften*). On the one hand, Ricoeur does not wish to identify interpretation simply with the role of understanding — which has tended to be associated with a type of psychological or aesthetic intuitionism. On the other, Ricoeur does not want to defer solely to explanation, which presumes that language is transparent and that interpretation is neutral. Ricoeur wishes that both understanding and explanation can be interactive partners in any act of interpretation. "I cannot accept the irrationalism of immediate understanding ... However, I am equally unable to accept a rationalistic explanation that ... gives rise to the positivist illusion of a textual objectivity closed in upon itself and wholly independent of the subjectivity of both author and reader. To these one-sided attitudes I have opposed the dialectic of understanding and explanation" (Ricoeur 1987: 378).

Anglo-American analytic philosophy and to a Christian world-view. A quick examination of many of the presently available textbooks gives evidence of this.[6] In contrast, phenomenology, in its more recent hermeneutical guise, is located within a broadly configured Continental philosophical approach with an emphasis on human experience. The main difference appears to be that, while philosophy of religion is concerned primarily with the use of rationality in relation to Christian faith and its justification, phenomenology, in its development from Edmund Husserl (1859–1938) to the hermeneutic qualifications by Paul Ricoeur (b. 1913), has become concerned with contextually based acts of knowing. Thus, these two philosophical approaches demarcate the act of knowing from very different positions that have significant repercussions. Unfortunately, at the present moment there is little if any contact, let alone dialogue between the two approaches of philosophy of religion and phenomenology. Rather, they tend to operate in mutually exclusive spheres of influence.[7] The attitude on the part of a majority of Anglo-American philosophers of religion is that phenomenological form of philosophy has nothing of a critically constructive nature to say. There are, as yet, on the part of philosophy of religion, no serious discussions that engage with phenomenology regarding the growing appreciation of the situated and interpretive nature of human experience and knowing.

The Problem of Truth

This situation is most clearly illustrated in the different relations of philosophy of religion and phenomenology to the notion of *truth*. Philosophy of religion, as a sub-discipline of philosophy, covers a vast range of topics, from the perennial question of the existence of (a good) God, to those that are dependent on this pre-eminent question, e.g., the problem of evil, life after death, ethics, and miracles. In one sense, philosophy of religion is a relatively new subset within philosophy, dating from the time of Kant, as a result of the demise of natural

---

6   A clear illustration of this can be found in the various editions of *An Introduction to the Philosophy* (1993) by Brian Davies, or in the old chestnut of John Hick entitled *Philosophy of Religion* (1989 [1973]) which still circulates unrevised. Though Hick is well-known for his work on religious pluralism, within philosophy of religion, his forays into religions other than Christianity seems mainly to be concerned with their truth claims. There are recent exceptions to this trend: Stump 1999 has one section on multi-cultural perspectives; Smart/Srinivasa Murthy, eds. 1996, is a reader of comparative philosophy, and Kessler 1999 is a textbook that includes readings from all religious traditions.

7   The division between Anglo-American and Continental philosophy does not necessarily have strict geographical demarcations. There are Continental philosophers who work within an Anglo-American ambit, and Anglo-Americans who do Continental philosophy.

theology, where it had been assumed that human beings could experience and have knowledge of God.[8] As such, it has nonetheless remained a distinctly Christian enterprise.[9] At the same time, philosophy of religion seems to have expended much of its energies into defining the notion of faith and its rational justification. In Anglo-American philosophy, truth thus pertains to an objective frame of reference, which is based on logical arguments and a correspondence theory of truth. As a result, theists and atheists have argued long and often on the particular merits of their positions. (Not to forget the in-fighting among theists themselves, who argue endlessly and vociferously as to who has the most consistent or logical argument on a particular topic.) There is little awareness or response to questions being asked by scholars who are critical of such a narrow perspective. As Grace Jantzen observes:

> The way in which the philosophy of religion as conventionally practised acts as a technology of powers stands out clearly in relation to the disciplinary boundaries that are drawn around it, the ways in which the topics which comprise it are disciplined. The same topics come up with predictable regularity: as Brian Davies says, philosophy of religion is about what philosophers of religion usually do! There is no indication in his work ... that the discipline has a history, that it is a social construction which has not always been constructed in the way that it is at present, and that what counts as philosophy of religion (and indeed as religion itself) is closely related to who is doing the counting. (Jantzen 1999: 23)

These observations certainly question the idea of truth as an objective rational ideal, untainted by its social and cultural contexts. Eugene T. Long, in his recent book, *Twentieth-Century Western Philosophy of Religion: 1900–2000*, which is a comprehensive survey of Western forms of philosophy and religion, describes in the General Introduction some of the interrogations that are being made today of philosophy of religion:

> Some philosophers argue that the philosophy of religion is too embedded in the eighteenth-century problematic of western theism at a time when persons are becoming more global in outlook and the boundaries of our histories are being expanded. Other philosophers argue that the traditional approach to philosophy suffers from unacknowledged ideologies which limits its scope and prevents it from taking into account the

---

8   For an informative treatment of the move from natural theology to philosophy of religion, see Collins 1967.

9   David Tracy, however, believes that in its beginnings, philosophy of religion, especially in the work of Kant and Hegel, demonstrated an intercultural interest, even if it was still governed by a superiority complex regarding Christianity. "A new narrative of origins of philosophy of religion may clarify how the 'founders' did in fact possess 'comparativist' interests, however inadequately those interests were executed by contemporary standards. This new narrative of origins could provide a new way to interpret the 'origins' of philosophy of religions so that the interdisciplinary and comparativist demands of contemporary philosophy of religion are encouraged" (1990: 15).

rich diversity of human experiences, purposes and social contexts. In some cases this
results in calls to expand the scope of western philosophy of religion. In other cases
philosophers call for the reconstruction of the philosophy of religion. At the root of
many of these challenges are deep questions involving the nature of philosophy itself.
(Long 2000: 2)

Long himself, however, does not respond to these challenges nor offer any
suggestions of ways of investigating or of implementing changes, though there
is a survey chapter on feminist philosophy in the book (2000: 495–521). Yet it is
of preeminent importance that these criticisms be heeded and addressed,
otherwise philosophy of religion will fail to advance beyond the limited methods of its Christian and Eurocentric perspective.[10]

In Continental philosophy, a contrasting appreciation of truth has developed, specifically within a phenomenological approach, beyond a definition
initially proposed by Husserl whereby an essence of an object (*Wesensschau*)
could be intuited. By way of Heidegger, Gadamer, and Ricoeur, a critical hermeneutics has developed, so that the act of knowing has come to be recognized
as intrinsically an interpretive act. Thus, there can no longer be an absolute idea
of truth or of essence as Husserl proposed. Of particular importance in this
development, especially with regard to texts, has been the work of Paul
Ricoeur. Ricoeur's appreciation is that truth, within an interpretative framework, is not a search for essences, but for probabilities that are in need of a form
of "validation." Validation is not verification in the way employed by
philosophy of religion. As Ricoeur observes: "To show that an interpretation is
more probable in the light of what is known is something other than showing a
conclusion is true. In this sense, validation is not verification. Validation is an
argumentative discipline comparable to the juridical procedures of legal
interpretation. It is a logic of uncertainty and of qualitative probability" (1981:
212). For Ricoeur, this validation would occur by dialogical exchange which
promotes a consensus rather than a correspondence theory of truth.[11]

---

10 There have been a plethora of books written on the topic of Eurocentrism and
    colonialism. However, these terms involve vast generalizations that need a more
    specialized discussion than this essay permits. There also need to be certain qualifica-
    tions that these are not monolithic entities with all-pervasive influences. My own use of
    the term "Western" in this essay requires such qualification. See Asad/Dixon 1984, and
    Amin 1989 for Eurocentrism. Also see Chidester 2000 for a cogent discussion of colo-
    nialism.

11 As Ricoeur observes: "The logic of validation allows us to move between the two limits
    of dogmatism and scepticism. It is always possible to argue for and against an interpre-
    tation, to confront interpretations, to arbitrate between them and to seek agreement,
    even if this agreement remains beyond our immediate reach" (1976: 79). In addition, for
    Ricoeur, this form of truth can also have ontological resonances. As his work pro-
    gresses from just the interpretation of texts, what becomes important is a person's own
    self-understanding, and the depth of his/her own awareness of the problematic nature

Ricoeur also emphasizes the epistemic shortcomings of human finitude, and the need for an on-going critical analysis of a self-reflexive nature in which a hermeneutics of suspicion plays a crucial role.[12] Such a critical modality of hermeneutics puts into question any claims to absolute truth. It is because of this admission of the limits of human knowledge that Ricoeur has been named a postmodernist, but this term and its superficial association with a form of destructive nihilism does not do justice to the multifaceted nature of the situation. I would caution that though critical and self-reflexive, Ricoeur's work is not of a nihilist orientation.[13] Pauline Marie Rosenau, in her book *Post-Modernism and the Human Sciences*, makes a distinction between two forms of postmodernism. She provides insight into two different ways that postmodernism can be understood. One way is that of a skeptical variety, which she describes as "the dark side of post-modernism, the post-modernism of despair, the post-modernism that speaks of the immediacy of death, the demise of the subject, the end of the author, the impossibility of truth, and the abrogation of the Order of Representation" (1992: 15). Rosenau contrasts this form with what she terms "affirmative post-modernism." She depicts adherents of this position as those who

> seek a philosophical and ontological intellectual practice that is non-dogmatic, tentative, and non-ideological. These post-modernists do not, however, shy away from affirming an ethic, making normative choices, and striving to build issue-specific coalitions. Many affirmatives [sic] argue that certain value choices are superior to others, a line of reasoning that would incur the disapproval of the skeptical post-modernists. (1992: 16)

This comparison is somewhat stark in its dualism, and discussion of post-modernism needs to be more differentiated, but for purposes of this essay, it

---

of any claims to knowing, especially those asserting that an absolute or objective truth has been attained.

12 Ricoeur introduced this notion in his work, *Freud: An Essay of Interpretation*, New Haven: Yale University Press (1970). Here he referred to Nietzsche, Marx and Freud as the "masters of suspicion." By this term, Ricoeur wished to indicate that these thinkers alerted us to the possibility that we may not be fully in control, because of external or unconscious influences, of what we say or do and that we harbor prejudices. Such a position would thus put into question most claims to the attainment of universal truth.

13 Ricoeur would understand a reflexive philosophy accordingly: "A reflexive philosophy is one that considers the most radical philosophical problems to be those that concern the possibility of self-understanding as the subject of the operations of knowing, willing, evaluating and so on" (1987: 370). However, he sees hermeneutic phenomenology as introducing a more suspicious dimension than that of Descartes or Kant whereby the presumed "ideal of the subject's transparence to itself" (1987: 376) can no longer be automatically assumed. This does not imply, however, that there is no subject.

will serve as an indicator of a basic functional distinction.[14] It would appear that Ricoeur has many traits in common with the approach of an affirmative post-modernism, in the sense that his view of philosophy as interpretation does not abandon meaning or values, but it certainly qualifies them, by means of a hermeneutics of suspicion. Ricoeur's brand of hermeneutic phenomenology allows neither for a self-satisfied sufficiency nor an automatic acceptance of past traditions and methods as privileged. As his terms of reference have broadened, Ricoeur's position has the potential to influence any perspective that is taken in relation to forms of otherness—be it that of a text, a person, or a religion. At the same time, Ricoeur is also equally concerned with the develop-ment of productive ways that surpass former limited categories of knowing. It is because of Ricoeur's unique combination of these critical and creative phases that I will focus on his potential contribution to the study of philosophy and religion.

My own position is that it is in the direction of these new possibilities and structures that religious studies now needs to turn, and not simply to rejoice that the fad of postmodernism is past;[15] that "objective" methods and theory of modernity can now be rightfully reaffirmed, and there will be a grateful return to the certainties of modernism. I do not think that this is any longer possible. The world community of today, with the problematic impact of technological innovation and globalization, and with a growing awareness of the issues of race, age, class, gender, and religion, as well as of indigenous, refugee, and homeless peoples, cannot but be conscious that momentous changes are occurring. Though there is no simple solution, modernism's assumptions of unity, neutrality, and presuppositionless inquiry can no longer hold firm. This, however, does not necessarily imply the death knell of modernism *tout court*. Nor need it imply that postmodernism, as it has been described by Jameson as the triumphant exemplar of American late capitalism/consumerism and globalization, has prevailed.[16] Things are far more complicated than positing a dichotomy of these two opposing "isms." Neither of the two movements is self-sufficient. It may well be that postmodernism could be described as a parasite of modernism; yet whatever description may best illustrate their relationship, the two are inextricably interlaced. Absolute knowledge or truth in its modernist form needs to acknowledge the charges of univocity, of inevitable prejudice,[17] of exclusivity, brought against them by postmodernism. At the

---

14   See Best/Kellner 1997 for a survey of the varieties of postmodernism.

15   See Marwick 2001 for a celebratory observation of the demise of postmodernism.

16   See Jameson's 1984 indictment of present-day capitalism as an expression of postmodernism.

17   Gadamer posits "prejudice" as an inevitable, i.e., inescapable, element of tradition and interpretation (1975), as a counter to the Enlightenment view of objective reason and its confidence in its ability to eliminate prejudices.

same time, postmodernism needs to answer to allegations of relativism, idio-syncratic subjectivism, and a seeming apolitical stance. This is not the place to present in detail the various claims of either side,[18] but to reflect on the current situation of knowledge itself, given this seeming divergence. Part of the problem is a recalcitrance on both sides to recognize the limitations of both modernism and postmodernism and to begin by exploring the intriguing new developments raised by their interrogative interaction with each other.

Philosophy of Religion

Philosophy of religion, as it has been described above, is basically Western, Christian and modernist in its orientation. Until recently, another undeclared presumption is that it has been a distinctly male enterprise. Any check of the table of the authorship in philosophy of religion texts vividly illustrates that most of the contributors to this enterprise have been male. Such an observation does not necessarily entail a polemic against "the patriarchy." Such a broad generalization no longer holds up to scrutiny. The historical contexts of all such abstract generalizations always admit to certain exceptions and subtleties of contextual interpretation, e.g., there have indeed been a number of women philosophers, though few in comparison to the numbers of men. Their numbers have been increasing in recent years, and thus it is valuable to take into consideration their work as they have begun to explore the relevance of philosophy for women and the reasons for the scarcity of women. Recent works by feminist philosophers of religion, Pamela Anderson (1998), Nancy Franken-berry (1998) and Grace Jantzen (1999), have challenged the apparent male monopoly and have suggested creative alternatives to the traditional concen-tration on rationality and its reifications. All of them are reacting to the way philosophy of religion seems to have spent much of its attention on defining the notion of *faith* and on its rational justification at the expense of other vital ways of understanding thought and experience.

Pamela Anderson (1998) is concerned about the form of foundationalism that is promoted by Anglo-American philosophy as it focuses on empirical realist forms of theism (1998: 13). Anderson's response is critical of the exclu-sion of women from such philosophic endeavors but she does not recommend the automatic inclusion of women in this existing enterprise. This is because female exclusion has taken two forms—both of which need to be addressed. One form of exclusion stems from the different types of mind/body dualisms

---

18   See Eagleton 1996 for a negative evaluation of postmodernism, and Lyotard 1984 as
      representative of the postmodern critique of modernism. Madan 1993 is an even-
      handed evaluator of these two opposed thinkers/positions.

that have been evident in philosophy from Plato, by way of Descartes, to the contemporary instrumentalist form of reason where the objective mind is privileged over the subjective, sensual and unreliable body. Thus, because of women's (socially constructed) affiliation with the body—not simply with its carnality, but also its erratic emotional aspects—they have not been regarded as sufficiently capable of reason. The body, particularly that of women, has, as Luce Irigaray observes, been virtually erased from Western philosophy.[19] Another development has been the relegation of women to the private, the aesthetic or to the natural world. This has been documented by Genevieve Lloyd who demonstrates that reason, in its definition by philosophers of different periods, has been associated with markedly "masculine ideals." As Lloyd states: "Our trust in a Reason that knows no sex has, I will argue, been largely self-deceiving ... The obstacles to female cultivation of Reason spring to a large extent from the fact that our ideals of Reason have historically incorporated an exclusion of the feminine, and that femininity itself has been partly constituted through such processes of exclusion" (1993: x).[20] As a result, Western philosophy of religion, where the mind has been concerned with examining the abstract (truth) claims as evidence for grounds of belief, has excluded both the minds and bodies of women, literally and figuratively. In this vein, Anderson claims that rationality, with its explicit emphasis on neutrality or objectivity has been gender blind. Anderson's specific aim is to enlarge the range of rationality itself, and thus to challenge its unstated assumptions about its own self-referential and self-sufficient nature.

Grace Jantzen's work *Becoming Divine* (1998) has similar critical evaluations of a male-identified mode of reason, but she worries that Anderson remains still confined within the ambit of rationality (albeit a modified one), especially with regard to the justification of beliefs as the central task of philosophy of religion. Jantzen is more concerned with "the work of a deliberate alternative to the areas of rational justification of religious beliefs" (121). The change Jantzen envisages for philosophy of religion, however, has even more serious implications, particularly with regard to sexual difference. This is because what she hopes to achieve is a rethinking of the nature of thought itself (of which rationality is but a part), and of understanding, from an embodied and experiential perspective, the nature of divinity and the issues associated with

---

19 Irigaray 1885: 185.

20 Lloyd describes the situation accordingly: "The pure Cartesian ego could readily be seen as opposed in its sexlessness to 'female' material sex difference. Neither the alignment of reason with maleness nor the opposition of the sexless soul to 'female' sex difference was of Descartes' making. But his influential dualism has interacted with and reinforced the effects of the symbolic opposition between male and female" (1993: xiv).

it.[21] Jantzen's approach can be observed in her discussion of the problem of evil. Instead of worrying whether evil and an omnipotent, loving God can co-exist, Jantzen responds: "A feminist approach to the 'problem of evil' is first of all outrage and bewilderment at the suffering and evil itself: how can the world be like this?"(1999: 263). She then continues:

> The issue is not so much "how can a good God permit evil?" as it is "how are the resources of religion, particularly Christendom, used by those who inflict evil on others? How are they used by people who resist?" ... It means also considering both how traditional theistic doctrines of power, mastery, and hierarchical patterns of domination feed into ideologies propping up the structures of domination and reinforce racism, sexism, poverty, and homophobia. The question of what religion has to do with evil and suffering is thus posed in much more concrete ways. (1999: 264)

Nancy Frankenberry (1998) is also troubled by the exclusion of women from Anglo-American philosophy of religion. As a process philosopher, she brings an alternative idea of philosophy of religion as involving a model of knowledge that is of an evolving and processual rather than a static nature.[22] From this position, Frankenberry questions the unexamined prerogatives of traditional epistemological categories.

> What has the status of knowledge? What gets valorized as worth knowing? What are the criteria evoked? Who has the authority to establish meaning? Who is presumed the subject of belief? ... What do we learn by examining the relations between power, on the one hand, and what happens as evidence, foundations, modes of discourse, and forms of apprehension and transmission, on the other hand? (1998: 192)

Thus, Frankenberry's reformative interrogations are mainly epistemological, querying the definition and values of rationality, but they also address issues of power, privilege and imperviousness to change. Both Jantzen and Frankenberry are not simply concerned with the absence of women's voices in philosophy, but also of those of other races, ethnic backgrounds, classes and, of course, religions. As Frankenberry observes, philosophy of religion has been largely "Eurocentric and Anglo-American in orientation" (193), so that there has been little consideration given to the fact that philosophy of religion could concern itself with other religions of the world. She states: "The next crucial stage of philosophy of religion will require engagement with and inquiry into a plurality of religions. Methodologically, this will mean taking as much account of history of religious and cultural anthropology as previous practitioners have of speculative metaphysics and practical theology" (194).

---

21 Jantzen's notion of the divine, however, is no longer affiliated with a transcendent notion of the divine, but with an immanent one, that is both generative and affirming of life. She makes a very strong case for pantheism (1999: 266–75).
22 For an excellent introduction to process thought, see Rescher 2000.

It is with this reference that Frankenberry brings into focus the obvious absence of discussions of race, class and culture, as well as of gender, that has kept most of philosophy of religion confined to white, Western, and Christian parameters. As she notes, while other areas in religious studies are moving in the direction of interdisciplinary and multicultural work, and paying attention to other religious traditions, including what could be termed as minority or even popular aspects of religion, Anglo-American philosophy of religion remains elitist in its unacknowledged presuppositions. Again, for Frankenberry, it is the unexamined notions of a predominantly Christian and Eurocentric orientation that prevails, though claims to neutrality and objectivity are still asserted.

Yet Frankenberry's reference to learning from history of religions, especially from a methodological perspective, is not without its own problems. Since 1978, when Edward Said published his book *Orientalism*, there has been a reluctant yet inevitable awareness that history of religions has not been without its own exclusions and impositions.[23] In his 1999 volume, *Orientalism and Religion*, Richard King, with specific reference to India and Hinduism, expresses his own evaluation of the changes needed in the prevalent colonialist approach of scholars of religion.

> What is required of the study of Indian culture and "religion" in a post-colonial context is an attempt to think across or beyond traditional Orientalist representations—to "transgress the boundaries" imposed by normative Western models of "religion." This must involve an interrogation of and displacement of Western (Judaeo-Christian/ secular) paradigms of what "religion" is, a problem that continues to dog the discipline of "religious studies," despite appeals to its apparently non-confessional and non-theological orientation. (1999: 210)

In my essay "Beyond a God's-Eye View" (2000), part of my project was to present the way the so-termed "Oriental" subjects, particularly Hindu women scholars such as Uma Chakravarti, Veena Das, Chandra Talpade Mohanty and Rajeswari Sunder Rajan are now defining their own positions with a self-

---

23 Said's work has not been without its critics over the years. Meyda Yeğenoğlu 1998 is one of the more recent ones. She faults Said on two counts: "1. Focusing on the epistemological dualism that Said sets between the 'real' Orient versus its representation, I suggest that although Said refutes an appeal to a notion of the 'real' or 'true' Orient as preceding its discursive constitution, his analysis is nevertheless bound to remain dualistic as he does not go beyond conceptualizing discourse as a linguistic activity … Although I follow in many ways the path that Said has opened up, I critically engage with his relegation of the questions of gender and of sexuality to a sub-domain of Orientalism. I suggest that the distinction Said makes between the *manifest* and *latent* content of Orientalism can be utilized as a useful guide for this purpose and can enable us to formulate the articulation of sexuality with Orientalism" (1998: 10).

reflexive awareness and theoretical sophistication that Western scholars in religion need to appreciate in order to move beyond their own unreflexive
authorial convictions.[24] As I also acknowledged there:

> There are various terms under which this challenge [to Eurocentrism] has been
> registered—Orientalism and postcolonialism, to name the most obvious. These terms
> are not synonymous, nor do their adherents have exactly similar views, but what they
> all focus on, from diverse perspectives, is the tendency obvious in Western thinking
> and cultural attitudes to a dualist division between the unified subject who is the
> scholarly enquirer, traveler, colonizer and the object/other (be it a person or a society)
> that is the recipient of imposed categories of difference—be they idealized projections
> or simplified reductions to a predetermined system of classification. (Joy 2000: 111)

In fact, within the ambience of religion, many of the peoples thus excluded and
categorized have now undertaken, from their postcolonial perspective, to define the theoretical approach and their own responses to this treatment. Musa
W. Dube provides insight into the situation: "The modern colonizer ... believed
in the superiority of his religion, race, economy, and culture. Such an ideology
was grounded in the beliefs of modernity, Christianity, and industrial
advancement. The colonized ... on the other hand, were imbued with the belief
that their own religion, race, economy, and culture were backward" (2002: 101).
In particular, she recognizes the situation of women with regard to religion was
even more problematic: "Postcolonial feminists recognize that the mechanisms
of subjugating women of the former colonies were often engineered by projects
that proclaimed themselves as redemptive, but which must now be subjected to
a decolonizing feminist analysis" (2002: 115).

Thus, while feminist, postcolonial and postmodernist theories are not
identical,[25] they do share certain critical commonalities in their reaction to the
imposition of generalized and inappropriate categories, especially those of a
rational variety. What is needed, according to a contemporary appraisal by
postcolonial scholars, is a state of critical awareness on the part of the scholar
who is involved in appreciating the culture and religion of others. In this
regard, no insight is innocent, qualified as it is with the intricate and often
subliminal subtexts of cultural norms involved. Such an incisive understanding

---

24 In this essay, I also reflected the concerns of certain of these writers who were worried
    that Western feminists in their work on non-Western women could also be guilty of
    committing "the ethnocentric sins of the fathers" (2000: 120).

25 For an excellent analysis of the terms "postmodernism" and "postcolonialism" and the
    differences of meaning involved, see Appiah 1991, Xie 1997 and Gandhi 1998. With
    regard to feminism and postcolonialism, there have been feminists who have endorsed
    the combination of postmodernism and feminism, e.g., Elam 1994 and Hekman 1990,
    while on the other hand, many have argued against it, e.g. Assiter 1989 and Weeks
    1988.

is in contrast to practices of the past, where the philosophical grounds of colonialist scholars was such that an investigator took for granted that his/her method was normative. Today there is a growing appreciation that any assertions of knowledge, made from such an uncritical position, cannot but be compromised.

In religious studies, contextual sensitivity to the basic phenomena of race, gender, and class, as well as to ethnic, indigenous, and non-Christian identities, needs to be incorporated into any act of knowing. Yet philosophy of religion has thus far been reluctant to undertake any committed self-questioning, or dialogue that could help to rectify these past omissions. It is with this in mind that I turn to phenomenology of religion to examine its contemporary status in religious studies.

Phenomenology of Religion

Edmund Husserl (1859–1938) is regarded as the father of phenomenology in its contemporary version.[26] Husserl's greatest concern was to return "to the things themselves," i.e., to phenomena, undistorted by historically dependent categories of rationality. Hence his adoption of the methodological procedure of *epoche* (bracketing off) of all presuppositions that could interfere with the act of knowing phenomena in themselves. As a result of this approach, Husserl posited that the *eidos* or essence of phenomena, which involves the self-evidence of physical objects, persons or mathematical truths, could be attained by an unmediated mode of intuition.

Although Husserl was not explicitly dealing with religion, the aspect of Husserl's thinking that had the most influence on religious scholars was his idea that it was possible to intuit essences of things. This was the aspect of his thought that was adopted by early phenomenologists of religion, such as G. van der Leeuw (1890–1950), who aligned his interpretation of Husserl's intuition with the term "understanding." Thus, it is van der Leeuw who is one of those responsible for the problematic status of the term "understanding" in religious studies. In his classic work, *Religion in Essence and Manifestation* (1963), van der Leeuw revealed his confessional stance:

---

26 Previous to Husserl's work, the term "Phenomenology" had been used by other philosophers, with different philosophical intentions from those of Husserl, e.g., Kant and Hegel. It is documented that the first use of the term "phenomenology" was by Johann Heinrich Lambert in *Neues Organon* (Leipzig, 1764).

The more deeply comprehension penetrates any event, and the better it "understands" it, the clearer it becomes to the understanding mind that the ultimate ground of understanding lies not within itself, but in some "other" by which it is comprehended from beyond the frontier. Without this absolutely valid and decisive understanding, indeed, there would be no understanding whatsoever ... In other terms, all understanding, irrespective of whatever object it refers to, is ultimately religious. (1963: 683–84)

But van der Leeuw is not the only guilty party of this imposition of a religious dimension,[27] as many other early scholars involved in the formation of the history of religions, while not equally strong Christian apologists, resorted to similar terminology in the service of metaphysical ideals.[28] Whether it was of a primordial and/or essential nature, a proto-Husserlian intuitive or speculative act of understanding was associated with a religious or sacred process and reality.

Joachim Wach (1898–1955) who introduced the discipline of *Religionswissenschaft*, as history of religions, to North America, employed a composite definition of understanding. It was influenced variously by the ideas of Dilthey, Husserl, Rudolf Otto, and Max Weber. He accepted the fact that, though religious experience was manifold, in its genuine form, Ultimate Reality was revealed. Understanding then situated itself as a means of appreciating the essence of these "genuine experiences," and in discovering (by induction) the structures that operate according to "strictly spiritual laws" and their own "phenomenological rules" (1961: 25). Mircea Eliade (1906–1986), Wach's successor at the University of Chicago, described his approach as phenomenological. Yet he has also been criticized for his similar imposition on phenomena of ontological presuppositions regarding the given status of the sacred or religious and its embededness in the world, which predetermine exactly what understanding will discern (Penner 1989). As Douglas Allen observes: "Controversies arise from criticisms that the Phenomenology of Religion is highly normative and subjective because it makes non-empirical, non-historical, *a priori*, theological, and other normative assumptions and because it grants an ontologically privileged status to religious phenomena and to special kinds of religious experience" (1987: 283).[29]

---

27 Van der Leeuw, like other religiously oriented phenomenologists, reinterpreted Husserl's intuition of essences as being of an inherently religious nature. Donald Wiebe (1999) has published a critical analysis of the work of van der Leeuw, and while I agree with his initial analysis, I differ with his recommendations for change.

28 For example, and C.J. Bleeker (1898–1983) sought the essence of religion by means of an *entelechia of phenomena*—which he proposed as a mode of phenomenology.

29 In his article on Phenomenology of Religion in *The Encyclopedia of Religions* (1987), Douglas Allen groups the users of phenomenology into four groups: "1. [P]henomenology of religion is used in the vaguest, broadest, and most uncritical of ways ... 2.

It is also unfortunate that none of the founding scholars in the history of religions employed either the term "phenomenology" or "understanding" in a consistent way. It is noteworthy that Ninian Smart in his book, *Worldviews* (1983), advised against the use of phenomenology because of the lack of consistency in its application (1983: 16), though he had used the term earlier in his own work. In this he is correct in that phenomenology, especially as it has been employed in the history of religions in connection with the term "understanding," has been the most problematic of words, as it is not immediately evident what it entails. In one sense, "understanding" has been consigned to a heritage of German idealist and romantic thought, with its strong individualist and speculative emphases. Thus, it tends to be aligned with a somewhat facile notion of empathy or intuition and regarded by realist thinkers as inferior to the more rational or the evaluative science-based approach. On such grounds, "understanding" tends either to be dismissed, or taken for granted, as it is by R. J. Zwi Werblonsky: "Little need be said here on the history of the concept of *Verstehen* and the philosophical discussions around it. The literature on the subject is by now classical" (1975: 146). My concern is to investigate how the meaning of the term "understanding" has developed since Zwi Werblonsky and Smart made their statements. It is time, I believe, to make a more detailed examination of understanding within the area of hermeneutics and to move beyond the often subjective and inconsistent way that it has been employed both by its supporters and detractors in the history of religions.

Hermeneutics

A certain amount of blame for the contemporary mistrust of understanding can be also be assigned to Wilhelm Dilthey (1833–1911), who was primarily concerned with hermeneutics. Dilthey was influenced by the work of Kant, Hegel and Husserl. The influence of the latter, however, did not have any essential or religious dimensions as it did in the work of van der Leeuw.

From the Dutch scholar, Chantepie de la Saussaye to … Geo Widergren and Ake Hultkrantz, phenomenology of religion has meant the comparative study and classification of different types of religious phenomena … 3. Numerous scholars, such as … Geradus van der Leeuw, Joachim Wach, C. Jouco Bleeker, Mircea Eliade, and Jacques Waardenburg have identified phenomenology of religion as a specific branch, discipline, or method within *Religionswissenschaft* … 4. A few scholars, such as Max Scheler and Paul Ricoeur, have explicitly identified much of their approaches with philosophical phenomenology" (1987: 273). With regard to phenomenology of religion, in addition to Allen's article, there have been a number of studies which are of an historical and/or theoretical nature: Capps 1995: 105–56; Ryba 1991; G.A. James 1985: 311–35; Waardenburg 1978: 89–137 and Hultkrantz 1970: 66–88 that explore the development of phenomenology.

Influenced by his study of Schleiermacher,[30] however, Dilthey had initially used *Verstehen*/understanding in a manner that was virtually identical with Schleiermacher's Romantic description of understanding as a form of psychological identification with the mind of the author. Dilthey has thus been associated with a type of "neo-idealist gnosis" and, according to Ermarth, as a result: "In the vast literature on *Verstehen* the 'intuitive' and 'divinatory' aspects have been stressed to the exclusion of Dilthey's equally strong emphasis on methodical rigor, empirical evidence and general validity" (Ermarth 1978: 241). In defense of Dilthey, Ermarth contends that Dilthey also adapted the term *Verstehen* from Kant's traditional use of *Verstand*.[31] To this must be added the further influence of Husserl, whereby "[t]o the subjective, experiential side of *Verstehen*, Dilthey added a new stress upon objective content, as distinct from psychic acts" (Ermarth: 255). It was in this way that Dilthey attempted to move from simply a descriptive psychological process to a more epistemologically and historically grounded one, that would be the basis of his hermeneutics.[32] Yet Dilthey differed from all these thinkers in that he also wanted to find an appropriate method for the human sciences (*Geisteswissenschaften*), as distinct

---

30 Dilthey's major early influence was Schleiermacher. In 1870, he published vol. 1 of his *Life of Schleiermacher*.

31 In this defense of Dilthey, Ermarth states: "*Verstehen* contains a normative property which has been obscured by exclusive attention to its logical and epistemological status. As Kant's theory of natural scientific *Verstand* pointed toward the transcendental ideas of moral reason, so Dilthey's theory of human scientific *Verstand* points towards immanent values of historical life and culture" (1978: 312). This view, however, relied on a double meaning of *Verstand*, whereby understanding referred both to "an ordinary or 'natural' (i.e., unreflective) form of human awareness and a method of inquiry into the human sciences" (245)—a somewhat problematic deployment of the term. Palmer has perhaps a clearer depiction of the situation: "In a sense Dilthey is continuing the "critical idealism" of Kant even though he was not a neo-Kantian but a "life philosopher." Kant had written a *Critique of Pure Reason* which laid the epistemological foundations for the sciences. Dilthey consciously set for himself the task of writing a "critique of historical reason" which would lay the epistemological foundations for the "human studies." He did not question the Kantian categories for the natural sciences, but he saw in space, time, number, etc. little possibility for understanding the inner life of man; nor did the category of "feeling" seem to do justice to the inner, historical character of human subjectivity (Palmer 100–101).

32 As Ricoeur states: "After 1900, Dilthey relied on Husserl to give consistency to the notion of interconnection. During the same period, Husserl established that mental life is characterized by intentionality, that is, by the property of intending an identifiable meaning. Mental life itself cannot be grasped, but we can grasp what it intends, the objective and identical correlate in which mental life surpasses itself. This idea of intentionality and the identical character of the intentional object would thus enable Dilthey to reinforce his concept of mental structure with the Husserlian notion of meaning" (1981: 50).

from that of the natural sciences (*Naturwissenschaften*).[33] In doing this he introduced a bifurcation between the terms understanding and explanation where he postulated that understanding alone was the relevant term for the human sciences. Richard Palmer describes Dilthey's approach:

> The key word for the human studies, Dilthey believed, was "understanding." Explaining is for the sciences, but the approach to phenomena which unites the inner and outer is understanding. The sciences explain nature, the human studies understand expressions of life. Understanding can grasp the individual entity, but science must always see the individual as a means of arriving at the general, the type. (1969: 105)

Thus, it was understanding alone that was to form the basis of an approach (*Geisteswissenschaften*, by which Dilthey determined to establish a distinct theoretical foundation for the human sciences, such as existed in the natural sciences (the domain of explanation). There remained, however, an inevitable tension in Dilthey's work between his effort to establish a distinct ahistorical epistemological foundation for the human sciences, and an historically contextualized, though individual act of knowing—understanding—which does not lend itself easily to be contained by fixed structures and general categories. Interpreters of Dilthey are divided in their estimation of his work and its implications. Ermarth would argue that: "*Verstehen* for Dilthey remains the elucidation of functional and structural relations rather than an intuition of essences—whether in the fashion of Husserl or Schleiermacher" (267). On the other hand, there are those such as Jean Grondin, who observe: "Nowhere does he show how interpretative psychology would validate the objectivity of propositions in the human sciences. In these respects ... Dilthey's project could not get beyond the merely programmatic stage" (1991: 86).

Yet it is on these basic ideas bequeathed by Dilthey—understanding in a historical context, and the relation of understanding and explanation—that contemporary hermeneutics continues to focus in attempting to revise hermeneutics so as to eliminate the dubious legacy of subjectivist psychological tendencies and the separation of explanation and understanding.

---

33   Makkreel describes the relation of Dilthey to Husserl: "[T]o whatever extent Dilthey may have been indebted to some of Husserl's phenomenological insights, he employed them only so far as they contributed to his own theoretical ends. Whereas Husserl considered phenomenology as the epistemological ground for all the sciences—the *Naturwissenschaften* and the *Geisteswissenschaften*—Dilthey looked to phenomenological analysis only as a means towards an epistemological foundation for the human studies which would at the same time distinguish them from the natural sciences" (Makkreel 1975: 275).

Hermeneutical Phenomenology

In the work of contemporary scholar, Paul Ricoeur (b. 1913) there is, for the first time, a unique blending of the phenomenological and hermeneutical streams.[34] This is because Ricoeur makes a definite qualification of the excessive claims made by proponents of Husserlian phenomenology to attaining objectivity by the bracketing of all contingent distractions (*epoche*), and to the subsequent intuition of an essence (*eidos*) (Ricoeur 1981: 105–12). Ricoeur, as did Heidegger in his criticism of Husserl, believes that it is impossible to avoid presuppositions—the task is to become aware of them. In an interview, Ricoeur provides an insight into his difference from Husserl: "I would say that in respect to Husserl the broadening of phenomenology within hermeneutics [as undertaken by himself] is also a kind of liberation of phenomenology ... In a sense Husserl remained within a framework of a theory of knowledge with the relation of subject/object" (Reagan: 104).

At the same time, Ricoeur's adds another dimension to hermeneutics. Though influenced by Dilthey, Husserl, Heidegger and Gadamer and their work on understanding, Ricoeur introduces an attempt to integrate understanding and explanation within an act of knowing. Such a modification permits an approach that does not subscribe to either of the opposed stereotypes of an unrestricted empathy/intuition (understanding, with its Romantic associations) and its reactive opposite, a reductionist objective stance (explanation, with its positivistic associations). Understanding is thus relieved of the major burden it has borne within a purely phenomenological framework, though it does not concede all authority to explanation. For Ricoeur, neither understanding nor explanation can operate independently, but need to be engaged in a mutually productive mode of interaction in the process of hermeneutics. Ricoceur thus reconciles two terms that have been regarded as mutually exclusive, which is perhaps the main reason that phenomenology and the term "understanding" have fallen on hard times in the history of religions, and in religious studies generally.

---

34 Heidegger's work is also characterized as hermeneutic phenomenology. As Palmer states: "Heidegger rethought the concept of phenomenology itself ... Heidegger asserted in *Being and Time* that the authentic dimensions of a phenomenological method make it hermeneutical ... His [Heidegger's] thinking becomes more 'hermeneutical' in the traditional sense of being centered on text interpretation. Philosophy in Husserl remains basically scientific ... in Heidegger, philosophical becomes philosophical, a creative recovery of the past, a form of interpretation" (1969: 1235–36). Ricoeur's work would be in agreement with this description, but he will add further theoretical developments.

While I would not presume that this model of Ricoeur will provide *the* solution to the problems I have described in philosophy of religion and phenomenology of religion, and history of religions, I do believe that phenomenological hermeneutics, with the further inclusion of a hermeneutics of suspicion, which is also developed by Ricoeur, is suggestive of one alternative approach that has as yet not been widely used or examined as a philosophical theory or method in the field of religious studies.

It is thus unfortunate that the work of Ricoeur, from both a philosophical and methodological perspective, would appear to have been rejected as just one more Christian figure whose work, even if not metaphysical in the traditional sense of the term, carries an agenda of faith that makes his work just as suspicious as Eliade's because of its religious presuppositions. Yet Ricoeur has made a clear distinction between his philosophical and his religious writings.[35] In proposing this version of hermeneutic phenomenology, Ricoeur does not have a vested interest in the maintenance of any ideal of religion as having a *sui generis* nature.[36] This is especially evident in the book of essays, *Paul Ricoeur: Hermeneutics and the Human* Sciences, translated and edited by John B. Thompson (1981).

It is in this book that Ricoeur describes this new aspect of hermeneutics:

> It is indeed my concern to avoid the pitfall of an opposition between an "understanding" which would be reserved for the "human sciences" and an "explanation" which would be common to the latter and to the nomological sciences, primarily the physical sciences. The search for a flexible articulation and a continual to and fro between the investigator's personal engagement with the matter of the text, and the disengagement which the objective explanation by causes, laws, functions or structures demands, is the guiding thread [of my work]. (1981: 36)

It is within this framework that Ricoeur defines his own appreciation of the role of understanding: "Understanding has less than ever to do with the author and his situation ... We are definitely prevented from identifying understanding with some kind of intuitive grasping of the intention underlying the text" (1981: 218). At the same time, he develops a model for the interaction of understanding and explanation:

---

35 Ricoeur has responded to a question concerning this aspect of his work. "I am very committed to the autonomy of philosophy ... I do not think, for example, that my treatment of metaphor or employment or my interpretation of historiography—which are in my recent works—or my latest reflections on the Other—use any religious arguments" (Reagan 1996: 125–26).

36 As Ricoeur observes: "between absolute knowledge and 'hermeneutics' one must choose" (1981: 193).

By understanding I mean the ability to take up again within oneself the work of structuring that is performed by the text, and by explanation the second-order operation grafted onto this understanding that consists in bringing to light the codes underlying this work of structuring that is carried through in company with the reader ... This specific manner of responding to the first task of hermeneutics offers the signal advantage, in my opinion of preserving the dialogue between philosophy and the human sciences, a dialogue that is interrupted by the two counterfeit forms of understanding and explanation that I reject. (1989: 378)

As an example of the interaction of understanding with explanation, particularly with reference to texts, Ricoeur discusses the form of structural analysis undertaken by Lévi-Strauss as a mode of explanation which can be used as an aid to a fuller understanding.[37] For Ricoeur, an objective analysis such as that provided by structuralism helps to provide insights into the meaning of the text, so that it does not remain at a level of an initial superficial reading. (Ricoeur would allow that many other forms of explanatory textual analysis would be helpful in a similar way.)

If ... we regard structural analysis as a stage—and a necessary one—between a naive and a critical interpretation, between a surface and a depth interpretation, then it seems possible to situate explanation and interpretation along a unique *hermeneutical arc* and to integrate the opposed attitudes of explanation and understanding within an overall conception of reading as the recovery of meaning. (1981: 161)

In this procedure, religion does not hold any special status or prerogative that would distinguish it from other human constructs. It is one worldview among others, and, by extrapolation, within the polymethodological framework of the discipline of religious studies, many different explanatory methods could be employed from various sciences to help clarify the elements that contribute to the construction of religious worldviews. In all such undertakings, however, ultimately for Ricoeur it is the interchange of understanding with explanation that forms a revised comprehension of the hermeneutical.[38] As Ricoeur re-

---

37 In structuralism, Lévi-Strauss undertakes a formal analysis of a text into its mythemes or structural thematic units, as a way of extracting the hierarchical and oppositional expressions of the text. According to Lévi-Strauss, these involve attempts to mediate concerns regarding human relations and the human condition itself. For Ricoeur, however, structuralism should not remain simply at this objective and impersonal analysis. In hermeneutics, there needs to be a mediation with understanding so that other resonances of the text can become apparent. "So if there is a hermeneutics ... it must be constituted across the mediation rather than against the current of structural explanation. For it is the task of understanding to bring to discourse what is initially given as a structure" (1981: 92).

38 Dilthey had previously defined this circle as the interaction of a person reading a text in a constant movement from the parts (words/sentences) to the whole (sentences/the

marks: "Ultimately, the correlation between explanation and understanding, between understanding and explanation, is the 'hermeneutical circle'" (1981: 22). Thus, for Ricoeur, phenomenological hermeneutics is not based on understanding alone, as it has been in hermeneutics thus far. Both understanding and explanation are necessary. Both are recognized as limited yet necessary perspectives within a hermeneutic framework.

While it appears from the above discussion that Ricoeur's work is directed primarily to textual interpretation, in a key essay, "The Model of the Text: Meaningful Action Considered as a Text," Ricoeur allows that this procedure can also be applied to the analysis and interpretation of human behavior.

> That the meaning of human actions, of historical events, and of social phenomena may be *construed* in several different ways is well known by all experts in the human sciences ... What seems to legitimate this extension from guessing the meaning of a text to guessing the meaning of an action is that in arguing about the meaning of an action I put my wants and my beliefs at a distance and submit them to a concrete dialectic of confrontation with opposite points of view. (1981: 213–14)

Though Ricoeur himself does not explicitly develop this move from understanding and explanation of a text to human activity, I would like to explore the rich and productive possibilities of making such a move. This could have distinct and important implications for philosophy and phenomenology of religion, especially in connection to methodology in history of religion. I propose that Ricoeur's work can be appreciated as supporting a move of hermeneutics from being solely a method that is applied to a text as other to a mode of hermeneutic phenomenology which inquires also into human behavior and interaction with other cultures and religions. Yet it would be difficult to undertake such a development simply within the parameters of understanding and explanation. It would seem necessary to include a further mode of critical self-reflexivity that would address the complex issues involved. It is for this reason that, before such a step can be taken in the direction of exploring a hermeneutics of human interaction, a further aspect of Ricoeur's work concerning the movement of distanciation needs to be investigated.

In his development of a hermeneutical phenomenology, Ricoeur does not stop with the dialectic of explanation and understanding, but also introduces another level of interchange that occurs between the modes of appropriation and distanciation. (In point of fact, this is parallel to, if not intimately interconnected to the exchange of understanding and explanation but, for purposes of exposition, Ricoeur separates this dialectic out as if it belonged to a further ordering in a progression of knowledge.) As Ricoeur observes: "The dialectic of distanciation and appropriation is the final figure which the dialectic of

---

entire text) and then, with further awareness of the overall meaning, returning to the parts *ad infinitum.*

explanation and understanding must assume" (1981:183). It is this movement of distanciation that is perhaps the most important step in the hermeneutic process, for it constitutes the moment of critique. "Distanciation, in all its forms and figures, constitutes *par excellence* the critical moment in understanding" (1981: 113). For Ricoeur, it is a movement which can employ a number of tools." Distanciation implements all the strategies of suspicion, among which the critique of ideology is a principal modality (1981: 113).[39]

Ricoeur makes this move because he is only too aware of the possibility of personal illusions and cultural distortions that can color all interpretations. It is because of this critical stance that I have employed Ricoeur in preference to Hans-Georg Gadamer as representative of the contemporary field of hermeneutics. Ricoeur's hermeneutical phenomenology requires a moment of suspicion that involves a specific critical dimension. While Gadamer, because of his notions of dialogue and fusion of horizons (1994: 302–307; 366–79), is frequently cited as a model of decentredness that would promote a non-reductive encounter with otherness (Halbfass 1988: 164–67; Dallmayr 1996: 49–58), his position as a form of simply legitimating tradition and prejudices as authoritative have been questioned.[40] The most well-known remains that of Jürgen Habermas (1977: 243–76),[41] who is highly critical of any position that accepts a cultural tradition without a critical moment does not expose the interests or, as Ricoeur would name them, prejudices/presuppositions involved (Ricoeur 1981: 66).

Ricoeur undertook a mediation of the debate between Habermas and Gadamer in an essay, "Hermeneutics and the Critique of Ideology" (1981: 63–

---

39   The term, "critique of ideology," comes from Jürgen Habermas, a Marxist scholar from the Frankfurt school influenced by *Ideologiekritik*. In this essay, when I use the term "ideology," I do not use it in exactly the same sense as Habermas, but rather Ricoeur's modified understanding of the term. Ricoeur has stated that "ideology is always an unsurpassable phenomenon of social existence" (1981: 231). That is to say that everyone lives on the basis of an ideology. Such an ideology can become distorted and associated with specific interests that dominate and control a society. See Ricoeur 1986: 1–18.

40   Part of the problem was that, at the time of the critique, Gadamer had not specifically addressed this issue. In a recently published set of interviews, Gadamer has clarified his position on this issue. He states: "Whoever appeals to authority and tradition will have no authority. Period. The same thing goes for prejudgments. Anyone who simply appeals to prejudices is not someone that you can talk with. Indeed, a person who is not ready to put his or her own prejudices in question is also someone to whom there is no point in talking" (2001: 44).

41   Ricoeur's following description is a summation of certain relevant aspects and terms of Habermas' thought: "According to the Marxist tradition, the critique of the subject is one aspect of the general theory of ideology. Our understanding is based on prejudices which are linked to our position in the relations of force of society, a position which is partially unknown to us. Moreover, we are propelled by hidden interests. Whence the falsification of reality. Thus the critique of "false consciousness" becomes an integral part of hermeneutics" (1981: 191).

100).[42] On the one hand, he was concerned that Gadamer, at that time, had not given sufficient attention to the fact that any encounter is a critical one. On the other, he was also concerned that Habermas' critique of ideology has its own regulative ideal, which could itself become an ideology. Ricoeur observed in the essay: "My aim is not to fuse the hermeneutics of tradition [Gadamer] and the critique of ideology [Habermas] in a super-system that would encompass both" (1981: 87). He stated that, instead: "I shall try to give a more modest meaning—a meaning less pre-emptive and less pretentious—to the notion of a critique of ideology, placing the latter within a framework of interpretation which knows itself to be historically situated, but which strives to introduce so far as it can a factor of distanciation into the work that we constantly resume in order to reinterpret our cultural heritage" (1981: 224).

There would seem to be a number of interrelated forms of suspicion involved in this movement of distanciation, and certain elements are connected to, but modified elements of Habermas' ideology critique. One of the central tasks of distanciation for Ricoeur is a demanding form of self-reflexivity or a critique of "false consciousness", that goes beyond the basic philosophical form of reflexivity described earlier in this essay. False consciousness has to do with the illusions of the self. One form it takes is a critique of presuppositions that one absorbs as a part of enculturation. Ricoeur observes: "Before any critical distance, we belong to a history, to a class, to a nation, to a culture, to one or several traditions. In accepting this belonging which precedes and supports us, we accept the very first role of ideology"(1981: 243). The other form has to do with the pretensions of the scholar. One needs to become conscious of what Ricoeur calls the imperialistic or narcissistic ego and its need for control. In its place, there needs to be an acknowledgement of the finite capacities of knowledge as well as the presumption of objectivity or neutrality on the part of the scholar. Another form of distanciation can be associated with the exercises of suspicion carried out by Freud, Marx and Nietzsche, who read the "text" of their culture, and critiqued the values and the interests involved. Thus, while distanciation is helpful in indicating the false-consciousness involved in various presumptions to knowledge, as a hermeneutics of suspicion it can also support a critical reading of texts, which indicts them insofar as they are products of a false consciousness, stemming from cultural biases that do not acknowledge the distortions, exclusions, and impositions involved.[43]

---

42 In an interview, Ricoeur gives his evaluation of this "mediation" (Reagan 1996: 102).

43 Richard Kearney gives a clear overview of the situation: "Ricoeur believes that the 'hermeneutics of suspicion' makes possible a new critique of culture … [I]t deals with falsehood and illusion not just in the subjective context of epistemological error, but as a dimension of our social discourse as a whole" (1986: 105). It was in this sense that the three hermeneutic masters of suspicion presented by Ricoeur served "[a]s reminders that there exist levels of signification removed from the immediate grasp of conscious-

In summarizing the contribution of Ricoeur, I would state that by his work in phenomenological hermeneutics, Ricoeur has clarified and expanded the notion of understanding (from its former quasi-psychological perspective) in phenomenology of religion and hermeneutics, both with regard to its application to matter of a text in an historical context and to the self-reflective dimension of knowledge.[44] Understanding is not to be separated from explanation, as the two together inform any act of knowing. At the same time Ricoeur promotes the view that knowledge has an important role to play in providing productive ways that engage with not just the present but with future dynamic changes that can result from critique. I believe that such a mediatory approach could lead to a more creative exchange that acknowledges diversification and difference and that provides grounds for critical evaluation without capitulating either to subjectivism or to an abstract philosophical standard with universal presumptions. Perhaps such an interactive model of knowing can help to move beyond the dualistic framework that has haunted most Western philosophic and religious theoretical undertakings. And while this approach does not demand that all scholars of religion be trained philosophers, it demonstrates the need for honest reflection of a philosophical nature. Specifically: "[I]t is the task of philosophical reflection to eliminate deceptive antinomies which would oppose the interest in the reinterpretation of cultural heritages received from the past and the interest in the futuristic projections of a liberated humanity." These two approaches must be mutually interactive, otherwise: "The moment that these two interests become radically separated, then hermeneutics and critique will themselves be no more than ... ideologies" (1981: 100).

Conclusion

From this perspective, the dialectic of understanding and explanation, as well as that of distanciation/suspicion, could provide a constructive alternative to the concerns raised above and those that I raised earlier in reference to phi-

---

ness. Freud, for example, dismantled the prejudices of the *ego cogitans*, by disclosing how 'unconscious' meanings can be organized and structured in a site beneath the jurisdiction of our sovereign consciousness. Similarly, Nietzsche showed how our so-called timeless concepts of value and reason are in fact 'genealogically' determined by the hidden strategies of the Will to Power. Finally, Marx's critique of ideology discloses how the meanings of human existence are often conditioned by socio-historic forces of domination which surpass the ken of the self-possessed subject" (1986: 104). As Kearney concludes: "All three were motivated by a common scruple of *hermeneutic doubt* which, observes Ricoeur, compelled them to demythologize the established codes in order to decipher concealed strategies of domination, desire or will (1986: 105).

44 In his more recent three volume work, *Time and Narrative*, Ricoeur has further refined these positions by a detailed recasting of the term *mimesis* (1984: 54–76).

losophy of religion and phenomenology of religion—specifically those that indicated a lack of self-reflexivity and cultural critique. The implementation of these hermeneutically influenced interactive and critical modes could also inform the quest for new modes and methods of knowing.

One primary task that could be undertaken in this direction is that of self-reflection and criticism. This would amount to the fact that, in a hermeneutical phenomenological approach, in adopting the stance of distanciation, a scholar needs to be aware of his/her own conditions of historical location and of cultural presuppositions. Ideally, there can no longer be an easy imposition by the scholar of a personal agenda, if there is a careful examination of any presumptions to truth claims and of the misapprehension of the transparency of a self and language. I see this as having two specifically dramatic applications with regard to philosophy and religion. The first has to do with the assumed scholarly impartiality and objective methods that have been employed in philosophy of religion. Thus far, within philosophy itself, minority challenges have been delegated to being the status rights issues, rather than acknowledged as constituting a challenge to the very structure and exercise of philosophy.

It is in phenomenology of religion, specifically as it has been employed in the history of religions, where such a hermeneutical phenomenology, particularly with reference to a revised notion of understanding and explanation, could have its most lasting and important impact. This is because here the encounter with the other is paradigmatic. Such encounters, be it with texts, other cultures or religions, present a situation where there has largely been a lack of critique of the vested interests and presuppositions arising from its Western biases. These need to be brought to consciousness and evaluated for the misrepresentations, omissions and exclusions that can occur in any interactive process that takes place between a scholar and other people or phenomena.

Too often, religious studies, including history of religions, in its study of other religions, has been content to stay within the confines of its own horizon, with the presuppositions or prejudices endemic to the historical constellation of the ideas that led to its foundation. This has led to the fact that the voice of the other has rarely been acknowledged or respected in its own right.[45] An interactive model should not be inferred (as it has been by some) to be an absolute deferral to the position of the other. Instead, it is an honest recognition that knowledge, in ideal circumstances, is a reciprocal venture, where the other's horizon brings to the engagement some information that may require not just a rearrangement of priorities on the part of the scholar, but a new position of openness that would effect a radical revision of the worldview that has thus far informed his/her categories, methods or epistemology. This could lead to a new

---

45   The work of Armin Geertz (1994) and his postulate of ethnohermeneutics is an endeavor to allow the indigenous interpreter/scholar a voice.

responsiveness and responsibility so that academic study of religion no longer imposes unilaterally its own frame of reference on those it deems alien or extrinsic to its customary terms of reference.

The final mode of critique—that of the hermeneutics of suspicion as a way of reading the cultural text and its traditions from an evaluative perspective, in the mode of Nietzsche, Marx and Freud—could also provide a contribution. This is because I place the critical interpretations of both feminist and post-colonial scholars as a form of a hermeneutics of suspicion. There have been allegations that these forms of critique are themselves just one more of ideology. When these accusations are made, however, usually the most extreme examples of a monolithic nature are employed as evidence. Such characterizations have to be qualified in the light of the manifold forms of both feminist and post-colonialist theories existent today.[46] Any careful reading of contemporary writings of feminists or post-colonialists will demonstrate that the respective theories are both acknowledged as resulting from multiple social, cultural and historical locations. At the same time, there is a definite awareness in both forms of critique that there is no place for a naïve idealism nor for any final resolution. A central part of any critique of a culture or a tradition involves both debate and constant self-critique. The results of such (self)-critique have been obvious in developments within Anglo/North American feminism as a result interrogations of by women of color, women of the second and third world,[47] who did not recognize their themselves in white, middle-class Anglo-American, professional accounts.[48]

Post-colonialist scholars today also acknowledge that they are inevitably implicated in the tradition from which they speak. There is no innocent, uncompromised position from which to speak. There can be no return to origins, to an uncontaminated past. The best that can be expected is that both they and those for whom they write acknowledge their complicity with the inevitable consequences of colonization. Rey Chow, a Chinese American scholar, endorses a critical position that is highly sensitive to cultural borrowings of any variety, while admitting their inescapable effects.

---

46 See Juschka 2001; Afzal-Khan 2000.

47 See Mohanty 1991.

48 Audre Lorde, a black American writer, is representative of the criticism leveled at white American women scholars: "As white women ignore their built-in privilege of whiteness and define *woman* in terms of their own experience alone, their women of Color become 'other,' the outsider whose experience and tradition is too 'alien' to comprehend ... [A]s long as any difference between us means one of us must be inferior, then the recognition of any difference must be fraught with guilt. To allow women of Color to step out of stereotypes is too guilt-provoking, for it threatens the complacency of those women who view oppression only in terms of sex" (1992: 50).

The task that faces Third-World feminists is thus not simply that of 'animating' the oppressed women of their cultures, but of making the automatized and animated condition of their own voices the conscious point of departure of their own intervention. ... [I]t also means that they speak with the awareness of 'cross-cultural' speech as a limit, and that their very own use of the victimhood of women and Third World cultures is both symptomatic of and inevitable complicitous with the First world. (Chow 1992: 112)

These complex and critical models, which themselves do not use the terms distanciation or "hermeneutics of suspicion" provide insights into the way that philosophical approaches to studying and theorizing religion could be modified from their traditional ways of operation. This is not to say that rationality itself as employed by philosophy of religion and phenomenology is fatally flawed, but that there is a need to acknowledge that reason has had a checkered history and that many present models, though assumed to be authoritative, are of recent development. These models have all been construc-ted, and their approaches would be better appreciated as being of an interpre-tative, not absolute nature. An interactive self-reflective mode of knowing still maintains demanding criteria of evaluation. The model that I have proposed is aware of the hubris of modernism, but it is not in favor of any relativism or of the complete undecidability of knowledge that is evident in certain forms of postmodernism. I would allow that, from a hermeneutical phenomenological perspective, knowing can provide a secure, though neither infinite nor universal ground for ethical and responsible knowledge.[49] Using this model, philosophy within religious studies could help people to understand their own inevitable implications and compromises. It could also illuminate how their social and belief structures, their institutions and its disciplines came to be framed with certain presuppositions in the first place. Unless philosophy in religion can encourage reflection on these issues, it will simply reflect both the implicit and explicit ideologies of the day, rather than questioning their pro-venance, exclusions and injustices.

Bibliography

Afzal-Khan, Fawzia/Seshadri-Crooks, Kalpana, eds. (2000), *The Pre-Occupation of Postcolonial Studies*. Durham, N.C.: Duke University Press.

Allen, Douglas (1987), "Phenomenology of Religion," in: *Encyclopedia of Religion*, ed. by M. Eliade. New York: Macmillan.

Amin, Samir (1989), *Eurocentrism*. Translated by R. Moore. New York: Monthly Review Press.

---

49   See Ricoeur 1992.

Anderson, Pamela (1997), *A Feminist Philosophy of Religion: The Rationality and Myths of Religious Belief.* Oxford: Blackwell.

Appiah, Kwame Anthony (1991), "Is the Post- in Postmodernism the Post- in Postcolonial?," in: *Critical Inquiry* 17: 336–57.

Asad, Talal/Dixon, J. (1984), "Translating Europe's Others," in: *Europe and Its Others.* Vol. 1, ed. by F. Barker et al. Colchester: Essex University Press.

Assiter, Alison (1996), *Enlightened Women: Modernist Feminism in a Postmodern Age.* London: Routledge.

Best, Steven/Kellner, Douglas (1997), *The Postmodern Turn.* New York: Guilford Press.

Bleeker, Claas Jouco (1963), *The Sacred Bridge: Researches into the Nature and Structure of Religion.* Leiden: Brill.

Cady, Linell Elizabeth/Brown, Delwin (2002), *Religious Studies, Theology and the University: Conflicting Maps, Changing Terrain.* Albany, N.Y.: State University of New York Press.

Capps, Walter H. (1995), *Religious Studies: The Making of a Discipline.* Minneapolis, Minn.: Fortress Press.

Chakravarti, Uma (1989), "Whatever Happened to the Vedic Dasi? Orientalism, Nationalism and a Script from the Past," in: *Recasting Women: Essays in Colonial History,* ed. by Kumkum Sangari/Sudesh Vaid. New Delhi: Kali for Women: 27–87.

Chidester, David (2000), "Colonialism," in: *Guide to the Study of Religion,* ed. by W. Braun/R.T. McCutcheon. New York: Cassell.

Chow, Rey (1992), "Postmodern Automatons," in: *Feminists Theorize the Political,* ed. by Judith Butler/Joan Scott. New York: Routledge.

Collins, James Daniel (1967), *The Emergence of Philosophy of Religion.* New Haven, Conn.: Yale University Press.

Dallmayr, Fred R. (1996), *Beyond Orientalism: Essays on Cross-Cultural Encounter.* Albany, N.Y.: State University of New York Press.

Das, Veena (1986), "Gender Studies, Cross-cultural Comparison and the Colonial Organization of Knowledge," in: *Berkshire Review* 21: 58–76.

Davies, Brian (1993), *An Introduction to the Philosophy of Religion.* Oxford: Oxford University Press.

Davis, Charles (1984), "Wherein There Is No Ecstasy," in: *Studies in Religion/Sciences Religieuses* 13 (4): 393–400.

Dilthey, Wilhelm (1976), "The Development of Hermeneutics," in: *Selected Writings,* ed. by H.P. Rickman. Cambridge: Cambridge University Press.

Dube, Musa (2002), "Postcoloniality, Feminist Spaces, and Religion," in: *Postcolonialism, Feminism and Religious Discourse,* ed. by Laura E. Donaldson/Kwok Pui-Lan. New York: Routledge: 100–20.

Eagleton, Terry (1996), *The Illusions of Postmodernism.* Oxford: Blackwell.

Elam, Diane (1994), *Feminism and Deconstruction: Ms. en abyme.* London: Routledge.

Eliade, Mircea (1959), "Methodological Remarks on the Study of Religious Symbolism," in: *The History of Religions: Essays in Methodology,* ed. by J.M. Kitagawa. Chicago: University of Chicago Press.

—— (1969), *The Quest; History and Meaning in Religion.* Chicago: University of Chicago Press.

—— (1987), *The Encyclopedia of Religion.* New York: Macmillan.

Ermarth, Michael (1978), *Wilhelm Dilthey: The Critique of Historical Reason*. Chicago: University of Chicago Press.

Ferré, Frederick (1967), *Basic Modern Philosophy of Religion*. New York: Charles Scribner's Sons.

Fiorenza, Francis Schüssler (1993), "Theology in the University," in: *Bulletin: The Council of Societies for the Study of Religion* 22 (2): 34–39.

— (1994), "A Response to Donald Wiebe," in: *Bulletin: The Council of Societies for the Study of Religion* 23 (1): 6–10.

Frankenberry, Nancy (1998), "Philosophy of Religion in Different Voices," in: *Philosophy in a Feminist Voice: Critiques and Reconstructions*, ed. by J.A. Kourany. Princeton, N.J.: Princeton University Press.

Gadamer, Hans-Georg (1994), *Truth and Method*. Translated by Joel Weinsheimer/ Donald G. Marshall. Second rev. ed. New York: Continuum.

— (2001), *Gadamer in Conversation: Reflections and Commentary*, ed. and translated by Richard E. Palmer. New Haven, Conn.: Yale University Press.

Gandhi, Leela (1998), *Postcolonial Theory: A Critical Introduction*. New York: Columbia University Press.

Geertz, A.W. (1994), "On Reciprocity and Mutual Reflection in the Study of Native American Religions," in: *Religion* 24: 1–22.

Gellner, Ernest (1992), *Postmodernism, Reason and Religion*. London: Routledge.

Grondin, Jean (1994), *Introduction to Philosophical Hermeneutics*. Translated by J. Weinsheimer. Yale Studies in Hermeneutics. New Haven: Yale University Press.

Habermas, Jürgen (1977), "A Review of Gadamer's *Truth and Method*," in: *Understanding and Social Inquiry*, ed. by F. Dallmayr/T. McCarthy. Notre Dame, Ind.: University of Notre Dame Press.

— (1978), *Knowledge and Human Interests*. Translated by J.J. Shapiro. London: Heinemann.

Halbfass, Wilhelm (1996), *India and Europe: An Essay in Understanding*. Albany, N.Y.: State University of New York Press.

Hekman, Susan J. (1990), *Gender and Knowledge: Elements of a Postmodern Feminism*. Longman Series in Feminist Theory. Boston, Mass.: Northeastern University Press.

Hick, John (1983), *Philosophy of Religion*. Third ed. Englewood Cliffs, N.J.: Prentice-Hall.

Hultkrantz, Åke (1970), "The Phenomenology of Religion: Aims and Methods," in: *Temenos: Studies in Comparative Religion* 6: 68–88.

James, Georges A. (1985), "Phenomenology and the Study of Religion: The Archaeology of an Approach," in: *Journal of Religion* 65: 311–35.

Jameson, Fredric (1991), *Postmodernism, or, the Cultural Logic of Late Capitalism*, Post-contemporary Interventions. Durham, N.C.: Duke University Press.

Jantzen, Grace (1999), *Becoming Divine: Towards a Feminist Philosophy of Religion*. Bloomington, Ind.: Indiana University Press.

Joy, Morny (1995), "What if Truth Were a Woman?," in: *Gender, Genre and Religion: Feminist Reflections*, ed. by M. Joy/E.K. Neumaier-Dargyay. Waterloo, ON: Wilfrid Laurier University Press.

— (2000), "Beyond a God's-Eye View: Alternative Perspectives in the Study of Religion," in: *Perspectives on Method and Theory in the Study of Religion*, ed. by A.W. Geertz/R.T. McCutcheon. Leiden: Brill.

Juschka, Darlene M. (2001), *Feminism and Religion: A Reader*. New York: Continuum.

Kearney, Richard (1986), "Paul Ricoeur," in: *Modern Movements in European Philosophy*. Manchester: Manchester University Press.

Kessler, Gary E. (1999), *Philosophy of Religion: Toward a Global Perspective*. Belmont, Calif.: Wadsworth.

King, Richard (1999), *Orientalism and Religion: Post-colonial Theory, India and the Mystic East*. New York: Routledge.

Kippenberg, Hans (2002), *Discovering Religious History in the Modern Age*. Princeton, N.J.: Princeton University Press.

Kitagawa, Joseph Mitsuo/Eliade, Mircea (1985), *The History of Religions: Retrospect and Prospect: A Collection of Original Essays by Mircea Eliade*. New York/London: Macmillan/Collier Macmillan.

Klemm, David E. (1986), *Hermeneutical Inquiry*. Vol. 1. AAR Studies in Religion 44. Atlanta, Ga.: Scholars Press.

Leeuw, Geradus van der (1963), *Religion in Essence and Manifestation*. 2 vols. New York: Harper & Row.

Lloyd, Genevieve (1993). *The Man of Reason: "Male" and "Female" in Western Philosophy*. Minneapolis, Minn.: University of Minnesota Press.

Long, Eugene Thomas (2000), *Twentieth-Century: Western Philosophy of Religion*. Dordrecht: Kluwer.

Lyotard, Jean François/Bennington, Geoffrey/Massumi, Brian (1984), *The Postmodern Condition: A Report on Knowledge*. Theory and History of Literature 10. Minneapolis, Minn.: University of Minnesota.

Makkreel, Rudolf (1975), *Dilthey: Philosopher of the Human* Sciences. Princeton, N.J.: Princeton University Press.

Marwick, Arthur (2001), "All Quiet on the Postmodern Front," in: *Times Literary Supplement*, February, 23, 2001: 13–14.

McCutcheon, Russell, ed. (1999), *The Insider/Outsider Problem in the Study of Religion: A Reader*. London: Cassell.

Mohanty, Chandra Talpade (1991), "Under Western Eyes," in: *Third World Women and the Politics of Feminism*, ed. by Chandra Talpade Mohanty/Ann Russo/Lourdes Torres. Bloomington, Ind.: Indiana University Press.

Palmer, Richard (1969), *Hermeneutics*. Evanston, Ill.: Northwestern University Press.

Penner, Hans (1989), *Impasse and Resolution: A Critique of the Study of Religion*. New York: Peter Lang.

Preus, James S. (1987), *Explaining Religion: Criticism and Theory from Bodin to Freud*. New Haven, Conn.: Yale University Press.

Rajan, Rajeswari Sunder (1993), *Real and Imagined Women: Gender, Culture and Post-colonization*. New York: Routledge.

Reagan, Charles E. (1996), *Paul Ricoeur: His Life and His Work*. Chicago: University of Chicago Press.

Rescher, Nicholas (2000), *Process Philosophy: A Survey of Basic Issues*. Pittsburgh, Pa.: University of Pittsburg Press.

Ricoeur, Paul (1967), *Husserl: An Analysis of His Phenomenology*. Translated by E.G. Ballard/L.E. Embree. Evanston, Ill.: Northwestern University Press.

— (1970), *Freud and Philosophy: An Essay on Interpretation*. Translated by D. Savage. Terry Lectures. New Haven, Conn.: Yale University Press.

—— (1973), "Ethics and Culture: Habermas and Gadamer in Dialogue," in: *Philosophy Today* 17 (2): 153–65.

—— (1981), *Hermeneutics and the Human Sciences*. Translated by J.B. Thompson. Cambridge: Cambridge University Press.

—— (1983), *Time and Narrative*. Vol. 1. Chicago: University of Chicago Press.

—— (1983–88), *Time and Narrative*. Translated by K. Blamey/D. Pellauer. 3 vols. Chicago: University of Chicago Press.

—— (1986), *Lectures on Ideology and Utopia*, ed. by George H. Taylor. Chicago: University of Chicago Press.

—— (1992), *Oneself as Another*. Translated by Kathleen Blamey. Chicago: University of Chicago Press.

Rosenau, Pauline Marie (1992), *Post-Modernism and the Social Sciences: Insights, Inroads, and Intrusions*. Princeton, N.J.: Princeton University Press.

Ryba, Thomas (1991), *The Essence of Phenomenology and Its Meaning for the Scientific Study of Religion*. Toronto Studies in Religion 7. New York: Peter Lang.

Said, Edward W. (1993), *Orientalism*. New York: Knopf.

Sarup, Madan (1993), *An Introductory Guide to Post-Structuralism and Postmodernism*. Athens, Ga.: University of Georgia Press.

Smart, Ninian/Srinivasa Murthy, B., eds. (1996), *East-West Encounters in Philosophy and Religion*. Long Beach, Calif.: Long Beach Publications.

Stump, Elenore/Murray, Michael J., eds. (1999), *Philosophy of Religion: The Big Questions*. Malden, Mass.: Blackwell.

Tiele, C.P. (1979), *Elements of the Science of Religion*. Gifford Lectures 1896. London: William Black & Sons.

Tracy, David (1990), "On the Origins of Philosophy of Religion: The Need for a New Narrative for its Founding," in: *Myth and Philosophy*, ed. by Frank E. Reynolds/David Tracy. Albany, N.Y.: State University of New York Press: 11–36.

Waardenburg, Jean Jacques (1978), "Toward a New Style Phenomenological Research in Religion," in: *Reflections on the Study of Religion: Including an Essay on the Work of Gerardus van der Leeuw*. The Hague: Mouton.

Wach, Joachim (1961), *The Comparative Study of Religion*, ed. by J. Kitagawa. New York: Columbia University Press.

—— (1967), "Introduction: The Meaning and Task of the History of Religions," in: *The History of Religions: Essays on the Problem of Understanding*, ed. by J.M. Kitagawa. Chicago: University of Chicago Press.

Weeks, Kathi (1998), *Constituting Feminist Subjects*. Ithaca, N.Y.: Cornell University Press.

Werblowsky, R.J. Zwi (1975), "On Studying Comparative Religion: Some Naive Reflections of a Simple-minded Non-philosopher," in: *Religious Studies* 11: 145–56.

Wiebe, Donald (1984), "The Failure of Nerve in the Academic Study of Religion," in: *Studies in Religion* 13: 401–22.

—— (1991), "Phenomenology of Religion as Religio-Cultural Quest: Geradus van der Leeuw and the Subversion of the Scientific Study of Religion," in: *Religionswissenschaft und Kulturkritik: Die Zeit des Geradus van der Leeuw*, ed. by H.G. Kippenberg/B. Luchesi. Marburg: Diagonal-Verlag.

—— (1994), "On Theology and Religious Studies: A Response to Francis Schüssler Fiorenza," in: *Bulletin: the Council of Societies for the Study of Religion* 23 (1): 3–6.

—— (1999), *The Politics of Religious Studies*. New York: St. Martin's Press.

Xie, Shaobo (1997), "Rethinking the Problem of Postcolonialism," in: *New Literary History: Cultural Studies: China and the West*. 28 (1): 7–19.

Yeğenoğlu, Meyda (1998), *Colonial Fantasies: Towards a Feminist Reading of Orientalism*. Cambridge Cultural Social Studies. Cambridge: Cambridge University Press.

Young, Robert (1990), *White Mythologies: Writing History and the West*. New York: Routledge.

Meaning and Religion

On Semantics in the Study of Religion

by

JEPPE SINDING JENSEN

Preamble: Meaning between Essence and Construction

It is common knowledge, among both "lay and clergy," that religions are generally considered to be meaningful phenomena in human affairs. But just what that assertion means is a matter of much contention—it has, in fact, been so for quite a long time. The religious point of view, that of the practitioners of religious traditions, is that the traditions and teachings etc. indicate the ways of things—what they are and have always been. A religious worldview furnishes human habitats with forms and modes of knowledge, with ascriptions of meanings, so that we may "know the world." Speaking in very broad and loose terms, a religious worldview will maintain that the knowledge we have is "given"—it consists of true propositions about the cosmos—and, in turn, the cosmos is only such because it consists of true propositions. There are of course many other aspects of religion and religious practice than assertions about the values of propositions, but let that rest for the moment since the main argument here concerns the status and functions of religions as semantic entities, whether these are seen as sanctified "givens" or as human inventions. The entire question concerns religion as a "meaningful" phenomenon and whether the "meaningfulness" of the phenomenon rests on conventions or on truths. As such, the question of meaning is intimately related to the case for or against "religious language," a problem which has been prominent in certain parts of the world and in their traditions' struggles with the processes of modernization.[1] In that process sanctified "givens" lose their "meaning;" that is, their reference is questioned and the remainder becomes an object of historical-critical commentaries. Certainly, positivists and logical empiricists could point to "religious language"

---

1   In this context "modern" refers to the loss of credibility of religious/transcendent/ metaphysic discourse and the loss of authority of its referents—so that revelations become "old books." "Modernization" is a common term for this process (in many ways akin to "secularization").

as being meaningless because it has no true and verifiable referent(s) in the systems of physicalist or naturalist conceptions of meaning, but others point to the possibilities of "religious language" as speaking about other matters which are (perhaps) more existentially true than the "truths" purveyed by the natural sciences. So, there could (perhaps) be more than one kind of truth. If religious language about god was somehow disqualified by lack of reference (i.e. "non-cognitive" in philosophical vernacular), then a possible candidate for reference could be the "human condition," and religious language could then be the expression of existential concerns.[2]

However, the present exposition of semantics in religion(s) is not primarily concerned with "religious language" and the ontological or epistemological possibilities of "god-talk" or "deep meanings" about human existence. Here, the object of concern is the investigation of what it entails to view religions as socio-cultural facts and thus as semantic phenomena. Socio-cultural facts are semantic because of the simple and compelling reason that there would be no human social or cultural "worlds" without communication, without symbolic and linguistic mediations—the products of our "semiosis"—our "sign-making." And all our historical knowledge points to religious traditions being the warrants of symbolic and conceptual stability in social systems—as well as being legitimators of schisms, violence and revolutions, but then that normally means re-instating a conceived "original" conceptual and symbolic state of affairs... This last aspect also discloses the fact that even the most stable and sanctified "givens" are the objects of human manipulation—even a death penalty for changing the traditional materials of myth does not "work" (van Baaren 1972: 200). The histories of religious traditions also present us with seemingly endless possibilities of religious innovations in schisms, sects, heresies and other modes of re-interpretation. The semantics of religious systems are as flexible and multi-facetted as are all other forms of semantics. The question seems to be whether there really is any such specific entity as "religious language" and/or whether the semantics of religious systems are just "plain" semantics of an order similar to other specialized terminological systems, those of, say, politics, sports or economics. When speaking of such more or less ideological systems as politics, sports and economics it is easy to see

---

2   These debates have been around for quite some time and they shall not be restated here, but see Frankenberry 1999 for interesting remarks on the "two level theories of truth." The contents of a majority of text-books on "philosophy of religion" seem to indicate that one major problem in that field is whether it is "rational to talk about god"—a typical legacy of analytic philosophy. I would say that it can be, but that does not "prove" anything concerning god's separate ontological status, but only that as a feature of our universe it is as rational to talk about god as about any other metaphysical entity, say "art." From a completely different angle it has been pointed out that religious representations have a high degree of "naturalness" (Boyer 2000).

"human hands at work" and the same applies to religions: that they are local knowledges and technologies concerning the many aspects of human social life, including the "invisible" worlds of traditional cosmologies. But such functional analogies are only possible because religious systems do "say" things, because they are expressive and communicative (they are also other "things" but these will be the topics of other contributions to the debate). Religion is "talk" but it is not idle talk, it is pragmatic and performative, in various degrees and shades, but nevertheless active in the sense that humans can employ the vocabularies and classifications of religious traditions as repertoires of rules and meanings as relevant to their own descriptions of their actions (including thought). As such, religions are ontologically no different from other socio-cultural systems of representations—the crucial difference lies in their purported reference to "otherworldly" agents but as long as we are concerned with religions in a semantic perspective (using texts and statements in whatever medium) that distinction makes no difference because a "semantic definition of religion remains at that same level of meanings represented by the texts and their related symbolic universes, without seeking validation or reference in theories about "something else," be it society, the psyche or the sacred" (Jensen 1999: 409). Why that is so will be a major underlying topic in the following presentation and discussion. It is also noteworthy that most works on theories of religion do not contain the word "meaning" in their lists of contents or subject indexes— and it could hardly be because they simply disregard the "meaning"-aspects of religion.[3]

1. What Is "Meaning" — the Scope of Semantics

"Meaning" is one of the most tricky words in the English language—a multi-referential one—which would have meant less if it were not such a central term. It is quite apt here (in case the reader not fully recalls or has it at hand) to quote a standard work of authority, *The Oxford Thesaurus*:

> meaning n. 1 sense, import, content, signification, denotation, message, substance, gist: *The meaning of the word 'lucid' is clear.* 2 purport, implication, drift, spirit, connotation, significance, intention: *You understand my meaning, so I need not explain.* 3 interpretation, explanation: *What is the meaning of my dream about being attacked by my philodendron?* (1997: 279).

---

3   Two examples are *Critical Terms for Religious Studies* (Taylor, ed. 1998) and *Guide to the Study of Religion* (Braun/McCutcheon, eds. 2000). The latter contains a contribution by Hans H. Penner, which relates to the issues—but it is not made explicit, nor does "meaning" appear in the index.

Although nouns, these "synonyms" are obviously members of quite different classes of terms, but most are concerned with actions (the list of synonyms of the verb to "mean" is much more extensive, ibid.) of either "intending" something, "pointing" to something, "expressing" something or of something "having importance" or "purpose." And it should come as no surprise then that the controversies over "meanings" are often traceable to a lack of definitional precision.[4] Consequently as meaning may have so many different meanings (in 1923 Ogden and Richards listed 22 definitions) I shall refer—henceforth—to "semantic content": that which is commonly meant by *word meanings*. Word meanings are concepts (most likely) and like other concepts they have two sides: *intensions* as contents in relations to other concepts and extensions as *referents*, that which they are about. These distinctions should, however, be treated with caution and only used as a rough guide as to what they "are about."[5] This is so because we cannot divide the world into one realm of things and another containing the words about the things, although that is what common-sense (a Cartesian legacy in this case) seems to suggest: Things are in the world and meanings are "in the head"—but that is not how it is anymore. There have been some momentous developments in the study and understanding of meaning, and much of that development was set in motion by the Czech priest Bernhard Bolzano (d. 1848) who may well be said to be the founder of the modern semantic tradition, as he was: "the first to see that the proper prolegomena to any future metaphysics was a study not of transcendental considerations but of what we say and its laws and that consequently the *prima philosophia* was not metaphysics or ontology but semantics." (Coffa

---

4   Simon Blackburn's *Oxford Dictionary of Philosophy* (1994) summarizes the problem like this: "meaning [bold in original] Whatever it is that makes what would otherwise be mere sounds and inscriptions into instruments of communication and understanding. The philosophical problem is to demystify this power, and to relate it to what we know of ourselves and the world. Contributions to this study include the theory of speech acts, and the investigation of communication and the relationship between words and ideas, and words and the world. For particular problems *see* content, ideas, indeterminacy of translation, inscrutability of reference, language, predication, reference, rule following, semantics, translation, and the topics referred to under headings associated with logic. The loss of confidence in determinate meaning ('every decoding is another encoding') is an element common both to postmodernist uncertainties in the theory of criticism, and to the analytic tradition that follows writers such as Quine" (235–36). Another possibility is to treat meaning as a metaphysical "primitive" and underived notion, as that which involves translatability and which founds human intentionality.

5   For instance: Intensions may serve as referents, because concepts cannot avoid also referring to other concepts, and referents can be the intensions of other intensions, which often happens in metaphors: e.g. a "white dove" is not just a bird but a symbol of peace.

1991: 23). And that suggests that a brief history of meaning might put certain matters in perspective.

1.1. A Very Brief "History of Meaning"

In philosophy most things begin with Plato and Aristotle and so it may here.[6] On the early history of "meaning" Dan Stiver says:

> The philosophical paradigm rooted in Greek philosophy that has predominated in philosophical thought until modern times has three components. First, meaning lies in individual words. Second, the meaning of words is primarily literal or univocal, which implies that figurative language must be translated into literal language in order to be understood. Last, language is instrumental for thought. The first point implies a kind of verbal atomism, often promoting a neglect of the wider context of words and their use. The second promotes the relegation of figurative language for the most part to secondary status, significant at best not for cognitive purposes bur for persuasive (rhetoric) or aesthetic (poetic) purposes. A corollary of Aristotle's approach thus was that the meaning of figurative language can be grasped only if it can be transposed or reduced to literal language … The third point recognizes the priority of thought. The idea was that thinking is in some ways a separate process from speaking, as evidenced by the common experience of seeking for the right word to express a thought. The effect also was to make language, philosophically speaking, secondary and less significant. (Stiver 1996: 11)

For centuries, the dominant theories of meaning were "correspondence theories"—based on the idea that meanings are "made" by correspondence between word and thing or concept. In religions, "sacred meanings" are those which corresponded to revelation and to gods' intentions. But such theories also center on the transparency of language, of words and their meaning in search for the corresponding referents, which could be (as in Platonism) the "eternal" forms to be "seen" more than spoken about. Language was an instrument of thought, and the ideals, from Antiquity to Descartes (and on…) were clarity and certainty. These would not, of course, always be the most prominent features of religious statements and thus Thomas Aquinas (d. 1274) held that religious language was analogical and purveyed not literal but a different kind of truth; as in the example of Jerusalem, which is literally a town on earth, allegorically the Christian church, topologically (i.e. ethically and morally) the soul and anagogically (i.e. eschatologically) the future heavenly city of God.

---

6   This is but a *very* brief overview—the "history of meaning" is also contained (and to some extent "hidden") in the general histories of semantics in philosophy and linguistics, of hermeneutics, semiotics etc.

1.2. Positivisms, Empiricism and Verificationist
Theories of Meaning

The predilection for the precise and empirical tracing of the meanings of words
was one of the hallmarks of historical philology: the meanings of expressions
were to be found in their genealogies and in their origins and such was also
commonly the practice of explaining ancient myths. Numerous are the exercises trying to explain what Greek gods "really" were in the beginning.[7] This
etymological approach culminated with Friedrich Max Müller and the "school"
of comparative and nature mythology. It was also largely driven by the discoveries in comparative Indo-European linguistics and thus paved the way for
both comparative and historical studies in which meanings are contextually
determined. To the philologians, theologians, and historians of religions in the
nineteenth century, "origins" were the most cherished objects of reconstructive
study, but the historicist paradigm also indicated that things were to be
understood in their historical context (in so far as these could be reconstructed).
The romanticist perspectives presented, simultaneously, the relations between
language, linguistic meaning and culture as larger entities (communities of
interpretation) and such a view laid a foundation for the much later ideas of
cultures as "systems of symbols."

A very different and strictly empiricist view of linguistic meaning was
introduced in the wake of positivism. The general impetus was to view and
model natural language (i.e. the form of language that ordinary humans speak)
along the lines of formal logic in philosophy and mathematics. This rigorously
positivist attitude to "meaning" reached its apogee in the theories of the logical
empiricists of the "Vienna Circle"—for instance Rudolf Carnap for whom
mathematical logic represented the grammar of the "ideal" language. Semantics analysis consisted in linking symbols with sense impressions and directly
observable empirical matter in the world. Judged from such a view, "natural
language" inevitably founders—and those parts concerned with moral, political and religious issues were considered "meaningless." Or, as it may also be
termed: "non-cognitive"—that is, about "nothing" (scientifically) real. The
doyen of empiricism, A.J. Ayer, can thus assert—on "religion as non-sense"—
what the difference is between saying that one sees "a yellow patch" or that one
sees "God." For, whereas the first concerns:

> a genuine synthetic proposition which could be empirically verified, the sentence
> „There exists a transcendent god" has, as we have seen, no literal significance. We
> conclude therefore, that the argument from religious experience is altogether
> fallacious.... The theist, like the moralist, may believe that his experiences are cognitive
> experiences, but unless he can formulate his „knowledge" in propositions that are

---

7   See e.g. the now "classic" works: *The Greeks and Their Gods* by W.K.C. Guthrie; *A
     Handbook of Greek Mythology* by H.J. Rose.

empirically verifiable, we may be sure that he is deceiving himself. It follows that those philosophers who fill their books with assertions that they intuitively „know" this or that moral or religious „truth" are merely providing material for the psycho-analyst. For no act of intuition can be said to reveal a truth about any matter of fact unless it issues in verifiable propositions. And all such propositions are to be incorporated in the system of empirical propositions which constitutes science. (1952: 119–20)

So much for "religious meaning."[8] The rather prolix and frustrated efforts of the positivists at formulating theories about possible criteria of meaningfulness for the natural languages in terms of verification of propositions and sentences slowly filtered out in the 1950s. But in the general (mostly Western) public the "scientistic" attitude persists, not least in regard to religion, which is often and in *toto* considered meaningless because of its lack of "verifiable reference."[9]

To positivists and empiricists, religious or other symbolic meaning belongs (if anywhere at all) "in the head": it is a psychological phenomenon pertaining to the realm of the subjective, a "something" as individual and private as are other entities of the world of (scientifically ungrounded) opinion and taste. It is true that meanings are not "things found glistening on the beach"[10] and this non-"thingyness" seem to prompt uneasiness in some of a more empirical persuasion. Even more so because meanings are but human ascriptions—they are not essences in objects, for meanings are *not in things*—meanings are produced or constructed. It is a human propensity and a decisive feature of our intentionality to endow meanings to whatever "there is" and to what we can imagine, but that does not make the study of meaning any less demanding. But empiricists are still uneasy about this and, for instance, Frits Staal has lamented the lack of direct empirical reference and verification for "meaning":

Although every zoologist knows that an elephant does not have meaning, students of the humanities and social sciences attach meaning to many expressions and mani-

---

8   Ayer does leave some space for the study of these matters, although not in philosophy: "one should avoid saying that philosophy is concerned with the meaning of symbols, because the ambiguity of 'meaning' leads the undiscerning critic to judge the result of a philosophical enquiry by a criterion which is not applicable to it, but only to an empirical enquiry concerning the psychological effect which the occurrence of certain symbols has on a certain group of people. Such empirical enquiries are, indeed an important element in sociology and in the scientific study of a language; but they are quite distinct from the logical enquiries which constitute philosophy" (1952: 69).

9   Edmund Leach's (now almost classic) remarks on this problem deserve mention: "Religious statements certainly have meaning, but it is a meaning which refers to a metaphysical reality, whereas ordinary logical statements have a meaning which refers to physical reality. The non-logicality of religious statements is itself 'part of the code,' it is an index of what such statements are about, it tells us that we are concerned with metaphysical rather than physical reality, with belief rather than knowledge" (1976: 70).

10   Clifford Geertz 1995: 62.

festations of humanity as if they were linguistic expressions ... Underlying such ideas is the assumption that man must make sense. To an unbiased observer, much of that sense seems arbitrarily assigned, evanescent, or due to chance. The available evidence suggests that man can make as much sense as he likes, but does not make intrinsic sense. (1989: 454)

Staal's problem is a very common one when meaning is conceived in the light of a particularistic and referential semantics: for where is meaning if not in the things themselves—as "intrinsic"? Where is the meaning of an elephant if not in the elephant? What is meaning if not a property of the object itself? Logically then, if the "foundation" of meaning is not in the empirically verifiable world of objects, it must be in the minds of actors and observers and so the only decent solution is to talk about meanings as "meanings for someone" inside their skulls. Thus for the frustrated "semantic empiricists" meanings become psychological entities. Furthermore, if and when it turns out that actors in rituals have no interpretative knowledge of the languages, spells and mantras employed—then there seems to be no meaning "at all." However, as it will be argued below, meaning and meaningfulness are not psychological entities or qualities, and actors' or participants' individual and conscious interpretations, exegeses or "points of view" do not furnish the criteria on which to judge meaningfulness as a property of human action. Meaning is not intrinsic in the objective world nor simply a phenomenon in the subjective world—it is "somewhere in between" and it is a third party which mediates between the two. For, as proponents of the "modern turn" would say: for a human to "inhabit" the world amounts to more than merely being physically present, it is also a consequence of our intentional stance—because we are always "making meaning" to ourselves and others and the primary medium for that activity is language. Thus, to inhabit a world also means to inhabit a language and vice versa.

2. The Modern "Turns"

The "modern" turn towards a conception of meaning as a public and inter-subjective phenomenon gained momentum in the first half of the twentieth century when the classical views of meaning as either intrinsic and universal properties or as mental and subjective contents were given up. This development corresponds with the above mentioned shifts of "first philosophy" from metaphysics to epistemology and Bolzano's realization that the next "prima philosophia" must be a philosophy of language and meaning. In retrospect, this movement towards the philosophy of language has been characterized as the "semiotic" turn in philosophy—later also as the "linguistic turn" by Richard Rorty. Responsible for this profound change were a number of key figures: Gottlob Frege (d. 1925) whose work on the distinction between sense and reference was ground-breaking.[11] Charles Sanders Peirce (d. 1914) who introduced the notion of "semiosis" as a designation for the human propensity for sign-making. Also important was the tradition in British analytic philosophy of the study of "ordinary language"—associated with names such as Bertrand Russell, Ludwig Wittgenstein, G.E. Moore and W.V.O. Quine. All of them combined interests in mathematics, science, logic and language—as it actually functions in human life. Their interest in religion, by contrast, was generally quite negative (in the vein of Ayer) so it is somewhat ironical that we now can see how they laid some of the foundations for much more adequate ways of understanding religious semantics and languages.

As important as the semiotic turn on language was the "social turn" towards conventions. When Durkheim and Mauss published their small book on *Primitive Classification* in 1903 no one could have foreseen the importance of their views: That classifications, and thereby also ideas, "senses," and meanings, were of a social nature and that meaning is thus also a species of "conventions." The main feature of conventions is that they are shared, for they need not be "epistemically" true to be effective in the world of collective representations. They are constructed by humans and in some sense "arbitrary." To which extent the ideas of Durkheim and Mauss were known by the linguist Ferdinand de Saussure is uncertain. However, his thoughts on language accord well with the theories of the two former because he not only sees language as a system but also as pertaining to the genus "social fact." Among his major theoretical achievements is the distinction between the two sides of a linguistic expression: between the "signifier" ("signifiant") and the "signified" ("signifié") and the realization that the relation between them is for the most part completely arbitrary. Only the contingencies of linguistic history explains why "arbre" in French is "Baum" in German etc. Saussure was also of the opinion that the theory of the systemic nature of language could be applied to other cultural phenomena as in the oft cited passage on a future "semiology," "which studies the role of signs as part of social life ... It would investigate the nature of signs and the laws governing them" (1993: 15).[12] Saussure was a linguist with

---

11   Very briefly: Frege "discovered" that the sense ("Sinn") of an expression is not determined by its reference ("Bedeutung"). Two expressions—in his example "The morning Star" and "The evening Star"—have the same reference (the planet Venus). Expressions may (re-)present references in multiple ways and these ways are then the sense(s) of the expressions which determine our thoughts about the matter, whereas the reference determines the truth-issue of the sentence. Important is also Frege's idea that "sense" is public. Most semantic theorizing has been indebted to his ideas, but not all philosophers do (of course) agree on this issue.

12   Further theorizing on this issue is presented and assessed in Paul Thibault's (1997) comprehensive account of Saussure's revolutionary contribution to the history of linguistics. See also Harris 2003.

a (primarily) structuralist interest in signs and sign-systems and he was less
concerned with the external or pragmatic aspects of actual language-use and of
linguistic change and history. However, it is not difficult to "supply" these
aspects to Saussure's thoughts, for they do not in any way preclude such "ex-
ternalizations"—they simply were not his primary concern, wherefore it is
"unjust" to charge Saussure of not supplying those aspects and therefore, as
some have done, consider his theory "static" or "abstract." Furthermore, it is an
epistemological premise that we have recourse to such systems in order to
perceive, understand and explain the flux of the world—we would be hard
pressed to explain a football game if we had no idea of the rules behind it.
Thus, Saussure's main accomplishment was to point to the systemic and rule-
governed aspects of language and thus indirectly also of other human socio-
cultural behavior as well as to the idea that any action (including speech and
thought) is always interpreted on the background of some sort of system of
which the action can be said to be an articulation. This does not imply that rules
and systems are causal, it is rather that they are constitutive and regulative for
our conceptions of what counts as a meaningful action or description of something. Saussure's work was truly ground-breaking and later it became the
foundation of structuralism.

2.1.1. Semantics and the Social Construction of Reality

The idea that meaning is exhibited by and through "language-in-use" was
primarily set forth by two very different scholars: the anthropologist Bronislaw
Malinowski and the philosopher Ludwig Wittgenstein. It was an accepted view
that when humans wish to convey information there are certain conditions that
must be met in order for them to be able to "make sense." Philosophers had for
long been debating these matters and one of Wittgenstein's major contributions
was to delineate the grounds on which humans can convey meaning. In
Alberto Coffa's words on Wittgenstein's project:

> A basic assumption of his project was that meaningfulness and meaninglessness are
> not merely relative to specific language systems; there are, in fact, general conditions
> that a system of signs must satisfy in order to qualify as a language and therefore also
> general conditions that determine the failure of meaningfulness. Once meaning is
> available, we can redistribute it at will, "by convention"; but we cannot originate sense
> by convention, since no act of semantic convention is possible in the absence of re-
> sources to express sense. The point is, in effect, that there is an objective factual
> difference between a representational system and a mere jumble of symbols, that there
> are conditions to be discovered—rather than agreed upon—such that fulfilling them is
> necessary and sufficient for being an information-conveying device. The emergence of
> sense is not the result of an act of the will but the outcome of acting in conformity with
> predetermined conditions of meaningfulness. (1991: 316)

Wittgenstein is famous for coining the idea of "language-games" to cover the function and use of language as rule-governed and self-contained — like a game. But, if like games they are performed for their own sake then that may lead to strong relativist assumptions, and on religious language-games it could perhaps also be said that if they are worthwhile activities for the participants then that settles the issue of their value and perhaps even "truth." This is the case when truth becomes a function of utility in the pragmatist view that religious people are rational in accepting religious beliefs because it enables them to deal with their existential concerns.[13] "Meaning is use" is another slogan associated with Wittgenstein. It implies that a word has the meanings which are warranted by its use — thus a theory about the meaning of words becomes a theory about use; that which the proponents of more formal theories of meaning would conceive of a second pragmative level. But, for the "use theorist" actual language use is the only way to solve the questions of meaning. What you do with a word will tell us how you understand it.[14] According to Wittgenstein, a description of the use of a word is a description of the rules for its use: "I can use the word 'yellow'" is like "I know how to move the king in chess," he has stated (1974: 49). Obviously, then, the rules for the production of meaning are also rules for doing things with words and this view counters the idealist (Platonist) ideas that objects have intrinsic meaning "in themselves":

> A better account is that to possess a concept is to acknowledge certain cognitive moves as justified. Grasping concepts is acknowledging norms. By analogy to the slogan that meaning is use, one may say that *concepts are cognitive roles* ... to possess a concept is to acknowledge a pattern of epistemic norms. (Skorupski 1997: 48)

A recognition that language produces more than meanings and that words have a pragmatic force also occurred to Bronislaw Malinowski during his field-work among the Trobrianders and especially in connection with his detailed

---

13   As one source — best left unmentioned — triumphantly declares in its final page: "The debate of whether religious beliefs are rationally acceptable is over." Nancy Frankenberry, in a critical assessment of "neo-pragmatism," very pointedly remarks: "The ways in which a particular religion may be shown to function in the benign and salutary manner approved by its adherents helps to obscure the fact that it may also function to express and reinforce superstition, irrationality, fanaticism, sexism, infantilism, and eschatological abstentions from real moral and political tasks" (1999: 519). Also, on rationality in and "on religion" see Jensen/Martin, eds. 1997.

14   On this aspect of the management of the Wittgensteinian heritage Avramides notes: "In contrast to the formal theorists, the use theorists put central emphasis on speakers and what they do in their account of meaning. They are not content to let mention of speakers and their intentions be relegated to the level of pragmatics. The debate is over the core; use theorists see themselves as offering an account of semantics ... According to these philosophers one cannot abstract away from the imprecision of natural language, but must study language in its natural habitat, so to speak" (1999: 62).

analyses of magical rituals. In his ambition to "grasp the native's point of view" in "his world" he emphasized the importance of context for the understanding of utterances and because context is more often than not a real, practical communicative situation, it was logical to conceive of language use as a form of social practice.[15] The primary function of language is not the expression of thought but its role as an active force in life and a basic precondition for concerted human action. This also entails that humans produce meaning while performing socially and that meaning is imbued in social action. For, as he says about myth: it is "a reality lived," "a narrative resurrection of a primeval reality," "a hard-worked active force," and "a pragmatic charter of Primitive faith and moral wisdom." (1948: 101). On the basis of Malinowski's view we may conclude that social action is—somewhat tautologically—only social action because it involves meaning and because it does so, we are in a position to understand the situation, context, other actors' intentions etc.

The view that language is a "force" was launched systematically by J.L. Austin in his now famous work on "How to Do Things with Words," posthumously published in 1962. He was tired of the prolix philosophical debates concerning the problems of truth and reference of words, meanings and utterances. So, Austin investigated what it is that we do when we speak, in "speech acts"—in "performative utterances"—which have "illocutionary force" because we do something "in the saying." For instance, when we "promise," we do not simply say that we promise, but we also *make* a promise. Such utterances contrast both with common "locutionary" utterances concerned with ordinary meaning and reference as well as with "perlocutionary utterances" which are intended to produce certain effects or functions. The theory (later to be developed e.g. by John Searle) is quite interesting for the study of religion because it makes us realize how much (to which extent) religious languages are not simply locutionary (descriptive) statements about the state of the world, they are often far more involved in expressing, creating and acting. Propositions and utterances in religious languages are more often either "illocutionary" in that they state "I/we herewith do" such and such, e.g. praying is not just talking, it is also an act or they are "perlocutionary" in the

---

15 These considerations also led Malinowski to reconsider the issue of translation and in his ethnographic theory of language, the requirements of translation include "the native's" contextual and practical considerations. See e.g. Duranti 1997, Ch. 7 on "Speaking as social action" (214–18 on Malinowski). Cf. also his view of the social context as the locus of the "real meaning" of myth: "It is clear, then, that the myth conveys much more to the native than is contained in the mere story; that the story gives only the really relevant concrete local differences; that the real meaning, in fact the full account, is contained in the traditional foundations of social organization; and that this the native learns, not by listening to the fragmentary mythical stories, but by living within the social texture of his tribe" (Malinowski 1948: 115).

sense that something could be achieved by the saying of such and such, e.g. in sacrificial discourse. A very interesting aspect in relation to the study of religions is that Austin saw how the illocutionary purport of an utterance should not be evaluated in terms of truth, but in what he termed the "felicity" conditions concerning how well an utterance fills in with other sentences in a certain set of actions and conditions. This is easily recognized as highly important in the use of religious and ritual language: the right things have to be said in the right circumstances, they are "framed" in a particular way because participants have a metapragmatic awareness about the well-formedness of the situation—even when they may not be able to provide any explicit rationale.[16] In a certain sense Austin's work can be seen as a pre-cursor for the later development of discourse analysis in its insistence on the importance of contexts and on what he terms the "condition of convention." Thus, the meaning of an illocutionary utterance depends on it being said or performed in the appropriate setting, and this in turns requires the recognition and mastery of sociocultural conventions—not only by the speaker as author but also by the audience and its tacit expectations and knowledge.

Given the view of the importance of convention, the realization of how linguistic meaning is a co-determinate factor in human constructions of their worlds is the next step. Two names are prominent in that respect, Edward Sapir and Benjamin Whorf, who became famous (or notorious) for their "linguistic relativity thesis" concerning the socializing force of language on culture and thought, i.e. on the causality of language on "worldviews" (including concomitant metaphysics). The theory states briefly that the forms and ranges of "meaning" in words and word-patterns in a language determine the ways in which its inhabitants think; thus it is also a theory of "linguistic determinism."[17] Language is the primary instrument which allows us to make sense of the world(s), that is, to ascribe meaning to it (them). We should, however, not do so in a "humpty-dumpty" fashion because no "concerted action" would then be possible. On the contrary, meaning ascription must be conventional and religious discourse is the prime example of that. The "fragility" of religious discourse is also a fact—one need only contemplate the innumerous schisms, sects, and other fractionings of religions and religious groups. For, characteristically, a specific group rallies around a specific discourse—that goes for Trobrianders as well as for Arminians…

---

16 Impressive ethnographic examples of such complex semantic situations have been provided by Victor Turner in a range of publications on ritual actions and processes, e.g. 1969.

17 The relativist "language at work" hypothesis entails, as Sapir stated, that the "worlds in which different societies live are distinct worlds, not merely the same world with different labels attached" (in Duranti 1997: 60).

2.1.2. Symbolic Studies

When religious "worlds" are conceived as symbolic constructs, the view of meaning becomes one of symbolic production and, extending contemporary metaphor, of symbolic capital management. The idea of "symbolic worlds" was, if not originally then influentially set forth by Ernst Cassirer (d. 1945) in his general theory of culture drawing on a variety of inspirations from the German philosophical tradition, not least from Immanuel Kant but also from a tradition of *Lebensphilosophie* which "taught the superiority of immediate experience over reflection, emotion over reason, synthesis over analysis, past over present, and so on" (Strenski 1987: 31). This ideal is found and expressed as an emotional and an experiential unity in the wholeness and coherence of myth and mythical worldviews, which, for Cassirer, are not so much rational but rather emotional expressions of a unity of feeling.[18] The importance of this view, not considering so much the problems it introduces, is displayed in the stress it puts on the relevance of experience in the construction and maintenance of socio-cultural systems of meaning—where semantic theories often seem to downplay the importance of semantic "practice" (because they separate semantics and pragmatics). It should be quite obvious that meaning may be obliquely displayed in many symbolic forms connected to, say, ritual activity and that the question of semantics involves much more than the piecemeal deciphering of meanings and truth-values of explicit propositions. Thus, according to Cassirer's *Philosophy of Symbolic Forms* it is a basic characteristic of humans that they build worlds in and through symbols and in different registers such as science, philosophy, art, religion etc. These different modes of knowledge are distinct, they have their own "range" and their own intrinsic function which all together contribute to a polydimensional understanding of the world and a "unity of cultural consciousness." Sympathetic and comprehensive as this view may appear it would also seem to suggest the existence of a set of mutually exclusive discourses: the view that there are separate languages for the various domains and the registers in which they are expressed, and that, in the end, they would become incommensurable and untranslatable. But, Cassirer avoids a normative judgment as to their epistemological status

---

18   As Strenski notes on *Lebensphilosophie*: "This feeling of the unity of life connoted an especially sentimental attitude to mindlessness perhaps unknown outside the tradition of German romanticism" (1987: 31). Nevertheless, this attitude had remarkably important consequences for the ways in which many scholars of religion conceive of their subject and its place in the academy as well in human life in general—for this attitude accords well with the view that religion(s) may, in the modern world, complement science as being more existentially "true" or "relevant." No further references should be required on this ... the number of scholars having expressed such views (which trace back to these "philosophical" assumptions) are legio.

and the "unity of cultural consciousness" assures the construction of a mean-ingful (and thus intrinsically semantic) world in and as a totality.[19] Similar reflections were advanced by Suzanne K. Langer, who combined aspects of Wittgenstein's philosophy of language with Cassirer's theories of symbols in a synthesis she termed the "new key." This was a linguistic-semiotic turn in the interpretation of culture(s) where she introduces an important distinction between discursive and presentational forms, rather similar to Peirce's dis-tinction between the iconic and the symbolic. This distinction is quite interesting in relation to the importance of more imagistic modes of religious representations in spectacular rituals or experiential ordeals in initiations—in situations where the discursive and semantic elements play a minor role (Whitehouse 2000). However, even such actions and experiences which are not linguistic, or non-semantic, are (or may become) objects of descriptions, expla-nations, and interpretation.[20]

The theories concerning religions as symbolic "worlds" are well-known and widely accepted. Although they come in various guises they all depend upon the semantic aspects, that is, on the realization that the "worlds" must inevitably be construed as worlds of meaning—whether the emphasis be placed on construction, re-production, or functions (etc.). In fact, the idea of human "life-worlds" seems to be one area in the study of religion where there is some cumulative growth of knowledge, i.e. the results, ideas, and perspec-tives of earlier theorists are not overturned as much as they are accepted, employed, and elaborated upon. More recently, the theories of Peter L. Berger and Thomas Luckman have demonstrated tenacity as a productive perspective. It is also well-known that a related view was introduced by Clifford Geertz in his program for the analysis of religion as a "cultural system." In short, "the lifeworld perspective" of religion as a semantic phenomenon is forwarded by a range of theorists from Pierre Bourdieu to Jürgen Habermas. This perspective may thus be characterized as a kind of "normal paradigm" (e.g. Paden 1988). It should be noted, however, that most of these theorists are more interested in functional analysis rather than the systemic properties of the "worlds"—but that and similar aspects are the subject matter of structuralist investigations.

---

19 The *Philosophy of Symbolic Forms* is no light reading—the reception of Cassirer has been scant and skewed in the study of religion and it could deserve a correction. See Capps 1995: 210–15 for a very brief overview.

20 This line of thought was later taken up also by Nelson Goodman in his *Languages of Art: An Approach to a Theory of Symbols* from 1976 and in *Ways of Worldmaking* (1978) where he states: "We can have words without a world but no world without words or other symbols." Goodman also notes that all "making" really is "re-making" — "from worlds already on hand" and "the search for a universal or necessary beginning is best left to theology" (1978: 7). He (rightly) considers "the search for a first world thus to be as misguided as the search for a first moment of time" (ibid., n. 8).

2.2. Structuralism

Structuralism was and still is a very strong "paradigm" in the human sciences. In some fields it has become more or less relegated to the history of theory—but for the study of religion it must be said that the productivity of structuralist thought is so impressive that this approach to religious materials is not likely to be given up or discarded. In fact, as religious "worlds" so aptly lend themselves to structural analyses it seems likely that a continued refinement of structuralist theorizing may in fact take place within the study of religion. The history and characteristics of structuralism in the study of religion, and in the human sciences in general, need not be rehearsed here, as they are amply accounted for elsewhere (e.g. Lechte 1994; Jensen 2000 for further references). In this connection the most noteworthy feature of structuralism is its insistence on the importance of analyzing semantic matter as a feature of relations, and it is thus a decidedly holistic approach. It is also important to note the systematizing and formalist ambitions of much structuralist theory and practice. And although these ambitions have sometimes been met with a critique (sometimes justified) of leading to sterile, static and intellectualist constructions, it must also be said that probably the most rewarding results of the structuralist endeavor are demonstrations of the systemic character of products of the human mind, be they language, mythology, or religion in general. In this sense, structuralists have contributed much to the "scientific" turn in the study of religion. The more formalist structuralist approaches are found in semiotics, where the heritage from linguists such as Roman Jakobson and Louis Hjelmslev has been expanded, transformed and turned into very productive analytical tools by e.g. Umberto Eco, Algirdas J. Greimas, Yuri Lotman and others. Being a formalist trend in the study of meaning, they have attempted to institute a "science" of meaning—with schemata almost resembling "periodic tables" of semiotic objects, and they have attempted to demonstrate how the construction and organization of meaning is constrained by features of these very same systems.[21] One of the problematic aspects of structuralist and semiotic theory was the relation to hermeneutics. At the most general level, a major issue of contention is concerned with the ontological and epistemic status of systems of meaning and their use and involvement in human interpretive practice. To most structuralists and semioticians, the status of such systems of meaning would be that they are objective features of the world, that they are imminent, self-contained, and exist *as such* irrespective of individual subjects' use of them. This is understandably hard to accept for those holding a subjectivist and individualist view of meaning, interpretation, and understanding. In an almost

---

21   For a more comprehensive introduction to these scholars Lechte (1994) is an invaluable guide. See also Peregrin 2001 and Caws 1997.

caricatured sense, we can say that for hermeneuticists it is we who, as human individuals, make meaning and for structuralists and semioticians it is meaning, as an intersubjective phenomenon, which makes us human individuals. In order to create meaning, to understand others as well as ourselves, we need these symbolic systems—pure introspection, if not dead, is at least seriously challenged.[22]

That humans are always "situated interpretants" and that interpretations are always pragmatically motivated has been stressed by later "post-structuralist" critics. The consequences of that criticism have probably been somewhat overrated. For it comes as no surprise that meanings are not stable, that everything that makes sense is only so because of human intentional practice and that this is again motivated and informed by power and all other kinds of interests. Some of the more interesting aspects of "post"-theories is their insistence on the reception-perspectives and on the ways in which meaning is pragmatically constituted and employed. To the study of religion, this move from the study of "origins" and later "developments" has been turned towards perspectives on use and meaning as products of effective history. It is a move from the comforts of the view that origins and essences have causal power as traditions which create history to the much more unstable view that humans exploit their symbolic resources (including "tradition") in order to make meaning and understand themselves, not only existentially but also in order to sustain power, dominate and generally further their own interests (which are, however, also constrained by the resources...). An interesting aspect of many "use"-, "reading"- and "reception"-theories is their demonstration of how meaning is always created in relation to preexisting patterns—all cultures favor certain constructions of meaning and downplay others. Cultures are in that sense "semantic processors" which set some limits for what can be said and understood. Cultures and religions speak in different modalities and they furnish the "grids" along which items and events may become intelligible.[23] These views are (evidently) functionalist—but that does not make them either false or trivial. Furthermore these perspectives make it possible to analyze the "politics" and "economics" of meaning(s)—what people do with words and what words do to them. That kind of analytic activity has now become familiar under the label of "discourse analysis"—which appears

---

22 One of main proponents of the combination of structuralism and hermeneutics is Paul Ricoeur—see e.g. the instructive volume edited by John B. Thompson (Ricoeur 1981).

23 As cultures and religions are models of and for the world, they are discursive systems, regulative of a number of aspects of social production and organization of meaning: on the epistemic (what can be known, assumed, doubted etc.), on the alethic (what is true, necessary, possible), the axiological (on values, what is good/bad) and the deontic (what is mandatory, prohibited, permitted). One does not need much familiarity with any religion to see that this seems to be the case.

as a promising direction for the study of meaning in relation to religion
(Albinus 1997).[24]

3. Semantics Currently: Meanings "Without Reference"/ "Anti-verificationism"

The idea of meanings beings meanings without having clear and explicit references to things "in the world" may seem counter-intuitive—and, indeed, it
is. Our "intuitive" semantics and linguistics repeatedly "convince" us that we
when we are offered coffee, we should not expect tea. A note of whatever currency refers to a certain amount and not to others. The label on a product refers
to what is inside the package. "Mother" means mother and "Ladies" means
that "Gents" should look for facilities elsewhere. Our "intuitive" ontologies and
semantics perceive the world in that way—words are referential and "deictic":
the objects that the words point to are their meanings. So, "sugar" is sugar, and
it does not matter one bit if you translate it into "Sucre", "Zucker" or whatever
it is called in Arabic or Hopi… and in this view, the meaning of a statement
consists in its verification. This "picture" theory of meaning goes well with the
intuitive assumptions of an "experiential realism"—the view that there is a
"phenomenological bedrock driven by perception and physiology that provides an interpretative anchor for the words we use, and enables us to understand each other" (Edwards 1997: 256).[25] Thus, it is problematic (to say the
least) to make the move from an analysis of language to an analysis of
"reality"—not least because our analysis of "reality" must be made through
language. There is no way in which we can understand the world apart from
any mode of describing it. We may also say that "theoretical concepts" in the
sciences do not directly refer to things that scientists have observed, rather that
these concepts enable scientists to analyze, discuss and produce coherent
accounts which we as humans are able to understand. That requires, more
often than not, that the world (all things included) must be narrativized, and it

---

24   Discourse analysis is a truly cross-disciplinary field—but like so many others it has
     hardly been communicated in the study of religion. A perceptive introduction by a
     major scholar in the field is Fairclough (1992).

25   As Hans Penner says—on the question of "meaning" in religion—we are mostly told:
     "to look for a reference. Words refer to things—you name it: sensations, certain stimuli,
     psycho-neurological states, needs, the numinous, the given and so on. Thus, if I can
     demonstrate what religion refers to I can tell you what it means. This is the famous
     correspondence theory of meaning, now also labeled as the 'realist' theory. It is the
     implicit theory in most studies of religion from Emile Durkheim to Victor Turner. This
     theory is critically wounded but has not yet been laid to eternal rest" (Penner 1999:
     474).

is thus fair to hold that scientific languages are purpose-specific extensions of natural language. Similarly, we could say that religious languages are extensions of ordinary language—and thus not of a wholly different nature. Some think that religious languages may be given or inspired by supernatural agents, gods (etc.) and that they are therefore of a "godly" nature; but it is probably more likely (we might imagine) that it is the gods who speak the languages of humans. At least, they must if "they" want to communicate with us humans.

3.1. Coherence Theory and Holist Semantics

The problem with human communication and language is that they consist in much more than just pointing to things and naming entities in physical space-time. Language may convey meanings about metaphorical assertions, imaginary situations, the future, a dream-time to which we have no access and—strangely enough—still be "meaningful." The possibilities of such sense-making seem puzzling. When the idea that meaning consists in verification of correspondence to matters of fact in the world or private states of mind has been given up, something else must be available for us to account for how meaning is created, used, discarded etc., and there is some agreement on *coherence* as being the necessary condition for sense-making: For any statement to make sense, it must be part of a pattern, network or system in which it makes sense—and so far this is a legacy from several sources, e.g. Saussure and Wittgenstein. The view that meaning is thus inherently dependent upon other meanings in a total pattern, network or system is habitually termed "holism" or "holistic." Hans Penner characterizes the theory in this manner: "Roughly and briefly, this theory rejects the principle of reference and emphasizes consistency and coherence of ideas, symbols, archetypes, and the like" (1999: 474). It is quite easy to imagine skeptic attacks on a holist semantics which emphasizes coherence above correspondence—in the sciences, it could lead to adherence to circularity and non-falsifiable hypothesis and (this has not so much been contemplated by philosophers) in the field of religion, it could lead to the defense of the "rightness" of religious beliefs. On the problem of the "coherence theory" Hans Penner states: "The flight into idealism is not the only problem here. The theory entails the shuddering thought that your beliefs could be completely consistent/coherent and totally wrong. The skeptics are now beginning to laugh" (1999: 474). The relativist menace is evident and imminent.[26] However, there is more to the theory than coherence among a set of

---

26   These issues have been the topic of heated debates among such well-known philosophers as Hilary Putnam, Donald Davidson and Richard Rorty—not least because the issues *are* very complex and difficult to access. Penner's contribution (1999)

beliefs. It involves the totality of beliefs, and it is, as Donald Davidson has emphasized, unlikely that we are all massively mistaken in our beliefs about the world. Neither are we so differently oriented in our conceptual schemes that they become radically alternative and untranslatable. Our general picture of the world cannot be totally mistaken, according to Davidson, for that general picture "informs" all of our beliefs, even those that may turn out to be false. The truth or falsity of beliefs is, to the semantic holist, not something that is given in relation to things in the world, as that is "mistaken." For as Penner explains (on Davidson): "The truth (meaning) of a sentence has nothing to do with reference, intermediary entities, or ideas, or bits of the world that make a sentence true" (1999: 479). Very briefly, the idea is that sentences are not true or false in virtue of extra (or non)-linguistic objects or "facts"—they have what meaning they have in relation to the totality of a language.[27] In relation to the study of religion this means that "religious beliefs and actions are to be studied as a system, a semantic structure. It makes no sense, for example, to speak of the meaning of *a* religious belief or action in isolation from the whole systems of beliefs, rituals, etc., of a religious tradition. Beliefs make sense only in relation with other propositional attitudes. Beliefs are holistically structured." (Penner 1999: 498).[28] Another version of semantic "anti-realism" is found in Michael Dummett's theory. He defines a speaker's knowledge of the meaning of a sentence—the speaker's understanding of the sentence—as knowledge of the conditions under which it can be asserted. This has become known as the theory of "assertability conditions."[29] As already noted, realist semantics would consider meaning to reside in the truth conditions of the sentence, that is, in verification of the facts which "make the sentence true." Dummett explains the differences between realists and "anti"-realists on their view of the truth of assertions:

> The anti-realist accuses the realist of interpreting those statements in the light of a conception of mythical states of affairs, not directly observable by us, rendering them true or false. According to the anti-realist, what makes them true or false are the

---

is a strong effort in trying to explain the consequences of holist semantics for the study of religion. See also my own contribution (Jensen 1999).

27   It is impossible to do justice here to the complexity of the argument. Besides Donald Davidson's own production on the issue, of which 1990 is instructive (and relatively accessible), Evnine (1991) should be mentioned.

28   Indeed, Penner also notes that this is not really so new: "Structuralist studies of myth and religion have stressed this warning for decades. I am afraid that it has yet to be taken seriously by most scholars who are full-time students of religion" (1999: 498).

29   This rendition of Dummett's semantics (mostly based on Frege and Wittgenstein) is almost unrecognizably condensed, which is all the more problematic because there is, among philosophers, general agreement on only one thing about his philosophy, and that is that it is difficult. Dummett's ideas are well presented in his anthology *Seas of Language* (1996).

observable states of affairs on the basis of which we judge of their truth-value. On the realist's interpretation, these merely provide *evidence* for the truth or falsity of the statements, or constitute an *indirect* means of judging them true or false; the anti-realist retorts that they are the most direct means there could be. (1996: 469)

Thus, "anti-realists" do not assert that there is no real world—or any such nonsense. Anti-realists are sensible people—who are "taking the sciences at full value" (as Nelson Goodman says), also when studying things that are not normally considered so realist. Being a form of "meta-language" the study of religion must treat religions as semantic systems in which it is culturally meaningful to speak of things that make little sense epistemologically. In that light, semantic anti-realism and holism appear attractive whether in Dummett's version or in Davidson's and Putnam's. These semantic theories may well be employed in the study of religion as they may assist us in ensuring that the course chosen is philosophically justifiable. However, the most uninteresting issue in philosophical debates about semantics, as viewed from the perspective of a scholar of religion, is the *truth question*, and that is, ironically, that which interests philosophers the most. Most scholars of religions—be they anthropologists, philologians or others—do not really care about *truth*, or, when they work on any number of mutually incompatible cosmologies, they tend to consider it a waste of time to discuss which local ontology may be more epistemologically defensible.[30]

As already noted in relation to Wittgenstein's notion of language-games, it is easy to slip from an idea of the autonomy and internal coherence of particular meaning-systems ("cultures") to an idea of incomparability or incommensurability. "Meanings" and interpretations not only differ from person to person but from culture to culture with no means of judging their importance—it would, in the end, be the "positivist's nightmare" revisited and the use of the term "meaning" might as well become meaningless and we shall all be dragged down the "hermeneutical vortex" (as some, e.g. Donald Wiebe, have already seen it becoming). One reaction to the apparent threat of subjectivity in the realms of meaning and interpretations is to limit talk to that which concerns the "factual." Apart from the fact that this (empiricist ambition) has been amply proved not to work in general or in scientific language, it certainly would have impaired any understanding of what religious and other normative "meanings" are about and how we may know them. It seems that "we can acknowledge that the normative is a domain of understanding, something we can judge of—but yet that norms are still like rules in this respect: we do not

---

30 However, in a world where religious traditions increasingly speak "for themselves" across traditional boundaries and in all media, it is not at all irrelevant that scholars of religion engage the truth-issue in relation to the validity of scientific versus religious discourse—see, e.g. Murphy 2000.

find them in the world. They are presupposed in cognition of a world" (Skorupski 1997: 54). That there are limits both to interpretation and of pragmatist license is quite obvious in many familiar settings—such as in visiting a restaurant where (this is part of the "frame") it is conventionally expected (even by the most post-modernist) that there be a high degree of correspondence between menu, orders, the food served (and tasted...) and the amount indicated on the bill.

3.4. Cognitive Constraints

Experience tells us, and scholars of religion know this more than many others, that the range of imagination of human minds seems quite limitless. And yet, for all its variability the same human mind appears (in what concerns religion) to revolve around or return to certain themes, and therefore there are limits as well as there are certain recurrent features in the sense that religions really do seem alike in many ways. These similarities may of course be the product of the scholar's own imagination so that we focus solely on things which "appear" according to a prefigured pattern: Religions look alike because we have determined that just such configurations as exhibit certain traits are labeled religion... and thus what we ensure is really just the circularity of our argument. That charge is, however, unavoidable, simply because (and this is somewhat overlooked) *when* we recognize something, it is a *model* which we *re*cognize and not an object "in itself." Given this precondition for recognition, however, we are still able to say that religions exhibit common and recurrent semantic (as well as cognitive) features and properties amidst all the observable variations at the surface level.[31] There are indications that we may legitimately theorize about universals in religions and that these universals are not bound to religious ontologies, as former generations of religiously motivated universalists would have it. Universals "in a new key" are, when it comes to religion, both of a semantic and of a cognitive nature (Jensen 2001).

Now, when it is agreed upon that religions "look alike," the next question will address the possible causes of the likeness. A likely answer to the question could concern some kind of general human psychological or mental mechanism, function or module which would then be responsible for the constructions and working of religious systems of meaning. In that respect the problem somehow resembles that more well-known problem concerning the origins and "causes" of language. The theories about modularity and the

---

31   In what concerns the cognitive aspects of this problem see Boyer 2000 which contains a
     very convincing analysis of how and what goes into the cognitive construction of
     religious representations.

"innateness" of language competence (primarily conceived by Noam Chomsky) have been met with mixed reactions. There are, however, other more interesting aspects of Chomsky's theory than the idea of innate modules, and that is his view of generative grammar. As first formulated (in 1957) it was a grammar of rules, of syntax only, but later criticism and developments led to the inclusion of semantics and an idea of a generative semantics has evolved for the purpose of explaining how "deep structures" may account for the construction of meanings at "surface" level. That is, the purpose is to elicit the mechanisms responsible ("transformational rules") for the ways in which semantic meanings are set forth. So, when it is also agreed that religions are semantic phenomena it is quite plausible that similar mechanisms can be elicited for religious behavior, including the production of meaning.[32]

3.5. Meaning and "the Mental"

As already mentioned, many of the contributors to the classical quandaries over "meaning" in the study of religion viewed meaning as a mental fact or property. That reaction was perfectly understandable as most of them developed their views on the basis and perspectives of subjectivist philosophies and psychologizing hermeneutics. Many of us (humans) tend to think that meaning is in our minds—it is an intuition, and seemingly a plausible one, for the meanings I have are mine—are they not? So where else could they be? It was argued above that this view is flawed for many reasons and the idea that meaning (in the semantic sense) is a mental property cannot be upheld. On the other hand, it is also obvious that things semantic are related to things mental— if there were no brains there probably would not be any languages or symbols (etc.) either. Languages also give indications of "how we think"—as witnessed in the work of e.g. George Lakoff (1987) on complex systems of linguistic and cognitive classifications. Now, although asking and, perchance solving, semantic linguistic questions, the "cognitive way" does amount to a theoretical reduction (that is: formulating the problems of one "domain" in the theoretical idiom of another), it is not quite so simple to answer the question whether and to which degree this kind of operation also implies an ontological or epistemological reduction. In one sense we may say that (semantic) meanings *really* are, simultaneously, inside minds as well as in language outside minds. It depends on the kind of description we use. For, we may say that they are

---

32 These advances in semantics have not fully been appreciated and applied in the study of religious semantics, but it seems that there is ample potential. The story about generative grammar and semantics is told and explained by Leech (1990: 343–59). A noteworthy example of the study of rules and syntax in ritual practice on an inspiration from generative grammar is Lawson/McCauley 1990.

ontologically independent, but also that they have some epistemological equivalence because we only know the mental through the domain of the linguistic and the semantic. That is, it is only as presented in "intersubjective semantic stuff" that we may gain and formulate knowledge about the cognitive and the mental. Furthermore, the state of the problem and the kind of discussion depends upon which kinds and levels of "meaning" are addressed. Some are more basic than others, for it may well be that "meaning at the most basic levels is supported and driven by general, not specifically linguistic, cognitive operations" (Fauconnier 1997: 190). But, then again, as Fauconnier also points out: "the simplest meanings are in fact not simple at all" (188).[33]

3.6. What and Where Is "Meaning" — on the (Emergentist's) Division of Labor

As witnessed by some of the previous notes it would be — by many — a welcome addition to our knowledge of ourselves and the world if we could *reduce* meaning and semantics to something more "basic" by means of which we could "prove" things and produce irrefutable evidence (the "scientific method" etc.). The only question is whether the results of such operations, favored by "semantic eliminativists" (as they are called), are still concerned with "meaning" or should they more likely be regarded as concerned with something else? Should the ambition of "reducing meaning" to nano-electric or micro-chemical (or some such) functions of/in the brain of an individual pronouncing the sentence "Rhubarbs are delicious" actually succeed some day (which it may — given the speed of scientific discovery), then the results of such analyses are more likely than not to be products of "meaning" in the semantic sense. On the other hand, as long as the results of these investigations would be communicated between humans and understood by them, the non-semantic would have to be translated back into semantic realms. Scientists involved could then re-examine by reduction their ideas about their reductions, and then they would never run short of matter to investigate.[34] It is or should be possible to

---

33 As Fauconnier further explains concerning simple meanings: "They rely on remarkable cognitive mapping capacities, immense arrays of intricately prestructured knowledge, and exceptional on-line creativity. They also rely on the impressive, and poorly understood, human ability to resolve massive underspecification at lightning speeds" (1997: 188). There is much more to be said on that point of view than may be referred to here, but Fauconnier's basic idea is that language primarily "serves to prompt ... cognitive constructions by means of very partial, but contextually very efficient, clues and cues" (ibid.).

34 A similar operation can be performed by the reduction of gastronomy into organic chemistry. The analyses of the constituents of nutrition would (probably) be correct under that new description, but "it" would cease to be gastronomy which still retains

retain the "level of meaning" as one which may both be reduced and *not* be reduced without the latter position being responsible for upholding some "mysterious" ontology for matters semantic. Facts about meaning and intention need not be reducible to other facts of a naturalistic (or "gravitational") kind — perhaps it is not even possible, for as Putnam states: "The problem, of course, is that what the semantic physicalist is trying to do is to reduce intentional notions to physicalist ones, and this program requires that he not employ any intentional notions in the reduction. But *explanation* is a flagrantly intentional notion."[35]

3.6.1. Linguistic Ontologies and Epistemologies

The ontologies of meaning are (so far) quite mysterious. It is obvious that languages exist and that they are different. Also, it turns out that they are translatable and anything described in one natural language can be described in another natural language with some degree of precision — as well as with some loss in precision. But, and this is the really mysterious part, the physical sounds "emitted" in linguistic practice are *not* meaning producing *in themselves*. They are only prompts and cues which make brains work in certain cognitively and culturally preconfigured ways. We cannot (so far) make an audio-spectral analysis of the meaning of a sentence, let alone of sentences embedded in social practice. But the question then apparently still remains whether it would be possible to reduce, and thus perhaps explain in idioms of current scientific practice, semantic meaning to something non-semantic? That idea depends on and proceeds from a dualism concerning things meaningful, or as formulated by Jane Heal:

> to the idea that the semantic arises from, or is constituted by, some kind of appropriate complexity in the non-semantic. For want of a better word, I shall say that he or she is committed to the reducibility of the semantic to the non-semantic. But it is to be remembered that what is involved is reducibility in some extremely broad sense. The difficulties of dualism have given a bad name to the whole idea of non-reductive

---

its own level of description (at least among, say, the French and Italians and other sensible nations).

35 As quoted in Hale/Wright, eds. 1997: 442. Putnam launches similar attacks on "meaning reductionists" in other places: e.g. against the idea of there being "innate semantic representations" he says: "A Chomskyan theory of the semantic level will say that there are 'semantic representations' in the mind/brain; that these are innate and universal; and that all our concepts are decomposable into such semantic representations. This is the theory I hope to destroy" (1988: 5). And: "Mentalism is just the latest form taken by a more general tendency in the history of thought, the tendency to think of concepts as scientifically describable ('psychologically real') entities in the mind or the brain … this entire tendency … is misguided" (1988: 7).

accounts of meaning (in the very broad sense of 'reduction' just gestured at). The bulk of philosophical writing on meaning (in the analytical tradition) has thus been concerned to pursue the radical interpretation strategy. But are dualism (in which a hidden and separate meaning is inferred *behind* the non-semantic surface) or a reductive materialist view (in which it is discerned *in* the patterns of the non-semantic) the only options? What if we abandon the assumption common to the materialists accounts and dualism, namely that meaning is not observable, while retaining dualism's commitment to non-reductionism? This gives us a view on which meaning is a public and observable property of certain sounds, marks or movements, but a non-physical one. But it is not part of the predominantly quantitative and value-free conceptual scheme we have built up for describing, predicting and explaining the behavior of inanimate objects; rather, it belongs to a different but equally fundamental area of thinking namely the one we use in our relations with other persons. This line of thought is favored by those with Wittgensteinian sympathies. If we accept this view it is likely that the idea of the imagined starting-point for radical interpretation, a starting-point in which a person knows plenty of non-semantic facts but no semantic facts at all, will come to seem incoherent. The starting point for any thinking is one in which we are observationally aware of the world as containing both semantic and non-semantic facts. (1997: 178–79)

These arguments presented by Heal indicate the difficulties in linking the mental as a stratum (or several such?) of neurological facts with the "level" of semantic meaning. And yet, there can be no doubt that such a level (or several?) are somehow connected to our physical capabilities as humans. The questions of how we install "culture in mind" and how culture, as a complex of semantic properties and function, works and what it "really" consists of, remain (so far) unsolved problems—although suggestions are not lacking—and some of them seem quite promising.[36] For instance, as pointed out by Terrence Deacon, different linguistic tasks are processed *more or less* in various regions in the human brain:

> Producing a metaphoric association requires selecting words with common semantic features, whereas producing a metonymic association requires shifting attention to specifically alternative features. This is why there may be a posterior cortical bias to metaphoric operations and a pre-frontal cortical bias to metonymic operations. (1997: 306)

Thus we may assume that: "The symbolic functions, the grammatical and representational relationships, are not processed in any one place in the brain, but arise as a collective result of processes distributed widely in the brain, as well

---

36   One very interesting suggestion comes from Bradd Shore in his *Culture in Mind. Cognition, Culture, and the Problem of Meaning* (1996). "Interesting" because Shore, as an anthropologist, is not unfamiliar with the kinds of problems facing the study of religion on "cultural models," "mental models," "instituted models" etc. It is beyond the scope of this presentation to elaborate further on Shore's work—but it deserves a more thorough application and testing in the study of religion(s).

as with the wider social community itself" (Deacon 1997: 309). But—whatever PET scannings reveal of brain activity, they will probably not (but who knows?) be capable of decoding such meanings as pass through the reader's mind when reading *just* these pages... Obviously, when speaking, listening, reading, writing and otherwise processing semantic materials, humans do employ their cognitive abilities; thus meaning-"metabolism" is a mental activity, and yet, that description does not exhaust the topic. Meaning is not only *in minds*, it is also, and perhaps more significantly, *between minds*, which then put together (or *synthesize*) the semantic materials in such ways that they engender meaningful events in our minds. Religious activities, imageries and utterances are prime examples of humankind's propensities and proclivities for such activities for it seems that these activities produce some kinds of "well-being," kinds of cognitive "flow," kinds of "blissful" effervescence on the more benign side but also, since religion is not just a "nice thing," on the side of the "tremendum": kinds of experience which satisfy thirsts for power, dominance, horror, violence, etc.

3.7. Levels of Semantics

To clarify what I think must be an inevitable stratification of matters semantic, I shall briefly refer to the concept of "downward causation." In a theory of "bottom-up" causation, things happen automatically at the higher levels—much as in chemical experiments. That being so, the other way of processing ("top-down") is much more interesting when we talk about meaning and semantics, for it is only in the presence of such functions that we can see more general information and intelligence at work. Translated to our discussion concerning semantics in religion, it could answer the question of how meanings effect social and cognitive "power," that meanings are more than "mere" epiphenomena—unable to influence the world (Jensen 2001: 256–59). It is in fact quite plausible that language, and thus semantics, is responsible for rather thorough "re-shaping" of not only cognitive contents, properties, and mechanisms but also of brains (as neuro-physiological and chemical etc. entities). As Mark Turner wrote:

> If we use the old metaphoric conception of the brain as an agent who "deals with" language or as a container that for a moment "holds" language while examining it for storage or discard, then it is natural to think of the biology of the brain as unchanged by its dealings with language. But if we use instead the conception of the brain as an active and plastic biological system, we are led to consider a rather different range of hypotheses: The brain is changed importantly by experience with language; language is an instrument used by separate brains to exert biological influence on each other, creating through biological action at a distance a *virtual* brain distributed in the individual brains of all the participants in the culture; early experience with language affects cognitive operations that go beyond language. (1996: 159–60)

What this means in terms of religion is that it lends theoretical credibility to the more old-fashioned idealist (but intuitively plausible) view that religions somehow condition the ways in which we think: that they as "semantic engines" are co-responsible for the ways in which we process information and construct meaning.[37] In most traditional societies, culture, religion and language have been learned ("installed") simultaneously so that meanings are multi-"meshed" in the classificatory architecture. As already pointed out above—languages (and semantic meaning) are concerned with and involved in much more than simple description. This is a field in which much remains to be done—thus there is ample space for "new approaches" along these lines. Although nothing retrospectively appears more antiquated than prophesying, it does seem that the fields of semantics and cognition appear as challenges to the study of religion, not the least in combination (Jensen 2002).

4. Religion as a Socio-"Cultural System"

What difference does all this make? It has been common-place for a long time to talk (with Clifford Geertz) of religions as "cultural systems."[38] In a more conventional view of these, they are pre-eminently semiological and of a thoroughly linguistic nature. Along the view of an objectivist semantics (such as Geertz'), these signs in life, which constitute the systems, are "as public as marriage and as observable as agriculture" (1973: 91). That these are public is a result of their being done, by their being "staged," by participants in whose conceptions of things they have to be made in a way that "counts as" something intentional

---

37 Gilles Fauconnier reaches a similar conclusion (although not about religion): "When meaning construction is taken into account, the fundamental cognitive issues of learning and evolution appear in a different light. Clearly, what children learn is not language structure in the abstract. They acquire entire systems of mappings, blends, and framing, along with their concomitant language manifestations" (1997: 189). An example from my own fieldwork: When Muslim mothers shout "Kafir!" (meaning: "unbeliever," "heathen") to children misbehaving they involve and invoke much more than a "no!"

38 It should be noted and remembered that Geertz' launching of the "cultural systems" program was a way in which to translate "the linguistic turn" in philosophy into anthropological theory and methodology. It has proved a very successful move although criticism was inevitable—against his idea that anthropology should become a primarily interpretive endeavor and thus, in the eyes of some, a less respectable scientific undertaking. However, after some decades of debate, it seems that the battle over "interpretation versus explanation" is (largely) over. Even the most empirically minded concede that interpretation is involved in all scientific activity and the most hermeneutically committed also acknowledge an element of explanation in interpretation.

(Searle 1995). In that sense the cultural and public displays of meaning are a way of objectivizing and projecting widely distributed cognitive models— including schemata, frames and "scripts." That is one of the ways in which symbols "have meaning" in religions, i.e. they "trigger" or evoke response by linking to other concepts "in the mind" among those who participate in the joint projects of having *those* concepts, values, and thoughts. In other words, those who share the "meanings" and the knowledge they amount to. Thus, when speaking about where we should "look for meaning" we may in fact look in more places—in the doings, writings, sayings that are publically available and in the heads of participants and interpreters as well. But since interior states are not always so easily accessible, the meanings and references of discourse are much more amenable and tractable at the public levels—such as in texts. Although not all, nor perhaps even many, participants of "cultural systems" have textual meanings "in their heads" they will always carry meanings that may be "text-ified," i.e. made into narrative and text. This a very simple corollary of the fact that we make sense of the world by talking about it and that knowledge which can not be transposed into some kind of narrative is (probably) not knowledge at all. So the "cultural systems" approach seems to be able to hold true and tractable for much more than religion (cf. also Geertz 1973, 1983).[39]

Throughout the history of philosophy one important topic of debate has been the relation between words and concepts. The question of meaning is intimately related to this debate and the same three (or four) positions are (logically) available. It is possible to transpose the stances on concepts to those on meaning and see how they may or may not make sense: 1) A "realism" concerning meanings according to which they would exist "in themselves" seems to be a non-sensical option; 2) an "empiricism" which derives meanings from experience is likewise questionable; 3) a "rationalism" positing meanings as psychologically or mentally "innate" fares a little better in light of advances in cognitive linguistics, at least as a necessary "sub-stratum, but 4) the "nominalist" view that they are the results of human intentionality, ascriptions which are defined as properties of their "relational" positions in comprehensive semantic systems and networks and thus "nothing but" conventional becomes the most probable solution to the problem. This holistic view in which mean-

---

39 In this I must confess to side with those who think it perfectly possible to study "externalized" linguistic and other "meaning-laden" facts in a theoretically informed way. Does this sound strange? Remember how Noam Chomsky "pushed" the study of language (back) into speakers' minds and made it a subdivision of psychology by saying that only internalized or "I-language" as "a structure in the mind" is the proper object of linguistic analysis. On the relations of such views to the study of, e.g. religious rituals see the discussion in Lawson/McCauley 1990, Ch. 4: "A cognitive approach to symbolic-cultural systems."

ings are eminently available as "externalized" objects in a collectivist methodology does not impair the view that meanings also exist and function as cognitive entities with "evocational" potentials. On the contrary, the first thesis
presupposes the latter. But, when the emphasis is strictly on the externalized
semantics that are available to us directly as articulations of discursive formations, the question of the individual appropriation of these systems of meaning
become somewhat less relevant. There is nothing wrong (inherently) with a
theory in favor of the study of externalized meanings and an "objectivized
semantics," for these are the meanings which "go into peoples' heads" (further,
the "internalist's" problem is that s/he cannot communicate the internalist point
of view except in externalist terms).[40] Obviously to many, a two-tiered model of
meaning(s) requires the problematic acceptance of a dualist ontology in which
there exist both meanings as semantic entities and cognitive entities as
properties of the mind and its functions.[41] But is it really so problematic? For,
when all is said and done, it also appears that a consequence could be that we
stop talking about meanings as something between and relating "words and
objects" but rather as a "something" which exists between words and historically situated humans — who use words to make sense of the world.

Concluding Remarks

Concerning, and in spite of, the importance of semantic questions in the study
of religion, it is noteworthy just how little attention the problem has attracted.
Perhaps this indicates the necessity of a "semantics of religion" as an addition

---

40 An interesting, but not too common feature in general in religions is the Muslim notion
of "Hafeez", meaning someone who has learned the Qur'an by heart, i.e. "internalized"
the whole body of semantic material in it as a text. The "argument from individual
appropriation" is not altogether fallacious, since what we are being told and what we
tell ourselves are really consequential for the way in which we react to new information. This should really not come across as anything new — but perhaps we are now
closer to presenting a credible account of how it is so. In order to elicit internal systems,
the analyst needs to construct external versions of, say, the internal competence and an
"idealized speaker's" competence in French — is most likely — to be found in French
grammar and syntax. The constructions of idealized speakers as well as of grammars
and syntaxes are all normative endeavors.
41 To what extent there really exist two (or more?) levels in an ontological sense is an
object of debate. In this relation I think there is good reason to support Donald
Davidson's idea of what he terms "anomalous monism": That there is but one reality
and that the various "layers" are related but in such ways that strict causal laws and
explanations are not applicable. See e.g. Evnine 1991 on this issue. A more modest
proposal is to view the two "worlds" of the mental and the semantic as epistemically
diverse or even that whichever parallels we posit are made so for heuristic reasons.

to the range of "new approaches." I, for one, think so.[42] For, the irony of the situation as described here—both historically and currently—is that we seem to be in a position where we are unable to account for that one matter, which appears to be responsible for the most crucial difference between humans and other creatures. It is so eminently intuitive for us to make sense, to simply "know" that there are things that are more or less meaningful in this world. Speaking about religion we may also conclude that religions are means and ways of making sense—more or less. This is a so much taken-for-granted intuition or so commonplace a conviction that it hardly qualifies as a theoretical position. But it should at least be acknowledged as a starting point for further theorizing. If we wish to go beyond the acceptance of meaning as what we could call a "trivial mystery" then we may have to revise our ideas of what science can be about and include within its range such things as "meaning." I— for one—think that this is the only way to make the study of meanings meaningful. Or, a scientific community which is unable to see the interesting challenge of providing us with an account of what it means to mean will simply remain meaning-less itself (just to toy a bit with the term). On the other hand, the study of religion which has always—as seen by most of its practitioners— been concerned with things meaningful could very well be in a position not only to learn from other fields or sciences but also to contribute directly towards a solution of the "mystery" because religion as well as "meaning" both seem to have been with the human species ever since the "symbolic revolution" eons ago. It is quite probable that religion is a product of the human propensity to "make meaning" and to make it in such a way that meanings appear as natural, intuitively available and—not least—stable, as if "given" so that religion becomes a warrant of semantic stability—or strife.

Many things point to religion as being a field of human activity which could lend itself to the most rewarding forms of inquiry in relation to these matters. So, where the modern empiricist would see religion as meaning-less and a result of human folly and superstition it may in fact be the opposite: that religion is such a powerful means of "making meaning" that it deserves serious attention. That is: serious scholarly attention. And then—the study of religion might also attract more and more serious attention from other fields—what it can hardly be accused of in its current situation. The "problem of meaning" is far from being solved but that only makes the study of it all the more meaningful—also within the provinces of the study of religion.

---

42   Fortunately, I find myself in limited but good company: Hans H. Penner (e.g. 1999) and Terry F. Godlove Jr. (1997, 1999) work along these lines.

Bibliography

Albinus, Lars (1997), "Discourse Analysis within the Study of Religion: Processes of Change in Ancient Greece," in: *Method & Theory in the Study of Religion* 9 (3): 203–32.

Avramides, Anita (1997), "Intention and Convention," in: Hale/Wrigth, eds.: 60–86.

Ayer, Alfred Jules (1952), *Language, Truth and Logic*. New York: Dover Publications.

Baaren, Th. P. van (1972), "The Flexibility of Myth," in: *Ex Orbe Religionum. Studia Geo Widengren*. Leiden: E.J.Brill: 199–206.

Boyer, Pascal (2000), "Functional Origins of Religious Concepts: Ontological and Strategic Selection in Evolved Minds," in: *Journal of the Royal Anthropological Institute* 6 (2): 195–214.

Braun, Willi/McCutcheon, Russell T., eds. (2000), *Guide to the Study of Religion*. London: Cassell.

Capps, Walter H. (1995), *Religious Studies. The Making of a Discipline*. Minneapolis, Minn.: Fortress Press.

Caws, Peter (1997), *Structuralism. A Philosophy for the Human Sciences*. Atlantic Highlands, N.J.: Humanities Press.

Coffa, Alberto (1991), *The Semantic Tradition from Kant to Carnap*. Cambridge: CUP.

Davidson, Donald (1990), "The Structure and Content of Truth," in: *Journal of Philosophy* LXXXVII (6): 279–328.

Deacon, Terrence (1997), *The Symbolic Species. The Co-evolution of Language and the Human Brain*. Harmondsworth: Penguin.

Dummett, Michael (1996), *Seas of Language*. Oxford: Clarendon Press.

Duranti, Alessandro (1997), *Linguistic Anthropology*. Cambridge: CUP.

Durkheim, Émile/Mauss, Marcel (1963 [1903]), *Primitive Classification*. Chicago: University of Chicago Press.

Edwards, Derek (1997), *Discourse and Cognition*. London: Sage Publications.

Evnine, Simon (1991), *Donald Davidson*. Cambridge: Polity Press.

Fairclough, Norman (1992), *Discourse and Social Change*. Cambridge: Polity Press.

Fauconnier, Gilles (1997), *Mappings in Thought and Language*. Cambridge: CUP.

Frankenberry, Nancy (1999), "Pragmatism, Truth, and the Disenchantment of Subjectivity," in: idem/Hans H. Penner, eds., *Language, Truth, and Religious Belief*. Atlanta: Scholars Press: 507–32.

Geertz, Clifford (1973), *The Interpretation of Cultures*. New York: Basic Books.

—— (1983), *Local Knowledge. Further Essays in Interpretive Anthropology*. New York: Basic Books.

—— (1995), *After the Fact: Two Countries, Four Decades, One Anthropologist*. Cambridge, Mass.: Harvard University Press.

Godlove, Terry F. Jr. (1997), *Religion, Interpretation, and Diversity of Belief. The Framework Model from Kant to Durkheim to Davidson*. Macon, Ga.: Mercer University Press.

—— (1999), "In What Sense Are Religions Conceptual Frameworks?," in: Frankenberry/Penner, eds.: 450–72.

Goodman, Nelson (1978), *Ways of Worldmaking*. Hassocks, Sussex: The Harvester Press.

Hale, Bob/Wright, Crispin, eds. (1997), *A Companion to the Philosophy of Language*. Oxford: Blackwell.

Harris, Roy (2003), *Saussure and His Interpreters*. Edinburgh: Edinburgh University Press.

Heal, Jane (1997), "Radical Interpretation," in: Hale/Wright, eds.: 175–96.

Jensen, Jeppe Sinding (1999), "On a Semantic Definition of Religion," in: Platvoet et al., eds., *The Pragmatics of Defining Religion*. Leiden: Brill: 409–31.

—— (2000), "Structure," in: Willi Braun/Russell T. McCutcheon, eds., *Guide to the Study of Religion*. London: Cassell: 314–33.

—— (2001), "Universals, General Terms and the Comparative Study of Religion," in: *Numen* 48: 238–66.

—— (2002) "The Complex Worlds of Religion: Connecting Cultural and Cognitive Analysis," in: Ilkka Pyysiäinen/Veikko Anttonen, eds., *Current Approaches in the Cognitive Science of Religion*. London: Continuum: 203–28.

Jensen, Jeppe Sinding/Luther H. Martin, eds. (1997), *Rationality and the Study of Religion*. Aarhus: Aarhus University Press.

Lakoff, George (1987), *Women, Fire, and Dangerous Things*. Chicago: University of Chicago Press.

Langer, Suzanne K. (1942), *Philosophy in a New Key. A Study in the Symbolism of Reason, Rite, and Art*. Cambridge, Mass.: Harvard University Press.

Lawson, E. Thomas/McCauley, Robert N. (1990), *Rethinking Religion. Connecting Cognition and Culture*. Cambridge: CUP.

Leach, Edmund (1976), *Culture and Communication. The Logic by Which Symbols Are Connected*. Cambridge: CUP.

Lechte, John (1994), *Fifty Key Contemporary Thinkers. From Structuralism to Postmodernity*. London: Routledge.

Leech, Geoffrey (1990), *Semantics. The Study of Meaning*. Harmondsworth: Penguin.

Lotman, Yuri M. (1990), *Universe of the Mind. A Semiotic Theory of Culture*. London: I.B. Tauris & Co.

Malinowski, Bronislaw (1948), "Myth in Primitive Psychology," in: idem, *Magic, Science and Religion and Other Essays by Bronislaw Malinowski*. New York: Doubleday: 93–148.

Murphy, Tim (2000), "Speaking Different Languages: Religion and the Study of Religion," in: Tim Jensen/M. Rothstein, eds., *Secular Theories of Religion. Current Perspectives*. Copenhagen: Museum Tusculanum Press: 183–92.

Ogden, C.K./Richards, I.A. (1923), *The Meaning of Meaning*. London: Routledge & Kegan Paul.

Paden, William E. (1988), *Religious Worlds. The Comparative Study of Religion*. Boston, Mass.: Beacon Press.

Penner, Hans H. (1999), "Why Does Semantics Matter," in: Frankenberry/Penner, eds.: 473–506.

Peregrin, Jaroslav (2001), *Meaning and Structure. Structuralism of (Post)Analytic Philosophers*. Aldershot: Ashgate.

Putnam, Hilary (1988), *Representation and Reality*. Cambridge, Mass.: The MIT Press.

Ricoeur, Paul (1981), *Hermeneutics and the Human Sciences. Essays on Language, Action and Interpretation*. Ed., trans., and introduction by John B. Thompson. Cambridge/Paris: CUP/Editions de la Maison des Sciences de l'Homme.

Saussure, Ferdinand de (1993 [1915]), *Course in General Linguistics*. London: Duckworth.

Searle, John R. (1995), *The Construction of Social Reality*. New York etc.: The Free Press.

Shore, Bradd (1996), *Culture in Mind. Cognition, Culture and the Problem of Meaning*. New York: Oxford University Press.

Skorupski, John (1997), "Meaning, Use, Verification," in: Hale/Wright, eds.: 29–59.

Staal, Frits (1989), *Rules without Meaning. Ritual, Mantras and the Human Sciences*. New York etc.: Peter Lang.

Stiver, Dan R. (1996), *The Philosophy of Religious Language. Sign, Symbol and Story*. Oxford: Blackwell.

Strenski, Ivan (1987), *Four Theories of Myth in Twentieth-Century History*. London: The Macmillan Press.

Taylor, Mark, ed. (1998), *Critical Terms for Religious Studies*. Chicago: University of Chicago Press.

Thibault, Paul J. (1997), *Re-reading Saussure. The Dynamics of Signs in Social Life*. London: Routledge.

Turner, Mark (1996), *The Literary Mind. The Origins of Thought and Language*. New York: Oxford University Press.

Turner, Victor W. (1969), *The Ritual Process: Structure and Anti-Structure*. Ithaca, N.Y.: Cornell University Press.

Whitehouse, Harvey (2000), *Arguments and Icons. Divergent Modes of Religiosity*. Oxford: OUP.

Wittgenstein, Ludwig (1974), *Philosophical Grammar*. Oxford: Blackwell.

Religion in Context

A Discussion of Ontological Dumping

by

Kirsten Hastrup

In anthropology we have been confronted with a number of more or (mainly) less elegant definitions of religion along with other social and cultural phenomena. Among the more elegant ones is Edward B. Tylor's definition of religion as "belief in spiritual beings" (1871). Less elegant is Clifford Geertz' attempt at locating religion in the social domain rather than individual belief; for him, religion is (or *was*, in 1966), "a system of symbols which acts to establish powerful, pervasive, and long-lasting moods and motivations in men by formulating conceptions of a general order of existence and clothing these conceptions with such an aura of factuality that the moods and motivations seem uniquely realistic" (Geertz 1966: 4). A century separates the two, and the difference in emphasis is a symptom of a particular development of anthropology, becoming increasingly sensitive to context and consequently ever more uncertain about its own terms.

My aim is neither to rehearse a series of definitions nor to trace a particular development, however, but to discuss why exhaustive definitions are epistemologically impossible, and why elegance may in fact prove a legitimate yardstick of individual concepts. Although I will use examples from the study of religion in both ancient and modern times, the discussion is theoretical rather than empirical, and should be seen in the light of general trends in anthropology, set within the larger horizon of the human and social sciences (K. Hastrup 1995, 1999). The principal object is scholarly understanding itself, that is the process by which we seek to comprehend and represent whatever part of human life we are currently studying.

My suggestion is that scholarship always works and advances by way of persuasive fictions or naturalized illusions one of which is "religion." To call it an illusion is not to claim it to be objectively false, but to point to the power of conceptual categories, including "religion." The idea is not to rehearse the old debate on nominalist versus realist definitions, nor to land us in yet another constructivist camp. The point of the exercise is to highlight the nature of scholarly understanding itself, by way of the study of religion. After the demise of modernism and the idea of metaphysical realism there is a lot to be gained from investigating the conceptual self-evidences of our predecessors, not to ridicule them but to learn more from them than mere concepts. Paraphrasing Pierre Bourdieu, I would suggest that at this age and day, the progress of knowledge presupposes progress in our knowledge of the conditions of knowledge (Bourdieu 1990: 1). Persuasive fictions are persuasive for a reason and my aim is to discuss why such notions as "religion" and "context" carry their own conviction along while still distorting the world they profess to describe.

Objectifying Religion

As a category, religion has defied definitive description in spite of numerous attempts, as implied in the above brief introduction of Tylor and Geertz. The defiance may be owed to the nature of religion itself as alluded to by Max Müller, in claiming that religion is "a struggle to conceive the inconceivable, to utter the inutterable, a longing after the Infinite" (Müller 1873: 18). Clearly, the attempt at walling in the inconceivable by means of words is doomed to failure. Yet this has not prevented scholars, including Max Müller himself, to write about religion in fairly self-confident terms, albeit with different emphases, amounting to what Melford Spiro has called "endemic definitional controversies concerning religion." Spiro suggests that "they are not so much controversies over the meaning either of the term 'religion' or of the concept which it expresses, as they are jurisdictional disputes over the phenomenon or range of phenomena which are considered to constitute legitimately the empirical referent of the term" (Spiro 1966: 87).

As for the empirical referent, Émile Durkheim, for instance, rejects the belief in supernatural beings as legitimate, because this would exclude the religion of primitive peoples, who do not distinguish between the natural and the supernatural (Durkheim 1976: 24–29). His advice is to free the mind of every preconceived idea, and to proceed to define religion "from the reality itself." He continues: "Let us set ourselves before this reality. Leaving aside all conceptions of religion in general, let us consider the various religions in their concrete reality, and attempt to disengage that which they have in common; for religion cannot be defined except by the characteristics which are found wherever religion itself is found" (ibid.: 24). And, as implied, the supernatural is not a shared feature as far as Durkheim is concerned. He sets forth, then, to encircle the essential nature of religion and he finds it in the "sacred." Uncharitable critics would be tempted to argue that he is merely substituting one obscurity for another, yet in the process he also introduces a social dimension, arguing simply that the sacred is whatever a society deems to be sacred. This is clearly a circumvention of a series of implicit semantic problems, that become even more acute when we consider the study of long dead religions of which we have only traces.

The religion of ancient Mesopotamia is a case in point. In a famous article, Leo Oppenheim (1964) answers his own question of "Why a 'Mesopotamian Religion' should not be written." He argues that conceptual distortion is an immanent feature of any study of religion, but in his own discipline it reaches prohibitive proportions. First, he considers the various textual and archaeological sources and find them somewhat wanting for a synthetic presentation of Mesopotamian religion; in this case, then, Durkheim's inductive method would be severely hampered from the outset. Oppenheim's main argument concerns the conceptual difficulties in understanding a polytheistic religion in a heavily stratified society, however, and the absence of centrality of any one deity or cult. He continues:

> This conceptual barrier, in fact, is more serious an impediment than the reason usually given, the lack of data and specific information. Even if more material were preserved, and that in an ideal distribution in content, period, and locale, no real insight would be forthcoming—only more problems. Western man seems to be both unable and, ultimately, unwilling to understand such religions except from the distorting angle of antiquarian interest and apologetic pretenses. For nearly a century he has tried to fathom these alien dimensions with the yardstick of animistic theories, nature worship, stellar mythologies, vegetation cycles, pre-logical thought, and kindred panaceas, to conjure them by means of the abracadabra of mana, taboo, and orenda. And the results have been, at best lifeless and bookish syntheses and smoothly written systematizations decked out in a mass of all-too-ingenious comparisons and parallels obtained by zigzagging over the globe and through the known history of man. (Oppenheim 1964: 183)

These are strong words, and they aim precisely at what we are discussing here: the nature of the objectification inherent in the study of religion, an objectification that is imbued with a long tradition of scholarship and temporary understandings.

Today, part of the problem in studying religion is precisely the heavy load of conceptual history, including the "religious" (or theological) basis of many theories of religion (cf. Jensen/Rothstein 2000). The concept itself preempts the nature of what can ever be seen as religious, yet as scores of ethnographers have noted over the years, reality often seems to challenge the words by which we seek to understand it. Authors of contemporary ethnographies of everyday religion in countries like Britain (Jenkins 1999) and Denmark (Rubow 2000), are at great pains to mediate the expansive and complex referents of local religiosity, not least because it seems at odds with the absolutely "modern" context. As Timothy Jenkins has it,

> In most contemporary accounts, "religion" is perceived as being confronted by its antithesis, "modernity", and as being in a process of intellectual attenuation and institutional decline. At the same time, and in the same perspective, it tends to be ascribed the minor qualities of each and every classificatory opposition: it belongs to the private

or personal as opposed to the public sphere, it is voluntary not obligatory, it concerns opinion not fact, it is emotive or affective, rather than cognitive, imprecise rather than exact, metaphorical not literal, and so on. (Jenkins 1999: 4)

The problem for a scholarly study of religion is very much related to this, in the sense that religion and science have themselves been defined also in opposition to each other (cf. Bell 2000). This historical coincidence apparently has exerted particular pressures on students of religion, who had to profess where their loyalty was; was one studying religion from the standpoint of science or the standpoint of religion. And why is it that this particular topic seems to demand a specific kind of either distantiation or empathy, while other topics of interest to the human sciences demands both at the same time? Further, why bother to rescue the category, apparently falling prey to its own referent, "the inconceivable," as identified by Max Müller? My point is to suggest that, in principle, "religion" is no different from any other category of thought that has become objectified in the social and human sciences in their never-ending quest for theorizing about the world. There is no particular delicacy or confession needed to study religion; all knowledge is positioned, and we must demand of all theories that they are self-reflexive for them to deserve the name in the first place.

Theories are sentences; they are suggestions as to how particular phenomena may be understood and explained, and as such they proceed through language (K. Hastrup 1995). The very use of language itself implies a degree of objectification. As Wittgenstein had it, the formal "clothing of our language makes everything alike" (Wittgenstein 1978: 224). In other words, the communicative quality of language hinges on a feature of generalization that often seems to belie the specificity of meaning and experience. The world-making quality of language rests on a cognitive impulse at impersonalization (Rapport 1997: 14–15). This does not mean that every individual attaches the same meaning to the shared categories and act according to a minimal common denominator; it simply means that people share a vocabulary in which to approximate each their individual experience. The closer our experiential worlds, the more likely are shared meanings, but it can never be taken for granted. This goes also for the category of religion, and when Oppenheim suggests that we cannot understand what it meant to the old Mesopotamians, this is largely because we cannot share their experience, nor do we know how to approximate it in words.

The question is how to "speak" about religion without preempting the content of the category; if language is the key link between the personal and the social, it is of acute importance in such slippery fields as "religion" (Jenkins 1999: 4). If it cannot represent, it can still communicate. It therefore gives access to people's thoughts, while also potentially distorting them and deluding the listener about his or her "understanding," not least because language is always

selective. This is not simply a feature of scholarly language and theoretical vocabularies, it is also a distinctive feature of "natural" languages, supporting
"cultural" tendencies "to notice some things about the world rather more than
others and to make more fuss about them" (Geertz 1995: 46).

For the humanities, the use of language is a cornerstone. There is no way to
present other histories, cultures, or attitudes save in words. We are, for better
and for worse, dependent on a language that is both unstable and ambiguous.
The lack of stability is owed to "new" understandings of phenomena that
cannot be properly captured in existing words; therefore, we introduce alien
notions such as mana and taboo into our language, and with time these concepts become emptied of their original ("real") meaning and become nominal
categories, at which Oppenheim (and others) may sneer.

While there is always an element of "taste" with respect to analytical
concepts, I would argue that the general process of incorporating new understandings by way of more or less alien concepts is not only a legitimate
procedure, it may also be the only one that allows new ontological knowledge
to actually surface in a given situation. Unprecedented concepts point to the
limits of traditional ones and open up new areas of interest. All scholarly work
is dependent on linguistic creativity; discoveries and the identification of new
categories are simultaneous. Truly, what begins as a tentative metaphor—understanding something by way of something different—may end up a dead
certainty; then it is time to move on, but there is no way to avoid a similar
process in the future.

An example from the incipient social sciences in the late nineteenth century
will illustrate the nature of this process, and take us also to its more limiting
implications. In his work on the sociological method from 1893, Durkheim
suggests that society should be considered as a "thing," a fact in its own right,
which must be studied as such by a new branch of scholarship. In other words,
he establishes a new analytical object, independent of both history and psychology, on the (by now) well-known assumption that society is more than the sum
of its individuals. Durkheim does not speak of states or other political or
territorial entities, but social wholes, whose nature as wholes is owed to the
division of labor and to collective representations and shared moral notions.
For us, the important issue is that in the process of understanding the nature of
social integration, a new *object* was born to the world. The object was to be
studied empirically through its symptoms, and gradually the invisible and in-
tangible "society" achieved logical and historical priority over those empirical
symptoms it was designed to organize in a comprehensive form in the first
place.

The point is that by announcing a new analytical perspective, a new social
fact or a new (material) phenomenon saw light; society, indeed, emerged as a
thing of no small material impact. Robert Paine has suggested that there are
two kinds of newness in the world, the newness of discovery and the newness

of invention (Paine 1995). The former implies that one discovers more of what is already known: a new star among stars or a new culture among cultures that are already classified and defined; in other words, extant categories can contain the new phenomena. By contrast, the new by invention implies that the new cannot be accommodated within existing categories; the phenomenon cannot be seen as an example of something that is already known, and one is forced to invent a new category. This is where something *ontologically new* emerges. It applies to Durkheim's concept of society as a moral whole. It began as an invention, or an analytical framework for understanding the connections and interdependencies of certain social phenomena, but it almost immediately came to be viewed as a "thing" in the world. One could say that the theoretical proposition made by Durkheim about a kind of structural logic preceding and determining individual acts was so successful that it became totally trusted. It became common sense that social structure had logical priority over social processes.

In other words, an epistemological relationship, that is a way of comprehending the world, was transformed into an ontological entity, or an objectively existing phenomenon, whose nature successive generations of scholars have had to explore. In a similar manner, a host of analytical objects that have been construed through time as epistemological concepts, have achieved status of empirical entities. It goes for culture, psyche, economy, language, law and religion etc., but it also goes for heat, light, distance, and speed and many more concepts that are normally seen as belonging to a completely different (physical) dimension of the world. But why would "speed" be more empirical than "culture" when it comes down to it? In both cases, it is a matter of words, that are but summaries of a vast variety of phenomena. Conversely, these phenomena can be said to find condensed expression in the words. These are reflections of the theoretical propensity to condense, simplify and tidy up what is in fact extensive, complex and disorderly. This is the beauty of theory in general.

If we look at Durkheim's theory of religion, the objectifying process and its huge epistemological implications become even more conspicuous. For him, religion was something eminently social (Durkheim 1976: 10), yet certainly also a thing in itself, a set of objectified sentiments (ibid.: 419). Religion consists, objectively, of two separate categories, as Durkheim calls them, that is beliefs and rites. The difference between them is the difference between thought and action. To operate with this objectified category of religion, Durkheim introduces a series of conceptual preconditions, such as a "bipartite division of the whole universe, known and knowable, into two classes which embrace all that exists, but which radically exclude each other" (ibid.: 40). The division is, as is well known, the division between sacred things and profane things, and Durkheim suggests that "religious beliefs are the representations which express the nature of sacred things and the relations which they sustain, either with each other or with profane things. Finally, rites are the rules of conduct which prescribe how a man should comport himself in the presence of these sacred objects" (ibid.: 41).

The objectification of religion, or of religious beliefs, is made possible because of another objectification, namely an absolute (material) distinction between the sacred and the profane. What we are witnessing is a process of naturalization, and it is a process that occurs also in everyday life. This process has been called a process of ontic (or ontological) dumping (Feldman 1987). In attending to the world, people (such as scholars) engage in epistemic (or epistemological) operations that reach out towards the new before it becomes the given (Rapport 1997: 14). In so far as language functions as a cognitive tool in this engagement, the epistemological operation implicitly entails a degree of objectification, and the result of the understanding is given ontological status. In short, the process of understanding itself transforms an inherently epistemological process to an ontological entity. If notions such as "society" or "religion" start as attempts at understanding specific and very varied phenomena, they end up as "things" or ontological entities, that scholars have a hard time dissolving afterwards. The hardness is related to the fact that the dumped categories have infiltrated "natural" language and become a given, a trusted entity. The "hardness" of facts, indeed, is a function of social agreement (K. Hastrup 1993).

In societies where church and nation are one, such as the Armenian society, the metaphysics of religion has the trusted power of an all embracing ontology, to the point even where time disappears as the referent of history (F. Hastrup 2000). In this case, the social agreement on matters religious makes them very hard facts, indeed. If this is a token of "traditional" security, even in a (post-) modern age, inevitably marred by ontological insecurity according to Anthony Giddens (1991), religion may still serve as a vehicle of creating "natural" ontologies that may or may not be in line with the specialist metaphysics, but which serve as temporary givens in a world with few trusted ideas. As shown convincingly by Rubow (2000), the ambiguous language of religion and church may serve as a vehicle of necessarily fluid ways of believing.

In scholarship, what is objectified (or ontologized) is also a (temporary) way of understanding reality. The process of objectification is vital in the cognitive economy of understanding in general, because it frees the mind to deal with urgent matters while leaving at least some stones on the path towards them unturned. If we had to speculate about the connection between each and every word and reality before we could begin to speak, the universe of thought would not only end, but *begin* in chaos. As Gregory Bateson (1972: 501) has emphasized, humans have to dump at least some concepts into a category of trusted ideas, that are immediately available for use without further reflection, in order to allow the consciousness some flexibility for dealing with new and unprecedented experiences and ideas. This process of dumping trusted ideas is related to what Bourdieu (following Marcel Mauss) has called habituation (e.g. Bourdieu 1990).

If we experience a degree of inertia in the world of scholarship it is not only owed to complacency and mental idleness, it is a feature of habituation in this very general sense. There is always something new in the making, but for the academic community to discard trusted ideas means also to question long established standards of value and quality judgment. These should not be taken lightly, if we want to maintain a degree of credibility also outside the world of scholarship. Habituation, as one outcome of ontological dumping, is not necessarily negative, then. It would be impossible to have all concepts and ideas up for inspection at any one time. We can only act in new ways on the basis of trusted ideas. Dumping is only a problem if we forget that the implied naturalization of phenomena is simply a consequence of a temporary mode of understanding. There are different temporalities in the different disciplines, but even the bounding of the disciplines themselves is a result of ontologically dumping particular understandings or perspectives as entities.

The notion of culture, owing largely to Johann Gottfried Herder and the neo-humanists of early nineteenth century, is a case in point. It gave rise to a host of "national" disciplines, and also to a comparative study of cultures, in some places known as cultural anthropology. As will be well-known, the notion of culture has been under heavy scrutiny along with other naturalized concepts from our rich modernist past. As Clifford Geertz writes: "Like most powerful ideas in the human sciences, this notion came under attack virtually as soon as it was articulated; the clearer the articulation, the more intense the attack. Questions rained down, and continue to rain down, on the very idea of cultural scheme" (Geertz 1995: 42). He ends the long list of questions and counter-questions by stating that "whatever the infirmities of the concept of 'culture' … there is nothing for it but to persist in spite of them" (ibid.: 43). As I read Geertz, he does not speak for a simple naturalized entity, but for a mode of comprehending diverse experiential worlds, implying a concept that we apparently can still not do without. Whatever the shortcomings of the concept of culture as used, we still need a notion for summing up the dimensions of the framework within which social life unfolds.

The practice of anthropology presupposes the possibility of human understanding across manifest difference; there is a basic assumption that people are imaginable to one another. We could also phrase it like this: people do not live in different worlds, they live differently in the world. Part of what we share is an experience of relativity; conceptual or epistemic relativity, that is, not ontological incommensurability. But because of ontological dumping, a fiction of incommensurability is introduced, also in matters of religious experience— and in the launching of particularly uncontaminated, *secular* theories of religion. We should realize that most of what we study in the human sciences are ontologically situated, *not* in the things themselves, but in our experience of them. Where are the objective entities of "religion," "aesthetics," or "culture" for instance, if not in our experience of their real, material, impact, summed up in the words, but not represented by them.

There is no fixed relation between the words we use and something which exists outside them, no direct reference, and no immediate representation, yet there is an experiential world that we may share, somewhere beyond the words. Generally, words relate to reality as the measuring rod to the measured; our realist concern must be located in the latter rather than in the former. This means that experiences, including religious experiences, have ontological priority over the words that are used to summarize them. Experiences cannot be measured or counted, but they can be identified, and communicated about in words. One could argue that while we may disagree on the definition of "religion" (as an allegedly ontological entity) both within and across "cultures," we could possibly agree on its capacity for summing up a variety of actually lived, "religious" experiences.

In general, the postmodernist avalanche of criticisms against modernist assumptions was a symptom of the (well-taken) will to question the trusted ideas; in other words it was a symptom of a process of de-ontologizing the social and cultural constructs that had led an untroubled existence as trusted ideas for the better part of a century. The problem is still that there is no way to address the world without a language that will by its nature pull understanding towards shared meanings and cultural givens (Daniel 1996). In contrast to action, language is of necessity collective and repeatable, and it therefore tends at featuring what can be shared. Language is, therefore, very badly equipped at dealing with fluid ontologies. We have to keep them in mind, however, and reserve at least part of the scholarly consciousness for dealing with the unprecedented in order to grasp (or suggest) the ontologically new.

The Positivity of Context

For a long time it has been almost a mantra in anthropology that social and cultural phenomena must be seen in context (Dilley 1999). The context authenticitates the ethnographic detail, yet by itself it is a (largely unacknowledged) theoretical by-product. If we refer back to Durkheim once more, it is clear that by establishing the sacred as whatever people agree to be sacred, his theory of religion co-produces a theory of a social context having primacy over the social facts. If, as I argued above, theories are sentences suggesting a particular understanding, they also suggest particular connections between phenomena identified as "things." A recent example from the study of religion will illustrate the point. Thus: "The theory of religion with which I work ... is that religion is (a) a social system (b) legitimated by claims to the authority of some superhuman power" (Martin 2000: 141). This definition not only has the beauty of combining the definitions offered by Tylor and Geertz quoted above, it also suggests a particular understanding of religion as one "thing" (a social system) connected to another (a superhuman power), and the connection itself qualified as "authority." At the same stroke, a cosmological context is produced, separating the social from the superhuman, and the religious from the secular. Text and context are mutually supportive.

Reference to context in general is a means of establishing links, making connections, and distinguishing relevances from irrelevances. Contextualization has been the hallmark of proper interpretation in anthropology and elsewhere (notably linguistics), and on the whole, context has been treated as self-evident; it has become (yet another) natural feature of the world. This is what Johannes Fabian calls "the positivity of context" (Fabian 1999).

Context is one of the prime persuasive fictions in anthropology (Strathern 1987); it is one of those categories that have been dumped in the process of the development of a series of disciplines, each of which can actually be seen as byproducts of the agreement on categories as ontological entities. Shifts in the designation of relevant contexts have made distinct paradigms in science; seeing events from the perspective of the agent or from the perspective of the analyst makes two distinct contexts (see e.g. Duranti/Goodwin 1992). As far as the study of religion is concerned, the context appealed to has been either historical, sociological, or metaphysical. Not even theologians have taken the position that religion can be absolutely self-contained, if nothing else they acknowledge a linguistic context of their interpretation of the canonical texts.

In anthropology, we have witnessed a good many monographs of religion testifying also to the different traditions or paradigms in anthropology, setting up each their salient context. Looking back, we have for instance *The Religion of the Chinese People* by Marcel Granet (orig. 1940; publ. 1975) being primarily an analysis of the social hierarchy in China, because this is what frames the analysis of religious sentiments, seen as far less tangible than the social classes; sociology is the obvious context of this analysis made by a (surviving) member of the Année Sociologique school, founded by Durkheim and largely erased by World War I, claiming the lives of many prominent members. Evans-Pritchard's work on *Nuer Religion* (1956) likewise is more of a study of classifications and worldview in general, the context being largely a system of meanings (as opposed to the system of functions of his immediate predecessor at Oxford, Radcliffe-Brown). The list can be extended in all directions, my point is simply that whatever context is appealed to, not only "frames" the analysis, but achieves ontological status by itself in the course of study. In more recent times, with the skepticism over notions like "culture" and "social system," framing has become more of a problem, and one tends to resort to anecdote. For all their lack of precision (and often their lack of apparent significance) ethnographical anecdotes, I would argue, are not necessarily a symptom of analytical or theoretical failure, but a means to keep the context unbounded. I shall give a brief example from my own fieldwork in Iceland (K. Hastrup 1998).

Along with the people I lived with, I participated in services in the local Church. Services were rare, because the vicar had several churches to attend to in the sparsely populated rural tracts. But when they happened, everybody went there, and I was invited along. Clearly, it was a "social event." I was told that "in the old days" people were always invited to the vicar's home after service, but now this had become rarer. However, in "our" *sveit* (tract) it was still done and it was much appreciated. Even my socialist woman friend and others, who could not be called "believers" in any traditional sense of the word, went for the occasion as did the ethnographer for whom it opened new doors of understanding. We were lavishly provided with "buttered bread" (with spreads of various kinds), cakes, biscuits, and the thinnest possible pancakes with whipped cream (thinness being highly praised and cream always being a token of wealth), and I realized the truth of what I had been told about the traditional "coffees."

The vicar's home was a "fine" one, according to my woman friend. The coffee (including the food) was lavish, and the rooms were beautifully equipped. There were embroideries, crystal vases and silver chandeliers etc. all over the place. On the armchairs, the elbow rests were covered in real lace, which also adorned the framed photos of children and grandchildren on display. In short, the home testified to the industry and skill of the vicar's wife; when we were back home at the farm, my friend remarked that she always felt so poor when returning. Her industriousness was not visible in the same way; yet she actually ran the local school with some fifteen pupils and was highly regarded in the community. The point is, that the visit to the vicar's home, served not only to mark the social space but also to emphasize particular values of family and gender.

At the vicar's, "we" automatically dispersed into three groups: the older men, the older women, and the younger women. Young men were conspicuously absent. It was this absence, which upon my inquiry was explained by themselves with a lack of faith, which made me realize why the young women came. It was not faith, either, which made *them* leave home on selected Sundays, it was sociability. If the older segment of the population possibly were believers—at least in tradition—the younger women with whom I debated the matter explicitly went for the being together. They enjoyed getting out of their homes, which were generally far apart, dressing up a bit, and talking, quite apart from the singing in church. In short, the church provided a place where one could practice the communal space. The service, the hymns and the language of the (religious) event, served as an entry into a larger unbound vocabulary of community and shared values. There was no clear boundary between text and context. Depending on analytical viewpoint, religion could be seen as either.

The point of this tale is to show that religious practice in the Icelandic countryside is impregnated with social meanings that make it well-nigh impossible to speak exclusively in terms of the category "religion," even if a religious feeling of sorts pervades the social gatherings. If the resort to the anecdotal form of exposition makes the definition of context supremely vague, it does pave the way for the wish to see figure and ground as somehow coincident and logically equal, in contrast to the implicit logical hierarchy between context and text as traditionally conceived. In this sense I follow Geertz, who says:

> Understanding a form of life, or anyway some aspects of it to some degree, and convincing others that you have indeed done so, involves more than the assembly of telling particulars or the imposition of general narratives. It involves bringing figure and ground, the passing occasion and the long story, into coincident view. (Geertz 1995: 51)

Figure and ground must be put into coincident view; that is the point, and the point, moreover, that will ultimately dissolve the notion of context as an "outer" frame. This is where we should not necessarily stop short of writing a "Mesopotamian religion" (pace Oppenheim), because evidently, there is lot of material that can be brought into coincident view. Instead of thinking in terms of ultimate definitions of religion (that may or may not include the figure we are currently investigating), we have to think in terms of a double hermeneutics (to paraphrase Giddens 1987), implying that theories themselves become part of their subject matter.

In acknowledging this, we arrive in fact to the point where the quest for understanding religion "in context," most often a social or cultural context, and giving up if we cannot establish the necessary distance between them, can be replaced by another one, namely that of seeing religion *as* context. At the empirical level, this is implied in a significant definition of religion offered by Jenkins, who suggests that "religion be understood as the expression of the human aspiration to flourish, or—to put it in another way—as the expression of the desire to be human in a particular form" (Jenkins 1999: 13). Starting from the ethnographic analysis of something that could be called a "religious event," Jenkins transcends the local context and brings religion back in *as* context in its own right: a context that by the choice of terms like "aspiration" emphasizes both "the sense of process and the sense of obligation that lies at the heart of human being" (ibid.). If "religion" is in itself a context of motivations, it need not be placed "in context." It is, one is tempted to say, a "total social fact," by being part of the definition of humanity itself through its will to ordering life according to particular notions of worth. The sacred is not an entity, it is a feeling of worth that surfaces from time to time. In the process of his analysis, Jenkins thus manages to rescue a dumped category from both naturalization and dissolution.

What is significant here, quite apart from the ethnographic authority that Jenkins achieves in such a slippery field as "everyday religion," marked by fluid signs more than anything else, is the renewed analytical confidence by which we may approach "religion." We need not waste time by recapitulating definitions and more or less obsolete typologies of "religion," before we can begin to discuss what goes on in the world. "Religion" may simply provide a relevant analytical context for studying certain actions, beliefs, or institutions that may or may not include all and sundry at all times.

As "context," clearly religion is not simply an "outer frame," but an intrinsic value given to some event or other by the participants. Too often, "frames" have been constructed that have little or no bearing on people's own view of their worlds; a recent one is the notion of the "global context," that means everything to some and nothing to most, and which cannot, therefore, be appealed to without discrimination as to place and person. Only by taking the agent's perspective can we contextualize events in a meaningful fashion, and bring figure and ground into coincident view.

This, incidentally, will also facilitate the shift from designative to expressive theories, to introduce a distinction suggested by Charles Taylor (1985: 218ff.). The former are relatively straightforward in their pointing out certain qualities of the object; with such theories, the object tends to be naturalized and meaning to be unmysterious. Such were the correspondence theories that we have now largely left behind, realizing that there is necessarily a discrepancy between the measuring rod (language) and what is measured (experiences). A more rewarding path is opening for us to explore, however, namely the path cleared by the development of expressive theories making the world manifest in embodying it. As an expression in this sense, anthropological theory may be partly enigmatic, and often present only a fragment of the reality it embodies. Yet, the point is that what is expressed is made manifest only by this expression. However imperfect, expressions cannot be replaced by other kinds of presentation. As expressive theory, the humanities maintain some of the mystery surrounding language as a field of indeterminacy.

Designative theories point to, and propose; expressive theories make manifest, and realize. No doubt, our general cultural strategies for coping with the world include both dimensions, just like our ways of using language are both propositional and evocative. For the human sciences to exploit its own full potential, it will have to cultivate the expressive dimension of its theorizing, thereby opening up new modes of understanding. Theories about human life are articulations of what is not otherwise said, and as such they may influence, confirm, or alter the constitutive self-description of particular people. In that sense, theories do not only make the constitutive self-descriptions explicit, they also extend, criticize and even challenge them. This makes social theory radically different from natural science, and poses distinct problems of validation.

Theories are public and open for inspection and dissent, and the degree to which theories are valid to a large extent hinges upon the extent to which they can be shared or agreed upon as a valid mode of understanding. Social theory must have some coherence with experience to be rationally acceptable. The sharing of significance is related to a sharing of experience; in anthropology this is the basis for learning from the cross-cultural encounter. There are other measures to theoretical adequacy, however, even when questions of reference (and ontology) have been defused. Theory, as an expressive practice, is not only about realizing something but also about inactivating the false implications of particular statements. Illusions have to be broken, presupposing that we have standards—if not for right and wrong then at least for better or worse inter-pretations.

Theories are not synonymous with the world, yet there are limits to license. No interpretation is wholly subjective, because meaning must in some ways be shared for it to be meaning at all. There are limits to which questions make sense in a community of conversational partners; language is always social and meaning cannot be wholly private. If theory summarizes reality in words, it still have to "resist" the trial of intersubjectivity and intertextuality. Theories (and we might wish to recall that they are but sentences) may be logically incompatible, yet still empirically equivalent, meaning that they may sum up experiences in equally acceptable ways. "Incompatibility" is often one of voca-bulary rather than reality, and it is related to the construction of evidence, and—indeed—context. Allegedly irresolvable rivalries between theories about human life often stem from a failure to acknowledge the nature of all theory as subject-referring and social, and as irrevocably underdetermined by the empirical (Quine 1992).

Once we have realized that most of what we see as significant data in anthropology and in other human sciences are ontologically not in the things themselves but in our experience of them, a principle of theoretical charity may result in a new creative dialogue between different kinds of experience that are not discredited a priori by reference to a particular (positive) context, but seen as other contexts, other ways of bringing figure and ground into coincident view.

Illusion in Scholarship

If we seem to have come a long way from the initial discussion of "religion," it is deliberate. I have wanted to broaden the perspective and to see religion as just a particular instance of a general problem of categorization, inherent in the scholarly process of understanding itself. If "religion" is largely an illusion, created through ontological dumping of a particular mode of understanding, this appertains to all analytical concepts used by academics. Scholarship of necessity works on the basis of ontological illusions. We have no choice but to create concepts that, if they are successful, produce their own dead certainties. This paradox should be explored further and put to creative use also in society, which rightfully expects scholars to suggest appropriate distinctions.

It has been noted with some force that so far much academic work, notably in the West, has perverted this ambition into a kind of intellectual terrorism, that by way of endless quotes of French philosophers mystifies the world while claiming it for themselves, thus perpetuating the colonial embrace (El Saadawi 1996). Without the French innuendo we know how a similar attitude has been criticized under the name of "Orientalism" (cf. Said 1979). Nawal El Saadawi raises the issue with particular reference to Egypt and makes the following observations:

> Egyptology is an example of cultural genocide or terrorism, in which a whole nation and its civilization and philosophy are violently reduced to a few stones or ruins. Egyptian philosophers have disappeared from history. One of them was a woman philosopher called Hypatia. She was killed twice: the first time in A.D. 415 by foreign invaders who killed her physically and burned her books together with the whole library of Alexandria in Egypt. The second time was in the nineteenth century when she was assassinated culturally and historically by the Egyptologists. (Nawal El Saadawi 1996: 168)

In face of such vehemence, scholarship might pack up and return to silence. One could argue that silence is sometimes better than speech, but when it comes to scholarship in general, the best way of testing a concept is "ceaselessly to return to it, critique it, ask new questions, hold it up to new contexts" (Johnson 1993: 9). This also goes for the concept of religion; by holding it up to new contexts the concept may explode from within—and transform into an analytical context in its own right. Similarly, it may not be Durkheim's use of the word "sacred" that is wrong, but the way in which the development of theories of religion has ontologized and contextualized it, to take another example (K. Hastrup 1996).

As we know from the long history of our learned institutions, the right to doubt old views and to suggest new ways of understanding, that will eventually entail new ontologies, must be cherished, lest we fall prey to inquisitions. A famous example was Galileo Galilei, who in the sixteenth century was accused of heresy when he suggested that the Earth was not the center of the Universe but simply a planet among others. While execution and inquisition are not as common as they used to be in this part of the world, we should not forget that:

> In every learned society there is power to censure what in the psychoanalytic tradition is called 'wild analysis'. And there must also, unavoidably, be an arbitrary exercise of institutional power. This is not a matter for merely abstract debate. To award a second-class degree instead of a first, to fail a Ph.D. dissertation—these are judicial acts with a real bearing on the future of the aspirants. (Kermode 1993: 62)

The standards are not immutable, but subject to interpretative norms that are both historically and culturally situated; this makes it necessary for scholars to reexamine their authority from time to time. However, the point is that in the learned societies, where such things as human values and legal norms are debated, there are always views that are marginalized. Even here, in the conversational community par excellence, there are right and wrong ways of looking at things; the more normative the science, the stronger the paradigm, the less openness to new terms. Wherever words are spoken, censorship is implicitly at work; the invisible third part in any conversation, society, may both inspire and block new ways of speaking about society. Yet words are all over the place, making distinctions, classifying people, noting differences, and adding up to theories that present us with the illusion of ontological knowledge.

Illusion is part of *la condition humaine*, as has been argued by Bourdieu in different works (e.g. 1990, 1993, 1996); *illusio* provides the necessary (allegedly "real") framework of whatever "game" or social action we are currently participating in. People have to agree on the reality of the illusion for their interaction to make sense; the illusion validates the feel for the game and the positioned interests and possibilities that it affords to individuals. Without this illusion of a naturalized context there is no way to act "in character" (K. Hastrup 2000). In short, the ontological dumping of concepts and the naturalization of context which I have claimed to be part of the scholarly process of understanding, is an inevitable consequence of scholarship being so profoundly (and provocatively) human.

In face of the immensity of the endless process of ontological dumping there is no reason to forget, however, that it is likewise part of what makes us human to remake ontologies that are at best temporary givens. For scholars this remaking is a vital part of their task of suggesting new understandings, and proposing new theories summing up relations in words that become naturalized as entities. If the theories resist the trial of time for a lengthier period, such as the naturalized concepts of culture and religion, it is because they adequately sum up a variety of experiences. When questioning those concepts and their "naturalized" connotations, as we must, we should not forget those experiences that are still in need of theoretical expression. For new expressive theories to take root, they should be both economical and elegant; the aesthetics of experience should be matched by concepts that are fulfilling the expectations of completeness (cf. Dewey 1997). To add yet another sentence to the cumbersome definition of religion suggested by Geertz in 1966 will not do the trick. Rather than expand on "religion" at the level of social life itself, and endlessly redefine or recontextualize it, we might want to rethink it as in itself a particular way of contextualizing humanity that presents itself as self-evident to some people, while dispensable to others. In this way, "religion" itself can be seen as a theory of worth, competing with other theories, and subject to epistemological investigation in the manner of all theory.

Bibliography

Bateson, Gregory (1972), *Steps to an Ecology of Mind*. New York: Ballantine Books.

Bell, Catherine (2000), "Pragmatic Theory," in: Tim Jensen/Mikael Rothstein, eds., *Secular Theories on Religion. Current Perspectives*. Copenhagen: Museum Tusculanum Press.

Bourdieu, Pierre (1990), *The Logic of Practice*. Cambridge: Polity Press.

— (1993), *The Field of Cultural Production*. Cambridge: Polity Press.

— (1996), *The Rules of Art*. Cambridge: Polity Press.

Daniel, E. Valentine (1996), "Crushed Glass, or, Is There a Counterpoint to Culture," in: E. Valentine Daniel/Jeffrey M. Peck, eds., *Culture/Contexture. Explorations in Anthropology and Literary Studies*. Berkeley, Calif.: University of California Press.

Dewey, John (1997), "The Aesthetic in Experience," in: Susan Feagin/Patrick Maynard, eds., *Aesthetics*. Oxford: Oxford University Press (Oxford Readers).

Dilley, Roy (1999), "Introduction," in: Roy Dilley, ed., *The Problem of Context*. Oxford: Berghahn Books.

Duranti, Allesandro/Goodwin, Charles, eds. (1992), *Rethinking Context: Language as an Interactive Phenomenon*. Cambridge: Cambridge University Press.

Durkheim, Émile (1893), *Regles de la methode sociologique*. Paris.

— (1976), *The Elementary Forms of Religious Life*. London: George Allen and Unwin (orig. 1915).

El Saadawi, Nawal (1996), "Dissidence and Creativity," in: Chris Miller, ed., *The Dissident Word. The Oxford Amnesty Lectures 1995*. New York: Basic Books.

Evans-Pritchard, E.E. (1956), *Nuer Religion*. Oxford: Clarendon Press.

Fabian, Johannes (1999), "Ethnographic Misunderstanding and the Perils of Context," in: Roy Dilley, ed., *The Problem of Context*. Oxford: Berghahn Books.

Feldman, Carol (1987), "Thought from Language: The Linguistic Construction of Cognitive Representation," in: J. Bruner/J. Haste, eds., *Making Sense. The Child's Construction of the World*. London: Methuen.

Geertz, Clifford (1966), "Religion as a Cultural System," in: Michael Banton, ed., *Anthropological Approaches to the Study of Religion*. London: Tavistock (ASA Monographs 3).

— (1995), *After the Fact*. Cambridge, Mass.: Harvard University Press.

Giddens, Anthony (1987), *The Constitution of Society*. Cambridge: Polity Press.

— (1991), *Modernity and Self-Identity*. Cambridge: Cambridge University Press.

Goodwin, Charles/Duranti, Allessandro (1992), "Rethinking Context: An Introduction," in: Allessandro Duranti/Charles Goodwin, eds., *Rethinking Context: Language as an Interactive Phenomenon*. Cambridge: Cambridge University Press.

Granet, Marcel (1975), *The Religion of the Chinese People*. Oxford: Blackwell.

Hastrup, Frida (2000), "Den Uendelige Historie. Religiøsitet og nationalitet i Amenien," in: *Chaos. Dansk-norsk Tidsskrift for Religionshistoriske Studier* 34.

Hastrup, Kirsten (1993), "Hunger and the Hardness of Facts," in: *Man* 28, no. 4, 19: 727–39.

— (1995), *A Passage to Anthropology. Between Experience and Theory*. London: Routledge.

— (1996), "Det hellige og det sublime," in: *Religionsvidenskabeligt tidsskrift* 29: 3–20.

— (1998), *A Place Apart. An Anthropological Study of the Icelandic World*. Oxford: Clarendon.

—— (1999), *Viljen til Viden. En humanistisk grundbog.* København: Gyldendal.

—— (2000), "Menneskelig handling. Illusion som dramatisk grundvilkår," in: *Tidsskriftet antropologi* 41: 5–22.

Jenkins, Timothy (1999), *Religion in Everyday Life.* Oxford: Berghahn.

Jensen, Tim/Rothstein, Mikael, eds. (2000), *Secular Theories on Religion. Current Perspectives.* Copenhagen: Museum Tusculanum Press.

Johnson, Barbara (1993), "Introduction," in: Barbara Johnson, ed., *Freedom and Interpretation. The Oxford Amnesty Lectures 1992.* New York: Basic Books.

Kermode, Frank (1993), "Freedom and Interpretation," in: Barbara Johnson, ed., *Freedom and Interpretation. The Oxford Amnesty Lectures 1992.* New York: Basic Books.

Martin, Luther H. (2000), "Secular Theory and the Academic Study of Religion," in: Tim Jensen/Mikael Rothstein, eds., *Secular Theories on Religion. Current Perspectives.* Copenhagen: Museum Tusculanum Press.

Müller, Max (1873), *Introduction to the Science of Religions.* London: Longmans.

Oppenheim, A. Leo (1964), *Ancient Mesopotamia. Portrait of a Dead Civilization* [revised ed. completed by Erica Reiner (1977)]. Chicago: University of Chicago Press.

Paine, Robert (1995), "Columbus and the Anthropology of the Unknown," in: *Journal of the Royal Anthropological Institute* I: 47–61.

Quine, W.V. (1992), *Pursuit of Truth.* Cambridge, Mass.: Harvard University Press.

Rapport, Nigel (1997), *The Transcendent Individual.* London: Routledge.

Rubow, Cecilie (2000), *Hverdagens Teologi. Folkereligiøsitet i danske verdener.* Copenhagen: Forlaget Anis.

Said, Edward (1979), *Orientalism.* New York: Vintage Books.

Spiro, Melford (1966), "Religion: Problems of Definition and Explanation," in: Michael Banton, ed., *Anthropological Approaches to the Study of Religion.* London: Tavistock (ASA Monographs 3).

Strathern, Marilyn (1987), "Out of Context: The Persuasive Fictions in Anthropology," in: *Current Anthropology* 28: 251–81.

Taylor, Charles (1985), *Human Agency and Language.* Cambridge: Cambridge University Press (Philosophical Papers 1).

Tylor, Edward B. (1971), *Primitive Culture.* London.

Wittgenstein, Ludwig (1978), *Philosophical Investigations.* Oxford: Blackwell.

Ideological Critique in the Study of Religion

Real Thinkers, Real Contexts and a Little Humility

by

IVAN STRENSKI

Among the newer approaches both to religion and to the methods by which we study religion is what one might call "ideological critique." By this, I mean a delving into the biographical, religious and ideological presuppositions shaping the theories of leading thinkers in the study of religion for the purpose of understanding those theories and bringing them to the bar of criticism. In essence, ideological critique attempts to understand theories in terms of the larger contexts in which they may be embedded — in the biographies and intellectual projects of theorists, in certain social and cultural contexts and strategies, in definite institutional settings.

We in the West are fortunate to live at a time when ideological critique and critical studies of knowledge have been among the most creative endeavors in the humanities. Consider the critical history of *mentalités*, begun with the *Annales* historians of the early part of the twentieth century, and in a way succeeded by historians like Michel Foucault and Edward Said.[1] They have, among many other things, made us consider the proposition that ways of seeing the world are themselves suitable subjects for critical investigation. No longer is history just about the machinations of diplomats or the movements of armies, but also about the categories we use to "think" things. Then one might also cite the revived historicism of the history of science, most often associated with figures like Thomas Kuhn or Paul Feyerabend for the natural sciences, but also carried forward by the University of Edinburgh's Science Studies Unit under the direction and inspiration of Barry Barnes. In areas more closely related to the study of religion, one can list Arthur Mitzman's classic study of Weber, *The Iron Cage*, Fritz Ringer's brilliant account of the genesis of philosophical and social thinking in turn of the century Germany, *The Decline of the German Mandarins*,[2] British historian of ideas Quentin Skinner's studies of

---

1   Said 1978 and Michel Foucault (1980), *Power/Knowledge: Selected Interviews and Other Writings 1972–1977*. New York: Pantheon.
2   Ringer 1969; Mitzman 1969.

Renaissance political theory, and historian of sociology, Robert Alun Jones'
numerous articles on the sociology of Durkheim.[3] My first book, *Four Theories of
Myth in Twentieth-Century History*, was an attempt to learn from these.[4] Without
passing judgment on their ultimate worth, here are researchers committed to
telling the story of the past *critically*—in telling how the past has been systematically, though sometimes unintentionally, constructed by the ideologies
and *methods* used to view or apprehend the past. We live in a time when we
should be sensitive to the ways our *beliefs* about the nature of religion and the
nature of the history of religion shaped what we in the West take religion and
its history to be. Said's work on orientalism, for instance, seems to me a good
example of how critical study of the study of religion can matter to the study of
religion—and in the "empirical" way for which I have argued. Primarily for the
case of our "knowledge" of Islam, Said attempted to show the wider cultural
and social significance of how European historians constructed the category of
the Islamic "orient" ready-made to be studied in a certain way, typically pre-
judicial to Islam. Whatever else Said achieved, he should make us cautious
about how our ideological commitments may shape the way we in the West
apprehend and conceptualize others, and thus how practical policies and social
attitudes may be informed as a result. Ideological critique such as practiced by
these founders of the practice presupposes such stocks-in-trade of today's
thinking as the idea that knowledge is "socially constructed" or culturally
conditioned.

In the present discussion, I would like to bring out some of the key
elements of "ideological critique" and reflect these off the criticisms that have
been and might be made against ideological critique. The good news about
ideological critique in the study of religion is that it has already attained a
degree of maturity. As will be clear from my mention of several books and
authors in the study of religion practicing "ideological critique," this approach
has made a good solid start. But, as far as the future or as far as "new approaches" to the study of religion go, ideological critique is ready to advance to
the next plateau of rigor, to a new level of maturity. Thus, the bulk of my
argument here involves showing how ideological critique can be more
successfully employed as the study of religion moves forward. In its present
forms, ideological critique does not always avoid crass or facile misuse. This is
because ideological critique can at times be a misleadingly easy approach to
religion and theories about religion. With an eye to the future, then, I shall
devote a good portion of the following discussion to the ways in which a more

---

3   Jones 1999; Skinner 1978.
4   Another fine example of this approach in religious studies is Harrowitz 1994. David
     Chidester has also set out on the same path, although I shall register some reservations
     about the way he does so. See his *Savage Systems* (Chidester 1996).

rigorous approach to ideological critique in the study of religion can be achieved.

Ideological Critique Is Post-Modern

The very term "ideological critique" itself buzzes with paradox, and hence cries out for explication. Not so long ago, when the modernist paradigm of inquiry reigned, the very idea of a "critique" which was at the same time "ideological" would *ipso facto* disqualify the project as hopelessly naive. Of course, all thinking is ideologically grounded! What is new in this? In a time when thinkers were not so impressed by or persuaded that the object of putatively scientific study was conditioned by the knower, the term "ideological critique" might itself seem a surd. But, for good or for ill, our fashion has become to believe that the subjective conditions of knowledge about religion—and everything else for that matter—are significant.

The problem is, however, that we may come to believe this proposition with as much vigor as previous generations of modernists believed in the "objectivity" of their knowledge of the world. We will have made a dogma out of the "working principle" that we should attend to the subjective determinants in the construction of scientific objects. If that were to happen, then the very prospects of ideological critique would be threatened. It would be in danger of inviting a sterility of thought issuing from its own methodological dogmatism. How can those who seek a future for ideological critique escape this fate?

In having devoted a considerable part of my career to ideological critique— to exploring the very "subjective" or "ideological" dimension of thought about religion characteristic of post-modern approaches to inquiry, I think I have learned a lesson or two about what it would take to advance the fortunes of ideological critique. In short, I think we need to insure that ideological critique proceeds with more rigor than has come to be common today. To achieve this higher level of rigor, we need, I shall argue, to be *empirical* about our criticism. We need to advance theses about the ideological content of theories that are testable and certainly falsifiable in appropriate ways. Accepting this principle entails that we should be skeptical of the main tenets underlying ideological critique itself—namely, we should retain a skepticism of declaring dogmatically that all knowledge is subjectively conditioned in significant ways. We need to be open to degrees in which knowledge is so conditioned not least of all because the statement itself that all knowledge is conditioned is putatively objective! At worst, it is thus not significantly subjective at all, but rather a way of "laying down the law" from a privileged position on high.

The more one reads the literature of ideological critique in the study of religion, as I shall show, the more convinced, I think, we will become of the need for the constructive refinements in method that I wish to spell out. Studying history of knowledge, for example, has a funny way of tempering one's conviction about epistemological certainties, such as about the bases of ideological critique itself. What really is the basis for our conviction that knowledge is "constructed," and that its construction matters, to mention only a pair of items in our list of present day certainties? Indeed, it is a humbling experience to read the works of otherwise great scholars only to stumble across what seem to us astoundingly obtuse views. Whether these are the more noxious racist opinions of our forebears or distant relatives now so widely exposed by scholars like David Chidester,[5] or their simple errors in reasoning, can we really put the certainties of our own time above such criticism itself? Odds are that we and our verities will look as foolish and full of ourselves to "them" as those of the past look now to "us." Anyway, one does not imagine some referee, endowed with God's eye vision, suddenly appearing on the scene to settle such arguments any time in the near future.

The only way I know to plan for this sort of potential embarrassment is to refine the sweeping generality of the claim inherent in ideological critique that, for example, all views are constructed, ideologically conditioned and that such a constructed nature matters. In this spirit, claims about the ideological intrusions into thinking about religion should be empirical, testable, falsifiable and the like. Let us proceed on a case by case basis, and see how and to what extent ideologies do in fact shape what our scholarship produces, and whether such intrusions really make a difference to the product.

In order, most instructively to make the case for the development and refinement of ideological critique, let us consider some cases where dogmatism has taken over and where the utility of ideological critique in the study of religion as a result suffers. My first examples come from the attempts of a range of recent neo-orthodox and liberal Christian theologians, both Protestant and Roman Catholic, to exploit the postmodern mood embodied in ideological critique to undermine the cognitive status of the study of religion in the interests of re-establishing the legitimacy of Christian theologizing within the secular university. Their attempts to re-theologize the study of religion will show those of us committed to religious studies how ideological critique can go very wrong and be turned against the study of religion.

---

5   David Chidester, "Anchoring Religion in the World: A Southern African History of Comparative Religion, " in: *Religion* 26 (1996): 141–60; Chidester 1996.

Post-Modernism and the Re-theologizing
of Religious Studies

Scientism's "myth of objectivity" seems long and well dead—at least among self-styled postmodernist critics of science. Notably, this critique of objectivity in science has been taken up lately by a range of Christian theological critics of religious studies. Without pretending to be exhaustive in my survey of these Christian re-theologizers of religious studies, I have selected a representative sample from among their number. These include a Barthian neo-orthodox figure like Garrett Green, liberal Protestant Delwin Brown and the Anglican John Milbank. Each of our re-theologizers is important enough both in their own academic circle as well as beyond. Green's manifesto for re-theologizing religious studies, "Challenging the Religious Studies Canon: Karl Barth's Theory of Religion," declares its intentions explicitly in a recent volume of a major University of Chicago journal, *The Journal of Religion*; Delwin Brown, of Iliff Theological College has been for many years a persistent and widely published advocate for "theology" within the secular university.[6] What knits two such different kinds of theologians together is the common grounding of their arguments for the inclusion of Christian theology in religious studies in what may be called principles of postmodernism linked to a certain construal of the method of ideological critique.

Green, for instance, wants Karl Barth's analysis of "religion as unbelief" as theoretical position on religion considered on a par with, say, the theories of Freud, Durkheim, Max Weber and so on. In classic postmodernist style, Green argues that since all viewpoints are grounded in relative positions, and no such thing as objectivity exists, then none exists in the so-called "sciences." Green thus embraces what he identifies as the "postmodern turn," saying that it "can be summed up in the oft-cited motto, 'all data are theory-laden.'"[7] For Green this means that all views, say, about religion "are socially and historically located and necessarily implicated in paradigmatic commitments to certain values, concepts, and methods."[8] Since this is so, the door is now wide open for including "theology" in the canon of religious studies.

Others in the theological camp like liberal Protestant theologian, Delwin Brown, have argued for the inclusion of "theology" (never identified by its sectarian nature) on similar grounds as Green. Like Green, Brown declares that the scientific pretensions of a "theory" of religion, such as Durkheim's, for

---

6   John Milbank, holder of a major named chair at the University of Virginia and author
     of the estimable, *Theology and Sociological Theory*, makes use of postmodern thought to
     undermine the scientific study of religion, although as a major voice from the side of
     contemporary Catholic theology; see Milbank 1990.

7   Green 1995: 473–86.

8   Ibid.: 473.

instance, is unwarranted. Sociology is thus no better than theology, since both are socially constructed discourses. Further, since religious studies cannot hope to "explain" religion, it must be more humble and accept the role of promoting "analysis" or interpretation. It is the ideal of interpretation, Brown believes, which gives theology its opening into the academy. The kind of knowledge for which the university should stand, in their view, is knowledge as understanding.

Critically for Brown, not only is all understanding interpretive, but all interpretive activity is "constructive" and transformative. The investigator is never free from the subject of investigation, since investigators bring to the subject their own subjectivities. And, since "theology" is interpretive as well, there should be nothing much objectionable in theology—at least a non-"confessional" theology[9]—bringing its presuppositions to the subject under study. It should be free to go about its constructive and transformative tasks in the public university, just like any other practitioner of interpretive methods in the humanities.[10] Fair is fair. Indeed, Delwin Brown would go beyond just recognizing "theology" as merely another interpretive discipline within a standard university curriculum. He aims to deploy his "constructive theology" inside the citadels of secular public learning like some sort of intellectual Trojan Horse, as an agent of radical change. Thus, Brown claims that what "we need now is not the retreat of constructive theology into the churches, but a methodological critique of the university discourses that, among other things, clarifies theology's location within them."[11] Brown thus assumes that "science" (so-called) or the interpretive activity long central in the humanities cannot claim epistemological privileges against "theology." For others sharing Brown's type of thinking, the constructive activity of the so-called social "sciences" really just masks their own ideologies, indeed "theologies."[12]

---

9   Brown 1993: 8. "Confessional theology" is one bound to the "conceptual symbols of particular traditions of inheritance."

10 Ibid.

11 Delwin Brown, "The Location of the Theologian: John Cobb's Career as Critique," in: *Religious Studies Review* 19/11 (January 1993): 14.

12 With Durkheim in particular in mind, Anglican theologian, John Milbank follows the script written by postmodernism. To wit, since all discourses are constructed by subjective interests, all discourses are, in effect, equal as cognitive entities. Tellingly, Milbank rather baldly asserts that "theology encounters in effect, in sociology only a theology, and indeed a church in disguise, but a theology and a church dedicated to promoting a certain secular consensus" (Milbank 1990: 4).

Learning from Said

Now, as stimulating as theological critiques of contemporary knowledge may be, they illustrate why ideological critique needs the kind of refinement and further development that I am trying to articulate. We need in particular to be alert to a serious drawback with the critical and skeptical attitudes encouraged by Foucault, Said, and others. Like the theologians, they seem to have spawned a new orthodoxy and risk laying the dead hands of dogmatism and cynicism on doing the study of religion. Thus, it is common enough, sad to say, in our "politically correct" academic world, to encounter on a regular basis the claim, that only members of particular subgroups can fairly write the history of those subgroups, and that those who are not, cannot. Made explicitly or implicitly, this amounts to saying that because a writer can be classified as one sort of person or another, this is sufficient evidence to justify the view that the work they do will be necessarily and seriously biased in terms of the interests of these societal subgroups.[13] While I can understand how such a shortcut saves the time and energy of actually reading and studying seriously the authors and works involved, one can hardly be pleased with such a sweeping writing off of writers. In particular, it would be well to recall that even Said himself distinguishes between historians of Islam such as Maxime Rodinson and Louis Massignon, both equally white, male and European from others he believes practice their craft in the classic orientalist style that he attacks.

Following the presumptions of the approach taken by Said and others, I thus believe that ideological critique of the study of the history of religion may help those committed to the study of religion to get purchase over their own conceptual framework—to take responsibility for their own concepts. Now I take it as a first principle that whenever we use theoretical notions, like "myth," "ritual," "mysticism," "religion" and so on, we should be clear how we are "conceiving" them. We can do this initially by simply introspecting or by analyzing our writing and speech—what passes as garden variety conceptual or methodological analysis in the study of religion. But, it is at this point where it becomes important to know about the historical "other." It is not enough to assume or guess or imagine what I would think if I were Durkheim, Eliade, etc., we must really have some grounds—the best grounds that we can have—for thinking we know what they meant when they proposed certain theoretical constructions round the term, "sacrifice," for example. I can think of no better grounds for understanding what a theorist meant than to understand their actual intentions, the meaning of their language and concepts in the context in which they wrote, the actual empirical *Sitz im Leben* of the theory or theoretical idea in question.

---

13   This question is discussed from many perspectives in McCutcheon 1999.

Further, at least some of the theological critiques owing their inspiration to the likes of Foucault, Said and others are self-refuting. Why should we grant plausibility, for example, to the view that the theory-ladenness of, say, Durkheim's theory of religion puts it into the same epistemological class as neo-orthodox Protestant—unless it be *objectively* true that "all data are theory-laden?" The question is painfully simple: are all data, in fact, theory-laden or are they not? Unless, this question can be answered in the affirmative, the principle of theory-ladenness really amounts to a new kind of dogma—relativism asserted absolutely. If the question as to the factuality of the theory-ladenness of data can be answered in the affirmative, then, as practitioners of ideological critique we need to get on with the job of exposing the actual ways in which thought is "laden" with actual theories. This excursus into some recent attempts to re-theologize religious studies by invoking features of the epistemology of ideological critique points out how very important, then, it is to prepare for a defensible, durable and creative program of ideological critique in religious studies. To reiterate, the claim of theory-ladenness means nothing unless it is seen as an *empirical* matter, a fact waiting to be either discovered or dismissed, rather than one of absolute principle, as, I believe, our relativizing theologians have done.

Refining ideological critique by bringing out the necessity of being empirical in our critiques is my belief that it is not worth doing ideological critique unless doing so *makes a difference*. The quest for theory-ladenness is about ferreting out real hidden agendas, actually agent, yet undisclosed, determinants in thought. What could the value of asserting theory-ladenness of some particular matter possibly be unless things would be different in the absence of the theory "laden" therein?

On Being Empirical about Eliade

Another way of showing how ideological critique should be refined along empirical lines is to focus on the temptations of an easy impressionism that sometimes afflicts our fledgling enterprise. Thus, some writers practicing what may seem like a form of ideological critique seem to think making allegations about the ideological determinants in a person's thought is sufficient unto the day. Put otherwise, they seem to imagine that just because one can "place" someone in a context that a given thinker *actually* occupied such a context. They further imagine that just because a thinker they may have occupied such a context, that their occupation of such a location was consequential for their thought—that it "made a difference." In order to secure the future of ideological critique, one must insist that ideological critique can never be a blanket excuse, allegation, accusation or smear. To illustrate my point, consider, take some attempts to bring the "life and letters" of Mircea Eliade before the bar of ideological critique.

For some years, it has been known that as a young man in Romania, Eliade had given his heart to the ideology of the radical "fascist"[14] Legion of the Archangel Michael. It is still deeply disquieting that a man so gentle, refined and deeply religious in person and manner seems to have published vicious political tracts in the religio-fascist Romania between the wars referring to the "pests brought to us (Romanians) by the Jewish invasion"[15] or, in a thinly veiled reference to Romanian Jews, to have called for the elimination of them from the body politic as so many "toxins"[16] — as one of Eliade's "ideological critics," Adriana Berger claims. If we accept all of the material which Adriana Berger has dug up here, the case for Eliade's vicious anti-Semitism seems overwhelming. If Berger is right about the actual "fascist" formation of Eliade's thought, then a devastating kind of ideological critique has begun — namely one which could in theory link Eliade's actual "fascist" ideology and thinking to other domains of his thought — such as Eliade's theories about religion — not hitherto recognized as related to an underlying political ideology like fascism.

I indeed attempted to do precisely this in my *Four Theories of Myth in Twentieth-Century History*.[17] There, for instance, I showed the remarkable parallels between the actual ideology of the Romanian Legion of the Archangel Michael — its Romanian "traditionalism," its adulation of the peasant, its "nostalgias for the archaic, cosmic and telluric" and so on — with familiar themes in Eliade's theory of religion.[18] I further showed that Eliade was personally linked at the highest levels with the leadership of this movement, and therefore that the parallels between his theory of religion and the ideology of the Legion of the Archangel Michael were no longer merely speculative, but indeed that the burden of proof rested with those who would assert that Eliade and his theory of religion were totally independent of this form of indigenous Romanian fascism. I had done as best I could to make my ideological critique of Eliade's theory of religion *empirical*. Moreover, my ideological critique made a palpable *difference*, as the numerous attacks and imitators of my position poured out from all quarters testified. If my arguments had made "no difference" to our

---

14 For a thorough and nuanced treatment of this notoriously misused term see Wiles 1969: 176. Cited in Strenski 1987: 213, n. 102.

15 Adriana Berger, "Mircea Eliade and Romanian Fascism and the History of Religions in the United States," in: Harrowitz 1994: 59.

16 Ibid.: 58.

17 Strenski 1987, chs. 4 and 5.

18 Ibid.: 102f.

evaluation, appreciation and understanding of Eliade's theories as they bore on religious studies, why all the fuss?[19]

Yet in any volume where moral and political elements so highly charge the atmosphere, the temptation to push things along is enormous. Berger occasionally fails to support claims with appropriate by citations, for example, in connection with Eliade's supposed endorsement of anti-Jewish laws.[20] And here, Berger's case is itself "tainted" by sometimes tendentious readings of the nature and extent of Eliade's participation in Romanian fascism. Her claims simply lack the kind of *empirical* grounding they need in order to make for good ideological critique. Berger thus asserts that Eliade wrote about the Iron Guard as a full formal member (a point of dubious importance anyway, as I shall argue), because he addressed a particular article to "the Christians outside the movement."[21] But although Eliade was quite likely what Berger says he was, it does not follow from the *empirical* evidence and arguments Berger presents here. For example, for Eliade to write as if he had intimate knowledge of the inner workings of the Iron Guard may only reflect Eliade's long and intimate association with the *spiritus rector* of the Iron Guard, Nae Ionesco, and indeed the whole crowd of "young generation" types he led, as I have argued in *Four Theories of Myth in Twentieth Century History*.[22] What matters for good ideological critique, in any event, is not formal membership, but actual intellectual and spiritual affinities. Did the Legion believe what Berger says it does; did Eliade do the same? Here, I think we have solid empirical evidence to make such connections. To wit, Eliade's closest friends were almost all deeply implicated in Guardist thought and politics; Eliade's intellectual and spiritual vision was moreover basically isomorphic with the structure of fascist thinking of the time as I have argued in *Four Theories of Myth in Twentieth-Century History*.[23]

---

19   Cave 1993 and Rennie 1996 may be listed among the most vociferous critics of *Four Theories of Myth in Twentieth-Century History*, while McCutcheon 1997 ranks as one of the most prominent imitators.

20   Adriana Berger, "Mircea Eliade and Romanian Fascism and the History of Religions in the United States" in: Harrowitz 1994: 59.

21   Ibid. 63f.

22   Strenski 1987, chs. 4 and 5.

23   Berger further leads one to suspect that her hold on the reality of the situation for Eliade and the Legion in Romania may not be very solid, and thus that her ideological critique may be mostly impressionistic and not as empirically grounded as it ought to be in order to "make a difference." She never, for example, puts up her case against the well-known and widely publicized, but admittedly abject, apologetics of MacLinscott Ricketts, Eliade's biographer and tireless defender. Ricketts strains normal credulity by claiming that Eliade could never have actually authored the anti-Semitic articles upon which Berger in key places relies. Berger at least should have noted this. But instead she does not even cite Ricketts at all! Having noted these infelicities in Berger's

I raise these points not only because Eliade is a well-known figure in religious studies, but also to make the point about what *good* ideological critique is. In the case of Eliade cited above, refining the way we do ideological critique requires distinguishing the many *actual* ways anti-Semitism *empirically* operates. To go beyond slogans, ideological critique needs to be a *critical* approach to theories and to resist the uncritical lumping of things that should be kept apart—that is if we want (and I certainly think we do) to understand how real—as opposed to fictional—anti-Semitic politics worked. Let me explain with another example drawn from the world of recent religion and politics.

Why Blame Luther?

It seems to me worth making a distinction between anti-Semitic thought which had *actual and direct* consequences for real Jews and that which did not. A critical ideological critique would want to understand, say, whether a given Christian theology or theologian was an anti-Semite of the sort who *directly* contributed to the death of Jews, or perhaps someone whose work may have been commandeered for anti-Semitic uses. Now, Eliade, Heidegger, and others all were involved in *deliberate and direct* ways with real policies which turned out immediately to be deadly to Jews—even if they were not lodged in the innermost centers of power in various ministries dealing with so-called Jewish affairs. In Eliade's and Heidegger's cases, they both reflected a fascist cultural reality and then contributed to articulating an ideological vision in which actual anti-Semitic policies flourished. Their thought both participated in the anti-Jewish spirit of their milieus as well as articulated deeper conception of a spirit unfriendly to Jews. In tracking these leads through their lives and thought, we are thus face to face with the real causality of anti-Jewish history. An ideological critique that grasped the historical reality of the *actual* situations of Eliade and Heidegger would then be contributing to the future of a durable ideological critique because uncovering the "fascist" ideologies to which Eliade and Heidegger *actually* ascribed would "make a difference" to any argument made thereafter that their academic and scholarly work reflected those political ideologies.

By contrast, although an egregious Jew-hater, Luther, by contrast, seems himself and in his theology to have had little or no effect on the lives of real Jews in the twentieth century. This was so not only because of the gap of time

---

treatment of Eliade, it is just important to maintain perspective. Thus while we may note that Berger overreaches or lacks nuance in the interest of moral outrage, her attacks are surely aimed in the right direction. The charge of Eliade's anti-Semitism now seems solidly established by the publication of Mihail Sebastian's wartime diaries (Dee 2000).

between him and us, but also because Lutheran tradition had concealed and suppressed Luther's anti-Semitism throughout its history. It was not until the Nazis recovered, rebroadcast and exploited it that "Luther"—the Nazi reading of Luther—entered the world of Nazi politics and ideology. Say what one will about Luther's anti-Semitism, in point of fact, Lutheran history is probably no more or less anti-Semitic say than Catholic or Calvinist history because of the things which Luther said against his Jewish contemporaries. If we are to believe Carter Lindberg's arguments, Lutheran history generally seems to have taken shape in respect to the Jews as if Luther had never uttered an anti-Semitic word at all![24] So, although Luther's anti-Semitism remains as deplorable as ever, it seems to have little to do with the role played by the Lutheran tradition and its theology in relation to real Jews and in particular to Nazi political policies to Jews as well. Just the opposite is true of Eliade and Heidegger.

In my judgment, the kind of second generation, refined (and thus, effective) ideological critique I am advocating, requires that more effort should be ex-pended on consequential thinkers like Eliade and Heidegger—on thinkers whose thought really "made a difference," who were actually part of an his-torical anti-Semitic politics. Thinkers of the distant past who became icons of Jew hatred do not seem to me priority targets of ideological critique. It is the *empirical* historical causality linking anti-Jewish thought and anti-Jewish poli-cies which I think deserves top priority as a "showcase" for a refined ideolog-ical critique. This does not in the least mean that I believe we should dismiss the power of the *symbolic* role of an anti-Semitic Luther. But, it would be immeasurably better to know more about the nameless, faceless, obscure, but consequential Nazi *Religionsforscher* who retrieved Luther for modern uses than to dwell on the prejudices of a man on the margins of the late middle ages. He, not Luther, "made a difference." A refined, second generation ideological criti-que would seek to undercover the hidden ideological foundations of his activity. How and why did he act as he did? Why did he know where to look? What politics was involved in getting his recommendations heard? Once made, in the case of Luther as well as in the case of Berger's Eliade, these distinctions let us paint a truer picture of the mind of the consequential anti-Semite.

Are these distinctions without a difference? I think not. If I have been persuasive, I hope I have convinced readers that ideological critique should place a premium on *actual historical* relation. Imagine how differently we would speak of Luther's anti-Semitism had his church not only kept his anti-Semitic teachings in full view, but had broadcast and reaffirmed them on their own? What matters is a sharp understanding of the kind of thinking which has effectively made our world inhospitable for our Jewish brothers and sisters,

---

24   Carter Lindberg, "Tainted Greatness: Luther's Attitudes toward Judaism and Their Historical Reception," in: Harrowitz 1994: 25.

even when that thinking may not be overtly or totally anti-Semitic, but only tainted with hatred of Jews.

Making a Difference in South Africa

Another, and even more prominent, example of how much more *close empirical* work we still need to do to attain a level of maturity and refinement in ideological critique emerges in David Chidester's *Savage Systems*.[25] In his pioneering exploration of the conceptualization of "religion" and its social consequences in southern Africa, Chidester seeks what we would all recognize as ideological critique of the history of various attempts—some deliberate, systematic and even academic, others haphazard, *en passant* and amateurish—to study religion in South Africa. Reflecting this variety of sources, Chidester surveys a vast corpus of writings from missionaries, explorers, travelers and scholars from the redoubtable Dutch (and German) language intellectual world, many of whom laid the bases for European theorizing about religion. In doing so, Chidester thinks he brings forth an ideological critique of the very discipline of religious studies. His thesis is in brief that "the study of religion was entangled in the power relations of frontier conflict, military conquest and resistance, and imperial expansion" and that "it arises out of a violent history of colonial conquest and domination."[26]

But at least two ambiguities afflict Chidester's claims. Both the notion of the actual empirical and historical nature of the "study of religion" and the idea of what is it to be "entangled in" or "to arise out of" the colonial enterprise lack empirical support. Thus, by "study of religion" Chidester says he means "comparative study of religion"—"a particular science."[27] That Chidester says he means a "particular science" gives the impression that he has in mind the likes of someone like Gerardus van der Leeuw, Mircea Eliade or Ninian Smart—someone who is both a professional academic and someone constrained by the norms of university institutional setting—someone with a (relatively) disinterested stake in the data. But, it is distinctly odd then of Chidester to include within this "particular science" the ragtag bunch whom he studies—the travelers or casual observers, to mention but one set upon whom Chidester lavishes attention. Nor would this "particular science" include others to whom Chidester gives his attention—those with explicit religious or political roles and agendas, such as Christian theologians and missionaries or British colonial administrators. Yet, Chidester applies the description, "study of reli-

---

25 Chidester 1996.

26 Ibid.: xii.

27 Ibid.: 1, 2.

gion" and "comparative study of religion" precisely to these sorts of folk—to precisely those with religious or political axes to grind, and not to so-called disinterested scholars going by the name of the discipline of "comparative studies of religion." In a bizarre wrenching of language in Chidester's hands, brazen Protestant mission theology is called either "Christian comparative religion"[28] or "Protestant comparative religion"—as if the undertakings of missionaries and scholars were on a par with one another.[29]

Thus, the main problem with these claims is that Chidester's ideological critique fails to identify the actual people or institutions and ideology against whom he claims to be offering a critique. Just on empirical grounds alone, Chidester's ideological critique seems to have missed its mark. Chidester aims his book at today's profession, religious studies. Yet, those who practice a real "particular science," called comparative students of religion, like Eliade or van der Leeuw or Smart, are not the same as those Chidester would indict. Chidester's attempt at ideological critique by identification of two such differently motivated modes of production needs, at the very minimum, some argument. Failing so to do, Chidester misrepresents both the colonial past and the study of religion. This is not to say that scholars never gave aid and comfort to colonial administrations, Christian missions, or apartheid governmental policy—often eagerly. Nor is it to say that they should not be criticized for doing so in the name of racist ideologies. It is only to say that he does not show that a general case can be made that the "particular science" of comparative study of religion does so.

It is unfortunately typical of Chidester, therefore, to labor the cases of people distant from the "particular science" of the comparative study of religion, but to silently assume that anyone comparing religions or studying religions *ipso facto* should be said to belong to the institution we have come to know as religious studies—to the "particular science" of comparative study of religion. One example is the way Chidester indicts two eighteenth century German travelers to southern Africa, Peter "Kolb" (sic) and Otto Friedrich Mentzel. Kolbe is particularly interesting in that he stayed on in southern Africa as secretary of the *landdrost* of Stellenbosch for about eight years, and wrote a reputedly influential book on life in the southern Cape. Now, while Chidester's case against Kolbe has initial plausibility, it misses the mark of indicting the "particular science" of comparative study of religion. While Kolbe was a tireless fieldworker and interviewer of Hottentot folk, and even attempted to construct a method of "self-conscious" comparative study, it hardly makes him

---

28   Ibid.: 37, 41.

29   Ibid.: 85. Note also how Chidester ignores the overwhelming role of the Dutch Reformed church missionizing in dealings with the native folk of southern Africa, even in a work Chidester cites for his own purposes. See Elphick/Giliomee 1979, especially articles by Elphick, Leonard Guelke and Martin Legassick.

the equivalent of Karen McCarthy Brown. Thus, while Kolbe is impressive in his practice of many skills which contain the makings of scholarship on religion, none of this marks Kolbe as someone representing "particular science" of the comparative study of religion. Kolbe, for example, operated alone, and outside the context of the university or research institute. Had Kolbe occupied a place like C.P. Tiele or Friedrich Max Müller, self-identified with a science of religion and with the institutions making such an enterprise possible, Chidester would indeed have a case. But Kolbe does not, nor do the countless individuals who have contributed to the study of religion, but who do not do so as part of any institutional scientific or professional community. It is at best anachronistic to project onto the informal scholarship of the eighteenth century the norms and identity of the professions of our own time. Put brutally, no such thing as "particular science" of the comparative study of religion existed in the time and place of which Chidester often writes.

Further, even if Kolbe can be identified with the "particular science" of the comparative study of religion, the question for a refined ideological critique is whether his book "made a difference." Chidester accuses Kolbe's book of having contributed to "the dispossession and displacement of Khoisan people in the Cape" by the publication of his book, in part because Kolbe expressed the view that the Hottentots had "religion."[30] He also tells us that Kolbe's book was influential in Europe and among ethnologists there. But Chidester says *nothing* about whether or not anyone with the power to "dispossess and displace the Khoisan people in the Cape" read it, or used it to justify such policies. He cites *no* sources of persons responsible for such policies of dispossession and displacement showing that they took into account what Kolbe said—no diaries, no official reports, no newspaper articles, no testimony of contemporaries to this effect—nothing! Even if it be granted that there is a formal congruence or even an affinity of values between what Kolbe wrote and the ideology of the colonial policies that Chidester rightly indicts, this would not show that Kolbe's book "made a difference" to colonial policy. Failing this ability to show that Kolbe's work "made a difference," we cannot resist wondering about the missing steps along the way connecting a book of the eighteenth century with the social policies of the nineteenth and twentieth centuries. No amount of textual analyses—something Chidester does excellently—will substitute for establishing the patterns of real causality Chidester claims. Once more, we can see how a failure at the level of making ideological critique "empirical," to demonstrate actual causality between ideologies in books and policies on the ground may undermine the efforts of the program of ideological critique for attaining the plausibility and long-term durability for which I have been arguing.

---

30   Chidester 1996: 71-72.

There is then a lesson to be learned here about insuring that our ideological critique really makes a difference. While so much of what Chidester writes is useful and worthy to be celebrated, a great deal more care is required so that ideological critique really "sticks." The context in which we try to "locate" a theory must *actually* be the context in which it is claimed to reside—and not, as I think Chidester has done in mis-locating the ideas he criticizes within a non-existent (at the time) location called "comparative study of religion." We also need to be sufficiently empirical in our location of ideologies and theories in order to show moreover that they "made a difference,"—that they actually informed the policies Chidester and other critics want to indict. We need to work harder to take the idea of theory-ladenness as an *empirical possibility*. That there are significant underlying intellectual strategies shaping thought is something for which we need to be prepared to test, and not simply to assume.

Getting Past the "Best" to the "Good"

A major moral emerging from the cases I have examined is that dogmatism or absolutism in ideological critique can lead us into many errors of mis-identification and mis-location of the thought under consideration. I have argued instead that sweeping claims about the ideological nature of thought require grounding in the facts of the situation—that an empirical and densely historical approach to the way thought is in fact shaped should be our ideal. If thought is conditioned by its biographical, religious and ideological locations, then discovering how it is should become a matter of *empirical* research. Thus, Chidester's confident "identification" of Kolbe's work as having lent itself to official mistreatment of native Africans fails, because Chidester provides no evidence that anyone is a position of power to mistreat Africans was informed by what Kolbe wrote. Furthermore, Kolbe's "location" in the "comparative study of religion" is at best an anachronism, since no such thing as this institution existed when Kolbe wrote. Further, the assumption of Luther's "place" in history as a proto-Nazi, because of his personal anti-Semitism likewise ignores the fact that the Nazis themselves had deliberately to reconstruct a Luther in their own image to achieve this effect. Berger's "situation" of Eliade in the front lines of the Iron Guard, while looking more and more likely as we discover more of Eliade's past, cannot be defended by the evidence Berger brings to bear.

From these examples alone, it should be clear that we might gain some confidence for moving beyond at least one more related dogma bedeviling the progress of ideological critique. This is the view that just because all viewpoints rest on assumptions, principles, axioms, and such that therefore all views are equally well or non-trivially "conditioned," "partial" and the like. Instead, I am arguing that ideological critique needs to move forward by accepting the provisional and corrigible nature of human knowledge, rather than lusting after absolutes. This is to argue that some "conditioned" or ideologically informed theories may be better than others. I should like to conclude my discussion then by coming round full circle by arguing why I have been so consistent in my assertion of the criterion of an *empirical* conception of what ideological critique can be—at least within the compass of the value world of the West.

While from an absolute or God's-eye or Buddhist Sunyata view, it may be correct that every human effort at knowledge is partial and inadequate, not many of us can successfully make the claim to be able to speak from so lofty a height or so profound a depth. We live in a world where we must at least assume as a first approximation that anything we say might in theory be reasonably contradicted or contested. To say we "know" in a strong sense would itself be to take the God's-eye view of absolute knowledge. But, living in this world where we can expect ideas to be contested and changed is not the same as living in a world in which views have no value, or in which every view has the same value in every context as any other view. Living in the world is not really served by in effect a wholesale delegitimizing or relativizing of all viewpoints. It may just be the case that some views in some contexts are to be *preferred* over others. Ptolemaic astronomy will not get the International Space Station positioned correctly, although modern astronomy will. I think the proposal that ideological critique ought to proceed *empirically* likewise makes for better ideological critique than other alternatives, such as those canvassed in the works of Berger, Chidester and others.

A wholesale delegitimizing of views because they rest on relative foundations, such as we saw with a neo-Orthodox Protestant theologian, like Green, for instance, also leaves us spinning our wheels in the nihilistic mud. This is not the future we want for religious studies, I would submit. While we want to continue to be alert to the ideological underpinnings of our programs, I am recommending that we ought not be too routinely nihilistic about it. Ideological critique, as I believe it ought to be practiced, does not require massive cynicism about theories. In religious studies, for example, we have many fine projects to accomplish; we have many fine efforts in which to enlist people. It is hard to see how human society of any sort could be possible were such positive and constructive values not in some way on the whole in the ascendent—at least as working principles.

In this everyday world, different communities make, often sheerly practical, decisions to value certain viewpoints. Indeed, part of what defines and constitutes communities at all are decisions about the "givens" of knowledge about the world. Bible-based churches, for example, are what they are because they take the Bible as axiomatic, as given, as "revelation"—criticisms of it (ideological or not) not withstanding. Some other text might occupy the place of the Bible instead—say the Vedas or Koran—and there may well be mutual knowledge of these different foundational literatures. So, the matter is relative and not absolute. But it still remains necessary to have some values, if life is to go on. Likewise, Euclidian geometry rests on certain axioms—treated for all intents and purposes as if they were absolute and uncontestable. Of course, we do have geometries in which parallel lines, for example, meet, and thus in which Euclidian axioms are violated. Other geometries are of course possible with a simple change of axioms. But the assumptions or axioms grounding such a new geometry are in a way still as (relatively) absolute *within that world* as the Euclidian axioms were in their world, given their circumscription of things. Religious studies ought not be the kind of community in which, say, the theological sophistry of a Karl Barth stands on the same footing as work done by such founders of the modern study of religion as a Max Weber, Louis Dumont, Ninian Smart, to name only a very small few. Although the work of these scholars will in time be superceded, and is in no way regarded as the "best" last word in the field, they have helped us move things along toward the "good." Thus whatever the ideological underpinnings of their work, they in no way delegitimate it in the way the Protestant apologetics of a Karl Barth would. All views are not equal, simply because they have ideological bases. It depends in part on the ideology at issue.

Now these practical considerations about getting on with life, about what Voltaire called preferring the "good" to the "best," are of the highest importance to the existence of civilized life even beyond religious studies. They are embedded in the epistemological principles undergirding our judicial and legal systems of the West—but not exclusively so.[31] Our Western judicial system, and thus Western culture, for example, assumes the foundational or axiomatic status of the priority of sense perception or empirical knowledge. Eye witness testimony, material evidence, even down to rarified DNA samples, all presume the foundational nature of empirical evidence, of knowledge through the senses. Extra-sensory perception, retro-cognition of past lives, so called "spectral evidence," the otherwise authoritative declarations of popes, gurus, buddhas or psychics—all are literally "ruled out of court." This does not, however, mean that popes, gurus, buddhas or psychics may not get to the truth, or that they might not someday become part of what we accept as "knowledge." Not at all. At the very least, however, their words are neither as "accepted" nor as foundational as, for example, the epistemological foundation of our legal and judicial systems. Drawing the line at the empirical, as we in the West do in our legal and judicial systems, is our *practical* way of getting on with having a civilized society.

There was a time, of course, in the history of the West when "spectral evidence"—literally the testimony of spirits or of those claiming to see or hear spirits—was acceptable in courts of law. The witch trials of county Essex and

---

31   Jayatillekee 1971; Villacorta 1972.

Salem in the sixteenth and seventeenth centuries all relied on such "evidence."[32] We in the West no longer do so. This decision to draw the line this side of the spirit world for such foundational parts of our civic life is our way of saying that we get along better in enabling life to prosper by doing so. Such a decision does not in itself mean that spirits do not exist. It only means that we have rejected everyday dependence upon a system which assumes that they exist. We in the West reject basing a legal system on evidence which would include the testimony of spirits or the testimony of those in communion with them—at the very least out of strictly practical considerations. Namely, we are in effect betting that it is not possible to have an orderly system of justice if we accepted "spectral evidence" into "evidence," as the development of a witch "crazes" attested. Given who we are, there are simply no reliable ways in which to check "spectral evidence." We in the West are not confident in being able to assess it, and thus what we call "knowledge" needs to have at least a strong *empirical* component.

For much the same reasons, our so called "secular" political systems in the West in a way rest on the wager that civilized society stands a better chance of success if we remove religion, or better yet, any single religion, from a foundational role in our society. We in the West learned from the various wars of religion of the sixteenth and seventeenth centuries that the social consensus necessary for a civilized society could not be based upon the kinds of transcendental beliefs over which people had been so fiercely divided. Such beliefs had to be declared neutral to the maintenance of our social life. Social peace was not possible, the wager stipulated, if religion was a matter of public civic contest. Such beliefs mattered far too much, and divided our populations too sharply to make them the measure of citizenship. Settling the score in favor of one or the other risked endless social unrest and violence.

Being Protestant in a state insisting upon Catholic principles of citizenship, for example, created a situation ultimately intolerable for Protestants. Social harmony is better served—again in a practical way—by eliminating religious tests or preferences as standards of citizenship. Better, again we in the West reasoned, as it were, to tolerate all religions, than to risk the potential for social disruption by privileging one.

Of course, social peace and a civilized society may not finally be preferable to living by the "true" religion—especially if there is one! These tensions are still with us. Everything from Operation Rescue to the Civil Rights Movement rests on the preference for "truth" over social peace. Even civilization's defining property—the rule of law—is flaunted in pursuit of a truth which offends existing social consensus and harmony, typical of these movements of reform and resistance. But, at least, as our societal "default," we in the West have

---

32 Thomas 1971: chapters 14–18.

opted for the rule of law and social peace over the continuous revolution promised by religious movements, marching as they do to the sound of often distant and different drummers. Likewise, what we in the West call "science" — including the scientific and interpretive study of religion—too rests on certain axioms or assumptions about what counts as knowledge. But this does not make it indistinguishable in this respect from other schemes of knowledge— including "theology."

For these and other reasons, I have proposed that *empirical* study and broadly scientific approaches should characterize ideological critique. While we may discover that these ways of governing ideological critique are not best, we must be on guard, as the saying goes, not to let our quest for the "best" become the enemy of the "good."

Conclusion

I have thus been arguing that the study of the ideological bases of the study of religion is part and parcel of the study of religion, and that we might just as well turn in our union cards as intellectuals, if we pass over it. How *could* an ideologically critical study of the study of religion *not* have *something* to do with the study of religion? How is it possible that any self-respecting thinking person in the study of religion could pursue academic goals in the present without some reference to the underlying ideological features of what they are doing— to the social and historic contexts of the work in question, to embedded ideologies informing the agendas of the research itself? Well, in conclusion, here are a few reasons why some might not go along with my attempts to advocate ideological critique. Let me speak to these objections.

To some students of religion, many of those inspired by theological interests, emphasizing the need to study the ideological bases of the study of religion will seem either irrelevant or offensive. They are often passionately *engagé*, and therefore contending with many pressing existential, political and social problems, such as race, gender, poverty, violence and so on. It is hard enough getting them interested in the comparative and phenomenological dimensions of religious studies as it is, without expecting them easily to become committed to the critical study of the ideological roots of religious studies. While I share their politics, the path to durable and long-term activism is not always as clearly marked as one may think. Their allergy to critical study comes from the kind of mentality that bent the study of the religions of India in the 1960s and 1970s into a concern either with Gandhi as a mentor for our own anti-war or non-violent political protest or toward an interest in yogic and mystical experience as confirmation for counter-cultural experimentation into drug experience—or just as often into "detoxing" from them. I would not want to gainsay these interests or efforts. Every time casts its spell on the things we do.

Furthermore, I shall be the first to admit that perhaps the *engagé* among us may have a point in not caring about the critical study of the ideologies informing religious studies. Are we really sorry, for example, that Martin Luther King, Jr. spent most of his time studying social ethics and Christian theology, rather than being critical of the ideologies underlying the study of religion? Like Martin Luther King, Jr. many of us too may be pressed with the demands of current social problems, and judged by our reactions to them in terms of present-day values. Thus, given the pull of such heady and heartfelt political and moral engagement, studying the ideological underpinnings of the history of religions seems only to rankle: those dead men of the past of the study of religion have the nerve now to insist that we use up our valuable youth paying attention to their aged interests and often discredited ideologies. Really! Who do these dead men think they are!?

To be sure, there may be other objections to engaging the ideological critique of theories in religious studies hailing from, those less inclined to being agents of social change than to advancing the study of religion in the humanistic or academic sense. They may agree with me about the need to understand the ideological roots of the study of religion, because their interests are primarily scholarly and rather than activist. But, still some of them may not be prepared to act upon my recommendation for the practice of the ideological critique of theories in religious studies. They might reply, "Sure, it would be *nice* to know the historical ideological circumstances lying behind the study of religion, just as it's *nice* to keep snapshots of our grandparents and great grandparents in some bureau drawer for occasional perusal. Thanks for the memories; and that's about it." For them, the question is whether or not being historically informed about the ideological roots of the study of religion *matters* in some significant way.

Then another group of nodders might add, "Oh yes, it would be *nice* to be critical of the study of religion's ideological roots—and it may even matter in some *significant* way for some purposes, but I want to get on with the primary task of studying *religion*, and if I am going to stray into second-order inquiry, my top priority there should be something practical such as *methodology*—what *methods* to use in studying religion. I don't want to spend my time learning about *how and why* religion *has been* studied in the past!" I mean, while physicists may read Newtonian physics, do they really care about the Newton's biography or about the world of English Puritanism and his immersion in it? Would we as a society and even as an academic discipline called religious studies be richer, say, in our knowledge of Islam or Buddhism because of historical sensitivity to the ideological commitments taken by those studying these religions in comparison, say, to the knowledge acquired about Islam or Buddhism thanks to Wilfred Smith or Stanley Tambiah directly? How much of the ideological background of the work of W.C. Smith or Tambiah will helps us understand how they studied religions?

To counter these arguments, we can always resort to the old saw that knowledge is good in itself. We can always say that being aware of the ideological commitments of those who study religion and of the ways they promoted the study of religions really needs no defense. For this reason, I have tried to argue for students of religion to be critical about the underlying ideological commitments behind the study of religion *empirically and historically*—in particular times and places. But, the more we engage in a socially and historically critical approach to the study of religion the more we learn how these so-called "ideological" substrata are in many cases religious themselves. What we do today rests on what *happened* yesterday, and also on what we *believe* happened yesterday and how we *conceptualize* both what we believe happened yesterday and actually did happen yesterday. These conceptualizations are often religious themselves, or at the very least kindred to religion in being "ideological."

For those who find themselves existentially committed, and want to change society, I hope to remind them of what they already surely know—the critical study of *culture, society and history* can reshape our definitions of the present, and thus become decisive in bringing about change in the present. This is why one often hears passionate complaints against those who would *re-write or revise* history. Or, more benignly, consider how recent work on women's critical study of Christianity in the West has armed feminist reformers with weapons for challenging religious institutions such as the male priesthood. For those others who are hell-bent to study their subject matter of religion with little or no dallying in the glades of critical methodology and history, I hope I have persuaded them to follow through on the idea some may widely embrace already—that the "religion" they seek to study, along with all the main concepts included in it—myth, ritual, magic, witchcraft, sacrifice and so on—are historically and culturally derived concepts. Those concepts and the ideologies behind them are especially worth studying critically in their real empirical settings.

Bibliography

Brown, Delwin (1993), "Constructive Theology and the Academy," in: *Bulletin of the Council of the Societies for the Study of Religion* 22 (1): 8.

Cave, David (1993), *Mircea Eliade's Vision for a New Humanism*. New York: Oxford University Press.

Chidester, David (1996), *Savage Systems: Colonialism and Comparative Religion in Southern Africa*. Charlottesville, Va.: University Press of Virginia.

Dee, Ivan R., ed. (2000), *Mihail Sebastian, Journal, 1935–1944: The Fascist Years*. Chicago: University of Chicago Press.

Elphick, Richard/Giliomee, Hermann, eds. (1979), *The Shaping of Southern African Society, 1652–1840*. Middletown, Conn.: Wesleyan University Press.

Green, Garrett (1995), "Challenging the Religious Studies Canon: Karl Barth's Theory of Religion," in: *The Journal of Religion* 75: 473–86.

Harrowitz, Nancy A., ed. (1994), *Tainted Greatness: Antisemitism and Cultural Heroes*. Philadephia, Pa.: Temple University Press.

Jayatilleke, Kulatissa Nanda (1971), *The Principles of International Law in Buddhist Doctrine*. Leyden: Academy of International Law.

Jones, Robert Alun (1999), *The Development of Durkheim's Social Realism*. Cambridge: Cambridge University Press.

McCutcheon, Russell T. (1997), *Manufacturing Religion: The Discourse on Sui Generis Religion and the Politics of Nostalgia*. New York: Oxford University Press.

— ed. (1999), *The Insider/Outsider Problem in the Study of Religion*. London: Cassell.

Milbank, John (1990), *Theology and Social Theory: Beyond Secular Reason*. Oxford: Blackwell.

Mitzman, Arthur (1969), *The Iron Cage*. New York: Grosset and Dunlap.

Rennie, Brian S. (1996), *Reconstructing Eliade*. Albany, N.Y.: SUNY.

Ringer, Fritz (1969), *The Decline of the German Mandarins*. Cambridge, Mass.: Harvard University Press.

Said, Edward W. (1978), *Orientalism*. New York: Pantheon.

Skinner, Quentin (1978), *Foundations of Modern Political Thought*. Vol. 1. Cambridge: Cambridge University Press.

Strenski, Ivan (1987), *Four Theories of Myth in Twentieth-Century History*. London: Macmillan.

Thomas, Keith (1971), *Religion and the Decline of Magic*. New York: Charles Scribners' Sons.

Villacorta, Wilfrido (1972), *Theravada Buddhism as a Value Standard of Attitudes towards International Law: Celyon and Thailand*. Unpublished Ph.D. Thesis, Catholic University, Washington, D.C.

Wiles, Peter (1969), "A Syndrome, Not a Doctrine," in: G. Ionescu/E. Gellner, eds., *Populism*. London: Macmillan: 166–80.

Gendering the History of Religions

by

Lisbeth Mikaelsson

The concept of gender points to culturally produced differences between men and women. It covers a wide range of phenomena as well as a scholarly discourse. Gender is a battleground of meanings where biological determinism is confronted with cultural relativism. The distinction between the biologically given and the culturally conceived is a fundamental characteristic of gender as a critical category. In the last decade feminist scholars have criticized the sharp distinction between biological sex and socio-cultural gender, or the so-called sex/gender model, which has been so prominent in feminist theory. The model is attacked for being too heterosexually oriented, for repeating the split between nature and culture, for not reflecting how much the body is a cultural construct, and for neglecting the corporeal dimension of meaning construction.[1] However, such warranted critique does not nullify the fundamental insight that socio-cultural gender structures cannot be explained by biological sex, but have to be assessed as historical and linguistic creations.

Religion is a main factor when it comes to how gender differences are produced and realized in people's lives. Religious mediation of gender happens through the interpretation of myths and symbols, as well as in their ritual, ethical and organizational enactment. Religious teachings legitimize gender hierarchies in society and influence personal gender identity. Gender research in the history of religions is important in society at large because it contributes to our understanding of how divisions between men and women are sanctioned and at the same time demonstrates how religion may structure people's lives in fundamental respects.

Although sexuality has figured as a phenomenological category in the shape of *hieros gamos*, sacred intercourse, gender has not been a central concern in the history of religions, to be compared with for instance myth, ritual, concepts of divinity, all of them phenomenological topics considered to belong to

---

1   Probably the most influential criticism of the sex/gender model has been launched by
     Judith Butler in her famous *Gender Trouble: Feminism and the Subversion of Identity* (1990).
     For recent overviews of different understandings of gender and discussions of religious
     studies in a critical gender perspective, see King 1995b; Morgan 1999; Warne 2000.

the very essence of religion. Instead, gender critique often subverts essentialist and metaphysical renderings of religion. In the same way, deconstructionist critique undermines the fixed gender dichotomies established by a great many religious traditions.

The critical category of gender entered the history of religions in the 1970s, in the wake of feminism. The category is rooted in feminist research and debates about gender difference.[2]

The Feminist Impulse

The history of the present feminist trend in religious studies can be traced to the 1960s, when female scholars started to ponder how religion is involved in the repression of women and besides, how scholarship made their own sex invisible.[3] During the 1970s this kind of questioning intensified and became widespread. This happened in the wake of the growing feminist movement's identification of how women in different fields of life were suppressed. Structures and procedures in the academy that make women invisible or marginal were seen as part of the multi-structured repression of women in society.

---

2   The concept of feminism should be thought of as comprising a wide spectrum of political ideas and social activities. One may profitably speak of several feminisms in the modern era, see Offen 1988 and 2000; Morgan 1999: 43.

3   Gender-critical work on religion in the second half of the twentieth century started in Christian theological contexts: Valerie Saiving's essay "The Human Situation: A Feminine View" appeared in 1960; Mary Daly's *The Church and the Second Sex* was first published in 1968; Kari Elisabeth Børresen's dissertation about St. Augustine's and Thomas Aquinas' views on women, *Subordination et Equivalence: Nature et Rôle de la Femme 'après Augustin and Thomas d'Aquin* came out in 1968; George H. Tavard's *Woman in Christian Tradition* was published in 1973, and Rosemary Radford Ruether's seminal edition, *Religion and Sexism. Images of Woman in the Jewish and Christian Traditions*, was available in 1974.

In the 1970s feminist criticism of the Christian tradition was a debated topic in several European countries and quite a number of books in native languages came out. Some early examples from my own country are the Norwegian publications *Kvinnen i kirken. Teori og praksis* (1977) by Marit Lindheim Gundersen; *Kloke jomfruer? Om kirke, kristendom og kvinnefrigjøring* (1978) by many authors; *Fra kirkens kvinneside* (1979), a committee report. An early Swedish pioneer treating gender ideology in the history of ideas is Asta Ekenvall's book, *Manligt och kvinnligt. Idéhistoriska studier* (1966), which was read in all the Scandinavian countries.

In the history of religions Mildreth Worth Pinkham's *Woman in the Sacred Scriptures of Hinduism* (1967) is an investigation of woman's status in Hinduism; Judith Plaskow and Joan Arnold's anthology *Women and Religion* (1974), and Rita M. Gross' 1977 edition, *Beyond Androcentrism: New Essays on Women and Religion*, are early exponents of the new feminist critique.

Women's studies, feminist research and gender programs have since developed during the decades between 1970 and 2000. This field of inquiry is at the same time interdisciplinary and distinctive for various subjects. Similar types of criticism, questions and insight are echoed in history, philosophy, cultural studies, and social studies. Gender is a cross-disciplinary category covering several common agendas which influence more discipline-specific discussions and opinions. At the same time there exist different theories of gender and fields of interest and topics of investigation which are characteristic for disciplines and subjects. Women's history for instance, has hitherto shown little interest in religion.[4] On the other hand, scholars from the history of religions and various theological disciplines, sharing a common interest in feminist topics, have collaborated and inspired each other. Generally sympathizing with the feminist movement, scholars have called for more focus on women's lives, experiences, and contributions to art, literature, religion, culture and society, besides demanding more female scholars in university departments. Fundamental questions about how the production of knowledge is affected by gender, race, and class have been discussed in these settings, with a view to integrate the stories of oppressed groups and understand the nature of their oppression. The topic of gender in a history of religions context must be understood in relation to this general situation.

Women's history, experience and products of many kinds have been at the center of attention for feminist scholars, and still even so-called gender studies mostly concentrate on women in one way or another. But from early on it was realized that a one-sided focus on women will not explain their status and allotted sphere of activity. The category of "woman" is culturally constructed in relation to the category of "man"; therefore women will have to be analyzed with a view to the social matrix which produces gender difference. In the 1970s the notion of gender became a framework in which socio-cultural differences between men and women were being conceptualized, and since then the concept has been in the center of feminist theorizing. One could imagine gender studies informed by other theoretical paradigms, but so far feminist discourse and feminist concerns have dominated in the humanities and social sciences. Research on men and masculinities, as well as the growing field of queer studies, are both deeply influenced by feminist thinking.[5]

---

4   The Swedish historian Inger Hammer has called women's history blind as regards the importance of religion, cf. Hammer 1998. Historical work on religion has tended, in North America at least, to be undertaken under the aegis of what has been called "Church History, " although it has now tended to distance itself from its confessional roots.

5   As to men's studies in religion, see Daniel Boyarin, *Carnal Israel: Reading Sex in Talmudic Culture* (1993) and *Unheroic Conduct: The Rise of Heterosexuality and the Invention of the*

Gender

The scholarly concept of gender is often used indiscriminately and without any theoretical intent. This even happens in religious studies, where gender sometimes covers topics relating to gender ideology, sex roles, goddesses, and the position of women in religion, without any attempts at explaining the operations of gender difference. However, the reason why gender has become a vital field of interest is feminist theorizing, which has made gender into a poignant critical and analytical category.

When religion is viewed from a critical gender perspective, universalist notions about *homo religiosus* and the patterns of the sacred are replaced by critical queries about gendered power structures and oppressive discourses. Gender critique contributes to orientating the history of religions away from the old phenomenological paradigm where religion is treated as a separate, sacred area of life to be assessed in terms of comparative, religious categories, to a paradigm where religion becomes part of culture and is seen as interwoven with the motive powers and ordinary affairs of human beings in various historical settings.

However, gender has the merit that it is an open and unbounded category, inviting many types of analytical perspectives as well as including an endless variety of data. Its range of vision comprises men, and in contrast to a negatively laden concept like patriarchy, it does not foretell the character of the structures investigated. Patriarchy, usually understood as men's power over women and men of inferior status,[6] is obviously a frequent structure in the world of religion; still, research is better served with a general category which does not universalize and totalize women's oppression and thereby prevents observing the privileges, power and influence of women, which can be considerable, even in patriarchal contexts.

Jewish Man (1997); Lawrence Hoffman, *Covenant of Blood: Circumcision and Gender in Rabbinic Judaism* (1996).

The anthology *Que(e)rying Religion: A Critical Anthology* (1997), edited by Gary David Comstock and Susan E. Henking, is a rich and manifold contribution to religious queer studies.

6   Sue Morgan defines patriarchy as "an institutionalized system of male power and dominance over women, subject men and the natural world as a whole" (Morgan 1999: 43). Bryan Turner's definition locates patriarchy to the household: "By patriarchy I mean a system of political authority, based upon the household, in which dominant property-owning males control and regulate the lives of subordinate members of the household, regardless of their sex or age." According to Turner the primitive patriarchal system became linked to monarchial power, and in turn transposed to the religious sphere, when divinity became a supreme, fatherly ruler (Turner 1997: 26). "Sexism", the ideology of patriarchy, is defined by Morgan as "a series of beliefs that sustain and reinforce the notion of male supremacy" (Morgan 1999: 43).

Gender is both an emic and an etic category, pointing at the same time to a gendered human reality as well as to our scholarly understandings and analytical
tools. Randi Warne has observed that gender is ubiquitous, but at the same
time it has often been invisible as an analytic category.[7] The emic-etic duplicity
which incidentally it shares with the category of religion, contributes in making
gender a very intricate matter. Its heterogenous field of reference is another
complicating factor. The lenses of gender can be directed towards large systems
as well as minor elements in social existence. Gender may refer to the individual person with her/his body, actions, feelings, speech, and so on, as far as
these elements are related to culturally established norms and meanings; it refers to social institutions, organizations and hierarchies, and to social discourse.
Gender operates in different cultural circumstances and meaning-constructing
processes, often in complex ways and intertwined with other agendas.[8]

Feminism argues that gender is interwoven with the social distribution of
power, but scholarly approaches to gender do not always focus on the power
aspect. However, to overlook the power element in the dynamics of gender
construction may result in a very incomplete understanding indeed, in religion
as in other areas. In fact, it can be argued that gender perspectives will not be
able to fundamentally change the history of religions unless the relationship
between religion and power is taken seriously. If this is going to happen, the
concept of religion as *sui generis*,[9] as something uniquely spiritual and symbolic
which should be assessed in a decontextualized fashion in order to bring out

---

7   Warne 2000: 141.
8   Randi Warne has presented a catalogue of the strategies and operations to which
     gender is subject and which may be combined in different cultural circumstances:
     ontologizing—ascribing to the level of Being;
     essentializing—positing as an essential (eternal) defining characteristic;
     cosmologizing—ascribing to a cosmic order;
     naturalizing—making something "natural", that is, free from (humanly constructed)
     conventions;
     reifying—converting something mental to a thing, that is, materializing;
     authorizing—sanctioning, giving authority;
     valorizing—imputing value;
     idealizing—exalting to perfection or excellence;
     normalizing—establishing as a rule, setting up a standard by which to judge deviation;
     pathologizing—naming as a disorder;
     problematizing—making into a problem requiring or implying a solution (Warne 2000:
     141).
9   Compare the following citation from Eliade's *Patterns in Comparative Religion*: "... a
     religious phenomenon will only be recognized as such if it is grasped at its own level,
     that is to say, if it is studied *as* something religious. To try to grasp the essence of such a
     phenomenon by means of physiology, psychology, sociology, economics, linguistics,
     art or any other study is false; it misses the one unique and irreducible element in it—
     the element of the sacred" (Eliade 1967: xiii).

the "purely religious" will have to be abandoned, as Rosalind Shaw convincingly argues in her essay "Feminist Anthropology and the Gendering of Religious Studies" (1995). Naturally religion (in some form or another) will be the central concern of the history of religions, but the main crux is to locate religion not as isolated from, but interwoven with other cultural processes and social formations.

Research cannot be done according to the principle of sexual equality, and a disproportionate emphasis on male religious elites and their creations may often be unavoidable. From a gender-conscious perspective however, the relevance of gender is not limited to the study of women. How the constitution of elites and male dominance in religion is related to the construction of masculinity is perhaps the key question in religious gender studies. On the other hand, a "perspective from below,"[10] focusing on lay people and folk traditions, will often be necessary if women's participation in religion is to be fully accounted for.

Feminist gender discourse even highlights power relations within the academy, like the power of established scholars to define what are the interesting topics and established standards of good research. Historian of religions Ursula King is not the only one who has been told that publications about feminism are not academically respectable.[11]

To sum up: The term gender covers a broad range of phenomena as well as a scholarly concept. Some of the main features of gender as an analytical category may be summarized as follows: 1) a distinction is drawn between biological and cultural genderedness; 2) gender is conceived as relational: there is a mutual dependence between masculinity and femininity, women must be understood in relation to men and vice versa; 3) the concept points to processes and structures (linguistic, ideological, religious, economic, legal) producing social asymmetry between men and women; and 4) gender is often thought of as a system, with levels of meaning structures interacting with and upholding each other.

While gender-related phenomena always have been studied in the history of religions, former descriptions generally lacked the critical, gender-conscious perspective typical of the last thirty years.

Gender and Religion: An Endless Variety of Data

Gender perspectives in religious studies have rich empirical material upon which to draw. Practically every aspect of religion can be analyzed from this analytical vantage point. Myths, symbolism, rituals, theological systems, ethics,

---

10   Shaw 1995.

11   King 1995: 25.

religious history, religious organizations, individual biographies, religious identity and experience all have important gender dimensions. In religion, conceptions of human gender become integrated in mythic dramas and cosmological visions. This wider web of opinions and symbolism, involving superhuman beings and often salvific messages, is the foremost characteristic of gender in a religious context. Human gender structures are reflected by gendered divinities and their actions, which again influence the discourse about human gender. Such dialectics between human and divine levels is very often the key to gender structures in religious organizations. Most religions constitute gender systems, specifying some sort of difference between the sexes, but varying as to the character and implementation of this difference. Besides, religious discourse is very often authoritative and absolute, and this feature also seems quite typical of religious attitudes to human gender.

Within religious frameworks, some gender topics are particularly prominent and influential. Tales about the creation of humanity, the so-called anthropogony myths, often represent a normative anthropology, delineating as they do the position of human beings in terms of their relations to divinities. Such stories frequently say something about gender hierarchies at the time they were produced. Their impact through long-lasting periods of time can be immense. The importance in the West of the Jewish-Christian creation myths and the story of Adam and Eve's relationship and fall can hardly be exaggerated. Since the time of Paul the Apostle, the drama has constantly been pondered and reinterpreted in Church history, from the Gnostic inversions of its biblical content to present-day feminist rereadings.[12]

The biblical foundation for female inferiority in the West was hotly debated in the nineteenth century, and it was highlighted by American feminist Elizabeth Cady Stanton and her collaborators when they published *The Women's Bible* in 1895 and 1898. The book is a commentary on biblical passages dealing with women. In this controversial work, which soon became a best-seller, the androcentrism of scriptural interpretation was exposed. The momentous two volume commentary edited by feminist theologian Elisabeth Schüssler Fiorenza in 1993 and 1994, *Searching the Scriptures*, is deliberately situated by the editor in the interpretative tradition of *The Women's Bible*.

The biblical coupling of sexuality and gender hierarchy demonstrates the centrality of sexuality in gender matters. Sexuality is an age-old, major theme in religion, symbolized in myths and celebrated in *hieros gamos* rituals. Procreation can be a sacred affair, sometimes involving gods and humans in the act, as is demonstrated by Christian dogma about Jesus Christ. However, religion is equally known for making sexuality a problem, to be regulated, mastered and

---

12   See Bird 1995; Boyarin 1998; Carr 1993; Gilhus 1983; Mikaelsson 1980; Phillips 1985; Ricoeur 1969; Trible 1978.

possibly avoided in lives of ascetism and celibacy. Gender boundaries are also at issue. Myths and symbols sometimes contain ideas of spiritual and bodily androgyny, and ritual castration is practiced in several traditions, thus the symbolic vision of what human gender purports is magnified.

Religious symbolism is extremely important in most societies, and symbolism is a constant source when it comes to cultural construction and reconstruction of gender. However, such general importance does not give us a clue to a general meaning or function of gendered symbols. Caroline Walker Bynum has emphasized the multivocality of symbols, and she has frequently been cited because of the following reminder:

> Gender-related symbols, in their full complexity, may refer to gender in ways that affirm or reverse it, support or question it; or they may, in their basic meaning, have little at all to do with male and female roles. Thus our analysis admits that gender-related symbols are sometimes "about" values other than gender. But our analysis also assumes that all people are "gendered". It therefore suggests, at another level, that not only gender-related symbols but all symbols arise out of the experience of "gendered" users. It is not possible ever to ask How does a symbol—*any* symbol—mean? without asking For whom does it mean?[13]

Bynum has criticized Victor Turner's influential theory of liminality and dominant symbols for being formulated from a male point of view.[14] On the basis of her research on spirituality in the European Middle Ages, more particularly the medieval narrative of the saint's life, Bynum argues that women's images and symbols do not invert or elevate them, as Turner's theorizing would predict; rather, their symbols emphasize continuity with the women's ordinary life experience. Bynum concludes that Turner's theory of religion is based (more than he probably was aware) on a particular form of Christianity that has been characteristic of male educated and aristocratic elites in the Western tradition, with its emphasis on world denial and inversion of images. In contrast to Turner, Bynum suggests that inferiors in society generally do not create images of reversal or elevation, and that liminality itself might be an escape for "those who bear the burdens and reap the benefits of a high place in the social structure."[15]

An intriguing question relates to the effects of divine gender. Religiously minded feminists in the West naturally find it unacceptable that Judaism and Christianity have more or less excluded the feminine from their concepts of divinity. Identification with the sacred symbol then becomes a male prerogative, a mythical sexism giving rise to questions concerning the relations between misogyny and symbolism. Everyone in this field must have heard the

---

13 Bynum 1986: 2–3.
14 Bynum 1992.
15 Bynum 1992: 32–34.

trumpet-call of former theologian Mary Daly's lacerating critique of God the Father, which she designates as male idolatry, and diagnoses as a keystone in theological and social misogyny.[16] Admittedly, it seems highly justified to examine possible correlations between exclusive, divine maleness and oppression of women in religious organizations and societies. Yet, whatever Western goddess worshippers in our time might presume, there is no general evidence supporting the belief that goddess symbols guarantee a better position for women in the societies where they are venerated.

The fact that all the major world religions are male dominated should not blind us to the fact that women sometimes do play leading parts in religion. In modern times we have several examples of women as founders of new religious movements, and the connections between the nineteenth century wave of feminism and movements like spiritualism and theosophy on the one hand and the Christian missionary movement on the other, is a fascinating, interdisciplinary topic which is very far from being exhausted.[17] Helena Petrovna Blavatsky (1831–1891), founder of the Theosophical Society and author of modern esoteric classics *Isis Unveiled* (1877) and *The Secret Doctrine* (1888), has become one of the most important religious leaders in the modern period through the lasting influence of her ideas in various theosophical offshoots and the New Age movement.[18]

The general topic of women and religion has occasioned a great many conferences and publications, drawing women from different disciplines and with various religious persuasions among them. Feminist theology is a vital branch of scholarship, demonstrated by the many well-known contributions by scholars like Rosemary Radford Ruether and Elisabeth Schüssler Fiorenza. An early landmark of feminist cooperation is the anthology *Womanspirit Rising: A Feminist Reader in Religion*, edited in 1979 by Carol P. Christ and Judith Plaskow, with contributions by historians of religions, theologians, witches and goddess-worshippers. *Womanspirit Rising* contains several seminal essays, among them the editors' introduction, Carol P. Christ's arguing in favor of the goddess symbol for women in "Why Women Need the Goddess: Phenomenological, Psychological, and Political Reflections," and theologian Valerie Saiving's 1960 pioneer essay "The Human Situation: A Feminine View," where she argues that the standard Christian interpretation of sin as pride or will-to-power does not fit with women's experience, which rather points to underdevelopment or negation of self as more typical feminine forms of sin. As recently as in 1996 Rita Gross characterizes *Womanspirit Rising* as "probably the

---

16 Daly 1973.
17 See Brouwer 1990; Okkenhaug 2003; Owen 1989; Dixon 2001; Huber/Lutkehaus 1999; McFadden 1999.
18 Hanegraaff 1996; Kraft 1999.

single most influential and widely used book in the field of feminist studies in religion."[19] In 1989 the same editors (changing their order) published a sequel to *Womanspirit Rising*, called *Weaving the Visions: Patterns in Feminist Spirituality*, which has also gained a wide-spread reputation. Ursula King's *Religion and Gender* (1995), is a similar type of publication, a woman-centered anthology dominated by feminist perspectives and including several essays dedicated to present-day Western women's spirituality and worship of the goddess. The impact of these volumes are therefore not just scholarly; they also nourish feminist spirituality and religious self-reflexion. Topics to be pondered by religious feminists include God-language and renamings of the sacred, gender inclusive language, ecological spirituality, and retrieval of women's religious history.

Whatever some people might like to think, attention to gender is not a diminishing trend in religious scholarship. New introductory books contain chapters about gender, thus proving the centrality of this issue.[20] Monographs and anthologies have come out since the 1970s and new ones are continually being produced.[21] It also has to be emphasized that scholarship in this field comprises far more than works written in English. Increasing internationalization and its foregrounding of English and North American scholarship reflects a power dimension which is also evident in religious studies scholarship on gender.

---

19   Gross 1996: 48.

20   See Boyarin 1998; Morgan 1999; Warne 2000.

21   Compare the following publications in English, which by the way document the continuous focusing on women and the feminine in this literature: Pat Holden, ed., *Women's Religious Experience* (1983); Clarissa W. Atkinson/Constance H. Buchanan/ Margaret R. Miles, eds., *Immaculate and Powerful: The Female in Sacred Image and Social Reality* (1985); Ursula King, ed., *Women in the World's Religions, Past and Present* (1987); Arvind Sharma, ed., *Women in World Religions* (1987); Nancy Auer Falk/Rita M. Gross, eds., *Unspoken Worlds: Women's Religious Lives* (1989); Paula M. Cooey/William R. Eakin/ Jay B. McDaniel, eds., *After Patriarchy: Feminist Transformations of the World Religions* (1992); Jean Holm/John Bowker, eds., *Women in Religion* (1994); Arvind Sharma, *Religion and Women* (1994) and *Today's Woman in World Religions* (1994); Kari Elisabeth Børresen, ed., *The Image of God: Gender Models in Judaeo-Christian Tradition* (1995); Ria Kloppenborg/Wouter Hanegraaff, eds., *Female Stereotypes in Religious Traditions* (1995); Rita M. Gross, *Feminism and Religion: An Introduction* (1996); Wendy Doniger, *Splitting the Difference: Gender and Myth in Ancient Greece and India* (1999); Darlene M. Juschka, *Feminism in the Study of Religion. A Reader* (2001). Judith Plaskow's *Standing Again at Sinai: Judaism from a Feminist Perspective* (1991) and Rita M. Gross, *Buddhism after Patriarchy* (1993) are feminist reconstructions from a believer's point of view. Feminist gender research on Islam has been carried out since the 1970s, for example the voluminous anthology *Women in the Muslim World* (1978), edited by Lois Beck and Nikki Keddie. Later works include Leila Ahmed, *Women and Gender in Islam* (1992), and Yvonne Yazbeck Haddad/John L. Esposito, eds., *Islam, Gender and Social Change* (1998).

On the other hand, it is not necessarily a given that gender-critical approaches are included in religious studies, even when their relevance is
evident. The fifteen volume *Encyclopedia of Religion*, published in 1987 with Mircea Eliade as general editor, has been criticized for its lack of interest in feminist
and/or gender-related topics. Only two articles of this kind are included in this
major work.[22] According to Ursula King, who has critically perused the
Encyclopedia of Religion, only about 17 per cent of the contributors are women
(approximately 227 out of a total of 1356), a stark reminder of the male
dominance of the discipline.[23]

One need not be a feminist or a specialist in gender research to find the
gender dimension of religious phenomena interesting and include it in one's
research. Many practioners in this field focus on gender only in some of their
projects, and then not necessarily making it a main concern. Neither is female
sex a requirement, though it has to be admitted that most gender researchers
are women. However, male scholars like Friedrich Heiler, David Kinsley,
Geoffrey Parrinder, Arvind Sharma and Daniel Boyarin have made significant
contributions to this field during the period of our study.

Homo Religiosus

Who lacks gender, age, class or race, but is all the same a male and belongs to
an elite? The answer is the famous *homo religiosus*—religious man—as this
concept has had a tendency to be constructed by historians of religions.

Homo religiosus—a variety of the generic masculine, which identifies the
male with the human—represents the very quintessence of the discipline's
problematic treatment of gender. In the first place *homo religiosus* has all to often
been construed as *vir religiosus*, neglecting *femina religiosa*. Men's leading part in
religious history has somehow emerged as a matter of course, while women
have been construed as subordinate, minor, or even invisible characters. To a
considerable degree women have been overlooked as religious actors and co-
producers of religious worlds. There is reason to ask if scholars have made
religious traditions more male-centered than they really are. In feminist
discourse the common term for such distortion and one-sidedness is
androcentrism. Rita Gross, an early critic of androcentrism in religious studies,[24]
defines it in the following manner:

---

22 Constance H. Buchanan, "Women's Studies," and Rosemary Radford Ruether, "Andro-
    centrism."
23 King 1995c: 235–40.
24 Gross 1974; 1977; 1987; 1996.

Briefly stated, androcentrism is a tendency to think and write as if men represent the normal, ideal, and central kind of human, whereas women are somehow peripheral and marginal to that norm. Androcentrism pretends that humanity contains only one gender, so that one might readily speak of androcentrism as a "one-sex model of humanity" ... Far more information is collected about men than about women, what men do is usually deemed more interesting and important than what women do, and society or religion is described as if it were solely the possession and creation of men.[25]

Homo religiosus implicitly understood as *vir religiosus* reflects a Western *doxa* of representative and primary maleness rooted in age-old paradigms. In the biblical Paradise narrative (Gen. 2:3), several motifs cooperate in presenting the male, Adam, as the primary human being. He is created first, and he is the bodily basis for the woman, Eve, when she is made of his rib. Adam's superiority is stressed in the important asymmetry of naming, when he pronounces the woman's names on a par with his naming the animals, while she silently submits to this act of subjugation. The motif can be said to epitomize men's exclusive right to shape the world under patriarchy, including the centering of the male sex while rendering women as "the other."[26] The idea of male primacy can also be related to how Christianity has combined gender and salvation. In antiquity salvation was seen as a realization of the spiritual essence in man [sic], which implied the denigration or renouncement of body and sexuality. The spiritual man that was saved by Christ was thought to be male, but somehow this maleness included women. If the Christian woman lived a celibate life, she became a spiritual male. This metaphor of sex change and transcendent androgyny was quite common in early Christian texts,[27] and the idea of the body-rejecting (male) androgyne has since been a powerful concept in Western religion. It entails a hierarchy of gender which allows the male to represent the female, but not the other way round.

From a postcolonial and poststructural point of view *homo religiosus*, even when *femina religiosa* is subsumed, must be dismissed as anything but an empty category. The questions *What is religious woman?* and *What is religious man?* cannot have any other universal import than a person who is sometimes preoccupied with religious matters. The moment *homo religiosus* is defined in terms of belief in divinities, piety, membership in religious organizations, ritual behavior, gender dichotomies or reaction to a *mysterium tremendum et fascinans*, *homo religiosus* has been essentialized in a way that bears the marks of a Western, Christian heritage. The androcentrism and parochialism that can be identified in many renderings of *homo religiosus* illustrate the poststructuralist

---

25   Gross 1987: 38.
26   Mary Daly suggests that the story is a paradigm of how the power of naming has been stolen from women in Western culture (Daly 1973: 8).
27   Meeks 1974; Vogt 1995; Boyarin 1998.

lesson that universalist discourse carries with it (hidden) negations and repressions. Also, the emphasis of difference in poststructuralism is most valuable in its problematizing of simple gender dichotomies as analytical tools. Contrasting *vir religiosus* and *femina religiosa* in a fixed or absolute manner is no better than defining *homo religiosus* as a pious creature. To overlook how class, race, ethnicity, education, time period, and so on, are factors creating differences within categories like "Christian man" or "Hindu woman" is no longer acceptable.

On this point, feminist criticism of the history of religions echoes a great many voices in other disciplines. Like the concept of gender, the concept of androcentricm is interdisciplinary. Androcentrism should be thought of as an institutionalized approach in scholarship, a paradigm of knowledge construction reflecting academic *doxa*. Women scholars may consequently be as androcentric as their male colleagues, and the latter group should not be accused of androcentrism just because of their sex.

Analytical Moves

Thus far, the fundamental change connected with feminism in religious scholarship is that women have become central objects of study. This development has contested hegemonic understandings of religious history and multiplied religious subjects worthy of attention. The centrality of women is brought out in many ways, i.e. in highlighting goddess symbols and images of femininity in sacred texts, in studying women's religious roles and status, in listening to women's religious experience, in investigating their religious activities and retrieving their religious history. Since androcentric descriptions of women have been content to elicit men's views on them, or to repeat religious or cultural stereotypes of femininity, inserting women's voices in religious history is an essential and necessary epistemological move. It is still a most important motive power in religious scholarship.

Experience, including the researcher's own experience, has been a critical point of departure for scholars in various disciplines. Its status and import is a fundamental feminist issue. In *Womanspirit Rising*, Carol Christ and Judith Plaskow relate it to women's consciousness-rising groups in the 1970s, where women learned to recognize and discuss their shared experiences. To these authors, the feminist naming of women's experience becomes the contrast to Adam's naming in the Genesis myth, and signifies a fundamental transformation of culture and religion.[28] The methodological import of subjective experience was acknowledged by Valerie Saiving when she used her own female experience as basis for criticism of male theologians' interpretations of

---

28   Christ/Plaskow 1979: 6–7.

the human situation. Judith Plaskow ascertains that women's experience is "the fundamental feminist methodological move."[29] Sue Morgan succinctly summarizes the centrality of women's experience as "the essential interpretative horizon of the feminist approach" which has "transformed both the subject of religious enquiry and the method of research."[30] However, following the argument of historian Joan Scott in a recent essay, it can be objected that experience cannot be the origin of explanation or be used out of hand as authoritative evidence, experience is vital, but it needs to be explained and historicized.[31]

Feminist identity politics related to experience has sometimes taken the shape of a universalizing discourse. Something of this sort can be seen in feminist theology, compare Marsha Hewitt's and Rosalind Shaw's attack on Carol Christ's "thealogy" and her appropriation of the experience of women in other times and places.[32] The well-known critique from women of color and women from non-Western cultures who refuse the idea of a common women's experience defined by Western, white feminists, is as relevant in religious scholarship as in other disciplines.

Still, experience is a fundamental matrix for interpretation and common understanding, also in comparative studies. The analytical potential of a comparative approach to gender was realized early on by Rita Gross. On the basis of her research on Australian religion, Gross sensibly advised scholars to look for parallel, male and female traditions of religious experience and activity, maintaining that Western scholars overlooked women's rituals and often made non-Western religions more male-centered than they really are. Ascertaining that women are excluded from men's rituals is not enough. Scholars should have in mind that there might exist patterns of mutual inclusion and exclusion between the sexes, treating males and females as co-equally modes of the human. Her ideas have been successfully applied by Richard Natvig in his investigation of the spirit possession zar-cult, which is dominated by women. Zar is not accepted by normative Islam, but it is an important folk tradition in several Middle-Eastern and Northeast-African countries, and the women themselves maintain that practicing zar is part of their Islamic identity. The zar-cult therefore demonstrates that men and women realize the Islamic religious universe in gender-differentiated ways.[33]

Gender in the history of religions may profitably be seen as a system, in the way suggested by Joan Scott in her by now classical essay "Gender: A Useful Category of Historical Analysis" (1986). Scott maintains that as a constitutive part of social relations, gender involves four elements systematically interacting

---

29 Plaskow 1991: 12.
30 Morgan 1999: 50.
31 Scott 1998: 6.
32 Hewitt 1993; Shaw 1995.
33 Natvig 1988; 1989.

with each other, i.e. cultural symbols, normative concepts, institutions and organizations, and lastly, subjective identity. While Scott thinks this model has a
very wide application, it is especially relevant in the history of religions when
analyzing gender in religious organizations. Churches, societies, sects and cults
are usually ideologically based on theological, normative interpretation of
myths and symbols, and implement their ideas in organizational structures,
while members absorb the same ideas in their personal identity construction.
Scott points out that symbols are socially important because they create identification with institutions, a fact widely attested by religion. In many cases
rather rigid and stable gender dichotomies are produced through religious
systems. However, a great analytical advantage of such a model is its categorical emptiness; it points to interconnected levels and processes, without
predicting the character and content of a specific, historical gender system.
Also, it is not presupposed that all four elements are equally important in all
cases, or that the gender system will necessarily be consistent. On the contrary,
one should expect paradoxes, suppressed ideas, and inconsistencies along with
normative versions. A great advantage of such a model is that men and women
are subjected to the same analytical perspective.

A most important development is the focus on the body (in both feminist
and other quarters) which is cross-disciplinary, theoretically advanced, and
attracting both male and female scholars.[34] In different branches of knowledge
the gendered body has lost its character as a natural, fixed or universal datum
of physicality. Instead it is conceived as an embodied self or a socially constructed artefact, the locus or intersection of various types of symbolism,
discursive processes and social development. Crucial Western dualisms of
flesh/spirit, body/soul, mind/matter are undeniably gendered; the association
of female with flesh, moral weakness, and irrationality and male with spirit,
moral strength, and rationality has had a long history in the Western world. In
analysis focussed on the body such dualisms are seen as inscribed on the body:
symbols and dogmas are accompanied by bodily transformations and regulations of diet, appearance, clothing, sexuality and movement; ideas of transcendence and sanctification are linked up with corporeal contrasts of de-
filement and decay. The wider context of such religious and cultural structures
are social power systems: the family, the state, the economic system, the
Church. The body becomes enmeshed in a complex web of cultural discourse
and social structure. At the same time this kind of analysis makes room for the
subject and its sexuality, desires, and strivings for self and identity. When

---

34 The literature on the body is enormous. See Coakley 1997 for a splendid anthology of
    religion and the the body. Caroline Walker Bynum has become widely known for her
    work on gender and the body in Medieval spirituality, see particularly her *Fragmen-
    tation and Redemption: Essays of Gender and the Human Body in Medieval Religion* (1992).

gender is inserted in this type of approach, it becomes as complex, problematized and polysemic as the body.

Feminist Spiritual Agendas and Scholarly Approaches

Prominent women researchers have argued that scholarship on gender and religion deeply involves them as spiritual subjects. Several feminist historians of religions have been drawn to the goddess movement, most notably Carol P. Christ.[35] Ursula King asks for a feminist study of religion involving "participatory hermeneutics," which produces new consciousness and new attitudes. In her opinion the feminist approach "elicit more empathetic involvement and personal concern in relation to one's studies,"[36] and she criticizes the ideals of objectivity and neutrality in the discipline, which in her view run counter to an alleged feminist paradigm shift.

Such enthusiasm is understandable, but nevertheless problematic, and the goddess spirituality professed by feminist scholars has probably made it easier for some to ignore the import of their overall critique. Feminist theology and spirituality has definitely been a significant branch of gender studies in the history of religions, but one may well ask if emphasis on researchers' religious subjectivity and demands for major changes in religion have worked against a general feminist paradigm shift in the discipline. Our discipline's traditional skepticism towards letting theological agendas, value commitments and subjective involvement determine research is deeply grounded, has stood its test for many decades, and is not likely to be fundamentally changed by feminist appeals or utopian visions. It is highly debatable whether critical insight into the gendered, local and temporal situatedness of research should be seen as an invitation to mingle one's scholarly, religious or existential concerns. The separation between personal involvement and professional outlook in scholarship is a porous, changeable line, in need of constant critique and reflection, but the intellectual and methodological value of such a distinction should not be underrated. A strong personal interest in the subject matter can indeed be a great resource in scholarship, but the quality of research and scholarly texts will nevertheless depend on theory and methodology. Actually there is no reason why gender research, even when fuelled by feminism, should not thrive in the discursive space typical of the history of religions, i.e. the combination of methodological empathy and religious non-involvement displayed by so many of the discipline's practitioners.

---

35   Christ 1979, 1997.
36   King 1995: 26–28.

Gender studies in the history of religions today are characterized by a pluralism of epistemological and methodological approaches. They may be woman-centered, man-centered, inclusive of both genders, or be more comprehensive, investigating the wide ramifications of engenderment and polysemic meaning construction in different types of religious and social phenomena. Feminist separatism, essentialism and theological reconstruction exist side by side with deconstructionist analyses of cultural undertakings and religious categories. One can hardly say that feminist perspectives have become a common horizon in the history of religion, but one may safely declare that gender is on its way to being established as a fundamental category of analysis and an integrated topic in many areas of research. If wide-ranging gender analyses still are few in number, it is increasingly being recognized that gender and religion is a field inviting a host of vital questions.

Bibliography

Ahmed, Leila (1992), *Women and Gender in Islam*. New Haven, Conn./London: Yale University Press.

Atkinson, Clarissa W./Buchanan, Constance H./Miles, Margaret R. (1985), *Immaculate and Powerful: The Female in Sacred Image and Social Reality*. Boston, Mass.: Beacon Press.

Beck, Lois/Keddie, Nikki, eds. (1978), *Women in the Muslim World*. Cambridge, Mass./ London: Harvard University Press.

Bowie, Fiona/Kirkwood, Deborah/Ardener, Shirlely, eds. (1993), *Women and Missions: Past and Present. Anthropological and Historical Perceptions*. Providence, R.I./Oxford, U.K.: Berg Publishers.

Boyarin, Daniel (1993), *Carnal Israel: Reading Sex in Talmudic Culture*. Berkeley, Calif.: University of California Press.

— (1997), *Unheroic Conduct: The Rise of Heterosexuality and the Invention of the Jewish Man*. Berkeley, Calif.: University of California Press.

— (1998), "Gender," in: Mark C. Taylor, ed., *Critical Terms for Religious Studies*. Chicago/London: The University of Chicago Press: 117–35.

Brouwer, Ruth Compton (1990), *New Women for God: Canadian Presbyterian Women and India Missions, 1876–1914*. Toronto: University of Toronto Press.

Buchanan, Constance H. (1987), "Women's Studies," in: Mircea Eliade, ed., *The Encyclopedia of Religion*. Vol. 15, New York/London: Macmillan: 433–40.

Butler, Judith (1990), *Gender Trouble: Feminism and the Subversion of Identity*. New York/ London: Routledge.

Bynum, Caroline Walker (1982), *Jesus as Mother. Studies in the Spirituality of the High Middle Ages*. Berkeley, Calif.: University of California Press.

— (1986), "Introduction: The Complexity of Symbols," in: Caroline Walker Bynum/ Stevan Harrell/Paula Richman, eds., *Gender and Religion: On the Complexity of Symbols*. Boston, Mass.: Beacon Press: 1–20.

—— (1992), "Women's Stories, Women's Symbols. A Critique of Victor Turner's Theory of Liminality," in: Caroline Walker Bynum, *Fragmentation and Redemption. Essays on Gender and the Human Body in Medieval Religion*. New York: Zone Books: 27–51.

Børresen, Kari Elisabeth (1968), *Subordination et Equivalence: Nature et Rôle de la Femme d'après Augustin et Thomas d'Aquin*. Oslo: Universitetsforlaget.

—— ed. (1995), *The Image of God. Gender Models in Judaeo-Christian Tradition*. Minneapolis, Minn.: Fortress Press.

Carr, David (1993), "The Politics of Textual Subversion: A Diacronic Perspective on the Garden of Eden Story," in: *Journal of Biblical Literature* 112 (4): 577–95.

Christ, Carol P. (1979), "Why Women Need the Goddess: Phenomenological, Psychological, and Political Reflections," in: Christ/Plaskow, eds.: 273–87.

—— (1997), *Rebirth of the Goddess. Finding Meaning in Feminist Spirituality*. New York/ London: Routledge.

Christ, Carol P./Plaskow, Judith, eds. (1979), *Womanspirit Rising: A Feminist Reader in Religion*. San Francisco, Calif.: Harper & Row.

—— (1979), "Introduction: Womanspirit Rising," in: Christ/Plaskow, eds.: 1–17.

Coakley, Sarah, ed. (1997), *Religion and the Body*. Cambridge: Cambridge University Press.

Comstock, David/Henking, Susan E., eds. (1997), *Que(e)rying Religion: A Critical Anthology*. New York: Continuum.

Cooey, Paula/Eakin, William R./McDaniel, Jay B., eds. (1992), *After Patriarchy: Feminist Transformations of the World Religions*. Maryknoll, N.Y.: Orbis.

Daly, Mary (1973), *Beyond God the Father. Toward a Philosophy of Women's Liberation*. Boston, Mass.: Beacon Press.

—— (1975 [1968]), *The Church and the Second Sex*. With a new feminist postchristian introduction by the author. New York: Harper & Row.

Dixon, Joy (2001), *Divine Feminine: Theosophy and Feminism in England*. Baltimore, Md.: Johns Hopkins University Press.

Ekenvall, Asta (1966), *Manligt och kvinnligt. Idéhistoriska studier*. Göteborg: Akademieförlaget.

Eliade, Mircea (1967 [1963]), *Patterns in Comparative Religion*. Cleveland/New York: The World Publishing Company.

—— ed. (1987), *The Encyclopedia of Religion*. 15 volumes. New York: Macmillan.

Falk, Nancy Auer/Gross, Rita M., eds. (1989), *Unspoken Worlds: Women's Religious Lives*. Second ed. Belmont, Calif.: Wadsworth.

Fiorenza, Elisabeth Schüssler (1984), *Bread not Stone: The Challenge of Feminist Biblical Interpretation*. Boston, Mass.: Beacon Press.

—— (1992), *But She Said: Feminist Practices of Biblical Interpretation*. Boston, Mass.: Beacon Press.

—— red. (1993–1994), *Searching the Scriptures*. Vol. 1: *A Feminist Introduction*. Vol.2: *A Feminist Commentary*. New York: Crossroad.

Fischer, Agnete et al. (1978), *Kloke jomfruer? Om kirke, kristendom og kvinnefrigjøring*. Oslo: H. Aschehoug & Co.

Fra kirkens kvinneside (1979). En utredning om kirken og kvinnen ved en komité nedsatt av Kirkerådet. Oslo: Andaktsbokselskapet.

Geertz, Armin W./McCutcheon, Russell T., eds. (2000), *Perspectives on Method and Theory in the Study of Religion*. Adjunct Proceedings of the XVIth Congress of the

International Association for the History of Religions, Mexico City, 1995. Leiden/Boston, Mass./Köln: Brill.

Gilhus, Ingvild Sælid (1983), "Male and Female Symbolism in the Gnostic *Apocryphon of John*," in: *Temenos* 19: 33–43.

—— (1994), "Trimorphic Protennoia," in: Fiorenza, ed.: 55–65.

Gross, Rita M. (1974), "Methodological Remarks on the Study of Women in Religion: Review, Criticism, and Redefinition," in: Judith Plaskow/Joan Arnold, eds., *Women and Religion*. Missoula, Mont.: Scholars Press: 153–65.

—— ed. (1977), *Beyond Androcentrism: New Essays on Women and Religion*. Missoula, Mont.: Scholars Press.

—— (1987), "Tribal Religions: Aboriginal Australia," in: Sharma, ed.: 37–58.

—— (1993), *Buddhism after Patriarchy. A Feminist History, Analysis, and Reconstruction of Buddhism*. Albany, N.Y.: State University of New York Press.

—— (1996), *Feminism and Religion: An Introduction*. Boston, Mass.: Beacon Press.

Gundersen, Marit Lindheim (1977), *Kvinnen i kirken. Teori og praksis*. Oslo: Land og kirke/Gyldendal Norsk Forlag.

Haddad, Yvonne Yazveck/Esposito, John L., eds. (1998), *Islam, Gender and Social Change*. New York/Oxford: Oxford University Press.

Hammer, Inger (1998), "Några reflexioner kring 'religionsblind' kvinnoforskning," in: *Historisk tidskrift* 1.

Hanegraaff, Wouter J. (1996), *New Age Religion and Western Culture. Esotericism in the Mirror of Secular Thought*. Leiden/New York/Köln: Brill.

Haraway, Donna (1988), "Situated Knowledges: The Science Question in Feminism and the Privilege of Partial Perspective," in: *Feminist Studies* 14 (3): 575–99.

Heiler, Friedrich (1977), *Die Frau in den Religionen der Menschheit*. Berlin/New York: Walter de Gruyter.

Helve, Helena (2000), "The Formation of Gendered World Views and Gender Ideology," in: Geertz/McCutcheon, eds.: 245–59.

Hewitt, Marsha A. (1993), "Cyborgs, Drag Queens, and Goddesses: Emancipatory-regressive Paths in Feminist Theory," in: *Method and Theory in the Study of Religion* 5: 135–54.

Hoffman, Lawrence (1996), *Covenant of Blood: Circumcision and Gender in Rabbinic Judaism*. Chicago: University of Chicago Press.

Holden, Pat, ed. (1983), *Women's Religious Experience*. London/Canberra: Croom Helm.

Holm, Jean/Bowker, John, eds. (1994), *Women in Religion*. Themes in Religious Studies Series. London: Pinter.

Huber, M.T./Lutkehaus, N.C. (1999), *Gendered Missions: Women and Men in Missionary Discourse and Practice*. Ann Arbor, Mich.: The University of Michigan Press.

Juschka, Darlene M., ed. (2001), *Feminism in the Study of Religion. A Reader*. London/New York: Continuum.

Kimmel, Michael S., ed. (1987), *Changing Men: New Directions in Research on Men and Masculinity*. Newbury Park: Sage Publications.

King, Ursula, ed. (1987), *Women in the World's Religions, Past and Present*. New York: Paragon.

—— (1990), "Religion and Gender," in: Ursula King, ed., *Turning Points in Religious Studies: Essays in Honour of Geoffrey Parrinder*. Edinburgh: T & T Clark: 275–86.

—— ed. (1995a), *Religion and Gender*. Oxford: Blackwell.

—— (1995b), "Introduction: Gender and the Study of Religion," in: King, ed.: 1–38.

—— (1995c), "A Question of Identity: Women Scholars and the Study of Religion," in: King, ed.: 219–44.

Kinsley, David (1987), *Hindu Goddesses. Visions of the Divine Feminine in the Hindu Religious Tradition*. Motilal Banarsiddass, Delhi.

Kloppenborg, Ria/Hanegraaff, Wouter J., eds. (1995), *Female Stereotypes in Religious Traditions*. Leiden: Brill.

Kraft, Siv-Ellen (1999), *The Sex Problem. Political Aspects of Gender Discourse in the Theosophical Society 1875–1930*. Thesis Submitted at the University of Bergen, IKRR, Department of the History of Religions, Bergen, February 1999.

McFadden, Margaret H. (1999), *Golden Cables of Sympathy. The Transatlantic Sources of Nineteenth-Century Feminism*. Lexington, Ky.: The University Press of Kentucky.

Meeks, Wayne A. (1974), "The Image of the Androgyne: Some Uses of a Symbol in Earliest Christianity," in: *History of Religions* 13: 165–208.

Mikaelsson, Lisbeth (1980), "Sexual Polarity: An Aspect of the Ideological Structure in the Paradise Narrative, Gen. 2,4–3,24," in: *Temenos* 15: 84–91.

—— (1987), "Hva kan kvinneforskningen tilføre religionsvitenskapen—fagteoretisk, metodologisk og kunnskapsmessig?" in: *Chaos* 7: 44–58.

Morgan, Sue (1999), "Feminist Approaches," in: Peter Connolly, ed., *Approaches to the Study of Religion*. London/New York: Cassell: 42–72.

Natvig, Richard (1988), "Liminal Rites and Female Symbolism in the Egyptian Zar Possession Cult," in: *Numen* 35, fasc 1: 57–68.

—— (1989), "Er kvinner hedninger? Om zar-kult og islam, om kvinner og menn," in: *Chaos* 11: 73–92.

Offen, Karen (1988), "Defining Feminism: A Comparative Historical Approach," in: *Signs* 14 (1): 119–57.

—— (2000), *European Feminisms 1700–1950. A Political History*. Stanford, Calif.: Stanford University Press.

Okkenhaug, Inger Marie, ed. (2003), *Gender, Race and Religion: Nordic Missions 1860–1940*. Uppsala: Studia Missionalia Svecana XCI.

Ortner, Sherry B./Whitehead, Harriet (1981), "Introduction: Accounting for Sexual Meanings," in: Sherry B. Ortner/Harriet Whitehead, eds., *Sexual Meanings: The Cultural Construction of Gender and Sexuality*. Cambridge: Cambridge University Press: 1–27.

Owen, Alex (1989), *The Darkened Room: Women, Power and Spiritualism in Late Victorian England*. London: Virago Press.

Parrinder, Geoffrey (1980), *Sex in the World's Religions*. London: Sheldon Press.

Phillips, John A. (1985), *Eve: The History of an Idea*. San Francisco, Calif.: Harper & Row.

Pinkham, Mildred Worth (1967), *Woman in the Sacred Scriptures of Hinduism*. New York: AMS Press.

Plaskow, Judith (1990), *Standing Again at Sinai: Judaism from a Feminist Perspective*. San Francisco, Calif.: Harper.

Plaskow, Judith/Arnold, Joan, eds. (1974), *Women and Religion*. Missoula, Mont.: Scholars Press.

Plaskow, Judith/Christ, Carol P., eds. (1989), *Weaving the Visions: Patterns in Feminist Spirituality*. San Francisco, Calif.: Harper.

Ricoeur, Paul (1969 [1967]), *The Symbolism of Evil*. New York: Beacon Press.

Ruether, Rosemary Radford, ed. (1974), *Religion and Sexism. Images of Woman in the Jewish and Christian Traditions*. New York: Simon and Schuster.

— (1975), *New Woman, New Earth: Sexist Ideologies and Human Liberation*. New York: The Seabury Press.

— (1979), *Mary: The Feminine Face of the Church*. London: SCM Press Ltd.

— (1983), *Sexism and God-Talk: Toward a Feminist Theology*. Boston, Mass.: Beacon Press.

— (1987), "Androcentrism," in: Mircea Eliade, ed., *The Encyclopedia of Religion*. Vol. 1. New York/London: Macmillan: 272–76.

Salomonsen, Jone (2002), *Enchanted Feminism. The Reclaiming Witches of San Francisco*. London/New York: Routledge.

Scott, Joan W. (1986): "Gender: A Useful Category of Historical Analysis," in: *The American Historical Review* 5: 1053–75.

— (1988), "Deconstructing Equality-versus-Difference: Or, the Uses of Poststructuralist Theory for Feminism," in: *Feminist Studies* 14 (1): 33–50.

— (1998) "Experience," in: Sidonie Smith/Julia Watson, eds., *Women, Autobiography, Theory: A Reader*. Madison, Wis.: The University of Wisconsin Press: 57–71.

Sharma, Arvind, ed. (1987), *Women in World Religions*. With an introduction by Katherine K. Young. New York: State University of New York Press.

— (1994), *Religion and Women*. Albany, N.Y.: State University of New York Press.

— (1994), *Today's Woman in World Religions*. Albany, N.Y.: State University of New York Press.

Sharma, Arvind et al. (1988), *Sati. Historical and Phenomenological Essays*. Delhi: Motilal Banarsidass.

Shaw, Rosalind (1995), "Feminist Anthropology and the Gendering of Religious Studies," in: King, ed.: 65–76.

Stanton, Elizabeth Cady (1985 [(1895–1898)]), *The Woman's Bible*. Introduction by Dale Spender. Edinburgh: Polygon Books.

Tavard, George H. (1973), *Woman in Christian Tradition*. Notre Dame, Ind./London: University of Notre Dame Press.

Trible, Phyllis (1978), *God and the Rhetoric of Sexuality*. Philadelphia, Pa.: Fortress Press.

Turner, Bryan S. (1997), "The Body in Western Society: Social Theory and Its Perspectives," in: Coakley, ed.: 15–41.

Turner, Victor W. (1974), *The Ritual Process. Structure and Anti-Structure*. London: Penguin.

— (1981 [1967]), *The Forest of Symbols. Aspects of Ndembu Ritual*. Ithaca, N.Y./London: Cornell University Press.

Vogt, Kari (1995), "'Becoming Male': A Gnostic and Early Christian Metaphor," in: Børresen, ed.: 170–86.

Warne, Randi R. (2000), "Gender," in: Willi Braun/Russell T. McCutcheon, eds., *Guide to the Study of Religion*. London/New York: Cassel: 140–54.

Critical Trends in the Study of Religion in the United States

by

RUSSELL T. MCCUTCHEON

1. Introduction

Despite the fact that the academic study of religion is well over one hundred years old in Europe and, in its most recent form, has been institutionally sanctioned in North America for nearly forty years, the problem of developing useful theories and methods—and by means of these, a secure institutional identity as part of the human sciences—continues to plague the field in the U.S.[1] I say "continues to plague" to signify that the current North American field is characterized by a long-standing split: between theologians and liberal humanists, on the one hand, and those more inclined to study religion in a social scientific manner, on the other. Whereas for the former group the study of religion is defined by its object, the latter group presumes that scholarly interests and theories comprise the organizing principles for any academic endeavor. For members of the former tradition, the object of study—variously termed God, the Sacred, the *mysterium tremendum*, ultimacy, religious experience, or simply Human Nature, the Human Spirit, or the Human Condition—cannot be grasped by the usual epistemological techniques and must therefore be deciphered by studying its varied expressions (e.g., myths, rituals, symbols). For members of the latter tradition, however, all such discourses on privileged discernment are facts of social life susceptible to the ordinary methods of study used throughout the human sciences.

Despite the fact that any description of some recent trends in the U.S. will inevitably be idiosyncratic and sadly partial (as the following surely is), such a

---

[1] I say "in its most recent form" because the North American field flourished but then died out prior to the first world war. Among the reasons commonly cited for the early field's demise is the turn to neo-orthodoxy among post-World War I Protestant theologians coupled with the fact that the early study of religion was too linked to lone, charismatic professors, thereby lessening the field's viability once they retired or died. On this see Shepard 1991.

description cannot help but examine the tension that has marked the long relationship between these two competing approaches. This chapter does just this, paying special attention to the practical implications of the liberal humanist approach that, today, has come to dominate the study of religion in the United States.

2. Impulses, Beliefs, and Convictions

In a 1994 special issue of the North American field's largest circulating periodical, *Journal of the American Academy of Religion*,[2] Sam Gill of the University of Colorado, offered the following blunt assessment:

> The emergence of an academic study of religion has been disappointing despite the boost it received thirst years ago when religion entered the curricula of state-sponsored American colleges and universities … As an academic discipline distinct from the religious study of religion, it has failed to advance any sustainable body of theory, any cadre of religion theorists, any substantial body of literature. (1994: 965–66)

In the same issue of this journal, Dartmouth University's Hans Penner echoed Gill's sentiment by flatly stating:

> When you review the theoretical status of the study of religion over the past decade I believe you will agree with me that not much, if anything, has happened. We speak and write metaphorically rather then theoretically, concerned with things like "thick descriptions." The academy, for the most part, continues to be interested in religious dialogue and experience rather than criticism. (1994: 977)

In his lament for the state-of-the-art, Gill goes on to observe that, at least in part, the budgetary problems experienced by many U.S. departments of religious studies during the 1990s can be traced to the inability of their members to articulate an overall, coherent theoretical basis for their field, a failure that has had ramifications for their failure to generate a continuing institutional identity (a position echoed in Smith 1995). Simply put, in Gill's estimate theories are not lofty, purely intellectual items. They have practical, institutional, and political implications.

---

2   The special issue's title was, "Settled Issues and Neglected Questions in the Study of Religion." Apart from the AAR's quarterly newspaper, *Religious Studies News*, close behind *JAAR* in terms of circulation is the *Bulletin of the Council of Societies for the Study of Religion* as well as *Religious Studies Review*, both published by the Council of Societies for the Study of Religion (CSSR)—an "umbrella" organization comprised of twelve professional associations, including the Catholic Biblical Association, the National Association of Baptist Professors of Religion, the North American Association for the Study of Religion, and the Society of Christian Ethics.

In the estimation of these writers, the conflation of the scientific study of religion (where "religion" is conceived as but an aspect of larger socio-cultural practices), with the study of religion conceived either as a liberal humanist or theologically ecumenical pursuit (what Penner termed "religious dialogue"), is one of the primary theoretical and institutional problems currently facing the U.S. field. Thus, any survey of recent trends takes place against this backdrop, for this is the Sisyphusean hill currently being climbed by a loosely knit collection of North American scholars intent on saying something new about both religion and the study of religion. So, to understand what—if anything—might be "new under the sun," we must first understand that, on many campuses throughout the U.S., the study of religion as a component of a liberal arts curriculum is conceived—and thereby justified—as the means whereby students will become "civilized," insomuch as they will learn of their own culture's supposedly deepest values as well as learn to understand, appreciate, and tolerate the "Other's" equally deeply held beliefs and values. The study of religion is thus sold to university administrators, and the general public as well, as a crucial aspect of nation-building. For example, a university where I once worked was recognized by the U.S.-based John Templeton Foundation[3] as one of the outstanding "character-building" schools in the U.S.—possibly a dubious distinction for a publicly funded school to receive since "character," much like "values," is generally a codeword for a very specific set of characteristics portrayed as universal and thus self-evident. As might be expected, at least the senior administration at this school seemed to understand the study of religion as one way to develop a student's "character," thereby making them a better

---

3   It is the Templeton Foundation which annually awards the £ 700,000 Templeton Prize for Progress in Religion. Quoting from their website: "The John Templeton Foundation was established in 1987 by renowned international investor, Sir John Templeton, to encourage a fresh appreciation of the critical importance—for all peoples and cultures—of the moral and spiritual dimensions of life. The Templeton Foundation seeks to act as a critical catalyst for progress, especially by supporting studies which demonstrate the benefits of an open, humble and progressive approach to learning in these areas. It is the Foundation's purpose to stimulate a high standard of excellence in scholarly understanding which can serve to encourage further worldwide explorations of the moral and spiritual dimensions of the Universe and of the human potential within its ultimate purpose ... Through its programs, the Foundation seeks to encourage the world to catch the vision of the tremendous possibilities for spiritual progress in an open and humble approach to life; encourage institutions of learning to incorporate training towards excellence in character in their efforts to prepare the next generation for service; to encourage growth in appreciating the potential of free societies; and to promote the understanding of the significant responsibilities associated with freedom in its several aspects, moral, spiritual, political and economic" (http://www.templeton.org/about.asp).

"citizen." The study of religion, then, is understood to have a redemptive and salvific quality, for both the individual and the nation.

Or, as another example, take a recent quantitative study of religion, and the academic study of religion, on U.S. campuses. The authors surveyed four representative schools,[4] finding that the "distanced objectivity" end of the teaching spectrum "seemed to be more sparsely populated than the opposite extreme" (outright religious advocacy) (Cherry/De Berg/Porterfield 2001: 11). Citing examples of professors who made claims in their classrooms concerning the religious value of the Hebrew Bible or the professor of Buddhism who "wanted his students to study Buddhism from the inside, gleaning religious truths from it for their own lives" (11), the authors refer to only one specific example of a professor who ruled such judgments out of bounds. Sadly, they provide no evidence for their conclusion that his "dedication to neutrality or objectivity had its limits" (12). Most revealing, perhaps, is their finding—long suspected by a number of professors, to be sure—that students, like their professors, see the religious studies classroom as a sacred site. "The academic methods and intentions of faculty aside," they remark,

> we discovered that for the students the religious studies classroom was often a site and resource for religious meaning and personal transformation. The line between the practice and teaching of religion thus could become blurred. In some instances, the blurring of the boundaries was invited by the faculty themselves. Even at the public university, where the transformation of the students' lives was a goal infrequently expressed by those who taught religion, students who were interviewed spoke of the important life issues raised in these courses, the all-night discussions they had about them, and the religious studies major as something undertaken for personal development rather than preparation for a specific career.

"In short," the authors go on to comment, "many students took religious studies courses because the courses forced them 'to think' and spoke to their search for meaning" (12). At the close of their article, the authors offer the following conclusion: "it is possible that religious practice and education have never been more connected with personal responsibility for society [i.e., good citizenship]. More clearly, our study reveals that the ethos of de-centered, diverse, religiously tolerant institutions of higher education is a breeding ground for vital religious practice and teaching" (13).

From the preceding it is clear that, in the U.S. at least, the category "religion" (often replaced by the now popular "spirituality") is often associated

---

4   Although not identified by name, the schools were: a large public university, a private Protestant (Lutheran) school, a private Roman Catholic institution, and a non-denominational, traditional African-American school (originally in the Presbyterian tradition). The article cited is an excerpt from the author's co-written book, *Religion on Campus* (Chapel Hill, N.C.: University of North Carolina Press, 2001).

with an utterly personal yet universal feeling, conviction, or moral disposition which is housed within the individual and which has lasting value for society as a whole. Perhaps this accounts for why Paul Tillich's vaguely subjective "faith in an ultimate concern" thus remains the definition of choice for many scholars, followed closely by Clifford Geertz's penchant for seeing religion as a system of "moods and motivations." Thus, ill-defined religious impulses, convictions, and interior states of emotion are presumed to reside somewhere deep in that which is shared by everyone, the all-inclusive "Human Nature"—an undefinable something to which scholars of religion are said to have access.

But such mythic inclusiveness is purchased at a high price. As phrased by Douglas R. Brooks in his *JAAR* article on the state of the study of Hinduism within North America's largest professional association for scholars of religion, the American Academy of Religion (AAR):[5]

> working without consensus about definitions and boundaries, scope and methods, and clearly stated agendas makes us fair targets for those who would accuse us of marginality, irrelevance, or unimportance within our institutions, or even within our larger guild. This may be a responsibility we cannot afford either to abdicate or delegate to others without risking further marginalization within institutions. (1994: 1192)[6]

The necessary parameters by means of which boundaries, scope, and methods—let alone institutional identity—are determined are thus largely absent from the study of religion *qua* interreligious dialogue on deeply personal moods and motivations. Moreover, the agendas that drive these vague and therefore misleadingly inclusive parameters are generally undisclosed.

A clarification is, perhaps, necessary at this point. The preceding's allusion to Clifford Geertz's classic 1966 definition, which defined religion in relation to "a system of symbols which acts to establish powerful, persuasive, and long-lasting moods and motivations" (1973), deserves some attention before we proceed. Some would argue that it is disingenuous to equate Geertz's work with that of such liberal Protestant theologians as Paul Tillich. For the purposes of this chapter, they are remarkably similar, however, insomuch as both are preoccupied with questions of such things as nonhistorical truth, value, and meaning, rather than with an examination of the thoroughly historical—and thus negotiable and contestable—structural conditions that make such things as

---

5   There has been no more vocal critic of the crypto-theological nature of the AAR than the University of Toronto's Donald Wiebe. His most recent collection of essays, *The Politics of Religious Studies* (1999) is by far the place to start for those interested in his assessment of the North American field, especially the formation of the AAR from the previously existing National Association of Bible Instructors.

6   Such blunt criticisms seem applicable to much of this very issue of *JAAR* insomuch as it continues to portray the study of religion as carried out in North America as a predominantly American, Christian, and theological enterprise.

truth, value, and meaning items of discourse. Although Geertz's work seems to have moved remarkably beyond the concerns of theologians, the continued popularity of his definition owes much to Geertz's concern with a hermeneutic; for in his work we find "an eminent anthropologist drawing on the cultural sciences ... [to] rescue religion from the ravages of positivism" (Frankenberry/ Penner 1999: 618). Geertz's enduring contribution to the study of religion was to assist his peers to shift the ground from disputing *truth* to ascertaining the *meaning* of cultural acts by means of a nuanced, or what he called thick, description of the practice. His goal, then, was not to explain these assorted practices, but merely to chronicle them and recover their meaning *as it was believed the participants themselves understood them*. As Frankenberry and Penner go on to conclude in their recent reappraisal of Geertz's early influence on the study of religion, "we suspect that the continued use of this definition of religion has gone hand in hand with a diminution of critical reflection on its central theoretical and methodological assumptions." This diminution, and its practical effects, is the critical trend of concern in this chapter.

Of the many problems with Geertz's definition that they examine in detail, take but one: the manner in which the definition assumes a correspondence or representational theory of truth. Symbols, he asserts in his essay, are any object, act, event, etc., that "serves as a vehicle for a conception—the conception is the symbol's meaning"; we find here the presumption of a one-to-one relation between nonempirical and thus pre-symbolic meanings and empirical symbols. This presumption relies on the same, virtually Platonic logic as the earlier phenomenological equation between a nonempirical essence and empirical manifestations. As Frankenberry and Penner convincingly demonstrate, neither Geertz nor his followers have ever investigated just what a conception might be or how it is that something can serve as a vehicle for one (1999: 619–26). Presuming a thoroughly historical setting for all human practices, including the study of human practices, they conclude, "there is no vantage point from which speakers [i.e., users of symbol systems] can transcend the symbolic language in which they are embedded in order to judge that the correspondence is indeed 'simulating,' 'imitating,' or in any other way representing some nonsymbolic reality" (623).

Confronted with the supposedly dehumanizing dangers of a mid-twentieth century positivistic, explanatory approach to the study of religion (in which "things religious" were completely reduced to other ordinary forms of human practice), while more than aware of the limitations of an explicitly theological and hence normative approach, this hermeneutic, middle path seems to have been tremendously appetizing to politically and theologically liberal scholars in the late 1960s and early 1970s. However, despite this apparent shift of attention, the presumption of a nonempirical reality and vantage point, either out there in the universe somewhere or lurking in the interior regions of the Human Condition, remained intact. Given the Church/State separation described in the first amendment to the U.S. Constitution, the latter, liberal humanist approach struck many people in the early field as nontheological (since it made no reference to God and, instead, referred to values and meanings). Thus, it was deemed acceptable in the confines of the then growing publicly funded study of religion.

A useful example of the appeal of this subtle shift is unwittingly provided by Robert Ellwood, a graduate of the University of Chicago's famous program and now well known for his many textbooks and reference works on religion, mysticism, and spirituality. In his recent book, *The Politics of Myth* (1999), Ellwood makes several autobiographical asides that provide interesting clues as to the appeal writers such as Mircea Eliade and Joseph Campbell held for students in the late 1960s, the generation that re-established the field in the U.S. The "Eliade effect"—which, if my students are any measure, continues unabated to this day—is evident at the outset of the book:

> One day [in 1962 while Ellwood was a U.S. Marine chaplain stationed in Okinawa], I came across a review of one of Eliade's books. Something about the account led me to believe it might help. I ordered the slim volume, read it, and suddenly the significance of a wholly new way of looking at religion arose into consciousness: not theological, but in terms of its phenomenological structures ... It was one of those books that make one think, 'This was really true all the time, but I didn't realize it until now.' Soon I left the chaplaincy and enrolled as a graduate student under Mircea Eliade at the University of Chicago Divinity School. (5)

Just what Ellwood needed "help" with was dealing with what he later terms "modernity's pluralism of space and time" (111). "I could not help but believe," he writes, "that some indefinable spiritual presence lingered in the lovely sylvan shrines of Shinto, or that there was more than mere atmosphere in the great peace that filled temples of the Buddha" (5). Jung, Eliade, and Campbell's works—not to mention Geertz—thus enabled readers in the 1960s and 1970s to depart from what they had come to see as their confining, sectarian perspective and embark on an equally salvific quest for what Ellwood calls "benign pluralism"—a truly liberal quest in which the utility of the comparative method is that it "enables one to experience vicariously the passions of other faiths as well as one's own, so leading to the enrichment of *total human experience*" (110–11; italics added). Simply put, the attraction of the field for those mid-twentieth century U.S. practitioners disillusioned with denominationalism was its ability to shift the ground from seemingly incontestable truth to infinitely variable symbols acting as ill-defined vehicles for elusive meaning—"and by meaning," Ellwood writes, "is denominated that which comes from a *universal source* but is congruous with one's own dreams and deepest significant fantasies" (177; italics added). Armed with what, at first glance at least, appears to be all things to all people, how could the history of religions fail to win converts in the U.S.? The attraction to studying such things as religion, myth, and ritual, then, is obvious for, expressing the core assumption of this tradition, Ellwood writes:

"Myth, like all great literature, can become universal, transcending particular cultural settings" (177).[7]

This liberal refashioning of dogmatic truth into elusive and all-inclusive personal meaning—a refashioning to which Clifford Geertz's hermeneutic anthropology contributed significantly—continues unabated in our field's general unwillingness to define religion in light of a specifiable set of observable human acts and institutions. Working without what Brooks terms a consensus about definitions and boundaries is puzzling, for without a commonly accepted definition of "religion"—some way of rather narrowly demarcating this category and the social domain to which it refers from such other categories and domains as "worldview," "belief system," "culture," "ideology," etc.—how do any of us know precisely what our colleagues are talking about when they make claims about this thing "religion"? Without a consensus on what in the inter-subjectively observable world counts as religion, and what does not, what, precisely, do members of our field study? More importantly, without an agreed upon manner for determining how it is that one goes about proposing, applying, testing and criticizing definitions, how will we know when anything "new" has happened in the field?

It is therefore understandable that when apologies for the academic study of religion are offered to our colleagues throughout the guild—let alone the reading public at large—more often than not they are written by people who conflate the role of the scholar of religion with that of the liberal, religious, if learned, devotee speculating on issues of ultimate meaning and inexpressible essences housed within a thing called "Human Nature"—all of which are "things" that hardly constitute legitimate data for scholars in the public university. As suggested by both Gill and Brooks, at a time of shrinking university budgets, such a conflation does not help us to offer persuasive justifications for the continued place of the study of religion within the public university. To repeat Brooks's conclusion: "This may be a responsibility we cannot afford either to abdicate or delegate to others without risking further marginalization within institutions."

Although this can easily be seen in the case of several of the articles that appear along with the previously cited quantitative study of religion on U.S. campuses—published in the journal of the Association of American Colleges and Universities (AACU), *Liberal Education*—two other examples of such troublesome apologies can be found in articles published in the U.S. periodical, *Academe*.[8] According to Martin Marty (1996), the University of Chicago's

---

7   It is to Ellwood's credit, however, that he immediately cautions his readers: "the mythologists ... did not always take into account that myth, like everything human, can be of quite varied moral worth ... [A]bstractions are not the solutions to problems."

8   *Academe* is the bi-monthly periodical of the American Association of University Professors (AAUP).

recently retired and tremendously influential liberal historian of U.S. religion, "religious faith" and "religious impulses" motivate and inspire human behavior; according to William Scott Green (1996), former editor of *JAAR*, religion or what he latter terms "religious conviction," "has become and yet remains a tremendously potent force in American social, political, and economic life." Because religious faith, impulses, and convictions are firmly housed within individual experience and private consciousness, they can only be expressed by the one who holds them and then, once made public, they can be described, translated, understood, and—in a mode of inter-religious dialogue—eventually appreciated by the observer. This leads to a field which, as already suggested by Penner, concentrates on recovering and then interpreting highly personalistic and non-empirical meanings (hence the continued popularity of Geertz's notion of "thick description" among scholars of religion) rather than theorizing on the empirically observable causes and consequences of such meaning systems.

Admittedly, the position represented by both Marty and Green is not limited to the U.S.; it may be likely that the private/public, belief/practice, or essence/manifestation rhetorics necessary for this viewpoint are among the more successful, and thus persuasive and pervasive, techniques employed within social formations for reproducing dominant forms of organization (more on this below). In the study of religion these rhetorics have a long history and can at least be traced back to the German Pietist theologian Friedrich Schleiermacher (1768–1834) who effectively protected—and thereby, some would say, simultaneously marginalized—those dimensions of social life then labeled as "religion" from what he saw as the cynical, prying eyes of Enlightenment rationality, by claiming that religion was essentially a personalistic, affective experience, somewhat akin to an aesthetic experience. Thus, the content of "religion" could not be observed or quantified, let alone explained. Just as for Marty and Green, so too for Schleiermacher: religious experiences are exclusively the causes of other things; they cannot be explained as merely the effects of other ordinary human behaviors. Such experience is understood as irreducible, primary, and utterly unique (i.e., *sui generis*).

But there is an equally long-standing tradition in the field that sees categories such as "religious impulse," "the sacred," "ultimate concern," and "faith" as so vague and subjective as to be of little or no theoretical use in studying the causes, functions, and consequences of human behavior and social organization. Traced back at least to the Scottish philosopher, David Hume (1711–1776)—and today represented in part by the members of the North American Association for the Study of Religion (NAASR)[9]—this tradition

---

9 Founded in Sidney, Australia, in 1985 by E. Thomas Lawson, Luther H. Martin, and
   Donald Wiebe, NAASR is the North American affiliate of the International Association

forgoes speculating on "deep" trans-historical meanings and pristine impulses. Instead, its representatives are generally interested in developing testable theories which are based in a shared rational discourse, theories on the workings of human cognition, the observable reasons and implications for human behavior, and the ways in which people construct and contest durable social identities.[10] Accordingly, the *claims* people routinely make about such "things" as the gods, trans-historical meanings, origins, and deeply personal, non-empirical realities turn out to be the objects of study for this type of scholarship on religion. In the words of Gary Lease, head of the History of Consciousness Program at the University of California at Santa Cruz, "the goals of evidence are not to replicate experience; not to validate as real this or that particular experience or claim; not to establish, in other words, exclusive norms or systems governing reality absolutely" (1997: 139). Shifting attention from appreciating and thereby reproducing the content of indigenous experiential claims (as in a previous era's phenomenology and morphology) to studying the causes, functions, and effects of the claims themselves gives this oppositional group its thoroughly anthropological focus.

What remains to be said is that such a shift does not, of course, mean that the study of religion has finally become the purely objective or non-biased activity once hoped for by those influenced by logical positivism. Such a dream is animated by the same drive that prompted efforts to determine the extra-historical truth or the deep meaning of religion. As with all human activity, it too is the product of certain contexts and thus open to critique and revision (as has resulted from the feminist critique that rightfully identifies the gendered presumptions that drive much scholarship on religion [see Juschka 1997, 2001]). But this shift does draw attention to the necessarily perspectival and thoroughly historical natural of all human systems of knowledge, a significant change from the effort to ascertain deep meanings associated with liberal humanistic scholarship on religion.

3. The Taxon "Religion"

Therefore, one of the most wide-reaching developments of the past twenty years is the interest among a small but productive group of writers in shifting attention from phenomenologists collecting supposed facts concerning the content of belief to historicizing the very tools, terms, and categories by which we

---

for the History of Religions (IAHR). Its quarterly journal is *Method & Theory in the Study of Religion* (published by Brill of the Netherlands).

10   See Jensen/Martin 1997 for essays from a conference at Aarhus University, Denmark, on the role of rationality in the study of religion. NAASR members are prominent in the collection.

discuss the issue—a shift in attention that may well be characteristic of the rebirth of theory or the "linguistic turn" found throughout the human sciences.[11]

Despite the fact that the term "religion" is used by many people to name certain of their own beliefs, behaviors, and institutions, scholars of religion have a history of defining the term in a very particular way, depending on the theory of religion they are using. As already suggested, folk or popular definitions of a term such as religion do not necessarily meet the standards of inter-subjectively available, cross-cultural data. Echoing Gill and Penner's assessment, for the Brandeis University anthropologist, Benson Saler, the general question that scholars of religion continue to face is how they can "transform a folk category into an analytic category that will facilitate transcultural research and understanding" (1993: 1). Despite a number of heated debates, such categorial retooling has successfully taken place over the past twenty years in literary studies (e.g., "literature," "author," "intention," and "text") as well as anthropology (e.g., "culture"), but, as Donald Wiebe has remarked, "it is clear that a generally accepted notion of 'religion,' upon which an understanding of the nature of the scientific study of religion can be based, and one that will be found acceptable to the majority of scholars in the field today, has not yet emerged" (1994: 104).

As a step toward retooling "religion," a number of scholars have looked to the term's etymology.[12] We know that it has equivalents in such modern languages as French and German; for example, when practiced in Germany the study of religion is known as *Religionswissenschaft* (the systematic study, or *Wissenschaft*, of religion); when practiced in France the field is known as *Sciences Religieuses* (e.g., Canada's main, bi-lingual periodical is entitled *Studies in Religion/Sciences Religieuses*). Even just a brief comparison of these and other related languages helps us to see that modern languages impacted by Latin possess something equivalent to the English term "religion." This means that, *for language families unaffected by Latin, there is no equivalent term to "religion"*—unless, along with liberal humanists, we pompously assert that our local word/concept captures something essential to the entire human species, thereby distinguishing local word from universal concept (i.e., "Although they do not call it religion, they still have *It*"), an assertion made all the easier by the long history of European influence on non-Latin-based cultures/languages by means of trade, coercion, and conquest. For example, although "religion" is hardly a

---

11   Indicative of this trend is the appearance of various wordbooks or handbooks on "key terms"; for example, see Taylor 1998 and Braun/McCutcheon 2000.

12   Although he is theologically inclined (insomuch as he prioritizes an inner and unseen "faith in transcendence" over religion, which he understands merely to refer to the observable "cumulative tradition"), the early and influential work of Wilfred Cantwell Smith (1963) cannot go unnoticed when discussing the history of the category "religion."

traditional concept in India, the long history of contact with Europe has en-
sured that modern, English speaking Indians have no difficulty conceiving of
what we might call "Hinduism" as their "religion"—although, technically
speaking, to a person we might call a Hindu, "Hinduism" is not a religion but
is, rather, *sanatana dharma* (the eternal duty/obligation/order). As might be
expected, despite its authoritative status in the history of textual studies, the
Christian New Testament is not much help in settling these issues, for its
language of composition—Greek—naturally lacked the Latin root word/
concept *religio*. Thus, English New Testaments will routinely use "religion" to
translate such Greek terms as *eusebia* (e.g., 1 Timothy 3:16; 2 Timothy 3:5), terms
that are in fact closer to the Sanskrit *dharma* (duty), the Chinese *li* (rules of
propriety and social rank), or even the Latin *pietas* (practices that maintain
proper social relations) than our term "religion."

Appeals to etymology are thus not much help in sorting out this problem in
taxonomy, for even in Latin our modern term "religion" has no equivalent—if,
by "religion," one means worshiping the gods, believing in an afterlife, or
simply being good. The closest we come when looking for Latin precursors to
our modern term "religion" are terms such as *religare* or *religere* which, in their
original contexts, simply meant such things as "to bind something tightly
together" or "to pay close or careful attention to something." So, where does
this linguistic turn leave us? Well, it leaves us with a lot of questions in need of
investigation: Just what do we mean by "religion"? If a culture does not have
the concept, can we study "their religion"? Is there such as thing as "the Hindu
religion" or "ancient Greek religion"? Is "religion" a supremely imperialistic
concept that "we" use to name "them"? Is cross-cultural, comparative analysis
of all such inevitably localized human meaning even possible? Or is "religion"
simply an arbitrary taxon some of us in the guild use to organize and talk about
aspects of the observable world that strike us as curious?

Although most often associated with the ground-breaking work of the
University of Chicago's Jonathan Z. Smith—particularly his widely read essay
collection, *Imagining Religion* (1982) as well as his most recent survey of the
concept "religion" (1998)[13]—I wish instead to focus on two other examples of
this sort of work: the often cited work of the anthropologist Talal Asad (1993)
and the more recent work of the scholar of Christian origins William E. Arnal

---

13 Smith famously wrote in *Imagining Religion* that there is no data for religion. In other
    words, he argues that, apart from its various folk usages among members of Latin-
    based language families, the very category "religion" when used as a technical term is a
    product of scholarly imagination, curiosity, and interests. The discourse on religious
    impulses and experiences found throughout the North American field may well, then,
    comprise an instance of the folk usage of the term, rather than a technical retooling of
    it. To this tradition of scholarship one can add Fitzgerald 1999; McCutcheon 1997b; and
    Saler 1993.

(2000). Taken together, they provide an example of how members of this oppositional tradition see the very rhetoric of private, religious experience as an
historical datum that can be studied without presupposing "things religion" to
be deeply personal, mysterious items of belief and deep conviction.[14] Thus, two
recent trends will simultaneously preoccupy us in the following: the
dominance of the liberal humanist tradition and its critique.

4. The Politics of Experience

In a move that would more than likely baffle those whose studies of religion
are limited to describing and comparing the manifestations of deeply held
personal beliefs in either this or that, both Asad and Arnal link the presumption
that "religion" connotes a disembodied, deeply personal experience to the
advent of the nation-state. (This thesis is directly applicable to the earlier
comments on the manner in which religious studies in the U.S. is today often
considered to have the effect of enhancing a student's character, making him/
her a better citizen.) The former group of scholars have thus become the object
of study for the latter.

As phrased by Asad:

> Several times before the Reformation, the boundary between the religious and the
> secular was redrawn, but always the formal authority of the Church remained pre-
> eminent. In later centuries, with the triumphant rise of modern science, modern
> production, and the modern state, the churches would also be clear about the need to
> distinguish the religious from the secular, shifting, as they did so, the weight of religion
> more and more onto the moods and motivations of the individual believer. Discipline
> (intellectual and social) would, in this period, gradually abandon religious space,
> letting "belief," "conscience," and "sensibility" take its place. (1993: 39)

After citing this very passage in an essay on the problems of defining religion,
Arnal goes on to comment:

> In other words, our definitions of religion, especially insofar as they assume a priva-
> tized and cognitive character behind religion (as in religious *belief*), simply reflect (and
> assume as normative) the West's distinctive historical feature of the secularized state.
> Religion, precisely, is *not* social, *not* coercive, *is* individual, *is* belief-oriented and so on,
> because in our day and age there are certain apparently free-standing cultural insti-
> tutions, such as the Church, which are excluded from the political state. Thus, Asad
> notes, it is no coincidence that it is the period after the "Wars of Religion" in the

---

14 Apart from "religion," this move to rethink our categories, and the role played by
    scholars in using them—a move often associated with the work of such "self-reflexive"
    anthropologists as James Clifford and George Marcus (1986)—can also be found in the
    study of "Buddhism" (Almond 1988; Lopez 1995), "Gnosticism" (Williams 1996),
    "Confucianism" (Jensen 1997), "myth" (Lincoln 1999), and "ritual" (Bell 1992).

seventeenth century that saw the first universalist definitions of religion; and those
definitions of "Natural Religion," of course, stressed the propositional—as opposed to
political or institutional—character of religion as a function of their historical context.

Arnal, then, concludes that

the very concept of religion as such—as an entity with any distinction whatsoever from
other human phenomena—is a function of these same processes and historical moments that generate an individualistic concept of it ... The concept of religion is a way
of demarcating a certain socio-political reality that is only problematised with the
advent of modernity in which the state at least claims to eschew culture *per se*. (2000:
31)

As suggested earlier, this seemingly well-meaning, benign, and all inclusive
discourse on "experience" and "belief" is more complex than it first appears.
Discourses on experience thus have a political effect, a means whereby alternative and therefore competing social worlds are privatized, ghettoized, and
thus governed. The rhetoric of "religious experience" is therefore what Wayne
Proudfoot, of Columbia University, once aptly called a "protective strategy"
(1985).

As the University of Michigan scholar of Buddhism, Robert Sharf, has recently phrased it in an article on the category of experience, "the term [religious
experience] is often used rhetorically to thwart the authority of the 'objective' or
the 'empirical,' and to valorize instead the subjective, the personal, the private"
(1998: 94). As argued by Arnal, the philosophically idealist rhetoric of
"experience" presumes that pristine, pre-reflective moments of pure self-
consciousness (or, along with Schleiermacher, we could call it "God-conscious-
ness") float freely in the background of the restrictive conventions of language
and social custom—what Jonathan Z. Smith, quoting Nietzsche, once called
"the myth of immaculate perception." It is a position comparable to that which
once fueled literary studies, insomuch as "Literature" was thought by some to
embody essentially transcendent themes and values that stirred the Human
Heart and expressed the meaning of the Human Condition.

Within the study of religion—specifically, the study of early Christianities—Smith has traced this Romantic rhetoric of pristine origins and pure
experience to what he terms "the regnant Protestant *topoi* in which the category
of inspiration has been transposed from the text to the experience of the
interpreter, the one who is being directly addressed *through* the text." After
identifying the anti-Catholic polemic the lurks within quests for original moments (as found in attempts to bypass the supposed tyranny of "popery" and
"tradition" by means of appeals to "the biblical witness" and "the historical
Jesus"—appeals eerily similar to some scholars of religions' appeals to the
authenticity of lived experience or the priority of the insider's viewpoint),
Smith concludes: "As employed by some scholars in religious studies, it must
be judged a fantastic attempt to transform interpretation into revelation" (1990:

55). Once contextualized within the wider geo-politics that characterized the period in which the modern concept of religion first arose in Europe ("wider" simply meaning outside strictly denomination rhetorics examined so well by Smith), Arnal concludes that

> one of the current political *effects* of this separation—one of the political ends served currently by it—is the evisceration of substance, i.e., collective aims, from the state. That is to say, the simple positing of religion is a covert justification for the modern tendency of the state to frame itself in increasingly negative terms: the secular state is the institutional apparatus by which the social body *prevents* the incursion by others into the personal and various other goals of individuals, rather than being the means of achievement for common projects and the collective good. This very definition of the modern democratic state in fact creates religion as its alter-ego: religion, as such, is the space in which and by which any substantive collective goals (salvation, righteousness, etc.) are individualized and made into a question of personal commitment or morality. (2000: 32)

As this critique makes clear, the rhetoric of experience has, to some degree, come under hard times in the U.S. Although there still exists a thriving industry in recovering the authenticity or immediacy of experience,[15] some scholars now understand so-called lived experience to be a thoroughly socio-political construct. Outside the study of religion, the work of the feminist historian, Joan Wallach Scott, comes to mind as another example of this critique of experience. In the conclusion to an essay entitled, "The Evidence of Experience," she writes:

> Experience is at once always already an interpretation *and* something that needs to be interpreted. What counts as experience is neither self-evident or straightforward; it is always contested, and always therefore political. The study of experience, therefore, must call into question its originary status in historical explanation. This will happen when historians take as their project *not* the reproduction and transmission of knowledge said to be arrived at through experience, but the analysis of the production of that knowledge itself. (1991: 797)

Or, as Sharf phrases it,

> the rhetoric of experience tacitly posits a place where signification comes to an end, variously styled "mind," "consciousness," the "mirror of nature," or what have you. The category experience is, in essence, a mere placeholder that entails a substantive if

---

15   Perhaps one of the more notable examples is provided by Karen McCarthy Brown's influential study of immigrant Haitian Vodou in New York, *Mama Lola* (1991). Helping to turn the tide toward a more self-reflexive, participatory form of ethnographic writing, Brown's book prompted heated debates in the study of religion. Chronicling her own growing participation in the life and rituals of the Brooklyn Vodou community, specifically her longtime, and ever deepening relationship with Alourdes—the priestess known as Mama Lola, whom she first met in 1978—the book's chapters alternate between more traditional ethnographic writing and fiction/short stories intended to uncover a deeper meaning or experience not communicable in ethnographese.

indeterminate terminus for the relentless deferral of meaning. And this is precisely
what makes the term experience so amenable to ideological appropriation. (1998: 113)

As counter-intuitive as it may at first sound, "privacy" is an item of public
contestation and claims that privacy has self-evident limits are evidence of a
political debate—ask former U.S. President Bill Clinton, whose "private" conduct while holding the "public" office of U.S. President made for some wonder-
ful rhetorical flourishes on both sides of the political divide. Like "privacy,"
then, "experience" does not come pre-packaged from the grocery store.

That two very different types of study of religion develop, depending on
how you talk about "experiences," should be evident. As suggested in the
opening lines to this essay, for some time these two fields have been, and
currently are, contesting each other. If we follow Asad and Arnal in seeing the
"private/public" distinction as a rhetorical technique crucial for making the
modern, large-scale social identities (i.e., the nation-state) possible, then it may
be a foregone conclusion that in the modern research university—but one
component of what is often referred to as the military-industrial-educational
complex—the discourse on pristine, pre-social experience has the home field
advantage.

5. The Politics of Tolerance

It may then make some sense as to why a brand of explanatory—what is most
often referred to, somewhat dismissively, as reductionistic or scientistic—
scholarship has not won the day in the U.S. Instead, as already observed by
Penner, scholars of religion who engage in various forms of liberal, inter-
religious dialogue continue to dominate the scene, setting the agenda in the
field's professional societies, the programs at its conferences, and providing the
public face of the field in the media.[16] Most recently, they have gone by the
name of "public intellectuals," a rather empty but rhetorically fertile designation (see McCutcheon 1997a). Due to the recent history of immigration that has
made much of North America an apparent cultural mosaic, we can easily see
the reason for the concern among such intellectuals with using the study of
religion *qua* deeply personal, private beliefs as a tool for resolving what Ellwood, somewhat abstractly, termed "modernity's pluralism of space and time."
This problem of observable cultural difference (the many) is resolved by
essentializing and dehistoricizing it within the heart of unseen yet universal

---

16 I think it fair to say that, over the past decade when a scholar of religion is interviewed
    in the mainstream, national U.S. media, more often than not it has been Martin Marty,
    who is most always identified as being both an ordained minister and a University of
    Chicago professor.

religious identity (the one). It may therefore not be a coincidence (though demonstrating a causal link must await another article) that the triumphant rebirth of this personalized discourse on religion in the U.S. roughly coincided with the Immigration Act of 1965, which, in the words of the literary critic Stanley Fish, "shifted [U.S.] immigration priorities from those Nordic European peoples who had furnished America with its original stock to Asian and African peoples from Third World countries" (1994: 83). Thus, the presence of a new "them" who could not simply be coerced or housed on reservations required new techniques to re-make what had previously seemed to be a seamless "us."

As but one example of this recent exercise in nation-(re)building, take Diana Eck's much heralded CD-ROM classroom resource, *On Common Ground* (Eck 1997).[17] In one of the web articles that states the goals of the project, Diana Eck writes: "Pluralism requires the cultivation of public space where we all encounter one another."[18] On one level this all sounds well and good for, as one might ask, "Who could ever be against a public space where we all *encounter* one another?" Despite the fact that, since the September 11, 2001, air attacks on New York City and Washington D.C., virtually everyone can easily imagine groups who might not wish to be included within such an ill-defined encounter, for the time being we can grant to the proponents of this kind of inclusive pluralism that they have well intentioned visions of some idealized, even cosmogonic, public forum where citizen-equals mount the proverbial soap box and freely "speak their piece." The infectiously quaint nationalistic paintings of the U.S. illustrator, Norman Rockwell, come to mind at this point, specifically, his "Freedom of Speech," a 1943 cover of the *Saturday Evening Post* magazine.[19]

Given Asad and Arnal's earlier comments, it is not now—nor ever was— quite as simple as this. The case of "free speech" zones come to mind: specific, public areas set aside on some U.S. university campuses in the late 1990s and early 2000s where protests or the distribution of materials not officially sanc-

---

17 The resource was produced by Harvard University's Pluralism Project, under Eck's direction. In this day and age of web-based teaching initiatives and laptop computers, such CD-ROM resources may very well comprise the future of the world religions textbook genre.

18 The article entitled, "Challenge of Pluralism," originally appeared in 1993 in *Nieman Reports*, "God in the Newsroom," 47 (2), but can be found on the web at: http://www.fas.harvard.edu/~pluralsm/html/article-cop.html.

19 This well known piece of Americana shows a proud but humble-looking, flannel-shirted, working class man standing alone, posed to "speak his mind" at what appears to be a small town hall meeting. He is surrounded by seated people stretching their necks to watch and listen to him. Two of the prominent figures in the painting are men who seem to be of a higher class insomuch as they are wearing jackets and ties.

tioned by or connected with the University are allowed to take place.[20] Although free speech is presumably a non-negotiable value in social democracies, the perceived need to have such set-apart zones makes it evident that there are obvious limits to what one can and cannot say. As reported in January, 2001, in the *Chronicle of Higher Education*:

> At the University of Mississippi, protesters are limited to demonstrating in front of Fulton Chapel, designated in 1997 as the university's free-speech zone. [Within two years two other zones were also created on campus.] Officials say a specified protest area is needed to prevent demonstrators from disrupting the business of the campus. Last August [2000], Arthur Baker, a student and cofounder of a conservative campus group, was arrested for failing to obey a police officer who ordered him to move his protest against the student newspaper to the area ... At New Mexico State, students can protest freely in three designated areas of the campus, but they must get permission from the university to demonstrate elsewhere. In September, Mr. Rudolph, a graduate student, was arrested for distributing a flier outside the zone without first getting permission from the university's student-affairs office. The flier was an advertisement for Mr. Rudolph's underground newspaper, which criticized the university's speech policy.[21]

As such, certain sorts of speech only exist in these specified areas, making evident that, despite the way it is used rhetorically, "freedom" is rather more structured and controlled than it first appears.[22] A related, anecdotal example

---

20 Such zones are becoming increasingly popular techniques for managing dissent. For example, they were used for protestors at the August, 2000, Republican National Convention in Philadelphia and, as of February, 2001, such zones were also planned for the 2002 Salt Lake City Winter Olympics. On the latter, see the February 13, 2001, article in *Sports Illustrated* (archived at http://sportsillustrated.cnn.com/more/news/2001/02/13/ aclu_complaint_ap/). At the time of writing this chapter it is not entirely clear how the attacks of September 11, 2001, will affect these zones. As of November 24, 2001, it was reported that four such zones will exist in Park City, Utah, one of the competition sites and one will exist in Salt Lake City itself (see the archived article from the *Park Record*, http://www.parkrecord.com/Stories/0,1002,8138%257E237707%257E122%257E,00.html).

21 This article, which appeared in the *Chronicle of Higher Education* (a weekly periodical that focuses on matters pertaining to higher education in the U.S.) on January 12, 2001, was entitled, "Promoting Order or Squelching Campus Dissent." The web archived version appears at http://chronicle.com/free/v47/i18/18a03701.htm. See also the *New York Times* article, "Student Life: Boxing in Free Speech," archived at http://www.uh. edu/admin/media/topstories/nytimes040901speech.htm.

22 Understandably, the existence of such sites has been contested, and contested successfully in some cases, prompting some university administrations to forgo the idea. One case in point is Iowa State University. On October 19, 2001, the student newspaper, the *Iowa State Daily*, reported that the University President "announced a proposal to allow broader use of university grounds and facilities by students, staff, faculty and the general public" (see the web article at http://www.iowastatedaily.com/ vnews/display.v/ART/2001/10/19/3bcfc9648bb89).

involves a U.S. university where I once worked. In the early fall of 2000 the campus's officially sanctioned gay and lesbian student association, BIGALA (the Bisexual, Gay, Lesbian Alliance) attempted to distribute a flyer to a campus-wide mailing list—at no cost to the association, since it was to be done through the campus mail system—which described what they saw to be the unethical, and perhaps illegal, activity of the Boy Scouts of America in "discriminating" against gays. Their flyer requested faculty members to protest by withholding their donations to the campus's annual United Way campaign (a national, non-profit charity organization, associated with the Boy Scouts, that holds annual fund-raising campaigns on many U.S. campuses). The flyer quickly caught the administration's attention. The administration understood the distribution of the flyer to be a grave misuse of campus mail, suggesting early on that it might have been an illegal act (U.S. postal regulations were cited by the administration). The episode prompted the formation of a task force to overhaul the campus mail policy, further restricting what can and cannot be sent legally through that university's campus mail.[23] Despite still routinely receiving flyers on such things as weight loss and belly dancing lessons sponsored by the Campus Wellness Center, these other sorts of flyers are now disallowed.

So, to return to Eck, precisely what does it mean to "encounter" each other? As in the case of free speech zones, or the case where one must obtain a government permit to protest the government (often disguised as a license to hold a "parade"), what undisclosed ground rules stipulate the nature and extent of this freedom to encounter? More than likely, the public square is not open to just anyone—e.g., it's likely not a coincidence that males naturally are the subject of Rockwell's "Freedom of Speech" portrait. To participate in any so-called public space one must already be operating by a set of socio-political values and rhetorical standards that make it possible, attractive, meaningful, and compelling to "encounter," "understand" and "appreciate" the Other in just this manner, in just this context, for just this end. Simply put, without giving prior, implicit assent to such an unseen structure, one might hold a revolution rather than a parade.

So it seems legitimate to ask whether one gets to be part of the religious pluralist's "we" and "public" if these generally unnamed values and rhetorics are not a priority? For example, if one does not see free market capitalism and a growth economy as the logical end point of human civilization—what we today call globalization—is one allowed into the big tent? While one may personally find it commendable to work toward some sort of social inclusion— much like being in favor of "freedom" or "family values," it is easy to be in

---

23   For minutes from the faculty senate meeting in which this issue was first raised, see
      http://www.smsu.edu/acadaff/fsenate/minutes/2000_Sept.htm.

favor of ill-defined inclusion—one would be terribly remiss if one understood
or portrayed the ground rules of such a supposedly inclusive, public forum as
somehow being ahistorical, self-evidently meaningful, commonly shared, and
utterly persuasive—as if free speech zones simply sprouted from the ground
overnight, fences and all. Presuming a disengaged "public" to which everyone
automatically and equally belongs, and to which everyone wishes to belong,
strikes me as already resolving in favor of some "our" the issue of "the many"
long before ever seriously entertaining the topic of diversity and contestation.
The sort of idealization needed to bring about such premature resolution is but
one instance of the technique identified by Arnal, whereby "religion, as such, is
the space in which and by which any substantive collective goals ... are
individualized and made into a question of personal commitment or morality."

To see the slippery nature of the logic that grounds the liberal dialogical
position so popular in the current U.S. field—a position that bears striking
similarities to the classic *Verstehen* tradition facilitated by Wilhelm Dilthey's
split between *Geisteswissenschaften* and *Naturwissenschaften*—consider the widely read book that preceded and, in many ways, is the basis for *On Common
Ground*, Eck's *Encountering God* (1993). There, Eck distinguished the pluralist
option from what she calls exclusivism and inclusivisim (168) and argued that
pluralism is more than the recognition of a plurality and is far more demanding
than mere tolerance of difference: one must *participate* within (i.e., encounter,
engage, etc.) a plurality to count as a pluralist, and the scholar of religion is in
the forefront of those who have skills to bring about such participation and
understanding. As rightly observed by Eck, tolerance is, after all, an expression
of privilege, and it therefore stands in the way of what she considered to be
true pluralism. As she argues,

> If as a Christian I tolerate my Muslim neighbor, I am not therefore required to under-
> stand her, to seek out what she has to say, to hear about her hopes and dreams, to hear
> what is meant to her when the words, "In the name of Allah, the Merciful, the
> Compassionate" were whispered into the ear of her newborn child. (1993: 192)

But there is a difficulty in seeing such a wide divide between, on the one hand,
exclusivism and pluralism, and on the other, between tolerance and pluralism,
a difficulty that liberal writers such as Eck and Martin Marty fail to recognize,
perhaps because their own hegemonic position blinds them to the contingent
basis of their common sense notions of engagement and understanding. What
they fail to recognize is that one cannot have it both ways: one cannot call for
an engaged pluralism among those committed to deep values while at the same
time arguing that this pluralism is more than mere tolerance, for the difference
between pluralism and tolerance is merely rhetorical. The only way to have
such co-existing differences is if "the Other" is already well on the way to playing one's own game, making the leftover, minor cultural differences something
the dominant group can easily put up with. Case in point: Eck's dialogue part-

ner in the above quotation—the proverbial Oriental "m/other" presented in her text in what at first appears to be a fashion far superior to those representations first critiqued by Edward Said in his book *Orientalism* (1978)— is busy whispering sweet nothings into a baby's innocent ear, not mounting a violent protest at, say, a world trade meeting or hijacking passenger planes. Her "Other" is thus a specifically *religious* Other and thus an idealized and safe Other whose differing—perhaps contradictory, incommensurable, even threatening—beliefs are so deeply held that they cannot be manifested in any form of public practice.

To those not usually acquainted with international news, after September 11, 2001, it is more than obvious that there are many "deeply held" and "real commitments" with which so-called encounter is, even for well meaning liberal sentiments, downright impossible. In working to find a discourse that is all things to all people, such liberals now seem to have little choice but to construct a discourse that, by means of such rhetorical devises as "evil," "fanatic," or "cult" separates what are understood as our sensible, deep commitments from those that actively challenge the foundational principles of our "free" social order. Following the air attacks on the U.S. this discourse was put into play surprisingly quickly by politicians and pundits, ensuring that those who acted on their dissent were understood as "terrorists" and "evil fanatics" while others equally identified with such cultural markers as Islam, the Arabic language and culture, etc., who either did not dissent or whose dissent did not prompt them to take violent action, were understood as "peaceful" and "tolerant." As characterized by Marty in his meditation on how the U.S. is able so productively to maintain its unified "one" amidst the contestable "many," so-called tribal life is exclusive and dangerous:

> the invention of modern weapons and the efficiency of communications now renders tribalism potentially lethal. Groups need only a few dollars for supplies and a few recipes for how to mix them to produce devastating explosives to advance their threats. ... Tribalism on the world scene in its extremist forms takes a monstrous human toll. (1997: 14)

For whatever reason (perhaps because they are attempting to reallocate actual resources, gain greater influence in regional or global politics, acquire increased material wealth, etc.), some people have little interest in encountering and understanding "us" (the ones who generally seem to do much of the owning); such people want to change the rules of the game by—at times—violent and coercive means. They choose not to "play nice" in the public square and this upsets liberal sentiments a great deal. That makes these so-called tribalists and extremists rather dangerous—not in some abstract sense but dangerous in a very practical way, dangerous to a very particular set of interests usually portrayed as universal and therefore neutral, along with a way of conceiving of the world and its socio-economic relations. However, in the above passage it seems as if Marty's conception of the world conveniently forgets just who usually sells the weapons and who designs the communication technologies that are being put to such dangerous uses. In other words, the critique of the extremist, dangerous "Other" all too easily avoids the kind of self-implication that comes with understanding that the performance of "our" mutual funds in part depend on a rather profitable worldwide trade in technologies.

If, as Eck asserts, "in a world of religious pluralism, commitments are not checked at the door" (1993: 193), then what do we do with those commitments which, for example, lead people to kill doctors who perform abortions or to work toward the violent overthrow of this or that regime? Are these commitments allowable in a pluralistic world, a world where we as scholars supposedly take seriously differences among competing core values? Or do such commitments deeply offend some obvious, standard of decency to which all humans—insomuch as they share some nonempirical human nature—give unconditional assent? Which commitments are to be left at the door, then? If *real* pluralism requires openness and commitment then, given the colorful ideological spectrum on today's political map, it is more than obvious that only a rather narrow party line of commitments will gain admission to this public square of open engagement. Specifically, they will be those commitments which occupy people's attitudes, their "hearts and minds,"[24] but which are not manifested in organized political action.

6. Conclusion

Anyone not in favor of these rules and the social world they make possible is, in suitably illiberal fashion, branded as an exclusivist, radical, militant, extremist, tribalist, belligerent agitator. Such name-calling strikes me as eliminating from serious consideration the very groups whom liberals claim to include in their pluralist umbrella, making the supposedly dialogical basis of religious pluralism surprisingly monologic. At this juncture, readers must be clear on one point, however: I am not offering a criticism of this tactic, only a description, following Arnal and others, of a particularly effective rhetorical technique that portrays self-beneficial, tactical maneuvers as timeless, abstract principles. As Fish has recently observed in his critique of the rhetoric of "principle," "[s]witching back and forth between talking like a liberal and engaging in distinctly illiberal actions is something we all do anyway; it is the essence of adhockery, which is a practice that need not be urged because it is the only one

---

24 In the phrasing of the U.S. Supreme Court, religion is a matter of "the citadel of individual heart and mind."

available to us" (1999: 72).[25] In arguing for an ill-defined engagement and an encounter that recognizes the necessity for "real commitments" that can inform action only if they happen to fall within a rather narrow party line, liberal scholars of religion fabricate a toothless "Other" whose seeming differences— "Look, dear, they call God 'Allah,' and we call God 'God'"—are easily resolved on "our" terms.

Religion, conceived as an undefinable, distinct, private experience of meaning, is thus the ultimate "Other" of the nation-state, useful in all acts of social formation insomuch as it is an empty concept. The seemingly unassailable zone of private experience it makes possible is thus the refuge and the end of dissent, for there, discord finds a safe haven but only insomuch as it is not acted upon. Indeed, the posited split between belief and practice, text and context—in the words of postcolonial critic Partha Chatterjee—enables anti-colonialism to create "its own domain of sovereignty within colonial societies well before it begins its political battle with the imperial power" (1993: 8). Such marginal groups, for whose members this concept religion "is an aspect of their culture, a valuable support in a hostile environment" (Sarup 1996: 3), thus obviously benefit from the ability to divide

> the world of social institutions and practices into two domains—the material and the spiritual. The material is the domain of the "outside," of the economy and of statecraft, of science and technology, a domain where the West had proved its superiority and the East had succumbed ... The spiritual, on the other hand, is an "inner" domain bearing the "essential" marks of cultural identity. The greater one's success in imitating Western skills in the material domain, therefore, the greater the need to preserve the distinctness of one's spiritual culture. (Chatterjee 1993: 8; quoted in van der Veer 2001: 69)

However, insomuch as this artful technique is successfully employed in housing marginal groups in alien and potentially hostile environments, such success is ironically evidence that these groups have succumbed to a larger hegemony. They have had to rethink and retool their own group identity and sense of self, in the process trivializing and privatizing that which previously had been public and taken for granted. For, insomuch as "Hinduism" comes eventually to be successfully portrayed as a "religion," with rights and obligations once reserved only for Christians, "it"—like Christianity before it—now falls under the governance of the State, ensuring that while private Hindu belief is indeed acceptable, the practice of, say, *sati* (so-called widow burning) is outlawed (as it was by the British in 1829) and the *caste* system ridiculed (as it most recently was in the liberal U.S. media during the boycotted, international

---

25   I am indebted to Fish's *The Trouble with Principle* (1999) for my analysis of Eck's and Marty's rhetoric, in particular Fish's chapter, "Boutique Multiculturalism" (56–73).

human rights conference held in 2001 in Durban, South Africa[26]). The discourse on religion thus provides a pivotal technique for housing a disparate and desperate citizenry's necessarily unrequited desires.

As should be clear from the preceding, when discussing critical trends in the study of religion we necessarily employ pairs of metaphysical concepts, such as sacred/secular and private/public, clean/unclean, us/them, even global/indigenous. They are concepts that, in themselves, are utterly meaningless but which, when held in varying degrees of tension, make meaningful worlds possible insomuch as they provide spaces in which squatters can reside or be contained, and where acts of comparison, conformity, and contestability can take place. The distance between these concepts is slippery and the social spaces they make possible are inherently negotiable. As Tim Fitzgerald has most recently phrased it, with regard to the modern sacred/secular pairing:

> This conceptual separation was a product of the struggle of new classes against the restrictions imposed by the church [understood, here, not as a religious institution but simply as among many institutions vying for control], its unaccountability, and its control of thought and action. Only by defining in a new way the realm of the "religious" and the realm of the "secular" could the separation of church and state be achieved and a bourgeois civil society be developed … It amounts, in effect, to the replacement of one ideological system by another. (2001: 111)

Contrary to the recent trend to study religion as something apart from politics, as something that helps to make a civil society, Fitzgerald, Asad, and Arnal draw our attention to the manner in which these two classifications—"religion" and "politics"—are used in ongoing contests over just what is and what is not understood as civil, and thus acceptable. Fitzgerald's own conclusion, then, aptly serves as the last word for this chapter: "the religion-secular distinction is the new ideological system in which the principles expressed by 'no taxation without representation' are central and definitive … [W]e cannot research 'religion' as though it were something distinct from, or independent of, the central democratic capitalist principles" (111).[27]

---

26 In January, 2002, an episode of the popular U.S. television talk show hosted by Oprah Winnfrey focused on the caste system and the untouchables. It was clear from the tone of the host, and her response to the personal stories from her "untouchable" guests, that institutions such as this ought not to exist in the twenty-first century.

27 Portions of this essay involve work elaborated in McCutcheon 2001, 2003, and 2004..

Bibliography

Almond, Philip C. (1988), *The British Discovery of Buddhism*. Cambridge: Cambridge University Press.

Arnal, William E. (2000), "Definition," in: Willi Braun/Russell T. McCutcheon, eds., *Guide to the Study of Religion*. London, U.K.: Continuum: 21–34.

Asad, Talal (1993), *Genealogies of Religion: Discipline and Reasons of Power in Christianity and Islam*. Baltimore, Md.: Johns Hopkins University Press.

Bell, Catherine (1992), *Ritual Theory, Ritual Practice*. New York: Oxford University Press.

Braun, Willi/McCutcheon, Russell T., eds. (2000), *Guide to the Study of Religion*. London, U.K.: Continuum.

Brooks, Douglas R. (1994), "The Thousand-Headed Person: The Mystery of Hinduism and the Study of Religion in the AAR," in: *Journal of the American Academy of Religion* 62 (4): 1111-26.

Chatterjee, Partha (1993), *The Nation and Its Fragments*. Princeton, N.J.: Princeton University Press.

Cherry, Conrad D./De Berg, Betty A./Porterfield, Amanda (2001), "Religion on Campus," in: *Liberal Education* 87 (4): 6–13.

Clifford, James/Marcus, George W., eds. (1986), *Writing Culture: The Poetics and Politics of Ethnography*. Berkeley, Calif.: University of California Press.

Eck, Diana (1993), *Encountering God: A Spiritual Journey from Bozeman to Banares*. Boston, Mass.: Beacon Press.

— (1997), *On Common Ground: World Religions in America*. New York: Columbia University Press [CD Rom].

Ellwood, Robert S. (1999), *The Politics of Myth: A Study of C.G. Jung, Mircea Eliade, and Joseph Campbell*. Albany, N.Y.: State University of New York Press.

Fish, Stanley (1994), *There's No Such Thing As Free Speech: And It's a Good Thing Too*. New York: Oxford University Press.

— (1999), *The Trouble with Principle*. Cambridge, Mass.: Harvard University Press.

Fitzgerald, Tim (1999), *The Ideology of Religious Studies*. New York: Oxford University Press.

— (2001), "A Response to Saler, Benavides, and Korom," in: *Religious Studies Review* 27 (2): 110–15.

Frankenberry, Nancy K./Penner, Hans H. (1999), "Clifford Geertz's Long-Lasting Moods, Motivations, and Metaphysical Conceptions," in: *Journal of Religion* 79 (4): 617–40.

Geertz, Clifford (1973), *The Interpretation of Cultures: Select Essays*. New York: Basic Books.

Gill, Sam (1994), "The Academic Study of Religion," in: *Journal of the American Academy of Religion* 62 (4): 965–75.

Green, William Scott (1996), "Religion within the Limits," in: *Academe* 82 (6): 24–28.

Jensen, Jeppe Sinding/Martin, Luther H., eds. (1997), *Rationality and the Study of Religion*. Aarhus, Denmark: Aarhus University Press.

Jensen, Lionel M. (1997), *Manufacturing Confucianism: Chinese Traditions and Universal Civilization*. Durham, N.C.: Duke University Press.

Juschka, Darlene (1997), "Religious Studies and Identity Politics: Mythology in the Making," in: *Bulletin of the Council of Societies for the Study of Religion* 26 (1): 8–11.

—— (2001), *Feminism and the Study of Religion: A Reader*. New York: Continuum Press.

Lease, Gary (1997), "Rationality and Evidence: The Study of Religion as a Taxonomy of Human Natural History," in: Jeppe Sinding Jensen/Luther H. Martin, eds., *Rationality and the Study of Religion*. Aarhus, Denmark: Aarhus University Press: 136–44.

Lincoln, Bruce (1999), *Theorizing Myth: Narrative, Ideology, and Scholarship*. Chicago: University of Chicago Press.

Lopez, Donald S., ed. (1995), *Curators of the Buddha: The Study of Buddhism under Colonialism*. Chicago: University of Chicago Press.

Marty, Martin (1996), "You Get to Teach and Study Religion," in: *Academe* 82 (6): 14–17.

—— (1997), *The One and the Many: America's Struggle for the Common Good*. Cambridge, Mass.: Harvard University Press.

McCutcheon, Russell T. (1997a), "A Default of Critical Intelligence? The Scholar of Religion as Public Intellectual," in: *Journal of the American Academy of Religion* 66 (2): 443–68.

—— (1997b), *Manufacturing Religion: The Discourse on Sui Generis Religion and the Politics of Nostalgia*. New York: Oxford University Press.

—— (2001), *Critics Not Caretakers: Redescribing the Public Study of Religion*. Albany, N.Y.: State University of New York Press.

—— (2003), "The Category 'Religion' and the Politics of Tolerance," in: Larry Greil, ed., *Defining Religion: Critical Approaches to Drawing Boundaries between Sacred and Secular*. New York: Elsevier Science Press.

—— (2004), *The Discipline of Religion: Structure, Meaning, Rhetoric*. New York/London: Routledge.

Penner, Hans (1994), "Holistic Analysis: Conjectures and Refutations," in: *Journal of the American Academy of Religion* 62 (4): 977–96.

Proudfoot, Wayne (1985), *Religious Experience*. Berkeley, Calif.: University of California Press.

Said, Edward (1978), *Orientalism*. New York: Vantage Books.

Saler, Benson (1993), *Conceptualizing Religion: Immanent Anthropologists, Transcendent Natives, and Unbounded Categories*. Leiden: E.J. Brill.

Sarup, Madan (1996), *Identity, Culture, and the Postmodern World*. Athens, Ga.: University of Georgia Press.

Scott, Joan Wallach (1991), "The Evidence of Experience," in: *Critical Inquiry* 17: 773–97.

Sharf, Robert H. (1998), "Experience," in: Mark C. Taylor, ed., *Critical Terms in Religious Studies*. Chicago: University of Chicago Press: 94–115.

Shepard, Robert S. (1991), *God's People in the Ivory Tower: Religion in the Early American University*. Brooklyn, N.Y.: Carlson Publishing Co.

Smith, Jonathan Z. (1982), *Imagining Religion: From Babylon to Jonestown*. Chicago: University of Chicago Press.

—— (1990), *Drudgery Divine: On the Comparison of Early Christianities and the Religions of Late Antiquity*. Chicago: University of Chicago Press.

—— (1995), "Religious Studies: Whither (Wither) and Why?," in: *Method & Theory in the Study of Religion* 7 (4): 407–13.

—— (1998), "Religion, Religions, Religious," in: Mark C. Taylor, ed., *Critical Terms for Religious Studies*. Chicago: University of Chicago Press: 269–84.

Smith, Wilfred Cantwell (1963) [1991]. *The Meaning and End of Religion*. Minneapolis, Minn.: Fortress Press.

Taylor, Mark C., ed. (1998), *Critical Terms for Religious Studies*. Chicago: University of Chicago Press.

Veer, Peter van der (2001), *Imperial Encounters: Religion and Modernity in India and Britain*. Princeton, N.J.: Princeton University Press.

Wiebe, Donald (1994), Review of Peter Byrne, *Natural Religion and the Nature of Religion* and Peter Harrison, *"Religion" and the Religions in the English Enlightenment*, in: *Method & Theory in the Study of Religion* 6 (1): 92–104.

—— (1999), *The Politics of Religious Studies*. New York: St. Martin's Press.

Williams, Michael Allen (1996), *Rethinking "Gnosticism": An Argument for Dismantling a Dubious Category*. Princeton, N.J.: Princeton University Press.

New Approaches to the Study of
Religion and Culture

by

MARK HULSETHER

No one can possibly read enough to have a complete handle on the subject of religion and culture. Everywhere in the literature, one finds agreement with Raymond Williams that "culture is one of the two or three most complicated words in the English language" (1983: 87). Stephen Greenblatt (1990: 225) comments that classic definitions of culture are "almost impossibly vague and encompassing, and the few things that seem excluded from [culture] are almost immediately reincorporated in the actual use of the word." Bruce Lincoln offers this capacious definition: "a people's communications, artifacts, and standard behaviors," especially as related to encoding and transmitting their aesthetic and moral "preferences"—that is, what are commonly called values. Lincoln's list of "serviceable alternatives" to the term includes "discourse, practice, ethos, habitus, ideology, hegemony, master narrative, canon, tradition, knowledge/power system, pattern of consumption and distinction, society, community, ethnicity, nation, and race." All of these "specify some part of what is encompassed in the broader but infinitely fuzzier category of 'culture'" (2000: 409).

Quite obviously, a comprehensive overview of new approaches to such a subject is out of the question. This remains true even if one delimits the discussion slightly—as we will do—to religion and the interdisciplinary network known as cultural studies. Intensifying this problem of focus, the very notion of having a clear fix on the subject of culture—a stable map of it or authoritative point of view on it—would be considered by many leading scholars as evidence that one has not digested the best scholarship on the subject. Much recent scholarship is more interested in destabilizing cultural boundaries and problematizing angles of vision for cultural analysis than in presupposing such boundaries and standpoints, however provisionally, and working within them. Simply by accepting an invitation to write something true, useful, and reasonably representative about culture, one might undercut one's credentials for doing the job in the first place—unless one sticks closely to deferring all stable meanings and calling for better deconstructive genealogies of these meanings in the future. However, such a stance is not appropriate for the current paper, which must address emergent debates about the degree to which such a deconstructive stance may produce diminishing returns in certain contexts.

Since all roads to a comprehensive overview of culture are blocked, let us reflect on two texts that offer a useful starting point for understanding trends in the overlapping territory between religious studies and cultural studies. First, we will consider the inaugural issue of *Culture and Religion: an Interdisciplinary Journal* edited by Malory Nye and a distinguished international editorial board (hereafter CR). Second, to provide a baseline for placing CR within a wider world of cultural studies, we will compare CR's distinctive emphases to those in the Blackwell *Dictionary of Critical and Cultural Theory*, edited by Michael Payne (hereafter DCCT). Along the way, we will relate both of these texts to articles in Mark C. Taylor's *Critical Terms for the Study of Religion* (1998) and Willi Braun and Russell McCutcheon's *Guide to the Study of Religion* (2000)— hereafter *Critical Terms* and *Guide*.

We begin from these texts not because they necessarily collect the highest quality, most sophisticated, work available—although their strongest contributions are state of the art—but because of the attractive combination of breadth and focus that they offer. The CR inaugural issue includes two symposia which can serve as rough barometers of emergent discussions: a programmatic editorial statement on religion and culture with responses from CR board members, and a wide-ranging exchange on method in the study of religion. The DCCT is an effort by a major press and more than one hundred contributors—many of them highly distinguished, such as Steven Connor, Simon Frith, Toril Moi, and Immanuel Wallerstein—to provide a "full and accessible reference guide to modern ideas in the broad interdisciplinary fields of cultural and critical theory, which have developed from interactions among modern linguistic, literary, anthropological, philosophic, political, and historical traditions of thought" (Payne 1997: xi). Although these texts cannot map new approaches to religion and culture in a comprehensive way, it is difficult even to imagine what such a way could be, given that culture takes in such a huge set of interlinked fields. Therefore, let us set aside aspirations for attaining what Linda Nicholson (1990) calls "God's eye views" and focus on developing a useful—if contestable—reflection on some key trends in this field from this vantage point.

Before we consider what CR's inaugural issue can teach about new approaches to religion and culture, we must clarify two preliminary problems. First, how can one discuss new approaches except in relation to approaches taken to be "old" or at least established? And second, since we will center our discussion within the field of cultural studies, can we develop a provisional definition of this field?

Clarifying the first matter is difficult. Gustavo Benavides notes in CR (2000: 120) that, for all the self-conscious innovation in recent writings about postmodernity, it is not always easy to distinguish the core arguments of postmodernists from the reflexive and self-critical aspects of longstanding modernist approaches. Nor it is easy to determine when modernity (with or without a "post") began. Many scholars trace the roots of the modern world system at least to 1492, and Benavides' article in *Critical Terms* (1998) discusses the contribution of ancient Greeks and various monastic movements to the rise of modernity. He asks mischievously whether the Buddha was a premature postmodernist. Benavides is admirably clear about how he himself uses these terms. For him modernity is a constellation of factors centering on historical reflexivity and classic Weberian themes such as bureaucratic rationalization and the rise of science and industry. None of these themes is unique to the West, although they came together in a distinctive way in eighteenth century Europe. From this point of view, much postmodern theory does not appear especially new, although it may be distinctive in significant ways. Overall, it represents hypermodernism more than a clean break with modernism. In this regard, Benavides' approach dovetails with neo-Marxian arguments by Jameson (1998) and Harvey (1990) about the fit between postmodernism and a global postindustrial economy.

Whatever one thinks of this approach—it is only one position within a tangled intellectual terrain that is beyond the scope of this article to map, the terrain of interpreting the condition of *postmodernity* and evaluating the myriad forms of *postmodernism* that actively clear space from things labeled modern in various discourses—the main point at hand is clear. Benavides exaggerates very little when he comments in CR that "there does not seem to be any position, theory, or author that cannot be labeled as modernist or postmodernist." He suggests that "the desire to place oneself in a putative 'post-modern' age has to do with anxiety driven by an intellectual market that constantly demands new products or ... new packaging" in response to job pressures in academia (2000: 118). Approaches to culture which are hyped as new may not improve significantly, if at all, on longstanding work in the traditions of Marx, Weber, Nietzsche, or Freud—or for that matter the Buddha.

Nevertheless there do remain recent trends worth noting, even after discounting for inflated hype about the latest market offerings. Elsewhere (Hulsether: 2005) I have offered a map of key trends in scholarship on culture during the past century, presenting it in two overlapping sections. One broad mode of analysis approaches cultures as whole ways of life; a notable example is the ethnographic tradition in anthropology that runs from Bronislaw Malinowski to Clifford Geertz—although it should go without saying that many other scholars are also relevant, including some that disagree profoundly with a Geertzian approach. Another mode approaches culture as valorized discourses in the arts; a notable example is the sort of literary work treated by writers like Raymond Williams. These two broad wings of the study of culture overlap extensively, despite efforts at boundary maintenance from both sides. Each is exceedingly complex and multilayered in numerous senses, including the ways that scholars grounded on either side may use the category of culture to reinforce dominant sociopolitical values and/or as a mode of cultural critique. Both wings have been trying for decades to strengthen their analyses by engaging more deeply with history—especially the history of Western colonialism—in response to concerns that literary critics and ethnographers have too often downplayed issues of cultural imperialism and change over time. Both wings have also been engaged with discourses about postmodernity and/ or postmodernism. They have sought both to clarify how their approaches relate to postmodern discourses, and to respond to a widespread assumption that postmodernity includes a breakdown in the ability to take for granted universal narratives about things such as reason or progress—a breakdown which is happening in many quarters whether or not one considers it warranted. Thus the evolving discourse of culture intersects not only with work by scholars such as Jameson and Harvey (whom we have already noted) but also people such as Michel Foucault in history, Jacques Derrida in literary studies, and James Clifford in anthropology. For the purposes of the current article, we will consider approaches such as Geertz's and Williams' (supplemented by "classic" postmodern interventions such as Clifford's) as the established approaches, the baseline against which we can identify "new approaches."

Let us turn to the problem of clarifying the term "cultural studies." Although there is little consensus about this matter, one can identify a few traits that are common among scholars identified with this movement—traits that may be helpful for locating the scholarly territory, as long as they are not understood as a boundary that marks a clear inside and outside for this proudly decentered network (Hulsether 1997; see also During 1999; Storey 1996). By cultural studies, I do not mean all studies of culture, but a particular network or scholarly movement, evolving but with identifiable emphases. It may be useful to use the letters of the word "simple" to bring these emphases into focus. The "S" stands for *symbolic* communication as the focus of analysis, and the "I" for an *interdisciplinary* approach to it, drawing on sociology, literary theory, and media studies among others. The "M" is for *Marxian*, or more precisely for a focus on how symbols relate to structures of power, when power is conceptualized within a broad neo-Marxian tradition (sometimes blended with a second M for *Michel* Foucault). Within the world of Marxian theory, cultural studies tilts toward the neo-Gramscianism of scholars like Raymond Williams and Stuart Hall who focus on civil society and the realm of ideas, and who expand and decenter the tradition by applying the concept of hegemony to issues like race and gender alongside class (see Morley/Chen 1996; Laclau/ Mouffe 1985).

Turning to the letter P, one might mention several terms that cluster around the theme of *postmodern problematization*. Cultural studies is highly suspicious of earlier scholarly work which posits the existence and/or desirability of cultural consensus—as opposed to multiculturalist and multi-perspectival approaches—or bases its analysis on single-factor models of power, whether these models are proposed by neo-Marxians or more mainstream scholars. Another "P" signals interest in *popular* and/or media culture, as well as a collapse of sharp distinctions between popular culture and canons of high culture.

More consistently than scholars in many other branches of cultural theory, scholars identified with cultural studies focus on concrete sociohistorical locations; they analyze culture in the context of coalition building and struggles for power. The L in our "simple definition" of cultural studies stands for this stress on critique grounded in *local* knowledge. This point deserves a varying stress, depending on which cultural studies scholars are in view and what alternatives one compares to them. From the standpoint of some sociologists and historians, cultural studies is alarmingly ungrounded (see Ferguson/Golding 1997). Nevertheless, scholars in the movement tend to focus more on situated knowledges (see Haraway 1988) than do literary theorists, philosophers, or grand theorists in the social sciences. Moreover, they tend to link such situated approaches to an "E" for *extracurricular engagement*, or a concern for how scholarship relates to sociopolitical processes larger than academic ones. Scholars in cultural studies seek to make their work count in public struggles for social justice, both inside and outside academia. Often this has taken the form of direct activism or cooperation with social movements, for example as expressed by the founding generation of cultural studies in a commitment to adult education and working class politics. Even when their particular research does not have direct relevance for specific activist agendas, scholars in the movement almost unanimously hope to advance cultural critique in some form.

If I were to risk one generalization about new approaches to culture and religion since 1980—bearing in mind the disclaimers above and noting that I work largely in English language sources from a North American base—I would make the following dual claim. First, postmodern critiques and cultural studies sensibilities (which in themselves are not new, since they were entrenched in many parts of the academy by the 1970s at the latest) have become increasingly established in the study of religion. But, second, their stress on theoretical destabilization and cultural difference—the sensibilities which weight our model of cultural studies toward postmodern problematization—have reached points of diminishing returns in some contexts. This does mean *some*, not all or even most contexts. Nevertheless there are contexts in which scholars are reasserting and/or refining established approaches such as Geertz's and Williams' as a counterweight and constructive rejoinder to postmodern and deconstructive approaches. At worst these interventions are more like backlash than new approaches; scholars do exist who engaged grudgingly and superficially with emergent arguments during the past three decades and now hope to dismiss them as a passing fad. However, this fact—which is also useful to postmodernists as a foil—does not erase the force of these second thoughts at their strongest. Thus it is better to approach such second thoughts as a shift of emphasis or reprioritization *within* postmodernity and cultural studies, rather than as a clean break with them or a failure to engage them. In this sense, the interplay between the dual themes we have noted—that is, the rising influence of cultural studies coupled with rising concerns about some of its themes—creates a newly distinctive dialogue, rather than a retread of earlier debates. Let us consider how the dialogues internal to CR's inaugural issue—as well as the relationships among CR, the DCCT, *Guide*, and *Critical Terms*—give a face and concrete texture to this emergent field of debate.

Problematizing Culture and Religion

Culture and Religion was born from the closing and reconstitution of the *Scottish Journal of Religious Studies*, and like the earlier journal it is produced at the University of Stirling. Its inside front cover states that it is no longer simply a religious studies journal, but one "seeking an engagement between scholars working across a range of disciplinary fields, including anthropology, cultural studies, critical theory, gender studies, and postcolonial studies." It seeks to explore how discourses on culture "intersect with (and are themselves intersected by) discourses on religious practices." For example, "is it necessary for cross-cultural debates on culture, power, and agency to locate a concept and practice of religion, and where do history and power reside in the coupling of the discourses of culture and religion?" (Nye 2000a: 5).

CR's inaugural issue has a strong consciousness of postmodern reflexivity from beginning to end. Editor Malory Nye sets the tone in the first paragraph of his introductory editorial. He cites Lila Abu-Lughod's argument that it is better to "write against culture" than to accept the assumptions enacted by taking the culture concept for granted. In the article Nye quotes, Abu-Lughod identifies these assumptions as positing (1) *stability and coherence*, as opposed to internal complexity and conflict, in the "cultural" group being analyzed, (2) the *timeless* or *ahistorical* quality of the notion of culture, as opposed to forms of analysis which focus on historical change and specificity, and (3) the *discreteness* of "cultural" boundaries, as opposed to the ways that real life is decentered and cross-cut by local and national practices, regional and international migrations, and global social flows which are lived in diverse ways at local sites (see Appadurai 1996; Clifford 1997). She arrives at the conclusion quoted by Nye: that to speak of culture radically oversimplifies the complexity of life and, more pointedly, is a form of simplification that "inevitably carries a sense of hierarchy" and naturalizes it. Culture "is the prime anthropological tool for making 'Other.'" (Nye 2000a: 5, citing Abu-Lughod 1991).

Such critiques have gained increasing support in religious studies. For example, in her article on culture in *Critical Terms*, Tomoko Masuzawa also denies that culture is a stable or neutral category that scholars can take for granted. Rather it is "an argument, a theoretical object that comes with a certain discipline, persuasions, and admonitions" (1998: 87). What does this argument argue? For Masuzawa, it is bound up with presupposing, and then reproducing through the process of analysis, the subject position of an Enlightenment observer in a colonial context. Such a subject must learn to screen out crucial things in order to perceive the coherence, timelessness, and discreteness identified by Abu-Lughod. To perform "cultural" analysis one must represent (for whom?) "the meaning" (translatable in terms of what?) of a "cultural whole" (related how to internal conflict and/or incoherence?). Researchers must learn to bracket how they are historically embedded—including the power dynamics of their ability to be present as interpreters among the people being studied— and remain relatively unconcerned about the hierarchical implications built into the notion of culture. In some cases scholars have functioned directly within institutions of political-military colonization, as in the case of E.E. Evans-Pritchard's work among the Nuer or as discussed in David Chidester's (1996) history of comparative religion in Southern Africa. Even if scholars deplore such precedents and seek to work against colonialism in the space available to them, they risk complicity with this history simply through being present among "others" and representing them in terms recognizable as "cultural." One shorthand way to summarize this problem is to say that it is difficult to speak about culture without complicity in Orientalism (Said 1978; Clifford 1988; King 1999).

Masuzawa suggests that such an "argument" or subject position builds on the intellectual legacy and emotional dynamics of Christian theology and missions. This finding is especially troubling for the type of religious studies scholar whose sense of purity and pollution is based on eschewing all overlap with Christian theologies. It is less decisive (although still interesting) for scholars whose top priority is counteracting Orientalism, who would focus on the *kind* of missionary or anthropological practice they are considering, approached in particular sociohistorical contexts. In any case, Masuzawa follows Christopher Herbert (1991) in arguing that missionaries laid the foundations for anthropology, often doing more thorough ethnographic study than anthropologists themselves, and that both the theological trail-blazers and the social scientists who followed in their footsteps found themselves writing about culture in relation to murky dynamics of cross-cultural desire. They first approached the problem of desire through the concept of original sin—a desire which might be disciplined and controlled through religion—but increasingly moved toward a secularized version of a similar idea: "anomie" which could be regulated by culture. For Herbert the idea of culture is "a complex and sometimes insidious reconfiguring of moral and religious ideas, in fact a whole sensibility, at a historical point of crisis" (1991: 42).

From this perspective it matters relatively little whether one quotes the Bible and sees others as heathens who need salvation, or whether (like Malinowski in his diary) one quotes Conrad's *Heart of Darkness* and acknowledges that one's "feelings towards the natives are decidedly tending to '*Exterminate the brutes*'" (Geertz 1988: 73–101; Clifford 1988: 105). Either way, consider the tension that results if a person undertaking a "cultural" interpretation starts with some such hierarchical standpoint linked to an ideal of keeping desire in check, yet at the same time feels sympathetic attraction to the people in question, and perhaps sees the goal of one's writing as presenting these people in a sympathetic light. For good measure, suppose that the researcher feels a personal attraction toward certain people in this culture, thus increasing the temptation to break the taboo of "going native"—an especially interesting dynamic in places where local mores permit greater sexual freedom than would be accepted back at home. One way to manage this sort of cognitive dissonance is to reduce to a minimum the researcher's personal presence in the analysis of culture. Scholars might try to produce transparent or objective accounts of culture as a complex whole, focusing on less emotionally fraught issues and leaving the underlying structural relations unremarked. Such an interpretation of the dynamics of anthropological practice might seem especially insightful to an outside observer who credits neo-Freudian insights about the far-reaching force of libidinal desires and the capacities of the psyche for repressing and redirecting them (Buhle 1998; DiCenso 1998). Such an observer would expect the repressed to return despite all efforts at ethnographic objectivity, and such a hypothesis is an intriguing way to help explain why so much writing on culture features eroticized and exoticized images of others across a boundary of continued social hierarchy.

Masuzawa sums up her case. Insofar as postmodern critiques discredit the notion of objectivity, and result in a situation in which "the position of the observer ceases to be ... hypercathected and fetishized," then "the gossamer reality of the 'complex whole' [that is, culture] will likely begin to appear no more substantial than the phrase itself" (1998: 88). Herbert presses a similar argument against the entire Durkheimian tradition, that stronghold of rational functionalist sobriety. He asks how scholars can confidently identify discrete cultural cores or explain the regulation of sin/anomie, based on categories so slippery and quasi-theological as "collective effervescence"? To Herbert it seems more accurate to speak about "superstitions of culture" fueled by the unconscious desires of Western scholars, than about objective social science.

These are examples of a growing sense among scholars on a "newer" cutting edge of religious studies that they should speak about culture—if at all—only in highly cautious ways that reflect a postmodern penchant for using words "under erasure" and experiencing the world as if it were in quotation marks. Nor is culture the only word that can be problematized in this way; for example, we could add scare-quotes almost anywhere in the previous sentence, until it speaks of "experiencing" "the world" as if "it" "should" "be" "in" quotation marks. For example, a key CR dispute to which we will return turns on the usefulness of just one of these words, "experience." Questioning Bryan Rennie's appeal to this term, McCutcheon (2000: 134) appeals to Robert Sharf's argument in *Critical Terms* (1998) which denies that "religious experience" is a valid category for religious studies. McCutcheon pairs Sharf's critique with an argument by Joan Scott that questions the political effects of appealing to women's historical experience. Now, despite certain overlaps between Sharf and Scott, one might also note the difference between Sharf's discourse about religious subjectivities such as mysticism, on one hand, and Scott's discourse about strategic essentialism in feminist politics, on the other. Are these scholars really addressing commensurate problems? And is it legitimate to appeal to experience at all—in any specified sense—in pursuit of an answer to this question?[1] Having posed such questions, one might spend a long time clarifying them, only to face further problems such as defining "world," debating whether there is just one world or a multiplicity of linguistically constituted ones (a problem flagged by Benavides 2000, in CR), and grappling with the status of the word "should" after the collapse of grand narratives. And we have not yet moved beyond unpacking Nye's first two sentences introducing CR— although we have captured much of the problematic that undergirds the whole issue.

The second paragraph of CR's inaugural issue turns from the concept of culture to the concept of religion and places it under equal if not greater scrutiny. It cites Talal Asad: "There cannot be a universal definition of religion, not only because its constituent elements and relationships are historically specific, but because that definition is itself the historical product of discursive practices" (Asad 1993: 29). As Jonathan Z. Smith argues in *Critical Terms* among other places, the abstract idea of religion is not a "native category" but a theoretical construct developed by scholars who approach it from the outside and must learn a certain standpoint and discipline in order to see it. Scholars have many suggestions for what this construct entails (see Wilson 1998). Without pre-

---

1   One might endorse Sharf's stance toward his key dialogue partners but ask whether these are the same people that Scott addresses. One might also pause over Scott's suggestion that "except for the 'catastrophic loss of grace in the wording' it makes far more sense for a feminist politics to have Sojourner Truth ask 'Ain't I a fluctuating identity?' and thereby recognize both the dangers and benefits of the collective consolidation implied in the category 'women'" (1995: 11). Scott prefers this to Truth's speech which (as popularly rendered) used the phrase "Ain't I a woman?" to demand equal rights. Despite the value of Scott's call for historicization and sophisticated nuance, the "loss of grace in wording" is not trivial for feminist politics. Also, one wonders when to stop. Should one also make "demands" for the "rights" of "women" to be "safe" from "discrimination" and "sexual violence"?

tending to survey this field, we must consider a suggestion that is pervasive in emergent writing on religion and culture: that "religion"—somewhat like "culture" in the works we have been discussing—also conveys perniciously modern and Western values.

Once again, let us pause to register some cautions from Benavides (2001) before considering this complaint directly. He underlines the narrowness and rigidity of some such critiques of Western discourse on religion, compared to the immense complexity of the field they seek to summarize. He also questions whether a cross-cultural domain like "religion" was really imagined for the first time only with Western colonialism. Nevertheless it is possible to make cautious generalizations about dominant themes in Western discourse on religion, as Benavides also makes clear in his *Critical Terms* article.

Commonly mentioned among such themes is the ability to speak about "religion" as a cross-cultural concept differentiated from other aspects of life. Just as a "cultural" whole can only be perceived from a subject position that itself represents a sort of argument, likewise "religion" can only be posited by learning to abstract from specific discourses and traditions, and by polarizing what CR calls "practice" (which is roughly what used to be called lived experience) into a secular realm and a privatized religious realm. Within worldviews informed by such thinking, practices identified as religious may be associated with whatever is being framed as the dead weight of pre-modern tradition.[2] In such forms, religions may continue into the present, but primarily as residual traditions living off momentum built in the past. Alternatively, religion may be recast ("modernized," "liberalized," reformulated to minimize its friction with reason or a modern political economy) in ways that keep it relevant as something more than merely residual, but limited to one side of an emergent Western religious-secular divide. If so—still assuming that religion is not a self-evident native category but a field of scholarly inquiry—arguments that naturalize such an understanding of religion may cause various problems.

For Asad, the key difficulty is that if one starts with this sort of modern perspective on religion—in which something called religion can be abstracted from the historical power structures in which it is embedded and interpreted as a matter of private meaning—and tries to map this understanding onto other times and places, the result may be fundamental distortions that impose Western understandings while screening out alternative ways that religions, discourses of selfhood, and structures of power fit together. The alternative Asad suggests—in another passage selected by Nye for the first page of CR—is that

---

2   What appears as "premodern" varies from one modern framework to another, so that finding the flip side of modernity is no easier than defining it positively. However, moderns have typically sought to set themselves off from things they conceive as tied to the past. Two classic patterns are Protestantism clearing space from Catholicism and secular rationalists clearing space from religion—or just Christianity—as a whole.

scholars should "begin [by] unpacking the comprehensive concept ... 'religion' into heterogeneous elements according to its historical character" (2000a: 5, citing Asad 1993: 54). In CR's first-ever article, Asad expands on this point, covering some of the same ground as his 1993 book, *Genealogies of Religion*. He explores diverse ways of constructing selfhood and agency in relation to suffering. He discusses approaches based on Christianity, Islam, and the Oedipus myth and contrasts them with Enlightenment approaches that he finds naïve, wherein transparent and autonomous modern subjects resist and progressively overcome pain external to themselves.

The problematization of "religion" is not solely relevant for translating between modern ways of seeing and alternative ways. As Janet Jakobsen and Ann Pellegrini (1999) point out, liberal conceptions of religion also cause mischief internal to contemporary cultural discourses. The Enlightenment sacred-secular distinction largely reworks a Protestant theology of the realm of grace versus the world. Moreover, the Enlightenment concept of reason came to occupy a similar conceptual space as God occupies in Christian theology—the role of overseeing a historical process that includes the realms of both grace/privatization/religion and world/public/secularity. From this perspective one might view the entire Western complex of *religion and secularism*—both of these correlative concepts in tandem—as a form of secularized Protestant theology. This quasi-theology in turn continually ties itself in knots. One problem bedevils both practitioners and critics of this way of understanding religion. Either way, definitions may vacillate between one conception of religion that is excessively privatized and another that is so sweeping and formless that it can barely distinguish religion from culture and/or reason at all. (Between these dual conceptions lies a continuum of practices with ample breadth to explain why neither religious apologists who use liberal theology to seek a private religious realm safe from the acids of modernity, nor critics who confine religion within such a realm to debunk it, can make their ideas of privatized religion completely stick.[3]) Jakobsen and Pellegrini also stress—not unlike

---

3   To pursue this point would require a detour through debates about secularization. Suffice it to say that scholars who stress privatization might argue that this has been a dominant trend in the secularization of the West—but this is an increasingly contested claim (see Casanova 1994; Warner 1993). Or they might assert that the more expansive pole of the vacillation we have noted, while it allows for talk about more than private religion, results in a field so vague that useful definitions of religion are forced in practice to treat religion as privatized—but this assertion does not demonstrate that all working understandings of religion within this field actually have been privatized in specific historical circumstances. Only by defining religion from the outset to screen out all non-privatized religion can they avoid this latter problem. At this point their argument no longer runs in harmony with Asad's concern, that liberal definitions of religion may be out of sync with lived practices in specific settings. It has turned into an *example* of the problem Asad identifies.

Herbert when he finds theological traces within "objective" theories of anomie
— that liberal ways of conceptualizing religion may prevent scholars in cultural
studies from perceiving the moral claims built into the disciplining role of
"value-free" reason. Secularism builds its claim to legitimacy upon clearing a
space free from the disciplinary power of theology, as well as defusing social
conflicts fueled by absolutized religious boundaries. Therefore, as Jakobsen and
Pellegrini put it, the ways in which modernity disciplines the body "feel like
freedom." However, as both Weber and Foucault show us, this feeling of freedom comes with the price of new specifically modern forms of discipline. It is
crucial for cultural studies scholars to grasp how alternative forms of value-
laden cultural discourses (including self-identified "religious" ones) may sometimes represent practices of freedom, not hegemonic constraint, in relation to
normalizing or disciplining aspects of the modern world.[4]

CR broaches the problem of defining religion and exploring how it relates
to culture largely through a symposium on McCutcheon's book, *Manufacturing
Religion* (1997). The symposium's range of positions will be useful for our purposes, but we must begin by clarifying the degree to which McCutcheon does,
and does not, represent a wider field. He attacks approaches that he finds
"regnant" in religious studies, which in a ideal-typical version might blend
several themes. The first is a concept of religion that stresses its privatized and
ahistorical aspects that we have noted, even to the extent that (as William Arnal
puts it in *Guide*) "the very concept of religion as such—as an entity with any
distinction whatsoever from other human phenomena—is a function of the
same processes and historical moments that generate an individualistic concept
of it" (2000: 31). The second is deploying such suspiciously privatized understandings not simply in efforts to identify "religious" aspects of specific
cultures, but also to search for the components (archetypes, ritual patterns, etc.)
of a least common denominator "human culture" across many times and
places—thus often abstracting from sociohistorical difference even more
severely than in the approach criticized by Abu-Lughod.[5] The third is the way

---

4   William Swatos (1999) conceptualizes a "new public religion" within a Habermasian
     distinction between system and lifeworld. He focuses not on safeguarding private
     realms from religion understood as part of the system. Rather, he sees religion allied
     with a lifeworld upon which the system (conceptualized in relation to globalization)
     encroaches. Insofar as the state intervenes within the lifeworld, efforts to defend private
     spaces may redefine the personal as political—his examples include some "family
     values" issues which would make Jakobsen and Pellegrini nervous—and move former-
     ly private religion into a public register.

5   Large-scale comparative schemes *can* function as frameworks within which to pursue
     concrete and fine grained analysis. However, McCutcheon accents the frequent failure
     of comparativists to do so with enough historical specificity. Sometimes this failure is
     hard-wired into the categories used for comparative work (see Friedman 1998) and
     McCutcheon attempts an especially sweeping indictment in this vein.

that upbeat humanist ideas about human universals or the pursuit of cross-cultural understanding may coexist with (supporting rather than contesting) neocolonial agendas on the ground. For McCutcheon, Mircea Eliade is a paradigmatic example of such problems because his methods abstract from issues of sociopolitical power and concentrate instead on a *sui generis* "religious experience" seated in private subjectivity. McCutcheon goes on to argue, fourth, that practices should not count as religious unless they involve perceived relations between humans and "non-obvious beings" such as gods or supernatural forces. Fifth, he assumes that these forces must be understood by religious people in terms incommensurate with Enlightenment reason. Insofar as a majority of these themes come together in particular instances of religious studies scholarship, the result is more like ahistorical theology complicit with neocolonialism, as opposed to publicly accountable critical thought.

We must approach this indictment case by case, since these five components are independent variables. We can find privatized religions without gods, gods articulated with anticolonialism, anticolonialists who appeal to humanist ideals, and so on—so that even though this ideal model matches much past work, it must often be unpacked into its own heterogeneous elements. Moreover, scholars by no means agree whether religions require a discourse about gods, and if so whether gods must be conceptualized in ways incommensurate with reason. Whereas McCutcheon interprets religious studies largely through Eliade, the field also draws on approaches that are harder to discount as ahistorical theology, from Durkheim and Geertz to postmodern and feminist approaches. In fact, McCutcheon echoes battles between idealist and functionalist approaches which Ortner (1994) sees anthropologists transcending as early as the 1970s—a point to which we will return since several CR authors follow Ortner on this point. Importantly, many people are convinced that some forms of religion are capable of perceiving the problems of religious individualism that Arnal calls "religion as such" and working from within religious discourses and communities to counteract these problems. Thus we must not prejudge questions about what José Casanova (1994) calls deprivatized religion, nor discourage concrete investigations of the diverse ways that a politics of nostalgia may function in relation to aspects of modernity. For all these reasons, McCutcheon's frame is not a definitive map of religious studies but one point within a larger map. Approached from this angle, CR's symposium is useful because of its *way* of opening the question of what lies elsewhere on the map—namely by interrogating the meanings of religion in relation to the concept of culture.

Bryan Rennie provides the symposium's most traditional argument, placing the "new" in sharp relief through defending the "old." He insists on the ongoing need to include subjective understandings of religion in analyses of religion and culture. For Rennie such investigation centers on traditional phenomenological approaches, and he sees his interests complementing other panelists' focus on religion, power, and history. Rennie grants the value of reductionist theories such as McCutcheon's for "reducing the total number of independent phenomena that we have to accept as ultimate or given." However, he worries about reducing this number excessively, and about who determines when this is happening. He will not accept an approach that "excises the subjectivity of the believer from [its] explanation entirely." Such a method would "positively discourage the understanding of the other" and might render the theory unfalsifiable if it "gives critics the right to impose whatever interpretation they feel is appropriate on any claims that the subject makes" (2000: 107–109). These are serious concerns for scholars both new and old, including those who take their cues from Asad. However, this is the point at which questions about deconstructing the term "experience" (as noted above) entered CR's discussion. Panelists faced the question whether Rennie's proposal was an outdated "liberal humanist critique" (2000: 134) incompatible with other panelists' concerns because of Rennie's appeal to an "experience" discredited by Sharf and Scott.

Suppose Rennie's solution to this problem does not qualify as a new approach; then what? For our purposes an especially interesting part of CR's symposium is Timothy Fitzgerald's essay based on his book *The Ideology of Religious Studies* (1999). He, too, indicts established discourses on religion. What makes him distinctive is his contention that Asad's unpacking of religion into its heterogenous elements should be a decomposition that goes all the way down, until no difference whatsoever remains between religious studies and cultural studies. More precisely, religious studies should split in two. One part that retains the term religion should either die or be exiled to confessional studies in seminaries, while the defensible part is subsumed without remainder into what Fitzgerald calls cultural studies. (He has in mind a broader set of mainstream social scientific approaches, as compared to the "simple definition" of cultural studies proposed above.) From this standpoint, Fitzgerald perceives limits to McCutcheon's definition of religion, which is loosely allied with Donald Wiebe's naturalistic arguments and largely parasitic upon positions it attacks. "We rarely get any sense outside of some vague and woolly references to 'belief in gods' what it is that requires a naturalistic explanation," Fitzgerald charges. Religion is not "located in relation to concrete ethnographic data or detailed 'on the ground' analysis" (200: 103).

Thus Fitzgerald questions McCutcheon's claim that religion remains a "useful heuristic tool" or "taxon" (2000: 132) at a descriptive level: that even though religion has "has no analytical value whatsoever" it remains useful for "distinguish[ing] talk of such non-obvious beings as gods or demons from talk of the family or … nation state" (1998: 57). Can McCutcheon evade Fitzgerald's charge that this approach to religion is too narrow and should be dissolved into culture? This depends on how we interpret McCutcheon—and here we approach a part of CR's symposium that is central for our analysis of culture and religion. On one hand, McCutcheon insists that different taxonomic schemes generate different "religions," so that the use value of this "useful taxon"—that is, the concept of religion—must be judged in terms of its utility for the goals of the people deploying it. On this side of his proposal—let us call it his postmodern side—religion is an intellectual construct which people may define and/or dissolve however they see fit. True, in his own practice such free play narrows abruptly because he discounts the goals and use-values of people classed as religious; he posits a gulf between first-order data about religious practice and second-order scholarly analysis, and he confines religious insiders strictly to the "data" category. However, there is nothing to prevent scholars from taking their cues from any working definition of religion they find helpful, including those developed in dialogue with insiders. If so, Fitzgerald's charge of narrowness dissolves—and by the same token we dramatize the instability of the category of religion and call attention to the need for clarifying and problematizing it.

On the other hand, we have noted how McCutcheon shares a widespread understanding of religion and critique of the sociohistorical functions it accomplishes—it is individualized, based on appeals to gods, used to legitimize social structures, and so on. He needs stable data and analytical leverage to make this case. Thus he focuses on first-order data such as "talk about the gods," suggests redescribing such talk as "a rhetorical mechanism in ongoing acts of social formation," and claims that the purpose of this rhetoric is to "portray the many as one and heterogeneity as homogeneity" in the interest of elites (2000: 137; 1998: 61). Against Fitzgerald's proposal to abandon the category of religion and replace it with culture (under a triple rubric of ritual, politics, and soteriology) McCutcheon claims that "politics can provide an explanation for both soteriology and ritual" (2000: 133). Insofar as this approach is illuminating for given cases, there is clear value in problematizing alternative approaches that are less critical about such matters. Yet insofar as other scholarly frames can identify forms of religion with other purposes that fall outside McCutcheon's purview, the charge of narrowness requires emphasis. Either way, once again we return to the need to problematize core concepts.

Various people (notably Arnal 1998) have noted how a drive toward reductive theories that rule out dialogue with what used to be called religious people (now redescribed as "data") coexists uneasily with postmodern appeals to reflexivity and multiple paradigms of reality. It is not clear whether scholars can ground naturalistic approaches in hard scientific data while also enjoying the boundless indeterminacy of postmodern social constructionism in which religion can mean whatever a scholar stipulates it to mean. McCutcheon is by no means the only scholar who has failed to solve this problem. On the contrary, a key reason why CR's symposium warrants our attention is that it dramatizes a dilemma faced by many theorists who are attracted by postmodern constructionism yet repelled by the epistemological and political implications

of relativism. Struggles to clarify this point are a key feature of emergent discussions of religion and culture, not only in CR's symposium but across a broad
spectrum of religious studies.

The Strengths and Weaknesses of Metatheory

The previous section used CR as an example of a larger drive to problematize
the two core concepts of this essay, culture and religion. All that was solid
melts into air, and whether postmodernism adds essential insight to this observation from Marx is not the main question. Rather it is where to go from here.
The current section switches the valance of our discussion. It stresses how,
against a background of critical reflexivity, CR identifies contexts in which
theoretical problematization may produce diminishing returns. No one at CR
wants to turn back the clock to a time—if there ever really was such a time—
when the critiques we have discussed could be disregarded. As long as substantial numbers of scholars in religion fail to reflect on how their categories
came into being and relate to power, work on this front will remain crucial.
However, Benavides' contribution to the CR symposium advances our discussion with its contention that, for all its importance, theoretical reflexivity holds
limited promise without another ingredient. This is historical thickness and
specificity: a process of testing theoretical and definitional frames against "raw
materials for manufacturing religion" which are roughly what Fitzgerald calls
"case studies with historical and ethnographic data taken from the whole
spectrum of the humanities and social sciences" (2000: 103). As Benavides puts
it, "if in an exaltation of theoretical hybris, metatheory is seen as an end in
itself, the result will be stagnation and boredom" (2000: 117).

Masuzawa's contribution to CR's symposium formulates this point in
terms especially useful for cultural studies. She shares the broad goal of
scholars like Asad to interrogate the relation between religion, Western discourses, and colonial power. She commends McCutcheon's efforts to build on
Jonathan Z. Smith, and exhorts scholars of religion to calm their fears that
emulating Smith's reflexivity might be tantamount to seeing their whole discipline sucked into a black hole. Rather they should move into this "hole" and
beyond it, exploring the relation between religion and more materialist
concerns than those typically treated in Smith's intellectual history, especially
related to colonialism. (Chidester 2000 makes related points.) However, Masuzawa worries that both options which McCutcheon suggests for defining
religion—an idealist approach which posits the existence of gods and other
"non-obvious" beings, and a social projection approach which accounts for
rhetoric about such gods in naturalistic terms—"would pin 'religion' up in the
sky, so the speak, as something that hangs over humanity ... as a real or
imagined pall of meaning" (2000: 125). She complains that many scholars

"prefer to circumambulate Smith's positions but not go any nearer" and notes that Smith's work is "positively overstuffed with historical details." Thus she suggests that "we gain little from continuing to deal in abstractions once we recognize that 'religion' has been imagined, invented, manufactured. Some of us should be dispatched to inspect the exact date of manufacture, the history, the process, the mechanism, the circumstances of this manufacture" (2000: 129). Moreover, Masuzawa insists that a reflexive approach is "independent of and ultimately contradictory and incompatible with" a firm commitment to naturalistic-reductionist approaches to religion (2000: 129).[6]

While stressing theoretical reflexivity and still presupposing her critique of colonialism (as discussed above), Masuzawa here opens the door to a grounded, dialogic, and multi-perspectival approach that has thus far been anathema not only to McCutcheon, but more importantly to a broad range of neo-Marxian approaches to religion in cultural studies. Her approach leads toward a greater role for approaches that we might call reflexive, subjective, or even theological, depending on how these terms are defined. Certainly it suggests a role for a group that Nye identifies as a core CR constituency: people who have "a sense for themselves that their cultural practice is also (to some degree or other) religious practice" despite a "genealogy that can be traced through colonial and neo-colonial histories and systems of power" (2000a: 6). Nye envisions CR as "a third space between phenomenology and reductionism, or between theological and secularist discourses"—a space that "goes beyond phenomenology to the contested ground between anthropology and religious studies" (2000a: 7, 11). Thus he echoes Rennie's worries about reductionist approaches, but frames this concern in terms more congenial for cultural studies.

For Nye, the term culture "signif[ies] practice (as the adjective or adverb cultural) rather than some essentialized entity which can be owned and described." He stresses that "cultures are done, they are practiced and manifest" and that CR seeks to explore "how religious practices arise out of and are part of cultural practices" (2000a: 6, 7; see also Nye 2000b, 2003). Having opened with an appeal to Abu-Lughod and Asad, he is not proposing an uncritical embrace of a static concept of culture. Rather he frames culture as a verb-like process of symbolic identity-formation that stresses the *non*-timeless, *non*-discrete, and *non*-static. It is an arena in which historical processes unfold and complex negotiations about social boundaries take place. Several responses from CR board members support this broad approach. For example, Ann Grodzins Gold (2000: 16) cites Marshall Sahlins and Sherry Ortner to argue that

---

6   The minimal implication, in relation to McCutcheon's project, is to place his naturalistic theories in metatheoretical scare quotes alongside other definitions, removing their privilege—thus pushing him toward the more "postmodern" horn of the dilemma posed above. McCutcheon concedes this point in his CR response to Masuzawa (2000: 136) while side-stepping some of her other critiques.

"processes covered by the term 'culture' continue even when its value qua term is rhetorically derided."[7]

A reading of Abu-Lughod and Asad supports Gold's point. Abu-Lughod's article in Ortner's *The Fate of 'Culture': Geertz and Beyond* (1999) uses a concept of identity formation that focuses on symbolic practices that Geertz would call cultural, despite Abu-Lughod's fascinating exploration of the cross-cutting flows of global, national, and local issues. Her article is better understood as complexifying certain reflexive aspects of Geertz's work than breaking with it. And although we must return to Asad's concerns about culture and agency, he strongly supports exploring concrete cases drawn from religious traditions (so-called), provided that this advances his goal of "historical anthropology that takes the cultural hegemony of the West as its object of inquiry" and explores how Western religious discourses "define forms of history-making" (1993: 24).

Against those who would abandon the term culture, Susan Hegeman argues that scholars need some way to move among complex dialectics between the global and local and across various disciplines. Although "the 'cultural' is not the only register in which we can imagine conceptual wholes," she sees it as one useful language to approach them—distinguishable from society, human life, and biological life—if used "provisionally" and self-critically. Its amorphous quality may function as a virtue if we understand culture as an arena for debate, or as a process through which symbolic contestation occurs. Hegeman sees "the intensity of debates surrounding the term as above all the measure of its continued rhetorical utility" (1999: 212–13). She offers a cautionary tale of what may happen if scholars give up on analyzing patterns of "cultural" difference (and/or some other form of human difference covering similar ground). This is the tale of Walter Benn Michaels, who attacks "culture" as a shadow concept for race and maintains that celebratory accounts of cultural difference are inextricable from racism. Unfortunately this leaves him with a problem of how to acknowledge patterns of human difference without drawing provisional boundaries. He winds up appealing to a sort of untheorized common sense about human diversity which (perhaps despite his intentions) becomes assimilated to mainstream liberal individualism without offering any tools to understand how this is different from other ways of being in the world. Extending a related criticism, Terry Eagleton stresses in *The Idea of Culture* (2000) that a radical-seeming "post" impulse, one committed to critique through destabilizing all fixed identities, may function much like garden-variety liberal individualism (see also Eagleton 1996).

---

7   Gold notes that Mary Daly (1973) pioneered the idea of religious practice as a verb; she might also have mentioned feminists less vulnerable to anti-essentialist critique like Welch 1990 or Chopp/Davaney 1997.

The CR contributing editor who is most emphatic about the drawbacks of metatheory is Ronald Grimes. He declares himself "post-post," insisting that this is not the same as pre-post, but simply reflects growing boredom with "post" themes that he has presupposed for years. Grimes asks scholars not to neglect theory, but to "write theory in a way that leads readers to care about it." They should throw sand in the gears of an academic reward structure in which publishable articles must "post at least three or four 'posts' to stake out the terrain." Instead they should adopt the motto that "Postmodernism is a window. Look through it, not at it. Think with it; don't write about it" (2000: 19–20). Grimes states that he has become "cranky," and one wonders if this has resulted from one too many discussions with post-theorists about whether his definitions were sufficiently problematized, or whether the provisional identities he was exploring were sophisticated enough. One can predict the direction in which such conversations are most likely to move: downward toward more arcane qualifications and outward into more dispersed micropolitics. If this process takes hold strongly enough, only the theory itself—like a purifying solvent if you like the outcome, or a cancer if you dislike it—will be left by the end. If one has enough experience with such dialogical journeys to envision at the beginning what lies at the end of the road, one might well ponder Grimes' advice to seek another route. Of course, there is a difference between doing so because one does not fully understand what is going on, and doing so because one understands all too well. In any case, it should not be ruled out as part of a repertoire of critical skills.

It is too early to say whether Grimes speaks for an emergent trend. There is room for concern that he may do so, but largely because his concerns dovetail (against his intentions) with a conservative backlash against cultural studies. Thus let us temper his complaints with three qualifications. First, there is no reason to single out problems with postmodern and postcolonial theory while remaining complacent about unreadable elitist jargon from traditional academic quarters. Many of the loudest complaints about cultural studies theory do exactly this. This is not an excuse for complacency about the concerns Grimes raises, but it points to the need for self-consciousness about the ways that anti-theoretical polemics function within larger cultural processes, such as debates about "political correctness" in the media. Second, there is nothing wrong with academic shorthand, technical vocabularies, or complex arguments. It is better to read a brilliant argument that needs editing than a mediocre one presented in a scintillating style. Nor should we underestimate the difficulty of challenging common sense assumptions, especially for writers who seek a hearing for new ideas at the highest levels of academia. The simple point is that it is a virtue, all else being equal, to write clearly in a way that respects readers, and that recent trends in cultural theory have been downward when judged from this point of view. Third—a corollary of the second—although impatience with jargon may be entwined with distaste for the ideas expressed through jargon, these two are separate issues. Consider Edward Said's complaint about theorists who use styles of "almost unimaginable rebarbativeness" and display an "astonishing sense of weightlessness with regard to the gravity of history" (1993: 278–79). Because these words ring so true as an indictment of much recent writing, they make it easy to forget that intellectuals who lack a sense of history may write beautifully (indeed neoconservative pundits with these traits are legion) while scholars with off-putting styles may contribute indispensable critiques of such pundits.

With these caveats, let us hope that Grimes' and Said's concerns—also voiced in cultural studies by Stuart Hall—do reflect an emergent trend.[8] However, it is unfortunate that Grimes uses "the hegemony of the term 'hegemony'" as his prime example of unproductive jargon (2000: 19). True, hegemony is a longish word used to speak about what in many ways boils down to the common sense and habitual practices of a group of people. True, students find it hard to pronounce, just as Grimes complains. Nevertheless it has earned its prominence in recent writing—at least if engaged at its strongest, rather than in straw versions.[9] Its value comes partly from being abstract enough to think in an integrative way about many different kinds of power and flexible enough to bridge Marxian and non-Marxian social theory. Above all, it helps keep a focus on the way that some forms of common sense uphold the interests of elites over non-elites in ways that cause unnecessary suffering. The difference between taking a cultural pattern for granted as common sense and analyzing it as hegemonic often amounts to the same sort of difference that

---

8   Some of Hall's work might be seen more as an example of this problem than a counterweight to it, but in a famous address to an international cultural studies conference, he expressed disquiet about the abstract "fluency" of recent theory. Earlier, addressing the matter of weightlessness about history, Hall excoriated theorists who "take it upon themselves to declare when and for whom history ends"; he suggested that "Baudrillard needs to join the masses for a while, to be silent for two-thirds of a century, just to see what it feels like" (Morley/Chen 1996: 273–75, 131–50).

9   Straw versions include those that posit a monolithic thing called "*the* hegemony" — whereas hegemony is a relation in which a "normal" taken for granted practice works to the advantage of one group over another. Many such relations co-exist in complex layers of identity, and such relations are not necessarily bad. Thus a teacher might have a proper authority in a class; the point is that the teacher's perspective on this issue might be suspect and the students' ability to imagine alternatives is a precondition for change. Hegemony is not only a matter of conscious ideology; it is also expressed through habits and the unconscious. Nor should scholars score cheap points against cultural studies by assuming that scholars who focus on cultural hegemony as one factor of power necessarily forget that other forms of power exist. I might add that insofar as Grimes objects to hegemony simply because too many scholars "write about it" rather than "think with it," we have little disagreement.

Said calls the ability to understand the world with, or without, a sense of weightlessness with regard to the gravity of history.

Hegemony theory has attracted other enemies besides Grimes. Neoconservatives attack it as faddish leftism, although not without adopting it for their own purposes (see Messer-Davidow 1993). Some Marxians contend that its usage in cultural studies has expanded beyond the point of apostasy, turning hegemony into a term that covers a *de facto* retreat from focused analysis of the interplay between cultural and economic processes. Meanwhile, many postmodernists consider even the most decentered hegemony theories to be tainted by past failures of Marxians to stress sexuality and race. For them hegemony is crippled by totalizing conceptions of power and romantic visions of progressive agency, somewhat like culture is hardwired to colonialism for Masuzawa; it carries a permanent stench of working class white maleness which makes it unsuitable for theorizing globalization and new social movements.

Nevertheless, let us recall Gold's comment that "processes covered by the term 'culture' continue even when its value qua term is rhetorically derided" (Gold 2000: 16). Something similar is true of contestation for hegemony. If cultural studies has any lingua franca for bringing diverse conceptions of power and practice into dialogue, it is hegemony theory that plays this role, along with associated concepts such as the distinction among residual, dominant, and emergent cultural formations, as well as the concept of articulation, or the process through which ideas and desires become linked to (articulated with) particular social formations engaged in struggles for hegemony. Among the more controversial of these concepts is the "structure of feeling" (see Williams 1977), which has been attacked somewhat like Abu-Lughod attacks totalizing concepts of culture, although also defended much like Hegeman defends cultural analysis. For better or worse, these concepts remain near the heart of cultural studies. Often they return through the back door in new packaging just as they are turned away from the front door as passé. If not these precise concepts, then we need something very much like them to explore CR's question about where "history and power reside in the coupling of the discourses of culture and religion" (Nye 2000a: 5).

By extension, we may need other theoretical categories—especially for people who are standoffish toward hegemony theory—to orient concrete analyses of the "raw materials for manufacturing religion" so that we do not produce mere descriptions or unwitting support for standing discourses of power. Whatever one thinks about the hegemony of hegemony, the larger issue at stake in the above two sections is not a zero-sum choice between sophisticated theoretical frames and grounded study, but rather how to determine the optimum form of interplay between them to address particular scholarly problems. Although we cannot map such interplay comprehensively through CR's discussions—nor through any other imaginable forum that is reasonably thick and focused—the general dynamics of CR's discussion are pervasive in wider emergent discussions.

Culture and Religion's Emphases within a Wider World of Theory

Recall our plan to use Blackwell's *Dictionary of Cultural and Critical Theory* to provide ballast for our argument and a benchmark to help gauge whether aspects of CR are idiosyncratic or unrepresentative. When comparing CR's inaugural issue to the DCCT, four points come into focus. Two can be treated briefly and two require more unpacking.

First, the DCCT offers ample evidence to support a point stressed by Nye in his rationale for CR, that cultural studies tends to downplay religious identities and practices. True, the DCCT has a few entries on topics like biblical studies, plus scattered comments about religion in articles on scholars like Said and Durkheim. However, on balance Nye's comment about cultural studies is also an apt summary of the DCCT's treatment of religion. Both cultural studies at large and the DCCT in particular largely assume a traditional Marxian approach "that perceives religion to be (at best) false consciousness and ideology. For the main, however, religion is invisible." If religions are noticed they are "subsumed within other frameworks" or approached as "a (relatively unimportant) form of cultural difference" that belongs near the end of lists beginning with race, class, and gender. A comparison of CR and DCCT also supports Nye's claim that "the concerns of those working in cultural studies are in fact often shared by those in the field of culture and religion." Unfortunately the effort to build bridges "so far seems to be a one-sided conversation" (2000a: 7–8). There is much to gain from cross-pollination and collaboration between the fields (Hulsether [forthcoming]; King 1999; Mizruchi 2001, Yancey 2001).

Second, one might suspect from reading CR that the DCCT would devote more space to theorists like Eliade, or to phenomenological approaches more generally. In fact this does not loom large amid the DCCT's concerns, despite exceptions to this rule centered on philosophical approaches such as Heidegger's. For whatever it may be worth to use the DCCT to identify leading cultural theorists who are also widely cited in religious studies—and who thus may be promising bridges between the two fields—the top prospects are Williams, whose fingerprints are all over the DCCT, and Geertz, who enjoys a prominent place in its introduction alongside Williams, Said, Foucault, Greenblatt, and Habermas.

Third, if Eliade is the sort of scholar that DCCT discusses *less* than we might expect from CR, what scholars does it discuss at *greater* length? Like cultural studies at large, DCCT is weighted more toward literature and language theory, compared to CR's greater tilt toward social science. Among the writers cited most often in its index, but addressed little if at all in CR, are Matthew Arnold, Roland Barthes, Walter Benjamin, and Ludwig Wittgenstein, among many others. In part, CR's relative inattention to aspects of culture that center on the arts and literature is an understandable reaction to a disproportionate stress on written texts in past scholarship on religion. Nevertheless it tends to place CR within a longer genealogy of "new approaches" to culture that have distanced themselves from perceived problems with older literary-canonical approaches. Let us recall a few forms that this dynamic has taken over the years. Matthew Arnold and T.S. Eliot, the top authorities for modern literary approaches to culture, congratulated themselves on moving beyond the parochialism and outmoded hierarchical thinking of Christian theology. Later, pioneers of the sort of anthropology that Geertz calls the "sweeping, up-from-the-ape, study-of-mankind sort of business" (1988: 146)—notably Edward Tylor and James Frazer—congratulated themselves for moving beyond Arnold's quasi-theological commitment to a regulative high culture and instituting a properly scientific study of "whole ways of life." (Inconveniently for this line of thought, Stocking 1968 argues that there was little difference between Tylor and Arnold that would interest contemporary cultural studies, unless Arnold gets an edge for being slightly less complacent about cultural critique.)

Also partaking in this dynamic was a later generation of anthropologists such as Boas and Malinowski who "came to focus on particular people as crystal wholes, isolate and entire" (Geertz 1988: 146). As they followed this path—the same path which (as noted above) Herbert later identified as having been blazed by missionaries—they congratulated themselves on ethnographic sophistication that placed their insight far beyond both missionaries and "armchair anthropologists" like Tylor. From the standpoint of cultural studies, this was arguably an advance that warrants some degree of congratulation because of their attacks on the racism of earlier evolutionary approaches and their defense of cultural pluralism. Unfortunately as this generation moved away from speculative panoramas of global evolution toward grounded study of specific cultures by ethnographers at one slice in time, it landed itself in the problems flagged by Abu-Lughod and Masuzawa: approaching cultures as coherent, timeless, self-contained, and abstracted from processes of colonialism.

If we consider emergent debates in light of this dynamic, we reach a sort of crossroads. One option is to work yet more rigorously to debunk the ways that written representations of culture naturalize hierarchies, and to decenter scholarship more relentlessly to distance our critical perspectives from inherited superstitions of culture. Momentum from this dynamic may help explain Abu-Lughod's passion for writing against culture, as well as why two of DCCT's entries on culture take a cool and nonliterary approach which echoes CR's most astringent social-scientific arguments.[10] DCCT's essay on cultural anthropology is far removed both from Matthew Arnold's approach to high culture as sweetness and light, and also from typical preoccupations of cultural studies such as popular music and contestation for hegemony. It describes culture as a breakthrough in evolution that explains "why humans put other species in zoos, aquaria, and conservatories" and not vice-versa, since culture enables superior adaptation to the environment through learned behavior rather than biological instinct. Meanwhile, DCCT's entry simply entitled "culture" stresses that the question at stake in cultural difference "may be one of having—or not having—oneself or one's relations recognized by another culture's definition of the human." Indeed "the definition itself is an act of violence, an invitation to potential if not actual genocide" (Payne 1997: 120, 128–29).

There is another option at the crossroads mentioned above, besides intensifying efforts to evade the risk that hierarchical values—up to and including invitations to genocide—may be encoded in artistic canons, transmitted through religious rhetorics, or reinforced through writing culture. Instead of escalating such fears even further, we might appeal to the open horizon of postmodernity to declare such risks inevitable, then redirect our suspicions toward single-minded quests to evade these risks. Scholars concerned about cultural critique might argue that in some contexts it is riskier *not* to acknowledge that human differences exist in intelligible patterns that can be interpreted. Or one might judge that art is part of what makes life worth living and makes struggles against unjust social hierarchies possible. (Of course for some people such art takes religious forms.) In line with the stress on local knowledges in cultural studies, one might approach such questions on a case by case basis.

One implication of this approach is abandoning a quest for critical perspectives uncontaminated by partiality, and embracing the inevitable narrativity of writing culture. Geertz offers a calm and confident version of this idea: "The moral asymmetries across which ethnography works and the discursive complexity with which it works make any attempt to portray it as anything more than the representation of one sort of life in the categories of another impossible to defend," says Geertz. "That may be enough. I for one think it is." He notes that anthropology has been "connected, if rather more complexly than commonly represented, both with the imperial expansion of the West and with the rise there of a salvational belief in the powers of science." Since such connections are now discredited, cultural analysis is left with the modest role of

---

10 Additional entries on "cultural studies," "cultural materialism," and "culture industries" complicate this argument because of their wider range of concerns and approaches. However, one might give priority to the essay on "culture" discussed in this paragraph since it was written by the DCCT's editor, Michael Payne.

"enabling conversation across societal lines—of ethnicity, religion, class, gender, language, race—that have grown progressively more nuanced." Its goal is to "enlarge the possibility of intelligible discourse between people quite different from each other" (1988: 144, 146–47). We must return to this argument, since what Geertz presents as confidence about making do with an inherited legacy through constructive engagement with the humanities, his critics denounce as liberal complacency. The point at hand is Geertz's cool stance— shared with scholars far less vulnerable than himself to the charge of political complacency—toward the tendency of social scientists to congratulate themselves for the superiority of their analyses compared to value-laden literary approaches. CR is invested more deeply than the DCCT in this dynamic. In this regard the DCCT's entries on culture which I quoted above are somewhat misleading. Its introduction strikes a more representative note when it showcases Geertz alongside Greenblatt and Said.

Masuzawa's article on culture in *Critical Terms* shares CR's relative disinterest, compared to larger spectrum of cultural studies scholarship, in valorizing literary and artistic approaches to culture. Although she draws heavily on Williams' *Keywords* (1976) and *Culture and Society* (1958), she presents his arguments primarily as a critique of a conservative Arnoldian concept of culture, rather than a meticulous argument for the multivocality of literary culture and its possible uses both for conservatism and counter-hegemonic practice. Lincoln's article on culture in *Guide* pays somewhat more attention to culture as a field of neo-Gramscian contestation, but also downplays the counter-hegemonic possibilities of aesthetic aspects of culture. At one point he states that culture with a "capital-C," anchored by dominant canons of high culture, is "nothing other than hegemony" (2000: 413). Later he wavers on this point, pondering whether high cultural texts (perhaps the kinds valorized by the Frankfurt School) can play a counter-hegemonic role in relation to culture industries like Disneyland. In the end he is skeptical about both elite and popular cultures, especially the subset of these cultures called religious. He suggests that the "defining characteristic" of religion is "to invest specific human preferences with transcendent status by misrepresenting them as revealed truths, primordial traditions, divine commandments and so forth" (2000: 416; see also Lincoln 2003). Insofar as he presents religious discourse as a field of hegemonic and counter-hegemonic contestation, he primarily sees it hardening lines of conflict and distorting issues, on an analogy with the European wars of religion. A debunking stance toward religion is his default approach for cultural critique.

My own sense of this matter, however—and the range of approaches in DCCT dramatizes this concern—is that genealogies of "culture" are too narrow, and in the end misleading, if they lean too heavily on narratives by social scientists about their tough-minded superiority to scholars of art and religious values. Hegeman argues that the emergence of a taken-for-granted gulf be-

tween anthropological and literary/aesthetic camps should not be presented as
we did above when discussing the self-perceptions of anthropologists. She does
not trace this divide to the establishment of non-judgmental approaches by
heroic anthropologists beginning in the nineteenth century—nor to the extension of their efforts by postmodern ethnographers who still quest for a sort
of "post-heroism," albeit in self-consciously ironic ways. For Hegeman, the
common wisdom that valorizes such heroic quests is itself an artifact of a
modernist sensibility which—like much else about modernism—appears
somewhat misleading in retrospect. In her telling, typical scholarly assumptions about this gulf should by no means be taken for granted. On the contrary,
the emergence of these assumptions should be traced to a regrettable set of
circumstances in the mid-twentieth century.

Developments at this time polarized what had previously been a fluid
interpenetration of literary approaches, anthropological ones, and cultural-
political interventions which were precursors of the activist tradition in cultural
studies. On one side, anthropology was captured by the logic of the postwar
social scientific academy and nearly swallowed up by structural-functionalist
influences and Cold War area studies. On the other side, scholars interested in
literary and artistic aspects of cultural critique—notably Frankfurt School intellectuals—became bitterly critical of mass culture in the wake of Nazism. To
say the least, they lacked confidence that commendable forms of culture could
emerge from middlebrow "whole ways of life"; in fact they approached these
ways of life through analogies with German mass culture and deemed them
conformist to the point of proto-fascism. Thus they held out for critique in the
realms of art and philosophy, hardening lines between high culture and
everyday life that recent cultural studies scholars have more typically sought to
dissolve. For Hegeman, both trends fit comfortably with the course of modernism in the early twentieth century. So do the cultural exchanges that stood
behind them—with complexities that may be obscured if one approaches them
in retrospect with a polarized interpretive frame pitting Cold War sociology
against Frankfurt school aesthetics—in which Eliot quoted Frazer in avant-
garde modernist poems, ethnographers and surrealist artists taught each other
about defamiliarization, pragmatism flowered as a philosophy and mode of
cultural critique, and U.S. citizens began to use notions like "middlebrow
culture" and "the American way of life" to interpret their experiences of dis-
location and change in a pluralistic urban landscape (see Clifford 1988; West
1989; Hutchinson 1996).

If we start from Hegeman's insights about culture as a "complexly modern"
concept, it raises a question: what adjustments are appropriate as we move into
a new millennium? Like many other scholars interested in writing culture—
including not only mild-mannered liberals like Geertz, but also vociferous
leftists such as Marcus and Fischer (1986) and Rosaldo (1989)—Hegeman
assumes that postmodern narrative theory discredits the idea of a sharp divide

between literary and anthropological approaches. Although she is aware of the dangers flagged by Abu-Lughod, on balance she presents "post-cultural" explorations less as an advance in political virtue, and more as an extension of elitist disdain for middlebrow culture. Her work does more than simply fuel doubts about abandoning the concept of culture (the context in which we introduced her above.) It also presses us to rethink standard genealogies of trends in cultural analysis with greater appreciation for the cross-pollination between the social sciences and literary/aesthetic cultural critique. Writing in CR, Nye notes that anthropologists are "jealous about the appropriation of the 'culture concept' which [they] consider to be 'their own'" (2000a: 8). Hegeman's argument powerfully extends and complicates this point, especially when we use it to frame the wider range of approaches in DCCT.

Let us consider one final point of contrast between CR and DCCT. The latter has drunk more deeply at the wells of structuralism and poststructuralism. This is true not only when it treats literary and linguistic scholars (Saussure, Derrida) but also anthropologists (Lévi-Strauss) and Marxians (Althusser). All these theorists loom larger in the DCCT. To be sure, CR shows some interest. Althusser's theories form part of the background for the McCutcheon symposium, although McCutcheon is equally prone to cite Althusser's arch-enemy E.P. Thompson.[11] CR's first review (Rapp 2000) showcases Derrida's efforts to bring Jewish and Christian negative theology into dialogue with poststructuralism. However, the most telling sentence appears in Nye's introduction, where he writes of "the obvious fact that people do cultures (or perform cultural action) rather than the other way around" (2000a: 6). Of course this point is not obvious to structuralists and poststructuralists at all. They would not write Nye's word "fact" without scare quotes, and they are more likely to think about human practices (or bodies, subjectivities, etc.) being constituted by cultural discourse than vice-versa. For structuralists such discourses are relatively stable and generalizable, while poststructuralists stress that meanings cannot be pinned down and subjectivities are fluid and unstable. Either way, discourses "speak" people rather than the other way around, and to think otherwise reflects a crippling liberal naiveté.

Asad's CR article underlines this point. We noted above how his article critiques liberal assumptions about agency; it explores approaches to suffering that are not based on Western discourses of individualism and upbeat progress. These arguments build on an earlier critique (1993: 27–54) in which Asad

---

11 McCutcheon 1998 draws heavily on Althusser, but since he also appeals to Thompson his major concern seems not to be structuralism so much as an attack on apolitical individualism. *Manufacturing Religion* models its critique of religion on Eagleton's flaying of Arnold and Heidegger in *Literary Theory* (1996). But although Eagleton draws on structuralism, he is cool toward it and quite hostile to poststructuralism; Williams emerges unambiguously as the hero of his recent book, *The Idea of Culture* (2000).

faulted Geertz for a static concept of culture which Asad calls "cognitive" rather than "communicative." Up to this point, Asad's point is similar to Nye's call for a verb-like notion of culture as practice. However, Asad would press Geertz harder for attention to underlying structures that set limits to cognition and interpretation. Asad suggests "taking Freud's project more seriously" in order to underline "our incomplete knowledge of and mastery over our bodies and desire" and to guard against overestimating our capacity for "conscious intention and controlled action" (2000: 30). "Choices and desires make actions before action can make 'history,'" he says. "But predefined social relations and language ... shape the person to whom 'normal' desires and choices can be attributed." To explore what agents can do, scholars "must also address the process by which 'normal persons' are constituted" (1993: 13).

Responding to this line of reasoning, Ortner (1994, 1999) proposes to continue exploring group agency and meaning, while simultaneously placing this inquiry in the context of larger structures of power. Any structural approach that cannot account for agency and resistance carries the burden of proof for her, not vice-versa. We might build a fairly broad consensus for this sort of abstract proposal—but the devil is in the details. Ortner pursues this approach by studying the relations between Sherpas and their Western employers within the context of the capitalist world-system, while underlining the role of meaning making by the Sherpas. However, in this case what she celebrates as "thick resistance" (1999) turns out to be too thin for the taste of some scholars. Asad states their concerns combatively when he writes— speaking not about Sherpas in particular but about scholars who focus on cultural resistance more generally—that "even the inmates of a concentration camp are able ... to live by their own cultural logic. But one may be forgiven for doubting that they are therefore 'making their own history'" (1993: 4).

Any treatment of new approaches to religion and culture must take account of such objections, and indeed underline them in many contexts. In cultural studies the classic form of the debate was a challenge to what became known as "culturalism"—a humanist form of hegemony theory associated with Williams and Thompson—by structural Marxists, among whom Althusser and Lacan were the most widely cited. Later, feminists influenced by poststructuralism such as Julia Kristeva (1996) and Judith Butler (1990) increasingly supplanted Althusser. As this became a leading edge of critique in cultural studies, it was often difficult to tell what was at issue in disputes pitting established male culturalists against poststructuralist gender theorists. Were they primarily arguing about disrespect versus respect for feminism, or about old-fashioned "experiences" of agency—including female agency—versus decentered subjectivities constituted by unstable discursive structures? Since there are feminist versions of nearly every position we have treated, battles can just as easily pit culturalist forms of feminism against anti-feminist versions of poststructuralism. Nye correctly notes that discussions of such issues—along with others in the overlapping territory between gender studies and cultural theory—are central to current debates on religion and culture. (See Boyarin 1998; Christian 1987; Chopp/Davaney 1997; Collins 1990; Nicholson 1990; and Warne 2000.)

In both structuralist Marxist and poststructuralist feminist versions, structural critiques forced a generation of cultural studies scholars to rethink the limits of their categories for human agency. Largely they moved in the direction of scaled-back optimism about agency, although it is difficult to generalize about this matter because some theorists came to stress the plasticity of human cultural performance, so that a sort of anti-humanist version of individual and subcultural "agency" (not named as such, but still inflecting categories such as performativity) returned through the back door. David Harris offers a sour assessment of the results of these disputations, an assessment related to Grimes' complaints about the hegemony of hegemony. Harris charts how neo-Gramscians responded to attacks from structuralists by beefing up their discussions of semiotics and reconfiguring hegemony theory to integrate these themes into their system. He describes the result as "a theory that is too political and partisan to be credible, and a politics that is too theoretical to be popular and effective" (1992: 198; see also Peck 2001). Meanwhile feminist scholars such as Nancy Fraser (1997) complain about a related process within academic feminism—one not attributable solely to semiotics but in which theory did have a role—through which much feminist theory became exceedingly abstract and ahistorical. Whether or not one agrees with Harris and Fraser (either in general or about specific writers) one outcome of these disputations is clear. By the end of the process, scholars in cultural studies who attacked earlier generations in the movement for privileging economic structures and working-class agency over other issues had gained a great deal of ground.[12] Ongoing disputes about how to evaluate this change are complex and contentious because some of the emergent approaches focused on dimensions of culture like race and gender which are easy to defend as analytical priorities alongside class, but others explored dimensions of more debatable importance. For example, much work overestimated the counterhegemonic potential of consumer culture.

---

12 This is an ironic result for a process that we can trace in part to Althusser, and it runs contrary to the intentions of many structuralists (insofar as their theory permits us to grant the relevance of intentions). In response many scholars have reasserted the importance of economic structures and sought to countervail against poststructuralists and multiculturalists whom they perceive underplaying class (see Palmer 1990). Nevertheless the trend we have noted remains dominant in cultural studies. This is a tangled issue because, just as feminists may conceptualize agency in many ways, there is more than one way to reassert the importance of class analysis. Both culturalists in Thompson's tradition and structuralists in Althusser's tradition do so.

It is difficult to judge how much space the culturalist versus structuralist debate in cultural studies deserves within an article of this kind. It is clear that the debate was foundational for cultural studies during the 1970s and is still reflected in the DCCT today, but it is less clear whether CR's relative tilt away from structuralisms or DCCT's tilt toward them best represents recent trends. By extension it is unclear how extensively we should treat other structuralist and poststructuralist scholars. In part, this is a place where we confront the massive disproportion between the field of religion and culture and what one can accomplish in one short article. For another part, the work within cultural studies that is most dedicated to exploring semiotics and answering objections from Althusser and Lacan may not be the most valuable parts of cultural studies to transmit to a new generation, especially insofar as these might be seen as "old approaches" centered in the 1970s. Scholars will have to judge this matter case by case.

In the end, can we agree with CR that "people do cultures ... rather than the other way around," even though this is not an "obvious fact" to stress in all scholarly contexts? It is not necessary to renounce this stance in order to understand that agency does not take place under conditions of our own choosing, but is constrained by forces from the world economy to the unconscious. Granted, this stance toward religion and culture may rouse suspicion from scholars whose standard mode of critique is to problematize assertions of religious and moral agency using structural methods. Yet it is not always clear how these scholars justify their own priorities. Are they not scholarly agents — or, if one prefers, are they not situated performatively within a scholarly subject position — with some range of choice about what projects to pursue? Must they place their scholarly agency in such deep scare-quotes, as to deny that they have some choice in this matter, and that some implicit moral calculus is at play in this choice? Most scholars take at least this much agency for granted, and it seems presumptuous to rule out analogous capacities (however differently constrained) in other aspects of life and among many of the (conventionally so-called) "religious" people we collaborate with or study.[13]

For most scholars in cultural studies, there is limited value in investigating how hegemonies, discourses, and structures constrain action, except as part of a scholarly practice which seeks leverage for counter-hegemonic critique. Of course this is only the beginning of analysis. It leads toward complex debates

---

13   It may be prudent to belabor the point that there is no contradiction between making this claim and grasping that these capacities are not free-floating and universal, but tied to specific historical discourses. To speak about "many people we study" is not to speak about all of them, and we should not underestimate how sociohistorical differences complicate this argument. Exploring whether practices are commensurate leads into dialogues which may or may not result in overlapping consensus ; they may equally well lead into profound conflict.

about how to identify counter-hegemonic values and determine which ones deserve priority in specific cases. This includes a question about when the most appropriate critiques should—and when they should *not*—debunk specific articulations of "religious" or "cultural" values. For example, let us assume that DCCT is correct that invoking cultural boundaries is potentially an "invitation to genocide." Is it equally appropriate to attack Nazi culture and Jewish cultural resistance to Nazism in such terms? And if a scholar claims neutrality on this point, is this not weightlessness with regard to the gravity of history? When Nye's introduction to CR identifies the "contemporary cultural practice" of academics—for example, within "culture wars" or human rights organizing—as a central feature of the field of culture and religion, it is because such questions, both explicit and implicit, are a major context for scholarship.

Conclusions

Can we derive any useful summary statements about new approaches to religion and culture from these reflections? It bears repeating that, although we have tried to offer a fair and reasonably representative picture of recent trends through the examples we have considered, we agreed to renounce aspirations toward an encyclopedic survey. Instead we sought to use CR and the DCCT as manageable points of reference for discussing a subject which is so immense that selectivity and risky generalizations have been inevitable. We began somewhat arbitrarily with a baseline of "old" approaches anchored by Geertz and Williams, and we partially supplemented this baseline along the way with Eliade and various structuralists. Against this background, we have discerned—at least inside CR and through CR's dialogue with texts that have some rough claim to representative status—a pattern of new approaches which interrogate the orientation to consensus, totality, and relative complacency about colonialism in Geertz, as well as the way Williams privileges a culture centered in relatively cohesive white working class communities. On all sides we found acute suspicions that pernicious Western ideologies and subjectivities are embedded in received understandings of culture and religion. New forms of interpretive anthropology "write against culture" and stress complex relations among culture, colonialism, and multiple forms of difference. Emergent cultural theorists embrace the decentered neo-Gramscianism of scholars like Laclau and Mouffe and poststructuralist theorists like Butler. Lively dialogues are ongoing among modernists and postmodernists, culturalists and structuralists, Marxians and non-Marxians, highbrow and lowbrow, phenomenologists and reductionists, feminists and anti-feminists, social scientists and literary critics, and a kaleidoscope of other tendencies from many disciplines.

We also found a growing number of people who argue that the acute sensitivity to difference and hyperinflation of theory that accompanied these trends has reached a point of diminishing returns in many contexts, despite its ongoing contributions in other areas. This point is highly contentious—indeed debates about it are themselves a major trend—since there is little agreement on what kind of "returns" scholars should look for in various contexts, or even whether asking about returns is appropriate. Nevertheless many people have begun to debate such questions, including several writers in CR along with kindred spirits such as Eagleton, Hegeman, and Said. "Post-post" sensibilities and efforts to revalorize supposedly "passé" categories like culture, class, experience, and religion are on the rise in many quarters.

It seems plausible that, a decade from now, we may look back on CR's call for a revitalized field of culture and religion which takes human agency for granted and seeks a third way between phenonomenology and reductionism. In retrospect we may see that CR's vision was part of an emergent movement that gained hegemony. However, even though this scenario is plausible, it is not probable. More likely the field will remain fragmented, with dozens of "new and improved" products on offer in addition to those available now. Scholars will continue to face the challenge of judging which of these approaches are worth their precious time and energy. In any case, whether or not everything comes clear in the future, no one can navigate *today* in a field as complex as "culture and religion" without facing such choices.

As I have reflected on this problem of prioritizing through my effort to write something worthwhile about this impossibly broad topic, I have often recalled Donna Haraway's comment: "Some differences are playful; some are poles of world historical systems of domination. Epistemology is about knowing the difference" (1990: 202–203). The purpose of knowing this difference, for most scholars in cultural studies, is not to underline the inevitability of the largest structures of domination, although appreciating their power is part of the task. The main point is to find leverage for cultural critique that can help to countervail against unnecessary suffering caused by these structures. It need hardly be said that religious practitioners, as well as the scholars who study them, often fail on this count. Nevertheless one can try to minimize such failures. If there has been an overall point to this study of emergent approaches to religion and culture, it has been a hope of contributing in some small way to this goal.

Bibliography

Abu-Lughod, Lila (1991), "Writing Against Culture," in: Richard G. Fox, ed., *Recapturing Anthropology: Working in the Present*. Santa Fe, N.Mex.: School of American Research Press: 137–62.
— (1999), "The Interpretation of Culture(s) after Television," in: Sherry Ortner, ed., *The Fate of 'Culture': Geertz and Beyond*. Berkeley, Calif.: University of California Press: 110–35.

Arjun, Appadurai (1996), *Modernity at Large: Cultural Dimensions of Globalization*. Minneapolis, Minn.: University of Minnesota Press.

Arnal, William (1998), "What If I Don't Want to Play Tennis?: A Rejoinder to Russell McCutcheon on Postmodernism and Theory of Religion," in: *Studies in Religion* 27 (1): 61–68.

— (2000), "Definition," in: Willi Braun/Russell McCutcheon, eds., *Guide to the Study of Religion*. London: Cassell: 21–35.

Asad, Talal (1993), *Genealogies of Religion: Discipline and Reasons of Power in Christianity and Islam*. Baltimore: Johns Hopkins University Press.

— (2000), "Agency and Pain: An Exploration," in: *Culture and Religion: An Interdisciplinary Journal* 1 (1): 29–59.

Benavides, Gustavo (1998), "Modernity," in: Mark C. Taylor, ed., *Critical Terms for Religious Studies*. Chicago: University of Chicago Press.

— (2000), "What Raw Materials Are Used in the Manufacture of Religion?," in: *Culture and Religion: An Interdisciplinary Journal* 1 (1): 113–22.

— (2001), "Religious Studies between Science and Ideology," in: *Religious Studies Review* 27 (2): 105–108.

Boyarin, Daniel (1998), "Gender," in: Mark C. Taylor, ed., *Critical Terms for Religious Studies*. Chicago: University of Chicago Press: 117–35.

Braun, Willi/McCutcheon, Russell, eds. (2000), *Guide to the Study of Religion*. London: Cassell.

Buhle, Mari Jo (1998), *Feminism and Its Discontents: A Century of Struggle with Psychoanalysis*. Cambridge, Mass.: Harvard University Press.

Burris, John (2002), *Exhibiting Religion: Colonialism and Spectacle at International Expositions, 1851–1993*. Charlottesville, Va.: University of Virginia Press.

Butler, Judith (1990), *Gender Trouble: Feminism and the Subversion of Identity*. New York: Routledge.

Casanova, José (1994), *Public Religions in the Modern World*. Chicago: University of Chicago Press.

Chidester, David (1996), *Savage Systems: Colonialism and Comparative Religion in Southern Africa*. Charlottesville, Va.: University Press of Virginia.

— (2000), "Material Terms for the Study of Religion," in: *Journal of the American Academy of Religion* 68 (2): 367–80.

Chopp, Rebecca/Davaney, Sheila Greeve, eds. (1997), *Horizons in Feminist Theology: Identity, Tradition, and Norms*. Minneapolis, Minn.: Fortress Press.

Christian, Barbara (1987), "The Race for Theory," in: *Cultural Critique* 6: 51–63.

Clifford, James (1988), *The Predicament of Culture*. Cambridge, Mass.: Harvard University Press.

— (1991), "Traveling Cultures," in: Lawrence Grossberg et. al., eds., *Cultural Studies*. New York: Routledge.

Collins, Patricia Hill (1990), *Black Feminist Thought: Knowledge, Consciousness, and the Politics of Empowerment*. New York: Routledge.

Connor, Steven (1989), *Postmodernist Culture: An Introduction to Theories of the Contemporary*, second ed. Cambridge: Blackwell.

Daly, Mary (1973), *Beyond God the Father*. Boston, Mass.: Beacon.

DiCenso, James (1998), "Religion and the Psycho-Cultural Formation of Ideals," in: Thomas Idinopolus/Brian Wilson, eds., *What Is Religion? Origins, Definitions, and Explanations*. Leiden: Brill: 15–25.

During, Simon, ed. (1999), *The Cultural Studies Reader*, second ed. New York: Routledge.

Eagleton, Terry (1996), *Literary Theory: An Introduction*, second ed. Minneapolis, Minn.: University of Minnesota Press.

—— (2000), *The Idea of Culture*. Oxford: Blackwell.

Ferguson, Marjorie/Golding, Peter, eds. (1997), *Cultural Studies in Question*. London: Sage.

Fitzgerald, Timothy (1999), *The Ideology of Religious Studies*. New York: Oxford University Press.

—— (2000), "Russell McCutcheon's *Manufacturing Religion*," in: *Culture and Religion: An Interdisciplinary Journal* 1 (1): 99–104.

Fraser, Nancy (1997), *Justice Interruptus: Critical Reflections on the 'Postsocialist' Condition*. New York: Routledge.

Friedman, Maurice (1998), "Why Joseph Campbell's Psychologizing of Myth Precludes the Holocaust," in: *Journal of the American Academy of Religion* 66 (2): 385–401.

Geertz, Clifford (1973), *The Interpretation of Cultures*. New York: Basic Books.

—— (1988), *Works and Lives: The Anthropologist as Author*. Stanford, Calif.: Stanford University Press.

—— (1995), *After the Fact: Two Countries, Four Decades, One Anthropologist*. Cambridge, Mass.: Harvard University Press.

Gold, Ann Grodzins (2000), "Everywhere You Go…," in: *Culture and Religion: An Interdisciplinary Journal* 1 (1): 13–18.

Greenblatt, Stephen (1990), "Culture," in: Frank Lentricchia/Thomas McLaughlin, eds., *Critical Terms for Literary Study*. Chicago: University of Chicago Press: 225–30.

Grimes, Ronald (2000), "Writing Against," in: *Culture and Religion: An Interdisciplinary Journal* 1 (1): 19–22.

Haraway, Donna (1988), "Situated Knowledges: The Science Question in Feminism and the Privilege of Partial Perspective," in: *Feminist Studies* 14 (3): 575–99.

—— (1990), "A Manifesto for Cyborgs: Science, Technology, and Socialist Feminism," in: Linda Nicholson, ed., *Feminism/Postmodernism*. New York: Routledge.

Harris, David (1992), *From Class Struggle to the Politics of Pleasure: The Effects of Gramscianism on Cultural Studies*. London: Routledge.

Harvey, David (1990), *The Condition of Postmodernity*. Cambridge: Basil Blackwell.

Hegeman, Susan (1999), *Patterns for America: Modernism and the Concept of Culture*. Princeton, N.J.: Princeton University Press.

Herbert, Christopher (1991), *Culture and Anomie: Ethnographic Imagination in the Nineteenth Century*. Chicago: University of Chicago Press.

Hulsether, Mark (1997), "Three Challenges for the Field of American Studies: Relating to Cultural Studies, Addressing Wider Publics, and Coming to Terms with Religions," in: *American Studies* 38 (2): 117–47.

—— (2005), "Religion and Culture," in: John Hinnells, ed., *The Routledge Companion to the Study of Religion*. New York: Routledge.

—— (forthcoming), "Bill Graham and Billy Graham: Why American Studies Should Pay More Attention to Public Religions," in: Janet Jakobsen/Ann Pellegrini, eds., *World Secularisms*. Minneapolis, Minn.: University of Minnesota Press.

Hutchinson, George (1996), *The Harlem Renaissance in Black and White*. Cambridge, Mass.: Harvard University Press.

Jakobsen, Janet/Pellegrini, Ann (1999), "Getting Religion," in: Marjorie Garber/Rebecca Walkowitz, eds., *One Nation Under God?: Religion and American Culture*. New York: Routledge: 101–14.

Jameson, Fredric (1998), *The Cultural Turn: Selected Writings on the Postmodern 1983–1998*. New York: Verso.

King, Richard (1999), *Orientalism and Religion: Postcolonial Theory, India and the 'Mystic East.'* New York: Routledge.

Kristeva, Julia (1996), *The Kristeva Reader*, ed. Toril Moi. New York: Columbia University Press.

Laclau, Ernesto/Mouffe, Chantal (1985), *Hegemony and Socialist Strategy: Towards a Radical Democratic Politics*. London: Verso.

Lincoln, Bruce (1998), "Conflict," in: Mark C. Taylor, ed., *Critical Terms for Religious Studies*. Chicago: University of Chicago Press: 55–69.

— (2000), "Culture," in: Willi Braun/Russell McCutcheon, eds., *Guide to the Study of Religion*. London: Cassell: 409–22.

— (2003), *Holy Terrors: Thinking about Religion after September 11*. Chicago: University of Chicago Press.

Marcus, George/Fischer, Michael (1986), *Anthropology as Cultural Critique*. Chicago: University of Chicago Press.

Masuzawa, Tomoko (1998), "Culture," in: Mark C. Taylor, ed., *Critical Terms for Religious Studies*. Chicago: University of Chicago Press: 70–93.

— (2000), "The Production of 'Religion' and the Task of the Scholar: Russell T. McCutcheon among the Smiths," in: *Culture and Religion: An Interdisciplinary Journal* 1 (1): 123–30.

McCutcheon, Russell (1997), *Manufacturing Religion: The Discourse of Sui Generis Religion and the Politics of Nostalgia*. New York: Oxford University Press.

— (1998), "Redescribing 'Religion' as Social Formation: Toward a Social Definition of Religion," in: Thomas Idinopolus/Brian Wilson, eds., *What Is Religion? Origins, Definitions, and Explanation*. Leiden: Brill: 51–71.

— (2000), "A Brief Response from a Fortunate Man," in: *Culture and Religion: An Interdisciplinary Journal* 1 (1): 131–40.

— (2001), *Critics Not Caretakers: Redescribing the Public Study of Religion*. Albany, N.Y.: SUNY Press.

Messer-Davidow, Ellen (1993), "Manufacturing the Attack on Higher Education," in: *Social Text* 36: 40–80.

Mizruchi, Susan, ed. (2001), *Religion and Cultural Studies*. Princeton, N.J.: Princeton University Press.

Morley, David/ Chen, Kuan-Hsing, eds. (1996), *Stuart Hall: Critical Dialogues in Cultural Studies*. New York: Routledge.

Nicholson, Linda, ed. (1990), *Feminism/Postmodernism*. New York: Routledge.

Nye, Malory et. al. (2000a), "Culture and Religion: An Editorial with Responses," in: *Culture and Religion: An Interdisciplinary Journal* 1 (1): 5–12.

Nye, Malory (2000b), "Religion, Post-Religionism, and Religioning: Religious Studies and Contemporary Cultural Debates," in: *Method and Theory in the Study of Religion* 12 (4): 447–76.

—— (2003), *Religion: The Basics*. London: Routledge.

Ortner, Sherry (1994), "Theory in Anthropology since the Sixties," in: Nicholas Dirks et. al., eds., *Culture/Power/History: A Reader in Contemporary Social Theory*. Princeton, N.J.: Princeton University Press: 372–411.

—— ed. (1999), *The Fate of 'Culture': Geertz and Beyond*. Berkeley, Calif.: University of California Press.

Palmer, Bryan D. (1990), *Descent into Discourse: The Reification of Language and the Writing of Social History*. Philadelphia, Pa.: Temple University Press.

Payne, Michael (1997), *A Dictionary of Cultural and Critical Theory*. Oxford: Blackwell.

Peck, Janice (2001), "Itinerary of a Thought: Stuart Hall, Cultural Studies, and the Unresolved Problem of the Relation of Culture to 'Not Culture,'" in: *Cultural Critique* 48, accessed on-line.

Rapp, Jennifer (2000), "On John Caputo, *The Prayers and Tears of Jacques Derrida*," in: *Culture and Religion: An Interdisciplinary Journal* 1 (1): 141–45.

Rennie, Bryan (2000), "Manufacturing McCutcheon: The Failure of Understanding in the Academic Study of Religion," in: *Culture and Religion: An Interdisciplinary Journal* 1 (1): 105–12.

Rosaldo, Renato (1989), *Culture and Truth*. Boston, Mass.: Beacon Press.

Said, Edward (1978), *Orientalism*. New York: Vintage.

—— (1993), *Culture and Imperialism*. New York: Vintage.

Scott, Joan (1995), "Multiculturalism and the Politics of Identity," in: John Rajchman, ed., *The Identity in Question*. New York: Routledge: 3–15.

Sharf, Robert (1998), "Experience," in: Mark C. Taylor, ed., *Critical Terms for Religious Studies*. Chicago: University of Chicago Press: 94–116.

Stocking, George Jr. (1968), "Arnold, Tylor, and the Uses of Invention," in: *Race, Culture, and Evolution: Essays in the History of Anthropology*. New York: Free Press: 69–90.

Storey, John, ed. (1996), *What Is Cultural Studies? A Reader*. New York: Arnold Press.

Swatos, William (1999), "The Public and the Pubic: Is Nothing Private Anymore?," in: William Swatos/James Wellman, eds., *The Power of Religious Publics: Staking Claims in American Society*. Westport, Conn.: Greenwood Press: 187–201.

Taylor, Mark C., ed. (1998), *Critical Terms for Religious Studies*. Chicago: University of Chicago Press.

Warne, Randi (2000), "Gender," in: Willi Braun/Russell McCutcheon, eds., *Guide to the Study of Religion*. London: Cassell.

Warner, R. Stephen (1993), "Work in Progress toward a New Paradigm for the Sociological Study of Religion in the United States," in: *American Journal of Sociology* 98 (5): 1004–93.

Welch, Sharon (1990), *A Feminist Ethic of Risk*. Minneapolis, Minn.: Fortress Press.

West, Cornel (1989), *The American Evasion of Philosophy: A Genealogy of Pragmatism*. Madison, Wis.: University of Wisconsin Press.

Williams, Raymond (1977), *Marxism and Literature*. New York: Oxford University Press.

—— (1983 [1958]), *Culture and Society, 1780–1950*. New York: Columbia University Press.

—— (1983), *Keywords: A Vocabulary of Culture and Society*, second ed. New York: Oxford University Press.

—— (1995), *The Sociology of Culture*. Chicago: University of Chicago Press.

Wilson, Brian C. (1998), "From the Lexical to the Polythetic: A Brief History of the Definition of Religion," in: Thomas Idinopolus/Brian Wilson, eds., *What Is Religion? Origins, Definitions, and Explanation*. Leiden: Brill: 142–62.

Yancy, George (2001), *Cornel West: A Critical Reader*. New York: Blackwell.

Section 3

Historical Approaches

Religion and the Internet

Presence, Problems, and Prospects

by

Lorne L. Dawson

A new dimension of unknown significance has been added to the study of religion: cyberspace. The Internet offers startling new opportunities to scholars of religion for research, the dissemination of information, collaboration with colleagues, and debate with rivals. But the religions of the world, great and small, have seized on the technical advantages of the Internet with even greater enthusiasm. Cyberspace is suffuse with religious content, of both a conventional and innovative kind. It presents new opportunities and challenges for all aspects of the study of religion, whether textual, historical, or field studies. Moreover, the Internet as a medium bears unique features that may well alter the global context of religiosity in which the academic study of religion operates. In intended and unintended ways a media revolution is well underway that is likely to change the face of religion by changing the social context in which religion happens. It is important that we seek to understand how and why this may be the case.

As with previous media revolutions, ranging from the invention of writing to television, we must recognize that the social implications are likely to be profound (e.g., Ong 1982). In many respects we have only begun to appreciate the religious implications of these past changes in communicative technologies. With the analyses of McLuhan (1965) and others in hand we now recognize that the medium is the message. Media are not neutral or passive conduits for the transfer of information. They mold the message in ways that crucially influence the world views we construct. They adjust our self-conceptions, notions of human relations and community, and the nature of reality itself. Unlike previous media, however, the Internet has blossomed almost overnight, and its astonishing growth is proceeding at an accelerating pace. Hundreds of millions of people have gained access to the Internet in less than ten years, and burgeoning nations like China, India, and Brazil have yet to come fully online. There is no precedent for this growth, which vastly out-strips the speed and scope with which literacy, electricity, the telephone, and television spread around the world.[1]

The religious uses of the Internet evoke parallels with television, with tel-evangelism and the earlier religious uses of radio in particular. In fact there are important continuities here yet to be explored. But there are important differences as well. At least three crucial differences come to mind: (1) the Internet is an interactive and not simply broadcast medium; (2) anyone can launch themselves onto the world wide web with relative ease and little expense; and (3), the Internet is truly global in its reach. With a comparatively small investment in time and money I can make my religious views known, at least potentially, to hundreds of thousands of others throughout the world. Television is the preserve essentially of a small cultural elite. The world wide web is open in principle and in practice to almost anyone. In posting my views I may be confronted with alternative opinions posed by people from lands and traditions quite alien to my experience, or enter into dialogue with high officials of my own religion. It is these key qualitative differences in the medium that have helped to generate the significant quantitative difference in the presence of computer-mediated communication, a difference that in turn magnifies the social and cultural significance of this particular media revolution.

In this essay I will quickly survey the presence of religion on the Internet, discussing the diversity of its forms and functioning. Then I will dwell on two of the many research problems that are emerging from this new field of study, and finally I will indicate how the rise of cyber-religion may be linked to certain broader patterns of religious change in contemporary society. The sociology of the Internet has raised certain focal issues with obvious relevance to the study of religion, issues that scholars of religion are only beginning to consider (see Dawson 2000; Dawson/Cowan 2004). In the second and largest section of this chapter I will provide an introduction to two of the most important and foundational issues: the potential impact of the Internet on the formation of personal identity, and the emergence of new kinds of communities (see Dawson 2000: 42–45 and Dawson 2001a for some consideration of additional issues, like the effects of the Internet on religious authority). Each issue is complex and inter-related, and they are considered separately here for heuristic purposes alone.

---

1   The number of Internet users worldwide is estimated to have been 16 million in 1995, 378 million in 2000, and more than 500 million in 2002 (Wellman/Haythornthwaite 2002: 11).

1. The Presence of Religion on the Internet

Religion is abundantly present on the world wide web and a host of Internet chat and news groups. Every major world religion is represented, every major and minor Christian denomination, almost all new religious movements, thousands of specific churches, and countless web pages operated by individual believers, self-declared gurus, prophets, shamans, apostates, and other moral entrepreneurs. In addition the net has spawned its own religious creations, from megasites of cyber-spirituality to virtual "churches," and strictly online religions. To this mix we can add numerous commercial sites wishing to turn a profit on our spiritual appetites, providing us with religious news, selling us religious paraphernalia, and acting as network nodes for links to hundreds of other sites. There are also many sites launched to educate the public or to pursue a diverse array of religious causes (e.g., sites based on university courses or anti-cult crusades).[2]

On the Internet people can read about religion, talk with others about religion, download religious texts and documents, buy religious books and artifacts, take virtual tours of galleries of religious art or the interiors of religious buildings, search scriptures using electronic indexes, locate churches and religious centers, participate in rituals, mediation sessions or pilgrimages, vote on organizational propositions, see images of their religious leaders, watch video clips, and listen to religious music, sermons, prayers, testimonials, and discourses. Soon they may even be able to feel the texture of objects appearing on their screen or smell the aroma of the virtual incense burning on the computer generated altar to their gods. The technology exists to simulate both.

The growth in the religious uses of the Internet is so extensive that the number of sites available exceeds the capacity of existing search engines and other specific online and offline guides. No one can keep pace with all the changes. There is a need, however, to begin to map the terrain better. We need to know more about what is on the net, who has put it there, and why. Some headway has been made with dozens of new books like Bruce Lawrence's *The*

---

2   World religion: e.g., www.dharmanet.org for Buddhism or www.fezana.org for Zoro-astrianism; Christian denominations: e.g., www.vatican.va for the Catholic Church or www.sbc.net for the Southern Baptist Convention; new religious movements: e.g., www.eckankar.org for Eckankar or www.sgi.org for Soka Gakkai; megasites of spirituality and virtual churches: e.g., www.godweb.org or the First Church of Cyberspace; online religions: e.g., the Church ov MOO, http://members.nbci.com/ gecko23/moo/; commercial sites: e.g., www.beliefnet.com; www.ibelieve.com; www.Christianity.com; educational sites: Jeffrey Hadden's course site, http://cti.itc.virginia.edu/~jkh8x/soc257/ profiles.html#top; the Ontario Consultants on Religious Tolerance site, http://www. religioustolerance.org/1st_visi.htm; the Academic Info site, http://www.academicinfo. net/nrms.html; anti-cult sites: e.g., Steven Hassan's site, www.freedomofmind.com or The Watchman Fellowship, www.atachman.org/cat95.htm.

Complete Idiot's Guide to Religions Online (2000), Lauramaery Gold's *Mormons on the Internet, 2000–2001* (2000), and Gary Bunt's *Virtually Islamic: Computer-Mediated Communication and Cyber Islamic Environments* (2000). Perhaps we will be able to fashion a useful typology of the religious uses of the Internet. To this end, though, a great deal of basic descriptive work must be done. We need to learn about the nature, origins, operation, and developmental history of religion online and online religions (see e.g., Bedell 2000; Helland 2000a; Horsfall 2000; Mayer 2000; Dawson/Cowan 2004; Hojsgaard/Warburg 2004). This should involve the content analysis of sites, as well as surveying and interviewing the creators, moderators, and users of specific web sites, MUDS (multiple user "virtual" domains), newsgroups, listserves, and chat rooms. We need to develop a more precise profile of the users of online religious materials and opportunities. We need to identify who actually is using the net in this way (i.e., their age, ethnicity, sex, occupations, geographic locations, religious backgrounds, etc.). What are their habits, their motivations, and the consequences of their actions? Does "virtual religiosity" exist already? If so, how, why, who is using it, and to what effect?[3]

A new forum has been added, then, for the comparative study of religion. At least in principle such is the case. At this writing, however, the sociology of the Internet is an overwhelmingly "Western" undertaking, geared to the assessment largely of computer mediated communication in North America and Europe—the parts of the globe most comprehensively wired into the world wide web at this time. In September 2000, for example, Nielsen/NetRatings reported that the United States and Japan had the largest populations of Internet users (137 million and 26 million respectively). Britain ranked third with 19.4 million users, and there were 62.6 million users throughout the rest of Europe (especially in Germany and Italy). Almost half of all American households were linked to the net by late 2000, and about one in five European households, including Britain in the calculation (*Globe and Mail* 2000). Consequently, the primary frame of reference of the findings and arguments presented in this chapter is the advanced industrial nations of the West. That is where the research available has been done. But the net is spreading elsewhere rapidly (see e.g., Bunt 2000), and hopefully we will soon see studies of its impact in other social and cultural settings (e.g., India, China, and Africa). But even in the Western context, with the exception of a few good case studies and limited surveys (e.g., O'Leary 1996; Zaleski 1997; Lovheim/Linderman 1998;

---

3   Some basic and important data has been made available by three studies produced by the Pew Internet and American Life Project (www.pewinternet.org): "Cyber Faith: How Americans Pursue Religion Online" (Dec. 23, 2001) and "America's Online Pursuits: The Changing Picture of Who's Online and What They Do" (Dec. 22, 2003). The executive summary of the former study is reprinted in Dawson/Cowan 2004. As this chapter was going into print, "Faith Online" was released, April 7, 2004.

Schroeder et al. 1998; Dawson/Hennebry 1999; Urban 2000; Campbell 2001; Helland 2001; Laney 2001; Linderman/Lovheim 2001; Brasher 2001; Dawson/ Cowan 2004; Hojsgaard/Warburg 2004; Lovheim 2004; Helland 2004), much of the most rudimentary research has yet to be done. All the same, from anecdote and personal experience we know that the means to be religious online exist, that some experiments are happening, and that some people have begun to significantly integrate the Internet into their religious lives. In 2001, the Pew Internet and American Life Project reported that approximately three million Americans turned to the Internet each day to meet their spiritual and religious needs (www.pewinternet.org). That was up from two million people in 2000, and constitutes one in four Internet users in the United States, or approximately twenty eight million people. By 2004 a third survey reported that 64% of online Americans, nearly 82 million, had used the Internet for religious or spiritual purposes.

2. The Research Problems Posed by Religion Online

Two themes have dominated the research done to date on the sociological consequences of the Internet: its impact upon our shifting conceptions of personal identity and on alternative forms of community. In both cases the focus stems from the fact that the Internet has been seized upon and legitimated as a new forum for the expression of human freedom (see e.g., Barlow 1996). The Internet presents us with an intrinsically sociological problematic, since studies of computer-mediated sociality have tended to dwell on the classic issue of conceptualizing the relations between the individual and society. In this regard, cyberspace is often portrayed as a new frontier. The analogy conjures up images of seemingly limitless new possibilities, escape from established restrictions, and the exhilaration of plunging into a new kind of wilderness (e.g., Rheingold 1993; Healy 1997). If any of this often utopian rhetoric holds up to scrutiny, the cyber-frontier is likely to have a significant influence on the future of religion.

In most instances religious ideas and practices continue to provide the ultimate framework of meaning within which people pose questions of identity and community. But the link between the Internet and religion, through experiments in the formation of identity and community, is dialectical and not causal. Religions have always exercised a profound influence on people's conceptions of self and sense of community. But if changes in the material conditions of communication facilitate new experiences or ways of thinking about the self and social relations on a massive enough scale, then the religious framework of ultimate social legitimation will have to change. Of course the changes induced will be resisted by others. In other words, the question is: has the Internet introduced a significant new dimension to the process of world construction associated with religion (Berger 1967)? Has it done so intrinsically, as seems to be presumed by the peddlers of a soft technological determinism? Or is the Internet a force to be reckoned with because it is synergistically aligned with some larger patterns of social change? I suspect the latter suggestion is more plausible, but then we must consider the interpretive options for gaining a sense of the relevant patterns of change. To date two primary interpretive frameworks have been preferred: various French postmodernists' insights or Anthony Giddens' conception of the consequences of modernity (Giddens 1990, 1991). From the postmodernist view the Internet is accelerating the decentering of the self. It is conditioning people to living as multiple selves, freed from the traditional constraints of geographically bound communities. It is fostering a measure of anarchistic transcendence of the modern social order. From the point of view of those influenced by Giddens, these claims are exaggerated and misguided. The Internet is not contributing so much to the dissolution of the self or the modern social order. Rather it is facilitating the more complete development of the self as the focus of social life under conditions of intensified reflexivity, while continuing the very modern expansion of the range of our sense of community to the globe itself. Before saying more, however, let us consider the more mundane grounds for suspecting that the Internet could serve as a mighty engine of change in people's conceptions of self and community, whatever ultimate interpretive frame work is employed.

2.1 Transforming the Self in Cyberspace

The structure and the diversity of the modes of interaction available through the Internet are augmenting the social experiences of increasingly large numbers of people in Western societies in ways that are having a reflexive impact on their understandings of their own nature—as individuals and as human beings. The changes in question are in line with those precipitated by the move from a rural and pre-industrial economy to the urban environment of advanced capitalism. Social relations are becoming increasingly numerous and diverse in kind, while the subjectivity experienced and the preference for subjectivism is deepening, and daily existence is becoming ever more segmented and modular. From the isolated comfort of their own homes, offices, and cars people are being pulled into the world, while simultaneously being encouraged to plunge ever deeper into their inner most states of mind. The Internet as a medium tends to reiterate and extend this bipolar pattern of development.

Large numbers of people are now spending many hours a day in cyberspace, doing everything from e-mailing, to engaging in synchronous chat with relative strangers, to assuming a well-crafted fantastic role in an ongoing virtual world. In all cases, though with notably varying degrees, the communication effected is marked by some distinctive features of the Internet that users may seek to mute or take advantage of, but which no one can avoid altogether. Some of these features are: anonymity, multiplicity, deception, and disembodiment. In practice all these features are almost inextricably intertwined.

The Internet is the first mode of mass communication that encourages anonymity by both technical and social convention (Myers 1987; Reid 1995). With the right technical knowledge, all but the most adept user can always be identified. But postings to electronic bulletin boards, news groups, Relay Chat rooms, and MUDs (multiple user "virtual" domains) are normally only done under the guise of a chosen, and usually fictitious, "screen name." Moreover, the mode of communication is textual. As such it is limited and far more subject to the control of the participants. It is clear, from Internet ethnographies (e.g., Turkle 1995; Markham 1998), that this anonymity is part of the appeal of these spaces for social interaction. It permits and often seems even to induce participants to engage in more risky behavior than they would entertain in so-called "real life" (Witmer 1998). People will more readily and completely express their views and feelings, running the full gamut from anger to erotic obsession. They will adopt imaginative identities and explore hidden or simply unexplored facets of their own social lives, personalities, and minds. They may do this in multiple ways in different online contexts simultaneously or serially. In each instance, by not being themselves, as conventionally defined, a space is paradoxically created for self-disclosure and discovery. Gender-bending is one of the most interesting and commonly discussed instances of such behavior (see e.g., McRae 1997; Danet 1998; Kornbluth 1998; Markham 1998: 159–60; Waskul/ Douglass/Edgley 2000). So is the entire discourse on "disembodiment" engendered by the Internet. For those uncomfortable with their physical appearance or abilities, or simply resentful of the restrictions placed on how people judge one another by social conventions, the Internet is seductively liberating (e.g., Markham 1998: 57, 175). Paradoxically, for some the strictly textual expression of self online can seem more real and fulfilling than their physical self offline (e.g., Markham 1998: 202).

Accordingly, one of the best known students of the Internet, the psychologist Sherry Turkle, proposes that the Internet may serve a therapeutic function. It may offer individuals a "moratorium" from some of the most distressing features of their real life, "an outlet for [working] through personal issues in a productive way," and "a space for growth" (1995: 196, 244, 263; see Waskul/ Douglass/Edgley 2000: 387–88 as well). For while one may be hiding part of one's self from others, one is nonetheless engaged in dialogue with others. Every forum stands, as Turkle notes (1995: 11), as an invitation to join in a collaborative and quite unpredictable act of collective writing or performance. In just "lurking" on the edges of the ongoing dialogue of others, lonely or stigmatized souls may experience a needed sense of connection, perhaps even community with others. And unlike the passive viewer of a TV soap opera, they can choose to participate at any time, and in the way they wish.

At the same time, however, Turkle recognizes the dangers posed by the conventions of anonymity and playing with multiple identities. Participants may exploit the net equally well to deceive others and themselves, in witting and unwitting ways. The rough and tumble dialogue that characterizes so many chat rooms and listserves may well be a protective social response to the lack of the traditional foundations of trust on the Internet (like the signs we normally give-off and make during face-to-face interactions; see Goffman 1959). The Internet provides a greater opportunity for new kinds of conversations with the self through the medium of new kinds of conversations with others. But some users may employ the multiple dimensions of the Internet simply to escape that self in favor of repetitively indulging in some maladaptive behavior with impunity. As the explosion of sexual activity of all kinds on the net reveals, the Internet is quite indiscriminate and sometimes undesirably double-edged (e.g., Branwyn 1994; Dibbell 1994; Ehrenreich 1998). Many may celebrate the freedom from repressive social conventions afforded by the Internet, but few can deny the debased nature of much of the interaction offered, sexual or otherwise.

Either way, Turkle provocatively suggests, computer-mediated forms of communication have become new "objects-to-think-with" or "test-objects" (1995: 22, 185) for experimenting with "the constructions and reconstructions of self" (1995: 180). Taking her cue from the French postmodernists (e.g., Lacan, Foucault, Derrida, Deleuze and Guattari), she proposes that our increasing comfort with technologically mediated forms of social interaction, with the generation of multiple selves online, is slowly conditioning us to a more performative and decentered sense of self. As we cycle in and out of so-called "real" and "virtual" worlds, the set and unitary self of modernist thought, the true self within, is giving way to a more composite and constructed sense of personal identity. The distinction between real and virtual life begins to blur as we become "increasingly comfortable with substituting representations of reality for the real" and are "explicitly turning to computers for experiences that [we] hope will change [our] ways of thinking or will affect [our] social and emotional lives" (1995: 23–26). Reverting to the more extreme views of Jean Baudrillard, other commentators talk of "hyperreality" and the loss of any real referents in the endless play of signs, of representations of reality, that is cyberspace (e.g., Nunes 1995, 1997; Rheingold 1993: 297–300; Urban 2000).

In an interview Baudrillard was asked whether he thought the rise of the Internet posed "great risks." His reply is typically obscure and provocative (Baudrillard 1996):

> I do not see a doom-laden phenomenon there. ... I don't think that it is possible to find a politics of virtuality, a code of ethics of virtuality because virtuality virtualizes politics as well: there will be no politics of virtuality, because politics has become virtual; there will be no code of ethics for virtuality, because the code of ethics has become virtual, that is, there are no more references to a value system ... Virtuality retranscribes

everything in its space; in a way, human ends vanish into thin air … One communicates, but as far as what is said, one does not know what becomes of it. This will become so obvious that there will no longer even be any problems concerning liberty or identity … The media neutralizes everything …

There is a measure of truth in this intriguing exaggeration, but it will be a challenge to sift it out. The challenge must be met with reasoned analysis based on sound empirical research into peoples' experiences online.

Turkle's observations are based on a limited sample of interviews with early and heavy users of the Internet, and only a minority of the participants in her study fit some aspects of the postmodernist profile. They may display either a typically postmodernist cynicism towards rationalistic and instrumental standards of truth, or a willingness to eclectically combine and derive meaning from a pastiche of cultural sources, or a disregard for the differences between high and low (or pop) culture, or they may celebrate the seeming fragmentation of the self playfully in their social relations and conversation. But for the vast majority of Internet users the situation is much more mundane. In her more calculated and careful ethnography of life online, Annette Markham (1998) draws conclusions that tend to bring the high-flying postmodernist speculations about cyberspace down to earth.

First, Markham argues, people experience computer-mediated communication "along a continuum" (1998: 20; see 85 as well):

> For some, the Internet is simply a useful communication medium, a *tool*; for others, cyberspace is a *place* to go to be with others. For still others, online communication is integral to *being* and is inseparable from the performance of self, both online and offline.

For most users the Internet is the first, a mere tool, and the third option holds as yet for only an exceptional few.

Second, users do not concern themselves much with the "reality" of their virtual activities, even when intensely engaged in disembodied communications through imaginary bodies in fantastic places. The real life/virtual life distinction, broached so often in academic discussions of the Internet, is sidelined by the experience that *"everything that is experienced is real"* [sic]. Notions of "reality" are shifting with the spread of the Internet, but in ways still grounded in the experiences of embodied selves in ordinary life (see Dawson 2001a for further discussion).

Third, Markham concludes (Markham 1998: 20), life online is very much about the exercise of control, and not its loss:

> participants go online, or remain there, in part because in cyberspace the self has a high degree of perceived control. Some users enjoy the capacity to control the presentation and performance of self in online contexts. Others talk about their increased ability to control the conditions of interaction and to control the extent to which people online

have access to the self. For almost every participant, control is a significant and meaningful benefit of online communication.

Users may be drawn, by intent or tacitly, into attempting to transcend the
constraints of social life, and maybe even their physical beings, through the
construction of forms of cyber-sociality. But over and again, Markham discovered, users recognize that the "reality" of online life cannot be separated
from offline life. Online life always works in a feedback loop with offline life,
and the strong satisfaction Markham's users expressed with their online control
of the presentation of the self is more characteristic of a modern than a postmodern mindset. Some may experience a fragmenting of the self online, but
they understand this to be but a graphic and true representation of their offline
existence under conditions of modernity. Consider the comments of one of
Markham's participants (1998: 194; see 163 as well):

> When I first joined Echo [an Internet community], I was advised to be 'myself,' and I
> couldn't really figure out what on earth that was. Was I supposed to be a graduate
> student, a sex worker, a bisexual woman, a family cancer survivor, a person who suf-
> fered from depression, or what? In time, I have learned to 'be' all of those things online,
> but there is a time and a place for each of these manifestations of personality. ... I don't
> think I've ever met anyone who had 'one self.'

Peoples' experiences on the Internet are not significantly discontinuous with
their offline lives. Continuity is more the norm, and recognition of this fact is of
greater social significance than paying attention to the differences. As I have
argued elsewhere: "The innovative potential of cyberspace for social relations is
circumscribed, it would appear, by a strong public desire to establish continuity
between the experiences of on-line and off-line social relations (see Blanchard
and Horan 1998, Fox and Roberts 1999, Parks and Roberts 1998, Rheingold
1993)" (Dawson 2000: 35). The relevant continuity, moreover, is not so much
with some emergent postmodernist social order (whatever that may be) as with
the conditions of late, high, or radicalized modernity, as delineated by Anthony
Giddens (1990, 1991) and others (see Slevin 2000).

The pivotal feature of this social order, with regard to questions of personal
identity, is the institutionalization of reflexivity. The self and the larger social
order are constitutionally open to continual revision in the light of new
knowledge. This revision is not just an occasional occurrence or possibility, it is
a daily expectation, and it introduces a crucial measure of "manufactured uncertainty" (Giddens 1990) into the lives of modern individuals (see Dawson
2000: 45–48), something their predecessors were spared. As the traditional
social order fades in the face of the information age people are experiencing
mounting moral and practical ambiguity coping with the many choices to be
made, choices for which the consequences are increasingly problematic in
societies of massive functional interdependency. It is important to realize, then,
that the claims made by Markham's Internet users are not necessarily made in

playful abandonment of the modernist quest for individuality. Rather, they are indicative of the personal struggle with modernist reflexivity. The users are employing the Internet to ameliorate, maybe even deny, the real experience of plurality with its incumbent risks, by instrumentally accepting and asserting control over a multifaceted, but still essentially unitary sense of self. As Markham has cause repeatedly to lament, the users she met consistently displayed a surprisingly naive, nonrelational, unidirectional, and even solipsistic view of communication (1998: 155–56, 175, 209, 213–15). They spoke of their control over the textual manifestations of the self online with little cognizance that others might be doing the same, or that the fuller and less controllable interactions of so-called "flesh meets" (i.e., face-to-face interactions) "play an important role in the construction of their own subjectivity" (1998: 124). Their engagement with cyberspace is, in other words, simultaneously a promotion of and cultural response against the dilemmas of personal identity posed by the heightened reflexivity and uncertainty of modern life—one made uniquely possible, however, by the mediation of this particular technology with its greater transcendence of the restrictions of time, space, and social distinctions.

So what will happen when people turn to the net to express and amplify their religious life? To some extent by virtue of their mere exposure to the medium they will be drawn into the dialectical interplay of changing conceptions of self in the light of changing patterns and frameworks of social interaction. In other words, religious involvement in the Internet will likely accelerate the need for largely pre-modern religious ideologies, practices, and institutions to adapt to the demands of a more radically reflexive social world, as well as the use of other features of this same technology to resist or even unconsciously subvert the consequences of this same social imperative. If the diagnosis of Giddens and company is on target, religions are of necessity adapting to these new realities already. The Internet just magnifies the effects and provides a new and perhaps more potent mechanism of adaptation. As such, study of cyber-religiosity might provide a unique window onto these larger changes and their implications for all forms of religious life. This also means that religious users of the Internet can only choose to be cognizant of the possible consequences of their activities, and not to avoid them altogether. All of the identity work in question, however, happens through interaction with others, so let us turn to a consideration of communal life of cyberspace, before returning briefly to a broader discussion of religion, the Internet, and the processes of social and religious change.

2.2. Creating Communities in Cyberspace

If there can be true communities in cyberspace, then presumably there can be religions in cyberspace. The question under debate is whether communities do exist, or at least in what sense do they exist? The rise of the Internet was rapidly heralded for providing a new means of overcoming the alienating effects of modern life (e.g. Berger/Berger/Kellner 1974). Virtual associations could replace the loss of traditional neighborhoods and small personal work environments, counter the deleterious effects of increasing social and geographic mobility, and so on. What is more, the Internet facilitates the formation of whole new kinds of communities, free of such limiting factors as ethnic stereotyping, class distinctions, and differences in time as well as space. People can reach out to each other twenty-four hours a day, from almost anywhere in the world (e.g., Rheingold 1993). "Synchronously and asynchronously," as Dave Healy states (1997: 60), "the sun never sets on the virtual community."

But, then, the sun of communal bliss may never have really risen on the net. The substitution of computer-mediated communication for the face-to-face variety may be symptomatic of the triumph of modern alienation, not its circumvention. It is important to ask if "most so-called virtual communities [are not] too specialized, largely ideational in content, and too intermittent or transitory to evoke the sense of we-ness commonly associated with the word community" (Dawson 2000: 38). Virtual communities may be nothing more than pseudo-communities (e.g., McLaughlin/Osborne/Smith 1995; Slouka 1995; Lockhard 1997; Barlow 1998). Of particular concern in this regard is the impact of computer-mediated communication on dialogue with "the other." True sociality grows out of the dialectical interplay of self and other, and we tend to presume that greater exposure to real others induces a more sensitive, reflexive, and hence enduring capacity to form communities. But how much otherness does one really experience seated solitarily before a computer screen? On the one hand the Internet facilitates "boundary-breaking" interactions (Kinney 1995: 770). People can readily enter into conversations to which they would never be exposed in the normal course of events, with people from the most diverse cultures and sub-cultures. On the other hand, the technologically limited connection provided inevitably attenuates the experience, and our extraordinary ability to control these contacts may render them more solipsistic than we are willing to admit (Foster 1997; Lockhard 1997; Willson 1997; Markham 1998). Paradoxically, in line with the rest of modernity, the communal promise of the Internet hinges on "cellularization of the population by workstation" (Holmes 1997: 16).

Identifying the real possibilities or limitations of community life online will tell us much about the possibilities for religious life online as well. Regrettably, as Wellman and Guila (1999: 170) and DiMaggio et al. (2001: 319) lament, truly systematic studies of communal life in cyberspace have yet to be completed. We lack either detailed ethnographies of established communities or survey research into who is using the Internet in this way and how. All the same, there are several empirical studies available that indicate that real relationships are forming online, with real consequences for peoples' lives online and offline (e.g., Rheingold 1993; King 1994; Turkle 1995; Markham 1998; Parks/Roberts 1998; Blanchard/Horan 1998; Fox/Roberts 1999; Miller/Slater 2000; Kendall 2002). People are establishing lasting friendships, forming business partnerships, providing therapeutic support, and even getting married online. Of course, each of these relationships requires the introduction of some crucial offline contact. In fact the evidence suggests the online relationships will not become the kind of lasting and more broadly based interactions we associate with community unless they migrate offline, for periods of time at least.

At least some nascent religious communities exist online and a few direct studies have been undertaken of these social experiments. Davis (1995), O'Leary (1996), and Lovheim and Linderman (1998) have looked at the "technopagans," Schroeder, Heather and Lee (1998) examine a virtual Pentecostal group, Dawson and Hennebry (1999) discuss a postmodernist cyber-religion called The Church ov MOO, and Helland (2000) describes an online UFO religion. But these efforts are largely exploratory and fragmentary. Sustained and systematic work, lending itself to worthwhile comparative analyses, has yet to be undertaken (or at least published). (For a more detailed and recent analysis of these issues see Dawson 2004a.)

In dealing with religious groups care must be taken to consider an additional factor. There is no obvious reason why many of the traditional activities of religious organizations cannot be done on the Internet, from posting announcements, studying scriptures, delivering sermons and hearing confessions, to providing counselling. But can the experiential core of religion be evoked online? Can rituals be performed in such a way that the states of mind (ecstatic, solemn or otherwise) commonly associated with religious practices are induced? Are technologically mediated religious experiences possible, and if so, how? The research community awaits a proper phenomenological and semiotic analysis of the experience of religion as delivered through the radio, television, or the Internet. If religion cannot be mediated technologically, its role in future societies is going to be circumscribed in new and telling ways (see Dawson 2001b and 2004b for further discussion of this issue).

In the end there can be little doubt that some measure of true communal life has emerged at some times in cyberspace. The organized group life in question often arises almost accidentally or incidentally, in response to the personal crises of members of an online group (e.g., the sick child or suicide discussed by Rheingold 1993) or a grievous disruption of the unspoken norms of interaction online (e.g., the cyber-rape discussed by Dibbell 1994). The community created, moreover, is likely to be characterized by a moderate level of interaction and commitment with regard, in most cases, to a fairly specific set of concerns. But this is in line with long recognized principles of group formation and solidarity (e.g., Coser 1956; Sherif 1966), and, as Wellman and Guila (1999) argue, most of modern life is marked by social bonds of "intermediate strength" at best. The net will neither restore the idealized Gemeinschaft of Toennies (1957), nor reverse our daily experience of "the lonely crowd" (Riesman 1950) in busy urban environments. It will facilitate, however, the development of new, true, and often quite unusual personal relationships (e.g., Bruckman 1996; Parks/Roberts 1998; Markham 1998).

From a religious perspective this is a mixed blessing. The anonymity of cyberspace allows religious relationships to be focused squarely on the religious, and as such embodies the age-old religious ideal of fellowship. Consider the following comment made by an Internet user (Lyles 1998: 114):

> Unlike the church, when I am in cyberspace, nobody really knows, unless I tell them, whether I am black, white, red, yellow, or even male or female, whether I am writing from a hovel or a palatial estate.
>
> Nobody knows my educational background or lack of it, or even my age. That doesn't seem to matter to anybody and this is the way church ought to be. We are a true community of seekers.

This possibility is reinforced by the democratizing tendencies of the Internet. By accessing a broader social world, people are exposed to novel knowledge, people, and circumstances, and in ways that allow them to safely compare, assess, and debate claims made by rival authorities. They are empowered to more readily "bypass certain intermediaries or gatekeepers who once managed and limited their access to information and their channels of communication" (Slevin 2000: 177).

But is this communion of cybersouls a sound foundation for religion? It flies in the face of the decidedly more social realities of religious life as it has been known for centuries (Durkheim 1965). The key dialectic, then, reiterates itself: the price of universal "brotherhood" is the reduction of self and social interaction to written language, facilitated by the actual physical isolation (if not actual isolation) of individuals. How does one begin to do a meaningful cost-benefit analysis of this apparent consequence of this new communicative environment? One factor that must be taken into account is whether religious life even should be so closely identified any longer with the formation and maintenance of social or relatively large group identities. Or, as James Beckford has ingeniously proposed (1989), is it possible that in the late modern context of Western societies we are on our way to the reconfiguration of religion as a relatively free-floating "cultural resource," geared more exclusively to the demands of personal identity? At this point there are more questions than answers, but this suggestion is in line with Giddens' reading of the social conditions of late modernity (see Dawson 2003). The institutionalized reflexivity of modernity is most prominently reflected in the preoccupation with the construction of personal identities in an environment of heightened uncertainty about the choices that must be made to fashion the identity. In part this is because the local and traditional social order, the source of identity in the past, is being displaced by global influences and points of reference. Religion is coming adrift from its conventional social moorings, just as our identity constructing processes in general are, and the Internet technically offers one of the few forums for the reflexive construction of identity by means of the inter-penetration of highly personal and more or less global concerns, issues, and resources.

3. Cyber-Religion in the Context of Religious Change

Whatever cyberspace is doing to people's conceptions of self and community, the impact of the Internet on religion needs to be conceptualized in terms of emerging conceptions of religious change in advanced industrial societies (e.g., Cimino/Lattin 1998; Roof 1999; Lambert 1999). The evidence at hand suggests that there is a synergistic link between the changes detected in people's reli-gious preferences and the capabilities of computer-mediated communication. Here I can only allude to the possible changes I have in mind. But these changes are not confined to the experimental fringes of religious life. Rather there are important commonalities between the "lived experience" of modern individuals from both the right and the left of the religious spectrum, as exemplified by the continuities Phillip Lucas detected between the Pentecostal and the New Age movements (Lucas 1992). It is not coincidental that both the so-called traditionalists and modernists have found a comfortable home on the Internet.

Drawing on the exploratory work of many others, I have argued elsewhere (Dawson 1998: 138–44) that a new religious consciousness is emerging in the Western world. This consciousness is marked by six features, and at least five are convergent with the social implications of doing religion in cyberspace (see Dawson 2000 as well). Religious life is characterized increasingly by an strong individualist orientation, both in terms of an emphasis on the primacy of personal identity issues and a tendency to find the sacred within (rather than in a transcendent realm). In line with this development, the traditional emphasis on doctrine and belief is giving way to a greater stress on the experiential dimension of religious life as mediated by simple faith and the felt effects of ritual or meditation. This development reflects in turn, and serves to reinforce, a more pragmatic approach to the attribution of religious authority, and to the engagement of individuals in specific religious practices. Experiential criteria are playing a bigger role in both choosing and sustaining religious commit-ments. This pragmatism inclines people to a much more tolerant, even syncre-tistic, understanding of other religious traditions and spiritual systems, and to an active preference for more flexible and open-ended organizational structures and involvements.

The Internet itself is marked by an implicit culture of romantic individu-alism, like that which pervades the computer sub-culture in general (Barlow

1998; Herman/Sloop 1999). This culture of individualism is technologically re-inforced by the physical isolation of cyber-communicants. Religions mounted online cater to and legitimate this individualistic orientation. As Markham found, individual control is perhaps the single most common and appealing aspect of computer-mediated social interaction.

The playful, multivocal, and disembodied character of Internet life also supports this heightened individualism, with its attendant focus on self cre-ation and modification. Extreme reflexivity, the condition of modernity, is magnified and glorified by the opportunities and the intrinsic limitations of the medium. Its creative exercise can become a mode of quasi-spiritual quest in it-self (see Markham 1998).

Likewise, as Markham (1998) found in trying to track and define how users conceive reality and virtuality, the Internet encourages an increased preoccupa-tion with the immediate and the experiential. Participants in her study were not much interested in contemplating the trumpeted blurring of boundaries between the real and the unreal in cyberspace (see Dawson 2001a). They were content to assert, explicitly or implicitly, that all that is experienced is real, in a manner highly reminiscent of Wouter Hanegraaff's (1996) and Michael Brown's (1997) careful observations of the New Age movement and the channeling community in America. Sincere and strong experience is taken as a key deter-minant of truth.

Certainly at present the net itself is fostering an unprecedented fusion of religious horizons by virtue of the simple and voluminous juxtaposition of diverse religious views. A search launched for information about any religious term is likely to produce some unexpected or unconventional results, exposing straight Catholics to the wonders of Tibetan mysticism or vice versa. Quick and ready exposure to diversity is endemic to the Internet, and highly syncretistic new religions (e.g., forms of neo-Paganism or American Buddhism) are full participants in the mix. Likewise the delivery of religious services through the net, and the creation and operation of online religions consummately satisfies the growing preference for more flexible and open organizational expressions of religion.

As must be apparent, however, the study of the Internet is in its infancy, let alone the study of cyber-religiosity. Detailed case studies are required of every aspect of the presence of religion on the net as well as statistical surveys of religious uses of the new technology (see Dawson/Cowan 2004; Hojsgaard/Warburg 2004). In scrutinizing the first wave of academic literature, though, a number of simple but very important conclusions emerge. On the one hand, it is best to discount the more utopian claims made on behalf of the Internet. The net is best seen as a social forum in continuity with the rest of social life. On the other hand, in treating the net more mundanely care must be taken to duly appreciate the role the Internet will play in fostering social, and hence religious, change. In either case, the key is to contextualize the net (Slevin 2000), to recognize its dialectical interplay with other larger social forces and patterns of change. Of course the challenge this presents is formidable, and in the process one must recognize that the Internet is not a monolithic entity. In fact there are many Internets, or aspects and modes of computer-mediated communication, with different interfaces with the larger world. With due hermeneutic diligence we must seek to balance the analysis of specific cyber-subcultures and experiences with an understanding of the global social transformations unleashed by the information age (Castells 1996).

References

Barlow, John Parry (1996), A Cyberspace Independence Declaration. Online at the website http://www.eff.org/~barlow/Declaration-Final.html.

Baudrillard, Jean (1996), Cybersphere 9: Philosophy. Baudrillard on the New Technologies: An interview with Claude Thibaut. Retrieved from http://www.egs.edu/faculty/baudrillard/baudrillard-baudrillard-on-the-new-technologies.html.

Beckford, James A. (1989), *Religion in Advanced Industrial Society*. London: Unwin Hyman.

Bedell, Ken (2000), "Dispatches from the Electronic Frontier: Explorations of Mainline Protestant Use of the Internet," in: Jeffrey K. Hadden/Douglas Cowan, eds., *Religion on the Internet*. Religion and the Social Order, vol. 8. New York: JAI Press: 183–203.

Berger, Peter L. (1967), *The Sacred Canopy*. New York: Doubleday.

Berger, Peter L./Berger, Brigitte/Kellner, Hansfried (1974), *The Homeless Mind: Modernization and Consciousness*. New York: Vintage Books.

Blanchard, Anita/Horan, Tom (1998), "Virtual Communities and Social Capital," in: *Social Science Computer Review* 16 (3): 293–307.

Branwyn, G. (1994), "Compu-sex: Erotica for Cybernauts," in: Mark Dery, ed., *Flame Wars: The Discourse of Cyberculture*. Durham, N.C.: Duke University Press: 779–91.

Brasher, Brenda (2001), *Give Me That Online Religion*. San Francisco: Jossey-Bass.

Bruckman, A.S. (1996), "Gender-swapping on the Internet," in: High Noon on the Electronic Frontier: Conceptual Issues in Cyberspace, ed. by P. Ludlow. Cambridge, Mass.: MIT Press: 317-25.

Bunt, Gary (2000), *Virtually Islamic: Computer-Mediated Communication and Cyber Islamic Environments*. Cardiff: University of Wales Press.

Campbell, Heidi (2001), *Connecting to the Sacred Network: A Look at Spiritual Communities within the Online Context*. Paper presented to the Religious Encounters in Digital Networks conference, University of Copenhagen, Nov. 1.

Castells, Manuel (1996), *The Rise of the Network Society*. Oxford: Blackwell.

Cimino, Richard/Lattin, Don (1998), *Shopping for Faith: American Religion in the New Millennium*. San Francisco, Calif.: Jossey-Bass.

Coser, Lewis (1956), *The Functions of Social Conflict*. New York: The Free Press.

Danet, B. (1998), "Text as Mask: Gender, Play, and Performance on the Internet," in: Steven G. Jones, ed., *Cybersociety 2.0: Revisiting Computer-Mediated Communication and Community*. Thousand Oaks, Calif.: Sage: 129–58.

Davis, Erik (1995), Technopagans: May the Astral Plane be Reborn in Cyberspace. *Wired*. Retrieved from: www.wired.com:80/wired/archives/3.07/technopagans_pr. html.

Dawson, Lorne L. (1998), "Anti-Modernism, Modernism, and Postmodernism: Struggling with the Cultural Significance of New Religious Movements," in: *Sociology of Religion* 59 (2): 131–56.

— (2000), "Researching Religion in Cyberspace: Issues and Strategies," in: Jeffrey K. Hadden/Douglas Cowan, eds., *Religion on the Internet*. Religion and the Social Order, vol. 8. New York: JAI Press: 25–54.

— (2001a), Doing Religion in Cyberspace: The Promise and the Perils. *The Council of Societies for the Study of Religion Bulletin* 30 (1): 3–9.

— (2001b), The Mediation of Religious Experience in Cyberspace: A Preliminary Analysis. Keynote Address delivered to the Religious Encounters in Digital Networks conference, University of Copenhagen, Nov. 1.

— (2003), "The Socio-Cultural Significance of Modern New Religious Movements," in: James R. Lewis, ed., *Oxford Handbook of New Religious Movements*. New York: Oxford University Press: 68–98.

— (2004a), "Religion and the Quest for Virtual Community," in: Lorne L. Dawson/ Douglas E. Cowan, eds., *Religion Online: Finding Faith on the Internet*. New York: Routledge: 75–89.

— (2004b), "The Mediation of Religious Experience in Cyberspace," in: Morten Hojsgaard/Margit Warburg, eds., *Religion in Cyberspace*. London: Routledge.

Dawson, Lorne L./Cowan, Douglas E., eds. (2004), *Religion Online: Finding Faith on the Internet*. New York: Routledge.

Dawson, Lorne L./Hennebry, Jenna (1999), "New Religions and the Internet: Recruiting in a New Public Space," in: *Journal of Contemporary Religion* 14 (1): 17–39.

Dibbell, Julian (1994), A Rape in Cyberspace: Or, How an Evil Clown, a Haitian Trickster Spirit, Two Wizards, and a Cast of Dozens Turned a Database into a Society," in: Mark Dery, ed., *Flame Wars: The Discourse of Cyberculture*. Durham, N.C.: Duke University Press: 237–61.

DiMaggio, Paul/Hargittai, Eszter/Neuman, W. Russell/Robinson, John P. (2001), "Social Implications of the Internet," in: *Annual Review of Sociology* 27: 307–36.

Durkheim, Emile (1965), *The Elementary Forms of Religious Life*. Translated by Joseph Ward Swain. New York: The Free Press.

Ehrenreich, Barbara (1998), "Put Your Pants on, Demonboy," in: Richard Holeton, ed., *Composing Cyberspace: Identity, Community and Knowledge in the Electronic Age*. New York: McGraw-Hill: 80–82.

Foster, Derek (1997), "Community and Identity in the Electronic Village," in: David Porter , ed, *Internet Culture*. New York: Routledge: 23–37.

Fox, N./Roberts, C. (1999), "Gps in Cyberspace: The Sociology of a 'Virtual Community.'" in: *The Sociological Review* 47 (4): 643–71.

Giddens, Anthony (1990), *The Consequences of Modernity*. Cambridge: Polity Press.

— (1991), *Modernity and Self-Identity*. Standford, Calif.: Stanford University Press.

Globe and Mail (2000), "U.S., Japan Top Web Populations." September 14, 2000: T2.

Goffman, Erving.(1959), *The Presentation of Self in Everyday Life*. New York: Doubleday.

Gold, Lauramaery (1999), *Mormons on the Internet, 2000–2001*. New York: Random House.

Healy, Dave (1997), "Cyberspace and Place: The Internet as Middle Landscape on the Electronic Frontier," in: David Porter, ed., *Internet Culture*. New York: Routledge: 55–68.

Helland, Christopher (2000a), "On-line Religion/Religion On-line and Virtual Com-munitas," in: Jeffrey K. Hadden/Douglas E. Cowan, eds., *Religion on the Internet*. Religion and the Social Order, vol. 8. New York: JAI Press: 205–24.

Helland, Chris (2000b), "Groundcrew/Plantary Activation Organization," in: James R. Lewis, ed., *Encyclopedia of UFO Folklore and Popular Culture*. Santa Barbara, Calif.: ABC-Clio Pub.

— (2001), "The Syncretic Inducement of Online-Religion: Charting the Paths of Religious Participation on the Web," Paper presented to the Religious Encounters in Digital Networks conference, University of Copenhagen, Nov. 1.

— (2004), *Religion on the Internet: A Sociological Inquiry into Participation and Community Online*. Unpublished doctoral dissertation, University of Toronto.

Hojsgaard, Morten/Warburg, Margit (2004), *Religion and Cyberspace*. London: Rout-ledge.

Holmes, David (1997) "Introduction: Virtual Politics—Identity and Community in Cyberspace," in: David Holmes, ed., *Virtual Politics: Identity and Community in Cyberspace*. London: Sage: 1–25.

Horsfall, Sara (2000), "How Religious Organization Use the Internet: A Preliminary Inquiry," in: Jeffrey K. Hadden/Douglas E. Cowan, eds., *Religion on the Internet: Research Prospects and Promises*. New York: JAI Press: 153–82.

Kendall, Lori (2002), *Hanging Out in the Virtual Pub: Masculinities and Relationships Online*. Berkeley, Calif.: University of California Press.

Kinney, J. (1995), "Net Worth? Religion, Cyberspace, and the Future," in: *Futures* 27 (7): 763–76.

Kornbluth, Jesse (1998), "{you make me feel like} A Virtual Woman," in: Richard Holeton, ed., *Composing Cyberspace: Identity, Community and Knowledge in the Electronic Age*. New York: McGraw-Hill: 76–79.

Lambert, Yves (1999), "Secularization or New Religious Paradigms?," in: *Sociology of Religion* 60 (3): 303–33.

Laney Michael J. (2001), "Christian Web Usage: Motives and Desires," Paper presented to the Religious Encounters in Digital Networks conference, University of Copen-hagen, Nov. 2.

Lawrence, Bruce B. (2000), *The Complete Idiot's Guide to Religions Online*. Indianapolis, Ind.: Alpha Books.

Linderman, Alf G./Lovheim, Mia (2001), "Young People, Religious Identity and Computer-Mediated Communication: Where Do We Go from Here?," Paper pre-sented to the Religious Encounters in Digital Networks conference, University of Copenhagen, Nov. 2.

Lockhart, Joseph (1997), "Progressive Poltics, Electronic Individualism and the Myth of Virtual Community," in: David Porter, ed., *Internet Culture*. New York: Routledge: 219–31.

Lovheim, Mia (2004), *Intersecting Identities: Young People, Religion, and Interaction on the Internet*. Unpublished doctoral dissertation, Uppsala University.

Lovheim, Mia/Linderman, Alf (1998), "Internet – a Site for Religious Identity Formation and Religious Communities?," Paper presented to Society for the Scientific Study of Religion, Montreal, Canada.

Lucas, Phillip C. (1992), "The New Age Movement and the Pentecostal/Charismatic Re-vival: Distinct yet Parallel Phases of a Fourth Great Awakening?," in: James R.

Lewis/J. Gordon Melton, eds., *Perspectives on the New Age*. Albany, N.Y.: State University of New York Press: 189–211.

Markham, Annette N. (1998), *Life Online: Researching Real Experience in Virtual Space*. Walnut Creek, Calif.: AltaMira Press.

Mayer, Jean-Francois (2000), "Religious Movements and the Internet: The New Frontier of Cult Controversies," in: Jeffrey K. Hadden/Douglas E. Cowan, eds., *Religion on the Internet: Research Prospects and Promises*. New York: JAI Press: 249–76.

McLaughlin, M.L./Osborne, K.K./Smith, C.B. (1995), "Standards of Conduct on Usenet," in: Steven G. Jones, ed., *Cybersociety: Computer-Mediated Communication and Community*. Thousand Oaks, Calif.: Sage: 90–111.

McLuhan, Marshall (1965), *Understanding Media*. New York: McGraw-Hill.

McRae, Susan (1997), "Flesh Made Word: Sex, Text, and Virtual Body," in: David Porter, ed., *Internet Culture*. New York: Routledge: 73–86.

Myers, D. (1987), "'Anonymity is Part of the Magic': Individual Manipulation of Computer-Mediated Communication Contexts," in: *Qualitative Sociology* 19 (3): 251–66.

Nunes, Mark (1995), "Jean Baudrillard in Cyberspace: Internet, Virtuality, and Postmodernity," in: *Style* 29: 314–27.

—— (1997), "What Space Is Cyberspace? The Internet and Virtuality," in: David Holmes, ed., *Virtual Politics: Identity and Community in Cyberspace*. London: Sage: 163–78.

O'Leary, Stephen D. (1996), "Cyberspace as Sacred Space: Communicating Religion on Computer Networks," in: *Journal of the American Academy of Religion* 64 (4): 781–808.

Ong, Walter J. (1982), *Orality and Literacy: The Technologizing of the Word*. New York: Routledge.

Parks, Malcolm R./Roberts, Lynne D. (1998), "'Making MOOsic': The Development of Personal Relationships On Line and a Comparison to their Off-Line Counterparts," in: *Journal of Social and Personal Relationships* 15 (4): 517–37.

Reid, Elizabeth (1995), "Virtual Worlds: Culture and Imagination," in: Steven G. Jones, ed., *Cybersociety: Computer-Mediated Communication and Community*. Thousand Oaks, Calif.: Sage: 164–83.

Rheingold, Howard (1993), *The Virtual Community: Homesteading on the Electronic Frontier*. New York: Addison-Wesley.

Roof, Wade Clark (1999), *Spiritual Marketplace: Baby Boomers and the Remaking of American Religion*. Princeton, N.J.: Princeton University Press.

Schroeder, Ralph/Heather, Noel/Lee, Raymond M. (1998), "The Sacred and the Virtual: Religion in Multi-User Virtual Reality," in: *Journal of Computer Mediated Communication* 4 (2). Retrieved from http://www.ascusc.org/jcmc/vol4/issue2/schroeder.html.

Sherif, Muzafer (1966), *In Common Predicament*. Boston, Mass.: Houghton Mifflin.

Slevin, James (2000), *The Internet and Society*. Cambridge: Polity Press.

Slouka, M. (1995), *War of the Worlds: Cyberspace and the High-Tech Assault on Reality*. New York: Basic Books.

Turkle, Sherry (1995), *Life on the Screen: Identity in the Age of the Internet*. New York: Simon and Schuster.

Urban, Hugh B. (2000), "The Devil at Heaven's Gate: Rethinking the Study of Religion in the Age of Cyber-space," in: *Nova Religio* 3 (2): 268–302.

Waskul, Dennis/Douglass, Mark/Edgley, Charles (2000), "Cybersex: Outercourse and the Enselfment of the Body," in: *Symbolic Interaction* 23 (4): 375–97.

Wellman, Barry/Guila, Milena (1999), "Virtual Communities as Communities: Net Surfer Don't Ride Alone," in: Marc A. Smith/Peter Kollock, eds., *Communities in Cyperspace*. New York: Routledge: 167–94.

Wellman, Barry/Haythronthwaite, Caroline, eds. (2002), *The Internet in Everyday Life*. Oxford: Blackwell.

Willson, Michele (1997), "Community in the Abstract: A Political and Ethical Dilemma?," in: David Holmes, ed., *Virtual Politics: Identity and Community in Cyberspace*. London: Sage: 145–62.

Witmer, Diane (1998), "Practicing Safe Computing: Why People Engage in Risky Computer-Mediated Communication," in: Fay Sudweeks/Margaret McLaughlin/Sheizaf Rafaeli, eds., *Network and Netplay: Virtual Groups on the Internet*. Cambridge, Mass.: MIT Press: 127–46.

Zaleski, Jeffrey (1997), *The Soul of Cyberspace*. San Francisco, Calif.: HarperCollins.

New Approaches to the Study of New Religions in North America and Europe

by

Jean-François Mayer

Foreword

While some concepts in the field of religious studies have already a long history, "new religions" have only recently emerged as a specific area of research. Consequently, it is certainly premature to want to distinguish between "old" and "new" approaches. However, there are two elements which should be kept in mind and may give to such an undertaking some legitimacy:

1. As we will see in this article, some definitions of the "new religious movements" tend to include some older "new religions" as well, i.e. groups which would usually have been labeled as "sects" by most scholars a few decades ago. One could emphasize the novelty of the current research efforts on new religions, but it is more advisable to understand how it has also built upon previous efforts to study religious sects and cannot be disconnected from that ancestry.

2. Research on new religions concentrates by definition upon a field which changes rapidly, and those rapid changes in the phenomena under study do certainly also have an impact upon research itself. It requires adjustments, revisions of some original theories—and new approaches. Unpredictable developments as well as the increasing opportunities for networking of scholars active in that field are bound to affect the ways research is being conducted.

Consequently, before describing the current approaches in the study of new religions in the Western world, this article will briefly examine the roots of current research work as well as the still unsolved problem of a definition of expressions like "new religions" or "new religious movements". Due to the lack of attention given to that problem, there is no current widely accepted definition, which means that two scholars studying new religions may actually have quite different ranges of groups in mind. This lack of definitional clarity is the main difficulty for writing an article like this and constitutes a potential source of misunderstanding for scholarly discussion as well.

Finally, as some other contemporary religious developments, new religions have also become an issue of public debate. Since academic research in a hot field cannot remain insulated, our analysis will have to take into account the wider social context too, and the way it has already affected or may affect scholarly pursuits.

1. What Is a "New Religion"?

At some identifiable point in history, mainline religious traditions such as Buddhism, Christianity or Islam have all been new religions. The emergence of distinctive religious beliefs and of organizations formed around those beliefs is nothing new. However, the sheer proliferation of religious groups today thanks to religious freedom and individualization of religious options as well as the opportunities offered by a globalized world (especially fast communications and means of transportation) have created a context that is unprecedented.

1.1. Definitions Remain Mostly Vague or General

When one reads works by a number of the leading academic experts who have studied new religious movements (NRMs), it soon becomes obvious that little space in most of their publications is devoted to the problem of defining what new religions or NRMs are. Bryan Wilson accurately observed in the early 1980s that "new religious movements are a phenomenon that taxes our existing conceptual apparatus" (Wilson 1982: 17). Neither the concept of *sect* nor the concept of *cult* seemed to be adequate. Wilson insisted that their newness should be seen in the context of an already existing tradition, since those movements supposedly offered something unavailable in that tradition. Well aware that NRMs were not limited to the Western world, but should be seen as a global phenomenon, Wilson prefaced a collection of essays suggesting several features which could be seen as characteristic of such movements in the West, among them: exotic provenance, new cultural lifestyle, high level of engagement, charismatic leadership, predominantly young and well-educated membership, emergence since the late 1960s (Wilson 1981: V). This indicated a clear focus at that time upon those movements originally thought to be associated with the counter-culture and (more widely) with the juvenile aspirations of the 1960s. This was a time when a German Lutheran minister could successfully launch in the German debate the expression of "youth religions" (*Jugendreligionen*) for qualifying such groups (Haack 1979). Such descriptions are however falling out of use and are no longer appropriate as young members of older NRMs grow older and new generations of NRMs continue to appear at a fast pace despite the changes in the social context.

However, our definitions of NRMs still remain—at least to some extent—marked by that original discussion. James Beckford rightly remarked that it was the emergence of a number of groups at the same time, in the 1960s and 1970s, which attracted the attention of scholarly observers (as well as of the wider public, but for partly different reasons). The perception would not have been the same if they had not appeared simultaneously, and it makes little sense to refer to one specific group as a NRM "in isolation from the wider phenomenon": "For it refers to them collectively—not separately" (Beckford 1985: 14).

During the 1980s and 1990s, one cannot say that the discussion has progressed much toward a more elaborate definition—perhaps because such a need is not really felt among scholars studying those groups. Eileen Barker suggest that "we can define new religions as groups or movements that are new in so far they *have become visible in the West in their present form since the Second World War*" (Barker 1998: 15). According to her, despite the dangers involved in any generalization, seven characteristics of these NRMs can be identified: small size, atypical representation of population (predominance of young people), first-generation membership, charismatic leaders, new belief systems, them vs. us divide, external hostility. But, she hastens to clarify, those characteristics are bound to change rapidly, and we are already able to witness changes on all seven points in a number of movements (Barker 1995). Perhaps, after all, "NRM" would be better understood as a description of a transitory status.

If we see NRMs as a global phenomenon, as an expression of unprecedented opportunities for religious creativity to flourish worldwide, we have also to consider NRMs from a much wider perspective, with manifestations which can be quite diverse. We should certainly not forget that expressions like "new religions" were used outside of the Western context even before most sociologists working on the European or American field paid attention to their burgeoning in their own culture. Missionaries paid attention to new movements emerging among those they were trying to convert, and mentions of new movements are not uncommon in some missionary periodicals. One of the first serious overviews of modern religious movements in India was produced by a YMCA official, who interpreted them as being actually more a revival of traditional religions (Farqhar 1915). Anthropologists observed movements which appeared in the most diverse colonial contexts, from Africa to the Pacific, and the concept of "new religions" actually appeared in an article published in 1913 (Chamberlain 1913). Such "movements of the oppressed" were seen as a direct result of a contacts between the native culture and the representatives of the intrusive culture; millenarian dimensions would be dominant in such groups. Some observers have attempted to delineate differences as well as similarities between those "two kinds of new religious movements" (Turner 1989). Some scholars working in non-Western cultural contexts have suggested to use the general category of NRMs for covering "the whole variety of collective (and distinctly religious) activities which amount to serious departures from pre-existent traditions or traditionalisms" over the last two centuries, whether in the West or in other places of the world (Loeliger/Trompf 1985: XI).

The expression of "new religions" had already a tradition of use in Japan, where it had become popular with the media after World War II for describing a wide variety of movements. There has been a great deal of research conducted on Japanese new religions, by Japanese as well as by foreign scholars (Laube 1995). Movements born over the last two centuries, or at least since the second half of the nineteenth century, are usually considered as "new religions." However, in a book published in 1957 on Tenrikyo (founded in 1838), a Roman Catholic scholar considered it as "a debatable point" if that movement should be described as a new religion, if only because it had already existed for many decades (Straelen 1957: 16). The fact that more recent generations of new religions are described today in Japan as "new new religions," for lack of a better distinction, also illustrates some of the difficulties inherent in the use of such an expression.

1.2. Sects, Cults, New Religions

While the expressions of "new religions" or NRMs may seem to emphasize the discontinuity between previously existing religious types and emergent groups, one should be aware that research on NRMs has never really been disconnected from the interest for religious non-conformity in general. In his famous book on religious sects, Bryan Wilson included some groups that would be considered as NRMs by the standards of a restrictive definition, and he applied his typology to those groups (Wilson 1970). Even if Wilson clearly emphasizes the differences between sects and new generations of religious movements, it is certainly not by chance that the same scholar studied both phenomena—and there is nothing strange in it, since they all represent groups perceived as marginal in relation to a religious mainstream. Similarly, another important figure of Western research on NRMs, Gordon Melton, began with an interest in the "smaller religions in America" in general (Melton 1995). His handbook of cults in America includes "the established cults" (from Christian Science and Mormons to Theosophy) and "the newer cults" (from Scientology to Krishna devotees and Neo-Paganism) (Melton 1992). He is not alone: an informative collection of essays gathers an even wider range of groups under the neutral heading of "alternative religions" (Miller 1995).

It must also be clearly said that the religious movements of the 1960s did not appear *ex nihilo* and that they were at least to some extent the expression of older trends; even if the movements were new, historians could identify some of their ancestors in the West (Ellwood 1979). While the expression "new religions" came in use after the publication of a book with that title by Jacob Needleman (1970), the older word *cult* was not abandoned immediately. Whether domestic or imported, cults "do not have prior tie [sic] with another established religious body in the society in question," which makes them different from sects (Stark/Bainbridge 1985: 25). The description fitted well most groups described as NRMs, even if research conducted in the 1970s still sometimes gave a prominent place to groups connected with Christian origins: for instance, an issue of the quarterly *Social Compass* devoted in 1974 to "New Religious Movements in the U.S.A." featured Jesus People, Pentecostals and Charismatics—unlikely to be cases of NRMs which would come spontaneously to the minds of most scholars today.

Due to their precise technical meaning in sociology of religion, words such as *sect* and *cults* are likely to remain in use in scholarly discussion. However, one finds them increasingly put between quotation marks. "Sociologists of religion have generally preferred the designation new religious movements (NRMs) to the concepts cults and sects for the very reason that the former does not carry negative connotations that are culturally ascribed to the latter." (Bromley/Hadden 1993: 7). Actually, some scholars have strongly recommended that "the term 'cult' should be severely limited in scholarly and other writings about religious groups" due to its negative connotations in the popular mind (Richardson 1993). Scholars advocating the avoidance of the word *cult* (sometimes to the extent of seeing it as "probably not salvageable") suggest that either other terms should be used or that those groups should more adequately be examined within the category of "new social movements" (Dillon/Richardson 1994).

Those views are not unanimously shared by scholars observing contemporary religious movements. Italian sociologist Enzo Pace has for instance advocated that, due to its long tradition, the word *sect* (which has in Latin languages negative connotations equivalent to those associated with *cult* in English) should continue to be used, and he applies it also to groups usually designated as NRMs not associated with the dominant religious traditions in the West (1997). But other scholars tend to go rather exactly into the opposite direction, using NRMs not only for emergent religions (as Ellwood suggested to call them), but also for describing the older sects, for instance those born during the nineteenth century.

This ongoing debate reflects at the same time the uncertainties surrounding the definition of "new religions" or NRMs, i.e. an academic debate, and concerns of a more "political" nature related to the heated controversies which have taken and are taking place in several Western countries around minor religious groups. In the same way the word *cult* has tended to be replaced by *NRM*, it cannot be ruled out that the latter will be superseded sooner or later by other expressions too. Considering the vagueness of definitions and the insatisfactions of many researchers with that expression, this seems even likely. But if such a development takes place, the inheritance of older terms such as "sects" and "cults" will still remain important in the discussion and continue to affect new theoretical elaborations.

1.3. New Religions or New Religious Movements?

However, especially from the perspective of history of religions, the emphasis on the newness of modern religious movements draws the attention to the phenomenon of religious creativity and also of differentiation between an emergent tradition and the preexisting tradition from which it has broken or drawn. Some historians of religion have suggested that the indistinct and inter-changeable use of "new religions" and "NRMs" was not appropriate. Many groups are not new religions, but new movements within a religious tradition which they recognize as their own. Some NRMs, however, may be the embryo of new, independent religious traditions, and not just new sub-sections within an already existing tradition (Mayer 1997: 463–67).

This is not unknown to history of religions, although it has rarely been as fully developed as it might be. In an article originally published in 1979, Kurt Rudolph had observed that some sects could develop into new religions, usually through a process of syncretism evolving into a new, original religious composition, giving the Bahá'í faith and the Vietnamese Cao Dai religion as examples of the contemporary creation of new religions (Rudolph 1992: 234). From this perspective, some sects could evolve into new religions.

It is not surprising that research on such issues has especially paid attention to syncretistic phenomena, as an obvious potential source for new, independent traditions. Beside those groups which could be understood in some sense as movements of revitalization of an already existing tradition or groups arising out of a crisis, there have also been what a researcher attempted to describe as "trans-traditional" new movements with universal claims (Colpe 1975: 487–95). Research on this line was later pursued by Johann Figl, who paid special attention to those universalist, inclusivist, syncretistic groups, which claim to reach what is supposed to be at the core of all religions; according to Figl's ana-lysis, this attempt to integrate deliberately all major religions—thereby actually relativizing each of them—constitutes a distinctive feature of such movements and at the same time poses a real challenge to traditional religions. Compared to classical religions, continues Figl, they are new in that they promote the religious experience of a teaching aiming at the unity of religions (Figl 1993: 183–84).

Reviewing publications by German historians of religion in the 1970s, Giovanni Filoramo remarked that it could be useful to pursue on the way opened by Günter Lanczkowski (1974) and to distinguish more accurately between NRMs and those few, but important movements which succeed in creating new and autonomous traditions (Filoramo 1979: 452). Strangely, research on this specific issue has not much progressed since, despite the obvious interest of such a perspective of the understanding of the emergence and differentiation of a new religious group, with the light which it could throw upon classical religions. Perhaps this is understandable due to the fact that many scholars interested in NRMs have more a sociological than an historical perspective—and for sociologists, a distinction between new religions and NRMs seems to be of little use and little interest.

Another and more fundamental problem would be to define theologically neutral characteristics for these groups. We have suggested taking into account factors such as the status of different sacred books in a group, the organizational pattern, and the distinctive ritual practices, amongst others, but this is still in need of refinement (Mayer 2004).

Perhaps, however, for most research issues, the adjective "new" should not be considered as being especially important. Its use may have led to misunderstandings assuming that this was a category with common characteristics—it is not, except for the (relative) novelty of the term. William Bainbridge suggests keeping the classical terms of *church*, *sect* and *cult*, and to speak simply of *religious movements* (without an adjective) for dealing with that infinite variety of groups attempting "to cause or prevent change in a religious organization or in religious aspects of life" (1997: 3). Bainbridge concludes that "religion will constantly renew itself through religious movements, indefinitely into the far-distant future" (1997: 395).

1.4. Taking into Account the Various Perspectives

Whatever the choices as well as distinctions made amongst terms, the problem remains to decide if "new" should be understood only in a chronological sense or if it should involve some significant departure from previous traditions. For historians of religions, movements which are less than 200 years old obviously remain still young and "new." Accordingly, in an historical perspective, expressions like NRMs may actually and legitimately incorporate a wide range of groups. In addition, those movements were born in the context of the modern world, and this may also produce features that appear novel, but on the other hand it is true that older religions have to adjust to those same circumstances as well.

It is not the purpose of this introduction on approaches to the study of new religions to argue either for a wide or restrictive definition for them. However, such choices cannot entirely be avoided, since it is necessary for deciding about what to include or not in this overview. Consequently, we will try to concentrate here upon those groups which have been understood as NRMs by most scholars, but taking into account their historical roots, which sometimes

predate the second half of the twentieth century. Basically, we will deal primarily with movements not connected with the mainline, classical religious
traditions of the West. However, we will not entirely exclude older movements
in the West (usually derived from Christianity), especially on those issues
which lead scholars to deal with several generations of movements. Moreover,
we will also try to take into account the issue of innovation itself, which may be
an important characteristic of older movements as well. This means that our
examination of various approaches and trends in recent research will not limit
itself to one of the definitions of new religions and NRMs.

2. Understanding New Religions

According to James Beckford, "[t]he relatively abrupt arrival of numerous new
religious movements … in the 1970s also sparked off one of the largest reorien-
tations of the post-war sociology of religion" (Beckford 1990: 53). It seemed to
be such an unexpected development in the eyes of many scholars—which
rather proves how much scholars can also be influenced by the changing
moods and fashions of their intellectual environment, and this must also teach
us caution before coming to hasty interpretations of contemporary religious
movements and their possible meaning. The appearance and development of
those movements has led to the production of a considerable amount of popular as well as scholarly literature over the past thirty years, and the yearly
production has been constantly growing. While it seemed still possible to keep
informed about most of the scholarly production until the early 1980s, this is no
longer an attainable goal today. This huge production is not confined to North
America or to English-speaking countries; a bibliography on NRMs in Western
Europe published in 1997 listed more than 1,800 entries, many of them in other
languages (Arweck/Clarke 1997).

2.1. General Works and Monographs

2.1.1. Surveys of New Religions

Many of the books which were produced on NRMs were very valuable
monographs of one specific movement or research works providing an examination of some specific topic based upon a limited sample of groups. But there
is obviously also a need for overviews of the variety of NRMs in encyclopedic
form. Due to the nearly unlimited diversity of groups across national and
cultural borders, not to mention the ever changing landscape which they represent, any attempt to produce such a picture at an international level would be
quite a difficult task and would probably have to limit itself to a representative

selection of groups. But it is not impossible to produce reasonably complete encyclopedic works on NRMs at the scale of a country or of a region.

One of the best examples of an encyclopedic work on religious groups (including NRMs) is the impressive volume produced by Gordon Melton on religious bodies in the USA, which has been constantly updated and improved throughout several editions (Melton 1999). Based upon decades of research, it comes probably closest to what the ideal national dictionary of religious groups should be, complete with descriptions and addresses, although its author is well aware that there are dozens of additional groups escaping his constant attention. There are few other equivalent attempts, although the more modest dictionary of religious bodies in the German-speaking countries of Europe produced by Reformed minister Oswald Eggenberger (1994) has proved quite useful too. It has been continued by a collective of authors, in the same format, but in a slightly different tone (Schmid/Schmid 2003). One could imagine that the proliferation of religious movements would act as a deterrent to those wishing to engage into similar pursuits, but this has not been the case. Melton himself has been trying actively in recent years to promote the idea of developing directories (and possibly similar encyclopedias at a further stage) for other areas of the world. As one example, the Center for Studies on New Religions (CESNUR) has compiled a well-researched encyclopedia of religious bodies in Italy (Introvigne et al. 2001) . At a more limited geographical level, a detailed and well-informed, 600 page long survey of the history, beliefs, organization and current situation of all religious groups (old or new) in the Swiss canton of Basel has been published and is being regularly kept up to date on the Internet (Baumann 2000). Since, there have been several other, similar undertakings on the local situation in Swiss or German cities. It is worth observing here that most of those remarkable attempts, even when they involve several researchers, derive primarily from the vision and dedication of one individual. This says a great deal about the strong motivation and fascination for the subject that can exist in those who enter that field. All the works listed above attempt to include all religious bodies in those countries or areas, which makes the task even a more formidable one, as NRMs are only part of the picture; treatment of other religious groups still predominate. There have been a few books trying to provide a general picture of NRMs in one country or area. For example, an historical and sociological study on NRMs in Switzerland, conducted in the late 1980s, is probably what comes closest to it for any Western country. It is not organized in a dictionary form, but this allows for a presentation of the wider context into which specific movements emerged (Mayer 1993). It can only be hoped that similar attempts will be conducted in other countries: especially if they do not limit themselves to present the situation at a given time, but rather attempt to develop a diachronic approach to show the local historical roots of the NRMs, thus counteracting an image of NRMs as ephemeral phenomena.

2.1.2. Research Works on Specific Groups

In-depth studies of specific groups can be invaluable. First, they provide the grounds for testing the adequacy of general theories. They also offer often fascinating insights on the religious life of a movement about which little may be known. As well, if an obscure group under study comes under the spotlight at a later stage, research conducted before it attracted attention becomes highly useful. Examples of this kind of work include John Lofland's early study on the Unification Church (1977) and Robert Balch's research on the group which would later become famous under the name of Heaven's Gate, a research initiated at the group's very beginning (Balch 1995).

Understandably, there have been many monographic studies on some of the most well-known groups. Some have taken quite original approaches, for instance the insightful research by anthropologist Charles Brooks (1989) on the Western Krishna devotees in the Indian town of Vrindaban, the way they have been perceived and have affected the local religious and social life. While the International Society for Krishna Consciousness is a relatively small movement considered statistically, its visibility has been high and there have been several research works conducted on it. By contrast, there have been few academic, satisfactory book-length treatments of Scientology since Roy Wallis' book (1977). This may seem puzzling, since it contrasts with the proliferation of journalistic or polemical reports on that movement in several countries, including a number of books which take this approach. It may be due to the hybrid nature of the movement; some observers, including academic ones, express doubts about its religious nature, while other ones conclude that it can be classified as a religion, though possibly "a secularized religion" (Wilson 1990: 267–88). However, the apparent reluctance to engage in-depth, independent research work on Scientology may be related not only to methodological problems (research in a controlled environment), but to more practical considerations as well, since the movement has shown a willingness to engage in legal battles when perceiving itself as "threatened." There have also been periods of intense interest for a group, followed by a decrease: for instance, there was a period of intense academic interest in the Unification Church—no doubt encouraged by the movement itself—which gave rise to books such as a classic study by Eileen Barker (1984). In recent years, publications on the Unification Church have been much less frequent, despite a few interesting works on the history, beliefs and practices of the movement (Chryssides 1991; Hummel 1998). Not only international and well-structured groups have attracted the interest of scholars, but also smaller groups without a central organization and developing rather as networks. Such is the case of the Neo-Pagan movement, which is extremely varied in its expressions, but has common forums where at least some sections of it meet (through periodicals, gatherings, and so forth). While the first books devoted to those movements tended to be rather journalistic treatments, there is now a network of scholars interested in those issues (some of them being actually themselves involved in the Neo-Pagan community), and a few valuable collections of essays on various aspects of modern Paganism are now available. Especially worth noticing, beside works on specific groups or general considerations about the Pagan "renewal," is Graham Harvey's attempt to summarize the practices and worldviews of the main trends of contemporary Paganism (1997). While such a degree of generalization is not easy to reach, it represents a necessary step in order to understand the worldview behind the multitude of small Pagan groups created during the last decades in various places in Europe and in the United States. Of course, despite its claims to a very distant past, Paganism is fundamentally a new religion, and as such constitutes an excellent example of the dialectic between the old and the new which can be observed in several other NRMs.

Given the considerable number of active NRMs today, it can safely be said that most of those movements have never been appropriately studied, even if we limit ourselves to those born and active in the West. There is a very wide field open for young and motivated scholars eager to feel the excitement of walking untrodden paths. A good example of a monograph on a little-known group is Phillip Lucas' book (1995) on the Holy Order of MANS, describing its evolution from a New Age order into an Eastern Orthodox group. Due to the relatively young age of most movements, any monograph on those appeared in the 1970s will necessarily have to give much attention to changes intervened during the first decades of existence of the group, even if changes are not always as radical as in the case of the Holy Order of MANS.

Generally speaking, it should be observed here that the study of some groups is just being undertaken, and this observation is not only valid for NRMs of recent years, but also applies to older generations of groups. It becomes especially obvious when one considers movements born in the nineteenth century which have reached approximately comparable dimensions by the end of the twentieth century. For example, here have been hundreds of scholarly publications on the Church of Jesus Christ of Latter-day Saints but, in strong contrast, there have been only a handful of research works at an academic level on the New Apostolic Church (see Obst 1996), despite the no less phenomenal growth of this movement. Apparently, there was no scholarly book or article on the New Apostolic Church in English between 1980 and 2000. There are several reasons for such a situation. A large amount of academic research on Mormonism is produced by Mormons themselves (whether still active or disaffected). Mormonism has always encouraged academic training and the Church of Jesus Christ of Latter-day Saints itself has set up academic institutions such as Brigham Young University. There are active academic societies devoted to research on Mormon topics, such as the Mormon History Association, and Mormon intellectual periodicals. Nothing similar exists in the New Apostolic Church. This seems to be one more indication that research on the history and developments of contemporary religious movements depends to a significant extent upon impulses coming from within the movements themselves. However, even this factor seems insufficient to justify the scarcity of research works on the New Apostolic Church. This striking example is by no way unique and shows the urgent need for monographs on a wide range of religious movements, not only small, recent ones.

2.1.3. Typologies

Bryan Wilson's typology of sects left a lasting mark on research about smaller religious groups in the West. Some scholars felt however the need to elaborate a typology more specifically adjusted to the study of NRMs. From the few attempts which were made, the most influential one has no doubt been Roy Wallis' (1984). Wallis defined three types of religious movements: the *world-rejecting new religion* (which views the prevailing social order as having departed substantially from God's prescriptions and plan), the *world-affirming new religion* (which sees the prevailing social order as possessing many desirable characteristics and aspires to develop the full potential of human beings) and the *world-accommodating new religion* (in which religion "is not construed as a primarily social matter," but "provides solace or stimulation to personal, interior life," possible consequences for society being largely unintended).

Another interesting distinction between various types of movements has been proposed by Rodney Stark and William Sims Bainbridge (1985: 26–30). Their distinction is based upon different levels of organization. They distinguish between: *audience cults* (i.e. mainly a consumer activity, people who gather to hear a lecture, read some kinds of books and magazines), *client cults* (the relationship between those promulgating the doctrine and those partaking of it is similar to the relationship between a consultant and a client, or a therapist and a patient) and *cult movements* ("full-fledged religious organizations that attempt to satisfy all the religious needs of converts").

Obviously, the purpose of those two typologies is not the same: the first one deals with organized religious groups, while the second one is rather interested in the continuum between a vague, non-committed interest, and active engagement into a movement. Consequently, the first one is more appropriate for an analysis focusing upon individual groups and their characteristics, while the second typology is especially appropriate for an attempt to put individual groups within the wider context of contemporary, multi-faceted religious seeking, in which highly structured group make only part of the picture. The highly disparate nature of NRMs probably explains why there have been no widely acknowledged recent attempts to develop a typology, as it would be difficult to go beyond the level of generality provided by a typology such as the one elaborated by Wallis.

There have also been some attempts to introduce distinctions amongst various types of experiences of "the sacred." For instance, Massimo Introvigne has proposed the interesting notion of "new magical movements" (1990: 7–43; 1995a: 45–60, 81–101), distinguishing them from NRMs due to their insistence on the acquisition and use of powers that can be controlled and manipulated. The category of "new magical movements" has not gained wide acceptance in the scholarly community, probably because its use of the definition of "magical" tends to remain limited to the historical family of Western movements with magical connotations rather than to treat it more broadly as a universally applicable type.

2.1.4. Periodical Literature

Scholars studying NRMs first published the results of their research in academic periodicals of various kinds. Due to the considerable participation of sociologists in that field, it is not surprising that sociological periodicals published a number of important articles on this topic. However, there has been a trend worth observing in recent years: the emergence of cross-disciplinary periodical publications specializing in the field of new religions. It is certainly an important indication of a growing importance (and possibly maturity) of the field. When one considers that, in many Western countries, non conventional religious movements were long considered as a not very serious topic, or at best a marginal one, the fact that high-quality scholarly periodicals now begin to be devoted exclusively to NRMs demonstrates the existence of a substantial research community. Among the few specialized periodicals which have been launched, the best example is probably *Nova Religio: The Journal of Alternative and Emergent Religions* (launched in 1997), which seems well on its way to become the leading reference in the field. At the same high academic level is found another periodical with a wider perspective, not exclusively devoted to new religions, although they usually make a large part of the content of each issue, the *Journal of Contemporary Religion*, originally launched as *Religion Today* in 1984 and published under its current title since 1995. The cross-disciplinary nature of those periodicals also reflects what one can observe at conferences devoted to NRMs; what unites participants is not a common methodology, but a common curiosity for emergent religious groups.

When dealing with periodical literature, one should not forget two other categories of periodicals which have proved to be valuable sources of information. First, there are Christian periodicals with an apologetic perspective, but providing important and usually well-researched information and analysis beside the more apologetic content. The best and oldest example of that kind is no doubt the German Protestant *Materialdienst der Evangelischen Zentralstelle für Weltanschauungsfragen*, formerly headquartered in Stuttgart and now based in

Berlin. It continues a tradition going back to a bulletin originally published in 1928, with a ten year long suspension between 1941 and 1951. It deals not only with non-conventional religious groups, but also more generally with contemporary worldviews and the challenges they may pose to the Christian faith. It has monitored several generations of emergent religious groups in Germany, from Christian sects to recent NRMs, which makes it a unique undertaking. Second, there are now also some periodicals which attempt to abide by academic standards and which are published by members of the groups themselves, while also open to scholars not belonging to those groups. An example of such a periodical is the *ISKCON Communications Journal* (launched in 1993), originally conceived as a channel for internal dialogue, but increasingly a forum for discussions open to academic outsiders. The emergence of such periodicals, discussing "hot" issues as well, tells a lot about the way in which some movements appeared over the last decades have evolved. The existence of that kind of literature is also bound to affect the inner life of the movements.

2.2. Disciplinary Perspectives and Research Issues

2.2.1. A Cross-disciplinary Field of Research

As we have already seen, scholars studying new religions belong to a variety of fields, including religious studies, sociology, history, psychology, theology, and anthropology (see Warburg 1995). Sociologists have played an important role, and every conference dealing with sociology of religion will today routinely include several workshops or lectures on NRMs. Sociologists have been especially intrigued by the sheer fact of such a proliferation in an increasingly secularized West. A crisis in values, decline of community, search for identity and other factors have all been evoked as factors contributing to the emergence of NRMs and certainly all make sense, without being however entirely convincing; in addition, there are serious risks of over-generalization (Hamilton 1995: 205–209). More than general explanations, sociological research has brought much to our understanding of conversions to religious movements as well as of interactions between those movements and society.

One would have expected history of religions to see in NRMs a privileged field of research, but this has often not been the case. As Peter Antes once observed, in a country with a strong tradition for history of religions such as Germany, for a long time there was only literature produced by theologians available for the study of such topics (Klinkhammer 1997: 242). There was often a hesitation to deal with groups which seemed not to be "serious religions" like the "great, historical" religions. This reluctance has not entirely disappeared, although there are more and more historians of religions willing to pay attention to those modern productions offering the opportunity to study religious movements in their original stages. Could there be a specific contribution of historians of religions and experts in comparative religious studies to that field, or should they do a work somewhat to the efforts of sociologists? Definitely, there is a specific place for history of religions in research on NRMs. First, history itself: even young movements usually do not come from nowhere. There are ancestors, there are borrowings from previous movements, there is reinterpretation of older material—the history of religious ideas has a role to play in assessing those dimensions. Then, there is the comparative approach between religious developments of various historical periods. Yet another important contribution is no doubt the analysis of sacred texts and of rituals: the theologies of NRMs deserve to be studied seriously. Despite all the social, economic and sociological explanations, it is likely that there are people who convert to NRMs because their doctrines sound attractive and convincing to them—because those doctrines give answer to perennial human interrogations about life and its purpose. Mary Farrell Bednarowski's research (1989) on the theological systems of six new religions is a good example of what can be done in that regard.

There are definitely methodological problems involved into such an undertaking; for example, not all NRMs have a clearly established set of sacred scriptures. In addition, doctrine is often still in a process of rapid development and change in a first generation new religion—consequently, those groups which are already older arguably make better candidates for study. Nor is studying sacred texts enough. It is mandatory to conduct at least to some extent participant observation in order to observe and understand how the doctrines are being understood and lived by the members of the religion. And finally, although this is highly subjective, there are texts which better fit the classical view which we have of what a sacred text should be like, while other ones may seem more perplexing and therefore, for some of a lesser interest. However, if sacred texts—whatever their literary merits or apparent spiritual quality— motivate people to commit themselves strongly to a religious cause and if those texts are able to inspire the creation of a religious movement, they are worthy of our attention.

Historians are also becoming increasingly interested in contemporary religious movements. According to one overview of trends in historiography, in the last few decades of the twentieth century there has been a fundamental shift—at least in the United States—in the historiography of sectarian communities, although "scholarly gains have not been uniform across all movements" (Stein 1997). As we have already mentioned, Mormonism is the most impressive example, and 1950 can probably be seen as the turning point in the emergence of a new, more professional Mormon history, involving many Mormon scholars, but several non-Mormon historians as well (Allen 1987). The intense activities in the field of Mormon history have produced valuable research, but also generated heated controversies in the Mormon community itself, with some people (including some in leadership positions) seeing it as a threat to the faith. When dealing with some sensitive topics, being both a Mormon and an historian writing about Mormonism may present difficulties (Quinn 1992). Those conflicts and tensions are not unknown in mainline religious bodies as well (history has many such examples), but these are new experiences in more recent religious movements.

It must be noted that serious historical work, considering the various dimensions of history, has only been conducted on a few NRMs. In other cases, historical works have been produced for internal consumption, and follow a simple chronological pattern—they are chronicles rather than analytical histories. Access to archives is also a problem with many NRMs; either they have archives, but are reluctant to give access to non-members, or they have little interest in history and have not kept archives. These difficulties aside, the field remains wide open for historical research. History has also inspired attempts to compare religious movements across centuries. The most famous such attempt has been Rodney Stark's book on early Christianity (1996b). A sociologist, Stark has applied insights gained from his study of religious movements to the rise of Christianity, and his research has led to debates among historians of primitive Christianity—an interesting example of the way in which research on contemporary movements can ultimately contribute to research in other periods and other disciplines. In a similar spirit, some specialists of ancient Christianity have tried to consider it as a new religious movement and to compare it with NRMs of the twentieth century, in order to identify common laws and characteristics. One of them comes to the conclusion that, "[a]s new religious movements evolve, the primary cause of dissension within them will be disagreement over the speed and course of deviation away from the parent movement and towards adaptation to the broader environment" (Sanders 1993: 257).

2.2.2. Thematic Research Works

This leads us to discussions regarding the future of contemporary religious movements. Could an analysis of past and current movements contribute to predict how they would develop, succeed or fail? An academic conference was convened in Berkeley as early as in 1983 in order to discuss those issues (interestingly sponsored by an association affiliated with Rev. Moon's Unification Movement, which did not control the choice of the participants, but certainly had some interest to know more about its potential future—another instance of the involvement of movements in encouraging research work!). While recognizing that the future obviously cannot be predicted, especially since so many unexpected factors can come to play a role, most participants did not foresee spectacular growth for the most widely known movements under observation, and even predicted a bleak future or decrease to several of them (Bromley/Hammond 1987). The work initiated at that conference has continued to bear fruit, as can be seen especially in the revised model for understanding the success or failure of religious movements proposed by Rodney Stark (1996a). Stark has attempted to propose a list of conditions for the success of religious movements: for instance, retaining a cultural continuity with the conventional faiths of the society in which they are active, having non-empirical doctrines, continuing to maintain sufficient tension with the environment, and the efficient socializing of youth. Obviously, testing models of development and growth on older NRMs which have already shown an ability to survive and grow seems to be an especially attractive option, and this is what Stark has done with Mormonism, convinced that it offers the possibility to study the rise of a new world religion (Stark 1999).

The late twentieth century has also seen the emergence of research works concentrating upon specific groups within NRMs. The development of gender studies is probably related to the fact that several books were devoted to women in NRMs (Palmer 1994; Puttick 1997), some of them also paying attention to their role in older NRMs or in traditional as well as new religions (Wessinger 1993; Puttick/Clarke 1993). The emergence of literature on children in NRMs cannot be separated from controversies surrounding the participation of children of members in some groups, as well as accusations of child abuse which led in some cases to widely publicized raids which did not always confirm that such abuse existed. (We will return to the problems connected with scholars becoming involved in controversies surrounding NRMs.) The interest in children in such groups is however also connected with questions of a more academic nature, such as socialization, future prospects for a group and results of educational experimentation (Palmer/Hardman 1999). Those works on specific groups in NRMs also contribute to illustrate the diversity of experiences which can be found in the same movement.

Some other issues, however, have been much less studied than one would expect them to be. Despite attention often given by media and public opinion to money when it comes to NRMs, relatively little work has been conducted on those issues. Aside from a few articles, there has been only one book devoted specifically to the economic dimensions of NRMs (Richardson 1988). The way a group chooses for financing itself has to be consistent, at least to a reasonable extent, with its ideology, and consequently experimentation with various ways of securing an income reveals much more than just economic dynamics.

NRMs tend more and more to spread worldwide, even more so after the fall of Communism in the Soviet-dominated areas, which opened new fields for missionary work (although some NRMs were already present clandestinely in Communist-dominated countries before 1989) (Brorowik/Babinski 1997). The presence of NRMs (including those of Western origins) in non-Western countries would go beyond the scope of this survey. However, there is another element which will certainly attract the interest of scholars in religious studies during the years to come: it is the constantly increasing number of spiritual teachers of Western descent claiming to be part of an Eastern tradition—a phenomenon which could be described as "white gurus." Most of those teachers "are not simply copies of the Eastern models," they represent "the flowering of the Western genius, which has discovered Eastern traditions, absorbed them and in the process changed them and has been changed by them," explains a researcher who has compiled a thick directory of such teachers (Rawlinson 1997: XIX).

2.2.3. Cultic Milieu and New Age—NRMs in Context

Colin Campbell's seminal article (1972) launched the key concept of "cultic milieu": cults must exist within a milieu which is highly conducive to the spawning of individual cults. While individual cults may prove ephemeral and transitory, the milieu is preexistent and will not only survive individual cults, but also absorb what they leave behind and create new generations of cult-prone individuals. Campbell suggested that it might be appropriate to take the milieu rather than individual cults as the focus of sociological concern.

The advice was wise, even if research has often continued to concentrate upon individual groups—which is anyway useful too, since case studies continue to be needed as well. In addition, it is true that a research on the cultic milieu presents serious methodological difficulties: Its boundaries are not clear, and there are no lists of members. Esoteric fairs or bookshops, various magazines and seminars, are some of the places in which one is able to observe the cultic milieu in action (Mayer 1999), but it is true that it is difficult to get a fully adequate picture. An interesting example of an exploration of the cultic milieu in a local context is provided by Danny Jorgensen (1992) and his exploration of loosely interconnected networks of practitioners and collectivities which constitute particular factions, segments, or alliances. Jorgensen was able to distinguish in the geographic area under study "three principal confederated networks of individuals and communities," according to their main spheres of interest.

Indeed, the cultic milieu is so diverse that it is necessary to identify subgroups, and also to examine how structured cults interact with more loosely connected networks. We have presented a specific example of a group in Central Switzerland in the 1980s, where a mixture of followers of UFO contactees, Indian gurus and readers of I AM literature all gathered together twice a month. Open in a non-judgemental way to a number of non-conventional beliefs, and reading the same literature and magazines, many of them had in addition their own practices or spiritual disciplines beside those regular meetings. Far from creating intense competition, those various messages tended to reinforce each other (Mayer 1993: 258–66). Whether such individual quests, even if they are pursued along with other people and contribute to each other's worldview, can lead to the emergence of a real community, remains a matter of debate. Michael Brown's exploration of the "channeling zone" (1997) has illustrated how, even if dreaming of community, "the majority of channels and their clients check in decisively on the side of privatized faith and the valorization of social interactions that qualify as mutually therapeutic" (1997: 140–41). One should remember that practices popular in the cultic milieu are not necessarily "religious" according to various definitions of this word, and one dealing with the cultic milieu has to reflect about those beliefs on the border between the sacred and the secular as well as about concepts such as "quasi-religion" (see Greil/Robbins 1994). Beside the concept of cultic milieu, close to it but not synonymous, sociologist Françoise Champion has developed the concept of *nébuleuse mystique-ésotérique* (1990). Champion's *nébuleuse* is very similar to Campbell's *milieu* (fluid and unstable groups, circulation of people across the groups, constantly changing contents...), but should rather be described as the current expression of a significant segment of the cultic milieu, resulting from the encounter between counter-culture, Eastern religions and older esoteric themes (1989: 158). His focus is the post 1970s' cultic milieu, the cultic milieu in an historical context, while Campbell's description rather refers to a cultural constant.

But which were the changes in the 1970s which could lead to such theoretical elaborations? The answer is the New Age. Despite the label "new," the New Age was definitely not new in many respects and reused to a large extent material already present in earlier movements. But it popularized those themes as possibly never before and—most of all—gave them a current identity, connected to supposed imminent radical changes. The success of the New Age theme, which became known in the wider culture and not just in the subculture of the cultic milieu, had positive consequences from the viewpoint of research too: there have been a number of valuable research works, including some which attempted to examine how the New Age might fit into the concepts used by sociology of religion (York 1995). Instead of just concentrating upon current manifestations of the so-called "New Age," several scholars were inspired to look for its historical roots and inheritance. Christoph Bochinger (1994) and Wouter Hanegraaff (1996) both produced extensive research works on New Age worldviews and their sources. Despite the heterogeneous nature of the New Age, Hanegraaff comes to the conclusion that there are elements in common across the New Age spectrum which make it more than just a convenient label for disparate products on the market. He emphasizes the New Age as *culture criticism* (all New Age trends are intended as alternatives to dominant ones) and as *secularized esotericism* (its roots are not found in the East, despite Oriental references, but in Western esoteric traditions). New Age religion has already been with us for decades, but it did not manifest itself as the New Age movement until the 1970s: "The New Age movement is the cultic milieu having become conscious of itself," writes Hanegraaf (1996: 522).

But what is the future of the New Age? If we understand it in a restricted sense, as a specific segment of contemporary alternative religiosity, several observers express the opinion that the decline of the New Age has already come, and that we will see a passage from the New Age to the "Next Age," i.e. the idea that the realization of individual transformation should take precedence over the expectation of planetary transformation—a dimension which, actually, has always been present in the New Age, despite the millenarian tones which it often took, now in decline in a post-utopian stage (Berzano 1999; Introvigne 2000). However this in no way means that alternative religiosity, of which New Age is a part and a manifestation, will decrease; it can rather be expected to take new forms, following the logic of a market which shows no sign of depletion.

3. New Religions, Scholars and Society

If NRMs would just be a topic for research, life would be much more simple for scholars dealing with those issues. However, the current reality of research on contemporary religious movements is quite different. We have to deal with controversial issues, and researchers sometimes become part of those controversies, willingly or not. In addition, since the 1970s, but especially during the 1990s in Europe, there have been a number of official reports in several countries dealing with "cults"—actually leading to various results, very cautious in some countries, militant in other ones. Official agencies entrusted with the monitoring of "cults" have even been set up in some European countries. In addition, during the 1990s there were several violent outcomes related to some small religious movements, which have created some anxieties and made law-enforcement agencies in several countries eager to know more about such groups. Scholars have to conduct their research in that environment, and they have also to be aware that the results of their investigations may be used by various, non scholarly actors, or interpreted as hiding a secret agenda.

It is consequently not surprising that those controversies in themselves have become a topic for research, and also for comparative perspectives on governmental attitudes toward NRMs in several countries (Beckford 1985).

3.1. Cult Controversies

3.1.1. The "Anti-cult Movement"

Historians are well aware that reactions against religious fringe movements are nothing new and that stereotypes are recurrent, even if emphasis on specific fears and groups will obviously change to some extent according to circumstances (Jenkins 2000). What makes the current controversies possibly new is that they tend to amalgamate an incredibly wide range of groups and that they take place in the context of societies where religion often does no more occupy the place which it used to have before.

The first groups critical of some NRMs appeared in the early 1970s in the United States, emerging within the next few years in several European countries as well. They were usually unconnected ventures, of a rather spontaneous nature, often formed by families concerned about the fate of relatives who had become members of newly appeared, radical groups. Opposition to NRMs soon also became a topic for research, especially since that opposition tended in its early years to take some radical forms as well, such as forced "deprograming" of members of NRMs (Shupe/Bromley 1980). The "anti-cult movement" (ACM), as it became known in sociological literature, had never been a unified movement, but included from the beginning a variety of components. Religiously based opposition to "cults" (which already had a long tradition) did not always follow the same goals and same ways of operating as those anti-cult groups formed by families who had "lost" a loved one to a "cult"; this made the ACM "a loose coalition" (Shupe/Bromley/Oliver 1984: 52). Massimo Introvigne has analyzed well the ideological differences between the secular *anti*-cult movement and the religious *counter*-cult movement (Introvigne 1995b).

As time went on, there was an increasing professionalization of several sectors of the ACM (Bromley/Shupe 1995). In the United States, the American Family Foundation (AFF) has published an academic periodical since 1984 entitled the *Cultic Studies Journal: Psychological Manipulation and Society*, turned, since 2002, into an Internet journal with a print version, the *Cultic Studies Review*. While relations between the ACM and a number of scholars have been and sometimes remain tense, since several scholars had been perceived as taking a side in the controversies, there have been noticeable improvements and serious exchanges between the AFF and several prominent researchers on NRMs over the past few years. Regarding research on the ACM, there still seems to be a lack of research works based on participant observation in anti-cult groups. Since there has been a lot of emphasis on the value of participant observation for seriously studying NRMs, it would certainly be valuable to have similar efforts for understanding better the dynamics of anti-cult groups.

3.1.2. Former Members and Brainwashing

Since much attention has been devoted to conversions to NRMs, it is not surprising that there have also been research works on reasons for which people would leave such groups. Religious disaffiliation is more than a topic of just a casual significance, argued David Bromley, and may contribute to help understanding religious group membership in processual terms as well as to gather some possibly significant information on the place of religion in contemporary society (Bromley 1988: 11). More recently, research has come to pay special attention to the role played by people who, after leaving a NRM, become actively involved in a fight against their former faith; several sociologists currently use the label of "apostates" for describing such figures (Bromley 1998).

The issue of disaffiliation is inevitably connected with the problem of free will. Did people become members of controversial religious groups due to an acquired inner certainty, or was their decision the result of a "mental manipulation"? That issue is a serious one, since there are even countries in which there have been discussions about the desirability of making "mental manipulation" legally punishable. If groups have developed techniques to help them to convert people without their informed assent, this is obviously a serious social problem. The issue of brainwashing has been a topic for scholarly discussion (see Bromley/Richardson 1983). While nobody would probably deny that mechanisms of social influence may play a role in a conversion, most scholars studying NRMs tend to reject the brainwashing hypothesis (Melton/Introvigne 2000). However, the discussion was revived when Benjamin Zablocki argued in two articles that the concept of brainwashing had not been given a fair scientific trial (1997 and 1998). A book presenting this debate as well as other issues of "objectivity in a controversial field" has been published (Zablocki/Robbins 2001).

3.1.3. New Religions and the Law

While European states as well as the United States and Canada proclaim their attachment to the principle of religious freedom, this does not mean that they can remain indifferent to what is happening in the religious field (Richardson 2004). Especially when groups become controversial or are criticized for allegedly dubious practices, state authorities have to pay attention. As James Beckford has observed, the management of such movements by the state may disclose broader issues of contention between religions and states in matters of control of social phenomena (Beckford 1993: 140–41). There have been several recent volumes on NRMs and the law in Europe (European Consortium 1999) or in specific countries (Messner 1999).

Beside the basic principle of religious freedom, the question arises to know if all groups are entitled to claim the benefits of religious freedom or if some actually make an abuse of it? As some observers have noticed, religion has become "a cultural resource over which competing interest groups may vie" (Greil 1996: 49). Scholars find themselves plunged in those debates and their definitions of what is religious or not may clash with other definitions: the purpose of a scholarly analysis is unlikely to be the same as the goal of a definition meant to solve legal problems (Introvigne 1999). This poses also the difficult problem of the situation of the scholar as expert.

3.1.4. New Religions and Violence

The renewal of controversies in recent years is not just the continuation of the earlier debates: it is also—at least to some extent—the consequence of some spectacular events involving small religious groups, such as the Branch Davidians in Waco (in 1993), the Order of the Solar Temple in Switzerland, Québec and France (in 1994, 1995 and 1997), Aum Shinrikyo in Japan (in 1995) and, more recently, the Movement for the Restoration of the Ten Commandments of God in Uganda (in 2000). While those groups—and other ones implicated in violent behavior—have little in common, each of them reinforced the perception of "cults" as being potentially dangerous for their members or even for the wider society. It has also justified some attention on the part of law-enforcement agencies (Kaplan 2002).

By the end of the twentieth century, several scholars were engaged in research on religious groups and violence, and this tends to an increase in comparative perspectives (Hall 2000; Wessinger 2000a), including collections of essays trying to take a look not only at contemporary groups, but also at historical cases (Wessinger 2000b). Since all those groups had a clear apocalyptic component, this has given an impulse to studies on millenarianism— which the coming of the year 2000 also encouraged. While several scholars tend to emphasize the role of conflicts with the environment as a primary cause of violent outcomes, other researchers give more importance to internal developments within the movements. Obviously, both elements can have an influence simultaneously as well. It remains to be seen how far such developments are predictable, i.e. if there are warning signs which may indicate that a movement is on its way to violence. All scholars agree however that those are exceptional cases, which affect only a tiny minority of NRMs (Mayer 2001).

3.2. Academic Integrity and Field Research

Finally, although it is not possible to enter into a detailed discussion of such issues here, it should also be mentioned that the involvement of scholars in a sometimes controversial field has also raised ethical questions, due both to the personal relations of researchers with the movements which they study and to public statements by some scholars regarding debated issues. Consequently, scholars themselves have sometimes become part of the field under study, or have come into competition with other interpretations in a context conducive to heated polemics.

Several of the questions raised in relation to those issues are not actually specific to the study of NRMs. Any person doing field research and participant observation is well aware that this kind of activity may also create personal links with people belonging to the group under study, and that critical distance has to be kept, but that is not something which can just be attained through the application of proper methodology. The realities of life and of fieldwork are always more complex, to find the proper balance requires constant efforts and adjustments (Poulat 1998). However, those issues became a matter of discussion especially when a few NRMs began to invite scholars to conferences and acted in a way which could sometimes be understood as using scholars for gaining social legitimacy (Horowitz 1978). Such issues have been repeatedly discussed at academic conferences, in scholarly journals such as *Sociological Analysis* (in 1983) or *Nova Religio* (in 1998) as well as in a book (Zablocki/ Robbins 2001).

One should not expect to find all scholars of one mind regarding the degree to which they should involve themselves in those debates, and this is unlikely to change. While several scholars have made no mystery of their advocacy for what they see as an issue of religious freedom, a few academics have also been highly critical of some NRMs. Those controversies have had consequences upon the work of a number of scholars or upon their research focus (Richardson 1991: 314). It only remains to be hoped that the heat of the controversies will not take researchers—whatever their opinion on specific groups—away from other topics which may be as much important and relevant for our knowledge of emergent religious groups.

Conclusion

Research on NRMs has been described as an emergent "sub-discipline" within the sociology of religion (Barker 1999: 206). As we have seen, however, research is by no means conducted only by sociologists of religion and, despite their dominant presence in that field, it would be more accurate to follow Gordon Melton's comment in his paper on "The Rise of the Study of New Religions" at the CESNUR conference in Pennsylvania in 1999: According to Melton (himself an historian), research on new religions emerged "at the point where religious studies and the social scientific study of religion converged," and has from its inception "been a multi-disciplinary venture held together by the subject matter rather than anything approaching a unified methodological approach." May we speak, however, of "New Religions Studies" as a "separate discipline," and is such an evolution desirable? As we have seen, there are increasing numbers of scholars working mainly on those topics. However, their roots in different disciplines serve to enrich this research. In addition, the full autonomization of such a field of studies might have the perverse effect of confining forever emergent movements to a kind of specific (and possibly "bizarre") category among religious phenomena. It is certainly a more fruitful approach to put them into the wider context of the history and contemporary developments of religions.

Bibliography

Allen, James B. (1987), "Since 1950: Creators and Creations of Mormon History," in: Davis Bitton/Maureen Ursenbach Beecher, eds., *New Views of Mormon History*. Salt Lake City, Ut.: University of Utah Press: 407–38.

Arweck, Elisabeth/Clarke, Peter B. (1997), *New Religious Movements in Western Europe: An Annotated Bibliography*. Westport, Conn./London: Greenwood Press.

Bainbridge, William Sims (1997), *The Sociology of Religious Movements*. New York/London: Routledge.

Balch, Robert W. (1995), "Waiting for the Ships: Disillusionment and the Revitalization of Faith in Bo and Peep's UFO Cult," in: James R. Lewis, ed., *The Gods Have Landed: New Religions from Other Worlds*. Albany, N.Y.: State University of New York Press: 137–66.

Barker, Eileen (1984), *The Making of a Moonie: Choice or Brainwashing?* Oxford: Basil Blackwell.

— (1995), "New Religious Movements: The Inherently Changing Scene," in: Irena Borowik/Przemysław Jabłoński, eds., *The Future of Religion: East and West*. Kraków: Nomos Publishing House: 73–92.

— (1998), "New Religions and New Religiosity," in: Eileen Barker/Margit Warburg, eds., *New Religions and New Religiosity*. Aarhus: Aarhus University Press: 10–27.

— (1999), "Taking Two to Tango: The New Religious Movements and Sociology," in: Liliane Voyé/Jaak Billiet, eds., *Sociology and Religion: An Ambiguous Relationship*. Leuven: Leuven University Press: 204–26.

Baumann, Christoph Peter (2000), *Religionen in Basel-Stadt und Basel-Landschaft*. Basel: Projekt "Führer durch das religiöse Basel."

Beckford, James A. (1985), *Cult Controversies: The Societal Response to the New Religious Movements*. London/New York: Tavistock.

— (1990), "The Sociology of Religion 1945–1989," in: *Social Compass* 37 (1): 45–64.

— (1993), "States, Governments, and the Management of Controversial New Religious Movements," in: Eileen Barker/James A. Beckford/Karel Dobbelaere, eds., *Secularization, Rationalism and Sectarianism*. Oxford: Clarendon Press: 125–43.

Bednarowski, Mary Farrell (1989), *New Religions: The Theological Imagination in America*. Bloomington, Ind.: Indiana University Press.

Berzano, Luigi (1999), *New Age*. Bologna: Il Mulino.

Bochinger, Christoph (1994), *"New Age" und moderne Religion: Religionswissenschaftliche Analysen*. Gütersloh: Chr. Kaiser/Gütersloher Verlagshaus.

Borowik, Irena/Babiński, Grzegorz, eds., *New Religious Phenomena in Central and Eastern Europe*. Krakow: Nomos.

Bromley, David, ed. (1988), *Falling from the Faith: Causes and Consequences of Religious Apostasy*. Newbury Park, Calif.: Sage.

— ed. (1998), *The Politics of Religious Apostasy: The Role of Apostates in the Transformation of Religious Movements*. Westport, Conn./London: Praeger.

Bromley, David/Hadden, Jeffrey K., eds. (1993), *Religion and the Social Order*. Vol. 3A: *The Handbook of Cults and Sects in America*. Greenwich, Conn./London: JAI Press.

Bromley, David G./Hammond, Phillip E., eds. (1987), *The Future of New Religious Movements*. Macon, Ga.: Mercer University Press.

Bromley, David G./Richardson, James T., eds. (1983), *The Brainwashing/Deprogramming Controversy: Sociological, Psychological, Legal and Historical Perspectives*. New York/Toronto: Edwin Mellen Press.

Bromley, David G./Shupe, Anson (1995), "Anti-Cultism in the United States: Origins, Ideology and Organizational Development," in: *Social Compass* 42 (2): 221–36.

Brooks, Charles R. (1989), *The Hare Krishnas in India*. Princeton, N.J.: Princeton University Press.

Brown, Michael F. (1997), *The Channeling Zone: American Spirituality in an Anxious Age*. Cambridge, Mass./London: Harvard University Press.

Campbell, Colin (1972), "The Cult, the Cultic Milieu and Secularization," in: *A Sociological Yearbook of Religion in Britain*. Vol. 5. London: SCM Press: 119–36.

Chamberlain, Arthur F. (1913), "'New Religions' among the North American Indians," in: *Journal of Religious Psychology* 6 (1): 1–49.

Champion, Françoise (1989), "Les sociologues de la post-modernité religieuse et la nébuleuse mystique-ésotérique," in: *Archives de Sciences sociales des Religions* 67 (1): 155–69.

—— (1990), La nébuleuse mystique-ésotérique: Orientations psychoreligieuses des courants ésotériques et mystiques contemporains," in: Françoise Champion/Danièle Hervieu-Léger, eds., *De l'Emotion en religion. Renouveaux et traditions*. Paris: Centurion: 17–69.

Chryssides, George D. (1991), *The Advent of Sun Myung Moon: The Origins, Beliefs and Practices of the Unification Church*. London: Macmillan.

Colpe, Carsten (1975), "Synkretismus, Renaissance, Säkularisation und Neubildung von Religionen in der Gegenwart," in: Jes Peter Asmussen/Jørgen Læssøe, eds., *Handbuch der Religionsgeschichte*. Vol. 3. Göttingen: Vandenhoeck & Ruprecht: 441–523.

Dawson, Lorne L. (1998), *Comprehending Cults: The Sociology of New Religious Movements*. Toronto/Oxford/New York: Oxford University Press.

Dillon, Jane/Richardson, James T., "The 'Cult' Concept: A Politics of Representation Analysis," in: *Syzygy: Journal of Alternative Religion and Culture* 3 (3–4): 185–97.

Eggenberger, Oswald (1994), *Die Kirchen, Sondergruppen und religiösen Vereinigungen. Ein Handbuch*. 6th ed. Zürich: Theologischer Verlag.

Ellwood, Robert S. (1979), *Alternative Altars: Unconventional and Eastern Spirituality in America*. Chicago/London: University of Chicago Press.

European Consortium for Church-State Research (1999), *New Religious Movements and the Law in the European Union*. Milano: Giuffrè.

Farqhar, J.N. (1915), *Modern Religious Movements in India*. New York: Macmillan.

Figl, Johannes (1993), *Die Mitte der Religionen: Idee und Praxis universalreligiöser Bewegungen*. Darmstadt: Wissenschaftliche Buchgesellschaft.

Filoramo, Giovanni (1979), "Nuove religioni: problemi e prospettive," in: *Rivista di storia e letteratura religiosa* 15 (3): 445–72.

Greil, Arthur L. (1996), "Sacred Claims: The 'Cult Controversy' as a Struggle over the Right to the Religious Label," in: Lewis F. Carter, ed., *Religion and the Social Order*. Vol. 6: *The Issue of Authenticity in the Study of Religions*. Greenwich, Conn./London: JAI Press: 47–63.

Greil, Arthur L./Robbins, Thomas, eds. (1994), *Religion and the Social Order*. Vol. 4: *Between Sacred and Secular: Research and Theory on Quasi-Religion*. Greenwich, Conn./London: JAI Press.

Haack, Friedrich-Wilhelm (1979), *Jugendreligionen. Ursachen—Trends—Reaktionen*. München: Claudius Verlag/Verlag J. Pfeiffer.

Hall, John R. (2000), *Apocalypse Observed: Religious Movements and Violence in North America, Europe, and Japan*. London/New York: Routledge.

Hamilton, Malcolm B. (1995), *The Sociology of Religion: Theoretical and Comparative Perspectives*. London/New York: Routledge.

Hanegraaff, Wouter J. (1996), *New Age Religion and Western Culture: Esotericism in the Mirror of Secular Thought*. Leiden/New York/Köln: E.J. Brill.

Harvey, Graham (1997), *Listening People, Speaking Earth: Contemporary Paganism*. London: Hurst.

Horowitz, Irving Louis (1978), "Science, Sin, and Sponsorship," in: Irving Louis Horowitz, ed., *Science, Sin, and Scholarship: The Politics of Reverend Moon and the Unification Church*. Cambridge, Mass./London: MIT Press: 260–81.

Hummel, Reinhart (1998), *Vereinigungskirche—die "Moon-Sekte" im Wandel*. Neukirchen-Vluyn: Friedrich Bahn Verlag.

Introvigne, Massimo (1990), *Il cappello del mago: I nuovi movimenti magici, dallo spiritismo al satanismo*. Milano: SugarCo.

—— (1995a), *La sfida magica*. Milano: Editrice Àncora.

—— (1995b), "The Secular Anti-Cult and the Religious Counter-Cult Movement: Strange Bedfellows or Future Enemies?," in: Robert Towler, ed., *New Religious Movements and the New Europe*. Aarhus: Aarhus University Press: 32–54.

—— (1999), "Religion as Claim: Social and Legal Controversies," in: Jan G. Platvoet/Arie L. Molendijk, eds., *The Pragmatics of Defining Religion: Contexts, Concepts and Contests*. Leiden/Boston, Mass./Köln: Brill: 41–72.

—— (2000), *New Age & Next Age*. Casale Monferrato: Edizioni Piemme.

Introvigne, Massimo et al. (2001), *Enciclopedia delle religioni in Italia*. Leumann (Torino): Editrice Elledici.

Jenkins, Philip (2000), *Mystics and Messiahs: Cults and New Religions in American History*. New York: Oxford University Press.

Jorgensen, Danny L. (1992), *The Esoteric Scene, Cultic Milieu, and Occult Tarot*. New York/London: Garland.

Kaplan, Jeffrey (2002), *Millenial Violence: Past, Present and Future*. London: Frank Cass.

Klinkhammer, Gritt Maria et al., eds. (1997), *Kritik an Religionen: Religionswissenschaft und der kritische Umgang mit Religionen*. Marburg: Diagonal Verlag.

Lanczkowski, Günter (1974), *Die neuen Religionen*. Frankfurt/Main: Fischer Taschenbuch Verlag.

Laube, Johannes, ed. (1995), *Neureligionen: Stand ihrer Erforschung in Japan. Ein Handbuch*. Wiesbaden: Harrassowitz.

Loeliger, Carl/Trompf, Garry, eds. (1985), *New Religious Movements in Melanesia*. Suva: University of the Pacific and the University of Papua New Guinea.

Lofland, John F. (1977), *Doomsday Cult: A Study of Conversion, Proselytization, and Maintenance of Faith*. Enlarged ed. New York: Irvington.

Lucas, Phillip Charles (1995), *The Odyssey of a New Religion: The Holy Order of MANS from New Age to Orthodoxy*. Bloomington, Ind.: Indiana University Press.

Mayer, Jean-François (1993), *Les Nouvelles Voies spirituelles: Enquête sur la religiosité parallèle en Suisse*. Lausanne: L'Age d'Homme.

— (1997), "Nuove religioni e nuovi movimenti religiosi," in: Giovanni Filoramo, ed., *Storia delle religioni*. Vol. 5. Roma/Bari: Editori Laterza: 463–88.

— (1999), "Le marché de la religiosité parallèle: visite d'une foire de l'ésotérisme," in: *Mouvements religieux* 226–27: 6–15.

— (2001), "Cults, Violence and Religious Terrorism: An International Perspective," in: *Studies in Conflict and Terrorism* 24 (5): 361–76.

— (2004), "Qu'est-ce qu'une nouvelle religion?," in: Jean-François Mayer/Reender Kranenborg, eds., *La Naissance des Nouvelles Religions*. Geneva: Georg: 5–22.

Melton, J. Gordon (1992), *Encyclopedic Handbook of Cults in America*. Rev. ed. New York/London: Garland.

— (1995), "The Changing Scene of New Religious Movements: Observations from a Generation of Research," in: *Social Compass* 42 (2): 265–76.

— (1999), *Encyclopedia of American Religions*. 6th ed. Detroit, Mich./London: Gale.

Melton, J. Gordon/Introvigne, Massimo, eds. (2000), *Gehirnwäsche und Sekten: Interdisziplinäre Annäherungen*. Marburg: Diagonal Verlag.

Messner, Francis, ed. (1999), *Les "Sectes" et le Droit en France*. Paris: Presses Universitaires de France.

Miller, Timothy, ed. (1995), *America's Alternative Religions*. Albany, N.J.: State University of New York Press.

Needleman, Jacob (1970), *The New Religions*. Garden City, N.Y.: Doubleday.

Obst, Helmut (1996), *Neuapostolische Kirche—die exklusive Endzeitkirche?* Neukirchen-Vluyn: Friedrich Bahn Verlag.

Pace, Enzo (1997), *Le sette*. Bologna: Il Mulino.

Palmer, Susan J. (1994), *Moon Sisters, Krishna Mothers, Rajneesh Lovers: Women's Roles in New Religions*. Syracuse, N.Y.: Syracuse University Press.

Palmer, Susan J./Hardman, Charlotte, eds. (1999), *Children in New Religions*. New Brunswick, N.J./London: Rutgers University Press.

Poulat, Emile (1998), "Sociologues et sociologie devant le phénomène sectaire," in: *La Pensée* 316: 93–106.

Puttick, Elizabeth (1997), *Women in New Religions: In Search of Community, Sexuality and Spiritual Power*. London: Macmillan.

Puttick, Elizabeth/Clarke, Peter B., eds. (1993), *Women as Teachers and Disciples in Traditional and New Religions*. Lewiston, N.Y.: Edwin Mellen Press.

Quinn, Michael D. (1992), "On Being a Mormon Historian (and Its Aftermath)," in: George D. Smith, ed., *Faithful History: Essays on Writing Mormon History*. Salt Lake City, Ut.: Signature Books: 69–111.

Rawlinson, Andrew (1997), *The Book of Enlightened Masters: Western Teachers in Eastern Traditions*. Chicago/La Salle: Open Court.

Richardson, James T., ed. (1988), *Money and Power in the New Religions*. Lewiston, N.Y.: Edwin Mellen Press.

— (1991), "Reflexivity and Objectivity in the Study of Controversial New Religions," in: *Religion* 21 (4): 305–18.

— (1993), "Definitions of Cult: From Sociological-Technical to Popular-Negative," in: *Review of Religious Research* 34 (4): 348–56.

— ed. (2004), *Regulating Religion. Case Studies from around the Globe.* New York: Kluwer Academic/Plenum Publishers.

Rudolph, Kurt (1992), *Geschichte und Probleme der Religionswissenschaft.* Leiden: E.J. Brill.

Sanders, Jack T. (1993), *Schismatics, Sectarians, Dissidents, Deviants: The First One Hundred Years of Jewish-Christian Relations.* Valley Forge, Pa.: Trinity Press International.

Schmid, Georg/Schmid, Georg Otto, eds. (2003), *Kirchen, Sekten, Religionen. Religiöse Gemeinschaften, weltanschauliche Gruppierungen und Psycho-Organisationen im deutschen Sprachraum.* Zürich: Theologischer Verlag.

Shupe, Anson D./Bromley, David G. (1980), *The New Vigilantes: Deprogrammers, Anti-Cultists, and the New Religions.* Beverly Hills, Calif./London: Sage.

Shupe, Anson D./Bromley, David G./Oliver, Donna L. (1984), *The Anti-Cult Movement in America: A Bibliography and Historical Survey.* New York/London: Garland.

Stark, Rodney (1996a), "Why Religious Movements Succeed or Fail: A Revised General Model," in: *Journal of Contemporary Religion* 11 (2): 133–46.

— (1996b), *The Rise of Christianity: A Sociologist Reconsiders History.* Princeton, N.J.: Princeton University Press.

— (1999), "Extracting Social Scientific Models from Mormon History," in: *Journal of Mormon History* 25 (1): 174–94.

Stark, Rodney/Bainbridge, William Sims (1985), *The Future of Religion: Secularization, Revival, and Cult Formation.* Berkeley, Calif./Los Angeles, Calif./London: University of California Press.

Stein, Stephen J. (1997), "History, Historians, and the Historiography of Indigenous Sectarian Religious Movements in America," in: Walter H. Conser/Sumner B. Twiss, eds., *Religious Diversity and American Religious History: Studies in Traditions and Cultures.* Athens, Ga./London: University of Georgia Press: 128–56.

Straelen, Henry Van (1957), *The Religion of Divine Wisdom: Japan's Most Powerful Religious Movement.* Kyoto: Veritas Shoin.

Turner, Harold W. (1989), "Two Kinds of New Religious Movements," in: G.J. Pillay, ed., *The Future of Religion.* Pretoria: Serva Publishers: 183–200.

Wallis, Roy (1977), *The Road to Total Freedom: A Sociological Analysis of Scientology.* New York: Columbia University Press.

— (1984), *The Elementary Forms of the New Religious Life.* London: Routledge & Kegan Paul.

Warburg, Margit, ed. (1995), *Studying New Religions.* Copenhagen: Institute of History of Religions.

Wessinger, Catherine, ed. (1993), *Women's Leadership in Marginal Religions: Explorations Outside the Mainstream.* Urbana, Ill./Chicago: University of Illinois Press.

— (2000a), *How the Millennium Comes Violently: From Jonestown to Heaven's Gate.* New York: Seven Bridges Press.

— ed. (2000b), *Millennialism, Persecution, and Violence: Historical Cases.* Syracuse, N.Y.: Syracuse University Press.

Wilson, Bryan (1970), *Religious Sects.* London: Weidenfeld & Nicholson.

— ed. (1981), *The Social Impact of New Religious Movements.* Barrytown, N.Y.: Unification Theological Seminary.

—— (1982), "The New Religions: Preliminary Considerations," in: Eileen Barker, ed., *New Religious Movements: A Perspective for Understanding Society*. New York/ Toronto: Edwin Mellen Press: 16–31.

—— (1990), *The Social Dimensions of Sectarianism: Sects and New Religious Movements in Contemporary Society*. Oxford: Clarendon Press.

York, Michael (1995), *The Emerging Network: A Sociology of the New Age and Neo-Pagan Movements*. Lanham, Md./London: Rowman & Littlefield.

Zablocki, Benjamin (1997), "The Blacklisting of a Concept: The Strange History of the Brainwashing Conjecture in the Sociology of Religion," in: *Nova Religio: The Journal of Alternative and Emergent Religions* 1 (1): 96–121.

—— (1998), "Exit Cost Analysis: A New Approach to the Scientific Study of Brainwashing," in: *Nova Religio: The Journal of Alternative and Emergent Religions* 1 (2): 216–49.

Zablocki, Benjamin/Robbins, Thomas, eds. (2001), *Misunderstanding Cults: Searching for Objectivity in a Controversial Field*. Toronto: University of Toronto Press.

New Approaches to the Study of the New Fundamentalisms

by

PETER ANTES

The consultation of two different theological encyclopedias in German leads to a very interesting discovery. In the article on fundamentalism in the *Theologische Realenzyklopädie*, published in 1983 (cf. Joest), the only subject dealt with is the American Protestant fundamentalism of the early twentieth century. This movement was strongly opposed to modern Christian theology, insisting on the fundamentals of faith without any compromise with either modern theology or the natural sciences. In contrast, in the fourth edition (1995) of the *Lexikon für Theologie und Kirche*, fundamentalism is described as a world-wide phenomenon found in all religions (cf. Beinert et al. 1995). The change in the use of the term may moreover be documented through reference to other encyclopedias published in German between 1983 and 1995. *Evangelisches Lexikon für Theologie und Gemeinde*, for instance, goes beyond confining the term to American Protestantism by acknowledging its broader use with reference to Catholic, Islamic, and Jewish groups, although the 1992 volume declares such terminology illicit and at variance with the original meaning of the term in its Protestant setting (cf. Holthaus). Such warnings, however, have largely been unsuccessful. The term is currently used widely, as demonstrated by the article in the *Lexikon für Theologie und Kirche* noted above. The question therefore is what has changed over the past decade or so to make fundamentalism a general term in use in the study of religions while previously it referred exclusively to a specific form of North American Protestantism. Moreover, what are the characteristics of such a fundamentalism in the world's religions, and how will this concept affect how data about those religions are perceived and analyzed?

1. The Development from a Special Term of a Specific Group towards a Broad Use of the Term in General

It is well known that the original meaning of fundamentalism in its American Protestant context signaled a strong opposition to both modern Christian

theology and scientific research, if those results contradicted traditional theological teachings. Such was the case for miracles and other historical claims
that seemed incompatible with non-Biblical source materials. Unlike modernist
Christian theology which tried to integrate these views into its interpretation of
the Bible, fundamentalists insisted on reiterating traditional positions in spite of
all the data that seemed to contradict the truth of Biblical texts. For example,
fundamentalists asserted the creation of the world in six days and God's direct
creation of human beings, modern cosmology and Darwin's theory of evolution
notwithstanding. The fundamentals of the creed, they believed, had to be
derived from the Bible, literally understood, and from teachings affirmed over
centuries within Christianity. Consequently, fundamentalism in this regard
may be seen as a dogmatic position in confrontation with modernizing trends
in Christian (more precisely Protestant) theology. It is political in the sense of
supporting policies that limit the exposure of young Christians to these modern
theories in their education. It upholds classical standards in theology and moral
behavior and is opposed to any changes in either of these areas.

Antimodernist positions were also found in Catholicism in the early years
of the twentieth century. Here, however, they became the leading position of
the church so that modernists were excluded and opposed until mid-century,
when under Pope Pius XII some antimodernist statements were eventually revised and modern exegesis entered Roman Catholic theology. Vatican II (1962–
1965) finally opened the way to modern exegesis in Roman Catholic theology
with the result that opponents like Bishop Lefebvre were then labeled as
"integrists" in order to stigmatize their antimodern attitudes. The previously
mentioned 1992 edition of the encyclopedia *Evangelisches Lexikon für Theologie
und Gemeinde* refers to Lefebvre and others as examples of Catholic conservatism, wrongly—according to the author of the article—called "fundamentalists."

A decisive step towards a broader understanding of fundamentalism was
taken when Ayatollah Khomeini came to power in Iran in 1979. That was a
shock to the whole Western world, that until the departure of the Shah from
Iran was convinced that modernization, as undertaken by the Shah and strongly supported by the West, would lead Iran to modern thinking in the best
Western Enlightenment tradition. It seemed inconceivable that such a process
of modernization could be stopped in the name of a religion that would effectively serve as an antimodernist force in the modern history of Iran. When the
Islamic Revolution succeeded against all expectations of both politicians and
trained scholars of different disciplines, the inexplicable had to be explained in
clear terms. Fundamentalism came to be seen as the most useful way to express
what had happened, namely a rejection of modernity and a return towards traditional concepts of religion as the guiding principle for politics.

Here the challenge was less that of reconciling dogmatic claims with
historical research and modern scientific understanding, than the claim that
politics should be shaped in a fundamental way by religious concerns and

obligations. This religious restructuring of modern politics was new and a significant expression of what was labeled as fundamentalism. Fundamentalism became a pejorative, negative term, a mark of extremely conservative religious thinking in its rejection of the modern claim that religion is simply a private matter, rightly kept separate from the organization of society overall.

Iran was not the only Islamic case where fundamentalism was described as an antimodern trend. Protest movements such as the Muslim Brothers in Egypt and Algeria were described in the same way, too, so that "fundamentalism" became a negative key term to designate opposition to Western concepts of a modern state. Differences amongst such opponents (for example, between the problems identified by Iranian, Egyptian and Algerian protesters, and hence the different remedies each offered) were not considered important. All protests in the name of Islamic religion were seen as expressions of fundamentalism, understood reductively as merely rejecting Western concepts of the modern state, rather than as an alternative reading of politics and the state in which religion has to play a decisive public role. This single-minded emphasis on what protesters opposed, rather than on their various understandings, proposals and goals, effectively suppressed those differences in subsequent debate.

The lack of differentiation with regard to proposals and goals noted above encouraged as undifferentiated application of the term in other contexts as well. A fundamentalist rejection of the modern state was now not exclusive to Muslims, but could easily be widened to include Hindus, for example, as in their protests of the 1990s against the loss of traditional values and norms due to the undue influence of non-Hindu traditions.

The broader use of the term in media and non-academic circles was paralleled by a scholarly attempt to study the phenomenon systematically. Conferences were organized and the results of these academic meetings were published in many Western countries. The most prestigious enterprise was directed by Martin E. Marty and R. Scott Appleby who made the fundamentalist challenge known to the academic world and declared its importance on a world-wide scale requiring scrutiny of all religious traditions. The need to satisfy the main interest of the project had a double effect: on the one hand, it was claimed that religions like Buddhism (cf. Donald K. Swearer in Marty/Appleby 1991: 628) and Judaism (cf. Gideon Aran in Marty/Appleby 1991: 265–344) did not easily yield data for the study, forcing the authors to look for substitute or comparable phenomena to replace the missing data; on the other hand, the fact that these religions were present in the study supported the notion that fundamentalism in this new sense is a world-wide phenomenon existing in all religious traditions. What was intended as a caution against using the term indiscriminantly thus had the counter-effect of suggesting fundamentalism's universal existence. Fundamentalism's development from a term designating a specific religious group within one religion, namely a specific form of Protestant Christianity, to a general tendency found in all religions has culminated in the term as described in the fourth edition of the German *Lexikon für Theologie und Kirche*. A term that once demarcated an internal distinction ("liberalism" or "modernity" from "the fundamentals" of the faith) has now become a way to describe groups from the outside.

The designation from the outside, however, did not remain unnoticed by those being referred to. They learned through publications on fundamentalism that they were not alone in their criticism of the negative effects of modernity. So, they started to use the label "fundamentalist" for themselves and took advantage of these studies on fundamentalism in order to get into contact with fundamentalists of other religious traditions so that a communication network was created that enriched the debate of most of these groups. In the Islamic Arab world moreover, the so-called "Islamicists" (in Arabic: *islāmiyyūn*, i.e. those who wish to make of Islam a political system) then called themselves "fundamentalists," using a literal translation of the term into Arabic by saying *uṣūliyyūn*. In connection with religion, this term is suggestive of "the principles of religion" (in Arabic: *uṣūl al-dīn*, a well known title for many medieval handbooks of Islamic theology) so that what was originally intended as a pejorative term for extremists took on very positive pious connotations. Subsequently, the debate took a different turn, accepting fundamentalism as a positive disposition that needed to be distinguished from fanatism and extremism in religion. Only the latter were associated with negative connotations while fundamentalism developed a much more positive image than previously, when it was exclusively associated with antimodern tendencies.

To summarize: a look at the history of the term fundamentalism (cf. Marty/ Appleby 1991: 823–33) showed that it was initially a self-referential term chosen by antimodern American protestants and only much later was used to designate Islamic protest groups rejecting negative consequences of modernity in their countries, notwithstanding the respective differences in their proposals and goals. A further step then was the extension of the term to other groups than Christians and Muslims, namely Hindus, so that the door was opened to finding fundamentalism in all contemporary religions. The consequence was academic research on the phenomenon as a world-wide tendency in religions that is seen as the major challenge to the modern state in international politics, this even more so since those groups themselves have started to refer to themselves in this way. In the Arabic case, moreover, fundamentalism developed positive connotations so that what was meant as a pejorative term became a mark of religious integrity, leaving only fanatism and extremism to be seen in a negative light.

The application of the term to different religious traditions was possible because they all had one point in common, namely their criticism of the modern state as a source of the loss of traditional values and as a producer of marginalization. It was neither in the center of the debate what these groups proposed, nor how they wished to overcome the difficulties they deplored. Here the differences between religions, and between certain trends within one and the same religion, would have mattered a great deal and would have made it impossible to interpret all these in the same way. The debate, however, concentrated the common point of protest and thus harmonized options rather than differentiating them. As a result, "fundamentalism" came to describe a general trend of opposition to the concept of the modern state. The following description of the characteristic elements of fundamentalism will show how this harmonization works and how it leads to a specific perception of the world.

2. The Characteristic Elements of Fundamentalism

The concept of a fundamentalist challenge that can be found in all religious traditions of the world today is based on the conviction that all the respective groups criticize the existing political situation of the countries in which they live. In terms of a definition, one may say: "*fundamentalists seek to replace existing structures with a comprehensive system* emanating from religious principles and embracing law, polity, society, economy, and culture" (Marty/Appleby 1991: 824). Their protest is directed against what was imported from, and supported by, the West, namely the concept of the modern state. The argument is that the modern state leads to a loss of the values and norms supported by traditional religious teachings. Therefore, a return to the application of these principles is imperative to avoid the negative consequences of their abandonment, as seen by many people in the country. Those who share these criticisms join the protesters and become members of so-called fundamentalist groups which, if they grow in number, are a real threat to political establishment, as it was the case during the last years of the Shah's regime in Iran or, during the 1980s and 1990s, in the less successful cases of Egypt and Algeria, and in Hindu circles of India.

The central point of these criticisms is not, as it is for American Protestant fundamentalism, a theological stance opposed to new scriptural interpretations and some of the findings of the natural sciences. It is the political claim for greater justice, interpreted according to classical values and norms, and mainly directed against global market strategies which are accused of being only profit orientated and of lacking respect for human beings. The solution, therefore, for Muslim protesters lies in Islamic economics and for Hindus, in a return to the classical caste system. The main argument is that these classical teachings set a social framework that needs to be respected in political decision-making, something that cannot be achieved if other priorities, such as profit, prevail.

The perceived economic and moral crisis of the country is, consequently, the driving force for the fundamentalists' criticisms of state policy. This has consequences for the understanding of religion in these criticisms, it has an impact on the followers and their interests, it sheds light on their opposition to modernity, and it delineates the political claims to overcome the crisis.

Religion is in this context not, as it is often depicted in English and American sociology of religion (cf. Kippenberg 1997: 239), an irrational stratum which has survived in spite of all attempts to achieve the rationality that is the hallmark of modernization. Instead, religion needs to be seen as a legitimate protest in the name of undeniable principles. It is used as a means to express the protest of those who consider themselves as losers in the battle with the West and who claim that, notwithstanding the great progress of Western technology, the value system of society should be the traditional one. They deplore that it is no longer respected, hence the crisis they describe. Nothing in that is irrational; the arguments are logically convincing if properly attended to. To insist that an argument in support of traditional religious values is irrelevant because irrational thoughts do not warrant attention, is simply an excuse not to enter the debate, making the conversation a one-sided and unequal one. On the one hand, there are those who claim to be rational because they allegedly make their decisions on the basis of market strategies alone, while on the other, there are those whose thoughts and claims are taken as irrational because, in the name of religion, they argue against the legitimacy of solely market-driven decisions by saying that these are not justified by traditional principles that need to be defended at any price.

The inequality of the partners in this confrontation sheds light on the followers of fundamentalist groups. In most studies on fundamentalism the founders and leaders of these groups as well as their publications are quoted to show how narrow-minded and irrational their lines of argumentation are. Even if this is so in many cases, it does not explain why these people have great success and find followers. A study on the fundamentalist "Front du Salut Is-lamique" (FIS) of Algeria gives evidence (cf. Ignace Leverrier in Kepel 1993: 25–69) that their followers all come from groups of society that are disadvantaged. This holds true for poor people who moved from the countryside to the capital and did not find what they had expected. This is so for students of technical sciences who know that after their studies are concluded they will not have any future on the job market. The fundamentlists offers of financial help and free medical care nourish the hope that after the victory of the FIS, a new phase of prosperous life will begin and ensure that all these marginalized people will have a real chance of full integration and participation in society, with much better lives than are possible for them now. Similar promises were made in Iran for the Islamic Revolution if successful, and it is well known that in the first years of Khomeini's rule in Iran poor families had a better income than under the Shah's regime. Consequently, religious fundamentalism in this respect has arisen to a large extent as a result of the social situation in the countries in which fundamentalists are on the rise. This explains also why the fundamentalist threat will continue to challenge Western interests as long as the socio-political situation of these countries does not improve.

The fact that many followers have been trained in technical sciences indicates that antimodern positions in these circles do not mean a rejection of modern technology as a whole nor does it imply—as has often been said—an irrational desire of return to premodern times, i.e. to medieval ways of life. It only means that the negative consequences of modernity are criticized, yet, quite often with the help of the most modern technological means. The departure of the Shah from Iran and Khomeini's return to the country would not have been possible without modern forms of communication such as tapes, cassettes, radio and TV. The Islamic Revolution was, in any case, more a result of modern mass media and high tech-technology than the effect of a simple call to antimodern lifestyles. A look at the Internet, moreover, shows that these groups make wide use of modern technology for self-presentation and do not hesitate to contact people via fax and e-mail as well as via satellite TV programs. However, in cases where, according to their interpretation, those means are harmful, they wish to impose appropriate forms of control to avoid that harm. If, on the contrary, information serves the interests of these groups, it is welcomed and recommended. Such an attitude is far from being against modernity or modern technology. The main attacks against modernity are directed against modern moral behavior as being too permissive and thus not respectful of traditional moral rules and standards.

Traditional teachings about moral behavior and justice are seen as the means to overcome the crisis. Respecting these is seen as a way to ensure a proper life and society, built on values and a normative framework that are inherently valid. The historical fact of past prosperity and welfare prior to the advent of modernity (i.e. the West) and the social marginalization which followed, is cited as an argument in support of this view. Descriptions of the deplorable conditions of those marginalized in contemporary society thus go hand in hand with a glorification of the past. Both are simplistic visions of reality but they continue to be attractive to desperate people who, with reference to their glorious past, regain a self-esteem that seems to heal the wounds of humiliation from which they suffer. That the explanation is simplistic is the source of its success and it is in this respect noteworthy that not only the followers but often the founders and leaders, too, are lay people in religious matters and not trained specialists of their religious traditions. They are precise in their descriptions of the crisis, they are powerful in their vision of how the world should be but they are often extremely weak in articulating how this aim can be achieved.

The desperate situation is often felt so acutely that many followers support the imminent overthrow of the political establishment, often without any concrete plans as to how a better world can be put into practice. Frustration is often so great that it leads to fanaticism and extremism which do not exclude violence as a legitimate means of political action. Though most of the groups are not extremists in this sense nor advocates of violence, the limits between softer and harder forms of protest are sometimes difficult to draw because of the general situation of society and the counterreactions of those in power to suppress any criticism whatsoever.

Fundamentalism, as shown here, is protest against social, economic and political developments that produce marginalization and are interpreted as consequences of disrespect for traditional values and norms. After so many failures of imported corrective systems like socialism and communism, fundamentalism is now the most recent attempt to combat neoliberalism in the economy and the political systems that make it possible. The goal is to establish greater justice and to maintain moral standards in society. The Western system is seen as being strong in technology but weak in its ability to ensure and defend justice, moral norms and values. The reference to religious traditions is consequently not an irrational, premodern type of survival of religion but a clearly conceived model of religion as a socio-political factor able to intervene where the fundamental rights of people are in jeopardy. What is common to all these groups is their obligation to be the voice of the voiceless in society and to formulate their protest against all forms of social, economic and political exclusion. Consequently, fundamentalism as a general term of protest in society with reference to religion concentrates more on criticisms of concrete situations than on proposals and goals for the future. It is thus a term that unites the groups under a common cause of protest instead of differentiating them with regard to their very different demands. As a result, "fundamentalism" is used to describe all kinds of protest groups in the various religious traditions of the contemporary world. This leads to the fear of the fundamentalist challenge as being present everywhere. It thus favors a certain perception of the world that needs to be looked at more closely.

3. The Perception of the World

Fundamentalism is an explanatory concept used to interpret empirical data. It is based on the conviction that in every religion today, two trends can be found: one, a rejection of modernity and the claim that traditional religious values and norms need to be maintained or restored; the other, in support of modernity, accepting changes in society as consequences of democracy and market strategies, leaving politics to rational planning and reducing religion to a private, individual matter. The latter fits perfectly into market policies while the former, in cases of conflict, gives priority to eternal religious principles instead of majority votes (i.e. democratic decisions). The latter is, consequently, manageable for market orientated economics and politics, while the former is incalculable and therefore a permanent threat to economics and politics as commanded by the market and democratic rule respectively.

For economists and politicians, the assumption of these two trends implies positive attitudes towards the second trend and negative ones towards the first. Therefore, there is opposition not to religion in general but only certain trends within religions. It, moreover, makes it easy to state which group stands for which trend. Empirical facts can thus be related directly to interpretative analysis. This viewpoint helps to bring order into a rather disordered reality. It provides simple explanations and systematizations with regard to complex situations. It offers a vision of the world in which things are clearly discernable in spite of the rather complicated and diversified nature of the cases at hand. Fundamentalism here becomes a key interpretive term in which the advocates of modernity are on the good side and the protesters are on the bad side.

From a hermeneutical point of view, fundamentalism is a good example of constructivism. It shows how empirical facts can be related to a concept of the world which as such is neither empirical nor the result of analyses, but rather preconceived and then enriched with data, even though it is unclear whether or not the data all should be grouped together in this way. Since protest and rejection of modernity as understood above are taken as the common denominators for the designation, fundamentalism comes to appear to be a world-wide tendency. If other denominators such as the particularities of specific religious claims in each of the religions were given more weight, this construction of the concept would no longer work.

To argue against fundamentalism by using the critical perspective of constructivism may seem odd to its defenders. It would indeed be so, if there were not other explanatory frameworks of the same kind, with somewhat different parameters. As examples in the field of religions and their importance for modernity one may think of two views that are also widely discussed. One is the Chicago *Declaration Toward a Global Ethic* of the Parliament of the World's Religions, held in 1993. This declaration was prepared by Hans Küng and tried to show that all great religious traditions of the world were able to cope with modernity, with none totally opposed to the modern world. The proposal advocated concentrating efforts to encourage particular tendencies in religions instead of always focusing on discouraging certain developments or elements. Rather than anxiously fearing fundamentalism, this perspective produces a much more positive description of the present world, and as well helps offset the possibility of producing self-fulfilling prophecies. The right answer to both is presumably to say that the data should be studied carefully in order to see whether the two tendencies do really exist and if so, what the balance is between them. Then it will be important to know how strong eventual collaborations are among groups of each tendency and how important the differences are between them that make common action unlikely. The question whether or not there are these two tendencies in each religion is relevant because the second example excludes internal divisions in religions as a basis for analysis. Such is Huntingtons's vision of "the Clash of Civilizations" for which these trends are irrelevant. What matters here is the idea that the world is dominated by areas in which dominant civilizations/religions make the decision about whether or not to embrace modernity and the Western concepts that go with it. The West is set up against the rest so that religions as a whole are judged by their willingness to accept or refuse Western standards. In this view, Islam is seen as the competitive counterpart of Western civilization and thus as the main threat to the Western world. In Huntington's view, it is not the case that, in addition to Muslim fundamentalists, there are Muslims who are open-minded and ready to accept modernity, as suggested by the *Declaration Toward a Global Ethic*. According to Huntington, Islam as such is a total rejection of modernity and so an enemy to the West. All the other civilizations/religions are in between these two positions, some tending more towards the West, others more towards Islam. The ideological bipolarity of East-West-block politics has thus been replaced by the Clash of Civilizations culminating in the bipolarity between the West and Islam.

Fundamentalism is not the only conceptual framework that can be used to describe the contemporary world. The *Declaration Toward a Global Ethic* offers a different view in its consequences, and Huntington's idea of the eventual Clash of Civilizations rejects the basic assumption of two rival tendencies within each civilization/religion and replaces it instead with a general position of each in favor of, or against, modernity so that civilizations/religions as a whole are seen within a perspective of conflict between two opposite poles: the West and its opponents, with Islam as the pivot of opposition to the West. Since all the three concepts, i.e. fundamentalism, the *Declaration Toward a Global Ethic* and the *Clash of Civilizations*, use empirical data to support their positions, it is obvious that the data itself is not self-evident, but is interpreted according to the per-ception of the world the observer has in mind. Data does not stand alone; only with reference to this vision of the world the empirical data become meaning-ful. That is what one may call constructivism in the field of religions and politics, as is also found in studies that describe recent developments in edu-cation and society. Scholars of religious studies do well to participate in the de-bate and to use the explanatory tools of the debate, but they also have the duty to point out the constructive side of the explanational concept in order to make clear the difference between its theoretical assumptions and its factual claims, or in other terms, what are the facts and what are the theories about them.

Conclusion

This article started by giving encyclopedia examples to document changes in the use of the term fundamentalism. This led to a look at the use of the term over time. It was found that originally the term was a self-designation used by American Protestant groups in early twentieth century, and only much later came to be used by outsiders to designate other religious groups in Catholicism, Islam, and Judaism. Its prominence began with the Islamic Revolution in Iran in 1979 and was from that moment onwards first widely used for all kinds of Islamic protest groups against the political establishment in countries with Islamic majorities, with particular reference to fanatic and extremist, and often also violent, Muslims. An even broader use came into play in the late 1980s and the 1990s when applied to Hindu groups and when research projects such as that of Marty and Appleby treated it as a trend existing in all religious traditions. The term proved to be so successful that it was picked up by academics and non-academics to describe what was and still is going on in many parts of the world. And the fundamentalists themselves, called so from the outside, became steadily more aware of this labeling and finally picked it up as a self-reference so that in some areas the originally pejorative term took on more positive connotations, and even prestige.

The great success of the term in its broader use is certainly due to the fact that it concentrated on protest in the name of religion against economics and politics of the political establishment in many countries in which social exclusion is strongly felt and on the rise. The common denominator is thus what is rejected and not what is proposed instead. Here differences between religions, as well as in interpretation of religious teachings in one and the same tradition, are obvious and hardly justify speaking of one general fundamentalist trend in religions. To interpret all these different forms of protest in the name of religion as the fundamentalist challenge to the modern world as has been done by Marty and Appleby (1992) is rather simplistic but very attractive to scholars, economists, and politicians. It provides the opportunity to see in this reappearance of religion on the public scene some irrational survival of religious thinking that does not require the attention of those who defend rational planning in economics and politics and insist that religion is a private matter for individuals. In fact, however, the fundamentalist challenge makes religion a social and political factor to be reckoned with.

Fundamentalism as a general tendency that is found in all religions is an explanatory concept that brings order to a rather complex reality. It helps to systematize empirical data with the help of an interpretative key that provides orientation by reducing various phenomena to basic options that seem to lie behind them. The fact that other descriptions of the world's religions such as those found in the *Declaration Toward a Global Ethic* or Huntington's Clash of Civilizations offer different interpretations, suggests that the interpretative frame is not the result of analyses of empirical data but a consequence of constructivism. The study of fundamentalism is thus, methodologically speaking, a new approach to the study of religion(s). In future it should concentrate essentially on patterns of interpretation and testing their validity as well as collecting further material about the fundamentalist groups and their ideas, in order to provide a more accurate account of what is actually going on in the world.

448 Peter Antes

Select Bibliography

Antes, Peter (1995), "Religiöser Fundamentalismus," in: Uwe Hartmann/Christian Walther, eds., *Der Soldat in einer Welt im Wandel: Ein Handbuch für Theorie und Praxis*. Mit einem Vorwort von Bundespräsident Roman Herzog. München/Landsberg am Lech: Olzog: 54–60.

— (1996), "Religions and Politics. Facts and Perspectives," in: *Religioni e Società. Rivista di scienze sociali della religione* 26, Anno XI: 5–13.

— (2000), "Fundamentalism: A Western Term with Consequences," in: Armin W. Geertz/Russell T. McCutcheon, eds., with the assistence of Scott S. Elliot, *Perspectives on Method and Theory in the Study of Religion: Adjunct Proceedings of the XVIIth Congress of the International Association for the History of Religions, Mexico City*. Leiden/Boston, Mass./Köln: Brill: 260–66.

— (2003), "The New Politics. History and History of Religions: The World after 11 September 2001," in: *Diogenes* no. 199, vol. 50 (3): *Identities, Beliefs, Images*: 23–29.

Beinert, Wolfgang, ed. (1991), *Katholischer Fundamentalismus: Häretische Gruppen in der Kirche?* Regensburg: Friedrich Pustet.

Beinert, Wolfgang/Müller, Hans-Peter/Garhammer, Erich (1995), "Fundamentalismus," in: *Lexikon für Theologie und Kirche*. Vol. 4. Freiburg/Basel/Wien: Herder: 224–26.

Etienne, Bruno (1987), *L'Islamisme radical*. Paris: Hachette.

Garaudy, Roger (1990), *Intégrismes*. Paris: P. Belfond.

Holthaus, Stephan (1992), "Fundamentalismus," in: *Evangelisches Lexikon für Theologie und Gemeinde*. Vol. 1. Wuppertal/Zürich: R. Brockhaus: 656–57.

Hottinger, Arnold (1993), *Islamischer Fundamentalismus*. Paderborn/München/Wien/Zürich: Schöningh.

Huntington, Samuel (1996), *The Clash of Civilizations and the Remaking of World Order*. New York: Simon and Schuster.

Jäggi, Christian J./Krieger, David J. (1991), *Fundamentalismus: Ein Phänomen der Gegenwart*. Zürich/Wiesbaden: Orell Füssli.

Joest, Wilfried (1983), "Fundamentalismus," in: *Theologische Realenzyklopädie (TRE)*. Vol. 11. Berlin/New York: Walter de Gruyter: 732–38.

Kepel, Gilles, ed. (1993), *Les politiques de Dieu*. Paris: Seuil.

Kienzler, Klaus, ed. (1990), *Der neue Fundamentalismus: Rettung oder Gefahr für Gesellschaft und Religion?* Düsseldorf: Patmos (Schriften der Katholischen Akademie in Bayern, vol. 136).

Kippenberg, Hans G. (1997), *Die Entdeckung der Religionsgeschichte: Religionswissenschaft und Moderne*. München: Beck.

Klemm, Verena/Hörner, Karin, eds. (1993), *Das Schwert des "Experten": Peter Scholl-Latours verzerrtes Araber- und Islambild*. Heidelberg: Palmyra.

Kochanek, Hermann, ed. (1991), *Die verdrängte Freiheit: Fundamentalismus in den Kirchen*. Freiburg/Basel/Wien: Herder.

Marty, Martin E./Appleby, R. Scott, eds. (1991), *Fundamentalisms Observed*. Chicago/London: The University of Chicago Press (The Fundamentalism Project, vol. 1).

— eds. (1992), *The Glory and the Power: The Fundamentalist Challenge to the Modern World*. Boston, Mass.: Beacon Press.

—— eds. (1993), *Fundamentalisms and Society: Reclaiming the Sciences, the Family, and Education*. Chicago/London: The University of Chicago Press (The Fundamentalism Project, vol. 2).

—— eds. (1993), *Fundamentalisms and the State: Remaking Policies, Economics, and Militance*. Chicago/London: The University of Chicago Press (The Fundamentalism Project, vol. 3).

—— eds. (1994), *Accounting for Fundamentalisms: The Dynamic Character of Movements*. Chicago/London: The University of Chicago Press (The Fundamentalism Project, vol. 4).

—— eds. (1996), *Fundamentalisms Comprehended*. Chicago/London: The University of Chicago Press (The Fundamentalism Project, vol. 5).

Meyer, Thomas, ed. (1989), *Fundamentalismus in der modernen Welt: Die Internationale der Unvernunft*. Frankfurt am Main: Suhrkamp.

—— (1989), *Fundamentalismus: Aufstand gegen die Moderne*. Reinbek: Rowohlt.

Mimouni, Rachid (1992), *De la barbarie en général et de l'intégrisme en particulier*. Paris: P. Belfond-Le Pré aux Clercs.

Newman, A.J./Jansen, J.J.G. (2000), "Uṣūliyya," in: *The Encyclopaedia of Islam*. New Ed. Vol. 10. Leiden: Brill: 935–38.

Parliament of the World's Religions (1993), *Declaration Toward a Global Ethic*. Tübingen: Stiftung Weltethos.

Pfürtner, Stephan (1991), *Fundamentalismus: Die Flucht ins Radikale*. Freiburg/Basel/Wien: Herder (Spektrum 4031).

Riesebrodt, Martin (1990), *Fundamentalismus als patriarchalische Protestbewegung: Amerikanische Protestanten (1910–28) und iranische Schiiten (1961–79) im Vergleich*. Tübingen: Mohr.

Rotter, Gernot, ed. (1993), *Die Welten des Islam: Neunundzwanzig Vorschläge, das Unvertraute zu verstehen*. Frankfurt am Main: Fischer.

Schermann, Rudolf, ed. (1990), *Wider den Fundamentalismus: kein Zurück hinter das II. Vatikanische Konzil*. Mattersburg/Bad Sauerbrunn: Ed. Tau.

Schmiegelow, Henrik, ed. (1999), *Preventing the Clash of Civilizations: A Peace Strategy for the Twenty-First Century*. [By Roman Herzog with comments by Amitai Erzioni, Hans Küng, Bassam Tibi and Masakazu Yamazaki.] New York: St. Martin's Press.

Tibi, Bassam (1998), *The Challenge of Fundamentalism: Political Islam and the New World Disorder*. Berkeley, Calif. et al.: University of California Press (Comparative Studies in Religion and Society, vol. 9).

—— (2000), *Fundamentalismus im Islam: Eine Gefahr für den Weltfrieden?* Darmstadt: Wissenschaftliche Buchgesellschaft.

Werbick, Jürgen, ed. (1991), *Offenbarungsansprüche und die fundamentalistische Versuchung*. Freiburg/Basel/Wien: Herder (Quaestiones disputatae 129).

Zen and the Art of Inverting Orientalism

Buddhism, Religious Studies and Interrelated Networks

by

JØRN BORUP

1. Introduction[1]

No single book has caused so much trouble and post-modern haunting in the fields of Orientalism as Edward Said's book of the same name from 1978. Though many books in the last few years go *beyond*, or simply negate the critique of Orientalism, Said (following Foucault) did raise some important issues to be continuously reflected upon. Apart from being an "exotic variant of the hermeneutical circle" (Faure 1993: 7), Orientalism in Said's eyes was a "Western style for domination, restructuring, and having authority over the Orient" (Said 1978: 2–3). The Orient in the hands of Orientalists was not so much a place, but a concept, a rhetorical means, where clichés about the passive, mystical, exotic, and corrupt Orientals could stand undisputed because they, being the silent Other, could not represent themselves.

In this article I do not intend to go into a general discussion of Said, his project, the critique having been raised against him, nor the almost inexhaustible row of problems which his own critique raises. Rather, I will put it into perspective by involving an often ignored aspect of the relationship between them and us, between emic and etic discourse, namely the others' response to, and systematic use of, what Said describes as the Orientalist project. I am not so much interested in the political as in the epistemological causes and consequences of "Orientalism" and its impact upon religious discourse.

As a starting point I assert that representation of others is not only a one-way construction. The process of representing and being represented is—and necessarily must be—a reciprocal communication process, with which the

---

1   Since this paper was originally submitted (1999), several articles, books, and conferences have further touched upon issues related to this article. See for instance Schalk 2003 and Snodgrass 2003.

critique of Orientalism also has to be put in perspective. There are also fusion of horizons as well as "Occidentalisms" and inverted Orientalisms.[2]

First I will describe how Buddhism was "written" in the West. This is followed by the description of an ideological and genealogical network within historical frames, leading towards the influential Japanese Zen interpreter and apologist D.T. Suzuki.[3] His representation of Zen and Buddhism is characterized by his focus on a decontextualized, transcendent and yet uniquely Japanese and Eastern concept. The historical relation and the sociology of knowledge around Suzuki is described to show that this Zen-interpretation is neither uniquely "native" nor independent of historical and discourse related contexts. On the contrary, Suzuki-Zen is a product of both a unique individual as well as of a unique interrelated network of ideas and persons.[4] As a counterpart to Said's Orientalists Suzuki-Zen represents reverse, or inverted Orientalism: it uses and structurally inverts Orientalist ideas and metaphors to its own advantage. Independently Bernard Faure (1993) and Robert Sharf (1993) have already brilliantly described and contextualized Suzuki and his Zen.[5] By using and extending their insightful observations and discussions this article intends to further underline and exemplify this traffic of ideas and persons behind the interesting relationship between the East and the West, as well as between emic and etic discourses. Suzuki-Zen is but one example of the (very important, but often ignored) inverted Orientalist response to postcolonial modernity in search of religious identity. A discourse only having been made

---

2   Carrier 1995 distinguishes between four related terms in a typology useful for illustrating the complex of problems. Apart from Orientalism (the West's essentialization of the others), he defines its contrast, "ethno-Orientalism," as "essentialist renderings of alien societies by the members of those societies themselves" (198), Occidentalism as "essentialist renderings of the West by Westerners," and ethno-Occidentalism as "essentialist renderings of the West by members of alien societies" (198). To further expand the confusion of ideas, see Lindstrom's (1995) introduction of the terms "auto-Occidentalism," "internal-Orientalism," "pseudo-Orientalism" etc. Probably Bernard Faure was the first to use the concept "reverse Orientalism" (1993: 53).

3   Though Said did not have much to say about this cultural and religious area the problems are naturally relevant—also in spite of the fact that Japan was never colonized, and Buddhism in general has always had a more positive image in the West, compared to the Islamic Middle East. See Lopez 1995 on postcolonial Buddhist studies.

4   Like Said, I also believe in the "determining imprint of individual writers upon the otherwise anonymous collective body of texts constituting a discursive formation like Orientalism," because "Orientalism is after all a system for citing works and authors" (1978: 23).

5   Faure, for instance calls it "Zen Orientalism" (1993: 52) and "secondary Orientalism" (1993: 5): "despite his nativist tendency, Suzuki relied heavily on the categories of nineteenth-century Orientalism. He simply inverted the old schemas to serve his own purposes" (1993: 64).

possible because of its inspiration from and cultivation in both "East" and "West." Inverted Orientalism and Suzuki-Zen are products of a cultural mixed marriage—just as Said is himself.[6]

2. Buddhism in the Western Mind

Buddhists have always studied and practiced what they have understood to be Buddha's way(s) and teaching(s). But as an object for systematic and scientific study, (the Orientalist construct) Buddhism was not born until the latter half of the nineteenth century.

Buddhism and the early *science of religion* were raised and cultivated in the dialectical relationship between the theoretical paradigms of universalism and evolutionism, between the rationality of enlightenment and the romanticist quest for spiritual truths. The Orient had been re-discovered in what Raymond Schwab calls the "Oriental Renaissance" (1984). Philosophers, poets, academics and interested laymen were fascinated by the revelation from the new spiritual dimension from the East. In spite—or because—of Western colonial power and suppression, the East became the missing link to a mental landscape, a projected Other World. The attitudes toward Eastern religions reflected different historical periods and thoughts in the West, placing them in—or structurally beyond—religious evolutionary schemes or ideas of universalism. The (especially French) enlightenment period had already raised Confucius as a rational gentleman, in opposition to the inferior, magical and ritualized "little tradition," Daoism, as well as against the contemporary European Christianity, losing its authority. Later (especially German) romanticism could use the "Hindus as mystics" and Hinduism as "undogmatic Protestantism" (Marshall 1970: 43–44). Both the rationalistic attitudes towards Chinese (Confucian) enlightenment and romanticist ideas of Indian mysticism were reincarnated in the discovery of Buddhism.

Buddha had variously been identified as an African and mongol, as Noah and Adam, as Osiris and Neptune, and even as Odin (Almond 1988). That he was also to be identified with Jesus and Luther and become a "true Victorian gentleman" (Almond 1988: 79) was due to the first serious reception and invention of Buddhism in the latter part of the nineteenth century. Edwin Arnold, who actually had been to India himself, and was "part of the late Victorian liberal/intellectual *avant-garde*—he was friendly with Darwin, Huxley, Herbert

---

6   In the words of J.J. Clarke: "The perceived otherness of the Orient is not exclusively one
     of mutual antipathy, nor just a means of affirming Europe's triumphant superiority,
     but also provides a conceptual framework that allows much fertile cross-referencing,
     the discovery of similarities, analogies, and models; in other words, the underpinning
     of a productive hermeneutical relationship (1997: 27).

Spencer, and John Stuart Mill" (Clarke 1997: 88)—wrote *The Light of Asia* in 1879, a poetic, romantic and Christian inspired[7] story of Buddha (later to be dramatized as theatre, opera and film) causing "an enormous upsurge in awareness of, and interest in, Buddhism" (Almond 1988: 1). It is said that reading Edwin Arnold was the reason Ananda Metteyya (Allan Bennett), the first known Western Buddhist monk, and the first Theravada monk to visit the West, became a Buddhist monk. He later made Edwin Arnold the first honorary member of his International Buddhist Society, *Buddhasāsana Samāgama*.[8] Some years earlier, in 1844, the French scholar Eugéne Burnouf wrote *L'Intro-duction à l'histoire du buddhisme indien*, the first detailed academic study of early Indian Buddhism. With him, Buddhist Studies had begun. Texts were collected, research carried out, Buddhism was interpreted, defined and revealed at the desks of energetic buddhologists. The search for the historical Buddha, the quest for the original de-mythologized Buddhism was most professionally organized in the (still existing) Pali Text Society. Created in London in 1881 by T.W. Rhys Davids, Pali was found to be the authentic language of early and essential Buddhism. Pali-canonic Theravada Buddhism was, by others, baptized "Protestantism of the East" (Almond 1988: 74), in opposition to the corrupt, "Catholic" Mahayana Buddhism (and Hinduism) with all its folklore, magic, superstition and idolatry.[9] To Victorian Protestants and the "Pali Text Society Spirit" (Faure 1991: 89), monastic life was not interesting, it expressed Catholic practice.[10] Meditation was often seen to express ritualized (and thus legitimate) laziness. Perhaps the most important quality of Buddhism was its status as "dead": Actual living Buddhism was looked upon as a false folk-religion, degenerated from pure and only existing "real" textual Buddhism. Living Buddhists were not true Buddhists, and they did not understand their own religion. Religious practice was considered to be a minor and false aspect of religious discourse.

From the outset there were built-in dichotomies in the approach to Buddhism; original versus degenerated, theory versus practice, doctrine versus

---

7 Arnold's main source of information on Buddhism was the Wesleyan missionary in Ceylon, Rev. Spence Hardy.

8 The branch (or support group) in England, the Buddhist Society of Great Britain and Ireland was later to have T.W. Rhys Davids as its president.

9 See Stcherbatsky 1977 (1923) for a comparison of these two "types" of Buddhism. To distinguish northern, Tibetan Buddhism from "true" Buddhism the concept "lamaism" has long been used to designate a further degenerated religious type.

10 To some Catholic missionaries, however, Buddhist monks were considered to be living (often degenerated) remains from earlier, often mythical, missionary efforts. The legendary founder of Chan Buddhism, Bodhidharma, for instance, was considered to be a misunderstood copy of the apostle Thomas (Faure 1993: 45.) When Xavier met the Japanese Buddhists he thought them to be fallen Christians—just as some of his opponents thought of Christianity as a strange Buddhist sect (App 1997).

ritual, spiritual essence versus material manifestation etc. —with the former part of the dichotomy having the hierarchical priority. Buddhism became an invented tradition, and a projected battlefield, reflecting the mind and culture of the "discoverer."[11]

3. Buddhism and Theosophy

The interest in Eastern religions as rationalistic and humanistic textual religions was, however, only one side of the coin. Mysticism and inner, subjective "spiritualism" were concepts appealing to the "romanticist" side of the Orientalists. The Theosophical Society played a major role in transmitting ideas of the exotic and "mystical East," of karma and reincarnation—and of Buddhism. Searching for universal religious "scientific" truths—somewhat inspired by Max Müller and his "scientific study of religion"—and esoteric wisdom, the society played a significant role in creating mental landscapes of geographic places. Egypt, India, Tibet, and in general "The East" manifested sacred space in theosophical cosmology. Based on the founder Madam Blavatsky's personal intuitive insight and magical powers, the Theosophical Society also reflected general thoughts of *fin de siècle*. They talked about a universal Wisdom Religion with an underlying essential religious truth, while also using evolutionary schemes— somewhat inspired by the social Darwinistic ideas of Herbert Spencer—tracing the purest manifestations and the source of all religion to Eastern religions, emphasizing a religious, cultural, spiritual and cosmic development, based on distinctions between esoteric truth and exoteric knowledge, between higher and lower mentalities and religions. Though anti-Christian, the theosophists often took over "Protestant" ideas and metaphors (inner individual spirituality and truths through texts versus outer ritualized and "degenerated" clergy-mediated religious practice) using them against Christianity itself and against the living religions of Asia. The theosophists, however, also helped create a more

---

11 King (1999: 144) suggests that "it is not clear that the Tibetans, the Sinhalese or the Chinese conceived of themselves as 'Buddhists' before they were so labelled by Westerners." The same counts to a large extent for Japanese Buddhists to which we will return later. That Buddhism as a concept was created (and later taken over by the Buddhists themselves) in itself is naturally not a problem, but expresses a phenomenological and conceptual necessity within the comparative study of religion. In this broad generalization it must also be stressed that some scholars were more scientifically minded than others. If early Buddhism is identified with the Pali canon—and this is a topic of discussion—it can of course also be argued that "the representation of early Buddhism as rationalist and free of ritual was not simply a creation of Westerners like Rhys Davids but reflected the attitudes of their Asian informants as well" (Nattier 1997: 471).

positive image of the northern Mahayana Buddhism with all its magic and mystery.

As her personal sources of inspiration to her knowledge on Asian religions and Buddhism, Blavatsky was at least familiar with the writings of Max Müller, William Jones, Eugéne Burnouf and Edwin Arnold. Regarding the respect for the latter, in her will she asked her friends to gather each year on the anniversary of her death day and read from his Light of Asia and from the Bhagavad-Gita (Cranston 1993: 429).[12]

Though the movement split and members publicly doubted Blavatsky's alleged spiritual and physical journeys to Tibet, since its foundation in 1875 the movement has had great impact on scholars'[13] as well as laymen's view of Buddhism. There was a theosophical subgroup of the Buddhist Society in London, the Buddhist Lodge, and prominent members of the Pali Text Society as well as other Buddhist scholars such as Christmas Humphreys, Edward Conze and Alan Watts were themselves Buddhists and somehow related to the Theosophical Society.[14] The first Western practicing Buddhist monks, as well as many practicing laymen, had their first impression about Buddhism from

---

12 Edwin Arnold was also influenced by Blavatsky, and he was impressed by the theosophical movement which has had "an excellent effect upon humanity" (Cranston 1993: 428). Light of Asia was even more widely known in America than in England, maybe because it was introduced through the Transcendentalist circle (Wright 1957: 73). Arnold was a personal friend of Emerson, whose name he gave to his youngest son.

13 Though being inspired by Buddhist scholars, however, many theosophists were against their too "theoretical" approach to religion—just as many academics (for instance Rhys Davids and Max Müller) were critical of the popular and amateurish approach of the theosophists. Olcott himself writes, after having met Max Müller, that they "agreed to disagree" on Buddhist matters (Olcott 1910, vol. 4: 59)—especially Müller insisted that esoteric teachings had no place in (Pali!) Buddhism. Emile Burnouf (cousin of Eugéne Burnouf), on the other hand, was more positive: "This [universal brotherhood] declaration [of the Theosophical Society] is purely Buddhistic: the practical publications of the Society are either translations of Buddhist books, or original works inspired by the teaching of Buddha. Therefore the Society has a Buddhist character" (quoted in Taylor 1999). Another source of inspiration for both Buddhists and theosophists was the Swedish Emmanuel Swedenborg: The first American Buddhist journals were "devoted to Buddhism in general, and to the Buddhism in Swedenborg in particular" (Loy 1996: 89).

14 Humphreys, who started the Buddhist Lodge in 1924, also wrote a book about, and forewords to some of the books by, Blavatsky. According to Mircia Eliade, Edward Conze, who thought of Buddhism as a kind of Gnosticism, admired Blavatsky's The Secret Doctrine, and thought she was the reincarnation of Tsongkhapa (Eliade 1978: 208).

theosophy and in general the reception and mental image of Buddhism in the West has gone through somewhat theosophical glasses.[15]

The most obvious theosophical impact on Buddhism itself, however, goes through Henry Steel Olcott.

4. Olcott, the White Buddhist

Henry Steel Olcott is a well known person in the Buddhist world. Without him, modern Buddhism might not have looked the way it does. He helped start the Theosophical Society as the charismatic Blavatsky's more "rational" partner. He soon found a particular interest in Buddhism, especially after having taken "refuge in the three jewels" in Ceylon in 1880 with Blavatsky—a ritual granting them the status of officially being the first Western Buddhists. Olcott was honored the "White Buddhist" and "the bodhisattva of the nineteenth century" by leading Buddhists, who saw the possibilities of the impact of this energetic man from the West, in a time where Buddhism was in deep crisis. Though "Buddhists were by no means dormant before the arrival of the theosophists" (Malalgoda 1976: 256), Olcott helped the Ceylonese revive—and invent—their religious and cultural tradition. He promoted and helped start Buddhist schools (modeled after missionary schools), a Buddhist Theosophical Society and a Buddhist response to YMCA, the Young Men's Buddhist Association.[16] He interceded with the British to have the birth, enlightenment and death anniversaries of the Buddha, Wesak, declared a public holiday (Amunugama 1985: 727). He helped design a Buddhist flag, still used today in the Buddhist world

---

15 Though later renouncing both, Ananda Metteyya was a member of the esoteric section of the Theosophical Society as well as the occult Hermetical Order of the Golden Dawn. Before turning Buddhist he was known to be a magician, and the teacher and friend of the occult master Aleister Crowley, who sponsored Metteyas travels to Ceylon and Burma (Harris 1998: 17). Other well-known Western Buddhists related to, or members of, the Theosophical Society include Nyanatiloka (Anthon Gueth), Govinda (Ernst Lothar Hoffmann), Alexandra David-Neel and Evans-Wentz. The present Dalai Lama had his first book published by the Theosophical Society, wrote the foreword to the 1989 edition of Blavatsky's *The Voice of the Silence*, and has visited and given speeches at the headquarters several times. In general the theosophists have also founded the way for what Donald Lopez calls "New Age-Orientalism" (1994), and many Tibetan lamas and authors can thank Evans-Wentz for the success of his strongly theosophically influenced book, the *Tibetan Book of the Dead* (see Lopez 1998).

16 The politically influential lay organization *All Ceylon Buddhist Congress* grew out of YMBA. Theosophically inspired politics is not unique: In India many of the founding members of the National Congress were theosophists, including Gandhi and of course Annie Besant. Interestingly, Gandhi was introduced to his beloved Bhagavadgita through Edwin Arnold's translation in his book *The Song Celestial* (Sharpe 1985: 60).

as an ecumenical symbol and as the official flag of the Worlds Fellowship of Buddhists. And he wrote his idea of how true spiritual, rational and textually founded Buddhism ought to be, the *Buddhist Catechism* (1881), to many having the status as a Buddhist Bible.[17] Olcott was interested in helping the national reform of Ceylonese Buddhism, but, being both a theosophist and a Buddhist, he was also a spokesman of a "United Buddhist World," and a "universal Brotherhood of Humanity." He was granted an official commission to conduct the ceremony of giving the refuges to Ceylonese Buddhists[18]—no layman had ever before been authorized such privilege[19]—and was asked by Burmese Buddhist priests to do missionary work in Europe. In Sri Lanka today, Buddhists are still celebrating "Olcott Day."

5. Dharmapāla—a Native Modern Buddhist

Anagārika (Don David Hevavitarana, 1861–1933) was born a Singhalese and a Buddhist, but was, since there were no Buddhist schools yet, educated in Christian schools. Through his family he knew well both Hikkaduve Sumangala and Mohottivatte Gunānanda, two of the leading Buddhist reformers in late nineteenth century Ceylon. High priest Sumangala was Olcott's personal friend, and one of the leaders of the Buddhist Theosophical Society. Gunānanda had founded the Society for the Propagation of Buddhism in imitation of the Society for the Propagation of the Gospel (Gombrich 1988: 181), and copying Christian rhetoric he victoriously discussed with (and humiliated) his Christian

---

17   According to Olcott himself, the catechism was used at Sorbonne, where he was an Honorary Member of the Société d'Ethnographie: the lecturer "told his pupils that they would find more real Buddhism in it than in any of the books published by Orientalists"(Olcott 1910, vol. 4: 276). Another Buddhist modernizer and early supporter of the theosophists, Gunānanda, who translated parts of Blavatsky's *Isis unveiled* into Sinhalese, a few years later wrote his own Buddhist catechism, inspired by, and as a rival to, Olcott's catechism (Malalgoda 1976: 252). A German convert, Subhadra Bhiksu (Friedrich Zimmermann), in 1888 wrote his *Buddhistischer Katechismus*, approved by Sumangala and later to be published by the Maha Bodhi Society.

18   The document was signed by H. Sumangala and W. Subhuti, the learned priest who was an instructor of T.W. Rhys Davids (Kirthisinghe 1981: 10–11).

19   Maybe this religious conduct had extra power due to his magical healing powers. Both monks, priests, laymen and Indian Brahmins were healed by Olcott's miracles—supposedly because of his *siddhis* (magical power) which he received through telepathic contact with the theosophical "masters," but probably also due to the fact that he was white. George Bond explains the related phenomenon that contemporary Sri Lankans accept Western meditation teachers, as the "Olcott complex"; "foreigners who espouse one's own tradition enhance its credibility and increase one's appreciation of it" (1988: 191).

opponents in public debates. Dharmapāla was deeply inspired by him, as he was by Colonel Olcott, whom he first heard when he was only sixteen years old. Later, through his friendship with Blavatsky and especially Olcott, he himself became a theosophist—his grandfather was already the president of the lay section of the society—a proud Buddhist and one of the founders of the Buddhist revival in Sri Lanka. Dharmapāla was not a philosopher, but "a propagandist, though in the best sense of the term" (Gokhale 1973: 35), a fact which made the British government put him in exile from Ceylon for some years.

Influenced by theosophy[20] and E. Arnold[21] (whom he often quoted), Dharmapāla wanted to define an authentic ("*Aryan*") Buddhism as scientific, human, rational and spiritual. He was in lead fighting the colonial power, Christianity and a corrupt priesthood. What Obeyesekere has termed "Protestant Buddhism" (1970) encompasses very well the characteristics of early Buddhist modernity, contained and expressed by Dharmapāla. Protestant Buddhism reacted against, and was deeply inspired by, the ideas, methods, and terminology of the Western colonial power and Christianity.[22] "The essence of Protestantism as we understand it lies in the individual's seeking his or her ultimate goal without intermediaries" (Gombrich/Obeyesekere 1988: 215). Other important keywords are universalism, individualism, egalitarianism, internalization and lay orientation.[23]

---

20 Blavatsky "acted as something of a mother figure to him" (Gombrich 1988: 189), and "in his eyes she was a Buddhist, and the agent of Masters who were also Buddhists" (Sangharakshita 1983: 29). Blavatsky advised Dharmapāla to study Pali and become a Buddhist missionary (Guruge 1965: 687). Before his later break with the movement, he apparently "considered himself more of a theosophist than a Buddhist" (de Tollenaere 1996: 277).

21 He visited him in London in 1893, and was deeply inspired by his book *Light of Asia*. Sangharakshita says he revered him as his "English Guru" (1983: 60).

22 Likewise, the religion of Dharmapāla's mentor, Olcott, has been described by Prothero as a "creolization" of liberal Protestantism: "While the lexicon of his faith was almost entirely Buddhist, its grammar was largely Protestant" (1996: 9). Dharmapāla, as well as his Indian counterpart Vivekānanda, were influenced by theosophical ideas of origination and evolution in their ideas of both Hinduism and Buddhism being the true roots of Christianity. Vivekānanda and his Neo-Vedantism used same ideas and metaphors in his "brahmanization" of Buddhism (King 1999: 144).

23 The concept "Protestant Buddhism," which has been further developed by Gombrich and Obeyesekere (1988: 202–41), naturally has been criticized for being an inadequate and ethnocentric term. As an analytical tool for making phenomenological analogies, as a concept "good to think with" personally I find it rather useful. The biased dichotomy between "Protestant" and "Catholic" has itself in Sri Lanka contributed to anti-Mahayana prejudice (Gombrich/Obeyesekere 1988: 220). Interestingly, "the Protestant missionaries who were the models for the first Protestant Buddhists were fundamentalists" (Gombrich/Obeyesekere 1988: 220).

Higher Buddhism is pure science. It has no place for theology, and ... it rejects the superstitions of an eternal hell and an eternal heaven, it rejects the idea of prayer to bribe the god, and it repudiates the interference of priests. (Guruge 1965: 658–59)

Dharmapāla searched for the true original Buddhism as exposed in the Pali literature (which he himself mainly read in English) and in the Ceylonese chronicles, in which he found evidence for the island being buddhicized and "civilized." Buddhist modernity was to him a return to origin, reform was the true purification of tradition, where the Sinhalese by actively supporting and following the Buddha's way could enlighten themselves here and now, and thus show the rest of the world the marvel of the East, compressed in Singhalese Theravada Buddhism.

His name "Anagārika" which originally in Pali and Sanskrit means "homeless," i.e. a monk's status, was by Dharmapāla (which means "Defender of the Buddhist doctrine") transformed to designate a status in between monk and layman.[24] He had long hair, wore white robes (the traditional layman's garb), but he also practiced celibacy and kept the eight precepts (normally only to be observed on *uposatha* days). In spite of his resistance towards the traditional priest- and monkhood, he became a monk himself in 1933, shortly before his death. Symbolically, he was buried in Sarnath, the place where the Buddha was supposed to have given his first sermon. Dharmapāla was in many ways a person "betwixt-and-between," a position in which his ideological stance as a "this-worldly ascetic," influenced from both East and West, took on a symbolic meaning.

In his homeland Dharmapāla, the "Lion of Lanka," became a national hero. He has streets named after him, and even a "Dharmapāla Day" was created, later to be subsumed in the National Heroes' Day. He was seen as a bodhisattva, "and he apparently considered himself to be one" (Gombrich 1988: 188). A Sri Lankan prime minister called him "one of the greatest men Ceylon has produced" (Guruge 1965: v), and many "political bhikkhus" who "sought to become reformers instead of renouncers" (Bond 1988: 69) were directly inspired by him. His *anagārika* role has "become virtually redundant because what it embodies has become so commonplace" (Gombrich/Obeyesekere 1988: 233). He is seen as a model for modern lay Buddhism, and especially he "initiated the fashion for lay meditation" (Gombrich 1988: 191), a religious practice hitherto reserved for monastic, ritual and textual Buddhism, now a symbol of true spiritual training in (almost) all modern Buddhism.[25] He taught himself meditation

---

24 Gombrich and Obeyesekere (1988: 217) suggest that his use of the *anagārika* concept was inspired by theosophical renderings of the Hindu *brahmacharin* role.

25 Dharmapāla also was influential in the later success of *vipassana* meditation—a technique and a movement, Sharf suggests it is an invented tradition (1995b: 242). Interestingly it became one of the most widespread forms of meditation in Sri Lanka—

by a book, which he found more authentic than learning it through the degenerated priesthood.

Dharmapāla was a main source of inspiration for Ceylonese Buddhist movements, for the father of Chinese Buddhist revival, Yang Wenhui (Welch 1968: 295 n. 19), and in India, being a theosophist, for helping activate Hindu revivals and, being a Buddhist, a Buddhist revival.

In the West, Dharmapāla had great success at the World Parliament of Religions 1893 (to which we shall return below),[26] and many potential Buddhist monks and laymen from the West saw Dharmapāla as a true ideal.[27] Though much more nationalistic than Olcott, he was inspired also by his quests for Buddhist universalism. He started the International Buddhist Union, (with Ananda Metteyya organizing the Western wing and other members counting Lama Govinda and Dwight Goddard), a project dying out some years later to be resuscitated in the form of the World Fellowship of Buddhists in 1950 (Humphreys 1968: 15), and in 1926 he established the still existing London Buddhist Vihara. A more successful endeavor with long-lasting effects was his establishing of the Maha Bodhi Society. With Olcott as director, Sumangala as president, and Edwin Arnold as one of the influential persons actively supporting this work, the society was a movement with the aim to actively recreate Buddhism physically and symbolically. Archeological (Western) restoration in the early nineteenth century had already turned the Maha Bodhi temple in Bodhgaya (the "Buddhist Jerusalem") into a symbol of the hidden past. But Edwin Arnold's[28] active support of giving the temple back to the Buddhists helped spark the revival and making it a renewed object of active pilgrimage. The still existing *Maha Bodhi Journal* was published the first time in 1892, one of several examples of the new way of actively using the press in propagating the Buddhist cause.[29] Dharmapāla, with the help of Olcott, is by some considered to be the earliest generator of what has come to be known as "socially engaged Buddhism" (Queen 1996: 20).

---

having been (re-) imported from Burma in its "original" (that is, "refined") form (1995b: 256).

26 C.T. Strauss, translator of Subhadra Bhikshu's (F. Zimmermann's) *Buddhistischer Katechismus*, received *pansil* from Dharmapāla at a ceremony held by the Theosophical Society in Chicago, thus being the first Westerner to become a Buddhist in the West.

27 During a lecture in 1903 William James, "founder" of psychology of religion, gave Dharmapāla his chair with the words "You are better equipped to lecture on psychology than I am" (Guruge 1965: 681).

28 When Arnold in 1886 arrived in Ceylon "the clergy turned out in crowds to honour him and hear him speak" (Wright 1957: 115).

29 Dharmapāla in 1906 also started his own Sinhala newspaper, "The Sinhala Buddhist" (Gombrich/Obeyesekere 1988: 207), and had earlier in 1898 published the Sinhala pamphlet, "The Daily Code for the Laity," containing general traditional Buddhist virtues and Western Protestant manners of conduct (Gombrich 1988: 193).

Later in Ceylon, both Olcott and the Theosophical Society lost influence and respect. It was criticized by especially monks and leading figures from the reform Buddhist movements—not all of whom enjoyed the power granted to, and taken by, lay Buddhism—for promoting own ideas instead of Buddhism.[30] Both Gunānanda, Sumangala and Dharmapāla eventually renounced Olcott and theosophy, the latter explaining in his diary of April 12, 1898: "Theosophists rose into prominence by borrowing Buddhist expressions. Their early literature is full of Buddhist terminology. Now they are kicking the ladder" (quoted in Malalgoda 1976: 253).

The intimate relation and mutual infiltration between theosophy and Buddhism criticized here was, however, the generative success of both parts. This success also inspired and influenced other Buddhist countries, waiting for international networks and useful discourses to clear the ground for a Buddhist survival and identification. Protestant Buddhism has had "long-term and probably irreversible trends" (Gombrich/Obeyesekere 1988: 203).

6. Buddhism Recreated in Japan

Buddhism in Japan had since the Meiji-restoration in 1868 endured hardships. Its close relationship with the totalitarian and feudal shogunate made the Japanese identify Buddhism with a decadent, old-fashioned culture. Buddhism, in the eyes of the critics, was foreign and anti-social, but also provincial, irrational and superstitious. Buddhism lost status, and was for a period persecuted. Buddhism needed a new face to survive. It needed its own "Buddhist modernity" with both rationalism, science, and spirituality. It needed a basis of legitimacy of both universal and local character.[31]

Apart from re-organizing the sectarian institutions and promoting lay societies there were also attempts to unite the Buddhist schools across sectarian boundaries. "Essentials of the Buddhist Sects" and "Buddhist Bibles" (*bukkyō seiten*) were written, and a unitarian "New Buddhism" (*shin bukkyō*) was attempted created by especially "young and restless Buddhist reformers ... often

---

30 Many theosophical ideas were simply not accepted by the Buddhists. For instance, only one monk in all of Ceylon believed in the existence of the "mahatmas" (Malalgoda 1976: 252). In reality, Malalgoda suggests, the Buddhist Theosophical Society "remained outside the mainstream of theosophy" (Malalgoda 1976: 254).

31 That the Tokugawa period was represented as dark and backward is only half a truth, politically and rhetorically legitimating the "new age." Naturally it is also problematic to one-sidedly focus on this process as a religious response to socio-historical factors. Internally Buddhism already during the Tokugawa period had started "modernizing." Ketelaar 1990 has thoroughly investigated Buddhism before, during and immediately after the Meiji-restoration.

referred to as 'the young Buddhists' (*seinen bukkyōto*)" (Thelle 1987: 195).[32] The united Buddhism was variously called the "Shaka Sect," "Mahayana Buddhism," "Eastern Buddhism," or simply "Japanese Buddhism" (Ketelaar 1990: 191).

The concepts of "East" (*tōyō*) and "West" (*seiyō*) found their way to the Japanese language with new connotations. "Western" universities were built, *keimo gakusha* ("scholars who illuminate the darkness") could enlighten Japan, and Buddhism and religion (*shūkyō*) became objects of study (*bukkyō gaku* and *shūkyō gaku*).[33] The approach to understanding religion in a new light was inspired by two influential theorists. Max Müller's "science of religion" signalled the idea of religion being rational and scientific and with an underlying universal "essence." Many young Japanese students or promising buddhologists went to Europe to learn science, philosophy and historical, philological and text-critical buddhology, primarily within studies of *original* Pali and Sanskrit Buddhism. The famous Nanjō Bunyō, among others, went to study Sanskrit under Max Müller, who, according to a missionary who visited him in the early 1880s, hoped that his Buddhist disciples "by receiving a purer form of Buddhism would be better prepared for the ultimate reception of Christianity" (quoted in Thelle 1987: 80). Another influential thinker for Meiji intellectuals, whom the Japanese "young men were eager for" (Brooks 1962: 4), was Herbert Spencer and his social Darwinism, placing the concept of religion within the cultural ladder of evolution. Two people who helped spread the ideas of Spencer were the Americans Ernest Fenollosa and Lafcadio Hearn, both being students of Edward Morse, of whom it was said, that "Japanese progress in virtually all the sciences had sprung" (Brooks 1962: 10). Hearn and Fenollosa were Buddhists,[34] and saw Buddhism as the best expression of Herbert Spencer's ideas, in which they were eagerly absorbed. They taught at Tokyo University in the last two decades of the nineteenth century inspiring many Meiji enlightenment thinkers and Buddhist modernizers. Among these were Okakura Kakuzo, an art historian interested in promoting an Asian spiritual

---

32 The concept and idea behind the "New Buddhism" (*shin bukkyō*) as opposed to the "Old Buddhism" (*kyō bukkyō*) was borrowed from the Japanese terms for Catholicism and Protestantism, "Old doctrine" (*kyū-kyō*) and "New Doctrine" (*shin-kyō*). See Thelle 1987: 194.

33 Especially after the World's Parliament of Religions, Chicago 1893 (to which we shall return later), *shūkyō* became a common concept of what is today known as "religion."

34 Fenollosa had converted to Buddhism in 1885. Hearn had his own personal way of using what he called "Higher Buddhism." Carl Jackson suggests that Edwin Arnold's influence on Hearn "seemed to hint an imminent conversion" (Jackson 1981: 225).

unity[35] and Inoue Enryō,[36] an influential philosopher and spokesman of Buddhism as the root of national spirituality.

Buddhist history was investigated and produced. A Chinese Buddhist "canon" was compiled between 1924 and 1932 (*Taishō Daizōkyō*, consisting of 85 volumes) by Japanese buddhologists—a standard edition for both Buddhists and scholars. Japanese Zen buddhologists (who at that time as well as today are often Zen Buddhists themselves) could define the supra-historical dharma-genealogy of the Zen tradition with the new scientific approaches. The study of Zen (*zengaku*) was created—already at that time there was a talk about a "Zen Boom" (Kirita 1996: 113)—as well as the idea of a Zen religion (*zenshū*) having roots in and a direct line to the original and pure Buddhism, while also being seen as the culmination of the evolution of Buddhism. In general, "Zen was, for young thinkers at the time, an extraordinarily intellectual religion" (Kirita 1996: 132).

International contacts promoted the Buddhist's case. Japanese Buddhists (monks, priests, laymen) went abroad to Buddhist countries to find other kinds of Buddhisms hitherto being outside the sphere of Japanese Buddhism.[37] One of them was Rinzai Zen-priest Kogaku Sōen (1859–1919), better known as Shaku

---

35 Okakura later visited India in 1901 meeting Hindu reformer Vivekānanda, whom he invited to attend a "Congress of Religions" in Japan, and with whom he hoped to arrange for a conference of Asian Buddhists (Hay 1970: 37). He joined Vivekānanda on a pilgrimage to Bodhgaya, where he hoped to obtain permission for Buddhists to build a rest home (Heehs 1994: 539). Okakuras book *The Ideals of the East* is said to have been an inspiration to India's budding young revolutionaries (Heehs 1994: 539); especially he made great impact on the Indian poet Rabindranath Tagore, who visited Japan in 1916 "with the express purpose of propagating the idea of a renascent Eastern civilization" (Hay 1970: 7). Also Vivekānanda, who later visited the country, had an ideal image of Japan as both materially developed and highly spiritual.

36 Inoue was the founder of the Buddhist School of Philosophy (*Tetsugakkan*, the present Tōyō University). He went to Europe to study Western philosophy, through which he could re-interpret and revive Buddhism. Inoue and other Buddhist revivers were anti-Christian, taking part in the religious discourse by means of the ideas and language of the enemy—just as in the case of Ceylon. Buddhism not only learned to express itself in Christian and "Western" terms. Several aspects of institutional and religious practice were inspired by Christianity. Arnold's book on Christ, *The Light of the World*, on the other hand, resulted in the "tendency of Christians to interpret Christianity by the help of Buddhism" (Thelle 1987: 308 n. 62). The conflict between Buddhists and Christians in Japan, however, later on turned into dialogue, see Thelle 1987. With regard to philosophy Shimomura says it was "a re-cognition, a re-interpretation of eastern thought as philosophy with the help of western philosophy" (1967: 21).

37 The *Japan Weekly Mail* in 1891 writes of the Nishi and Honganji sects in Kyoto having "sent priests to China, Siam, India, Thibet and Turkey to report on the history and progress of the faith in these countries, and thus to furnish material for a Japanese history of foreign Buddhism" (quoted by Dharmapāla in Guruge 1965: 824).

Sōen (*Shaku* being a Buddhist honorary name). Shaku Sōen has later been known for his role in modernizing Zen and Buddhism in Japan, being one of the leading generators of the "New Buddhism" and lay Zen Buddhism. After graduation at Keiō University (where he studied English and Western philosophy[38]), he went to Ceylon in 1887 where he stayed until 1890,[39] to find the original (*konpon*) Buddhism, and, as he said, to "hide myself from the world of name and fame" (Senzaki 1978: 97). Though already ordained a Zen monk and having trained at Myōshinji and Engakuji,[40] he was ordained as a Theravadin monk with the Ceylonese name Panna Ketu. He was taught Pali by Panna Sekara, a disciple of the theosophist and Buddhist modernizer Hikkaduve Sumangala. Sōen (with other Japanese monks) studied at one of the "cradles of Protestant Buddhism" (Gombrich 1988: 185), the Buddhist ecclesiastical college Vidyodaya Pirivena, where Sumangala was principal, Dharmapāla was in the management committee, where Edwin Arnold (whom he later met in Japan) the year before had been received as an honored guest, and where Olcott had given lectures on Buddhism and theosophy. In his diary Sōen copied excerpts from the latter's Buddhist catechism as if they were words of wisdom to be remembered or reflected upon (Sōen 1941). In Ceylon Sōen was in contact with Shaku Kōzen (1849–1924).[41] Kōzen was a disciple of the Shingon priest and Buddhist "modernist" Shaku Unshō. He came to Ceylon in 1886 and took the precepts through the afore-mentioned high priest Sumangala, and with his new name Gunaratana, he became another of the first Japanese-born Theravada monks. Kōzen had close relations to Dharmapāla with whom he went on a pilgrimage to Bodhgaya. With Kōzen, Sōen visited Dharmapāla and attended his lectures in Colombo, and Kōzen also helped him with his Pali studies—later on he was also to be the Pali teacher of a certain D.T. Suzuki (Senzaki 1978: 93).[42]

---

38 Among the Western thinkers Sōen was presented to was Herbert Spencer and his social Darwinism (Nishimura 1993).

39 Among the subscribers supporting his trip was the Meiji intellectual Fukuzawa Yakuchi, the founder of Keiō University (Tsunemitsu 1994: 221), and one of the "members" of the intellectual circle Meirokusha which promoted "civilization and enlightenment" (*bunmei kaika*) along Western models.

40 At Engakuji he got the certification of the seal of dharma transmission, *inka shōmei*, by Kōsen Sōon, better known as Imakita Kōsen (1816–92). At Engakuji he later became a well-known abbot. See Sharf 1993 and Furuta 1967.

41 The name has been transcribed as alternatively Kōzen or Kōnen.

42 On his return, Kōzen wanted to transplant original Ceylonese Buddhism to Japan, especially the practice of taking (and keeping) the precepts. For this purpose he founded the *Shakuson Shōfukai* ("Buddha Right-style Assembly"). He escorted Ceylonese monks to Japan and helped Japanese monks to go to Ceylon to become Southern monks. Kōzen also actively took part in a *seinenkai* (YMBA) with Unshō. On Shaku Kōzen, see Tsunemitsu 1968 and Fujiyoshi 1968.

Perhaps inspired by Ceylonese and theosophical ideas of a unified Buddhism, mixed with the general Meiji-Buddhism unification trend, upon his return to Japan in 1890 Shaku Sōen participated in the *Bukkyō Kakushō Kyōkai* ("Buddhist Transsecterian Cooperation"), and among five other leading "new Buddhists" from other sects, he co-edited the "Essentials of the Buddhist Sects" (Ketelaar 1990: 197; Nishimura 1993: 73). Sōen in Ceylon also must have been generally inspired to his efforts in modernizing and internationalizing Buddhism. He has been ascribed the role of establishing lay Zen (*koji zen*) in Japan (Furuta 1969: 90), and with Dharmapāla he was later to represent Buddhism at an important event, to which we shall return later. An exchange of Ceylonese and Japanese monks—which to a certain extent is still kept alive today—was established, through the early modernist pioneers of Japan.

7. Buddhism and Theosophy in Japan

There was, however, also another important factor in these international Buddhist relations. Having been invited, and sensing the time to be ripe for a United Buddhist World (revived through the Theosophical Society), Olcott and Dharmapāla in 1889 went to Japan to propagate for a Buddhist revival. These journeys are given three chapters of over sixty pages in Olcott's *Old Diary Leaves*, and he is certainly not afraid to mention the successes their visit caused all over the country. Olcott held speeches in Buddhist temples, bringing with him an appeal from Sumangala to justify Olcott's status and missionary work. He was met by thousands of Japanese Buddhists, waving with their Buddhist flags, every paper seem to have had interest in his person, he was made an honorary member at the Tokyo Club, he met influential persons (Fenellosa, Bigelow, the prime minister etc.). Olcott helped establish a Japanese Theosophical Society (*Reichi Kyōkai*, or *Shinchi Kyōkai*), YMBAs and YWBAs, modeled on the Ceylonese (and Christian) associations—a Women's League Movement even managed to have the emperor's aunt as president. In 1903 an international union of the YMBAs was formed in Tokyo. Because of Olcott, a Japanese Buddhist said, "Buddhists began everywhere to undertake the revival of their ancient faith" (Olcott 1910, vol. 4: 160).

Olcott did something no Buddhist had ever done before. He assembled not only the different sects in Japan to a General Council of the heads of all the Sects (Olcott 1910, vol. 4: 104), he also, on a later journey to the country in 1893, secured signatures from all the sects (except the Jōdō Shinshū) of Buddhist Japan, thus representing the Mahayana part of the Buddhist World. These signatures—one of them representing Japan was Shaku Kōzen—approved a fourteen-point "Buddhist Platform," on which all Buddhist wheels and major countries could now vote for. On paper at least, Olcott had gathered all Buddhists to one common idea, expressed by Olcott's private project.[43] In 1932 the American Dwight Goddard wrote his "Buddhist Bible." This book was an inspirational source for the "Teaching of the Buddha," published and meant to be a Buddhist Bible by the Federation of All Young Buddhist Association of Japan in 1932. He was, as Prothero (1996: 130) writes, "no longer merely the 'Father of the Sinhalese Buddhists,' he was now revered as 'The Apostle of Asia.'"

Dharmapāla also had success in his private project. Four times he went to the country, which he regarded as "an example of how the Buddhist heritage could contribute to modernization without Westernization" (Bond 1988: 56). Interestingly, (though later) turning images of where to find "authentic Buddhism" upside-down, he described how "the ancient Buddhist civilization although lost to India … is still visible in Japan, and it is possible, if necessary, to reconstruct the pure Aryan form of Buddhism from the Japanese storehouse" (Dharmapāla 1927: 192). Both Arnold—who spent some of his last years in Japan—and Dharmapāla were engaged in establishing a Maha Bodhi Society in Japan.[44] An Indo-Buddhist Society (*Indo Busseki Kōfuku Society*), in cooperation with the Maha Bodhi Society, sent Buddhists to Bodhgaya to carry on the Buddhist propaganda in India. Bodhgaya was seen as a symbol of Buddhist revival, but also a projected image of Japanese Buddhist revival itself. When a Japanese Buddha image was presented to the Maha Bodhi temple in Bodhgaya, it caused some trouble with Hindus, who did not want "their" shrine further buddhicized, and it became a strong symbol of the united Buddhist struggle for identity. The Ōbaku-affiliated Zen priest Kawaguchi Ekai[45] entered Tibet in

---

43 Inspired by Olcott's unifying attempts, the theosophist and founder of the Buddhist Society in London, Christmas Humphreys, some years later succeeded in gathering the largest Buddhist sects in Japan to accept his "Twelve Principles of Buddhism." However, neither in Japan nor in other Buddhist countries (to which they were also directed) these principles—like Olcott's project—ever had any practical significance in the long run. Whether D.T. Suzuki through his close friendship with Humphreys was also involved in constructing the principles or in organizing the implementations of them is still to be found out.

44 Arnold, who was later given the Order of the Rising Sun (as well as other orders from Asian countries), lectured to groups of priest about Bodhgaya arousing "enough interest in his audience so that a society was formed to promote interest in Gaya among Japanese Buddhists" (Wright 1957: 117). Shaku Sōen did not visit Bodhgaya until 1905 on his return trip from America. Dharmapāla, showing his admiration for Japan, had hoisted the Japanese flag beneath the *bodhi* tree at Bodhgaya, side by side with the Buddhist flag (Sangharakshita 1983: 52).

45 Kawaguchi was a scholarly disciple of Nanjō Bunyō and Buddhist modernizer Shaku Unshō, and among some of Kawaguchi's own disciples counts Myōshinji abbot Yamada Mumon. Kawaguchi was described as "Shramana" by Olcott (Olcott 1910, vol.

1899 in order to bring back texts from an unspoilt Buddhist country. In 1899 he met a "Singhalese gentleman" (Kawaguchi 1909: 25), Anagārika Dharmapāla, in Bodhgaya, with whom he had "a very interesting conversation" (Kawaguchi 1909: 25). In Maha Bodhi Society in Calcutta, he met other Japanese students, priests and modernizers on pilgrimage to Bodhgaya, among whom was Inoue Enryō.

Among many other Buddhist national and more or less international associations from this period, the Buddhist Propagation Society (*Kaigai Senkyōkai*, "Overseas Missionary Society"[46]), was established, with branch offices in London in 1890 (Thelle 1987: 110). Not all had relations to the theosophists. And though the Theosophical Society was "regarded as an effective means of Buddhist expansion in the West" (Thelle 1987: 110), it could not take all the credit for international Buddhist relations. In the long run, Olcott's missionary work "led to just one lodge, which fizzled out a few years later" (de Tollenaere 1996: 65). Maha Bodhi Society was popular, but it has lost its vigor, and theosophy in Japan, as well as the names of Olcott and Dharmapāla, are only relics today.[47] But they took part in, and were inspiring generators of, an ambitious project. In this sense, it can be argued, that one specific event took over and indirectly accomplished (or laid the ground for accomplishing) their goals: the successful revival of the East, of Buddhism, and of (Zen) Buddhism. Buddhism was about to be re-created in Asia.

4: 6). D.T. Suzuki was informed about Kawaguchi's Tibet travels. In a letter from America he asked for a copy of his *Chibetto Ryokōki* (Inoue 1989: 292–93). Whether the fact that his book *Three Years in Tibet* (1909) was published by the Theosophist Office in Madras indicates more personal interests in, and relations to, the society is still to be found out. He was, however, also acquainted with Sarat Chandra Das, whom both Blavatsky, Olcott and Dharmapāla knew, and who, it has been speculated, might have been model for one of the "mahatmas." See Lopez 1998: 235 n. 12. Also, Kawaguchi in 1908 visited Indian poet and "mystic" R. Tagore, and was one of the influencial persons from Buddhist Japan to invite him to his stay in the country the year after.

46 The society was first called *Ōbei Bukkyō Tsūshinkai* ("The Society for Communication with Western Buddhists"), when it was created in 1887 (Thelle 1987: 110). It probably had its inspiration from the Society for the Propagation of Buddhism in Ceylon, which was later run by the Buddhist Theosophical Society.

47 Mahabodhi Society is still existing in Japan, run by a Buddhist priest. It still has relations with Bodhgaya, where the *Indosan Nipponji* is part of the International Buddhist Brotherhood Association, and represents Japanese Buddhism with their own temple. Both Bodhgaya and Sri Lanka are still destinations of pilgrimage and places of respect.

8. Turning the Dharma Wheels—the World's Parliament of Religions, Chicago 1893

The World's Parliament of Religions held in Chicago in 1893 was in many ways signal event in the religious dialogue between East and West.[48] The meeting was a culmination of the interest in the East and in universal religious truths. It was also an opportunity for the different religions to strategically display and compete for public positions at the evolutionary ladder. While Christians saw the event as a possibility to finally beating the other religions in public, for the Orientals it was a welcome chance to manifest themselves through the battle against Christianity and the West, and—seen retrospectively—to use those orientalist stereotypes as instruments in their own religious identification and international marketing.

Dharmapāla was chosen by Sumangala as the delegate of the southern Buddhists[49]. Especially he and the Hindu delegate Vivekānanda impressed the audience and the press, while the Japanese representatives had to wait a little with their success until after the Parliament. These had all somehow been involved in modernizing and reviving Buddhism. They were from different sects (Rinzai Zen, Shingon, Tendai, Jōdō Shinshū and two lay representatives) but were on the same trans-sectarian track, heading for a common goal; national identification through international recognition.[50] Shaku Sōen, representing Rinzai Zen, spoke of Zen Buddhism as a universal religion in harmony with science and philosophy. His paper in the original Japanese was a "precise and well-handled technical exposition of the Buddhist doctrine of co-dependent origination" (Ketelaar 1990: 151). However, the terms used in Chicago, translated by D.T. Suzuki, were "taken directly from language current to contemporary theosophical discourse" (Ketelaar 1990: 151). This form of more or less conscious "expedient means" (*upāya*) might have been the most proper way of communicating Buddhist ideas to the spirit-seeking audience. The two lay-participants and translators Noguchi Zenshiro and Hirai Kinza were both theosophists. They had been engaged in bringing Olcott to Japan (Olcott 1910, vol. 4: 78 and 82), and were both leading members of the Young Men's Buddhist Committee (one of the YMBA's). Another bridge to communication

---

48 Fader 1982, Ketelaar 1990 (136–73), and Sharf 1993 examine the influence of the Parliament on Zen in the West.

49 Guruge (1965: xxxvi) suggests that the invitation was due to the international success of the *Maha Bodhi Journal*, which Dharmapāla had created and edited.

50 During the Parliament the delegates held public meetings, handed out tens of thousands of pamphlets on Mahayana Buddhism as "missionary efforts, the first ever by modern Buddhists" (Ketelaar 1990: 163). On religious dialogue, Ketelaar (156) says: "The invited Buddhists, like the hosting Christians, saw and heard precisely what they desired."

was through Sōen's contact with Paul Carus (1852–1919), an American philosopher and chief editor of the journals *The Open Court* and *The Monist*. Born, raised and educated in Germany, Carus was both a "rationalist" and inspired by the romanticist interest in the Orient. His later goal in America was to find the universal truths of all religions in a "New Religious Era," and to prove that true religion—of which he found Buddhism to be a prime example—was in accordance with both science, rationality, psychology and spirituality. Carus later became friends with Dharmapāla, and founded a branch of the Maha Bodhi Society in America, the first Buddhist center in the West. Carus and Sōen could use each other. Carus could use Sōen's Buddhism for his own "science of religion." And Sōen could use Carus' fascination with Buddhism as an incentive to his endeavors in spreading Japanese Buddhism abroad and thereby of its prestige at home.[51] In Japan the "champions of Buddhism" (*bukkyō no championra*) were seen as legitimators of the New Buddhism, being both modern, rational and universal, and yet uniquely Buddhist, Oriental and Japanese.[52] Carus' book *The Gospel of Buddha* was an attempt to constitute a united Buddhism. He partly succeeded. It was sponsored by Sōen and translated by D.T. Suzuki to Japanese in 1895. Sōen also wrote a preface, in which he describes the superiority of Buddhism in the hierarchy of religions, indicating the lack of Western (capability of) knowledge of Buddhism (Snodgrass 1998: 325).[53] The *Gospel of Buddha* was "aimed to rival Edwin Arnold's famous poem, *The Light of Asia* ... but with the academic validation that Arnold's work lacked" (Snodgrass 1998: 323). It was later used—not so much for its "reliability as a source of knowledge concerning Buddhism" as for its "strategic value" (Snodgrass 1998: 340–41)—in Buddhist schools in Japan, Ceylon and other Buddhist countries. Even today the book is sold as an introduction to Buddhism.

The Parliament in Chicago was symptomatic of the time. It was a battle ground for religions, but also a foreign and neutral meeting place for "Eastern religions" that otherwise would have no reason to talk to each other. Through the Parliament Sōen and Dharmapāla met in USA, just as the Buddhist sects had met through Olcott and theosophy in Japan, or Buddhists had met each other through Western interpreters or books. The Parliament itself also inten-

---

51 In Japan Carus was "respected as an authority on the West and on Western philosophy" (Snodgrass 1998: 334).
52 Shaku Sōen and D.T. Suzuki in 1896 arranged a Buddhist-Christian conference, the "Little Parliament of Religions" (Thelle 1987: 226).
53 Sōen was, however, conscious about the Western contribution to the understanding and popularity of Buddhism; "Swedenborg came to Buddhism through his interest in mysticism; Arnold through his elegant poetic vision; Olcott through his interest in superior intellect; Müller through his interest in the refined Sanskrit language" (quoted in Snodgrass 1998: 330).

sified the tendencies within the intellectual life of the time. Especially because of one single person.

9. D.T. Suzuki and the West

Suzuki Daisetsu Teitarō (1870–1966) was Japanese, and strongly influenced by the West. He has been described as a researcher, translator, religious thinker, philosophical psychologist, spiritual mentor and popularizer (Fader 1986: 95). Cultivating his academic career, he was registered as a special student in the literature department of the school of humanities at the Imperial University, where he studied English and philosophy. He was introduced to modern Western science and intellectual life,[54] and he became engaged in the early Meiji New Buddhism. With his English translation of the text *Awakening of Faith in Mahayana* and as a co-author of a Zen "minimal canon" (Faure 1993: 52), he hoped to contribute to a united, universal Buddhism. As a layman (*koji*)[55] he was instructed in Zen Buddhist philosophy and meditation at the Rinzai monastery Engakuji in Kamakura under Shaku Sōen, through whom he later came to America. Although he had already written articles and his first book before his departure, Suzuki's actual scholarly background was cultivated in America. From 1897 to 1908 he worked for Carus in La Salle, translating and writing articles. He was later on employed at different American and Japanese universities, and became author of more than a hundred books (most of them in Japanese) on religion, Buddhism and Zen. Especially the first years with Carus strongly influenced the Zen interpretation that Suzuki was later to be known for.[56] He eagerly read books on religious thought, psychology of religion (especially William James and his focus on the religious experience),[57] Buddhist studies, Arnold's *Light of Asia*, the American Transcendentalists (he thought Emerson—who was inspired by Swedenborg and Eastern "mysticism" himself—to have taught Zen [Kirita 1996: 114]), and naturally Carus' science of religion. According to Suzuki's close friend and "secretary" Okamura Mihoko,

---

54   Kirita (1996: 115 and 130) suggests that Suzuki must have read and been inspired by both Inoue Enryō and Herbert Spencer.
55   Sōen gave him an honorific Buddhist name, *kojigo*, but not, as sometimes presumed, an institutionally sanctioned certificate of enlightenment, *inka shōmei*. Also the famous writer Sōseki Natsume trained under Sōen as a layman.
56   On the relationship between Suzuki and Carus, see Sharf 1993.
57   James himself was inspired by theosophy and was familiar with Swedenborg. His ideas of unmediated experience influenced not only Suzuki but also the philosopher Nishida Kitaro.

he highly respected Anagārika Dharmapāla.[58] He also read and was deeply impressed by Swedenborg, whom he called "Buddha of the North" (Loy 1996: xv). At the request of the Swedenborg Society he translated three of his books into Japanese and wrote a book about him, and in Japan he was later to become a member of a the Order of the Star, a sub-group of the Swedenborg Society, who met at Suzuki's home in the 1920s (Sharf 1995a: 144). He was also deeply fascinated by theosophy. He believed that "undoubtedly Madame Blavatsky had in some way been initiated into the deeper side of Mahayana teaching" (Suzuki 1970d: xiii), and, having seen a picture of Blavatsky, he said "[s]he was one who attained" (Cranston 1993: 84). Having read Blavatsky's *The Voice of Silence*, he sent it to Miss Beatrice Lane, a theosophist who was later to become Mrs. Suzuki, with the words "Here is the real Mahayana Buddhism" (Cranston 1993: 85). According to a Theosophical Yearbook, Mrs. Suzuki established the Mahayana Lodge of Theosophists in Kyoto in 1924, she did "enthusiastic work" in spreading theosophy in Japan, and both Suzukis greeted theosophical visitors to Japan, including the international president, C. Jinarajadasa, in 1937.[59] Later, Suzuki also hosted the famous Tibet-adventurer and theosophist Alexandra David-Neel. According to Okamura Mihoko, Suzuki read a lot about theosophy, and was a host at meetings of theosophists (see note 58). At the Buddhist Society in London he lectured on Zen and Buddhism. Here he met Ananda Metteyya in 1908, and later met and strongly influenced the Buddhist scholars (and theosophists) Christmas Humphreys, Edward Conze and Alan Watts, who because of meeting Suzuki not only became interested in Eastern Buddhism, but also changed focus from "Buddhist meditation" to "Zen meditation" (Humphreys 1968: 78–79). With Omori and Anesaki he was a participating member as one of the Japanese delegates of the Third International Congress for the History of Religions in Oxford 1909 and later in 1936 he was invited to the World Congress of Faiths in London. Again in the 1950s he was in America for long periods, lecturing at universities and almost becoming a religious cult-figure for a whole beat-generation. In this period Suzuki also was in contact with influential individuals in Europe related to (the study of) psychology, mysticism, and theology. Rudolf Otto and Suzuki had already inspired each other since the 1920s, and Suzuki's friendship and professional correspondence with C.G. Jung, shows a mutual interest in several themes, especially the religious experience.[60] Suzuki also participated in the Eranos

---

58 Interview in Kyoto, March 1997. Strangely, it seems not, however, that the two actually ever met.

59 Ellwood 1979: 182 n. 1. 1924 was also the year when the same Jinarajadasa helped Humphreys establish the subgroup of the Theosophical Society, the Buddhist Lodge.

60 Apart from his friendship with several Orientalists (and a general knowledge of their writings) Jung was himself influenced by the theosophist's understanding of Eastern

conferences in Switzerland, where the "essence" of religion was discussed by contemporary influential theologians, psychologists and scholars of religion (e.g., C.G. Jung, M. Eliade, M. Buber, P. Tillich etc.). With several of these he was later to have a relationship of mutual inspiration, just as the "East-West dialogues"[61] and Buddhist studies have used his personality and ideas. Until some years ago Suzuki-Zen monopolized the presentation of Zen Buddhism in the West, and most practicing Zen Buddhists in the West started out their spiritual quest after having read D.T. Suzuki.[62] The many popular books on Zen can thank Suzuki for their existence, among these the amount of books with the title *Zen and the Art of ...*

10. Suzuki's Influence in Japan

Like Dharmapāla, Suzuki wrote many of his works in English, and in that sense, his audience was to a large extent foreign readers, or the ("Western") educated intellectuals. But he also wrote and spoke in his local tongue. He was and is recognized in Japan. And although Zen Buddhism in Japan and East Asia has a much wider theoretical and practical reference than "Suzuki-Zen," he has had lasting influence on Japanese Zen Buddhism. Suzuki was (and to some extent, still is) a living symbol of the modern (mostly intellectual, reform) Zen.

As an expression of his general, official recognition he was honored by Japan Academy, he was appointed as professor at different universities, he received a cultural medal from emperor Shōwa, who also presented him with the post-humous title Senior Grade of the Third Court Rank. Among his many

---

religion. On Tibet, theosophy and the psychologization of Buddhism, see Pedersen 1997.

61 Suzuki was active in or indirectly an inspirational force behind for instance the East-West Conferences in Hawaii and the Buddhist-Christian dialogues and exchanges of monks (Zen and Catholic). Most of the many Christian priests or theologians with theoretical of practical interest in Zen, also were inspired by, or in contact with, Suzuki. Thomas Merton, in gratitude to Suzuki, compares him with Einstein and Gandhi (1967: 3–9).

62 For instance the first Westerner to become a Zen priest in Japan, Ruth Fuller Sasaki—late in life married to Sōkei-an/Sasaki Shigetsu, a dharma heir of Shaku Sōen—was introduced to Nanzenji and Daitokuji in Kyoto through Suzuki and Mrs Suzuki, both of whom she knew. It was Suzuki who had given her instruction in *zazen*, before attending "real" monastic life. Sasaki later edited Suzuki's *Essays in Zen Buddhism*, and founded the First Zen Institute of America in Japan at Ryōsen-an, Daitokuji, giving this temple a revival. Here scholars-to-be (such as Yanagida Seizan and Philip Yampolsky) as well as intellectuals and "beatniks" (such as Gary Snyder) met to discuss, read and practice Zen Buddhism.

lecture tours in Japan, he also lectured for the emperor (later to be published as
The Essence Buddhism. The Doctrine of No-Mind). The foreign ministry and the
ministry of education sponsored the publications of a few of his books as well
as some of his travels to the West, and Japan Society for the Promotion of
Science published his book *Japanese Spirituality*. He had many readers of his
books and articles, and many "common people" listened to his lectures, have
seen or heard him in TV or on the radio. His ninetieth birthday, his death and
the thirtieth anniversary of his death (posters announced him as a "cosmopolitan Japanese") was commemorated in publications and exhibitions by
Japanese and international scholars, priests and friends.

Suzuki was first of all known as a "thinker" (*shisōka*). He was not really an
academic, though he wrote many books, forewords and articles on more or less
academic issues to several different Japanese journals related to Zen, Buddhism
or religion (for instance *Shūkyō, Zenshū, Zen Bunka, Daijōzen, Hansei Zasshi, The
Young East, The Cultural East*). With his close friendship and intellectual relationship with the famous philosopher Nishida Kitarō (1870–1945) he directly
influenced the "Kyoto School," whose "members" (Nishida, Nishitani, Abe etc.)
because of Suzuki-Zen have used Zen Buddhism as a means and expression of
Japanese philosophy.[63]

Within the Japanese Zen world—first of all Rinzai Zen—Suzuki has received respect and recognition.[64] His collected works are highly esteemed[65] and
are part of most Japanese Buddhist universities. At the Rinzai Zen Buddhist
Hanazono University in Kyoto students of Buddhism, many of whom will later
become temple priests, are expected to have read him, and many students from
Kyoto University end up getting an interest in Zen Buddhism through having

---

63   The Kyoto School and The New Kyoto School has generally been engaged in dialogue
     between (Zen) Buddhism and Christianity, between Western and Eastern philosophy.
     In the recent years, however, the nationalistic tendencies of these schools have been
     criticized, and it has been suggested, that the "dialogue" has been used as a rhetorical
     promotion of the uniqueness of Japanese culture, mentality and thinking—a discourse
     known as *nihonjinron*. See for instance Faure 1993 and 1995. Bernard Faure calls these
     Suzuki-inspired schools for "Zen Occidentalism" (1995: 270) and "reverse Orientalism"
     (1995: 245).

64   As Suzuki had an almost sectarian approach in favouring Rinzai as opposed to Sōtō, he
     has not had the same significance within the Sōtō world. However, some of the English
     publications from the Sōtō Headquarters (*Sōtōshu Shūmuchō*) has definitely borrowed
     the terminology of Suzuki-Zen. Sōtō priest Kōhō also approves: "the work of Dr.
     Suzuki has been phenomenal" (1960: 85).

65   Fujioka (1994: 24) comments on the introduction to the Japanese editions of Suzuki's
     collected works: "it shows the high esteem in which he was held in Japan. Few
     Japanese have received such extravagant praise."

studied the philosophy of the Kyoto School and Suzuki.[66] He is treated by most Zen scholars (Yanagida, Ueda, Abe, Nishimura, Kirita, Furuta, Fujioka, etc.), as well as intellectual laymen (Hisamatsu, Akizuki etc.). The "Zen Boom" of the last decades in Japan (where "boom" is, however, used more frequently than the English term might suggest) directly or indirectly has been influenced by Suzuki. Because

> his style of writing in Japanese was extremely plain, clear, and readable ... generally speaking, his books not only stimulated those in the temple, but also helped common people appreciate Zen as a traditional asset benefiting their own lives. (Kondo 1967: 92)

Many Japanese have either read him, or "come to regard Zen more highly because of the attention it has received in the West" (Victoria 1980: 61).[67]

A great part of modern Japanese Zen Buddhism has been democratized and lay-oriented, thanks to the Suzuki "tradition," beginning with his masters Imakita Kōsen and Shaku Sōen.

Though journalists and writers mistakenly have called Suzuki a *rōshi* (master) or *jūshoku* (priest), though he has been called a bodhisattva and compared to the thirteenth century Zen master Dōgen, Suzuki was "only" a devoted and professional layman, a *koji* (layman), a *sensei* (teacher), a *hakushi* (doctor) and a *shisōka* (thinker).

Suzuki-Zen did, however, also leave certain impressions on the monastic world. Several *rōshis* or temple priests (for instance Shibayama, Morimoto, Omori, Nanshinken) knew Suzuki personally or his ideas and writings.[68] On several occasions he also lectured in Zen monasteries, and as the former priest of a Daitokuji sub-temple wrote: "One of the main achievements of Dr. Suzuki was his success in communicating the incommunicable" (Kobori 1967). The

---

66 Interview with Tanaka Sōyō (formerly student at Kyoto University) from Nagaoka Zenjuku, a Zen monastery for laymen, where Morimoto Shōnen was formerly a *rōshi*.

67 The Vietnamese Thich Nhat Hanh, who in the West in many ways has received the same status as Suzuki, says about the phenomenon: "Because Westerners are interested in Zen, many Asians have returned to their spiritual tradition" (1995: 159). It is interesting, however, that no "Zen Boom" apparently has struck the ethnic Japanese in the USA (Tagami 1986).

68 Sharf (1993) does not believe Suzuki had any significance for the monastic and institutional world; he was too intellectual, and, if we accept the assertion, that Suzuki-Zen is a kind of "Protestant Zen," it is only natural, that institutional and monastic Zen Buddhism would have to negate an approach in no need of a clergy, of rituals, of institutions. However, though it is naturally problematic to measure indications for such influence, my general impression (through Japanese sources and talks with Zen scholars and priests) is that Suzuki in the Zen monastic world was not at all counted as being "marginal," though a bit to the "intellectual" side—that he is not revered as a true master in the monastic world is because of his essential nature of "only" being a layman (*zaike*), and not a true "renouncer" (*shukke*).

Sanbō Kyōdan movement is a direct outcome of Suzuki-Zen, the East-West meeting and Buddhist modernity in Japan.[69]

Apart from his adventures and cult-status in the West, Suzuki has also been more directly influential in terms of international propagation from Japan. Together with his wife he founded and edited the Buddhism-promoting journals *The Eastern Buddhist* and *The Young East*,[70] and they were counsellors in the International Buddhist Society (*Kokusai Bukkyō Kyōkai*). Through Suzuki's status and relations, Zen priests and *rōshis* were invited to the Buddhist Society in London, and through Suzuki's paving the way, already in the beginning of this century Japanese Zen monks went abroad to America. The Zen Studies Society was founded in 1956 in order to help Suzuki introduce Zen to the West. It has been managed by influential Zen Buddhists, and has created relations between Japanese and American Zen studies and practices. At the International Zen Center in Kyoto and other places in Japan, where Westerners are invited to join the Zen practice, Suzuki's books are part of the literature visitors can read or buy. The Suzuki-inspired layman's Zen organization FAS (founded by Hisamatsu) is situated in a sub-temple of Shōkokuji (Kyoto), and some Zen priests also have attended the regular meditation sessions.

Suzuki invented Zen in the West. But, to a certain extent, he was also influential in re-inventing it in his home country.[71]

11. Protestant Buddhist Pizza-effect with a Taste of Zen

Suzuki's recognition and influence in the West as well as in his home country is not only due to his publications and personality, but also to his place in history. As a product of East and West in a time where both worlds needed a spiritual bridge-builder and mediator, Suzuki managed not only to get Zen to the West,

---

69   Sanbō Kyōdan is an independent Zen sect with elements from both Rinzai, Sōtō and Western Zen. Sharf (1995c) calls it a new religious movement, and equals its relationship to Japanese Zen with that of Jehova's Witnesses and Christianity in the West. An interesting counterpart to Dharmapāla's lay Buddhism is the way in which Sanbō Kyōdan uses texts as authority and bases the religious practice on taking the texts at face value. See Sharf 1995c: 427. Many recognized masters and institutionally high ranking priests from the Rinzai sects have trained under Harada and Yasutani, who might have been controversial but certainly not as marginal as Sharf suggests.

70   *The Young East* saw itself as the successor of the *Bijou of Asia*, the journal published by the *Buddhist Propagation Society*. It also compares its role as propagator of Buddhism with that of *The Eastern Buddhist* (Takakusu 1929: 254).

71   As with the case of Dharmapāla (and other national "universalists" like Vivekānanda) it might be argued that the rhetoric of internationalization were slogans in promoting own nationalistic feelings—Sharf 1993 focuses on this approach to understanding Suzuki.

but also had an important role to play in getting it back to Japan—not in its "original" shape, but in a transformed form. What Bernard Faure has called the "Suzuki-effect" (1993: 54), corresponds (in its Japanese effect) in an interesting way to what Agehananda Bharati called the "pizza-effect" (1970: 273): In its home country the pizza was a simple bread, a snack, but was later imported and transformed into a main dish by the Americans, an individual meal in many different sizes, with different tastes and shapes. The point of the pizza-effect is the fact, that this Americanized form was re-imported by the Italians themselves. The pizza as a meal and concept got a new shape and meaning in its home country after having been transformed abroad. Another metaphor is the "Hollywood-effect"; the meaning and shape of for instance an "original" fairytale being "Americanized" and re-imported to European children who think that the fairytales of Hans Christian Andersen are actually supposed to have a happy Hollywood ending. To extend the metaphor, one might even talk of an "inverted" pizza-effect, when "unique European philosophers" (for instance Heidegger) appear to have been significantly inspired by Eastern thought—an Eastern thought itself presented through "Protestant" or "Western" eyes. This transformation is naturally not a unique phenomenon in religious studies, where interpretations, re-interpretations and inventions are seen as common characteristics of religion.[72] Invented, and inverted, traditions are also real traditions to be studied as such.

12. Zen and the Art of Inverting Orientalism

The historical context and the religious discourse of which Suzuki was a part is important for understanding his project. He played and systematically reversed the game of Orientalism.[73]

Especially from his time with Carus, Suzuki was obsessed with proving Buddhism as a unified tradition to be scientific and in accordance with modern,

---

72 For related subjects, see also Ketelaar 1990: 137 (on "strategic Occidentalism"), Bharati 1970 (on neo-Hinduism and its use of Orientalism), Lopez 1996 (on the way both Chinese and Tibetans use Orientalist clichés to own advantage), Kopf 1985 (on the way Shakto-Tantrism was negated or de-sexualized and later idealized in India in response to Orientalist puritanism and Western sexual emancipation), Sharpe 1985 (on Western interpretations of the Bhagavadgita and Indian responses and re-interpretations). As an illustrative example of the fact that mutual reflection is not just a Orient/Occident incident, but rather a general expression of the way religions work, see Kohn 1995 (on ways Buddhism and Daoism use each others' ideas and myths to identify and legitimate themselves).

73 It is not my intention to reduce Suzuki's numerous literature to this "project." Suzuki had much higher ambitions, but Orientalism can be seen as the frames, within which Suzuki-Zen could and had to operate.

universal culture. And like his Victorian predecessors, he rejected all ritualistic activity as merely symbolic (or as a spiritual gesture towards the unenlightened folk believers). Only meditation (or rituals enacted "meditatively") is the correct soteriological and spiritual "means of attaining truth" (1970a: 94). Suzuki often uses the etymological identification between Zen and meditation, justifying Zen practice and the Zen school as being truly spiritual, spirituality being seen as a complementary counterpart to rationality and science. Zen meditation is the symbol of Zen modernity, it is both "scientific" (as a non-ritual technique to "pure experience" of reality, direct and unmediated) and "spiritual" (what is experienced is beyond language and conceptual knowledge). Zen is therefore also irrational (or anti-rational), and can only be experienced subjectively: "To study Zen means to have Zen experience" (1967: 123).

Suzuki's "Zen" is not the Zen of the Zen sect (or school, *Zenshu*) as an institutional and living religion. "True Zen" is defined through its (classical) texts, taking them at face value to represent (an idealized) reality. Zen becomes a concept, a transcendent essence, underlying Buddhism and all religions in their different manifestations. Zen study therefore is the way to "Zen" (Kirita 1996: 114). Zen is the quintessence of the "religious consciousness of mankind" (1970a: Preface), of "the human spirit" (1970c: 347) and—though Rudolf Otto seems to have been more inspired by Suzuki than the other way round—Zen gets a taste of "The Holy." Suzuki can therefore also find "Zen" in Buddhism, Christianity, Islam, Daoism and Confucianism, and among Swedenborg, Emerson, Blavatsky, Eckhart and other Western mystics.

Suzuki found Zen perfectly suitable to modernity. Or rather, he found modernity perfectly suitable to Zen. But—like the spiritual theosophists, the romanticists, the mystical depth psychologists, the essentialist historians of religion—Suzuki could only sustain this spiritualism by rejecting or complementing modernity and universalism. He also finds a more evolutionary model suitable to envelope Zen, and systematically inverts Orientalist ideas, dichotomies and metaphors.

First, Suzuki inverts the Western Orientalist idea of the "original," southern, canonic and "true" Buddhism, being opposed to a degenerated Mahayana Buddhism.[74] He regards the first as a "primitive Hinayana," while Mahayana is seen as not just "the genius of the entire East," but also as "a great monument of the human soul" waiting to be excavated (1921: 85). But Suzuki

---

74 The ideas of Mahayana as more developed or subtle than Hinayana is of course a rhetorical division within the Buddhist traditions themselves. A Buddhist hierarchical system of classification was developed further in China (*panjiao*), which has also been used in Japan by different schools. But it is Suzuki who must be credited for having transformed the equalization or favoring of Mahayana to the West, where the southern Buddhists' own presentation of originality and authority had traditionally been accepted.

goes further. Zen Buddhism represents not just true Buddhism (the "essence of Buddhism" being transmitted without faith and words) but is the goal of a teleological development, "the culmination of the development of Buddhism" (1970d: 13). Suzuki also later negates the relation between Zen and mysticism, as the concept of mysticism cannot cover the unique Zen spiritual essence (see Faure 1993: 60), or at least "Zen is a mysticism of its own order" (1969b: 45). Also a scientific and rational analysis will be mistaken; "our so-called rationalistic way of thinking has apparently no use in evaluating the truth or untruth of Zen" (1930: 20), a critique directed towards the Chinese (Suzuki-critical) Chan/Zen scholar Hu Shih's historical approach. In his "dialogue" with Christianity, he clearly places this Western religion below Zen. Christian faith is a dualistic faith in God, while Zen is faith in oneself (1969a: 79), Christians are looking heavenwards, Zen Buddhists are looking within themselves (1969a: 81). Zen has neither rituals, ceremonies nor gods (1969b: 39). In many ways, Suzuki's Zen seems more "Protestant" than the Christianity with which he (also) describes Zen.

Especially in his later works, Suzuki more aggressively explains this religious teleologically closed evolution by differences in culture and mentality. Zen is unique for "the original mind" (1970a: Preface), for the "Far Eastern Culture" (1970b: 91), it expresses the "spirit of the East" (1970c: 347), in Zen (though at other times being non-philosophical) "all the philosophy of the East is crystallized" (1969b: 38). Though Chan/Zen as a distinct school originated in China, the true spirit of Zen is uniquely Japanese. "The Zen life of the Japanese came to full flower in Japanese spirituality" (1972: 18–19), "it has been due to the Japanese that its technique has been completed" (1967: 122). He talks about the "Zen character of Japanese spirituality," and in his book *Zen and Japanese Culture* (1959b), he explains everything Japanese—from culture, mentality, personality character, love of nature, to the samurai-spirit—to be "Zen-like." In other words, those attributes Zen might have in common with other "Japanese things" by metaphorical association are ascribed an essential quality, revealing a relation of assigned identity. This metaphorical association is transferred to more general differences between "East" and "West," two essential phenomena and concepts from the discourse of Orientalism, now in an inverted qualitative relationship. To underline the Oriental qualities Suzuki inverts and transforms the traditionally negative stereotypes into positive characteristics.[75] Thus,

---

75 In this article I have only exemplified from Suzuki's English works. Among some of the titles of his many books in Japanese are *Building a Spiritual Japan, East and West, The Mind of the Orient*; see Hisamatsu et al. 1970 for a translated list of content of *The Complete Works of Suzuki Daisetz*.

> In many ways the East no doubt appears dumb and stupid, as Eastern people are not so
> discriminate and demonstrative and do not show so many visible, tangible marks of
> intelligence. They are chaotic and apparently indifferent. (Suzuki et al. 1960: 6)

The West becomes *The Other*, being characterized by a "relative ego" versus the
"transcendental Ego" of the East (1957: 131), the West uses logic, the East uses
intuition (1959b: 219), Westerners are alienated towards nature, the Orientals
are close to nature (Suzuki et al. 1960: 2), and "the idea of conquest (nature) was
imported from the West" (1958: 141). Christianity is an "autocratic, domi-
neering power," but Buddhism a "religion of peace" (1957: 138). And:

> The Western mind is … analytical, discriminative, differential, inductive, individu-
> alistic, intellectual, objective, scientific, generalizing, conceptual, schematic, impersonal,
> legalistic, organizing, power-wielding, self-assertive, disposed to impose its will upon
> others. (Suzuki et al. 1960: 5)

The East is

> … synthetic, totalizing, integrative, non-discriminative, deductive, non-systematic,
> dogmatic, intuitive (rather, affective), nondiscursive, subjective, spiritually individu-
> alistic and socially group-minded. (Suzuki et al. 1960: 5)

The differences are not of degree but categorical and essential. In an interview
with Hisamatsu Shin'ichi, Suzuki says that he has neither met nor heard of
Westerners having understood Zen (Shore 1986: 19–23). "Zen is the keynote of
Oriental culture; it is what makes the West frequently fail to fathom exactly the
depths of the Oriental mind" (1969b: 35).

The hermeneutical circle seems hermetically closed to Westerners.

13. Zen, Inverted Orientalism and the Art of Studying
Buddhism in Religious Studies

D.T. Suzuki transmitted Zen to the West — and to some extent back to Japan. As
a product of both East and West he acted as a translator of cultures, as a
spiritual bridge-builder and "midwife," and had he been a mythological figure,
he could have been called a culture-hero. Suzuki did not transmit Zen in a one-
way directly transmitted "objective" way. He was not alone in constructing
"Suzuki-Zen." He was part of a well-defined discourse, an almost neutral part
of a fine-meshed interrelated network, a human sign among a web of signifiers,
an infinite frame of reference where ideas, ideals and metaphors were part of a
communicative living tradition.

This network — from Meiji Buddhists, to buddhologists, theosophists,
Swedenborgians, spokesmen of religion-as-science, psychologists of religion,
theologians, Zen practitioners from the West — should not be understood as
pearls on a string (as the idea of the Zen patriarch's transmission "from mind to

mind"), but as a genealogical network, as a "hybridization process" (King 1999: 202), of interrelated individuals whose personal relations and mutual influence of ideas (rooted in different paradigms such as universalism, evolutionism, spiritualism, rationalism and "Protestant" anti-ritualism, etc.) in many ways seem more homogenous than the Zen tradition he wanted to reveal.

Suzuki-Zen is thus also a performative network of active individuals, creating the discourse, constituting the tradition itself. D.T. Suzuki could therefore also step out of the discourse to create his own personal account of Zen. By taking over and transforming ideas and metaphorical dichotomies (East/West, Mahayana/Hinayana, Japan/Asia, Zen/Buddhism, wisdom/belief, meditation/ ritual, spiritualism/materialism, up/down, in/out, doctrines/beyond doctrines, etc.), Suzuki structurally inverted and invented religious parameters pointing at a new cultural and religious hierarchy. Instead of a de-mystification and de-Orientalization of the Orient (as Said asked for), Suzuki-Zen is an expression of a project, a "strategic Occidentalism" (Ketelaar 1990: 137) which through Orientalism could re-mystify, re-mythologize, re-essentialize and re-Orientalize the Orient (and, especially Japanese Zen).

D.T. Suzuki has been criticized by a new generation of academic Zen scholars. As an interpreter of Zen and Buddhism he had many inaccuracies. Since Suzuki, time has changed. Many descriptions and approaches to the study of Zen still have to be re-written and re-considered in the post-Suzuki-Zen study, which need not see previous renderings as "mere mistakes which would have better been avoided, but [as] necessary and salutary turnings of the hermeneutical wheel" (Clarke 1997: 190). Suzuki was not, and did not see himself as being, a historian of religion. Suzuki-Zen is not primarily (as often understood in the West) describing or writing *about* Zen, but performatively prescribing an idealized Zen and Buddhism, being more a model *for*, than a model *of* Zen and Buddhism.

Suzuki is primarily to be seen as an apologetic voice of the tradition, he interpreted and "revealed." As such he was unique, but also a product of a cultural communication, a fusion of horizons in a creative "mirroring" reciprocity of ideas and mental images. D.T. Suzuki can still be read as a creative thinker, a Zen theologian with many enlightening thoughts. As an "emic voice" he is not "wrong." Judging his existential and religious ideas as right or wrong would repeat the old ethnocentric and "Protestant" dichotomies of true and essential versus misunderstood and degenerated Buddhism. As the Platform Sutra says about the mirror, "how can there be dust?"

Suzuki-Zen is an interesting expedient means (*upāya*) for self-reflection. Suzuki-Zen has forced the study of Zen Buddhism to see and acknowledge the hermeneutical web of relationships between emic and etic discourse, between "us" and "them." Just as their apologetic religious discourse has colored our interpretations (as the case Suzuki is a prime example of), so our descriptions of them are "an act, a performance" (Faure 1993: 146) with ideological and herme-

neutical consequences for them. The blurred overlappings between Oriental-
ism(s), inverted Orientalism(s) and Occidentalism(s) have not made it easier to
represent them (as the "others"), nor to understand ourselves. Acknowledging
these conditions, however, there might be a point in polishing the mirror, after
all. By distinguishing (though not transcending) the emic-etic discourses, by
revealing the sociology of knowledge behind certain ideological and methodological differences might reveal that some models, after all, are more useful
than others. In retrospect Suzuki opened doors to another world—but he also
made us see it in blinkers. In his apologetic attempt to elevate, transcend and
essentialize Zen, he reduced it, with the effect that until recently studies on
institutional, social, ritual and in general "religious" aspects of Zen Buddhism
have been virtually ignored.

Studying religion is not like looking through a window. It is necessary to
see with glasses, to use models and maps to see religion not as a metaphysical
truth to be perceived, but as a cultural phenomenon, itself a construction, a
living reality. Though both constructivism and processes of relational intercon-
nectedness are also keywords within Buddhist discourse, our "constructions"
need not be in harmony with theirs. But ideally they need to be potentially
reflecting each other. Though a mirror can be used for reflection and illumination, the images reflected in the mirror are not the thing itself.[76] Historians of
religion are not supposed to reveal a "truth," but to reflect on an always ongoing discourse about their truths—and on our own discourse. Suzuki-Zen and
related case stories—with or without the discussions on Orientalism—are good
opportunities to keep polishing our mirrors.

Bibliography

Almond, Philip (1988), *The British Discovery of Buddhism*. Cambridge: Cambridge University Press.
Amunugama, Sarath (1985), "Anagarika Dharmapala (1864–1933) and the Transformation of Sinhala Buddhist Organization in a Colonial Setting," in: *Social Science
Information* 24 (4): 697–730.
App, Urs (1997), "St. Francis Xavier's Discovery of Japanese Buddhism. A Chapter in
the European Discovery of Buddhism, part 1," in: *The Eastern Buddhist* 30 (1): 53–78.

---

76 Sharf: "[L]ike Narcissus, Western enthusiasts failed to recognize their own reflection in
the mirror being held out to them" (1993: 39). Extending the metaphor by borrowing
Barbara Babcock's reflexion from a different context also fits the dilemma: "Narcissus'
tragedy then is that he is not narcissistic enough, or rather that he does not reflect long
enough to effect a transformation. He is reflective, but he is not reflexive—that is, he is
conscious of himself as an other, but he is not conscious of being self-conscious of
himself as an other and hence not able to detach himself from, understand, survive, or
even laugh at this initial experience of alienation" (1980: 2).

Arnold, Edwin (1879), *The Light of Asia: Or the Great Renunciation, Being the Life and Teaching of Gautama*. London: Routledge & Kegan Paul.

Babcock, Barbara (1980), "Reflexivity: Definitions and Discriminations," in: *Semiotica* 30 (1–2): 1–14.

Bharati, Agehananda (1970), "The Hindu Rennaissance and Its Apologetic Patterns," in: *Journal of Asian Studies* 29: 267–87.

Blackburn, Anne M. (2002), "A Cosmopolitan in Colombo: Hikkaduve Sri Sumangala's Nineteenth-Century Transnational Buddhism." Paper presented at the AAR annual meeting in Toronto.

Bond, George (1988), *The Buddhist Revival in Sri Lanka. Religious Tradition, Reinterpretation and Response*. Columbia, S.C.: University of South Carolina Press.

Brooks, Van Wyck (1962), *Fenollosa and His Circle*. New York: Dutton.

Carrier, James G. (1995), *Occidentalism. Images of the West*. Oxford: Clarendon Press.

Carrithers, Michael (1983), *The Forest Monks of Sri Lanka: An Anthropological and Historical Study*. Delhi: Oxford University Press.

Clarke, J.J. (1997), *Oriental Enlightenment. The Encounter Between Asian and Western Thought*. London/New York: Routledge.

Cranston, Sylvia (1993), *HPB. The Extraordinary Life and Influence of Helena Blavatsky, Founder of the Modern Theosophical Movement*. New York: Putnam.

Dharmapala, Anagarika (1927), "An Appeal to Japanese Buddhists," in: *The Young East* 3 (6).

de Tollenaere, Herman A.O. (1996), *The Politics of Divine Wisdom. Theosophy and Labour, National, and Womens's Movements in Indonesia and South Asia, 1875–1947*. Uitgeverij Katholieke Universiteit Nijmegen.

Eliade, Mircia (1978), *No Souvenirs Journal 1957–69*. London: Routledge and Kegan Paul.

Ellwood, Robert S., Jr. (1979), *Alternative Altars. Unconventional and Eastern Spirituality in America*. Chicago: University of Chicago Press.

Fader, Larry A. (1986), "D.T. Suzuki's Contribution to the West," in: Masao Abe, ed., *A Zen Life: D.T. Suzuki Remembered*. New York/Tokyo: Weatherhill: 95–108.

Faure, Bernard (1993), *Chan Insights and Oversights. An Epistemological Critique of the Chan Tradition*. Princeton, N.J.: Princeton University Press.

—— (1995), "The Kyoto School and Reverse Orientalism," in: Charles Wei-hsun Fu/ Steven Heine, eds., *Japan in Traditional and Postmodern Perspectives*. Albany, N.Y.: State University of New York Press: 245–82.

Fujioka, Daisetsu (1994), "Suzuki Daisetz 1870–1966," in: Yusen Kashiwahara/Koyu Sonoda, eds., *Shapers of Japanese Buddhism*, transl. by Gaynor Sekimori. Tokyo: Kosei Publishing Co.: 241–50.

Fujiyoshi, Jikai (1968), "Sairon ni okeru Sōen Zenji," in: *Zen Bunka* 50: 29–37.

Furuta, Shokin (1967), "Shaku Sōen: The Footsteps of a Modern Zen Master," transl. by Kudo Sumiko, in: *Philosophical Studies of Japan* 8: 67–91.

Gokhale, Balkrishna Govind (1973), "Anagarika Dharmapala: Toward Modernity through Tradition in Ceylon," in: Bardwell L. Smith, ed., *Tradition and Change in Theravada Buddhism: Essays on Ceylon and Thailand in the 19th and 20th Centuries*. Leiden: E.J. Brill: 30–39.

Gombrich, Richard (1988), *Theravada Buddhism. A Social History from Ancient Benares to Modern Colombo*. London/New York: Routledge.

Gombrich, Richard/Obeyesekere, Gananath (1988), *Buddhism Transformed. Religious Change in Sri Lanka*. Princeton, N.J.: Princeton University Press.

Guruge, Ananda, ed. (1965), *Return to Righteousness. A Collection of Speeches, Essays and Letters of Anagarika Dharmapala*. Colombo, Ceylon: Ministry of Cultural Affairs and Education.

Hanh, Thich Nhat (1995 [1973]), *Zen Keys. A Guide to Zen Practice*. London: Thorsons.

Harris, Elizabeth J. (1998), *Ananda Metteya. The First Emissary of Buddhism*. Kandy: Buddhist Publication Society.

Hay, Stephen N. (1970), *Asian Ideas of East and West. Tagore and His Critics in Japan, China, and India*. Cambridge, Mass.: Harvard University Press.

Heehs, Peter (1994), "Foreign Influences on Bengali Revolutionary Terrorism 1902–1908," in: *Modern Asian Studies* 28 (3): 533–56.

Hisamatsu, Shin'ichi/Susumu, Yamaguchi/Shokin, Furuta, eds. (1968–1970), *The Complete Works of Suzuki Daisetz (in Japanese)*. Tokyo: Iwanami Shoten; announced in: *The Eastern Buddhist* (New Series) 3 (2): 146–48.

Humphreys, Christmas (1968), *Sixty Years of Buddhism in England*. London: Buddhist Society.

Inoue, Zenjō (1989), *Suzuki Daisetsu Mikokai Shokan*. Kyoto: Zen Bunka Kenkyusho.

Ishii, Kōsei (2002), "Thoughts and Genealogy of Ultranationalists Strongly Influenced by Buddhist Philosophy: The Exchange of Japanese Nationalists and Ceylonese Buddhists." Paper presented at AAR annual meeting in Toronto.

— (2004), "Dharmapala's Activities in Japan." Paper presented at Duke University.

Jackson, Carl (1981), *The Oriental Religions and American Thought. Nineteenth-Century Explorations*. Westport, Conn.: Greenwood Press.

Kawaguchi, Ekai (1909), *Three Years in Tibet*. Madras: The Theosophical Office.

Ketelaar, James E. (1990), *Of Heretics and Martyrs in Meiji Japan: Buddhism and Its Persecution*. Princeton, N.J.: Princeton University Press.

King, Richard (1999), *Orientalism and Religion. Postcolonial Theory, India and The Mystic East*. London/New York: Routledge.

Kirita, Kiyohede (1996), Young D.T. Suzuki's Views on Society. *The Eastern Buddhist* 29 (1): 109–33.

Kirthisinghe, B.P. (1981), "Colonel Henry Steel Olcott, the Great American Buddhist," in: B.P. Kirthisinghe/M.P. Amarasuriya, eds., *Colonel Olcott. His Service to Buddhism*. Kandy: Buddhist Publication Society: 1–20.

Kobori, Sohaku (1967), "The Enlightened Thought," in: Nishitani Keiji/Sakamoto Hiroshi, eds., *In Memoria, Daisetz Teitaro Suzuki 1870–1966. The Eastern Buddhist* 2 (1): 99–109.

Kohn, Livia (1995), *Laughing at the Tao. Debates among Buddhists and Taoists in Medieval China*. Princeton, N.J.: Princeton University Press.

Kondo, Akihisa (1967), "The Stone Bridge of Joshu," in: Nishitani Keiji/Sakamoto Hiroshi, eds., *In Memoria, Daisetz Teitaro Suzuki 1870–1966. The Eastern Buddhist* 2 (1): 90–98.

Kopf, David (1985), "Sexual Ambivalence in Western Scholarship on Hindu India. A History of Historical Images of Shakto-Tantrism, 1800–1970," in: Bernard Lewis/Edmund Leites/Margaret Case, eds., *As Others See Us. Mutual Perceptions, East and West*. New York: International Society for Comparative Study of Civilizations.

Lindstrom, Lamont (1995), "Cargoism and Occidentalism," in: James G. Carrier, ed., *Occidentalism. Images of the West*. Oxford: Clarendon Press.

Lopez, Donald S. (1994), "New Age Orientalism: The Case of Tibet," in: *Tibetan Review* May: 16–20.

— ed. (1995), *Curators of the Buddha: The Study of Buddhism under Colonialism*. Chicago: University of Chicago Press.

— (1996), "'Lamaism' and the Dissappearance of Tibet," in: *Comparative Studies in Society and History* 38 (1): 3–25.

— (1998), *Prisoners of Shangri-La. Tibetan Buddhism and the West*. Chicago/London: University of Chicago Press.

Loy, David (1996), "The Dharma of Emanuel Swedenborg: A Buddhist Perspective," in: *Buddhist-Christian Studies* 16: 11–35.

Malalgoda, Kitsiri (1976), *Buddhism in Sinhalese Society 1750–1900*. Berkeley, Calif.: University of California Press.

Marshall, P.J. (1970), *The British Discovery of Hinduism in the Eighteenth Century*. Cambridge: Cambridge University Press.

Merton, Thomas (1967), "D.T. Suzuki: The Man and His Work," in: Nishitani Keiji/ Sakamoto Hiroshi, eds., *In Memoria, Daisetz Teitaro Suzuki 1870–1966. The Eastern Buddhist* 2 (1): 3–9.

Nattier, Jan (1997), "Buddhist Studies in the Post-Colonial Age," in: *Journal of the American Academy of Religion* 65 (2).

Nishimura, Eshin (1993), *Suzuki Daisetsu no Genfukei*. Tokyo: Okura.

Obeyesekere, Gananath (1970), Religious Symbolism and Political Change in Ceylon. *Modern Ceylon Studies* 1 (1): 43–63.

Olcott, Henry Steel (1910), *Old Diary Leaves. The Only Authentic History of the Theosophical Society, Fourth Series, 1887–92*. London: The Theosophical Society.

Pedersen, Poul (1997), "Tibet, die Theosophie und die Psychologisierung des Buddhismus," in: Thierry Dodin/H. Räther, eds., *Mythos Tibet: Wahrnehmungen, Projektionen, Phantasien*. Cologne: Dumont: 165–77.

Prothero, Stephen (1996), *The White Buddhist. The Asian Odessey of Henry Steel Olcott*. Bloomington, Ind.: Indiana University Press.

Queen, Christopher (1996), "Introduction: The Shapes and Sources of Engaged Buddhism," in: Chr. S. Queen/Sallie B. King, eds., *Engaged Buddhism. Buddhist Liberation Movements in Asia*. New York: State University of New York Press: 1–44.

Said, Edward (1978), *Orientalism*. London: Penguin Books.

Sangharakshita, Bhikshu. (1983), *Anagarika Dharmapala. A Biographical Sketch*. Kandy: Buddhist Publication Society.

Schalk, Peter, ed. (2003), *Religion im Spiegelkabinett. Asiatische Religionsgeschichte im Spannungsfeld zwischen Orientalismus und Okzidentalismus*. Uppsala: Uppsala Universitet.

Schwab, Raymond (1984), *The Oriental Rennaissance: Europe's Rediscovery of India and the East, 1680–1880*. New York: Columbia University Press.

Senzaki, Nyogen (1978), *Like a Dream, Like a Fantasy. The Zen Writings and Translations of Nyogen Senzaki*, ed. and with an introduction by Eido Shimano Roshi. Tokyo: Japan Publications, Inc.

Sharf, Robert (1993), "The Zen of Japanese Nationalism," in: *History of Religions* 33 (1): 1–43.

—— (1995a), "The Zen of Japanese Nationalism," in: Donald Lopez, ed., *Curators of the Buddha: The Study of Buddhism under Colonialism*. Chicago: University of Chicago Press.

—— (1995b), "Buddhist Modernism and the Rhetoric of Meditative Experience," in: *Numen* 42: 228–83.

—— (1995c)," Sanbokyodan: Zen and the Way of the New Religions," in: *Japanese Journal of Religious Studies* 22 (3/4): 417–58.

Sharpe, Eric (1985), *The Universal Gita. Western Images of the Bhagavadgita, a Bicentenary Survey*. London: Duckworth.

Shimomura, Torataro (1967), "The Modernization of Japan, with Special Reference to Philosophy," transl. by John R. McEwan, in: *Philosophical Studies of Japan* 8: 1–28.

Shore, Jeff (1986), "Zen in America and the Necessity of the Great Doubt: A Discussion between D.T. Suzuki and Shin'ichi Hasamatsu," in: *FAS Society Journal*: 19–23.

Snodgrass, Judith (1998), "Buddha no Fukuin. The Development of Paul Carus's Gospel of Buddha in Meiji Japan," in: *Japanese Journal of Religious Studies* 25 (3-4): 319–44.

—— (2003), *Presenting Japanese Buddhism to the West. Orientalism, Occidentalism, and the Columbian Exposition*. Chapel Hill, N.C.: The University of North Carolina Press.

Sōen, Shaku (1941), *Seiyō Nikki*. (Facsimile reprint). Tokyo: Kamakura Matsugaoka Tōkeiji.

Suzuki, D.T. (1921), "Editorial," in: *The Eastern Buddhist* 1 (1): 80–85.

—— (1930), *Living by Zen*. Tokyo: Sanseido.

—— (1957), *Mysticism: Christian and Buddhist*. New York: Harper.

—— (1958), *Zen and Japanese Buddhism*. Tokyo: Charles E. Tuttle Company

—— (1959), *Zen and Japanese Culture*. London.

—— (1967), "An Interpretation of Zen Experience," in: Charles A. Moore, ed., *The Japanese Mind. Essentials of Japanese Philosophy and Culture*. Honolulu: 122–41.

—— (1969a), *The Field of Zen*, ed. by Christmas Humphreys. London: The Buddhist Society.

—— (1969b), *An Introduction to Zen Buddhism*, ed. by Chr. Humphresy, foreword by C.G. Jung. London: Rider & Company.

—— (1970a [1949]), *Essays in Zen Buddhism. First Series*. London: Rider.

—— (1970b [1949]), *Essays in Zen Buddhism. Second Series*. London: Rider.

—— (1970c [1953]), *Essays in Zen Buddhism. Third Series*. London: Rider.

—— (1970d [1969]), *The Field of Zen. Contributions to the Middle Way, the Journal of the Buddhist Society*. New York/London: Buddhist Society.

—— (1972), *Japanese Spirituality*, transl. by Norman Waddell. Tokyo: Japan Society for the Promotion of Sciences.

Suzuki, D.T./DeMartino, Richard/Fromm, Erich (1960), *Zen Buddhism and Psychoanalysis*, New York: Harper.

Tagami, Taishu (1986), "The Internationalization of Zen—Problems and Perspectives," in: *Zen Buddhism Today* 4: 72–80.

Takakusu, Junjiro (1929), "The Young East in a Sad Plight," in: *The Young East* 4 (8): 254–61.

Taylor, Richard P. (1999), Blavatsky and Buddhism. Http://www.blavatsky.net/forum/taylor/tibetanSources1.htm

Thelle, Notto R. (1987), *Buddhism and Christianity in Japan. From Conflict to Dialogue, 1854–1899*. Honolulu: University of Hawaii Press.

Tsunemitsu, Kōnen (1968), *Meiji no Bukkyosha*. Vol 1. Tokyo: Shunjusha.

—— (1994), "Shaku Sōen (1859–1919)," in: Kashiwakara Yusen/Sonoda Koyu, eds., *Shapers of Japanese Buddhism*, transl. by Gaynor Sekimori. Tokyo: Kosei Publishing.

Victoria, Daizen (1980), "Japanese Corporate Zen," in: *Bulletin of Concerned Scholars* 12 (1): 61–68.

Welch, Holmes (1968), *The Buddhist Revival in China*. Cambridge, Mass.: Harvard University Press.

Wright, Brooks (1957), *Interpreter of Buddhism to the West: Sir Edwind Arnold*. London: Bookman Associates.

The Study of Western Esotericism

New Approaches to Christian and Secular Culture

by

WOUTER J. HANEGRAAFF

1. Introduction

Defining "Western esotericism" is precisely as difficult as defining "religion," and for very similar reasons. In both cases, scholarly disagreements about the precise nature and demarcation of the field are bound up with basic and far-reaching theoretical and methodological differences, resulting in a variety of disciplinary approaches which are competing for academic priority (Hanegraaff 1998a: 11–61; 1999: 337–78). In the study of Western esotericism, as in the study of religion, it is therefore impossible to sidestep questions of method and theory in order to restrict oneself directly to the field of study "in itself": there simply *is* no such field of study unless and until it is construed as such in the minds of scholars and scholarly communities. Likewise, and for the same reasons, terminological preferences are subject to ongoing academic negotiation: that these respective fields of research should be referred to as "religion" and "Western esotericism" is not obvious, but constitutes a choice which may be disputed on various grounds, perhaps in favor of alternative labels.[1]

And yet, in spite of such cautionary remarks, the study of religion and the study of Western esotericism both take their departure from the assumption that there does exist some kind of reality (according to at least some meaning of "exist" and "reality") to which the labels refer. To claim that Islam is definitely "religion" does not need to imply any essentialist or *sui generis* approach to religion, but may merely reflect the understanding that the label "religion" (according to whatever definition happens to be used) is useful as a means of demarcating certain types of human experience and practice. Likewise, the study of Western esotericism emerges from the understanding that in Western

---

1 For "religion," itself obviously a Western term, see e.g. the modern tendency to replace it by terms such as "the sacred" (discussion in Hanegraaff 1999a: 337–78, esp. 364–68 and 373–375). For "Western esotericism," see discussion of various alternative terminologies in Hanegraaff 1998a: 11–61.

culture we find certain types of human experience and practice which display a sufficient degree of similarity and specificity to be set apart—for pragmatic reasons at least—as a domain of research. Such an understanding has existed in Western culture at least since the end of the seventeenth century and arguably since the end of the fifteenth, as will be seen. While the field in question was originally referred to by general terms such as "platonic-hermetic Christianity" and "Christian gnosis," the substantive "esotericism" (*l'ésotérisme*) is not attested earlier than 1828 (Laurant 1992: 19).[2] By that time—and increasingly over the following decades—the intended category had already come to be expanded, so as to include not only currents and movements from the fifteenth to the seventeenth centuries but also more recent ones of a similar nature and historically connected to earlier ones. In the wake of the Enlightenment, some manifestations of esotericism were already in a process of emancipating themselves from the Christian context which had been self-evident prior to the eighteenth century; and as this process continued during the nineteenth and twentieth centuries, Western esotericism increasingly came to be perceived as a countercurrent or subculture more or less set apart from the mainstream. We will see that such a perception is misleading: it is essential to understand that Western esotericism is all of a piece with the general history of Christianity until deep into the eighteenth century, and that the autonomization of non-Christian types of esotericism since that period is quite as inextricably interwoven with the general processes of the secularization of religion in Western culture. Indeed, the social, cultural and epistemological watershed of the eighteenth century constitutes what is arguably *the* central challenge to a general definition of Western esotericism (as well as of religion generally, see Hanegraaff 1999a: 364–75): while the existence of strong historical connections and continuities from the Renaissance to the present is not in any doubt, Western esoteric currents have nevertheless been changed so dramatically under the impact of secularization processes that one might legitimately wonder how much there is still in common between pre-Enlightenment figures such as e.g. Giovanni Pico della Mirandola or Jacob Böhme on the one hand, and their post-Enlightenment counterparts such as the theosophist Helena P. Blavatsky or—to stretch the comparison to an extreme—the New Ager Shirley MacLaine on the other.

It has been noted that the perception (under whatever name) of Western esotericism as a specific domain of human experience and practice goes back at least to the late seventeenth century.[3] Serious research in this field has been

---

2   On the history of the term esotericism (*l'ésotérisme*), see also Laurant 1993: 7–13 and Riffard 1990: 63–137.

3   See in particular the polemics of Ehregott Daniel Colberg against platonic-hermetic Christianity (Colberg 1690–1691) and the defense of the same currents by Gottfried

done at least since the first decades of the twentieth century and has been increasing exponentially since the 1960s. Nevertheless it is only recently—essentially since the 1990s—that this research has begun to be recognized by the academic community as constituting a field in itself. This belated recognition is largely due to the residual influence of theological models and presuppositions in the modern study of religion in general and the study of Christianity in particular. While the study of religion as such has been emancipating itself from Christian theology ever since the nineteenth century and increasingly during the twentieth, scholars of religion have unfortunately been quite uncritical in adopting crypto-theological perceptions of Western esoteric currents—often referred to by means of loaded terms such as "magic" and "the occult"—as marginal heresies and contemptible superstitions unworthy of serious investigation (cf. Styers 1997, 2004 and Hanegraaff 1998b). The resulting marginalization has been aggravated by the fact that scholars of religion have tended to concentrate on non-Western religions while leaving the study of Christianity to church historians and theologians;[4] the latter, in turn, have tended to perpetuate research paradigms which are essentially normative rather than historical, and from the perspective of which esoteric currents were bound to remain neglected. Finally, with respect to esoteric currents since the eighteenth century, the marginalization of the field has been even further aggravated by the fact that the study of this domain was long dominated by the sociological study of "New Religious Movements": a field of obvious importance, but the representatives of which tended to concentrate exclusively on the sociological dimension while neglecting historical research. Again, it is only quite recently that the study of New Religious Movements has begun to be more attentive to history.[5] In sum: again and again, and from various perspectives, the study of Western esotericism has found itself caught between a rock and hard place. The result is a very serious lack of academic expertise in this domain, which is only now beginning to be corrected.[6]

Arnold (Arnold 1700). Cf. Hanegraaff 1999c: 507–508, with special reference to Gilly 2000.

4   As succinctly formulated by Monika Neugebauer-Wölk (2000: 323): "die Arbeitsteilung zwischen den Theologien und der Religionswissenschaft ist ja traditionell dadurch bestimmt, dass die Religionsgeschichte des christlichen Abendlandes theologisch bearbeitet wird, nur aussereuropäische Kulturräume religionswissenschaftlich erforscht werden."

5   See, e.g., the writings of scholars like J. Gordon Melton, Massimo Introvigne, and Jean-François Mayer.

6   This correction results not just from the recent development of Western esotericism as a field of research, but also from a major reorientation that is taking place in the study of religion in the West. As summarized by Neugebauer-Wölk (2000: 323): "Die Religionswissenschaft hat die europäische Religionsgeschichte entdeckt und mit ihr deren Vielfalt." With reference to an important programmatic article by Burkhard Gladigow,

2. A Short Historical Overview

While human thinking and behavior is far too fluid and complex to be caught in neat theoretical categories, such categories can nevertheless be useful as a means of orientation through the jungle of history. In order to get a grip on the field of Western esotericism as well as to understand the reasons for its traditional marginalization, it is useful to distinguish between three general strategies which have been used in Western culture in order to find "truth" (van den Broek/Hanegraaff 1998: vii–x). It is important, however, to understand that these three strategies are of an ideal-typical nature, i.e., that they are not mutually exclusive and should not be reified. How important this caveat is for a correct understanding of the nature of Western esotericism will become evident below.

A first strategy relies on human reason, observation, and argumentation: this is the approach basic to rational philosophy and scientific research. A second one relies on the authority of a collectively-accepted divine revelation, which is believed to transcend mere human wisdom: this approach is essential to established religion and doctrinal theology. A third one, finally, relies on the authority of personal spiritual experience or interior enlightenment: this approach may conveniently be referred to as *gnosis*, and has always had a problematic relationship to the first two approaches. The fact that its adherents look for truth "beyond reason" has made them look like obscurantists in the eyes of rationalist philosophy and science; and the fact that they believe to have personal access to divine revelation has evoked the suspicion that they are bypassing the authority of established religion and its collectively recognized sources of revelation. In short: those who have relied to a considerable extent on this third approach tend to be suspected of irrationalism and excessive individualism, while they in turn blame their opponents for relying on religious authoritarianism and excessive rationalism.

Undoubtedly the most famous manifestation of this third perspective in late antiquity is known as Gnosticism. But far more important for the study of Western esotericism as understood here—although less important from the perspective of early Church history—is another movement of the same period which relied on *gnosis*, and is known as Hermetism. Originating in Hellenistic

she explains the centrality of Western esotericism with respect to the new emphasis by historians of religion on the "europäische Markt an Sinnangeboten" (Gladigow 1995: 22), i.e. on *pluralism* as a fundamental characteristic of the history of religion in Europe since the Renaissance. Along these lines, see especially the recent work by Kocku von Stuckrad (2004).

Egypt, and flourishing in the second and third centuries CE, this current derives its name from a mythical and quasi-divine founder, Hermes Trismegistus (i.e., the "Thrice-Greatest Hermes"). Among the many writings attributed or linked to Hermes, most important and influential have been the collection known as the *Corpus Hermeticum*, and a longer text entitled *Logos Teleios* but known in its Latin translation as *Asclepius*. The *Asclepius* was known in the Latin West throughout the Middle Ages; but the *Corpus Hermeticum* only became widely known after it had been translated by the Florentine neoplatonic philosopher Marsilio Ficino in 1463 (printed in 1471).

This translation has proved to be of pivotal importance for the development of alternative "esoteric" spiritualities in modern and contemporary Western society. Foundational Renaissance thinkers such as Ficino (1433–1499) and Giovanni Pico della Mirandola (1463–1494) saw in Hermes one of the earliest and hence most authoritative sources of a *prisca theologia* or ancient theology. This primordial wisdom had supposedly been revealed by God to Adam, but had declined after the Fall. It was kept alive, however, by a succession of divinely inspired sages, beginning with Zoroaster and Hermes Trismegistus (Walker 1972; Stausberg 1998). Since this primordial wisdom had been revealed by God himself, it was necessarily consistent with the most profound mysteries of the Christian faith and could be seen as a prophetic announcement of it. This in itself accounts for the great spiritual authority attached to the *Corpus Hermeticum*, and, since Hermes was believed to have lived around the same time as Moses and much earlier than Plato (and some authors, such as Lodovico Lazzarelli, even went as far as claiming that he had flourished many centuries before both), the hermetic philosophy could be seen as a means to reconcile philosophy and Christianity, reason and faith. An important corollary of the authority attached to "Hermes" was a new appreciation of the so-called "occult sciences": magic, astrology and alchemy. The *Corpus Hermeticum* contains a spiritual philosophy with very little reference to occult sciences; but since these sublime teachings were supposedly written by the same author to whom had long been attributed a wide array of magical, astrological and alchemical writings, the latter were bound to be perceived in a new and more positive light. As a result, the "hermetic philosophy" of the Renaissance came to be linked from the very beginning with a revival of the occult sciences. In the writings of authors such as Cornelius Agrippa (1486–1535), Francesco Giorgi da Veneto (1466–1540), Giordano Bruno (1548–1600), Paracelsus (1493/94–1541), and many others, the outlines appeared of a new type of religious syncretism: a mixture of Christianity, Neoplatonism, Hermetism, Magic, Astrology, Alchemy as well as an important new phenomenon: Christian reinterpretations and adaptations of the Jewish Kabbalah. The latter current derived its essential impulse from Giovanni Pico della Mirandola's *900 Theses* (1486), which included 47 "kabbalistic conclusions," and was continued by a great number of influential authors such as Johannes Reuchlin (1455–1522), Guillaume Postel (1510–1581), and many others in the centuries to come.[7]

During the sixteenth century, a basic "referential corpus" of writings thus came into existence which, in spite of variations and divergences, clearly displays a common direction. While the Hermetic writings are certainly not its only source – see also, for example, the authority of the Chaldaean Oracles, incorrectly attributed to Zoroaster (Stausberg 1998: 35ff)—the authority attached to "Hermes" is certainly sufficient to refer to this new syncretism as "Hermeticism" in a general and encompassing sense (as distinct from "Hermetism," which is taken as referring specifically to the teachings of the *Hermetica* and its commentaries). This phenomenon of Renaissance Hermeticism is the historical foundation of what is now commonly referred to as "Western esotericism." As the main modern and contemporary representative of the "third component" referred to above, its representatives emphasize the importance of personal religious experience or *gnosis*; and since such types of experience are hard or impossible to express discursively and logically, they display a marked preference for mythical and symbolic language. More specifically, the worldview of traditional Western esotericism has been defined as a "form of thought" characterized by four intrinsic elements and two non-intrinsic (i.e. not strictly necessary) ones: (1) a belief in invisible and non-causal "correspondences" between all visible and invisible dimensions of the cosmos, (2) a perception of nature as permeated and animated by a divine presence or life-force, (3) a concentration on the religious imagination as a power that provides access to worlds and levels of reality intermediary between the material world and God, (4) the belief in a process of spiritual transmutation by which the inner man is regenerated and re-connected with the divine, (5) the belief in a fundamental concordance between several or all spiritual traditions, and (6) the idea of a more or less secret transmission of spiritual knowledge (Faivre 1994: 10–15).

In 1614, after doubts about the pre-Christian origins of the Hermetic writings had been expressed by scholars for over four decades (Mulsow 2002), the Swiss scholar Isaac Casaubon provided conclusive proof that the *Corpus Hermeticum* dated not from a remote antiquity but from the first centuries after Christ, thereby exploding the Renaissance myth of Hermes Trismegistus. However, while this discovery eventually weakened the authority of the Hermetic writings among intellectuals, it did not prevent religious currents originating in Renaissance Hermeticism from continuing during the seventeenth century and beyond (Assmann 1999). Of particular importance in this respect is the so-

---

7   The best introduction to Renaissance Hermeticism (but to be read with caution) remains Yates 1964. For the Christian Kabbalah and its later developments, see e.g. Secret 1985 and Kilcher 1998.

called Rosicrucian furore caused by the anonymous publication, in Germany and beginning in the very same year as Casaubons book, of two manifestoes— the *Fama Fraternitatis* (1614) and *Confessio Fraternitatis* (1615)—which claimed to be messages from a mysterious brotherhood of the Rose Cross. A year later they were followed by a third text which, although its form and character is quite different, is usually regarded as the third manifesto in the series: a symbolic novel of initiation known as *The Chemical Wedding of Christian Rosenkreuz* (1616). We now know that all three manifestoes have originated in Tübingen, in a circle of friends around the Paracelsian doctor Tobias Hess (1558–1614), and that their principal author was the Lutheran pastor Johann Valentin Andreae (1586–1654) (Edighoffer 2005). Due to the exited discussions caused by these pamphlets, the image of a "Rosicrucian brotherhood" took hold in the popular imagination, as seen for example in the work of much-discussed authors and self-proclaimed "Rosicrucians" such as Michael Maier (1568–1622) and Robert Fludd (1574–1637). While there is no evidence that a Rosicrucian brotherhood actually existed in the seventeenth century, various movements claiming to be its heirs would come into existence during the eighteenth century. The strongly paracelsian and alchemical type of Hermeticism typical of the Rosicrucian current generally flourished in Baroque culture, giving rise to a speculative tradition characterized in particular by its rich production of emblematic and allegorical imagery.

Parallel to the Rosicrucian current, the writings of the great visionary philosopher Jacob Böhme (1575–1624) laid the foundations for another highly influential Western esoteric tradition known as Christian Theosophy, the influence of which was to continue throughout the century with representatives such as Johann Georg Gichtel (1638–1710), John Pordage (1608–1681) and Jane Leade (1624–1704). The current continued into the eighteenth century with authors such as Dionysius Andreas Freher (1649–1728), William Law (1686–1761) and Friedrich Christian Oetinger (1702–1782); and from there into the heart of the German Romantic movement, with representatives including Franz von Baader (1765–1841) and Louis-Claude de Saint-Martin (1743–1803). Christian Theosophy came to be closely linked to the emergence of German *Naturphilosophie*, including a strong interest in magic and the "occult" phenomena associated with "the Night-Side of Nature" (Crow 1848). It flourished, finally, in the so-called Illuminist current of the later eighteenth and the early nineteenth centuries, partly linked to new initiatory societies modeled upon or connected with Freemasonry such as the theurgical Elus Coëns, the Illuminés d'Avignon, the Rectified Scottish Rite, the Order of the Gold and Rosy Cross and the Asiatic Brethren. The existence and influence of a popular as well as a learned Hermeticism during the Age of Reason, partly linked to Freemasonry and the general surge of secret societies in this period, has recently been receiving more attention from historians, and challenges received ideas about the nature and history of the Enlightenment (Neugebauer-Wölk 1999).

Western esotericism emerged as a syncretistic type of religiosity in a Christian context, and its representatives were Christians until far into the eighteenth century. From about the middle of that century, however, the complicated historical processes that may be referred to under the general heading of "secularization" began to have their impact on Western culture and religion generally, and they naturally affected esotericists as well. If we understand the term "secularization" as referring not to a process in which religion declines or vanishes but, rather, to a process of profound *change and transformation of religion* under the impact of a combination of historically unprecedented social and political conditions (Hanegraaff 1999a), we may speak not just of a "secularization of religion" but also, more specifically, of a "secularization of esotericism" during the nineteenth century. The result of this process was a new type of esotericism that may be referred to as *occultism,* and comprises all attempts by esotericists to come to terms with a disenchanted world or, alternatively, by people in general to make sense of esotericism from the perspective of a disenchanted secular world (Hanegraaff 1996: 422).

Early signs of a secularization of Western esotericism may be perceived in the perspectives of the Swedish visionary Emanuel Swedenborg (1688–1772) and the German physician Franz Anton Mesmer (1734–1815), both of whom have exerted an incalculable influence on the history of esotericism during the nineteenth and twentieth centuries (Hanegraaff 1996: 424–35). Theurgical practices, spiritual manifestations and "psychic" phenomena of a type already present in some esoteric societies of the later eighteenth century as well as in the popular practice of "magnetic healing" achieved mass popularity in the second half of the nineteenth century, in the occultist movement *par excellence* known as Spiritualism. Spiritualism provided a context within which a plethora of more or less sophisticated occultist movements came into existence. Among these manifestations of alternative religiosity, the Theosophical Movement founded in 1875 by the Russian Madame Helena P. Blavatsky (1831–1891) is certainly the most important in terms of its influence, and the basic metaphysical system of modern Theosophy may be considered the archetypal manifestation of occultist spirituality at least until far into the 1970s. Side to side with modern Theosophy, and connected with it in complex ways, appeared a variety of occultist currents with an emphasis on magical practice. Of particular importance in this respect is the influence of the French author Alphonse-Louis Constant (1810–1875), better known under his pen-name Eliphas Lévi. Among the more important manifestations of occultist magic in the second half of the nineteenth century one might mention the occultist milieu that flourished in fin-de-siècle France, around figures such as Gérard Encausse (1865–1916), known as Papus; and organizations such as the English Hermetic Order of the Golden Dawn. Finally, popular practices of "magnetic healing," also referred to as "mesmerism," reached the United States as early as 1836 and spread widely in the following decades, eventually providing a popular basis for the emergence of the so-called "New Thought" movement of the later nineteenth century. Each one of these various currents—Spiritualism, Modern Theosophy, Occultist Magic, and the American New Thought movement—has taken on a multitude of forms, and their representatives have mingled and exchanged ideas and practices in various way. The result of all this alternative religious activity was the emergence, during the nineteenth century, of an international "cultic milieu" with its own social networks and literature; relying on an essentially nineteenth-century framework of ideas and beliefs, this cultic milieu has continued and further developed during the twentieth century, eventually to provide the foundation after World War II for the emergence of the New Age movement.

3. Western Esotericism and Secularization

The occultist milieu of the nineteenth and twentieth century differs from traditional Western esotericism in at least four crucial respects. Firstly, esotericism was originally grounded in an "enchanted" worldview where all parts of the universe were linked by invisible networks of non-causal "correspondences" and a divine power of life was considered to permeate the whole of nature. Although esotericists have continued to defend such an enchanted "holistic" view of the world as permeated by invisible forces, their actual statements demonstrate that they came to compromise in various ways with the "mechanical" and "disenchanted" world-models that achieved cultural dominance under the impact of scientific materialism and nineteenth-century positivism. Accordingly, occultism is characterized by hybrid mixtures of traditional esoteric and modern scientistic-materialist worldviews: while originally the religious belief in a universe brought forth by a personal God was axiomatic for esotericism, eventually this belief succumbed partly or completely to popular scientific visions of a universe answering to impersonal laws of causality. Even though the laws in question may be referred to as "spiritual," nonetheless they tend to be described according to models taken from science rather than religion (Hanegraaff 1996: 421–42; Hammer 2001: 201–330).

Secondly, the traditional Christian presuppositions of modern Western esotericism were increasingly questioned and relativized due to new translations of oriental religious texts and the emergence of a "comparative study of the religions of the world". Oriental religions began to display missionary activities in Western countries, and their representatives typically sought to convince their audience by using Western terms and concepts to present the spirituality of religions such as Hinduism and Buddhism. Conversely, since occultists had always believed that the essential truths of esoteric spirituality were universal in nature and could be discovered at the heart of all great religious traditions East and West, it was natural for them to incorporate oriental concepts and terminology into already-existing Western-occultist frameworks. One excellent example is the concept of "karma" that was adopted by Blavatsky from Hinduism, as a welcome alternative for Christian concepts of divine providence, whereas Blavatsky's basic understanding of reincarnation depended on Western-esoteric rather than oriental sources (Hanegraaff 1996: 442–62).

Thirdly, the well-known debate between Christian creationism and the new theories of evolution became highly relevant to occultism as well, and in this battle occultists generally took the side of "science". But although popular evolutionism became a crucial aspect of occultism as it developed from the nineteenth into the twentieth century, and although this evolutionism was generally used as part of a strategy of presenting occultism as scientifically legitimate, the actual types of evolutionism found in occultism depended less on Darwinian theory than on philosophical models originating in German Idealism and Romanticism. The idea of a universal process of spiritual evolution and progress, involving human souls as well as the universe in its entirety, is not to be found in traditional Western esotericism but became fundamental to almost all forms of nineteenth- and twentieth-century occultism (Hanegraaff 1996: 462–82).

Finally, the emergence of modern psychology (itself dependent partly on Mesmerism and the Romantic fascination with the "night-side of nature") has had an enormous impact on the development of occultism from the second half of the nineteenth century on. While psychology could be used as an argument against Christianity and against religion generally, by arguing that God or the gods are merely projections of the human psyche, it also proved possible to present Western-esoteric worldviews in terms of a new psychological terminology. Most influential in this respect was the Swiss psychiatrist Carl Gustav Jung (1875–1961), whose spiritual perspective was deeply rooted in the esoteric and occult currents of German Romantic *Naturphilosophie* but whose theories could be used to present that spirituality as a "scientific" psychology. Apart from Jung, the "pop psychology" of the American New Thought movement has been a major influence on the mixtures of occultism and psychology typical of contemporary New Age spirituality (Hanegraaff 1996: 482–513).

To these four main aspects of the "secularization of Western esotericism," perhaps a fifth one should be added that became dominant only after World War II, and is fully characteristic of the New Age movement of the 1980s and 1990s: the impact of capitalist market economy on the domain of spirituality. Increasingly, the New Age movement has taken the shape of a "spiritual supermarket" where religious consumers pick and choose the spiritual commodities they fancy, and use them to create their own spiritual syntheses "fine-tuned" to their strictly personal needs. The phenomenon of a spiritual supermarket is not limited to the New Age movement only, but is a general characteristic of religion in (post)modern Western democracies. Various forms of New Age spirituality are competing with more traditional forms of religion (including the Christian churches as well as other great religious traditions such as Islam or Buddhism) and with a great number of so-called new religious movements, popularly referred to as "cults." However, in this universal battle for the attention of the consumer, the New Age movement enjoys certain advantages over most of its competitors, which seem to make it the representative *par excellence* of the contemporary "spirituality of the market." Whereas most other spiritual currents that compete for the attention of the consumer in modern society take the form of (at least rudimentary) organizations, enabling their members to see themselves as part of a religious community, New Age spirituality is strictly focused on the individual and his/her personal development. In fact, this individualism functions as an in-built defense mechanism against social organization and institutionalization: as soon as any group of people involved with New Age ideas begins to take up "cultic" characteristics, this very fact already distances them from the basic individualism of New Age spirituality. The stronger they begin to function as a "cult," of even as a "sect," the more will other New Agers suspect that they are becoming a "church" (i.e., that they are relapsing into what are considered old-fashioned patterns of dogmatism, intolerance and exclusivism), and the less will they be acceptable to the general cultic milieu of New Age spirituality (cf. Hanegraaff 1996: 12–18). Within the present social context of a democratic free market of ideas and practices, the New Age's strict emphasis on the Self and on individual experience as the only reliable source of spiritual truth, the authority of which can never be overruled by any religious "dogma" or considerations of solidarity with communal values, functions as an effective mechanism against institutionalization of New Age religion into *a* religion (Hanegraaff 1999a; 1999b; 2000). This essential individualism makes the New Ager into the ideal spiritual consumer. Except for the very focus on the Self and its spiritual evolution, there are no constraints *a priori* on a New Ager's potential spiritual interests; the fact that every New Ager continually creates and re-creates his or her own private system of symbolic meaning and values means that spiritual suppliers on the New Age market enjoy maximum opportunities for presenting him or her with ever-new commodities (Hanegraaff 1999b).

4. Approaches to the Study of Western Esotericism

The ideologically-charged battles over methodology which have characterized the emancipation and professionalization of the study of religion since the nineteenth century are mirrored in the far more recent professionalization process in the study of Western esotericism. In both fields, the insistence by academics on value-free historical, empirical and analytical approaches has been criticized by those who believe that the field should be approached from internal esoteric and religionist perspectives. For anyone familiar with the history of the study of religion, current theoretical and methodological debates about the proper way of studying Western esotericism will frequently evoke feelings of *déja vu*, since they largely amount to a repetition of the same well-known arguments. However, they also contain dimensions which are quite specific to the field in question. In order to get a grip on these debates it is useful to distinguish between five main categories of authors: (1) perennialists or traditionalists, (2) religionists, (3) historians of science and philosophy, (4) specialists on specific currents, and (5) generalists in the study of Western esotericism (cf. Hanegraaff 2001).

The immediate parallel to dogmatic theology in the study of Western esotericism is known as *Perennialism* or *Traditionalism*, linked to the names of authors such as René Guénon, Ananda Coomaraswamy, Frithjof Schuon, Julius Evola, and Seyyed Hossein Nasr.[8] Here we are actually dealing with an approach to the comparative study of religion generally, but one which becomes relevant to the study of Western esotericism because its representatives believe that the great religions of the world share a common "esoteric" dimension. In that respect they are heirs to the *prisca theologia* or *philosophia perennis* associated with Renaissance Hermeticism. Modern perennialists approach religion from an explicit and uncompromising doctrinal perspective based on metaphysical "first principles," which they oppose wholesale against the values of "the modern world." Various approaches basic to academic research—such as the primacy of historic research over metaphysical speculation, and the importance of the social sciences in the study of religion—are rejected by them as wholly misguided. Predictably, therefore, perennialism in its openly doctrinal manifestation has not been accepted by the academy; but its influence on major figures in the study of religion—implicitly for example in the case of Mircea Eliade, explicitly in the case of Huston Smith—should not be underestimated. The comparatively strong influence of perennialist perspectives on the current study of Western esotericism—particularly in France and the United States—might be considered somewhat bizarre, given that perennialists explicitly do not understand "esotericism" as referring to any specific historical currents (such as those listed in section 2, *supra*) but as referring to a metahistorical and metaphysical dimension of reality as such. The fact is, however, that many present-day students in the field simply never stop to ask themselves what they mean exactly when they categorize certain currents and ideas as "esoteric"; just as some students of religion work from the assumption that "everybody knows" what religion is, quite a number of students of esotericism seem to assume the same about their subject. Quite frequently this lack of interest in definitions leads to a naive adoption of (crypto)perennialist assumptions within studies of specific historical Western-esoteric currents, resulting in an essential vagueness about what the authors of such studies mean when they refer to these currents

---

8   For a good overview of this current, see Faivre 1999.

as "esoteric." Obviously such vagueness—usually combined in these cases with clearly "spiritual" rather than scholarly agendas—has the effect of confirming existing prejudices and stereotypes about the field. Quite clearly therefore, although it must be recognized that studies of Western esotericism on perennialist assumptions constitute a far from insignificant section of the existing literature, and although parts of that literature can be profitably used by scholars, the perennialist study of Western esotericism as such is a religious pursuit which does not fit within the framework of modern academic approaches to the study of religion (Hanegraaff 2001).

While perennialist approaches to the study of Western esotericism are openly dogmatic in their insistence on specific metaphysical doctrines, the dogmatism of *religionist approaches* remains largely or wholly implicit. The single most important background to religionist studies of Western esotericism lies in the specific approach to religion associated with the famous *Eranos* meetings in Switzerland since 1933. Without for a moment denying the genuine scholarly substance of these meetings (see e.g. Wasserstrom 1999), *Eranos* as such may be interpreted as a specific type of a "cultic milieu," the corporate identity of which was based upon a specific and innovative type of modern esotericism (Hanegraaff 2001; cf. Hakl 2001). In truly syncretic and eclectic fashion, this cultic milieu adopted aspects of Perennialism, German Romanticism and Idealism, Christian Theosophy (incl. Swedenborgianism), Christian Kabbalah, and Jungian depth psychology. In so doing, *Eranos* has laid the foundations for a new type of modern, non-denominational spirituality which proved congenial to the countercultural sentiments of the 1960s and found a mass audience by means of highly popular authors such as Mircea Eliade and Joseph Campbell. While the *Eranos* approach to religion has gradually been losing academic prestige since the 1970s, it has been adopted enthusiastically by a popular readership interested in a non-denominational spirituality referred to by the code word of "the sacred" (Hanegraaff 1999a); indeed, as formulated by Steven Wasserstrom, it is the New Age to which much of the spirit of History of Religions has fled (Wasserstrom 1999: 238). Religionist approaches along the lines of Mircea Eliade and Henry Corbin have exerted a major influence on the study of Western esotericism particularly since the 1960s. This is evident even in the writings of the doyen of the study of Western esotericism Antoine Faivre (see below), whose authoritative oeuvre is solidly grounded in historical research but whose writings of the 1970s and 1980s also clearly display the characteristic flavour of *Eranos*.

Until the 1960s, *historians of science and philosophy* had mostly adopted a whiggish modernist approach as summarized by George Sarton in his *Introduction to the History of Science*: The historian of science cannot devote much attention to the study of superstition and magic, that is, of unreason ... Human folly being at once unprogressive, unchangeable, and unlimited, its study is a hopeless undertaking (Sarton 1975: 19). This unproductive attitude was changed due to the influence of a book published in 1964 by the intellectual historian Frances A. Yates, *Giordano Bruno and the Hermetic Tradition* (Yates 1964). Since the 1930s, Italian researchers such as Kristeller and Garin had begun to call attention to the importance of hermetism in Renaissance culture (Kristeller 1938; Garin 1954), but the impact of this research had remained limited to the circles of specialists. As a gifted and imaginative writer, Yates was able to present "the Hermetic tradition" to an English-speaking audience in a manner that struck her readers as a revelation: an entire forgotten tradition, marginalized by the theologians and suppressed by mainstream science, suddenly seemed to have been brought to light. Moreover, in an influential article published in 1967, Yates went beyond her book on Bruno in making far-reaching claims about the Hermetic Tradition as an essential, almost causal factor in the emergence of the scientific revolution (Yates 1967), and this led to vehement academic debates all through the 1970s and beyond.[9] Nowadays the extreme idea of the Hermetic Tradition as a causal factor in the emergence of modern science is no longer accepted by historians, although weaker versions of it remain widely current; but the debate fueled by Yates' provocative theses had the highly positive effect that the importance of the "hermetic" dimension in the seventeenth-century scientific and intellectual discourse is now generally recognized.[10] Thus the study of hermetic currents is now well-established and recognized by historians of Renaissance philosophy and of the Scientific Revolution.

The new interest in "the Hermetic tradition" has also had its effects outside the domain of history of philosophy and science. Since the 1960s there has been a rapid development of research, from a variety of disciplinary perspectives, into a large range of *specific currents and personalities* belonging to the field of Western esotericism as understood here. While part of this research has been inspired by perennialist and religionist motivations, a large part has been historical and empirical in nature. Such studies have increased exponentially during the 1980s and 1990s but, surprisingly perhaps, this has not led to academic recognition of Western esotericism as a specific field of research in the humanities. In other words: the scholarly study of Western esotericism has been flourishing for decades, but it has done so *invisibly*, carried by the individual efforts of essentially isolated individuals, rather than by an internationally organized academic discipline with its own research paradigms, scholarly journals, congresses and symposia, academic chairs, and so on. This failure—until quite recently—of Western esotericism to gain academic recognition as a field of research has to do essentially with the influence of perennialist

---

9   For synthetic overview of the debate, see e.g. Copenhaver 1990 and Cohen 1994: 169–83.

10   See e.g. the cases of Newton (Dobbs 1991) and Boyle (Principe 1998).

and religionist approaches, which were correctly perceived (and hence rejected) by academics as religious rather than scholarly in inspiration. The public "image" of the study of Western esotericism in the 1970s and 1980s came to be dominated by explicit or implicit countercultural ideologies in which Yates' grand narrative of "the Hermetic Tradition" was interpreted from religionist perspectives reflecting the *Eranos* approach (Hanegraaff 2001). As a result, students of Western esotericism tended to be suspected of being krypto-esotericists rather than academic scholars, and such perceptions are still current. Predictably, therefore, many specialists of specific currents and person-alities still prefer not to be associated with the label "esotericism," perceived by them as tainted with overtones of the New Age. Understandable though such an attitude may be, it has the adverse effect of discouraging interdisciplinary contact and exchange between specialists whose fields of study have much in common.

The number of *generalists in the study of Western esotericism*—scholars whose research may obviously be of a specialized and detailed nature no less than in the previous category, but who perceive the study of Western esotericism as their general discipline—is still relatively small.[11] The explanation is quite simple: the existing lack of academic positions has made it very difficult for any scholar to devote him- or herself entirely to this field, and the lack of general in-ternational academic structures and organizational bodies has worked against the development of a critical academic debate, productive exchange of views and ideas, and the formation of basic research paradigms. During the 1990s, however, several new developments have taken place which inspire confidence in the development of Western esotericism into a recognized academic disci-pline. These will be discussed in the next section.

5. A New Discipline in the Study of Religion

5.1. Academic Positions

The world's first academic chair in the field, entitled "History of Esoteric Christianity," was established at the fifth section of the *École Pratique des Hautes*

---

11   The category includes e.g. Antoine Faivre, the late James Webb, Joscelyn Godwin, Arthur Versluis, Gerhard Wehr, Christopher McIntosh, Jean-Pierre Laurant, Jean-Pierre Brach, Olav Hammer, Nicholas Goodrick-Clarke, Andreas Kilcher, Kocku von Stuckrad, Marco Pasi, and the author of this article. Of course not all these authors cover all periods from Renaissance to present in their actual research; but even if they concentrate on a more specific area, their approach demonstrates that they perceive their work primarily as contributions to the study of Western esotericism in a general sense.

Études (Sorbonne) in Paris in 1965. It was held by François Secret from 1965 to 1979, when he was succeeded by Antoine Faivre, and the title was changed to "History of Esoteric and Mystical Currents in Modern and Contemporary Europe"; Faivre was succeeded in 2002 by Jean-Pierre Brach, and the title was changed to "History of Esoteric Currents in Modern and Contemporary Europe." Until 1999 this has remained the only chair in the world. Like the other chairs in the E.P.H.E., it is essentially a research position, the teaching load consisting of a weekly two-hour seminar which is not part of the general student curricula of the Paris universities.[12] As a result, while the previous chairholder has exerted a major influence on the study of Western esotericism by means of his many publications as well as by supervising doctoral and Ph.D. theses, he has not been in a position to establish a formal "school" or research tradition integrated in the French university system.

In 1999 a second chair, devoted to "History of Hermetic Philosophy and Related Currents," was established at the University of Amsterdam (the Netherlands). It is connected with a new subdepartment of the same title, which also includes two full-time lecturer/researchers, two Ph.D. students, and secretarial staff. Wouter J. Hanegraaff was appointed full professor on this chair, and two lecturer/researchers were appointed for the period Renaissance-eighteenth century and nineteenth-twentieth century respectively. For the former position were appointed Jean-Pierre Brach (2000–2002) and Kocku von Stuckrad (2003–present); for the latter Olav Hammer (2001–2003) and Marco Pasi (2004–present). The subdepartment offers a minor "Western Esotericism" as part of the B.A. program religious studies, and an English-language M.A. program "Mysticism and Western Esotericism" open to international students has been offered since 2003 in a one-year and a two-year variant (full and up-to-date information can be found on http://www.amsterdamhermetica.com). The presence in the same city of the world's best collection of hermetic literature, the *Bibliotheca Philosophica Hermetica*, provides excellent conditions for collaboration, so that Amsterdam may be expected to play an important role in the future development of the discipline. The new chair has elicited positive reactions internationally, and there is reason to expect that the example set by the University of Amsterdam will be followed by other universities in the years to come.

---

12   The function of Directeur d'Études (professor) at the the École Pratique des Hautes Études has an adjoined position referred to as Chargé de Conférences. Chargés de conférences are appointed on a temporary basis and receive no formal salary; their task involves the teaching of a weekly seminar.

5.2. International Organizations and Meetings

In 2002, a new "Association for the Study of Esotericism" (ASE) was established in the United States under the presidency of Arthur Versluis, and a first conference was organized by this association in June 2004 (Michigan). Preparations for a European Association are now in an advanced stage. In the meantime, apart from a plethora of regional conferences organized by various groups and networks in Europe and the United States (partly devoted to subdomains of the field), international meetings intended to bring scholars into contact with one another and establish the study of Western esotericism as a comprehensive discipline have increasingly been organized during the 1990s. Of particular importance in this respect are the meetings in the context of the American Academy of Religion (AAR) and the International Association for the History of Religions (IAHR).

The study of Western esotericism at the annual meetings of the AAR can be traced from 1980. The history of these sessions (which are organized in a number of formats, known as panels or round tables, consultations, seminars, and groups) should one day be written down in detail, since it provides fascinating insight into the development of the discipline. Originally the influence of perennialism and religionism was paramount, but tensions developed with more historically and empirically-oriented scholars, leading to an internal split around 1988 followed by a discontinuation of most esotericism sessions in 1990. A new beginning was made by James Santucci in 1994, with a seminar on "Theosophy and Theosophic Thought" which has run for five years and has been followed since 1999 by a consultation titled "Western Esotericism from the Early Modern Period." This consultation is empirico-historical in orientation, and therefore represents the emergence of properly academic research from a previous perennialist and religionist context.[13]

---

13   The main outlines of the AAR sessions may be summarized as follows (info as provided by A. Faivre to the author). Three panels organized by a group consisting of James Cutsinger, Seyyed Hossein Nasr and Robert McDermott: "Modern Western Esotericism" (1980), "The Spiritual Significance of Alchemy in the Modern West" (1982), "Esotericism Today: The Example of Henry Corbin" (1983). Then a two-year consultation "Esotericism" organized by the same group: "Esoteric Anthropology" (1984) and "Secrecy" (1985). The consultation got up to group status in 1986, under the title "Esotericism and Perennialism": "Religion and the Evolution of Consciousness" and "Is there a Transcendent Unity of Religions" (1986), "Perennial Philosophy and Hierarchy" and "Secular and Sacred Science" (1987), "Body, Nature, the Feminine" and "The Work of F. Schuon" (1988), "Metaphysical Assumptions in Esotericism" and "Hierarchy and Cosmologies" (1989), "Imagination and Transformation in Esotericism" and "Methodologies of the Esoteric" (1990; with the general group title changed to "Esoterism"). From 1991 to 1998 an independent seminar on Swedenborg has been organized by Jane Williams-Hogan; and an isolated panel "Perennialism" was organized

At the seventeenth quincentennial congress of the IAHR (Mexico City, 1995), a large symposium "Western Esotericism and the Science of Religion" was organized, the proceedings of which were published three years later (Faivre/Hanegraaff 1998). This initiative was continued at the eighteenth quincentennial congress (Durban, 2000), with an even more extended program "Western Esotericism and Jewish Mysticism." Both symposia, and the second one in particular, have been of foundational importance in creating a podium for the discipline in the context of the most important world organization for the academic study of religions, and in putting on the agenda basic questions of a theoretical and methodological nature. The nineteenth quincentennial congress (Tokyo, 2005) again contains a series of sessions devoted to the study of Western esotericism. It is a clear sign of how fast the field is developing that, this time, so many applications of high quality were submitted that over half of them had to be declined in spite of their generally high level of quality.

5.3. Journals and Publication Series

Quite a number of journals and yearbooks devoted to, or immediately relevant to Western esotericism, have been in circulation since the 1960s. Many of them (such as e.g. the American series *Alexandria* [since 1991] and *Gnosis* [1985–1999], the French *Cahiers de l'Université de Saint-Jean de Jérusalem* [1975–1985] and the German periodical *Gnostika* [since 1996]) have been partly or predominantly representative of the religionist currents described above. Among the strictly scholarly journals devoted to Western esotericism or specific aspects of it, most are either restricted to subdomains or have a limited distribution and geographical scope. Mention should be made at least of *Ambix* (published by the Society for the History of Alchemy and Chemistry since 1937), *ARIES* first series (1985–1999), *Theosophical History* (since 1985), *Chrysopoeia* (again focused on the history of alchemy, 1987–2001), *Politica Hermetica* (since 1987), *Charis: Archives de l'Unicorne* (since 1988), and *Accademia* (since 2000). In addition, special mention should be made of the new electronic journal *Esoterica* (www.esoteric.msu.edu; since 1999).

A professional academic journal devoted to the study of Western esotericism generally, and widely distributed across linguistic and geographic boundaries, was lacking until 2001. Since January of that year, E.J. Brill academic publishers are publishing *Aries: Journal for the Study of Western*

---

in association with the "Platonism and Neo-Platonism" group in 1993. The historico-empirical development begins with James Santucci's seminar "Theosophy and Theosophic Thought," which ran for five consecutive years from 1994–1998. The new consultation "Western Esotericism from the Early Modern Period" has run since 1999.

Esotericism. Accepting articles and book reviews in four languages (English, French, German, Italian), *Aries* sees it as its mission to reflect and stimulate the establishment of the study of Western esotericism in an academic context.

Among the major monograph series devoted to Western esotericism, mention must be made of the series "Western Esoteric Traditions" published by State University of New York Press (Albany), "Bibliotheca Hermetica (Alchimie—Astrologie—Magie)" published by Denoël & Retz (Paris), "Bibliothèque de l'Hermétisme" published by Dervy (Paris), and "Gnostica: Texts & Interpretations" published by Peeters (Louvain).

5.4. Two Disciplinary Paradigms

The grand narrative of "the Hermetic Tradition" created by Frances Yates in her influential writings since the 1960s provided the study of Western esotericism with its first major research paradigm. This "Yates Paradigm," which has remained dominant through the 1970s and only gradually began to wane during the 1980s, has two main characteristics. First, "the Hermetic Tradition" (and by implication, Western esotericism generally) is presented as a quasi-autonomous counter-tradition pitted against the mainstream traditions of Christianity and rationality. Second, the presentation of this Hermetic Tradition is inextricably linked to modernist narratives of progress by means of science. Yates' grand narrative was based upon an exciting paradox: she claimed that the "great forward movement" of the scientific revolution, from which the modern world has emerged, was crucially indebted not to rational traditions but—of all things—to the hermetic magic epitomized by figures such as Giordano Bruno. In other words: precisely this forgotten hermetic counterculture of the West, long decried as merely superstitious and reactionary, had supposedly been the true motor of progress. This message made Yates' writings irresistible to the spiritual heirs and sympathizers of the 1960s counterculture, who added to her narrative the new suggestion (unthinkable for Yates herself) that the worldview of the Renaissance magi could and should now be revived in contemporary society. Such countercultural hopes for a "new renaissance" on spiritual foundations have been central to religionist currents in the study of Western esotericism. Below I will argue that the basic assumptions underlying the "Yates paradigm" can no longer be upheld; and above I have argued that the religionist approach to the study of Western esotericism is based upon religious rather than scholarly foundations. The development of the discipline therefore requires us now to move beyond the Yates paradigm.

During the 1990s, an alternative paradigm appeared on the stage, based upon Antoine Faivre's definition of Western esotericism as a "form of thought" identified by four intrinsic and two non-intrinsic characteristics (see summary *supra*). Originally formulated in 1992, this definition has enjoyed a rapid career particularly due to the English translations of Faivre's writings which began to appear in the same decade, and several of which repeat his definition in only minimally different formulations. A rather long list could be made of publications in which the authors apply Faivre's definition to a wide range of currents and personalities, in order to decide whether or not these qualify as "esoteric." Many of these publications demonstrate a problem of general importance, i.e. the tendency among scholars of esotericism to understand definitions in an essentialist rather than nominalist fashion. Actually, however, since all definitions are scholarly constructs, no answer is possible to the question of "whether movement x is *really* esoteric"; we can only know "whether movement x qualifies as esoteric according to definition y." Obviously this makes the exercise of applying Faivre's definition as a lithmus test for their "esoteric" nature rather futile; and the frequency of such attempts illustrates the continuing—but often barely conscious—influence of *sui generis* assumptions among methodologically less sophisticated students of Western esotericism. As for the value of Faivre's paradigm if properly understood as based upon a scholarly construct, its heuristic value is undeniable, but as foundation for a disciplinary paradigm it creates some problems when applied to post-sixteenth and particularly post-eighteenth century currents. Since Faivre's definition is based upon the original "referential corpus" of Renaissance hermeticism, it is only partly applicable to a series of new and unprecedented developments that appeared during the seventeenth and eighteenth centuries; in the context of Faivre's paradigm the latter's "spiritualist"/pietist dimensions in particular can never become more than a non-intrinsic variable, even though one might well argue that they are in fact intrinsic to a phenomenon such as Christian Theosophy (Hanegraaff 1996: 401–403). The problem becomes all the more pressing if one applies the definition to post-eighteenth century "occultist" currents. Precisely Faivre's first—and arguably central—intrinsic characteristic, the worldview of correspondences, was severely compromised, to say the least, under the impact of a "mechanical" and positivist worldview based on instrumental causality. Obviously this is not to deny that doctrines of "correspondences" may be encountered in various nineteenth- and twentieth-century forms of esotericism. The point is that the disenchantment of the world may cause the meaning of "correspondences" to get thoroughly reinterpreted; one might even go as far as suggesting that at least some nineteenth- and twentieth-century "esoteric" currents reflect a (neo)positivist "form of thought" adorned with some of the trappings of pre-Enlightenment esotericism, rather than the reverse. In sum, it seems that Faivre's paradigm runs the risk of ignoring or minimizing the creative innovations and transformations of Western esotericism under the impact of secularization, in favor of a "grand continuity" on phenomenological foundations.

5.5. The Emergence of a New Research Paradigm

The fall of the Berlin wall in 1989 may be seen as symbolic of a subtle but clearly perceptible change in how scholars tend to approach historically-based research in the humanities. Whether one wishes to use or rather to avoid fashionable labels like "post-modern," it is hard to ignore the evidence for a widespread disaffection in contemporary intellectual life with the grand narratives of modernity and their ideological underpinnings. The emergence of a *neue Unübersichtlichkeit* was analyzed by the leading proponent of modernity Jürgen Habermas as early as 1985, and has become increasingly characteristic of the cultural *Zeitgeist* in Western intellectual life since the 1990s (Habermas 1985).

The implications of this shift for the study of Western esotericism are far-reaching. The confidence with which authors like Sarton could dismiss the study of magic as self-evidently useless, as well as the enthusiasm with which Frances Yates presented hermeticism as a force of progress, are both equally based upon a firm belief in the grand narratives of modernity. This confidence is no longer widely shared today. It has become evident to historians that the story of the emergence of modern science is much more messy and complicated than suggested by the old narratives (i.e., progressive scientific rationality either breaking free triumphantly from the reactionary forces of superstition and the occult, or coming into its own after having first received its essential impetus from hermetic magic). Likewise, the perception of the eighteenth century as the "Age of Reason" in which humanity at long last emancipated itself from the deceptive lures of irrationality is fundamentally questioned by current research, which again brings nuance to the traditional picture by emphasizing the actually highly complex patterns of interaction between esotericism and the Enlightenment (e.g. McIntosh 1992; Neugebauer-Wölk, ed. 1999). The general decline of faith in the grand narratives of modernity goes hand in hand with a new interest in—indeed curiosity about—the historical currents and ways of thinking that have been left out of the normative picture and were neglected by historiography. The study of Western esotericism is therefore regarded as timely and relevant, precisely because it challenges received opinions about the nature and development of Western culture.

Contrary to religionist-countercultural projects, the currents surge of academic interest in Western esotericism is not inspired by the search for a new ideology but, rather, by a profound distrust of all ideologies. As a result, to a much larger extent than before, Western esoteric currents now tend to be studied simply out of scholarly curiosity, and from a perspective of ideological neutrality. Much such research is inspired by a hermeneutics of suspicion with respect to modernist historiography: a wish to "fill in the gaps" left by earlier generations and become familiar with hitherto unexplored dimensions of Western religion and culture. In addition to such purely historical research, there is a new interest in conceptual analysis of the relation between Western esotericism and historical processes of modernization/secularization. The basic incompatibility between the two, stipulated by modernist narratives, seems to be contradicted by the facts: rather, the evidence suggests that Western esoteric currents have a remarkable ability to survive by means of adaptation and assimilation.

Obviously, if Western esoteric currents do not represent an essentially static worldview but are continually transformed by means of adaptation to new circumstances, this again brings up the question of how to define and demarcate the field. From a strictly historical point of view, the matter is unproblematic: Western esotericism comprises—as formulated in the title of the Amsterdam chair—"the hermetic philosophy and related currents." Along the lines of a Wittgensteinian concept of family-resemblance, contemporary New Agers may have little or nothing in common with fifteenth-century Renaissance hermetists (not to mention the hermetists of late antiquity), and yet be historically connected to them by means of many intermediary links. Such a pragmatic approach may be sufficient for demarcating the field, but will leave the theoretically-minded scholar of religion unsatisfied. If we wish for a more theoretical definition, the distinction between three basic strategies of knowledge which I proposed at the beginning of section 2 (*supra*) may be of some limited use.[14] It is indeed hard to deny that an emphasis on *gnosis*, rather than on rationality or the reliance on religious authority, is quite typical of the currents and personalities usually considered as falling under the heading of "Western esotericism"; and one may add that a marked preference for mythical and symbolic rather than logical and discursive language follows naturally from these premises. The great risk of such a definition consists in the frequent tendency to misunderstand its ideal-typical and heuristic nature, and use it in a reductionist fashion. The ideal types of "reason," "faith" and "gnosis" do not in fact make their appearance in concrete historical reality (where one invariably finds mixtures, with only a relative emphasis on one of the three strategies), and one and the same historical current or personality may very well shift emphasis over time or according to circumstances and the demands of the moment. For example, Frances Yates' figure of the "Renaissance magus," representing the type of "hermetic gnosis," is a non-existent entity. Authors such as Ficino, Pico della Mirandola, Agrippa, Bruno or Dee were in fact highly complex figures who are misunderstood if they are reduced to the straightjacket of the "magus," at the expense of their interest in e.g. mainstream Christian theology, scholastic philosophy, or contemporary physics, astronomy and mathematics. Obviously this is not to deny the great, even central, im-

---

14   For a theoretical development of this approach, see Hanegraaff 1994; and cf. my self-criticism in Hanegraaff 1998: 42–43.

portance of magic and hermeticism in their thinking. The point is that their intellectual world cannot reasonably be reduced to that factor only, and (most importantly) that one does not correctly understand *even* the very nature of those magical and hermetic dimensions in their work if one does not take into account the complex ways in which these are interwoven with non-magical and non-hermetic dimensions. It is precisely that interwovenness—and not any "purely hermetic" worldview—that makes the study of Western esotericism such a challenge for the study of religion in the West.

As reflected by Habermas' formula *neue Unübersichtlichkeit*, the key word in historically-based research in the humanities since the 1990s is *complexity*. Like other disciplines, the study of Western esotericism must avoid—or rather, overcome—the traditional mistake of reifying the domain of "Western esotericism" by perceiving it as a quasi-autonomous "counterculture" or "undercurrent" set apart from the dominant currents of Western mainstream culture (and accordingly of little relevance to them). The challenge of the field lies precisely in the opposite direction: that of exploring the complex interwovenness of "Western esotericism" with the general development of Western religion and culture since the Renaissance. In other words: rather than as a quasi-autonomous counterculture or undercurrent, Western esotericism is more profitably understood as a neglected dimension of modern Western religion and culture itself, which needs to be explored in order to better understand the latter's nature and development. This is why the present article is subtitled "New Approaches to Christian and Secular Culture." In the end, to study pre-Enlightenment manifestations of Western esotericism means quite simply to study pre-Enlightenment Christian culture[15] while concentrating on dimensions which have not received sufficient attention. Likewise, to study the development of Western esotericism since the eighteenth century means quite simply to study the Western process of secularization of religion while again concentrating on dimensions which have only been cursorily treated by earlier generations.

---

15 The assumption made here (obvious to the historian of religion, but unfortunately still far from generally appreciated) is that the phenomenon of Christianity can in no way be restricted to its doctrinal-theological dimension only, nor to a church history concentrating merely on the established churches, important though the latter may be. As a cultural and religious system, Christianity has a variety of dimensions—e.g. ritual, magic, various experiential practices and phenomena, folklore, art, and so on—which are increasingly attracting the interest of historians but still tend to be neglected by theologians (on this point, cf. Hanegraaff 2004).

6. Western Esotericism and the Study of Religion

Apart from its innovative potential with respect to the history of Christianity and the secularization of religion, the study of Western esotericism may contribute to the development of new theoretical approaches in the study of religion generally. In particular, it can play an important role in overcoming the eurocentric heritage of the study of religion so as to contribute to a globalization of the study of religion in the twenty-first century.

Obviously the modern study of religion emerged in the modern West, and its specific methodological assumptions are deeply indebted to the Enlightenment heritage. The latter's critical/analytic, empirical and potentially reductionist approach has been criticized by theologians and religionists ever since the nineteenth century, and is now being criticized anew by new generations of scholars born and raised in the non-Western developing countries.[16] There exists a fear among some Western scholars that a thorough globalization of the study of religion may lead to a new prominence of the religionist and kryptotheological perspectives which the discipline has fought so hard to overcome. Accordingly, they hold that the study of religion is bound and should remain bound—for better or worse and even in non-European academic contexts—to its Western intellectual foundations, although this inevitably implies a certain degree of imperialism and ethnocentrism. The problem with such an approach is that it may be insufficiently critical of its own intellectual foundations in Western culture, and as a result may remain blind to certain intellectual biases and uninvestigated presuppositions which are ideological rather than scholarly in nature. Formulated positively: the Enlightenment project is not complete if it does not apply its basic principle of intellectual *criticism* to its own historical and intellectual foundations.

For our present purposes, the implications of such criticism and the relevance to the study of Western esotericism may be illustrated at the example of the old Tylorean/Frazerian triad "magic—religion—science" and its remarkable persistence in the contemporary study of religion. Although contemporary scholars of religion will generally hasten to emphasize that classics such as *Primitive Culture* and *The Golden Bough* are long outdated, current published research on magic in Western and non-Western cultures demonstrates that actually their basic ideas remain very much alive. When contemporary academics discuss "magic," the assumptions which guide their understanding of it are essentially variations on Tylor's and Frazer's intellectualist theories, Mauss' and Durkheim's functionalism, and Lévy-Bruhl's theory of participation. These theories may be mixed and combined in various more or less interesting ways;

---

16   For a short introduction to the debate, see Chitando 2000; and cf. various contributions to Platvoet/Cox/Olupona 1996.

but practically without exception this is done *within* a general context that is more basic than the theories themselves, and the validity of which remains largely unexamined. This context is and remains essentially the Tylorean/ Frazerian triad. Its point of departure is that "religion" (however defined) is clearly something essentially different from modern science and rationality. That relatively unproblematic distinction having been made, it is followed by the observation that there exists a certain class of phenomena in human culture and history which are likewise quite clearly different from modern science and rationality, but which somehow do not quite seem to fit the model of "religion" either. This third category is then referred to by a variety of names, the very abundancy of which already demonstrates that it is in fact a waste-basket filled with left-overs: "magic," "the occult" (resp. "occultism," "occult science"), "superstition," "mysticism," "esotericism," "the irrational," "primitive thought" (cf. "fetishism," "idolatry"), and so on.

Tacitly assuming such a triad, scholars of religion have usually been in favor of "science and rationality," respectful at least towards "religion," and quite negative about "magic and the occult." Now, a first and basic thing to observe is that the very insistance on distinguishing between the last two categories (religion and magic) does not originally follow from any critical scholarly argumentation but simply adopts the historical usage long known to Western Christian culture. In its original historical manifestation, religion meant "true (i.e., theologically correct) Christianity" while magic meant demonic worship and pagan idolatry. The discussion became more complicated since the thirteenth century, with the emergence of the idea of *magia naturalis*: magic understood as "occult science" based on the hidden (i.e. occult) forces of nature, and therefore easier to legitimate theologically (Kieckhefer 1989: 1–18; Hanegraaff 2005). As a result, with the emergence of modern science since the seventeenth century *magia naturalis* increasingly came to be attacked from all sides: the Protestant reformation gave a revived sense of urgency to anti-magical arguments, many theological critics failed to be convinced about natural magic being non-demonic and continued to accuse practitioners and theoreticians of the occult sciences of trafficking with the devil, and they were now joined by modern scientists and philosophers who accused them of obscurantism and irrationality. This second line of attack was taken over by the Enlightenment tradition, adopted by E.B. Tylor, and continued by scholars throughout the twentieth century.

The core irrationality in most academic theories of magic since Tylor consists in the fact that they *continued* to make a sharp distinction between religion and magic, in spite of the fact that this distinction belongs to the domain of theological polemics internal to Christianity, and cannot claim any scholarly foundation.[17] The lack of such a foundation has not sufficiently both-ered scholars of religion. They uncritically adopted a purely theological notion, which eventually assumed the role of an unexamined guiding intuition in their discussions: an assumption too basic even to be perceived, and too self-evident to be in need of arguments. Political and social factors have played a significant role in this process: after all, the perception of "magic" and "the occult" as something sharply different from religion came to play an important role in the colonial enterprise. To the extent that the vestiges of true "religion" (conceptua-lized as "animism" in the wake of Tylor) were encountered among primitive peoples, these were capable of being redeemed and purified by being channeled towards Christianity. For the "magic" of the primitives, however (branded by Tylor as a contemptible superstition and as one of the most pernicious delusions that ever vexed mankind [Tylor 1871: 112–13]), such redemption was neither wished-for nor needed: it had to be rooted out by education or use of force. In its—ultimately fruitless—attempts to do so, the missionary enterprise merely repeated the early Christian missionary attempt to free Europe from pagan superstition (see e.g. Flint 1991). In sum: scholarly theory about magic served as theoretical justification for converting non-European peoples from primitive magic to Christianity and an Enlightened worldview; but this theory itself was merely a reformulation of Christian-theological polemics against paganism. In the post-colonial period Western scholars have become more sensitive about issues of ethnocentrism and Eurocentric arrogance, but this has not led to the logical step of discarding the category of "magic." Many authors opt for half-way solutions such as speaking about "magic" while admitting that is a form of "religion," but without ex-plaining in what then relies its specificity. Others make it easy on themselves by using adjectives such as "magico-religious," but again without specifying in what respect this category is different from "religion" pure and simple.

In a stimulating article, H.S. Versnel observed that you cannot talk about magic without using the term magic (Versnel 1991: 181). This paradox nicely puts the finger on the right spot and points out the core of the problem: even prior to any conscious attempt to apply our theories and terminologies to human practices and beliefs, the latter *already* appear to us pre-categorized in the terms of our own cultural conditioning. We do not need any theory to explain to us that what we perceive is a magical practice: we *know* that it is magic, because we recognize it as such! No amount of deconstruction, no sophisticated theory, can possibly make us question what we observe with our own eyes: that this practice over there is not just "religion" but something

---

17 Tylor himself, with characteristic intellectual honesty, recognized this later in his life (Hanegraaff 1998b). But this shift of opinion came too late to have an impact on his followers, and has been generally ignored.

different, both more specific and more vague, and somehow more discon-
certing.

Precisely this type of cultural pre-conditioning is, I suggest, a major but
greatly underestimated problem in the systematic study of religion. How can
we be confident that our interpretations, analyses and explanations have any
objective validity, if the practices and beliefs we study already appear to us
prepackaged by our cultural conditioning so as to be readily digestible by our
theoretical apparatus?[18] It seems to me that if there is any way out of this
dilemma it must be based upon recognition of the historicity—and hence, the
future flexibility—of the discipline of the study of religion. The discipline
emerged and developed under quite specific historical, social, and geographic
conditions, and this heritage remains part of its present identity. Crucial to that
identity is the methodological principle of *criticism* (whether applied to
historical sources, empirical evidence, or existing theories and interpretations)
basic to the Enlightenment project. But in theory at least, that very principle
allows us to deconstruct the patterns of cultural bias by means of which we
automatically perceive practice x as "magic" and practice y as "religion," practice q as "irrational" and practice z as "rational," and to become conscious of
the fact that the phenomena of human culture might also be categorized
according to entirely different criteria. Given the undeniable fact that ingrained
magic-religion distinctions are not just culture-specific but clearly bound up
with normative ideologies, which have a religious rather than a rational or
scientific foundation and are therefore likely to distort the evidence under investigation, such an attempt at re-categorization can be expected to lead to
significant advances in the study of religion. Admittedly, that new alternative
categorizations will be entirely free from cultural bias is highly unlikely; but the
very exercise of deconstructing ingrained traditional categories may sharpen
our sensitivity to the slipping-in of new ideological distortions. In any case it is
necessary at least to make the attempt, if the global study of religion in the
twenty-first century does not wish to get trapped in a fruitless recycling of
nineteenth-century European obsessions.

With respect to the magic-religion problematic specifically, it may be expected that significant advances towards more adequate scholarly approaches
will come from two main directions: historians of Western esotericism, on the
one hand, and at least some non-Western academics studying the religion of
their own countries, on the other. The reason for such an expectation is quite
simply that these two groups are studying practices and beliefs which have

---

18 To be sure, the problem of cultural pre-conditioning and its methodological implications has been a continuing theme in the academic study of religion. But I am not
aware of attempts to apply it, in the way I am doing here, to the perception of certain
types of belief and practice as "magic."

suffered most strongly from the impact of eurocentric theorizing about "magic and the occult." As for the study of Western esotericism: analyzing in detail the development of Western polemics pro and contra esotericism, in the Christian context as well as under the impact of secularization, allows us to trace the historical emergence and historical transformation (from *emic* to *etic*, as well as the reverse) of concepts which have become basic to the modern study of religion. A systematic deconstruction of those concepts as academic tools will have profound consequences not just for the study of Western esotericism but for our general understanding of religion, in the West and elsewhere. Only if the usage of terms such as "magic" or "the occult" will be consistently restricted to their occurrance as *emic* terms used in the polemical interplay between believers/practitioners and their critics, while new and academically-neutral terms and concepts are developed for *etic* discussion of the beliefs and practices concerned, will it become possible to envision an unbiased and sufficiently nuanced perspective on the historical dynamics of Western religion. Such a task of historical deconstruction will likely be performed by scholars of religion in the West (since that is where the terminology in question developed), and here the historical study of Western esotericism has an important role to play. The construction of *new* theoretical frameworks, to replace the old ones, is most likely to come from those non-Western scholars who are studying religious practices in their own countries that have been perceived as "magic" by the Western mind.

7. Conclusion

The moral of this overview should be clear. Western esotericism is more than just another previously-neglected domain of study in need of being recovered for academic research. In addition to this, it is a discipline which happens to hold great innovative potential for the study of religion generally. This is true on the purely historical level as well as on the level of theory and method. As for the former, the study of Western esotericism indeed requires the development of new approaches to Christianity and secular culture, leading to a significant revision of traditional views. As for the latter, it opens a perspective on the development of new frameworks for analysis and interpretation which might well revolutionize the study of religion. The potential is there; but needless to say, it will only come to fruition if scholars will recognize its presence and take up the challenge.

Bibliography

Arnold, Gottfried (1700), *Unpartheyische Kirchen- und Ketzer-Historien: Vom Anfang des neuen Testaments bis auf das Jahr Christi 1688*. Frankfurt am Main: Thomas Fritsch.

Assmann, Jan (1999), "'Hen kai pan': Ralph Cudworth und die Rehabilitierung der hermetischen Tradition," in: Neugebauer-Wölk, ed., *Aufklärung und Esoterik*: 38–52.

Broek, Roelof van den/Hanegraaff, Wouter J. (1998), "Preface," in: Roelof van den Broek/Wouter J. Hanegraaff, eds., *Gnosis and Hermeticism from Antiquity to Modern Times*. Albany, N.Y.: State University of New York Press: vii–x.

Chitando, Ezra (2000), "African Christian Scholars and the Study of African Traditional Religions: A Re-Evaluation," in: *Religion* 30 (4): 391–97.

Cohen, H. Floris (1994), *The Scientific Revolution: A Historiographical Inquiry*. Chicago/London: The University of Chicago Press.

Colberg, Ehregott Daniel (1690–1691), *Das Platonisch-Hermetisches* [sic] *Christenthum, Begreiffend Die Historische Erzehlung vom Ursprung und vielerley Secten der heutigen Fanatische Theologie, unterm Namen der Paracelsisten, Weigelianer, Rosencreutzer, Quäcker, Böhmisten, Wiedertäuffer, Bourignisten, Labadisten, und Quietisten*. 2 Vols. Frankfurt/Leipzig: M.G. Widmann.

Copenhaver, Brian P. (1990), "Natural Magic, Hermeticism, and Occultism in Early Modern Science," in: David C. Lindberg/Robert S. Westman, eds., *Reappraisals of the Scientific Revolution*. Cambridge: Cambridge University Press.

Crow, Catherine (1848), *The Night-Side of Nature. Or, Ghosts and Ghost-Seers*. Repr. Wellingborough: Aquarian Press 1986.

Dobbs, Betty Jo Teeter (1991), *The Janus Face of Genius: The Role of Alchemy in Newton's Thought*. Cambridge: Cambridge University Press.

Edighoffer, Roland (2005), "Andreae, Johann Valentin," in: Wouter J. Hanegraaff, ed., *Dictionary of Gnosis and Western Esotericism*. Leiden etc.: E.J. Brill.

Faivre, Antoine (1994), *Access to Western Esotericism*. Albany, N.Y.: State University of New York Press.

—— (1999), "Histoire de la notion moderne de tradition dans ses rapports avec les courants ésotériques (XVe–XXe siècles)," in: *Symboles et Mythes dans les mouvements initiatiques et ésotériques (XVIIe–XXe siècles): Filiations et emprunts* (ARIES special issue). Archè/La table d'Émeraude: Paris.

Faivre, Antoine/Hanegraaff, Wouter J., eds. (1998), *Western Esotericism and the Science of Religion: Selected Papers presented at the 17th Congress of the International Association for the History of Religions, Mexico City 1995*. Louvain: Peeters.

Flint, Valerie I.J. (1991), *The Rise of Magic in Early Medieval Europe*. Princeton, N.J.: Princeton University Press.

Garin, Eugenio (1954), *Moyen Age et Renaissance*. Paris: Gallimard 1969.

Gilly, Carlos (2000), "Das Bekenntnis zur Gnosis von Paracelsus bis auf die Schüler Jacob Böhmes," in: Roelof van den Broek/Cis van Heertum, eds., *From Poimandres to Jacob Böhme: Gnosis, Hermetism and the Christian Tradition*. Amsterdam: In de Pelikaan: 385–425.

Gladigow, Burkhard (1995), "Europäische Religionsgeschichte," in: Hans G. Kippenberg/Brigitte Luchesi, eds., *Lokale Religionsgeschichte*. Marburg: diagonal-Verlag: 21–42.

Habermas, Jürgen (1985), *Die neue Unübersichtlichkeit*. Frankfurt am Main: Suhrkamp.

Hakl, Hans Thomas (2001), *Der verborgene Geist von Eranos: Unbekannte Begegnungen von Wissenschaft und Esoterik. Eine alternative Geistesgeschichte des 20. Jahrhunderts.* Bretten: Scientia Nova.

Hammer, Olav (2001), *Claiming Knowledge: Strategies of Epistemology from Theosophy to the New Age.* Leiden/Boston, Mass./Köln: E.J. Brill.

Hanegraaff, Wouter J. (1994), "The Problem of 'Post-Gnostic' Gnosticism," in: Ugo Bianchi, ed., *The Notion of "Religion" in Comparative Research: Selected Proceedings of the XVI IAHR Congress.* Rome: "L'Erma" di Bretschneider: 625–32.

— (1996), *New Age Religion and Western Culture: Esotericism in the Mirror of Secular Thought.* Leiden/New York/Köln: E.J. Brill [U.S. edition: Albany, N.Y.: State University of New York Press 1998].

— (1998a), "On the Construction of 'Esoteric Traditions,'" in: Antoine Faivre/Wouter J. Hanegraaff, eds., *Western Esotericism and the Science of Religion*: 11–61.

— (1998b), "The Emergence of the Academic Science of Magic: The Occult Philosophy in Tylor and Frazer," in: Arie L. Molendijk/Peter Pels, eds., *Religion in the Making: The Emergence of the Sciences of Religion.* Leiden/Boston, Mass./Köln: E.J. Brill: 253–75.

— (1999a), "Defining Religion in Spite of History," in: Jan G. Platvoet/Arie L. Molendijk, eds., *The Pragmatics of Defining Religion: Contexts, Concepts and Contests.* Leiden/Boston, Mass./Köln: E.J. Brill: 337–78.

— (1999b), New Age Spiritualities as Secular Religion: A Historian's Perspective. *Social Compass* 46 (2): 145–60.

— (1999c), "Gnosis II," in: Christoph Auffarth/Jutta Bernard/Hubert Mohr, eds., *Metzler Lexikon Religion.* Vol. 1. Stuttgart/Weimar: J.B. Metzler: 506–10.

— (2000), "New Age Religion and Secularization," in: *Numen* 47 (3): 288–312.

— (2001), "Beyond the Yates Paradigm: The Study of Western Esotericism between Counterculture and New Complexity," in: *Aries* 1 (1): 5–37.

— (2004), "The Dreams of Theology and the Realities of Christianity," in: J. Haers/P. De Mey, eds., *Theology and Conversation: Towards a Relational Theology.* (Bibliotheca Ephemeridum Theologicarum Lovaniensium 172). Leuven: Peeters: 709–33.

— (2005), "Occult/Occultism," in: Wouter J. Hanegraaff, ed., *Dictionary of Gnosis and Western Esotericism.* Leiden etc.: E.J. Brill.

Kieckhefer, Richard (1980), *Magic in the Middle Ages.* Cambridge: Cambridge University Press.

Kilcher, Andreas (1998), *Die Sprachtheorie der Kabbala als ästhetisches Paradigma: Die Konstruktion einer ästhetischen Kabbala seit der frühen Neuzeit.* Stuttgart/Weimar: J.B. Metzler.

Kristeller, Paul Oskar (1938), "Marsilio Ficino e Lodovico Lazzarelli: Contributo alla diffusione delle idee ermetiche nel rinascimento," repr. in: Kristeller, *Studies in Renaissance Thought and Letters.* Vol. 1. Roma: 221–47.

Laurant, Jean-Pierre (1992), *L'ésotérisme chrétien en France au XIXe siècle.* Lausanne: L'Age dHomme.

— (1993), *L'ésotérisme.* Paris: Cerf.

McIntosh, Christopher (1992), *The Rose Cross and the Age of Reason: Eighteenth-Century Rosicrucianism in Central Europe and Its Relationship to the Enlightenment.* Leiden/New York/Köln: E.J. Brill.

Mulsow, Martin, ed. (2002), *Das Ende des Hermetismus.* Tübingen: Mohr Siebeck.

Neugebauer-Wölk, Monika (1999), "Esoterik im 18. Jahrhundert: Aufklärung und Esoterik. Eine Einleitung," in: Neugebauer-Wölk, ed., *Aufklärung und Esoterik*: 1–37.
— ed. (1999), *Aufklärung und Esoterik*. Studien zum achtzehnten Jahrhundert 24.
Hamburg: Felix Meiner.
— (2000), "Esoterik in der frühen Neuzeit: Zum Paradigma der Religiongsgeschichte
zwischen Mittelalter und Moderne," in: *Zeitschrift für historische Forschung* 27 (3):
321–64.
Platvoet, Jan/Cox, James/Olupona, Jacob, eds. (1996), *The Study of Religions in Africa:
Past, Present and Prospects*. Cambridge: Roots and Branches.
Principe, Lawrence M. (1998), *The Aspiring Adept: Robert Boyle and his Alchemical Quest*.
Princeton, N.J.: Princeton University Press.
Riffard, Pierre (1990), *L'ésotérisme*. Paris: Robert Laffont.
Sarton, George (1975), *Introduction to the History of Science*. Vol. 1. Huntington, N.Y.:
Robert E. Krieger.
Secret, François (1964), *Les kabbalistes chrétiens de la Renaissance*. Repr. Neuilly-sur-
Seine/Milano: Arma Artis/Archè.
Michael Stausberg (1998), *Faszination Zarathushtra: Zoroaster und die Europäische
Religionsgeschichte der frühen Neuzeit*. 2 vols. Berlin/New York: Walter de Gruyter.
Stuckrad, K. von (2004), *Was ist Esoterik? Kleine Geschichte des geheimen Wissens*.
München: C.H. Beck.
Styers, Randall Gray (1997), *Magical Theories: Magic, Religion and Science in Modernity*.
Ph.D. dissertation, Duke University.
— (2004), *Making Magic: Religion, Magic, and Science in the Modern World*. Oxford etc.:
Oxford University Press.
Tylor, E.B. (1871), *Primitive Culture: Researches into the Development of Mythology,
Philosophy, Religion, Language, Art, and Custom*. Repr. London: John Murray 1913.
Versnel, H.S. (1991), "Some Reflections on the Relationship Magic–Religion," in: *Numen*
38 (2): 177–97.
Walker, D.P., *The Ancient Theology*. London 1972.
Wasserstrom, Steven M. (1999), *Religion after Religion: Gershom Scholem, Mircea Eliade,
and Henry Corbin at Eranos*. Princeton, N.J.: Princeton University Press.
Yates, Frances A. (1964), *Giordano Bruno and the Hermetic Tradition*. London/Chicago:
Routledge and Kegan Paul/University of Chicago Press.
— (1967), "The Hermetic Tradition in Renaissance Science," in: Charles S. Singleton,
ed., *Art, Science and History in the Renaissance*. Baltimore, Md.: Johns Hopkins Press:
255–74.

List of Contributors

PETER ANTES (1942), Dr. theol., Dr. phil., Habilitation for "Religionsgeschichte und Vergleichende Religionswissenschaft," Professor and Chair of the Department for the History of Religions (Religionswissenschaft), University of Hannover, Germany. Research interests: Islamic ethics, methodology in the study of religions and world religions in education.

JØRN BORUP (1966), Ph.D., Current teaching positions at the Department of the Study of Religion and the Department of History and Area Studies, Aarhus University, Denmark. Research interests: Modern Japanese Zen Buddhism; Buddhism in the West.

LORNE L. DAWSON (1954), Dr. phil., Chair of the Department of Religious Studies, Associate Professor of Sociology, University of Waterloo, Canada. Research interests: New religious movements; religion and the internet; theory and method in the study of religion.

ARMIN W. GEERTZ (1948), Dr. phil., Professor in the History of Religions at the Department of the Study of Religion, University of Aarhus, Denmark. General Secretary of the International Association for the History of Religions (IAHR). Research interests: Hopi Indian religion (based on fieldwork since 1978); the religions of indigenous peoples; method and theory in the study of religion; cognitive theory in the study of religion; and new religious movements.

WOUTER J. HANEGRAAFF (1961), Dr., Professor of History of Hermetic Philosophy and Related Currents at the Faculty of Art, Religion and Culture of the University of Amsterdam, the Netherlands. Research Interests: History of hermetic and related currents, especially since the Renaissance; Western esotericism; religion and the arts; method and theory in the study of religions.

KIRSTEN HASTRUP (1948), Dr. phil., Dr. scient. soc., Professor, Institute of Anthropology, University of Copenhagen, Denmark. Primary research interests: Icelandic history and society; anthropology of theater; theoretical anthropology; historical and philosophical foundations of scholarship.

MARK HULSETHER (1957), Ph.D., Associate Professor of Religious Studies and American Studies, University of Tennessee, Knoxville, Tenn., USA. Research interests: Religion, culture, and society in recent US history.

JEPPE SINDING JENSEN (1951), Dr. phil., Associate Professor, Department for the Study of Religion, University of Aarhus, Denmark. Research interests: Semantics and cognition in religious narrativity; myth and cosmology; method, theory and the philosophy of science in the study of religion.

MORNY M. JOY (1948), Ph.D., Full Professor in the Department of Religious Studies, University of Calgary, Alberta, Canada. Principal areas of research: Philosophy and religion; women in the religions of the world.

PRATAP KUMAR (1952), Ph.D., Professor, University of KwaZulu Natal, Durban, South Africa. Research interests: History of Srivaishnavism, South Asian diaspora, religious pluralism and methodological issues in the study of Hinduism.

JEAN FRANÇOIS MAYER (1957), docteur en histoire, Lecturer in Religious Studies, University of Fribourg, Switzerland. Research interests: New religious movements; religion and politics; religion and the Internet; missions and proselytism.

RUSSELL T. MCCUTCHEON (1961), Ph.D., Associate Professor and Chair of the Department of Religious Studies, University of Alabama, Tuscaloosa, Alabama, USA. Research interests: History of the study of religion, method and theory, and the politics of classification systems.

LISBETH MIKAELSSON (1942), Dr. phil., Professor, Department of the History of Religions, University of Bergen, Norway. Research topics and fields of interests: Norwegian foreign mission; new religious movements; religion and gender; religious autobiography; religion and locality; pilgrimage and religious tourism; theory in the history of religions.

BÜLENT ŞENAY (1966), Ph.D., Associate Professor of History of Religions, Uludag University, Bursa, Turkey. Research Interests: Early and contemporary Christianity, method and theory in the study of religion, Muslim-Christian relations, religion and identity.

IVAN STRENSKI (1943), Ph.D., Holstein Family and Community Professor in Religious Studies, University of California, Riverside, Calif., USA. Recent Books: *Theology and the First Theory of Sacrifice* (2003); *Contesting Sacrifice: Religion, Nationalism and Social Thought* (2002) and *Durkheim and the Jews of France* (1997).

Current research interests: the role of religion in shaping modern political and economic structures.

ABDULKADER I. TAYOB (1958), Ph.D., Professor of Social Processes in Modern Islam, University of Nijmegen, International Institute for the Study of Islam in the Modern World. Research interests: Islam in Africa; modern Muslim intellectual history.

GARRY WINSTON TROMPF (1940), Ph.D., Professor in the History of Ideas, Department of Studies in Religion, University of Sydney, Australia. Books on Western macrohistory, Pacific Island religions, and theories of religion.

RANDI R. WARNE (1952), Ph.D., Professor and Chair of the Department of Philosophy/Religious Studies, and Coordinator of Cultural Studies, Mount St. Vincent University, Halifax, NS, Canada. Research interests: Gender; religion and culture; method and theory in the study of religion.

Index of Names

Index of Subjects